BUSINESS COMMUNICATION

BUSINESS
COMMUNICATION

FRANK J. DEVLIN
Associate Professor of Business Administration
Assistant Dean, School of Business
John Carroll University

1968
RICHARD D. IRWIN, INC.
Homewood, Illinois

Library of Congress Catalog Card No. 67–17040

Printed in the United States of America

PREFACE

What are the chief needs that a book on business writing should be expected to fill? This was the task-setting question confronting me as I began to outline this book, *Business Communication*. The answer, as I perceived it, embraced three points:

1. The book should contain dependable theory.
2. It should be workable as a college-level textbook.
3. It should be adaptable either as a continuing reference book for a person after he has finished using it as a textbook—or as a handbook for a businessman in actual practice.

My planning, therefore, centered on incorporating these features into the book. Numerous other points are, of course, included. Some of these even represent breakthroughs or innovations—but they are used to support, not increase, the features already mentioned as important.

From the standpoint of theory, there was first of all the necessity of finding a bed-rock base. Many of the existing textbooks suggest a "teacher knows best" philosophy which does not provide satisfactory reasons to support the instruction given. The learner can imitate, but he is not fully capable of transferring his skills to new situations. He lacks the solid theory that would provide a universal weapon to cope with all foreseeable challenges.

Some of the textbooks have been developed along the line of an "approach." Thus, we have had various approaches emphasizing letter form, letter "types," letter "situations," language expression (Business English), and so on. These emphases are rather superficial at best. Actually, no business letter or report exists as one part to the exclusion of any or all of the others. It is a composite of all the essential parts—a final document, the effectiveness of which depends on the proper handling of *all* the parts. There is a danger, therefore, that something may be overlooked when a specialized "approach" is used. If so, the finished product could fall short of doing the job intended by the writer.

In *Business Communication*, no part of the letter or report is emphasized, no part slighted. Each is given its proportionate share of attention so that the final document, or transmittable communication, can be up to standard in all respects. The entire operation is placed on the solid foundation of communication in general. "Business communication" is then shown to be a specific adaptation of the communication process—and thus subject to all the requirements set forth in communication theory. Then, business communication is recognized as the transacting of business through the written word. As such, it is also subject to all the requirements that amount to good business relations. The foundation has now been laid. The various important components of a business communication—content, language, and form—must comply with the requirements of both good communication and good business practice. If any part does not so comply, it gives rise to a kind of noise, an interference with the smooth flow of the business communication.

Akin to the matter of theory are two other details which I have long felt to be lacking in many textbooks. One of these is that highly subjective area dealing with the writer's attitude toward his reader. Some textbooks discuss this matter under "semantics"; others cover it under the special heading of "basic principles." Either way, the learner is shown the problems that exist but is usually left to develop a "finger to the wind" instinct for solving them. In *Business Communication*, I have limited the subdividing of this area to just three components. I have reduced each of these components to a definable state, and have provided a method of testing the suitability of each within the confines of a given sentence. It is hoped that these efforts will mark the beginning of positive, objective control over qualities heretofore regarded as too elusive to define and attainable mostly as a practiced art.

I have made a diligent attempt also to adhere to a consistent use of terms. In this book, for example, "tone" means but one of several possible things. Whenever it is used in a later place, it has the same meaning as it had when it was first introduced. The learner is not required to adjust to a new usage—rather, new terms are found to keep distinctions clear. Moreover, the selection of terms has been made carefully, so that the most usual meanings have been followed. Even persons whose experience has been with "sliding" terminology should find this standardization a welcome change.

In considering the use of this book as a college-level textbook, I had to take into account both the educational stage of the typical student and the traditional teaching patterns of business-writing instructor. As a first course in functional writing, Business Letters (or Business Letters and Reports) is undoubtedly an offering at the undergraduate level. In the junior colleges, it is likely to show up during the second year; in the senior colleges, in the third or fourth year. In either case, at least one year of college-level English (or Business English) will probably precede it. Thus, the student should be somewhat refreshed on the mechanics of expression by the time he enters the course in business writing; but he still will be only partially conversant with the complexities of business practice. His textbook, therefore, should relate the specific instructions for writing to the problems which typically arise in business practice. A necessary minimum amount of background should be provided along the way to place these problems in their proper business setting.

Traditionally, teachers of business writing have found it expedient to plan their syllabi along the following lines: general principles (attitude toward the reader), mechanics of expression, form, business letters (by types), and, if included, business reports (informal and formal). By catering to this traditional approach, a textbook can introduce its improvements and contributions with only a minimum of adjustment required of the teacher. It can help the teacher preserve and refine his own techniques, whereas an unconventional approach might undermine his position and make him overly dependent upon the textbook.

To be sure, new and improved teaching methods are to be encouraged. Not only should they represent forward steps but they should also be easily assimilated by the main stream of teachers in the field. For instance, in recent years recognition has been given to the existence of basic business letter "situations" as opposed to letter "types." This development is an important advance in the identification of basic models for request letters, inductive-order letters, and deductive-order letters. Unfortunately, it has led to the influx of various textbooks in which "types" are more or less abandoned. In their place are sections devoted to each of the newly recognized "situations." As orderly and logical as such a treatment of the subject matter may be, it provides neither the ideal business atmosphere for the learner nor an effective sequence of material for the teacher.

Business Communication has been prepared along traditional lines to help both learner and teacher. Also, it stresses sound, rational instruction. Illustrative materials are on the positive side, showing always the recommended ways of writing business communications (never the disapproved ways).

Last, but not least, is the potential value of the book apart from its use as a college textbook. Can it be beneficial to a learner once he has left the classroom—or to an established businessman who may never have had a formal course in this field? To this end, I have organized the book according to coordinated sections, each of which contains an associated grouping of chapters.

A unique feature is the presentation, at the end of each chapter, of a summary or capsule of the chapter content. This feature is designed to effect instant recall on the part of the user without his having to reread the entire coverage of the chapter. Its presence should encourage the learner to retain his copy of the book. Its use later on should have its rewards for both the learner and the teacher—in that the "recall" will tend to revive the invaluable personal contribution which the teacher has made through his presentation of the course.

An effort has been made to compose each chapter so that it can be read beneficially independent of any of the other chapters. The topical nature of each chapter makes it possible for either an old or a new user of the book to find a desired piece of information through the table of contents as well as through the index. Supplements provided at the end of the book provide handy source material on language skills, stenographic matters, and the terminology of the business communication field.

Needless to say, this book did not just happen. It is the outgrowth of nearly two decades of living, breathing, and teaching business writing. For its development, I am truly indebted to an undeterminable number of persons. Included in their ranks are my own teachers and advisers, as well as co-workers, colleagues of the American Business Writing Association, and business friends. I could scarcely begin to acknowledge them individually—indeed, the passage of time has even obscured the precise contribution made by many of them. In fairness to them all, I can but express my total and heartfelt gratitude.

FRANK J. DEVLIN

Cleveland
December, 1967

TABLE OF CONTENTS

PART I
·················

BUSINESS COMMUNICATION
PRINCIPLES

In the first section of this book, we shall discuss the basic principles to be used in writing business letters and reports. The communication process is examined as a means of putting the discussion on a sound base.

Chapter 1 considers the mission of communication in general and the different viewpoints that have been taken of it, both ancient and modern. An up-to-date communication model is constructed to depict the combination of message and technology. In Chapter 2, attention is turned to a specific variety, "business communication," with emphasis on how its goal goes beyond the minimum requirements of communication in general. A model is worked out for business communication showing the component parts and stages of development used by the writer, and in reverse order, the extracting of the message by the reader.

The next three chapters examine each stage in the development of the business letter. Chapter 3 considers the message—the content of the letter at the planning stage. Four distinct business letter situations are recognized, and the basic requirements of each are pointed out. Since planning requires an understanding of *how* we should express the points in our letter as well as *what* we should include, we acquaint ourselves with the matter of finesse and devise a means of testing for its presence.

In Chapter 4, the discussion moves to the language of the business letter. In this area, there are two aspects to be observed—readability and mechanical accuracy. Both aspects are important, because language is the encoding process by which a message is put into transmittable shape. When readability requirements are observed, it is possible to write even to an absolute stranger with the likelihood that he will be able to extract the message effortlessly. And, sticking to the generally accepted standards of language mechanics (spelling, vocabulary, grammar, sentence structure, and punctuation) not only earns the respect of the reader but also enhances the clarity of the message.

Finally, Chapter 5 covers the matter of letter form. This aspect of a business letter really performs three jobs in the communication process. To begin with, form is the transmitting instrument; then, it is the channel which carries the message to the reader; and, in the end, it is the reader's receiving instrument. Although from a writing viewpoint form might be rated the least important of the three basic components of a letter, it is still very essential. Thus, there is a need to examine the standards, conventions, and good taste to be used in presenting a message on paper. Form is approached as a means to an end, not as an end in itself.

....

CHAPTER 1

GENERAL
COMMUNICATION
THEORY

In this book, we are going to investigate many of the aspects of business communication. We are going to examine the topic as to its scientific and artistic aspects. We shall try to lay a dependable foundation upon which to build a communication message, no matter what might be the situation or the external form involved. Above all, we shall relate business communication to managerial leadership.

COMMUNICATION DEFINED
....

As a first step, however, it would be well for us to become acquainted with the basic concepts of communication. By ordinary dictionary definitions *to communicate* means "To make known; recount; to give by way of information." *Communication* means "intercourse by words, letters, or messages; interchange of thoughts or opinions; correspondence." We can see, therefore, that the aim of communication is to transfer a thought of some kind from one person to one or more other persons. Of importance to us, at this point, is to understand something about how such transfer of thought is achieved.

AN EARLY VIEWPOINT

Attempts to explain the communication process are anything but new. For example, the philosopher Aristotle (384–322 B.C.), who studied virtually everything known to man during his era, had some definite thoughts on communication. Because his approach was to set up all things scientifically, we are indebted to him for a basic scheme of explaining the communication process. In model form, we can depict it as follows.

We can appreciate Aristotle's insight even today, some 2300 years later. But in light of what we now know, we should also be able to see certain limitations and inadequacies. Briefly, these are:

1. The system is subject-oriented. It does not provide adequately for the transference of the message from one person to another. It is valid mainly for vocal communication. It does not well suit other possibilities, such as written documents, visual signals, and the many electrical and electronic systems available today.
2. The phraseology of the model is limited, although in harmony with the vocal communication concept. If words of a more neutral nature were used, greater flexibility of application would be possible.
3. The system includes but one subject (or message). As we shall soon see, a representative communication model would include at least two, and even as many as four messages.

A MODERN VIEWPOINT

All about us today, we see the results of man's efforts to find new and improved methods of communication. That area which concerns itself with the *means* of communicating—that is, the actual transmission—has identified itself by the designation, *communications*.

In relatively recent times, we have had the development of the telegraph, the telephone, radio, public address systems, office intercoms, teletype, television, and even electronic computer hookups whereby machines communicate with machines. These devices all have the advantage of speed in communicating over long distances. As communications satellites become firmly established, we can expect worldwide networks to spring up.

We should realize, however, that these innovations have their problems. As man-made devices, they are prone to imperfections and breakdowns. Our research engineers are constantly looking for refinements. Obviously they need a dependable, scientific base upon which to operate.

Such a base emerged in 1948 as a result of the efforts of the late Norbert Wiener and those of Claude Shannon. Through their contributions, we have been given a communications model of the following type.

This model is readily adaptable to any of the available methods of communicating. It shows that information at the source must be put into a state which can be sent through the given channel, be picked up by the receiver, and finally be returned to its original state at destination. It is oriented to the matter of *communications*, however—that is, to the method. Using this base, our engineers have concentrated on the technology of relaying the message from source to destination. They have not concerned themselves with the message itself. To them it need not even be intelligible; it need only get through to its destination with the highest possible degree of fidelity.

One of the major problems confronting communications engineers is a matter they refer to as "noise." This is a jargon-type word, but also imaginative and useful. It can be defined as any disturbance (something committed or omitted) which interferes with the process of communications. Thus, a malfunction in either the transmitter or the receiver would constitute a kind of noise. So would interference in the channel—such as static on a radio, a loose connection on a telephone call, or loss of power on a long-distance call. Moreover, noise can apply to a visual disturbance also. We can see a good example of this type of noise in a television receiver.

1. If the set does not work at all, possibly because of a loose power connection, the trouble (noise) has completely blocked reception of the telecast.

2. If the set lights up, produces the sound and voices of a telecast, but does not produce a picture, noise has again interfered.

3. If the picture produces lines instead of a picture, noise is still dominant.

4. If only a fluttering picture can be brought in, noise is still disrupting the reception.

5. If both picture and sound come through reasonably well, noise would be controlled. Even so, a blurry, or light, or dark picture would still indicate some amount of noise.

This kind of "noise" is symbolic; but it is just as disturbing to the person or persons at destination as would be audible noise. In fact, the absence of all sound—as in the instance of a dead telephone line—is nevertheless an example of what we can regard as noise.

All in all, our engineering function has done a commendable job in holding noise to a minimum. Transmitting and receiving equipment, in both radio and television, has been constantly improved. Airwave static has been countered by FM radio. New potentials have been opened up in telephone service by the introduction of microwave transmission.

While new discoveries themselves are susceptible to new kinds of noise, our research staffs are alert to blocking it out. We now confidently expect our communications devices to render service with a high degree of fidelity.

A MERGER OF CONCEPTS

If we are to depict communication in a representative manner, we must combine both of its basic components—the message and the means. The first step is to restate the message-oriented model in general terms. Thus, our model could take the following form.

It is now necessary for us to recognize something overlooked in the ancient, message-oriented model. The fact is that there are really *two* messages involved. One is the message intended at the source; the other is the message extracted at the destination. Ideally, these messages should be the same; but in practice they are usually not exactly the same. For example, suppose we wish to communicate a message to someone about a tree. This seems a simple thing; but our concept of "tree" is an abstraction which embraces an infinite number of particular trees. If we wished the message to specify a certain pine tree, and our listener imagined some other kind of tree, certainly the intended and extracted messages would be different. To illustrate:

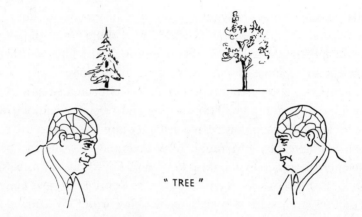

" TREE "

Some message words will not cause such difficulties. Perhaps we do not need to be specific. If we are asked, for instance, "Are those bushes or trees?" the response, "Trees," is all that is necessary. It may be so with many messages in which *yes, no, hello, goodbye, sixteen, tomorrow,* are the only responses called for. On the other hand, such "pure" abstractions as *love, honesty, truth,* can evoke so many shades of meaning that communicating exactly what we have in mind will be much more difficult than is the case with our one, specific tree.

What happens if we restrict the meaning of "tree" by the use of modifiers (adjectives)? While we do tend to limit the possible interpretations, we still do not always reduce them to the absolute *one.* Suppose we expand the message to "bushy pine tree." If we are thinking of an outside pine tree and the words cause our listener to envision an indoor Christmas tree, we again have two messages instead of one.

" A BUSHY PINE TREE "

Carrying the illustration further, we could make an entire sentence of our intended message. In a sentence we can describe the tree as either something in action or something acted upon. By that form of message, we can limit the possible interpretations even more. For instance:

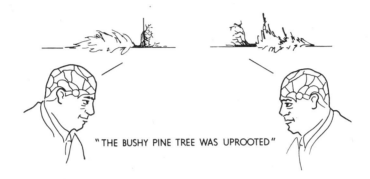

"THE BUSHY PINE TREE WAS UPROOTED"

Now, both we and our listener are reasonably close with regard to the message. We both envision an outside, bushy pine tree which has been toppled over, its roots pulled out of the ground. But still there could be differences between our intended message and his extracted message. These differences would involve such incidentals as the direction in which the tree fell, the damage to the branches, the manner in which the roots are exposed, and so on. If we have seen the tree, we know the facts; our listener can only imagine them at this point.

To reflect the concept of two messages (theoretically or ideally the same, but in practice somewhat different), we shall expand our methodless communication model as follows.

We now are ready to combine this model with the messageless communication model.

In making such a merger, we can see that "source" and "destination" are common to both original models. Each need appear but once in the combined model. Also, since we must begin at the source with the message intended, we should show this concept on the base line with the other steps forming a "bridge" across to the destination.

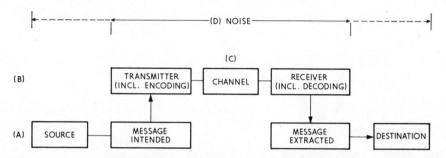

This combination finally gives us a flexible model to depict the full process of communication (message and method stages). A glance at the three levels of activity shows us:

A. *The message aspect.* The source has a message it intends to send to a destination. When extracted at destination, the message may or may not be the same as the message intended. We can usually expect some differences—thus, the concept of two messages.

B. *The intermediate steps*—before and after the act of sending the message. These we call the *encoding* and *decoding steps*—that is, casting the message intended into a transmittable state and later converting it back to a message state. There is the possibility of further slippage from the message intended during both encoding and decoding. Therefore, we might consider whether these steps give rise to sufficient distortions as to cause third and fourth messages to come into being!

C. *The physical hookup*, or *bridge*, between the source side and the destination side of our communication model. Here the encoded (sendable) message is sent from one point to another by some method. Our model is flexible enough that it can be fitted to any method now in use.

D. *The problem of noise.* From an engineering standpoint, the chief difficulty is with noise. The reduction or elimination of all disruptions and interferences along the channel hookup, therefore, is a continuing goal of our research scientists and engineers. Upon the merger of the two models, however, we no longer can confine noise to the channel only. If noise is considered to be any disturbance which interferes with the process of getting the message from source to destination, then it could enter anywhere along the entire circuit. This would include the message itself as well as the other steps in the process. Thus, such matters as sequencing, phrasing, and correctness would have a definite bearing on the message extracted. We could consider them to be either noisy or noiseless, as the case might be. Naturally, a smooth-flowing, agreeable, accurate message at the source would have a good chance of being extracted properly at destination. It is up to us who compose messages, not the channel-oriented engineers, to exclude noise in our phase of the communication process.

SUMMARY

We may subdivide the general area of communication into two aspects: the message and the method. Man has from early days given thought to this process. In more recent times, our emphasis has been on the method, particularly in improvements to reduce or cut out disturbances called "noise."

In any full treatment of the communication process, however, we must take into consideration both message and method. A diagram or model of the complete process shows us that there are at least two messages involved: the message intended and the message extracted through communication. In strict theory, these messages would be the same—but in practice, they probably are not. In fact, because the message has to be encoded and decoded (that is, placed in a form that can be transmitted and later reconverted), there is the possibility of additional distortions of the message intended.

In the process of communication we face the threat of noise—a disturbance of some kind which would interfere with getting our message across. Our research scientists are working to control noise along the channel. We, the issuers of messages, must strive to control noise in our phase of the work—that is, in the message itself.

QUESTIONS

1. In general, what is the aim of *communication?*
2. What are the shortcomings in Aristotle's model of communication which have been imposed by the passage of time?

3. What can be done to remove these shortcomings in Aristotle's model of communication?

4. Distinguish between the two fields, *communication* and *communications*.

5. What is to be observed about Aristotle's handling of the *means* of conveying a message?

6. What is involved in the concept of *two messages* being present in a given communication attempt?

7. What important element is missing from the model depicting technology-oriented communications?

8. What are the requirements of a model capable of showing the full process of communication?

9. In the field of communications technology, what is meant by *noise?*

10. Under the technology-oriented model, at what points is the process supposedly vulnerable to noise?

11. How is the responsibility for noise shared, under the model depicting the full process of communication?

12. Is the problem of noise expanded or contracted, in general, when the *methodless* and *messageless* models are fitted together?

2

· ·

BUSINESS
COMMUNICATION
THEORY

So far we have made an informal inquiry into the essentials of general communication theory. The resulting composite model, including both the message and the means of transmitting it, can be applied to any communication process. All that is ever needed is a slight adjustment of the "channel" concept to fit the given situation. For example, in open television we must have audiovisual equipment (a transmitting device) capable of picking up and broadcasting the message (scene and sound); and at another point, we must have another piece of equipment (a receiving set) to re-create a facsimile of that message. In closed-circuit television, we use the same basic principle, but carry the message impulses to their destination by means of a special cable. In oral communication we make audible sounds, and the listener extracts our message from these sounds. And, when we write, we place our message on paper and forward it to a reader, who picks up the message by eye.

TYPES OF BUSINESS COMMUNICATION
· ·

In a broad sense, we could communicate in business by any of the available methods. But, because some of the methods are impractical or difficult to use, and others are as yet too expensive, we still find that speech and writing are our mainstays. By word of mouth—either in person or by telephone—we customarily issue commands and instructions to our subordinates, render minor reports to superiors, and give explanations to customers. We have meetings and conferences at which all sorts of business is discussed. By written word we send letters to suppliers, customers, and clients. We send commands by memorandum to those below us in the organization chart; we send reports, informal and formal, to those above us.

Oral communication has certain on-the-spot advantages over written documents. For one thing, we are often in the presence of the listener. We can use gestures and facial expressions to good advantage. In any event, we can use voice inflections to help get our message across. For another thing, we can use repetition whenever we detect that our listener is not extracting the message we intend. Also, we are in a genuine conversation with our listener—that is, we can adapt our message to his on-the-spot responses, questions, objections, or suggestions. The chief disadvantage in oral communication is that the message is not "on record." This lack leads to a gradual deterioration of the message extracted by our listener, without the possibility of reinforcement through exact repetition at a later time (as a written document would provide). It also leads to possible disagreement between the speaker and the listener, later on, as to what was really said.

On the other hand, something which we write, while it offers the advantage of permanency, is relatively limited as regards dimensions for clarity. For this reason we must do our best at the outset to be accurate, clear, and complete. We do not have a way of bolstering the reader if he becomes puzzled. Repeating the message in different ways is not satisfactory, because if the reader understands it the first time, he will probably consider the rest as a waste of his time. As our reader is likely to be at a distant point, he is in a poor position to question us as to our meaning, if he should wish to. For these reasons, clear thinking, good planning, correct use of words, proper spelling, sensible punctuation, acceptable sentence formations, and the like must be put into our writing efforts. Probably because many persons cannot effectively handle all of these ingredients at one time, we find the business world appealing for better training toward developing the important talent of writing.

THE STRUCTURE OF BUSINESS COMMUNICATION

In our study of business communication, we need to make a point clear from the very beginning. Our emphasis is on the conduct of business by means of communication—specifically, written communication. While this communication function will operate according to the general concepts we have already seen, we are primarily *doing business* with our reader. Therefore, whatever would be good business practice for us apart from our written document must still be observed. We use a written communication to help us get a job done. The written material is not an end in itself; it should not even attract special attention to itself. In short, it is merely our means to an end in a given situation.

Before trying to turn out letters and reports, we shall first look into the structure of business communication. We shall see how it parallels the structure of general communication, and what incidental differences are to be found. Also, we shall make a first acquaintanceship with the terms and concepts of the business communication process.

THE MESSAGE INTENDED

As in general communication theory, business communication theory begins with a source (the writer). The writer has a message which he intends to send to the destination (the reader). This message concerns a business relationship between the writer and the reader. It has two basic aspects—a program (working outline) and the matter of finesse.

By way of definition, we shall consider a *program* to be a list of topics and subtopics, arranged in a sequence attuned to the psychological needs of the reader, to guide the writer in composing his message. Basically, it is the same concept as an outline, except that in an outline the sequence may be suited to the needs of the writer only. Once either a program or an outline has been worked out, however, the writer follows it, step by step.

In business writing, we must size up both the situation and our reader, and prepare a program that will arrange the parts of our message in a sequence acceptable to our reader. We shall go into the matter of programming thoroughly when we take up specific business writing situations.

If we can visualize the program of a business communication as being the "what," we can regard the matter of finesse as being the "how." By *finesse* we mean the adroitness, flavor, persuasiveness, polish, semantics, strategy, and subtlety which we can apply in transforming our program into a full-blown composition. By knowing the potentialities of finesse, therefore, we are in a position to make use of the proper "touch" when we compose a written message.

Finesse is decidedly an art or sense of direction; it defies a precise definition; it is learned chiefly through practice and experience. In attempts to explain the matter to beginners, some analysts have subdivided it into many narrow components. For our purposes, however, it will be enough to partition finesse into three segments only: diplomacy, service attitude, and positiveness.

Diplomacy is that quality of written expression which shows proper respect both for the reader and for ourselves. On its active side, it includes the courtesies of "please" and "thank you" when they are the reader's due, and, in general the trying to "get along" on a businesslike basis with our reader. On its passive side, it is the softening of a blow, steering clear of adverse criticism, abstaining from accusations and scoldings, and shunning a direct dispute with the reader. We must remember that business thrives on goodwill, which in turn depends on good personal relationships.

Service attitude, often called the "you" attitude, is that quality of written expression which emphasizes values of interest to our reader. By its use we slant our message so that it will win his approval. Moreover, if our message contains a request, we work in some motivation—that is, we persuade or induce him to act. And, if the desired action can be helped along by detailed instructions and/or physical aids, we include them, too. While *we* stand to gain by the reader's acceptance of our message, we are careful not to let this fact peek through our words. We are performing as salesmen, in effect, when we apply the service ("to you") attitude.

Positiveness is that quality of written expression which stresses the good, favorable, or pleasant side of a situation. By its use we strive to make the flavor of our communication agreeable to the reader. We must be on guard, therefore, to recognize things which would not be of a satisfying flavor to him. We must try to express ourselves on such matters in a way that will play up whatever brightness can be found—

or at least neutralize every bit of the gloominess. In so doing, we tend to win psychological approval from our reader. He feels a minimum of uneasiness or discouragement, if any, as he extracts our message.

All in all, our intended message must be planned carefully before it is written. By constructing an appropriate program, we order our thoughts in a sequence which has the best receptive flow to our reader in the given situation. By knowing the elements of finesse, we control the phrasing of our message so that it will be polite, convincing, and agreeable to our reader.

THE ENCODING STEP

In written business communication, the step that parallels "encoding" in general communication theory is the placing of our message into words. This step may be accomplished either by writing a draft or by dictating the intended message to a stenographer or to some kind of recording device. In any event, our message should follow the selected program and be guided by the matter of finesse. Also, our attention must be directed toward two new matters which enter the business communication process at this point. These are:

1. A level of writing that can be absorbed easily by our intended reader.
2. The mechanics of language.

We should strive for a level of writing that is simple and clear, that can be decoded effortlessly by the reader. We must avoid such bad habits as using overly technical words, or jargon; falling back on long, stilted words or phrases we may have heard used; or wandering into involved, unclear sentence structures.

If we know our reader very well, we can generally fit our writing to his tastes, special interests, knowledge in a particular field, and so on. Much of the time, however, we will be writing to someone we do not know, or to a varied audience. We might well compare our situation to that of the journalist, who knows his readers are "doctors, lawyers, merchants," housewives, students, ball players—who, in short, must write about many specialized matters without assuming anything but generalized knowledge in his readers. A good business writing style will similarly aim at standard, general usage, easily understandable to the great majority of possible readers.

Reasonable accuracy in handling the mechanics of language is also a matter that helps the reader extract our message. We are expected to write according to the generally accepted rules. If we do not abide by them, the reader may have difficulty in getting our message; and he may also get provoked or disgusted with us for being so careless.

The mechanics of language may be handily subdivided into five areas: spelling, punctuation, use of words, grammar, and sentence structure. Of these areas, spelling and punctuation are often the contribution of our typist. But, since we take responsibility ultimately when we sign a message, we should examine the final copy to be sure that these details are correct. If we let the message go out with misspellings, we run the risk of annoying the reader and creating an unfavorable impression of us and of our firm. As for punctuation, we must appreciate the work it is supposed to be doing for us. In oral communication, we do not have punctuation as such. We use voice inflections to indicate statements, questions, and exclamations; and we use pauses of various lengths to set off phrases, clauses, and sentences. In writing, we must rely on punctuation marks, each with its own purpose, to achieve proper reception by our reader.

The other areas of language remain our responsibility from beginning to end. We must select words which correctly encode the thoughts we are trying to communicate and which may easily be decoded by the reader. In addition, we must be careful to detect and avoid "stereotypes" —words or phrases which communicate well enough, but, because of being overworked, tend to be boring or repulsive to most readers. As for grammar, we must express our thoughts with verbs agreeing with their subjects and pronouns with their antecedents, with verbs in their proper moods, with correct idioms, and so on. In the matter of sentence structure, we must pay attention to such things as parallel construction and to the proper positioning of modifying words, phrases, and clauses.

THE TRANSMITTING STEP

Our message, once encoded, must be transmitted by some method. Each method of transmission has some bearing on the type and extent of the encoding that precedes it. As we have progressed so far, we have considered the composing of a message for our reader. Now, how do we get it to him? At this stage our message is probably in the form of a longhand draft, shorthand jottings in a stenographer's notebook, or grooves on a plastic tape.

A written communication (letter, report, newspaper, book, or the like) is different from the other types of communication. Here, the document itself—not an image of it, an electrical impulse, a dot-dash sound, or a blink of light—is presented to our reader. The functions of transmitter and receiver are therefore performed by the selfsame device; and the channel operates merely as a physical carrier. Little or no noise can be introduced by the channel in this type of communication process. Noise occurs only as distractions built into the message by ourselves (which we try to avoid) and those which surround our reader at destination (over which we seldom have any control).

Under these conditions, the preparation of the document—that is, our message in transmittable form—becomes our final consideration. The overall approach here is to select a form that lies within the tolerance limits of convention. In that way, we transmit our message without attracting our reader's attention to the form. If we were to use a strange or unconventional form, we would risk arousing questions or causing distractions in the reader's mind. In effect we would be introducing some noise along with our message. It is better to direct the reader's full attention to the all-important message, none of it to the form we happen to use.

Form is a combination of two elements, one objective, the other subjective. Objectively, form is what we see when we look at a written document—say, a letter. If we were to catch a glimpse of a letter at a

distance that is too far away to permit us to read the words, we could still recognize it to be a letter. We could see the black-on-white markings that make up the letterhead, date, inside address, salutation, paragraphs, complimentary close, and signature parts. If the form adhered to ordinary conventions, we would probably not give it a second thought. But what if it were in a strange arrangement, or off-balance, or crowded to the top of the sheet? The chances are that we would begin to wonder about it.

Even though form is in proper objective order, we must also consider its subjective variables. It would jar a male reader if we were to use the salutation, "Dear Madam." Yet, objectively, it is a salutation, is it not? A frequently confused combination is the addressing of a letter to a business firm but using the salutation, "Dear Sir." That also is a salutation, is it not? The measure, by subjective standards, is that our form not only look authentic, but that it make sense to the intended reader. Otherwise, a form of noise enters into the communication process to distract him.

A MODEL FOR BUSINESS COMMUNICATION

Having examined the elements which comprise a business communication, we may now prepare a specific model to depict it. Such a model would be as follows.

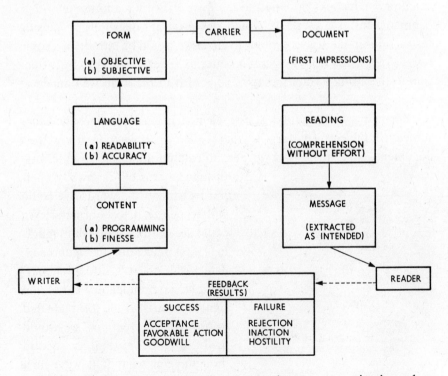

We can see from this illustration that business communication takes shape in an upward movement. First, we have a message in mind to transmit to our reader. We program our message according to the psychological needs of our reader in the given situation, and we alert ourselves to the matters of finesse. Next, we move up to the composing stage—draft or dictation—where we express our message in readable and accurate language. Finally, we place our composition in the form of a specific document (say, a letter) which is transported to our reader.

As far as the reader is concerned, his receiving of our message proceeds in the reverse order—a downward movement.

At first he is confronted with objective form—the envelope and the document he removes from it. As he begins to read, he becomes aware of subjective form. These details either make for favorable first impressions or fail in the attempt.

After passing the salutation, the reader begins on our encoded message. If it is written in conformity to the recognized rules of language and at a level suitable for him, our reader will be able to proceed effortlessly.

And, because the flow of thought was programmed, with his psychological needs in mind, our message should unfold to him with smoothness.

Also, because we applied the various aspects of finesse as we wrote, the reader should find our message cordial, convincing, motivating, and acceptable.

At the bottom of our business communication model is shown an additional feature, "feedback." By feedback, we mean an indication, direct or indirect, of how effective our message has been. A direct feedback is rarely experienced, since by that we would understand a return message from our reader in which he would comment favorably on the message itself. An indirect feedback is more likely to occur, although even it might be a long time coming or be somewhat less than conclusive.

Generally speaking, however, we tend to regard our message as a success if it results in a favorable response by the reader. If the message seems to produce whatever results were desired—for example, if the reader acts favorably on a request we have sent him—we consider that we have succeeded. In some cases, however, our goodwill may have suffered; and we could be blissfully unaware of it until much later. (Perhaps the reader was unfavorably impressed, but not deterred from practicing his finesse and "you attitude" on us!)

On the other hand, if we receive objections from the reader or do not get the action requested of him, we can classify our letter as failing in its mission. Even more of a failure would be a letter which caused the reader to take some hostile action against us. After all, good business requires constant attention to goodwill. Customer goodwill, especially, leads to more sales; and increased sales mean more profits.

SUMMARY

Business communication theory is basically the same as general communication theory. The incidental differences are as follows:

(1) The message must appeal to goodwill. Thus, our planning must include a program (outline) geared to our reader's psychological needs and must be graced with finesse.

(2) Only a partial encoding is needed—from thoughts to a composition. But we must pay attention to effortless reading as well as the mechanics of language.

(3) The form of the document (such as a letter) should be conventional and sensible, so that it will not take any of our reader's attention away from our message.

(4) The transmitter and receiver are identical. They are our finished document (letter or report), which is simply transported to our reader.

On the sending end, we perform our task in the order of steps just enumerated. At destination, our reader extracts the message by proceeding in the reverse order. Sooner or later, through our reader's words or behavior, we can expect to learn something about the success or failure of our message. While part of our purpose is always to promote goodwill, feedback on goodwill is usually slow in coming.

QUESTIONS

1. What types of thought transferal are the mainstays of business communication?
2. What are the chief advantages of oral communication over the written variety?
3. State the chief disadvantage of oral communication.
4. Why, despite all the information available on how to handle written communication, does the business world continue to appeal for more training in this area?
5. What is the proper role of business communication?
6. Give the two major components of an intended message.
7. In general, what is a writing *outline?*
8. What would be a suitable explanation of the term *program?*
9. Explain what is meant by *finesse.* What are its components?
10. Define:
    (a) Diplomacy.
    (b) Service Attitude.
    (c) Positiveness.
11. What constitutes the *encoding* step in the case of written communications?
12. Identify two important matters which enter the business communication process at the encoding stage.
13. In what physical state is our message likely to be immediately after the encoding stage?
14. How does written communication differ from other varieties (telephone calls, television shows, radio broadcasts, etc.) at the transmitting step?
15. In written communication, what is the transmitting instrument and what is the receiving instrument?
16. In written communication, what is the likelihood of noise entering by means of the *channel?*
17. Without discussing details, state what is meant by *form* in written communication.

18. What is meant by *subjective form?*
19. What is the general production sequence used by the writer of a business communication? Does the reader follow this same sequence?
20. Discuss *feedback* and how it can signal the success or failure of a communication effort.

....

CHAPTER 3

THE WHAT
AND HOW OF
THE MESSAGE

Because we look upon written business communication as the transacting of business through writing, we see that it involves more than the mere act of communicating a message. Our business communication should do as much as we would do in person-to-person dealings with a customer, client, supplier, employee, or whoever else is concerned. Our aim should always be to cater to that person's goodwill and to win his acceptance of our message; at times, our aim may be higher still—that is, to get favorable action on a request we are making.

In preparing a written communication for delivery to our intended reader, we pass through three stages of development. The first stage is the planning of our message—the content of the communication. The second stage is the expressing of message in words—the language of the communication. The last stage is the preparation of the document—the physical substance or form of our communication—which can be sent to our intended reader, and from which he can read our words and extract our message.

THE MATTER OF PROGRAM

Let us turn our attention first to the planning stage of the communication. In all kinds of writing, we find it helpful to have a plan before we try to put our thoughts into words. Called an outline, such a plan contains the various points we intend to include. Also, it is arranged in a sequence which we should like to follow. Thus it serves to guide us as we write: to assure us of including all the points we set out to cover, and to keep us on the orderly track we selected for a satisfactory flow of thought.

In business communication, we make use of this same general concept—with one important variation. It is not enough for our business communication to follow an orderly flow of thought. We must make certain that the sequence we use will be virtually incapable of having an adverse impact on our reader. The writing guide we set up for ourselves to follow should not be based on "author's choice," as the traditional outline might be. Instead, to be effective, our guide should anticipate the psychological needs of our intended reader and be sequenced accordingly. Therefore, to recognize this difference, we shall call our business communication guide a program instead of an outline. Our definition of this term, *program,* is: a list of topics and subtopics to be covered in a business communication (e.g., letter or report), arranged in a sequence suited to the psychological needs of the intended reader, to guide the writer in the presentation of his message.

MANAGERIAL ASPECT

The matter of sequence suggests an important concept from a managerial standpoint—that is, the exercising of leadership. People generally, including the readers of our letters and reports, prefer to do things because they see the light rather than because they are bossed into action. Thus, by selecting the proper points to be discussed in a given situation and by placing them in a sequence to which the reader will be receptive, we are leading rather than pushing. The fact that the sequence is in tune with his psychological needs helps the reader to go along with the flow of ideas as we have put them in our letter or report. We have already made an important start on eliciting the kind of response we want.

IDEAL CONDITIONS

The cardinal rule concerning the formation of a program is that we should fit it precisely to the psychological needs of our reader. It follows, therefore, that the better we know the reader, the better chance we have of preparing a program that will fill his needs. If our reader is an associate, friend of long standing, or a client, for example, we probably know quite a bit about him. We are in a favorable position to cater to his likes, his moods, and his sensitivities; to include or exclude certain points, as would be best for him; and even to take certain liberties with him which might not be taken with anyone else. In short, we can do a specialized job in planning our com-

munication for this reader. As a matter of fact, not only our programming but our entire writing job becomes clear-cut. Our level of language, application of finesse, and all other subjective elements can be directed at a definite target. The matter of choice is simplified almost to a matter of certainty.

ORDINARY CONDITIONS

Because of the rise of the great manufacturing corporations, the far-flung chains of retail outlets, and the large department stores in modern times, we usually find that the ideal writing conditions just cited do not exist. Too often, we who must write business communications do not know much about our intended reader. At best, we know the person's name, sex, address, and his business relationship to us. In some cases, because we are answering a letter he sent to us, we might have a clue to his mood or temperament. But in general, our knowledge of him is hazy at best; and writing the best possible communication to him is a decided challenge.

What can we do about programming a business communication under these conditions? Our solution lies in the recognition of a safe approach—one which is based on a standard sequence of points, but adjusted in keeping with what shreds of information we are able to find out about our intended reader. It is an adaptation of the mass communication concept to a specific individual. It is useful for writing both letters and reports. For convenience of discussion, however, we shall confine our attention at this point to the topic of business letters.

In our efforts to select a safe approach, our first step is to recognize that all business letters can be divided logically into two varieties. The first variety is the *single-purpose* letter, which is simply a message of goodwill. The other is the *multipurpose* letter, which also caters to goodwill but which has at least one additional purpose for being written. Functionally, however, there are three distinct types to be found within the multipurpose variety: one that asks our reader to fulfill a request; one that conveys a pleasant message; and one that delivers a not-so-pleasant message. Most of our business letters will be representative of the multipurpose types. Some situations will even be representative of a combination of these types—for example, a letter in which we may have to give both good news and bad news in connection with the same business transaction.

For discussion purposes, we cannot do much with the terms single-purpose and multipurpose. They are too vague for us to use in a comparative analysis. Our examination of basic types of business letters will therefore center on a four-way classification: simple goodwill letters, request letters, good-news letters, and bad-news letters.

Goodwill

Simple goodwill letters can be summed up as messages we write over and above the ordinary letters required in business. As alert businessmen, we can take advantage of certain occasions and events to drop a friendly, thoughtful letter to someone with whom we should like to form a better business relationship. Such letters include public relations messages of various kinds—such as letters of appreciation for favors performed or, seasonally, for business transacted with us. They include congratulations on some happy event—such as an appointment, promotion, election victory, marriage, birth of a child, and graduation from school or college. They also include letters of condolence or sympathy in the event of a serious illness, death in the family, rampage of nature, or other misfortune befalling someone we know.

The advantage we can gain by sending out such letters is great. Although these letters could be written on a strictly personal basis, we choose to prepare them on our company letterhead so that the effect created will be of goodwill value in our business. There is no question that our reader will be impressed; the fact is, most people tend to feel that they have never received enough letters of this variety. Our competition will likely be slim; human inertia will whittle down the minority who will even have the inspiration to write. Thus, our letter will likely be all the more appreciated and our goodwill relationship strengthened. Moreover, our reader will be inclined to save this kind of letter. If he

does, it will have renewal value every time he comes across it in the future.

In preparing a simple goodwill letter, we must bear in mind that a good performance is necessary. If we cannot write a suitable letter for the situation at hand, we run a serious risk of defeating our intended purpose.

We might do better to send an appropriate greeting card. At least, we would be showing thoughtfulness without the danger of creating ill will. But no card can do the job of an individually and well-prepared letter typed on our own company stationery.

If we are to do a good job in composing a simple goodwill letter, we should be aware of three necessary characteristics of such letters. The first of these is good timing. Accordingly, we must not let too long a time elapse between a person's accomplishment and our sending him a congratulatory letter regarding it. Otherwise, the effectiveness of our letter might drop off drastically. The same is true of a letter of condolence or sympathy we should like to send to someone who has had a bereavement or some other unfortunate experience. Our letters of appreciation for special favors should be prompt also—preferably right after the receipt of such favors—if they are to do their best job for us. If we make use of public relations letters containing seasonal themes, we should make sure that our mailing schedule is in agreement with those themes. For example, we should not come out with a Christmas theme in the summer—or with a Thanksgiving theme at Christmas.

The second characteristic of a simple goodwill letter is sincerity. We should be sure to keep the tone of our letter compatible with the occasion or the overall theme. For example, our letter of congratulations will ring true if it is enthusiastically presented. It would be a dud if it were to be written in drab tones, or would give our reader the slightest hint that we could be envious of his achievement. Similarly, when we send a sympathy letter, we should write with the dignity and compassion that befits the occasion—not in some flippant or offhand manner. If we keep in mind exactly what we are trying to do, and follow that through logically, we can turn out a letter which will be prized by our reader. This principle applies to all varieties of simple goodwill letters.

The third important consideration is unity—that is, oneness. It means that our simple goodwill letter should be just that—a goodwill gesture, nothing else. In such a letter, we will not directly try to transact any business or even bring our reader up to date on ourselves. We will thank him, or congratulate him, or sympathize with him, perhaps add a few kind words to cement the goodwill, and that is all. We will not try to match his success with ours, ask favors, collect money, sell our product or services, file a claim, or seek employment. Any attempts of this kind would most certainly spoil the goodwill effect our letter was intended to create. We must leave such topics, no matter how timely they may be, to a separate letter.

Request

Request letters (good will plus a request) may be either letters we originate or letters we send in answer to letters received. Examples of originating letters are favor-requests, inquiries, orders of goods or services, claims and complaints, promotions of goods and services, collection appeals, and job applications. Requests of the answering type arise because someone who wrote to us stated a request of his own in an unclear or unsatisfactory manner. For example, we might receive an order letter in which some portion of the description material is unclear or missing. Or, a claim-type letter does not tell us what its writer really wants us to do. Or, a credit applicant omits financial data or names of references—details we wish to have before deciding on his request. In such instances, we can but write back with a request of our own, seeking the information needed.

Because request letters are multipurpose letters, we can generally expect that their construction will be more complex than those of the simple goodwill variety. Our request letter must, of course, cater to goodwill—but it must also contain a minimum number of parts aimed at the fulfillment of our request. The sequence of these parts is not particularly important, but their inclusion in our letter is vital. Failure of our request letter is almost certain if we omit any of these parts. On the other hand, we cannot guarantee ourselves success merely by including these points in our letter. After all, many other factors—timing, appearance, level of language, finesse, and so on—have their bearing on the success or failure of a letter.

One very important ingredient of a successful request letter is a definite request. We might think that this point would be automatic. Yet, if it were, we should never have to write for additional information in connection with an order letter or with any other kind of request we receive. The fact of the matter is that we do have to write for clarification—and more often than just once in a while. With some people it is forgetfulness; with others, it is carelessness; and with some, it is timidity—a hesitancy to come right out with what they want us to do. As letter writers, therefore, how can we expect a reader to fulfill our request if he does not know what we really want? It is our duty to see that this point is made clear.

Another important point to be included in a request letter is ample motivation. This element means providing our reader with a reason or reasons, in terms of his own self-interest, for complying with our request. It has its basis in the psychological fact that he is more concerned with his problems than he is with ours. A reader is usually not moved by sympathy in a business situation. Thus, he must be "sold" on the value of doing what is asked of him; and it is our job as petitioners to do the necessary persuading. Of course, not all situations require us to apply motivation with equal vigor. Some letter situations are virtually self-motivating—for example, orders for merchandise and inquiries about one's product. Some requests call for a nominal amount of motivation, such as the promise of appreciation (which should appeal to our reader as an opportunity for strengthening goodwill). Other requests, however, call for much stronger motivation than the mere promise of our appreciation. We might have to find something of direct benefit to our reader to use as leverage. Depending upon the circumstances, therefore, we can win his approval by variously promising him publicity, secrecy, reciprocity, reimbursement, social status, comfort, peace of mind, health, security, and so on.

The third basic requirement of a request letter is ample assistance. Like motivation, the amount of assistance needed will depend on the situation involved. But it stands to reason that, if we ask our reader to do something for us and provide him with sufficient motivation to make him inclined to do it, we should not leave—or place—roadblocks in his way.

In preparing request letters we should look for ways in which we can help our reader help us. The concept of ample assistance implies that whatever help a given situation calls for should be given. If it is sensible to do so, we could even provide more than the bare minimum that seems to be indicated.

Some situations, of course, do not require that we do anything special. We may have made action sufficiently easy by giving a clear, definite statement of our request and providing the necessary motivation to our reader. In fact, there might not be anything else appropriate for us to do. Other situations could require us to include our telephone number for our reader's convenience, or to provide an address for forwarding a package, and so on—details which can be given in the phrasing of the letter. Still other situations might call for something of a physical nature—for example, an order blank and a return envelope in the case of a sales letter. Our rule for ample assistance is therefore flexible: we should do whatever is necessary to make the desired action easy.

Good–News

Good-news letters (goodwill plus a pleasant message) are frequently letters we write in response to someone's request; but sometimes they are notifications originating with us. In such letters, we must not only include the necessary points, but we must also arrange the points in a sequence that is in tune with the psychological needs of our reader. What, then, are these basic points and their preferred sequence?

Experience shows that people are generally in a hurry to get things over and done with. They do not like unnecessary explanations or beating around the bush. They do not like to have the pleasure taken out of a piece of good news by some sermonizing or moralizing on the part of the informant. Once they have heard the good news, they usually do not want to be bothered with unnecessary explanations—they already have what they were interested in getting.

From these behavioral observations, we can establish a basic framework for a good-news letter. This letter should come out early with the notification of good news and follow with a minimum amount of explanation, if indeed any at all is needed. If we sense that some explanation is desired by our reader, or some instruction, or some helpful suggestion beyond his actual request, we should convey it to him. But it should come after his real request has been fulfilled. Goodwill is taken care of to a major extent by the very fact of our giving the good news. It can be enhanced, however, by helpful "extras" and by means of a courteous ending to our letter.

Bad–News

Bad-news letters (goodwill plus an unpleasant message) also may be either answers or original notifications. Just as with good-news letters, we must adhere to a definite sequence for the sake of the psychological impact on our reader. But here the points to be included and their sequence are different. We need to give our reader a patient explanation, a delayed notification of the bad news, and some effective words of encouragement—in that order of presentation.

The reasoning behind this approach is as follows: If we were to announce the bad news early in the letter, our reader would have his answer—definitely. Whatever we might say thereafter would not change that answer. Our reader, therefore, would tend to close his mind to our attempts to reason with him. He might not even bother to read our explanations; or, he might look upon them as excuses and read them with hostility. Thus, our explanations, instead of being persuasive, would become targets for him to attack and destroy. On the other hand, by giving our explanations first and discussing the issues with our reader, we can apply persuasion while he still has an open and reasonable mind.

The process of giving a convincing explanation before announcing the bad news helps us soften the impact on our reader. Yet, we must realize that no matter how gentle that process is, our reader will feel somewhat let down by the bad news. To close our letter at this point would not be in the best interests of goodwill. We should try to start our reader on an upward or rebounding psychological curve before we close our letter. To this end, it is usually possible for us to make some kind of helpful suggestion—such as a different source of information, a remedy, an alternate plan, or a lead to a source of supply. At least, we can offer to help him in some other way or at some other time—to show that the bad news is limited to the subject of this letter and is not indicative of any lack of friendship toward him.

THE COMMON DENOMINATOR

The basic requirements of the four distinct kinds of business letters are still not to be considered as our programs or working outlines needed for the task of writing. Development of such programs must take into account the incidentals of the situation at hand. We shall work out such specialized programs when we discuss letter-writing situations in later chapters of this book.

Despite the identifying characteristics of each of the four kinds of business letters, there is one feature that is common to them all. This is the aspect of goodwill. We see it as the whole embodiment of the single-purpose (simple goodwill) letter, and as an ever-present ingredient of the various multipurpose letters. A request letter is strengthened by our catering to our reader's goodwill; it is virtually ruined by our incurring his ill will. A good-news letter has a mild, automatic likelihood of goodwill built into it, but very often we can help it along by exercising a little constructive effort. A bad-news letter, as a result of its unpleasant message, tends toward a lowering of goodwill; it is up to us to change the direction of our reader's feelings by putting in something that promotes goodwill.

Our aim in every letter should be to create, enhance, preserve, or rebuild goodwill, whichever is the challenge. In dealing with someone for the first time, we try to create goodwill. Later on, in writing to this person, we try to enhance goodwill or at least preserve the high degree of goodwill that has come to exist. Once in a while, because goodwill may have suffered unavoidably, our job is to renew or rebuild goodwill. But never in a properly executed business letter should we consciously destroy goodwill.

The following illustrations show the psychological reactions we should strive for in connection with the various possibilities of catering to our reader's goodwill.

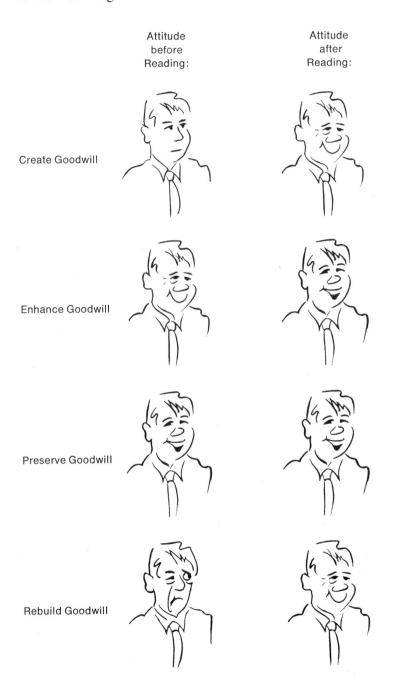

Attitude before Reading: Attitude after Reading:

Create Goodwill

Enhance Goodwill

Preserve Goodwill

Rebuild Goodwill

Our aim should always be that our reader will like us, after reading our letter, as much as or better than he did at the moment he picked up our letter.

THE MATTER OF FINESSE

As we have noted earlier, we exercise leadership in eliciting a favorable response from the reader when we include the proper points and sequence in our letter. By catering to his psychological needs, we reduce his resistance and enhance our opportunity to be persuasive. In a simple manner of speaking, the devising of a program is planning *what* to do; the matter of finesse is *how* we will do it.

Finesse is the final touch, the polish, the art of words we apply to make our message agreeable, persuasive, and acceptable to our reader. It is the lubricant, as it were, which makes our communication machinery run smoothly. Finesse has its roots in our basic attitudes toward people and life in general, and toward our intended reader here and now. It calls for the quality of empathy—that is, our ability to see the situation as our reader will see it. We must sense his conscious and unconscious needs, and phrase our thoughts in harmony with all that is involved. We want to be sure that our statements cannot be misconstrued by our reader.

Admittedly, finesse takes form during encoding—that is, the actual putting of our thoughts into words. But since we want to turn out letters in a minimum amount of time, without having to rewrite them, we must consider finesse at the planning stage. We should know the components of finesse, understand them well, and be able to anticipate which ones are likely to be most important in a given letter situation. We should be fully prepared, before writing or dictating, to add "plus" values of finesse wherever they will be needed and to steer clear of any pitfalls in the area of expression which are waiting to trap us.

Regardless of the situation, the effectiveness of a business letter depends on its finesse, which consists of three somewhat intangible qualities known as diplomacy, service attitude, and positiveness. If we can develop an appreciation of these qualities and master them, we will be well on our way to becoming talented letter writers. It is by reason of their inability to handle these qualities that many persons find themselves limited to mediocrity as business writers.

Although these three qualities are extremely elusive and difficult to pin down by precise definition, the following discussion will be helpful in understanding them.

DIPLOMACY

Our writing is diplomatic when it portrays our good manners and

STICK 'EM UP !

... PLEASE ?

self-respect. It is the kind of writing that is guided by such phrases as "please" and "thank you," and by the overall spirit of politeness. Diplomacy is something we practice to make our message agreeable. It does its best job for us when it is smooth, natural, and subtle—not ostentatious of insincere.

We violate the quality of diplomacy when our writing suggests a lack of social awareness on our part. In such a case, our writing may fall into one or more of the following classifications: (1) discourteous, (2) scolding, (3) unnecessarily apologetic, (4) arbitrary, (5) tactless, (6) condescending, (7) insincere.

The following situations will help illustrate how we might observe diplomacy instead of being trapped into violating it:

1. *Discourteous or Courteous?* A customer ordered and received prompt service from our company. Now, we find that he has not kept up his installments although he has been billed regularly. In a collection letter to him, we could be blunt and challenge his good faith. But, for diplomacy, we should cite our company's excellent service to him, and put the question to him persuasively:

   ```
   Won't you please complete the bargain by meeting your
   monthly installment?
   ```

2. *Scolding or Businesslike?* In the foregoing situation, it is also

necessary that we resist a tendency to pout and scold—that is, to tell the customer that we cannot understand why, after all we have done for him, he has kept us waiting. We should politely ask him for cooperation.

```
Won't you please complete the bargain by meeting your
monthly installments?
```

3. *Overly Apologetic or Businesslike?* On the other hand, in trying to be diplomatic, we should not get things so turned about that it appears that we are in the wrong. Thus, a collection appeal beginning with, "We don't want to bother you, but . . ." will not keep the issue in its proper perspective. It is much better to be direct, but polite.

```
We haven't received any payments on your account, however,
for over three months. May we have your prompt attention
to this matter, please?
```

4. *Arbitrary or Reasonable?* A customer has requested a quantity discount. Our company policy does not permit discounts—we have one price to all customers. But such an explanation is lame and arbitrary from our customer's viewpoint. After all, if we set a policy, we can change it. Hence, we had better say something that is true, but less arbitrary.

```
As a retailer we are unable to adjust the price--but, we
stand behind our merchandise with a 90-day service
warranty.
```

5. *Tactless or Tactful?* A customer has written that an article he purchased from us is defective. It would be tactless for us to answer him with such phraseology as "which you claim is defective," "which you say is . . . ," "which you report to be . . . ," etc. These constructions cast aspersions on his honesty and imply that we do not admit that there really is any defect. If the article must be referred to, we should use a description that is not controversial.

```
. . . the Elica 35 camera which was returned.
```

6. *Condescending or Gracious?* When granting a concession, we should be careful that our wording is literally correct. It is condescending to seem to be granting something that is already within our reader's area of competence, such as "We will allow you to buy . . . ," ". . . allow you to pay . . . ," etc. We should use a friendly, businesslike approach.

> We can change the terms for you during this emergency.
> May we suggest that you pay only half the amount now and
> the remainder in monthly installments?

7. *Insincere or Sincere?* There is also the possibility that in trying not to offend we may overcompensate, and thus appear to be applying "soft soap." Phrases such as "more than glad," "only too happy," and "wonderful customer" are representative of this fault. A sincere, straightforward statement of fact is usually sufficient.

> We are granting you a 30-day extension of time.

SERVICE ATTITUDE

Our writing has service attitude when it is slanted toward our reader —conveying the impression of "service to you," "benefit to you," "solution to your problem," and so on. We make use of service attitude to win the approval of our reader. While we as businessmen stand to gain by our reader's acceptance of our message, we must earn that acceptance. To be successful we must subtly play up the values which are of importance and interest to him—and play down those which concern us. On the other hand, we violate service attitude when (1) our writing emphasizes our desires rather than those of our reader and (2) we fall short of rendering the full amount of assistance needed by our reader.

There are two tests (one objective, the other subjective) which we can use to measure service attitude. The objective test is easy to apply, but it is a surface measure and is not particularly reliable. It consists of checking for a favorable balance of "you" constructions as against "we" and "I" constructions. In many instances, such an emphasis coexists with real (or subjective) service attitude. The subjective test is applied by our playing the role of intended reader. Thus, we read our own letter as the recipient might read it. We try to judge whether it has a sufficient motivating spirit to promote interest, acceptance, and (if applicable) ease of response or compliance. Is it as helpful as possible—in word, deed, and attitude? If anything, we should have tried to do more than the minimum expected, because these extra signs of sincerity and desire do help motivate our reader.

The following situations will help illustrate how we might achieve service attitude by slanting our message toward our reader:

1. *Our Desires or Yours?* A woman customer from out of town has requested an exchange of a defective ceramic vase. It is apparent that the customer has given the article rough handling. However, the value involved is low; and this customer does make regular purchases in our store. We realize that a regular customer is a valuable asset, and we certainly want this woman to continue as a regular customer. We have decided, therefore, to make the exchange for her. Now—we should do so without exposing our line of reasoning. Since we have already made our decision, we should settle down to the task of telling her the good news.

   ```
   You will receive a new vase immediately . . . [And, if
   necessary, we might go on to rebuild her good will toward us] . . .
   because you are entitled to full value, always, at
   Milton's.
   ```

   Our Desires or Yours? A collection letter is to be written to each of our delinquent customers. The fact is that their slow-pay performance has begun to hurt our cash position, and our own creditors have begun to press for payment. But we should be unwise to use this fact as a collection appeal. Broadcasting the word on our tight financial position might cause our own creditors to put additional pressure on us. It might induce some of our delinquents to put off payment longer than ever. And, unfortunately, our problems are of so little concern to others that the approach of need would not serve to collect an appreciable amount of money. What we should apply is some motivation—a reason why it is good for the delinquent customer to clear up his overdue balance. So, we can use service attitude by helping him see the light.

```
Remember--a good credit rating is simple to hold, but hard
to regain. Protect your good credit now by sending your
check today.
```

2. *Hindrance or Help?* A customer has written our company a letter in which he has ordered some merchandise. One item is a pullover sport shirt which comes in three colors: blue, green, and tan. The customer has neglected to specify his color preference. Our job is to acknowledge his order and request clarification of his choice of color. It would be an easy matter for us to ask that he write us a letter; but it would not be a wise course to take. After all, we do want to complete the sale and should have enough sense to go after it. Moreover, writing a letter will not have a great amount of appeal to our customer, who has already erred in his first letter. For the sake of proper service attitude, therefore, we should enclose an easy-to-use form on which the customer can check off his color preference, and include a reply envelope for the return trip. Our wording could go something like this.

```
Just check your choice of color on the enclosed card,
slip it into the postage-paid envelope, and mail. Your
shirt will be on its way to you the same day we receive
your card.
```

POSITIVENESS

Our writing has positiveness when it is cheerful, direct, and specific —ever striving to treat of things that will be pleasing to our reader. Positiveness is a flavor which, like diplomacy, we use to make our message agreeable. Thus, we should play up pleasant values whenever the possibility exists. In good-news letters, we have the opportunity ready made.

" YOU MAY HAVE ANY ONE OF
SEVERAL LAKE - FRONT LOCATIONS ... "

Even though a given situation may be gloomy (as in a bad-news letter, a claim letter, an adjustment letter, or a collection letter), our letter need not be negative. If something unpleasant must be referred to, we should minimize it as much as possible (mention it in neutral terms, take the sting out of it, remove the bitter taste, soften the blow).

We violate the quality of positiveness when our writing (1) introduces an unpleasant thought, (2) elicits a contrary response from our reader, (3) is weak when strength is expected, (4) deals with "minus" values instead of readily available "plus" values, (5) uses double negatives.

The following situations will help illustrate how we can make a proper choice between positiveness and negativeness:

1. *Unpleasant or Pleasant?* We are members of an accounting firm. An audit report mailed to an out-of-town client proved to be incomplete. Our client had to postpone an important meeting while our staff prepared a corrected report. We are now ready to submit it to him; and to avoid any additional delay or inconvenience, we will send it air mail. Suppose that we are also sending him an advance notification. To play up the positive values and to steer clear of the original unpleasantness, we should write:

   ```
   The new report is being sent to you by air mail so that
   you may be assured of having it on Friday.
   ```

   Unpleasant or Pleasant? Our company engineers have developed an alarm clock that we guarantee to awaken a sound sleeper without startling him. This is all well and good; but if we were to talk about "startle" in a sales letter, we might cause our reader to develop an unfavorable attitude toward *all* alarm clocks. Accordingly, we should play up only the positive or pleasant thing to be experienced.

```
At the time you set, your clock will put in a gentle
first call. Five minutes later, if need be, it will try
again--a little higher up the scale.
```

2. *Disagreeable or Agreeable?* The expert salesman knows that he can get his prospect warmed up by telling him bits of humor and things he is sure to agree with—never things with which he will disagree. Thus, an atmosphere conducive to putting across the main point is created and receptive thought channels are opened. The same principle holds for sales letters. Yet some writers succeed only in triggering a hostile response from their reader when they try to begin with what they consider to be a clever, attention-getting statement. (Examples: "You don't want to waste money when you paint your house." "Would you deliberately overdraw your checking account?" "Do you want to make a profit in your business?") A statement just does not have positiveness if it suggests something undesirable to the reader, or appears to be foolish or ridiculous. Positive versions will either gain affirmative response or cause the reader to desire more information.

```
You want your money's worth when you paint your house.

One moment, please--before you sign that check!

Here's a way to boost your profits--and do it on your
present investment.
```

3. *Weak or Strong?* Suppose we are writing a sales letter for one of our company's products. After showing our reader how this product fills one or more of his particular needs, we reach the "action" stage. Although our call for action could in theory be phrased a number of ways, it is probably best psychologically that we use an appropriate command. In a sales situation, despite our service attitude, our reader knows what we are trying to do —and it always aims at separating him from some of his money. During our sales talk, he tends to build up defenses and re-

sistance. Hence, a weak action statement at a time when a strong, decisive statement is really expected becomes, relatively speaking, a form of negative. It shows a lack of confidence on our part. (Examples: "If you are interested in this equipment, we hope you will contact our regional office." "Why not come downtown and see this furniture for yourself?") Our reader will get the impression that we are withdrawing from the sales effort and leaving all initiative up to him. It is better that we retain the leadership position and state definitely what is to be done.

```
To get more information on this valuable equipment and on
what it can mean to you, send the postage-free card today!
```

```
See this stylish furniture in our downtown store--this
week, for sure!
```

4. *Unable or Able?* Practically every situation has its good side and its bad side. Some people tend to look at the gloomy side of the situation and thus construct their thoughts—and resultant messages—so as to stress negative values. Suppose that we were an agency for insurance. A prospective customer for life insurance has finally decided to take out a policy—and, of course, wants immediate service. The company we represent cannot issue the policy until he has passed a physical examination. If we must inform him of this fact in a letter, we should play up the positive value—what we *can* do.

```
We'll be able to issue your 20-year endowment policy just
as soon as the doctor's clearance comes through.
```

5. *Double Negative or Positive?* Some people believe that two negatives make a positive, and carry this belief into their thinking and writing. Perhaps they choose a double negative to hedge a statement or to achieve some diplomacy, but more than likely such people are not really aware of what they are doing. In any event, the danger lies in the fact that a negative does not absolutely do away with another negative; both are present for the reader to see. Such usage merely sets up a "straw man" and then tries to knock it down. It not only wastes words but tends to leave the reader with a feeling of misgiving.

There are several formations of double negatives. One is the grammatical form, which is the most obvious because of the presence of offsetting negatives in the literal sense ("An increase in gross sales is not unlikely."). Another is the partially obscured double negative, which combines a grammatical negative with a conceptual negative ("Don't hesitate to let us know."). Still another form is the obscured double negative, which uses a conceptual negative to offset one or more other conceptual negatives ("To avoid delay and inconvenience, . . ." "To spare you needless worry, . . ."). As a general rule, we should be on guard to detect and recast such constructions into a positive form in order to have the best possible effect on our reader.

```
An increase in gross sales may be expected.

Please let us hear from you.

To assure prompt delivery.

For your peace of mind, . . .
```

ANALYSIS OF FINESSE

In the foregoing sections, we kept the concepts of diplomacy, service attitude, and positiveness separated so that we could discuss the identifying characteristics of each. In an actual communication, these three qualities of finesse will exist in combination with each other.

As far as our overall message is concerned, our reader should have, at the close, a feeling of satisfaction and an attitude of goodwill toward us that is at least as good as he had at the beginning. It follows, therefore, that the various components of our message—that is, each sentence that we write—should be simultaneously in harmony with all three of the qualities of finesse. If we are out of tune with any or all of these qualities in a sentence, we are heading for some kind of disapproval from our reader.

We should realize, too, that the three components of finesse differ in importance. Diplomacy ranks as the most serious. If our letter is undiplomatic at any point, our reader is likely to become antagonized. His reaction will then be to resist rather than yield to our efforts to win his approval. His goodwill toward us will be diminished rather than being preserved or strengthened. If diplomacy is observed throughout our letter, we can consider that we have put our reader into a receptive frame of mind. Our next concern is to convince him that our message is the best one under the circumstances that exist. Here is where the service attitude assumes its importance. Our reader will more readily agree with what we say if we show him that there are values afforded to him. We should not merely let him guess at such values—nor should we stress the values of importance to us. Positiveness, important though it is, rates last among the components of finesse. We should strive to express our thoughts as pleasantly as possible, of course. But some situations require us to give out bad news or to refer to unhappy events, and many of these cannot be converted into pleasant messages. Thus, while positiveness is a quality which will brighten our letter, it may not be fully attainable. Unavoidable negatives accompanied by diplomacy and service attitude are usually acceptable to our reader.

It is one thing for us to realize that "something" is wrong with the finesse of a given sentence, and another thing to be able to identify the trouble area and make the necessary correction. Sometimes the sentence must be entirely done over; sometimes only a portion (sequence of words) need be revised; and at other times only one word replaced or deleted can be enough.

Sentences

In connection with sentences, a number of relationships may exist concerning finesse. As regards diplomacy, we might find that a given sentence has either plus values or minus values because our reader is involved with what is being said. But, we might also find that the sentence is neutral on this quality. Such would be the case when information, statistics, or other purely factual data are being given. Similarly, we might find that service attitude in a given sentence rates as a plus, minus, or neutral value. Thus, the inclusion of certain facts for the benefit of the reader (a part of programming) might give the letter some service attitude; but it might not give service attitude to the sentence in which it appears. The latter will depend on the manner of the wording. We need not build a plus value of service attitude into every sentence we write; it is frequently enough that we keep our own motives out.

When it comes to positiveness, we have a slightly different situation. There are two kinds of positives: the grammatical positive and the conceptual positive. In finesse, we are chiefly interested in conceptual positiveness—the stressing of the pleasant and the agreeable. But we do include the preference for forceful phrasing (when expected by our reader) and specific phrasing (when pleasant or helpful to our reader). Hence, the grammatical positive or negative gets into the picture with the conceptual positive or negative. Grammatically, however, there is no "neutral"; a sentence is either positive or negative. The possibility of a neutral value for positiveness, in the same sense that it exists for diplomacy and service attitude, seems to be nil. Even a negative sentence, in the conceptual sense, that has been neutralized by rephrasing would appear to be positive.

In some instances we may be justified in writing what might be regarded as a negative sentence in either the grammatical sense or in the conceptual sense. After all, there are times when we must turn down a request made by our reader. Although we may try to get by with an implied refusal, we must expect that many times our only recourse is to tell him the bad news. There are also times when we must initiate some bad news, as in a claim letter when we notify our reader that something adverse has happened. Because the use of a negative is forced upon us in such instances, we do not consider a grammatical negative harmful per se. We should do our best, though, not to bombard our reader with more negatives than are necessary to communicate the essential message. Going a step further, we may even choose to use a grammatical negative to accomplish another purpose—say, for example, diplomacy. A request can be made polite-sounding to our reader, as well as persuasive, when it is stated as a negative question: "Won't you help in this important study by answering the few, easy questions enclosed?"

We can see that we are confronted with a tricky decision: how should we judge a sentence in which a negative is forced upon us by the circumstances, or in which we place a grammatical negative to achieve a plus value in another area? The answer might be reasoned out as follows: Any negative should be viewed with suspicion. But if a given negative is necessary or is chosen in order to create a better overall effect, it may be regarded as "harmless." A harmless negative is not a violation of the concept of positiveness. Nor is it really positive; "neutral" would be the more suitable description.

Having determined that a given sentence may be regarded as having a good, poor, or neutral value in each of the three components of finesse, we see that it is mathematically possible for that sentence to appear in any one of 27 combinations. It might be good on all three; it might be poor on all three; it might be neutral on all three; it might be good on one, poor on another, and neutral on the third; and so on. Nineteen of these combinations would be more or less in violation of the niceties of finesse, as they would contain at least one poor value. The other eight combinations would be acceptable; being either entirely of good values or of a mixture of neutral and good values, they would not be in violation of finesse. These 27 combinations are shown in the following illustration (+ = good, 0 = neutral, — = poor).

DESIRABLE *(no violations)*

Diplomacy	+ + + + 0 0 0 0
Service Attitude	+ + 0 0 + + 0 0
Positiveness	+ 0 0 + + 0 + 0

UNDESIRABLE *(one or more violations)*

Diplomacy	+ + + + + 0 0 0 0 0 — — — — — — — — —
Service Attitude	+ — 0 — — + — 0 — — + 0 + 0 + — 0 — —
Positiveness	— + — 0 — — + — 0 — + + 0 0 — + — 0 —

The odds, we can be sure, are definitely against our leaving the matter of finesse to mere chance. We should anticipate the part finesse is to play in our letter and prepare for it when we are still in the planning stage.

It is axiomatic that if we find a sentence which violates any of the three components of finesse, we should correct it. In practice, we often find that a sentence does not have the right flavor or touch; but do we really know what is wrong? If we can identify the trouble area, we can be on our way to working out a solution. To this end, we should make a thorough analysis of each doubtful sentence to establish its rating with regard to diplomacy (D), service attitude (S), and positiveness (P). The following table contains the major points to be considered in each area of finesse for rating a sentence as good, poor, or neutral.

Component of Finesse	Good (+)	Poor (−)	Neutral (0)
Diplomacy (D)	Uses expected courtesies. Sidesteps possible antagonism.	Omits expected courtesies such as *please* and *thank you.* Uses antagonism, or overshoots diplomacy.	Is simply a factual statement or a necessarily firm request.
Service Attitude (S)	Slants statement as a value to the READER. Gives ample assistance.	Distorts statement as a value to the WRITER. Omits ample assistance.	Is simply a factual statement or a request.
Positiveness (P)	Plays up pleasant side. Uses direct phrasing; gets to the point. Shows strength, confidence. Is specific on *harmless* facts. Is vague on *harmful* facts.	Plays up gloomy side. Uses double negatives unnecessarily. Shows weakness, lack of confidence, or timidity. Is vague on *needed* facts. Is specific on *harmful* facts.	Uses necessary or desirable (therefore "harmless") negative constructions.

Now, let us apply this approach as we analyze the following three sentences.

To avoid further delay, we are sending the new contract by air mail.

D—Neutral, if the writer was at fault; undiplomatic, if the reader was at fault.
S—Good service attitude.
P—Poor; negative suggestion (revives memory of old trouble); contains a form of double negative.

Correction procedure: Replace opening phrase with a clause or phrase that states a positive reason for the action indicated in the main clause.

Please write and tell us which color of sweater you prefer.	D—Good; polite enough (note "Please"). S—Poor service attitude—not enough assistance given to the reader. P—Good; sufficiently positive.

Correction procedure: Use a different approach: make action easy by giving the reader an easy-to-use form on which to check his preference; provide for return mailing.

As we are urgently in need of cash, we hope that you will respond by sending us your check.	D—Good; sufficiently polite; not blunt. S—Poor service attitude; mentions only our needs. P—Poor; weak, for a collection request.

Correction procedure: Use a different approach; this may entail revising parts of the letter preceding this sentence. State the request politely but firmly.

Portions of Sentences

We begin to see that the violation of a component quality of finesse sometimes applies to only a portion of a sentence instead of to the sentence as a whole. In the first of the three preceding examples, we can salvage the sentence by giving it a positive beginning. The second and third examples, however, are beyond redemption. In each instance, we would have to rewrite the sentence using a completely different approach. Probably we would find that more than one sentence has to be used to effect the desired change.

As a general rule, we can expect a violation of service attitude to require an extensive overhauling. But violations of diplomacy and positiveness often can be corrected by rephrasing only a portion of the sentence. The chief offenders in the area of diplomacy are (1) the omission of courtesies (such as "please" and "thank you") when they are expected or desired and (2) the use of untactful word sequences involving "you" and "your" (such as "Can't you . . . ?" "you claim," "you failed," "your carelessness," and "your reluctance"). In most of the word sequences the antagonism is obvious if we look at them as our reader will. We should find neutral words, at least, to add the diplomatic touch. Further, in some of the verb sequences, we can remove the antagonism by changing over to the passive voice; and this technique may be used upon occasion. We can even use the passive voice to neutralize some of the "I" and "we" constructions and thereby gain a slight relative increase in service attitude.

While many of the undiplomatic word sequences could also be cited for violations of service attitude and/or positiveness, we usually do not carry our analysis out that far. We have already singled out these sequences because they are untactful or insulting in nature. Our corrections to make them diplomatic will usually remove the side taints as well.

High on the list of offenders in the area of positiveness are the "double negatives." Unlike a simple grammatical negative which is sometimes needed, the double negatives are never needed and are always a waste of words. They tend, therefore, to introduce an off-brand flavor; they often hinder the reader because they interfere with the direct flow of thought. Although some writers use double negatives to achieve diplomacy, the end does not really justify the means. It is sufficiently easy for us to be diplomatic and still abide by the concepts of positiveness.

Individual Words

Since sentences and portions of sentences are composed of words, we can even narrow down to individual words in analyzing for violations of finesse. It is unlikely, however, that we could determine much about service attitude by considering just one word. This quality becomes more apparent as longer segments of writing take form.

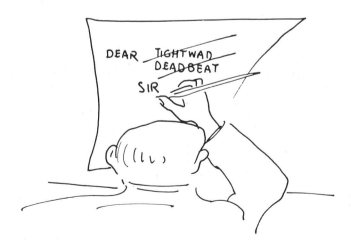

In the area of diplomacy and especially in the area of positiveness, the situation is different. Here, we can detect a violation at the level of the individual word and direct our efforts at keeping objectionable words out of our writing. Included in this classification would be verbs, adverbs, common nouns, adjectives, proper nouns—any word that would produce noise for our reader. Such words might be clearly unpopular, gloomy, distasteful, or annoying—or they might simply be distractive. In any case they would have an adverse effect on the rapport which should be maintained between our reader and ourselves.

A sampling of negative words would include such universals as: accident, blame, complaint, damage, dishonest, fault, ignorant, mistake, neglect, policy (rule), substitute, wrong. Words of this order—regardless of whether the precise form is a verb, noun, adjective, or adverb—are suggested to us by the very facts of a situation we are attempting to handle. It is our job to find neutral-sounding words to submerge the negativeness.

The better we know our intended reader, the easier it is for us to adjust exactly to his needs. In some reader's minds, the mention of certain names or places might be enough to cause negative reactions. So might words pertaining to religion or politics. And, of course, there may be some words this reader just does not like, even though most people might find them ordinary enough. Our guiding principle should be to write in harmony with our reader's needs when we know them; otherwise, to play it as safe as possible.

SUMMARY

The first step in the development of a business communication is the planning of our message—the content of our letter or report. It includes both what points will be embodied in our message and how these points will be put across to our reader.

If we were working under ideal conditions, we could expect to know our reader rather thoroughly. It would be easy for us to select our points and to sequence them in a manner exactly suited to his needs. Expressing ourselves in a most agreeable manner would also be relatively easy. The fact is, however, that we often know very little about our reader and must fall back on a safe, standard approach when we are writing to him.

PROGRAM

Narrowing down to the business letter, we find that there are four basic classifications: the simple goodwill letter, the request letter, the good-news letter, and the bad-news letter. The simple goodwill letter is a single-purpose letter—we intend it only for goodwill purposes. The other three types are multipurpose letters—that is, they aim at good will and something else besides. Our common denominator, therefore, in all business letters is goodwill—to create, enhance, preserve, or rebuild it.

Each basic type of letter has its own necessary characteristics.

Simple goodwill letter—good timing, sincerity, unity.
Request letter—definite request, ample motivation, ample assistance.
Good-news letter—prompt notification, minimum explanation (in that sequence).
Bad-news letter—ample explanation, delayed notification, encouraging ending (in that sequence).

A given letter which we are composing will be identifiable with one of these basic types. Our task is to form our writing program or working outline in accord with the basic type that applies. We are then reasonably protected against having an adverse impact on our reader.

FINESSE

Having decided what points and what sequence are needed in our letter, we must also consider how our thoughts will be expressed. We want to be sure that our statements cannot be misconstrued by the reader. To this end, we concern ourselves with the matter of finesse— the subtle strategy needed to make our letter agreeable, persuasive, and acceptable to our reader.

Finesse is composed of three somewhat intangible qualities known, in order of importance, as diplomacy, service attitude, and positiveness. The values we seek in each of these three components of finesse are as follows:

DIPLOMACY: Our statement should be courteous, tactful, polite, appreciative, sympathetic, or properly apologetic. It may be neutral, but it should not be in conflict with these values.
SERVICE ATTITUDE: Our statement should signify a benefit, service, or

something else that is good for our reader. It may be neutral, but it should not emphasize our interests or desires.

POSITIVENESS: Our statement should use phraseology that is cheerful, pleasant, or direct. It should be specific in stating necessary facts; vague or general, when acknowledging unpleasant happenings. It may be neutral; but it should not use gloomy or unpleasant phraseology, nor should it revive memories of unfortunate events.

Our objective with regard to finesse is that each of our statements should rate as good, or as a mixture of good and neutral, on each of the three component qualities. We should evaluate each statement in our letter to satisfy ourselves that it does not violate diplomacy, service attitude, or positiveness. Of 27 possible combinations for good, poor, and neutral, 19 are to be considered unsatisfactory because of the presence of one or more ratings of poor. The remaining eight combinations are acceptable. They are increasingly desirable to the extent that they include good ratings for finesse rather than neutral ratings.

QUESTIONS

1. In what way does the proper sequencing of a business communication program have managerial value?
2. Ideally, what conditions are desirable for planning or programming a business communication?
3. How does a writer proceed when he does not have personal knowledge of his intended reader?
4. In a strictly logical classification, what are the two varieties of business letters?
5. Define and give the general requirements of a simple goodwill letter.
6. Is a simple goodwill letter a frequently written type?
7. Define and give the general requirements of a request letter.
8. What requirement of a request letter is highly relative to the circumstances of a given case?
9. Define and give the general requirements of a good-news letter.
10. Does a good-news letter by its very nature enhance goodwill?
11. Define and give the general requirements of a bad-news letter.
12. In which of the four basic letter situations is a prescribed sequence of steps needed?
    (a) Simple goodwill letter.
    (b) Request letter.

    (c) Good-news letter.

    (d) Bad-news letter.

13. What is the underlying characteristic of all four basic letter situations?

14. When the writer tries to cater to the reader's goodwill, what are the four possible objectives from which he must choose in order to solve the problem he faces?

15. Although *finesse* has been assigned to the planning of the message (along with *program*), at what stage of the communication process does it actually emerge?

16. Under what conditions does *diplomacy* do its job best?

17. What purpose is achieved by including *service attitude* in a written business communication?

18. Does an abundance of "I" constructions mean that service attitude has been violated?

19. In the context of finesse, what does the term *positive* mean? What does the term *negative* mean?

20. What is a *double negative*?

21. Which of the three components of finesse is the most crucial in catering to goodwill?

22. How many possible combinations are there for good, neutral, and poor ratings on all three components of finesse?

23. Would a sentence which rated neutral on all three components of finesse be considered satisfactory?

24. Would a sentence which rated good on diplomacy, poor on service attitude, and good on positiveness be considered satisfactory?

25. Which components of finesse are sometimes vulnerable to defeat if even one ill-chosen word is used in a sentence?

EXERCISES

3–1. Set up the following column headings on a sheet of paper:

    Sentence   *Diplomacy*   *Service Attitude*   *Positiveness*

Next, list numbers from 1 through 10 under the column headed *Sentence*. Finally, analyze the components of finesse in each of the following sentences. Indicate your analysis of these components under the column headings, in the space opposite each sentence number. Use the following symbols: + (good), 0 (neutral), and − (poor).

    1. Your order dated February 19 arrived today. − 0 +

    2. The office supplies will be sent by parcel post this afternoon and should not take more than three days for delivery. 0 0 −

3. The copy of *New Tax Developments,* however, cannot be sent unless you provide some additional information. *0* —   —

4. You did not state in your letter whether you prefer the cloth-bound or the paperback edition of this book. — *0* —

5. The prices are $4.00 and $1.98, respectively. *0* *0* +

6. Either price paid is includable as a deduction by anyone who itemizes such matters on his income-tax return. *0* *0* +

7. Drop us a line stating your preference; we'll be standing by to process your order.

8. We realize that a satisfied customer is a valuable asset—so we want you to be satisfied.

9. To avoid delay and inconvenience, we will send your book special delivery as soon as we hear from you.

10. Please don't hesitate to call on us, for we are always glad to be of service to you.

3–2. On a sheet of paper, set up seven answer forms similar to the one shown below:

D_____ _____

S_____ _____

P_____ _____

Use the symbols, + (good), 0 (neutral), and − (poor), to rate each component of finesse in the following sentences. Place the symbols on the short lines after D, S, and P; and, on the long lines, state the reason for your rating.

1. He has completed his study of the sales campaign.

2. We have an untarnished record of always doing right by you, our customer.

3. Continued good luck to you in your new position!

4. Please write and tell us the style of jacket your prefer.

5. Your dishes will be delivered to you as soon as our new stock arrives.

6. This shaver will give you good service if it is used correctly.

7. To be assured of complete satisfaction, please check off your preference on the enclosed business reply card and mail it to us.

3–3. Set up the following column headings on a sheet of paper:

Sentence   Diplomacy   Service Attitude   Positiveness

Next, list numbers from 1 through 10 under the column headed *Sentence.* Finally, analyze the components of finesse in each of the sentences appearing in the following letter of introduction. Indicate your analysis of these components under the column headings, in the

space opposite each sentence number. Use the following symbols:
+ (good), 0 (neutral), and − (poor).

Dear Mr. Kemphurst:

(1)   This letter will introduce Mr. Louis J. Speck, who is
vice president of Vita-Steel Products Company here in
Pittsburgh.

(2)   Mr. Speck is a former associate of mine at National
Steel and is still a very close friend. He is presently

(3) in charge of all personnel divisions at his firm. His

(4) reputation for friendliness and executive ability is
becoming well known.

(5)   Mr. Speck will be in Washington on October 24 and 25.

(6) He hopes to visit four business firms, including yours,
in order to gather ideas on setting up a pension plan.

(7) He is due to be at your office at 10:00 A.M. on October
25.

(8)   Will you assist Mr. Speck in his work? He is partic-

(9) ularly interested in anything along the lines of deferred
compensation and tax-sheltered annuity plans.

(10)   We'll greatly appreciate your talking to Mr. Speck
and passing along to him any suggestions you may have.
Sincerely yours,

3–4. Analyze the components of finesse in the following acknowledgment
letter. Follow the instructions given for Exercise 3–3.

Dear Mr. Maxwell:

(1) Your first order came in this morning. We appreciate
this expression of confidence in us, and we shall cer-

(2) tainly try our best to live up to our reputation for
good service.

(3) As we want you to have your initial stock of Sports-Wear
at once, we're sending the shipment this afternoon by

(4) Terminal Truck Ways. The invoice will follow by mail.

(5) In order that we may be ready to take care of future
orders promptly and on open-account terms, it will be
helpful if you will send us the usual financial state-

(6) ment to complete your credit file. Perhaps, rather than
prepare a special statement, you will prefer to fill out
the enclosed form and return it in the postage-paid
envelope we have provided.

(7) However you submit this confidential information, you
may be sure that it will be used only to help us cooperate with you effectively.

(8) Thanks for this first order. It is a pleasure to have

(9) you as a distributor of our merchandise. We'll be ex-

(10) pecting your financial figures soon, so that we can
open a trade account with you.
Yours very truly,

3–5. Analyze the components of finesse in the following adjustment letter. Follow the same instructions given for Exercise 3–3.

```
     Dear Mr. Walters:
(1)     Your complaint to our Denver office has been for-
(2)  warded to me. Please accept my apology for the damage
(3)  which was done to your suitcase. You may have the suit-
(4)  case repaired and send the receipted bill to me. A refund
     will be mailed to you promptly.
(5)     Your remarks about our handling methods are well taken.
(6)  But in view of the large volume of luggage we handle, we
     must be realistic and expect that accidents will some-
(7)  times occur. We are making a concerted effort, however,
     to cut down the number of accidents involving luggage.
(8)  Studies are constantly being made to find better handling
     methods.
(9)     Thank you for writing as promptly as you did. We are
(10) looking forward to making your next trip a thoroughly
     satisfying experience.
                              Yours very truly,
```

3–6. Set up the following column headings on a sheet of paper:

Sentence   Diplomacy   Service Attitude   Positiveness

Next, list numbers from 1 through 10 under the column headed *Sentence*. Finally, rate the suitability of the components of finesse in each of the following sentences. Indicate your rating of each component under the applicable column heading, in the space opposite each sentence number. Use the following symbols: OK (suitable for use) or X (unsuitable for use).

1. Your size of shoe is temporarily out of stock, but will be available again within one week.

2. The watch which you say is defective is made by a dependable manufacturer.

3. Answer the questionnaire and return it to me in the courtesy envelope enclosed.

4. You are perfectly right in complaining about the late delivery of the lumber.

5. Please do not hesitate to contact us if we can be of further help.

6. Your order for one dozen ball-point pens was received today.

7. We'll appreciate your taking the trouble to show Mr. Brown through your plant.

8. Why not be the first in your area to own one of these symbols of status?

9. Please write and tell us the style of gloves you prefer.

10. We are unable to quote a price on this job until our estimator has submitted his report.

. . . .

CHAPTER 4

ENCODING
THE MESSAGE

A business communication starts out as a thought we wish to convey to an intended reader. During the planning stage, we select and organize the component topics we are going to include in such a message. We also tune in our thinking processes to anticipate the likes and dislikes of our reader and to be aware of the opportunities for using finesse. Two important steps still remain. One is to express our message through language; the other is to place the expressed message into the form of a document that can be delivered to our reader.

In terms of basic communication concepts, the language step is the encoding of our message so that it can be transmitted. As yet we have no better way than to use the body of symbols and rules we call language. In some cases, we find it convenient even to recode language to accommodate a given method of transmission—such as the dot-and-dash coding of the telegraph. But first our thoughts are either written down or spoken to some kind of recording facility.

Language is an intermediate step between the message as it exists in our mind and the appearance of the message in a final document (say, a business letter). Our reader will not know what is in our mind except as he is able to extract it from our message as it appears in the document he receives. Thus, if we do not express our thoughts completely, if we use a somewhat unconventional kind of language, or if we write at a level that is difficult to understand, we tend to defeat the purpose of communication. Our reader should know effortlessly what we are saying and what we want him to do. He should not have to be a mind reader or a decoding expert, nor should he be distracted by a pretentious style of writing. The language phase of communication is, after all, merely a means to a desired end.

To serve its purpose best, our language should be understandable to our reader. An often-heard suggestion is that we should write conversationally and approach the task of communicating as though we were going to talk rather than write. Advice of this nature is pointed in the right direction; but, of course, it cannot be followed too literally. There is a significant difference between writing and talking. Writing is necessarily a one-sided activity, the communicator having the floor from beginning to end. Conversation is essentially two-sided; each party has his turn at speaking, listening, questioning, repeating, rephrasing—doing whatever is required to fill the needs of communication. Tone of voice, pitch, gestures, and facial expressions can be used to bring out desired moods and meanings. Such fundamental distinctions between writing and speaking techniques would seem to make the patterning of one after the other a rather impossible task.

Furthermore, there is a reasonable doubt whether the language used by many people in conversation could be advantageously used in their business writing. Much of conversational language is exceedingly lax in organization, logic, and direction of thought. It is often plagued by poor grammar and sentence structure—if, indeed, complete sentences are actually used. It is riddled with pauses, stammerings, and annoying mannerisms (such as "I mean," "you know," and "huh?") which are tossed in at every opportunity. For some people, conversational language must contain a generous sprinkling of profanity and other unacceptable discourse. Surely, no one seriously advocates that such individuals should write in the same manner that they talk!

What is correctly meant by advice to be "conversational" is the indication it gives as to the tone and style of our language. We are conducting everyday business affairs in business letters. We should use the same kind of direct, simple, clear language we would use in face-to-face encounters. Good general language usage is relatively informal; natural in tone (though free of our "natural" faults in mechanics or in organization); certainly never pompous, ostentatious, or stilted. Business letters we write along these lines will be read comfortably and understood easily.

READABILITY

We begin to see that to be understandable our writing should be at a readable level and be properly executed. There is a relationship between these qualities. We might say that a well-executed message, from a language mechanics approach, is still not necessarily an easy message to read. But a well-executed message incorporating the various means available for helping our reader is almost certain to be functional and readable. It is important that we know something about the things that can help make reading easy.

TONE: PERSONAL OR IMPERSONAL?

When we attempt to communicate, we have a choice of two tones of language. There is the personal tone, which is often thought of as "I-and-you" language. It is fully in step with the concept of conversational language. There is also the impersonal tone, which uses no first-person constructions and few, if any, second-person constructions. It is generally cast in third-person constructions only and is often referred to as "bookish." The question is which tone should we select for a business letter?

While impersonal language is factual in tone and assumes an aura of impartiality, it is relatively lacking in reader interest. Most readers become interested when the subject matter is people rather than concepts or things. They become even more interested when they are brought right into the communication by the means of "you-and-I" or "you-and-we" constructions. Whether they realize it or not, by this increased interest they tend to be just a little more active or cooperative in extracting our intended message. The readability of our communication is accordingly improved. At the same time, from a writing standpoint, we find it easier to be persuasive and to apply service attitude when we phrase our message in the personal tone. Thus, the personal tone helps both reader and writer, and makes an excellent choice when tone is optional. It is the tone we should prefer for our business letters.

VOICE: ACTIVE OR PASSIVE?

Another consideration, closely related to tone, is the matter of voice. The English language has two voices: the active voice, in which the subject of the sentence performs the action indicated by the verb; and the passive, in which the action indicated by the verb happens to the subject. The active voice is the more positive of the two. Its effect on the sentence is that of forward movement. The passive voice is relatively weak and, therefore, of lower interest value. Its effect on the sentence is that of starting to move forward, then of casting back to let the action happen to the subject, and then of moving forward again. This behavior requires some extra effort on the part of the reader. This effort, combined with the lessened interest value, tends to make reading more difficult. Thus we risk introducing a slight disturbance—a bit of noise—when we change to the passive voice. The recommended procedure is to select the active voice and to stick with it as much as possible.

There are two good reasons, however, why we should consider switching to the passive voice at times. One is that the passive voice can take the sting out of "you" word sequences which would be undiplomatic otherwise. For example, if we must say something along the lines of telling our reader "you didn't . . . ," the passive voice will remove the scolding tone. "Such-and-such wasn't . . ." neutralizes the possible antagonism. It blocks out a louder noise than it creates; our reader is relieved, unconsciously perhaps, that he is not being blamed for an error. He is psychologically willing to accept the phrasing and read on without a noticeable snag.

The second reason we might make use of the passive voice is to give a slight improvement to service attitude. A first-person subject does not of itself go against the concept of service attitude. The true measure is whether we slant our thoughts, whenever possible, toward our reader—that is, present them in a way that has meaning within his set of interest values. Yet if we compose our letter mainly of sentences using "I" or "we" as subject, we again are risking noise. Our reader may get the feeling that, although his interest values are being discussed, the discussion is not slanted his way. He would then become aware that we are viewing the topics from our side, whereas he would prefer our seeing them from his vantage point. If we detect a large proportion of first-person sentences building up as we write, we can begin holding back. We can give some sentences fresh subjects and retain the active voice. We also can convert certain sentences to the passive voice and thus avoid the ones with too much first-person phrasing. For example, we do not need to use the active voice to inform our reader of something routine. If we are sending him a return envelope, we can use the passive voice to tell him: "A business reply envelope is enclosed for your convenience in answering."

STYLE: INFORMAL OR FORMAL?

When we write a business communication, we usually must decide upon a style suitable for our reader and our purpose. We can generally expect that the informal style will go well with the personal tone and active voice. It is an ideal choice for use in business letters and in many business reports. On the other hand we make a good combination of the formal style and impersonal tone (with both active and passive voice) when we wish to sound highly factual. It is the style we will choose for certain kinds of business reports, particularly formal reports.

The informal style in writing is in large part what the people who advocate "conversational" style are actually trying to say. As we have already seen, however, we can only go so far toward "writing as we would talk." We are limited in using that approach, and the informal style is about the extent of it. Aside from the fact that personal tone lends its own bit of informality, we have two additional degrees of freedom.

1. We may use common, everyday contractions. In this category we include:

aren't	I've	wasn't
can't	isn't	we'd
couldn't	it's	we'll
didn't	she'd	we're
don't	she'll	we've
hasn't	she's	who's
haven't	shouldn't	won't
he'd	that's	wouldn't
he'll	they'd	you'd
he's	they'll	you'll
I'd	they're	you're
I'll	they've	you've
I'm		

(and informal, shortened words such as *auto, phone, teletype, TV*, etc.)

The question of whether any other contractions would sound natural or artificial would have to be answered at the time we considered using them. The main thing is that we should not insert contractions just to have them—or even to have more of them. The informal style lets us use contractions, instead of requiring us to spell everything out in full.

2. We may use natural-sounding slang. It would be next to impossible to fashion a list of natural-sounding slang expressions, because slang is an ever-changing thing. Yet there are many phrases which would be frowned upon by language purists, but which make for excellent and easy-to-read communication. Here are a few examples.

```
He made his pile on Wall Street.

From the looks of these bills, we'd better apply the
brakes on our expenses.

That's a lot of money just for spare parts.

Here it is--hot off the presses.
```

We can easily appreciate the color and sparkle that can be built into our message when we use such down-to-earth words and phrases. We must be careful, of course, to use slang in good taste and with sound judgment. Objectionable words and phrases might offend our reader; and localized slang, not universally understood, would interfere with communication. If we were to use the wrong kind of slang, we would be introducing noise—instead of blocking it out.

Slang, however, even when used judiciously, is not an end in itself. If we find that we have written a letter and have used no slang, there is little point in our going back to put some in. We should "be ourselves" when we write; we should not be imitators of other people. If we do not ordinarily use slang, we may actually worsen our presentation by trying to force some into our written work. As with contractions, the license to use slang does not mean that we must use it.

In contrast, the formal style of writing sticks closely to the rule book. When we write in the formal style, we usually elect to use the impersonal tone also. To be sure, we do not use contractions or slang. Our communication therefore takes on an air of impartiality—factual, "official."

Because concepts and inanimate things, instead of people, are often the subjects of our sentences when we write formally, we do not give our reader much in the human-interest category. In addition, the absence of conversational-type writing tends to hold our message at a distance from our reader. We do not involve him in the discussion as we do when we use the personal tone and the familiarities of contractions and slang. We seem to cast him in the role of an onlooker instead of making him somewhat of a participant. As he becomes less active in extracting our intended message, our own responsibility for getting through to him rises proportionately.

Good writers can communicate effectively in either the informal or the formal style. In fact, many of them have come to prefer the formal style once they have mastered it. But, in the final analysis, what is best for our reader should really be our basis for making a choice. Unless we have a clear-cut indication, by requirement or circumstance, to do otherwise, we should favor the informal style for business writing.

WORDING: FAMILIAR OR STRANGE?

Although studies have been made proving rather conclusively that words by themselves have a bearing on readability, most of us could have surmised that fact anyhow. When we read, we can move along rapidly and effortlessly if the words we encounter are familiar to us. Whenever we come to a strange or infrequently used word, we slow down. Perhaps the meaning of the word pops into our mind, and we can again resume our regular pace. Sometimes we must pause a while and puzzle over the intended meaning—or even decide to move on in the hope that the meaning will eventually become clear. But, in any event, we have been subjected to a form of noise—a disturbance in the communication process. In proportion to the seriousness of that noise, we tend to lose touch with the train of thought. In extreme cases, we might even have to go back and try to regain the continuity. Obviously, when it is we who are doing the writing, we should ease our reader's task by sticking to familiar words.

"NOW, WHAT'S THAT ALL ABOUT?"

.... SO AS TO SURMOUNT THE ENERVATING AND OFTEN DELETERIOUS OBFUSCATIONS ....

A word of caution is appropriate at this point. We should realize that there is such a thing as using words and phrases which are overly familiar—that is, words overused in business writing. Such words and phrases are referred to as "stereotypes" or "rubber stamp" words. Users of such words show a lack of imagination and originality. It is as though the writer owned a special typewriter keyed with ready-made words and phrases—or, similarly, a rack of rubber stamps. Whenever something of a recurring nature is needed, the writer draws upon these pat expressions. The trouble is, he has accumulated these expressions either from messages he has received or from files of old correspondence. This is the same procedure used by other unthinking people. Thus, with a great number of writers using substantially the same phrasing, it often happens that much of a reader's mail will appear hackneyed and unsavory. What is wrong is not the presence of unfamiliar words in this case; rather, it is the presence of *noticeably* familiar words. In truth, other familiar words (such as articles, conjunctions, personal pronouns, and prepositions) are used more frequently than the so-called stereotypes; but they do not draw attention to themselves annoyingly.

Still another matter for us to consider is the length of the words we use. Other things remaining equal, we can help our reader by using short words, whenever possible, instead of long words. We can appreciate that there is a relationship between shortness and familiarity of words which makes for easier reading than the contrasting combination, length and strangeness. But we should not rely wholly on the expectation that shortness means familiarity and that length does not. Our choice should be based on familiarity, first and always; shortness, if possible. For example, let us consider the following sets of words.

	Short Word	*Long Word*	*Better Choice*
(1)	use (verb)	utilize (verb)	use
(2)	fete (noun)	festival (noun)	festival

In the first set of words, we see that the meanings are close, that both words are rather familiar, but that *use* has one syllable as against three for *utilize*. In such a case, our choice would ordinarily be *use*. In the second set, we see that the shorter word, *fete,* is not so familiar as *festival*. Therefore it does not communicate quickly and effortlessly. It is even capable of causing our reader to receive *feat,* an entirely different concept. Despite its three-syllable length, *festival* would be our better choice of word.

Sometimes we have little, if any, choice concerning the length of word to use. We cannot always readily find a substitute for certain long words—nor can anyone else. For example, we may need to use *ambassador, automation, basketball, government,* or *university*—and there are no handy short words to fall back on. Fortunately, we can use such long words with the expectation that they will be familiar enough to our reader not to be troublesome. In fact, many people read long words *in toto,* that is, as units or symbols rather than as series of syllables. It is only when they read aloud or encounter a strange word that they are actually concerned with the syllables.

In essence, our job with regard to readability is to help our reader go through our message at a comfortable pace. Our words can either help or hinder. Short, familiar words are the best choice we can make. Long, familiar words may be used—sometimes they must be used; but they have a tendency to slow our reader down. Strange words, short or long, can stop him in his tracks. As a type of communication noise, they disrupt our reader's continuity of thought and lessen the effectiveness of our message.

DIRECTION OF THOUGHT

For clearness—and therefore for ease of reading progress—our message should move in what we might call "a straight line." We do, of course, control this matter in the overall flow of thought by first preparing and then following a program (working outline) for the problem at hand. But control of the overall direction is not enough. Our thoughts are expressed through relatively small units of composition—individual sentences. It will be helpful to our reader, and increase communication, if our thoughts flow in a straight, forward direction insofar as possible within each sentence, as well as from sentence to sentence.

"THIS PATIENT SUFFERS FROM INVERTED CLAUSES."

In a basic classification, we have our choice of three kinds of sentences. There is first of all the simple sentence, in which there is essentially one clause (the "subject, verb, object" concept). Next, there is the complex sentence, which consists fundamentally of a main clause and a subordinate clause. Lastly, there is the compound sentence, which is typified as two main clauses (independent sentences, actually), connected together, and punctuated as a single sentence.

From the point of view of a straight-line direction of thought, the simple sentence definitely fills the requirements. For a number of valid reasons, however, we may well hesitate to use only simple sentences when we write. Among these reasons are the tendency toward choppiness that often results from a continuous run of simple sentences and the fact that such a technique is a drastic departure from the everyday styles of writing. It would be more prudent for us to use a blend of various kinds of sentences—favoring first simple sentences, then complex sentences, and finally compound sentences.

The reason for preferring complex sentences over compound sentences can be readily explained. A complex sentence may move in a slightly indirect line, but it still contains one main thought. The secondary thought is relegated to the dependent clause and is subordinated (held down below the main thought). In the compound sentence, there are two "main" thoughts—at least, there are two thoughts grammatically equal. This condition results in two subjects, two verbs—in fact, two distinct actions—being merged into one sentence. Sometimes these actions are in different directions, even in conflict with one another in relation to the message. They also tend toward sentences of a rambling nature which grow in length and confusion.

The following illustrations show how two simple sentences, although easy to read, can be restated as a complex sentence. A possible choppiness of the original sentences is smoothed out, and the new sentence is still an easy one to read.

Simple Sentences:	In the afternoon we began to compute the payroll. Suddenly, the electrical power failed.
Complex Sentence:	In the afternoon, as we began to compute the payroll, the electrical power suddenly failed.

The two simple sentences could also have been combined into a compound sentence, as shown in the next illustration. But here there seems to be a zig-zag movement of thought and very little smoothing out of the original choppiness.

Compound Sentence: `In the afternoon we began to compute the payroll, but suddenly the electrical power failed.`

In the complex sentence, the reader is given the clue that the main thought concerns "electrical power." But he has no such clue when both "we" and "electrical power" are assigned equal rank. So, while compound sentences do have their place, we are well advised to use them sparingly.

MECHANICS OF EXPRESSION

Even though we have made the recommended choices under each of the areas just discussed—tone, voice, style, wording, and direction of thought—we still cannot assume that our writing will be easy to follow. We have yet to face the problems of the mechanics of expression. We must use language in a correct and conventional manner if we are to be understood effortlessly by our reader.

Mechanics of expression will be examined in greater detail later in this chapter. But we should consider how this area affects readability. If our writing contains misspelled words, incorrectly used words, poor grammar, faulty sentence structure, and improper punctuation, our reader is going to be hard pressed to understand it. He may be able to fathom our message; but then, he may not. In either case, he will be put through needless effort—perhaps an amount of backtracking and rereading. We could never incorporate enough personal tone, active voice, informal style, easy words, and simple sentences to compensate for a broadside of language blunders. They would still be there as noise —stumbling blocks in the path of communication.

On the other hand, the purest of language is not necessarily the easiest to read. A vast number of textbooks, reference books, professional articles, and scientific papers can be cited as examples of works that are mechanically well written but not easily read. Such works usually presuppose a keen interest and desire on the part of the reader, if not also a highly specialized background. In the business world, however, we operate on a different base. We wish to reach as many people as possible, in a clear and effective manner, and with a minimum of effort required on the part of our readers. We can succeed in our purpose by using correct language and by exercising good judgment with regard to the various options open to us.

EYE APPEAL

Ordinarily, the matter of eye appeal, or general attractiveness of a business letter or report, comes up in the discussion of form. Yet there is a degree of overlap which puts a portion of it, at least, into the category of readability.

To begin with, a document can appear to be either inviting or forbidding as soon as it strikes the eye. Such a first impression, whichever kind it may be, could have an important effect on the person who is supposed to read the document. In some instances it could even be the basis for the receiver's decision to read or not read the message. The inviting document, therefore, is the one with built-in positive psychology. It looks easy to read, even before the reader has given it a try. It is the one that we should try to produce.

Aside from the recognized conventions of form, there are certain things we should strive for in the production of an inviting document. Ample margins, short and medium-length paragraphs, tabular presentation of important points, and the two-part document (covering page with an enclosed chart, graph, or table) are helpful aids for eye appeal. All of these things add horizontal white space to the document; and the last three also spread out the wording vertically. By their use our document is spared the dense or "heavy reading" look that can dampen our reader's enthusiasm.

The open or uncluttered look is inviting and tends to keep the reader's interest from bogging down. The reader's eye can keep signaling his brain that what is coming along next does not appear to be heavy reading. The technique of numbering points and putting them in a list has added benefits when it comes to reviewing the document or answering such points in a response. The two-part letter or report permits a separation of the personal message from the factual data presented, and this is sometimes desirable. Since neither part is absolutely controlled by the other, a seemingly shorter message, the best choice of eye appeal for each part, and a detachable fact sheet are all made possible.

In certain kinds of letters—sales letters, for example, and some of the modern collection letters—the addition of colors is used to gain eye appeal. The purpose is, as always, to keep interest high so that the reader will be drawn in to participate in the communication process. The reader is thus able to read our message with a lesser degree of conscious effort.

MEASUREMENT OF READABILITY

During the past two or three decades, a number of psychologists and communication consultants have conducted experiments aimed at analyzing the readability of written material. Some valuable information has been compiled and some theories confirmed as a result of their studies and research. For instance, it has been demonstrated that sentence length contributes to reading difficulty. The longer a sentence is, the more effort must be exerted by the reader to carry the thought. He has a much easier reading experience when he is provided with relatively short sentences. Also, it has been found that the length of words has a bearing on readability, short words being easier to read than long ones. Apparently, the greater number of familiar words are short words. Probability therefore favors the coincidence of short words being familiar to the reader, as contrasted with the long words in our language. On the other hand, it has been learned that certain words have high ratings with regard to human interest. These words are psychologically capable of attracting the reader, of making him extra desirous of getting the message, and of converting him into an active participant in the communication effort. Such human-interest words have been identified as the personal pronouns and their actual or potential antecedents. The overall effect of such words in a message is to make the message easier to read.

It is not surprising that such findings should lead to the formulation of various systems for measuring readability. Although some of the systems are more elaborate than others, the general philosophy behind them is the development of a quantitative, or numerical, value for a sample of writing. This value or "score" is then compared to a preestablished standard to see whether the sample qualifies as being readable writing. If its rating shows that the sample would be difficult for the intended reader, the author can make revisions to lower his composition to the reader's level. Obviously, such measuring devices hold forth the promise of valuable help to a person who is called upon to write business letters and reports.

Upon close examination, however, we usually find that each system of measuring readability has some kind of limitation or disadvantage. The easy-to-apply systems may make their evaluation on the narrow basis of but one of the many factors affecting readability—for example, on the length of words. The harder-to-apply systems often take into consideration two or three factors, but become intricate because of weights assigned to each factor. One early system went so far as to refine the assigned weights to four decimal places, even though the approximate ratio of $2:1:1$ was practically self-apparent. Some of the systems require the user to make unnecessary calculations. These are in the nature of an adjustment to the readability score computed from the data, the purpose being to make the score fit neatly on a predetermined table. Strangely enough, this type of adjustment consists of a standard amount to be subtracted from the computed score—or of a fixed percentage to be taken of the computed score. It would seem that a better approach would be simply to recast the table so that the score arrived at under the system could be evaluated directly. Finally, most of the readability measurement systems have been set up to serve all kinds of authors writing to all levels of readers. The purpose is to permit the author in any field to adapt his composition to the reading level of his audience. In business writing, however, we do not always know very much about our reader or readers. We strive for a level of writing that will be "businesslike"—that is, clear and effortless to the kind of person we are apt to deal with in the marketplace. We should probably prefer a readability measuring system, if we are inclined to use one, which is specifically prepared for business writing.

On the strength of the foregoing analysis, we can establish the following criteria for a system to measure the readability of a piece of business writing:

1. It should be oriented particularly to business writing.
2. It should incorporate as many readability factors as experimentation and research have been able to reduce to quantitative measurement.
3. It should be easy to understand and apply.
4. It should be free of complicated steps, such as the assigning of weights to the factors under consideration.

5. It should be free of extra steps over and above the computing of a "score" from the quantified factors.

6. It should permit direct reading of the computed score on an evaluation table.

7. It should provide dependable interpretations for the guidance of the user.

The system which is described later in this section has been especially constructed in accordance with these criteria. Those of us who might some day wish to check the readability of something we have written will be interested in how this system fulfills the requirements just stated.

1. The evaluation table is fashioned along the lines of a quality-control chart. The middle segment of values—rated as "businesslike"— is bracketed by upper and lower control limits. Scores within this range are considered readable for business-writing purposes, with lower scores being more desirable than higher scores as a general rule. Danger limits are also included to sound a warning that scores falling between them and the control limits could be trending too high or too low.

2. The system measures the interaction of three readability factors which have identifiable objective characteristics. These are the same factors used by most of the highly sophisticated systems devised for measuring readability. They are: sentence length (a measure of straight-line direction of thought), word length (a measure of the use of familiar words), and human-interest words (a measure of the personal tone).

3. The score computed under this system will fall either inside or outside the control or tolerance limits. If it is inside the limits, the sample of writing is judged suitable for the typical business reader. If it is outside the limits, it is considered to be unbusinesslike. The system is thus held to a simple *yes-no* decision regarding readability.

4. The numerical value of each factor is left unweighted—or, if we wish to be technically accurate, it is assigned the weight of one.

5. The numerical values for sentence length and word length, being measures of difficulty factors, are added together. The numerical value for human-interest words, being a measure of a factor that assists the reader, is subtracted during the computation of the word-length figure. It lowers the score to be carried to the evaluation table.

6. The evaluation table is in the form of a control chart. The danger and control limits have been established empirically—that is, from ob-

servations obtained through the use of systems which combine the same three readability factors. The segment of the control chart lying within these limits is ready to accept the score as it is arrived at under the system. It already compensates for the lack of weighting and tail-end adjustments, and thereby simplifies the work required of the user.

7. This system is about as reliable as any present-day system can be. It reflects the interplay of the readability factors which research has shown to be quantitatively measurable. It contains an evaluation table which is as valid as those offered by even the most sophisticated systems. This table gives the same *go-stop* signal to the user that other systems would give for the same piece of writing; yet it does so strictly within the context of business communication.

To use this system of measuring readability, we simply examine a piece of our business writing (say, a letter or a representative sample of a report) and perform the following general steps:

1. We determine the average length of our sentences. We do this by dividing the number of words by the number of sentences.
2. We add to this figure the index of word length, using the theory that the allowable rate is one syllable for a regular word and two syllables for a human-interest word. Thus, our total syllables minus the allowable syllables (number of words plus human-interest words) equals the excessive syllables. This excess divided by the number of words equals the proportion; the proportion multiplied by 100 equals the index.
3. We then record the resultant total on the readability control chart to find whether it fits inside or outside the tolerance limits for business writing.

To see this system in operation, let us examine some statistical data relating to three business letters. These letters were written by an individual who has a good mastery of language. When he wrote the first letter, he believed that his letters had always been good examples of business writing. He was aware of the value of human-interest words and used them generously whenever he wrote.

An analysis of the first of his three letters revealed the following facts.

Sentences	6
Words	157
Human-interest words	17
Syllables	252

The readability score was worked out in the following manner.

```
Average number of words in a sentence:
    157 ÷ 6 ...............................................  26
Plus: Index of word length:
    Syllables  .........................................  252
        Credit for number of words ...............  −157
        Extra credit for human-interest words ........  −  17    −174
        Excessive syllables ...............................  78
        Proportion: 78 ÷ 157 ...........................  .50
        Index: .50 × 100 ..............................   50
Readability score .....................................   76
```

The score of 76 was inserted on a readability control chart in the space provided for Sample No. 1, as shown on page 80. A dot was marked below it at the 76 level of the scale. Since the segment of the control chart which measures "businesslike" is in the range of 33–67, this first letter, at 76, was decidedly too high. The letter would not likely make for effortless reading on the part of the person for whom it was intended.

What caused the score to be so high? Some of the difficulty can be attributed to the length of the sentences, which average out to 26 words. Generally accepted research, however, has led to the conclusion that the ideal average for sentence length is somewhere in the range of 15 to 20 words—probably about halfway between. This guideline does not mean that each sentence should come out that way. But a blend of sentences of varying lengths, averaging out slightly below 20 words, would be desirable.

In the letter under study, we can see that the score is 26 points above the center line of the businesslike segment of the control chart. This fact means that, with only about 7 to 10 points caused by excessive sentence length, some other important influence must be at work. Obviously, it is the long words that are causing the trouble. Even with the extra credits allowed for 17 human-interest words, the index of word length stands at 50. The index probably should be in the range of 30 to 40 in a readable business letter; and it should not be dependent upon so many human-interest words.

Now, if this had been our letter, we should certainly want to make some changes to put it at an effortless, businesslike reading level. There are four steps we can take to lower the readability score of something we have written. They are:

1. *Remove superfluous words and phrases.*   Most of us find that we can cut down on the wordiness of our written work. Of course, we  are entitled to our own way of writing — but this does not mean we should be redundant, tautological, or excessively wordy. Such usages have a tendency to creep into our work, especially during dictation when we are thinking ahead in our program but trying to keep the flow of words from shutting off. Thus, we should be on guard against "nothing" words—those which do not add to the message value. Sometimes we can simply delete one or more words from a phrase without changing the meaning. Here are some examples.

ORIGINAL PHRASE	DELETION	REMAINDER
at the present time	the...time	at present
cooperate together	together	cooperate
enclosed herein	herein	enclosed
identical in every way	in every way	identical
inasmuch as	inasmuch	as
in order to	in order	to
one and only	one and	only

At other times, we may be able to use a single word to replace a cluttered phrase. Examples follow.

ORIGINAL PHRASE	ONE-WORD REPLACEMENT
don't hesitate to	please
for the reason that	because
in the amount of	for
in the event that	if
previous to	before

Whenever we can practice such economies, we lessen the work of our reader. By keeping him from tiring as he reads, we help him retain his interest and thereby aid our own cause of communication.

2. *Break up the long sentences.*   If we can increase the number of

sentences in our message, without materially adding to the number of words used, we will reduce the average length of the sentences. The compound sentences, being really two or more full sentences punctuated as one sentence, are a fertile area for this kind of improvement. Sometimes we can revamp complex sentences so that we arrive at two simple sentences instead of one long sentence with a main clause and a dependent clause. But there is a practical limit to this entire approach. Once we bring the average sentence length below 20 words, the further improvement to be derived is probably not worth our time and effort. For example, if we have written five sentences containing a total of 150 words, we could expect the following improvements as we proceeded to break up the longer sentences.

CONDITION OF MESSAGE	SENTENCES	WORD AVERAGE	IMPROVEMENT
Original state	5	30	
1st sentence break	6	25	5
2d sentence break	7	21	4
3d sentence break	8	19	2
4th sentence break	9	17	2

From this point on, we could not gain much improvement by breaking up sentences. In fact, it is doubtful that we could find any more sentences suited for such treatment. Our better approach would be to turn to some other means of improving readability.

3. *Replace long, strange words by short, familiar words.* From the standpoint of computing the readability score, only one syllable is permitted without penalty for each ordinary word we use. Beyond this allowance, excessive syllables begin to accumulate as a weighty contribution to the score. Therefore, we reduce our score when we substitute short words for long words. But since the real measure of effortless reading is more the familiarity of our words than length, we should not carry this substitution process to a ridiculous extent. We should be selective, and choose the short word when it is also the familiar word. We also should remember that we are striving for a word-length index in the range of 30 to 40—not something like 0 to 10, which would cause problems of another kind.

4. *Increase the number of human-interest words.* When we com-

pute our word-length index, we allow ourselves an extra credit for each human-interest word we have used. Since this procedure lessens the influence of the index, it also reduces the readability score. Thus, if we have not been using human-interest words (personal pronouns and other words that refer to people) or very many of them, we can improve our score by adding some to our message. The chances are, however, that a natural-sounding, inconspicuous rate would be an average of about one such word to each sentence used—or possibly three such words for every two sentences. An overdose of human-interest words would become obvious to our reader and tend to work against our communication effort as a form of noise.

These four pointers were brought to the attention of the person who had scored 76 on his letter. In his next letter-writing effort, he tried to incorporate the first three of these pointers and to discontinue his practice of overloading the message with human-interest words. An analysis of his second letter showed the following.

Sentences	6
Words	115
Human-interest words	5
Syllables	168

The readability score was computed as follows.

Average number of words in a sentence:
115 ÷ 6 19
Plus: Index of word length:
Syllables 168
Credit for number of words .... −115
Extra credit for human-interest words .. − 5   −120
Excessive syllables 48
Proportion: 48 ÷ 115 .... .41
Index: .41 × 100 41
Readability score 60

This second letter, scoring 60, earned the classification of "businesslike." Although the human-interest words totaled but five in six sentences, the difficulty factors of sentence length and word length were reasonably low. The score of this letter was recorded and plotted on the readability control chart, as shown on page 80.

A third letter by this same author was examined also. The statistical facts concerning it were as follows.

Sentences 7
Words 129
Human-interest words 7
Syllables 181

The readability score was worked out as follows.

Average number of words in a sentence:
    129 ÷ 7 18
Plus: Index of word length:
    Syllables 181
        Credit for number of words .... −129
        Extra credit for human-interest words . − 7 −136
        Excessive syllables 45
        Proportion: 45 ÷ 129 .... .35
        Index: .35 × 100 35
Readability score 53

This time the score reflected a further improvement in the author's writing level. Six of the seven points that marked the improvement were removed from the index of word length, and one point from the average length of the sentences. As with the other ratings, this score of 53 was recorded and plotted on the control chart shown on page 80. Lines were added connecting the plotted points of the three scores as an aid in appraising the progress of the improvement. Since this writer was now scoring within the tolerance limits, his main task henceforth would be to develop the knack of doing so as a matter of habit. Of course, occasional testings would always be helpful.

In the preceding discussion, we began with statistical data taken from three business letters. In actual practice, it would be necessary for us to obtain these data from the letter being scored. Although the work involves merely counting, we must do it carefully if we are to get a reliable score. First of all, in this work, we are concerned with the message only—the body of the letter, not any of the other parts. Then, we should be alert to the different challenges involved in the counting of different things. Counting the number of sentences is very easy. Counting the number of words is a bit more difficult—every word is included; there are no exceptions. We must take care to get an accurate count. We run into still greater difficulty with the human-interest words. There will be a relatively small number of such words and they will be scattered throughout our message. Yet we must be careful to include all of them.

Counting syllables is not overly difficult, although a dictionary might be needed at times. Most of the words—at least two thirds of them—will be one-syllable words. The main thing is that we make an accurate count of the syllables, and this will be somewhat more difficult than the counting of the words.

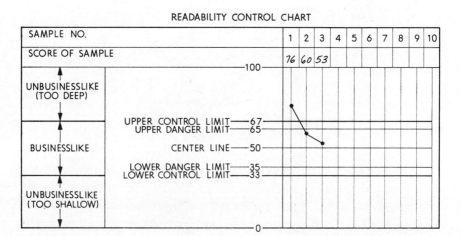

READABILITY CONTROL CHART

SAMPLE NO.		1	2	3	4	5	6	7	8	9	10
SCORE OF SAMPLE		76	60	53							

```
                                                    ─100─
UNBUSINESSLIKE
(TOO DEEP)
                        UPPER CONTROL LIMIT──67─
                        UPPER DANGER LIMIT──65─
BUSINESSLIKE                  CENTER LINE──50─
                        LOWER DANGER LIMIT──35─
                        LOWER CONTROL LIMIT──33─
UNBUSINESSLIKE
(TOO SHALLOW)
                                                    ─0─
```

Let us follow the procedure through from beginning to end. In the letter shown below, there are six sentences. The number of words typed on each line has been noted in the left-hand margin, and a total taken. Each human-interest word has been underscored; seven such words are used. The syllables have been noted in the right-hand margin, and a total taken.

WORDS		SYLLABLES
	Gentlemen:	
10	The Tree Tomato plant, which I ordered from you on	13
11	April 19, arrived here in Orlando last week. I'm sorry to	17
11	report that it did not manage to survive the trip south.	14
11	Although it was still green in color and had a small	13
11	leaf at the end of the stalk, the plant was exceedingly dehy-	16
11	drated and limp. I did everything possible to revive it, but	16
12	apparently it had crossed the point of no return. Now it is	16
8	a dried-up twig, a brownish bit of straw.	10
7	Since your offer carried a 90-day replacement guar-	14
12	antee in case of such an occurrence will you please send me	15
7	another plant, to the address shown above?	11
111		155

Yours very truly,

An analysis of this letter gives us the following facts.

Sentences 6
Words 111
Human-interest words 7
Syllables 155

Put to work in our readability measurement system, these facts show the following.

Average number of words in a sentence:
   111 ÷ 6 19
Plus: Index of word length:
Syllables 155
   Credit for number of words .... −111
   Extra credit for human-interest words . − 7   −118
   Excessive syllables 37
   Proportion: 37 ÷ 111 .... .33
   Index: .33 × 100 33
Readability score 52

The score of 52, when plotted on a readability control chart, lies almost at the center line of the "businesslike" segment. If our own writing regularly tests out at such a level, we can conclude that we have cleared an important hurdle on our route to effective business writing.

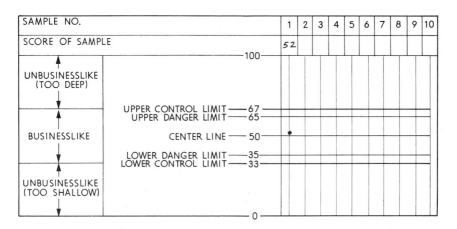

Finally, we should heed a word of caution. Present-day readability measurement systems, including the one we have just examined, are far from being perfect. Not only are they limited, measuring only some of the factors that bear on readability, but they depend on the assumption that the factors not measured are being handled properly. A person who is inept at writing cannot redeem misspellings, faulty vocabulary, poor grammar, and other language blunders simply by attaining a "business-like" readability score. And, it takes only a fool to "beat the system" by writing gibberish although using short sentences and short words together with a generous sprinkling of human-interest words.

To be of value, a readability measurement system must be used with discretion. It should be an extra tool for the person who has writing ability, who uses good judgment in the things that cannot be measured, and who is sincerely trying to communicate.

MECHANICS OF EXPRESSION

We can appreciate by now that effective business communication requires a definite preparation on the part of the writer. He must be well versed in business affairs, especially in dealing with people. In business communication, he is first of all transacting business; he is writing because that happens to be the expedient way of doing business under a given set of circumstances. But, undeniably, he is writing—and that fact requires that he be reasonably proficient at it.

We might as well face an important truth right now. If we are going to be business executives, we are going to have to write business letters and business reports. These messages will have to be written in acceptable language. There is no getting out of it. And, not only must we write well, but we must be able to exercise sound, critical judgment on the written work submitted to us by people down the line.

To do a good job in everything—be it an art, a skill, or a trade—we must be equipped with the proper tools. For the job of business writing, we need to accumulate a workable set of tools—some general, some specialized in nature. Among the general items should be at least a competent dictionary and a book on English grammar. Among the specialized items should be a style manual, an easy-to-use reference book on business writing, and a spelling dictionary. Our individual needs will indicate whatever other aids should be included. We should, however, include only items which we need and which we will actually use. This collection is not intended to decorate our desk or impress visitors.

While it is not our purpose here to give training in language matters, some helpful suggestions are given in the following pages. A more detailed coverage of the mechanics of expression is presented as a special supplement in the back of this book.

SPELLING

Of all language blunders, misspellings are clearly the most obvious. Even school children and other poor spellers themselves can usually detect misspellings, especially if more than a very few occur. And the matter is rather cut and dried; little is left to the writer's discretion or opinion.

We are given no credit for spelling our words correctly. Our reader expects it of us. Yet if we misspell words, we begin to irritate him and create doubts about us in his mind. In extreme cases, we could even destroy the confidence he has had in us, our company, and our product or services. For example, what judgment might be made in connection with a drug manufacturer that sends out letters with carelessly spelled words? Are its compounds and medicines being formulated with this same kind of attention? Often, our reader is seeing his first sample of our work when he gets a piece of business writing from us. A great deal can be at stake during this first encounter.

So, we had better be sure that words are spelled correctly in our business writing. Whether we are good or poor at spelling, we can turn out work that is free of misspelled words. First of all, we have the many spelling rules to guide us. But, such rules apparently benefit the good spellers among us more than they do the poor spellers—or else why do we continue to have poor spellers? Next there is the regular dictionary, which carries the spelling, syllabication, and pronunciation of all the words we are likely to use in our kind of writing. Such a book is a boon to both the good speller and the poor speller. Also, there is the special type of dictionary which lists only the spelling and syllabication of words. As it does not contain definitions, it is compact in size and time-saving in use. It is especially valuable for the poor speller, who may need to refer to a spelling aid frequently.

Some of us may be reluctant to use either a regular or a special dictionary, in the belief that such use is an admission of weakness. The truth is that we are simply showing good sense by using the pertinent tools of our trade. In the case of other fields, do we scoff at a lawyer who consults his law books? Or at a mathematician who refers to a table of logarithms? Or at a tax consultant who uses a table of tax rates? Of course not!

In our own lives, do we drop a dime into a pay telephone and then  dial what we merely guess is the number we wish to call? That certainly would be an expensive practice—yet how much more costly the practice of misspelling can be! The course of action is clear: use a telephone directory to find the correct number to call; use a dictionary to find the correct spelling of any word we are not absolutely sure about. A bit of trouble arises, though, because some of us do not know when to refer to a dictionary. We rely on our recollection of the correct spelling, and memory lets us down.

The following four categories of words can help us know when to use our dictionary. These categories are not all-inclusive, but they do bracket a sizable number of misspelled words. If we form the habit of looking up words in these areas, however, we should find it increasingly easy to expand the habit to other words besides.

1. Words requiring a choice between *a* and *e*; examples follow.

> countenance
> independent
> maintenance
> prevalent
> subsistence

Words of this type are always difficult for poor spellers and should be checked in a dictionary.

2. Words containing a combination of *e* and *i*; examples follow.

CEI	CIE	EI	IE
ceiling	ancient	foreign	achieve
conceive	conscientious	forfeit	believe
deceive	financier	leisure	chief
perceive	legacies	neighbor	grievous
receiver	scientist	weight	siege

We all have heard the rule (subject to many exceptions) offered as an aid for spelling words that combine *e* and *i*. But can we recognize it at

work in the words listed above? Yet, these certainly are not to be classified as rare words. For all of us, reference to our dictionary will be worth
the effort whenever there is any doubt in our mind.

3. Words possibly containing double letters; examples follow.

accommodate	occupied
acquitted	occurrence
basically	parallel
equipping	personnel
installment	questionnaire

In words of this type, poor spellers are open to many kinds of mistakes.
Single letters might be doubled; letters that should be doubled might not
be; where more than one set of double letters is needed, just one set
might be used; and so forth. The only solution is to look up the word
in the dictionary.

4. Words containing an *s* sound. Among the letters and combinations of letters causing this sound are: *c, ce, cs, s, sc, se, ss, ts,* and *ze.*
Examples of such words include the following.

prophecy	miscellaneous
prophesy	misspell
advice	presence
advise	presents
facsimile	analyze

Certainly the dictionary can save us much grief in spelling the words in
this category.

Related to spelling and worth noting at this point is the division of
words at the end of a line of copy. We can find rules on this subject in
many typewriting manuals, thesis manuals, and similar sources. Some
of these rules are in agreement; others are specialized for local purposes.
Some are minimal; others are carried out to a high degree of refinement.

In business writing we are neither overly strict nor overly lax. Common sense and good judgment enter into our decisions about dividing
words, but so does the limitation of time. We can generally get satisfactory results by using the following approach:

1. We should divide words only when necessary to avoid a seriously
   uneven margin.
2. We should divide a word only between syllables—and only after
   verifying the syllabication in our dictionary. We should never guess

at the syllabication. For instance, *knowledge* is divided *knowl-edge*—although not many persons might guess it correctly.

3. We should never divide either a one-syllable word or a two-syllable word with a one-letter first syllable. Accordingly, the words *should* and *about* are never to be divided.

4. We should avoid dividing a word before a two-letter final syllable. Sometimes we can make an exception, especially if another unit of typewriting—such as a comma, period, or parenthesis—follows the last letter.

5. We should avoid dividing words on consecutive lines and from one page to another. However, we do see these practices occurring because of necessity in even the best of publications.

WORD CHOICE

Even though our words are correctly spelled, it is necessary for us to make certain both that they will be understood by our reader and that they convey the meaning we intend. Here again is where our dictionary, some alertness, and good judgment can come to our rescue.

There is no denying that a large vocabulary is a valuable asset. We have heard this fact aired throughout our years in school—the period during which most of our lifetime vocabulary is developed. In our daily life, too, we come across features in magazines and newspapers urging us to "increase word power." Having a large vocabulary is especially helpful to us in reading. The more we can read and understand, the more knowledgeable and intelligent we become. Our mind, which is seemingly unlimited in its storage capacity, is more and more enriched as we accumulate knowledge. We are increasingly better able to solve problems and rise to the occasion in emergencies.

While a large vocabulary may help us gather knowledge, we must learn how to control it. Our position in relaying information is like that of an intermediary handler who repackages a product for the consumer. Our inflow of facts may have hinged on our large vocabulary, but our outflow to our reader should be based on an understanding of the facts. If we really understand what we are trying to communicate, we should be able to express our message in words that are easy to follow. In that way, we are able to get the facts across to our reader and, in many cases, render him a distinct service.

In the matter of word choice, we should be guided by the following suggestions:

1. Use ordinary words whenever possible. Even though we happen

to be at home with the vocabulary of a specific activity or profession, we may not assume that our reader is equally well versed. So, unless we know our reader to be on the same technical level, we should translate our thoughts into ordinary words when we write to him. In some instances we might have to use a technical word for the lack of a substitute —or we may believe that our professional standing would be jeopardized were we to go too far afield. Such situations do not become dilemmas, however. We can resort to a clear definition of the term, and then use it consistently within that meaning. To be avoided also are the nonprofessional words which are difficult for the ordinary person to understand. The fact that we read such words—or even do our thinking with them—has nothing to do with our reader. He depends on his own vocabulary when he tries to read what we have written. He is not likely to view our request letter, sales letter, or application letter as "required" reading. If such a message is troublesome to read, he may not choose to continue the effort.

2. Use words within their precise meaning. One of our aims in communicating is to make sure that we cannot be misunderstood. To this end, we must be careful in the use of slang and jargon. Also, we must be careful to keep our use of conventional words under proper control. Over the years some words and phrases have become widely used in meanings which are not accurate. While they may get by in the sense of communicating, such words and phrases tend to tattle on us when they are seen by the discriminating segment of our readers. If we stick to ordinary words and use them accurately, we should be clear to all our readers without the danger of appearing substandard to any of them. Some frequently misused words are listed below.

WORD	REMARKS
advise	is used excessively and often incorrectly. It implies giving advice. Specific words should be used when other meanings are intended: *explain, inform, state, tell.*
amount	is singular in concept; it should not be used in place of *number.*
between	refers to two things only; *among* should be used when we are referring to more than two things.
can	is used to denote power or possibility; *may* is used to ask or grant permission.

WORD	REMARKS
claim	means to demand as a matter of right. We should not use it in place of *allege, assert, say,* or *state.*
further	is used to signify degree, quantity, or time. To indicate spatial distance, we should use the word *farther.*
if	should be used to introduce a condition or a sup- position. We use *whether* (sometimes followed by *or, or not, or whether,* etc.) to indicate an alternative of some kind.
less	refers to a bulk concept (amount, degree, quantity, and the like). We should use *fewer* when we refer to a plural concept.
locate	should be used to signify something in a particular place. A different word, *find,* means to come upon or discover.
per	is best limited to Latin phrases, such as per annum, per capita, percent, per diem, and per se. In an English phrase, we should use *a* or *an.*
providing	the present participle should not be used to mean *if.* We could use *provided*—but *if* would still be our better choice.

3. Use words which will not cause distractions. Such words, al- though they are of the ordinary type and are used correctly, turn out to be poor choices. At times, the reason is a side meaning or connotation which gets our reader onto a thought tangent.

As an example of such a possibility, let us consider the word "strike," as in "strike a match."

A present or former baseball pitcher might find his mind drawn (pleasantly enough) to some incident in which he blazed a fast ball past a blinking batsman.

But, a baseball slugging star might begin reenacting an argument with the umpire who called him out on strikes with the bases loaded in the ninth inning.

A mining engineer might have all sorts of pleasant mental pictures upon seeing this particular word.

Yet, a labor-relations officer of a threatened company might easily be channeled into unhappy thoughts about the current situation.

At other times, words are used in a way that may indicate either misspelling or an incorrect meaning; at any rate, it is apparent that we are using a word we do not really know how to handle. Rather glaring examples are "renumerate" for "remunerate," or "momentum" for "memento." Examples of other cases where we must distinguish follow.

WORDS	REMARKS
affect—effect	*Affect* is a verb meaning either to influence or to pretend. *Effect* as a noun means result; as a verb, it means to accomplish, or produce as a result.
imply—infer	The speaker or writer *implies* (hints at, suggests) something; the listener or reader *infers* something from what is said or written.

WORDS	REMARKS
principle—principal	*Principle* refers only to a tenet, rule, assumption, an underlying idea. *Principal* means first or main; a leading person; or a sum of money in various usages.

The examples given are only a few of many possible ones; and indeed, we know from our studies in language and usage that even "authorities" disagree on some matters. It is unlikely that we could ever be aware of all the possible unpleasant connotations—probably the majority of words have had some such association sometime, somewhere, to someone.

We must strive to be as correct as possible. We should be sensitive to the use of certain words in addressing certain particular groups. And if we are careful to observe the matters of diplomacy, service attitude, and cordial tone, we can be confident that this will overcome any unintentional shortcomings in word choice.

GRAMMAR

From the selection of the words to be used, we move to the task of putting these words together to convey the message we have in mind. We should abide by the rules of grammar to achieve clearness and to keep our reader's attention focused on the message. The following guides will help us handle grammatical matters in a satisfactory way.

1. Agreement of Case and Number

a) Basically, we should use a singular verb with a singular subject; a plural verb, with a plural or a compound subject.

> He expects our answer by noon on Monday.
>
> They want to know our warehouse manager's name.
>
> The sales manager and his assistant are attending a conference in Chicago.

b) But we must be able to recognize the true subject of the sentence. When we associate words with the subject through the use of such phrases as *in addition to, together with, as well as,* etc., we do not cause a compound subject. Thus, we do not affect the number of the verb to be used.

> A debenture issue, in addition to the first-mortgage bonds already approved, is being studied.

> This textbook, together with its homework forms, is available at the bookstore.

> Our company, as well as other manufacturing firms in the area, favors the highway proposal.

c) Sometimes we use a collective noun as the subject of a sentence. Then, we must make up our mind on the meaning we wish to convey (singular concept or plural concept) and use the corresponding number of the verb.

> The board is meeting in a private session.

> The board are talking informally while coffee is being served.

d) When we use nouns as objects, we retain the regular form. But when we use many of the pronouns as objects, we change them to the objective case.

> I gave him the monthly payment.

> He issued us a receipt.

> They did not invite her to the meeting.

But, *you* and *it* are the same in the objective case.

> We recognized you the moment you opened the door.

> I thought I had lost it; but there it was, exactly where it belonged.

e) When we use a pronoun, we should make certain that it agrees in number with its antecedent; its case depends on its position in its own clause.

> Here are the prints; they are the best I can make.

> Here are the prints; please send them to the engraver's.

f) If we use a pronoun to refer to a collective noun, we should be consistent in making both the verb used and that pronoun agree with the collective noun.

```
Maston's is making this offer to its charge-account
customers.

Maston's record is that they always have made good on
their promises.
```

g) We should distinguish between *who* (also, *whoever*), the subjective case of that pronoun, and *whom* (also, *whomever*), the objective case. When we introduce a subordinate clause with such a word, we should notice how it behaves within its own clause. If it is the subject of the clause, we use *who*; if it is the object, we use *whom*. How that clause in turn behaves in the full sentence is beside the point.

```
Notify those who you think will be interested.

Notify whoever is available.

Notify whomever you meet.
```

h) Because certain words—such as *each, every, everybody, everyone, either,* and *neither*—are singular concepts, we should use a singular verb when such a word is our subject.

```
Each of these applicants meets the minimum requirements.

Everybody knows that the regulation is unfair.

Either place is a suitable location for our new plant.

Neither is able to keep up his payments.
```

i) When *either* is coupled with *or* in a subject (also, *neither* with *nor*), we use the number of the verb agreeing with the portion of the subject that is nearer the verb.

```
Either Billings or Tuttle is available to help you.

Either the workers or the supervisors have misinter-
preted the agreement.

Neither the boxes nor the merchandise was damaged.

Neither the merchandise nor the boxes were damaged.
```

j) When we use the collective pronoun *none* as subject, we must choose the proper number of the verb. If *none* refers to a singular or bulk concept, we should use a singular verb; if it refers to a plural concept, we should use a plural verb. In general, if we can handle *all,* we can also handle *none.* (*Some, any,* and *most* are treated in the same manner.)

```
All of the merchandise has arrived.

None of the merchandise has arrived.

All of the packages have been mailed.

None of the packages have been mailed.
```

k) Ordinarily, we do not have much of a problem with the possessive case. For people and living things, we usually form the possessive case by adding *'s* (singular) or *'* (plural). Proper names of one syllable and ending in *s* usually take the *'s.* Through accepted usage, personifications and certain other words also take *'s.* But inanimate objects, strictly speaking, do not "possess" and should take the genitive construction, *of the.*

```
We found the woman's purse.

The dog injured its paw.

Credit this payment to Mr. Black's account.

Mr. Jones's desk has been repaired. (BUT Mr. Williams').

Our advertisement appeared in Saturday's newspaper.

This is today's assignment.

The spring of the lock is broken.
```

Our chief concern in using the possessive case of pronouns is that the number (singular or plural) agree with that of the antecedent. As for form, an apostrophe is not used with any of the personal possessive pronouns; one is used with an indefinite pronoun (such as *one, everyone, nobody,* etc.).

```
My secretary has already finished her work.

The roofers will begin their job on Wednesday.

This is my first experience with an electronic computer.

Everyone's assignment is listed in the memorandum.

That report is nobody's business but ours.
```

In a specialized usage, we couple the possessive case with a gerund.

```
We'd appreciate your taking Mr. Brown through the
factory.
```

2. Proper Form of Words

a) Our regular manner of discourse is carried on in the indicative mood; but when we state a supposition that is contrary to fact, we switch to the subjunctive mood.

```
If I were you, I should consult a doctor.
```

But not every supposition is necessarily contrary to fact.

```
If he was at the meeting, I did not see him.
```

b) In our most formal writing, and in reading literary works which conform to that style, it is useful to know that some writers use *shall* (or *should*) to denote simple futurity in the first person, and to denote a sense of determination in the second and third persons.

```
I shall gladly support your plan.
They shall not pass.
```

However, good general usage in the United States today, particularly in the relatively informal, personal tone that is preferred for business writing, indicates the use of *will* to indicate simple futurity in all three persons.

```
I will appreciate your comments on this proposal.
I would say that this is the best plan.
```

We can also, informally, use the contractions.

```
We'd appreciate your cooperation.
I'll gladly support your plan.
```

c) Sometimes we have a problem with modifying words. Articles and adjectives are used to modify nouns; adverbs are used to modify verbs, adjectives, and other adverbs. We have three articles in our language: the indefinite articles *a* and *an,* and the definite article *the. A* is used with words beginning with sounded consonants and with the vowel *u* when it carries the sound of "you." *An* is used with words beginning with a silent consonant followed by a vowel (e.g., *hour*) and all words beginning with *a, e, i,* and *o,* as well as the vowel *u* when it carries the sound of "uh."

```
It is a good offer.

This is an active stock.

Mr. Jensen has been here an hour or more.

The accounting department is short of help.

I recommend that we buy the property.
```

When we use adjectives and adverbs, we should be careful to use the proper form for our purpose. Often, adverbs are derived from adjectives through the addition of *-ally* or *-ly*.

```
Our delivery man is a careful driver.

Our delivery man drives carefully.

He seems to get real enjoyment from his work.

He takes a really keen interest in his work.

It is a basically sound idea.

They very quietly entered the room.
```

3. Idiomatic Expressions

Apart from strict grammar, we are often guided by what is called idiomatic usage. Certain combinations of words are customarily used for certain purposes and become the established phraseology. This is particularly apparent in the use of specific prepositions with specific objects.

```
We advertise in magazines throughout the country.

Last year we advertised on radio.
```

If we use two idiomatic expressions of exactly the same form, we may express the preposition only once; but if we use two different idioms, we must express both prepositions.

```
We advertised in magazines and newspapers.

We advertised in magazines and on radio.
```

SENTENCE STRUCTURE

In addition to the grammatical formation of a sentence, there is the matter of proper placement or positioning of the various parts. As we have noted before, in business writing it is not enough that our message can be understood; our message should be incapable of being misunderstood. Thus, we should always place modifying words, phrases, and clauses within our sentences in such a way that the reader cannot misinterpret our meaning. Usually, we accomplish this by positioning the modifiers as near as possible to the words they modify. Also, when we join two or more parts of a sentence by conjunctions, we should provide for our reader's ease in following our thoughts. This we do by casting each such part of the sentence into a similar pattern or construction.

1. Modifiers

a)   When we use individual modifying words (adjectives and adverbs), we should, if possible, place them adjacent to the words they modify.

```
I have time for only one more interview.

He has paid almost half of his installments.

I only heard the collision; I did not see it happen.
```

In the case of adverbs, we sometimes achieve a desired effect by placing them away from the verb they modify. In such cases, we often use a comma, or commas, to set the adverb off from the rest of the sentence.

```
Ordinarily, marked-down merchandise is not returnable
for a refund.

It would be a good idea, ultimately, for you to
diversify your product line.
```

When we modify an infinitive, we should ordinarily place the adverb either in front of or after the whole infinitive, but not between the sign of the infinitive (*to*) and the continuation. Smoothness and naturalness are the criteria on whether to split an infinitive.

```
The rule is to weigh carefully all material that is
delivered to the construction site.

I want you especially to read the paragraphs that have
been checked in red ink.
```

b)   When we use modifying phrases, we should place them as close as possible to the words they modify. Phrases introduced by the present participles of verbs (called participial phrases) are particularly troublesome. Our clue to correctness is whether the word just after such a phrase, or just before it, can logically be modified by that phrase.

```
Seeing that business was slack, we decided to close the
store earlier than usual.

The general manager, realizing that production was be-
hind schedule, called a meeting of the department heads.
```

c) In the use of modifying clauses, we must be on guard especially with those which modify nouns. *Who* and *whom* are high among our clue words. Because more than one person may be mentioned in our sentence, a "who" clause should be as near as possible to the word it modifies.

```
Mr. Vickers, who was hired on Monday, has already made
a valuable suggestion to the office manager.

He is a trainee whom we are recommending for promotion
ahead of the rest of his group.
```

The same caution holds true for *which* (things) and *that* (people or things). Moreover, we must sometimes provide a summary word for the clause to modify, so that the meaning will be clear.

```
We are granting you credit for the goods returned, an
adjustment which we hope will be satisfactory.
```

d) Sometimes we use what is called an "elliptical clause." This is a clause in which the subject and part of the verb are omitted. In such a case, we must take care that what comes either immediately after the clause, or immediately before it, is the understood subject of that clause.

```
While storing the boxes, you may be able to count the
number on hand.

When repaired, this machine should be almost as good as
new.

This machine, when repaired, should be almost as good
as new.
```

2. Parallel Construction

a) When we join two concepts with the conjunction *and,* we should be careful that we put both concepts in the same grammatical formation. This technique permits our reader to absorb our message smoothly. We may join two nouns, two adjectives, two verbs, two adverbs, two infinitive phrases, two participial phrases, two clauses, two sentences, and so on. But we should not pair a noun and a verb, a noun and a clause, a phrase and a clause, or any other dissimilar formations.

> A tablet and a pencil were placed on each desk.
>
> Remove all the bent and broken pieces from the bin.
>
> Please stamp and mail these letters.
>
> When you enter, go cautiously and quietly.
>
> He is in New York to attend the various style shows and to buy a selection of dresses for our stock.
>
> This machine can be used both for producing goods and for repairing tools.
>
> Because some stores give trading stamps and we do not, we have had to emphasize the value of our merchandise and service.
>
> Mr. Cardwell wanted to sign the papers today, and he was waiting in his office for the lawyer to arrive.

b) Included in this category, but sufficiently troublesome to warrant separate attention, are the combinations *and who, and which,* and the like. To be parallel in construction, our sentences should contain these combinations only when we have used a respective *who, which,* and the like in an earlier part of the sentence.

> He is a man who is able to come and who would be happy to help.
>
> The box contained the shirts which I had ordered in May and which I had expected to receive more than a month ago.

c) Sometimes we use correlative conjunctions (*either . . . or, neither . . . nor, not only . . . but also,* and so on) to join concepts. In such a case, we should be careful that the concept adjacent to one correlative conjunction is in the same grammatical formation as the concept that is adjacent to the other correlative conjunction.

> We learned that we could borrow the money from either a bank or a loan company.

```
He is neither rich nor poor.

They carry not only a full line of men's suits but
also a wide variety of shirts.
```

d) At times we wish to connect more than two concepts. Such an arrangement, called a series, should be kept parallel, also. We should use all nouns, all verbs, all sentences, etc.—not a mixture of different parts of speech and/or different grammatical formations.

```
They specialize in making bolts, nuts, and washers.

Each piece must be machined, enameled, and baked.

The Bactrian camel has two humps, the dromedary has
one hump, and the llama has no hump.
```

PUNCTUATION

An area of language expression which is important to us in business communication, and yet which is somewhat troublesome to many of us, is punctuation. The difficulty apparently lies in our looking at punctuation as a body of rules governing the different marks of punctuation. Perhaps it would be wiser for us to relate punctuation to the functions it is trying to perform.

In our spoken language we seldom, if ever, give a thought to punctuation. We change the pitch of our voice, we speed up, we slow down, we pause, we stop. At times we use facial expressions and gestures to add meaning and emphasis to what we are saying. Even our eyes can help in putting across our message. In writing, however, we have no opportunity to use these methods; our words are merely two-dimensional symbols appearing on paper. But we have at our disposal a limited number of signals, called punctuation marks, which we use to let our reader know when he should pause, stop, imagine a rising inflection, and so on. These signals do not produce as dramatic a result as we could have done orally, but they do help the reader get the most out of our written message. In fact, properly guided, our reader can extract our message almost as though he were listening to us speak.

Our approach to punctuation should be that of extending the effectiveness of our spoken language into our written language. We should, of course, use the regularly accepted signals so that our reader will understand how he is to go about his task of reading. We want him to extract effortlessly from our communication the same message that we have written into it.

1. Sentences

a) Perhaps the chief marks of punctuation are those which we use to indicate the ends of sentences. We have a distinct punctuation mark for each of the three main types of sentences: the period (declarative sentence), the interrogation mark (question), and the exclamation point (exclamatory sentence).

> There is a position open in our accounting department.
>
> Mr. Hendry did not come to work that day.
>
> How soon do you expect the catalogue to be published?
>
> Of course you want your money's worth!

b) At times we may use an elliptical sentence—one in which an important part is not expressed in our writing, merely left to the understanding of our reader. If such a sentence is a question, we use an interrogation mark to punctuate it. In other kinds of sentences, we probably should use an exclamation point. This punctuation mark either will show the enthusiasm we wish to convey, or at least will signal our reader that the omission was an intentional act, not a blunder.

> Two for the price of one?
>
> Congratulations on your promotion to manager!
>
> Yes, today!

c) Under ordinary rules, we may state a polite command in the form of a question, but use a period as the end punctuation. In business writing, however, we do well to use the question mark after any sentence that is phrased as a question. The reason is that our reader then cannot misinterpret our sentence as being bossy or officious. The politeness of our message is protected, and nothing is really sacrificed.

> Will you please send these items immediately?

d) If an abbreviation occurs at the end of a declarative sentence, we use one period to punctuate both the abbreviation and the sentence. If the abbreviation occurs at the end of any other kind of sentence, we should use a period for the abbreviation and the appropriate end punctuation for the sentence.

```
As you directed, we mailed the book to Edgar Rawlins,
M.D.
```

```
Which is the order from Selby Brothers, Inc.?
```

```
Hurrah for the U.S.A.!
```

2. Clauses

a) Independent clauses (main clauses) occurring in the same sentence are regularly separated by a semicolon. The truth is that such clauses could be punctuated as separate sentences. Therein we have a clue: under ordinary conditions, a semicolon is the proper punctuation when both what precedes it and what follows it are capable of being separate sentences.

```
Mr. Radcliffe was not at the meeting; he was at our
suburban store in Eastwood.
```

```
Our final report is due on September 1; therefore,
every departmental report must be submitted by August
15.
```

```
I doubt that we can reach so high a quota; however, I
believe we shall set an all-time record for this area.
```

If we use the conjunctions *and, but, or,* or *nor,* we use a comma as the separating punctuation between independent clauses—provided we have not used a comma elsewhere in the sentence. If we have used a comma elsewhere, we use a semicolon between clauses.

```
Construction costs were high at the first location we
checked, and labor shortages were acute at the second.
```

```
There is a flaw in the veneer, but it is not a serious
defect.
```

```
As a result of the storm, a short circuit developed in
the transformer; and all operations were halted for
three hours.
```

```
Our driver can pick up the dress on Thursday; or, if
you prefer, you may bring it to our service desk on
your next visit to the store.
```

b) We should think of a dependent clause (subordinate clause) as a modifier of some part of a main clause. It is not a full sentence and therefore does not call for the use of a semicolon. If we place the subordinate clause in front of the main clause (an arrangement called the inverted order), we use a comma after it.

    When you finish taking inventory, you may quit for the
    day.

    If I am right in my estimate, we have already surpassed
    last year's total.

    Because the shipment was late, we could not hold the
    sale we had advertised.

If we place the subordinate clause after the main clause (an arrangement called the natural order), we choose between using or not using a comma according to whether the clause is restrictive (essential) or nonrestrictive.

    I intend to invest, hoping that the business climate
    will remain favorable.

    I intend to invest if the business climate remains
    favorable.

If we use *as, for,* or *since* to mean *because* when we introduce a dependent clause after a main clause, we use a comma to precede it.

    We had to make allowances for his work, as this was
    his first day on the job.

    They were surprised to see Mr. Jennings at his desk,
    for he had been given permission to go home.

    I've begun to worry about our credit policy, since this
    is the fourth consecutive month that our sales have
    declined.

We must distinguish between restrictive and nonrestrictive clauses. A restrictive clause is considered essential to an identification of the word it modifies; thus, we do not set it off by punctuation. A nonrestrictive clause merely adds further description to a word that has already been identified; since it is not essential, we set it off by commas.

    He is the man who formerly managed the Scott Company.

    Mr. Lewis, who formerly managed the Scott Company, is
    our new president.

3. Phrases

a) Another subsection of a sentence which often requires us to use punctuation is the phrase. This is a thought unit composed of two or more words, but it is not so forceful as a clause. It comes in four main varieties: the prepositional phrase, containing a preposition and its object; and three kinds containing verb formations, the participial phrase, the infinitive phrase, and the gerund phrase. When such phrases are part of the continuous thought of our sentence, we do not use punctuation with them.

```
He opened the door and walked into the office.

She is hopeful of getting a position with a commercial
bank.

Mr. White entered the hospital to receive a thorough
physical examination.

Running a sales office can be a worthwhile experience.
```

If we use phrases merely as additives (explanatory or non-essential wording), we indicate this fact to our reader by setting them off by commas.

```
In short, he doesn't want any more delays.

Knowing your need for this piece of equipment, we have
given your order top priority.

Mr. Newalt, to make sure that the installation will be
done right, will personally supervise the job for you.
```

4. Words

a) Since words are our basic thought units, we ordinarily are not concerned with punctuation marks in front of or behind them. Usually one word follows another in the development of a larger thought segment, such as a phrase, clause, or sentence. There are times, however, when individual words are to be read with pauses; and in these instances, we regularly use commas to indicate the pauses. Examples are adverbs which we have placed away from the words they modify and certain conjunctions, after which our reader is supposed to make a brief pause.

Generally, the parking ban does not apply after regular
working hours.

This is a main part of the plan, however; we must not
ignore it.

The accident was held to be unavoidable; therefore,
the operator was not accused of negligence.

He plans to drive to Louisville; and, if you wish to
go along, he will be glad to take you.

b) Sometimes we use two or more adjectives consecutively. To help
our reader get the precise meaning intended, we often need to
separate these words by a comma. One way of deciding is to
examine the noun that is being modified. If the modifier next to
the noun can properly be considered a part of the noun concept,
only the remaining modifier or modifiers are behaving as adjectives. We then do not need a comma until we have three
words (apparent modifiers) in front of the noun.

Please use the stamped return envelope for your answer.

We are enclosing a convenient, stamped return envelope
for your answer.

If all the adjectives in the sequence modify the noun itself, then
we use a comma between each adjective.

He brought us a big, ripe mango from Florida.

Please use the addressed, stamped envelope which we
have enclosed.

c) In a series of three or more words, we should use a comma after
each item in the series, except the last.

The colors of our flag are red, white, and blue.

Hospitalization, retirement deposits, and insurance
premiums are the other items handled through payroll
deductions.

Some of the people applauded, some cheered, and some
wept as the rescuers brought the last miner out of the
tunnel.

When we already have a comma in one or more of the items of
the series, we use a semicolon for each of the major separations.

```
The dates of our three orders were December 10, 1965;
January 25, 1966; and March 7, 1966.
```

d) Sometimes common nouns, people's names, and the like are used in apposition to some other word in a sentence. When this occurs, we set off such appositives by commas. State names, and years in dates, are set off by commas.

```
The man in charge, the chief clerk, gave me a receipt.

The manager of their company, Mr. Paul Engels, will
meet you at the airport.

I met him in Denver, Colorado, last September.

He was hired on November 6, 1964, and has worked for
us ever since.
```

e) Sometimes we form compound words by hyphenating. These may be nouns, verbs, or adjectives. Generally, adjective forms are connected by a hyphen when they precede the word modified, but not hyphenated when they follow it.

```
Proper follow-up makes a big difference.

Single-space the lines in this report.

He is a well-known man in our city.

He is well known.
```

Compounding is a complex subject, and there is wide variation in usage. The most important point to remember is to be consistent within any one document, and in words that we use consistently in our regular correspondence. In doubtful cases, we must use a dictionary or consult the special section within the dictionary dealing with compounds. As a generalization, it is useful to realize that good modern style tends to minimize hyphens. Very common combinations, whose use is well understood as a single concept, may be made into one word (buildup, commonsense, overall, nationwide) or used as two words without a hyphen (data processing, key punch, public relations). Similarly, the trend is to "close up" (not hyphenate) the common prefixes and suffixes: co-, non-, re-, pre-, etc. Fractions are hyphenated as adjectives (a one-fourth interest), but not as nouns (two thirds of the business).

5. Enumerations

a) When we wish to enumerate a series of items, we regularly use a colon to introduce them.

> We want the complete outfit: the projector, the screen, and the extension cord.
>
> His reasons for dieting were three, namely: (1) a dislike of being teased by his associates, (2) a fear of high blood pressure, and (3) a desire to look trim.

6. Insertions

a) Occasionally, we insert a side thought or point of clarification during the progress of a sentence. The insertion may be a word, a phrase, or a clause. The traditional punctuation for this purpose has been parentheses; but the modern trend is to use dashes, except when parentheses are obviously the better choice.

> Often—almost every day, in fact—we must turn down an applicant for credit.
>
> If they get the order—heaven forbid!—they will have taken over our best territory.
>
> In poor weather—for example, when there is snow or ice on the ground—our location is not very accessible.
>
> During the previous year (1964), our profits had continued to rise.

b) In rarer instances, we may wish to insert an entire sentence within the sentence that contains our main thought. Unless it has to be capitalized for another reason, the first word of such an inserted sentence is not capitalized. If it is a declarative sentence, it does not call for a period at the end. But if it is a question or an exclamation, it does call for its own ending punctuation.

> He is one of the guiding forces—in fact, he is the leading banker—of our city.
>
> The man who wore the tan suit—do you know his name?—is the one who impressed us most.
>
> Professor Smith—I remember him well!—could add the figures as rapidly as we could read them off.

7. Quotations

a) We handle the punctuation of quoted matter in business writing the same as we do in regular composition work. Quotation marks are used immediately before and after the quoted matter. Commas and periods used with closing quotation marks are always placed inside the marks, but other marks are placed inside only if they are part of the quotation.

> As the saying goes, "There is no time like the present."
>
> "Who wrote this report?" the office manager asked.
>
> To test for a possible "slide," divide the difference between the debit total and the credit total by nine.

b) If we use only a part of a quotation, we put in ellipses (. . . at the beginning or middle of a quotation, and . . . . at the end of the quotation) to inform our reader of our intentional omission.

> The regulation clearly states, "Failure to comply with the foregoing requirements will result in the suspension of the driver's license of the operator . . . for a period of three years. . . ."

LANGUAGE TEAMWORK

From this discussion of readability, and especially of the mechanics of expression, emerges a significant fact. As we apply the various influences which make our writing easier for our reader to absorb, we also make the mechanics of expression easier for ourselves to handle. And, as we handle our writing mechanics with greater accomplishment, we make our message still easier to read. This interaction certainly seems worthy of being set into motion.

Readability is predicated on correct language expression. But it goes far beyond mere correctness. It requires that we write at a level which the typical business reader can understand effortlessly. Thus, we are encouraged to write in the personal tone and in the informal style for the purpose of sharpening our reader's interest. We are told to favor a mixture of sentences which average out to a moderate length. We should prefer the use of simple sentences to other types, and especially prefer to cut down on compound sentences. In selecting our words, we should keep our specialized and technical vocabularies under control and use short, familiar words as much as possible.

In following such guides, we discover that most of the problems of language expression have been avoided. By selecting short, familiar words, our spelling task is simplified; and so is our job of using words correctly and precisely. Problems of grammar, sentence structure, and punctuation are at a minimum when we express our thoughts in simple sentences. It is usually in connection with complex and compound sentences that we begin to have such problems as straying subjects, lost antecedents, dangling participles, mixed constructions, and all sorts of confused punctuation.

The simpler our writing is, the easier it is to handle correctly. If our writing is handled correctly, it is easier for our reader to follow. There is, consequently, a kind of teamwork or beneficial exchange going on between good readability and correctly handled writing.

SUMMARY

Language is the encoding aspect of business communication. It is viewed from the angle of readability, particularly as it relates to the mechanics of expression.

Readability pertains to the ease with which our reader can extract the message from our communication. Seven factors contribute to the readability of a piece of business writing: tone, voice, style, wording, direction of thought, mechanics of expression, and eye appeal. Several readability measurement systems, including one suggested in this chapter, have been devised to help the writer know how well his work will be understood. These systems should not be relied upon exclusively. All of them are limited in that they measure only a few of the factors that have a bearing on readability.

The mechanics of expression should be mastered before we try to write business communications. But guides and summary reviews can often refresh us in this area. The principal divisions are spelling, choice of words, grammar, sentence structure, and punctuation. For clear communication, we must handle our language expression in accordance with the generally understood rules.

Fortunately for us, the mechanics of expression, when executed properly, aid readability in a sort of circular progression. The steps that lead to readability make language expression easier for us to handle. Correct language expression, in turn, makes our writing additionally easier to read.

QUESTIONS

· · · · · · · · · ·

1. In the preparation of a written communication, what constitutes the *encoding* of the message? *language*

2. Is writing conversationally a desirable usage in business communication? *limited*

3. What is meant by *readability*? *reading gets same message in decoding*

4. Although the active voice is to be preferred, what two reasons exist for occasionally using the passive voice?

5. Distinguish between the formal style and the informal style of writing.

6. What is implied in the suggestion that short words be used in place of long words in order to enhance readability?

7. What kind of sentence is best for fulfilling the requirements of a straight-line direction of thought?

8. Discuss the value of eye appeal in enhancing readability.

9. What are the criteria for a system to measure the readability of a business communication?

10. Identify the influences on readability which are used in the measuring system presented in this chapter.

11. Explain what is meant by *human-interest words.*

12. What steps can be taken to improve the readability score of a given piece of writing?

13. Suggest some of the advantages arising from a readability control chart such as the one described in this chapter.

14. What shortcomings exist in connection with readability measurement systems?

15. Identify four classes of words that are known to be troublesome to spell.

16. What are the criteria for dividing words at the end of a typewritten line?

17. What is the proper viewpoint concerning a large vocabulary?

18. What suggestions are offered as ways of controlling vocabulary?

19. List the language considerations which this chapter has assigned to the area of *grammar.*

20. List the language considerations which this chapter has assigned to the area of *sentence structure*.

21. What is used in oral language in place of the punctuation marks which appear in written language?

EXERCISES

4–1. Determine the following data concerning the letter which appears below (body only).

Number of words . . . . ____

Number of sentences . . . . ____

Number of syllables . . . . ____

Number of human-interest words . . . . ____

NOTE: Simplify your work by counting words and syllables one line at a time. Enter the count for each line in the marginal columns at the left and right. Total each column for the final count. For human-interest words, underline each one that appears in the body of the letter, and then count the words you have underlined.

WORDS   SYLLABLES

Gentlemen:

____   This letter will introduce to you Mr. Sidney   ____

____   Blake, who has become our new buyer of industrial   ____

____   chemicals. He is replacing George Walters, who has   ____

____   retired to a life of leisure in Tucson, Arizona.   ____

____   Mr. Blake is new at his present work, but he   ____

____   has had the benefit of three years' experience in   ____

____   our purchasing office. He is very pleasant to be   ____

____   with and eager to succeed. Best of all, he comes   ____

____   personally recommended by George Walters.   ____

____   Mr. Blake will be in to see you at 9:30 A.M.   ____

____   on May 12 to discuss the renewal of our chemical-   ____

____   supply contract. We have always been pleased by   ____

____   your cooperation in the past and are confident that   ____

____   you will receive Mr. Blake warmly on this, his   ____

____   first visit to your company. We hope that you will   ____

____   work with him in settling the terms for the coming   ____

____   year.   ____

____

____   Very truly yours,   *total 205*

4–2. From the data arrived at in Exercise 4–1, compute a readability score for the letter and evaluate it in terms of the control chart shown in this chapter.

4–3. Following the procedure outlined in Exercise 4–1, compute a readability score for the letter shown below (body only). Evaluate the score on the basis of the control chart shown in this chapter.

WORDS   SYLLABLES

       Dear Mrs. Auburn:

_____   I can readily share your feelings at not being   _____

_____   able to serve the candy you had planned on having   _____

_____   at your daughter's birthday party. Likewise, I am _____

_____   grateful that you informed us of this situation.   _____

_____   Enclosed is a check for the full amount of the _____

_____   candy, postage, and handling charges. And, as a   _____

_____   birthday token to your daughter, a Bonnie Lass   _____

_____   doll will be arriving shortly after this letter.   _____

_____   I am sure that in the future we will serve you   _____

_____   most adequately from our large selection of can- _____

_____   dies. Please let us know whenever we can be of   _____

_____   assistance to you.   _____

_____   Cordially yours,   _____

4-4. Following the procedure outlined in Exercise 4–1, compute a readability score for the memorandum shown below (body only). Evaluate the score on the basis of the control chart shown in this chapter.

WORDS   SYLLABLES

_____   TO: Mr. Andrew A. Crawford, President   _____

_____   FROM: Vincent D. Fallon, Personnel Director   _____

_____   SUBJECT: Recommendation of Manager for Cincinnati   _____

_____   Branch Office   _____

_____   The purpose of this memorandom is to recommend the   _____

_____   person best qualified to fill the position of man-   _____

_____   ager at our branch office in Cincinnati. I am rec-   _____

_____   ommending Charles R. Kope for this position.   _____

_____   My decision is based on an analysis of information   _____

_____   contained in the personnel records of the three   _____

_____   leading candidates. My findings are as follows: _____

_____   1. Charles R. Kope, my choice, has been em-   _____

_____   ployed by Burns-Ohio for five years. A   _____

_____   graduate of Great Lakes University, he has   _____

_____   always scored high on our management apti-   _____

_____   tude tests. At age 30, he has served three   _____

_____   years as assistant to our Sales Manager.   _____

_____   His performance ratings are excellent.   _____

_____   2. The second candidate, Wilbur D. Moss, has   _____

_____   had 10 years' experience in sales—four of   _____

_____   them with Burns-Ohio. He holds a business   _____

_____   degree from Babson College, but has never   _____

_____   had a high score on any of the management   _____

_____   aptitude tests. On the other hand, he has   _____

_____   the best sales record of all our salesmen.   _____

_____   It would appear that he will best serve   _____

_____   Burns-Ohio and himself by continuing as   _____

_____   a salesman.   _____

_____　　3. The third candidate, Gregory W. Holton, has　_____
_____　　　been employed in our purchasing office for　_____
_____　　　the past six years. He is 28 years old and　_____
_____　　　has not yet completed college. He has been　_____
_____　　　working toward a liberal-arts degree during　_____
_____　　　the evenings. Although his scores on our　_____
_____　　　management aptitude tests and reports from　_____
_____　　　his department manager are very favorable,　_____
_____　　　Mr. Holton probably is not quite ready ·to　_____
_____　　　take over a branch office.

_____　Through this comparison, therefore, I believe that　_____
_____　Charles R. Kope makes the best choice to carry out　_____
_____　the policies of Burns-Ohio and to direct activities　_____
_____　in the Cincinnati branch.
　　　　　　　　　　　　　V.D.F.

4–5. Presented below is an excerpt from a government agency report to a group of trade-union representatives. It attempts to explain the government's attitude toward revising priorities then in effect on strategic raw materials.

Following the procedure outlined in Exercise 4–1, compute a readability score for this excerpt. Then evaluate the score on the basis of the control chart shown in this chapter.

WORDS　　　　　　　　　　　　　　　　　　　　　　　　　　SYLLABLES

_____	We are now peaking our program philosophically,	_____
_____	but it is naive to assume the allotment program is	_____
_____	an equity program unless the allotments are so	_____
_____	abysmally low that they permit the agency to relax	_____
_____	and allow market determination as a percentage of	_____
_____	base period, sidetracking military return with	_____
_____	adjustments.	_____
_____	This is based on use levels proportionately and	_____
_____	is in the market test sense. We have a quantitative	_____
_____	framework with marginal qualitative reallocations	_____
_____	to formalize the procedure for further refining and	_____
_____	implementing of our objectives.	_____

4–6. Each of the following sentences contains a word which is either incorrect or a poor choice. Rewrite each sentence, replacing the questionable word with another of similar but more precise meaning.

1. Their annual rate for absenteeism averages about two days per employee.

2. Under the terms of sale, we can take up to six months to pay our bill.

3. I could not locate you at your office yesterday.

4. We do not know if this is the beginning of a new era in sales promotion.

5. They ~~claim~~ that this detergent will give the best results. *say*

6. ~~Less~~ men will be needed after the new equipment has been installed. *fewer*

7. We will buy the goods, ~~providing~~ shipment can be guaranteed by Friday. *provided*

8. Please ~~advise~~ us of your preference. *inform*

9. The distance was ~~further~~ than we had estimated. *farther*

10. We saw a large ~~amount~~ of people gathered near the truck. *number*

4–7. The following sentences contain grammatical errors. Rewrite these sentences; use correct grammar throughout.

1. When I applied for a charge account, they told me that my credit rating was excellent.

2. Burns-Ohio is always ready to serve their customers.

3. The vote favored postponing the meeting until the next day, which we did.

4. Everybody in our office have their own telephones.

5. None of the machines was damaged in the fire.

6. Neither the merchandise nor the boxes was to be found.

7. This is the man whom I thought was recommended.

8. The matter should be kept confidential between you and I.

9. If I was you, I would consult a lawyer.

10. We will be glad to serve you on a cash basis.

11. He appreciates you showing Mr. Allison the factory cafeteria.

12. Because snow had been expected was not a valid reason for staying home.

13. Give this warning to whomever is in the foundry.

14. The price of this lamp is only $14.95 apiece and may be obtained at either of our suburban stores.

15. All of the merchandise on this order, as well as our invoice, were sent to you on March 12.

4–8. The following sentences contain faulty sentence structure. Rewrite these sentences so that the structural defects will have been corrected.

1. Knowing that you wanted them as soon as possible, the goods were sent by air express.

2. It is too early to definitely tell what the outcome will be.

3. He will either pay for the merchandise by check or cash.

4. Mr. Hadley is going to Florida for his vacation and to visit many of our dealers in that state.

5. Our accountants are alert, inquisitive, and often make worthwhile suggestions.

6. He is the man chosen by our employees and who will head our charity drive this year.

7. Before reaching a decision, we suggest that you review the cost estimates.

8. To get the best performance from this calculator, a contract for monthly service is advisable.

9. The pipe was too lengthy to store it in the tool shed.

10. When painted, you will say that the truck could pass for new.

11. We only sell our product to dealers.

12. Upon retirement, your pension will amount to $212.50 a month.

13. Careless granting of credit may cause losses to your company, which does not seem likely at present.

14. He not only works hard all day, but putting in extra hours is commonplace with him also.

15. Each tube is placed inside a cardboard box, and then they are packed into a corrugated paper case.

4–9. Something is defective about the punctuation used in the following sentences. Rewrite these sentences, using correct punctuation throughout.

1. They have gone back to the method of straight-line depreciation; the system we used when we first started our business.

2. The driver found the house door locked, so he left the parcel inside the garage.

3. Before signing your letter be sure that there are no misspellings in it.

4. Included among the articles were watches, bracelets, and some unfinished gems, however nothing was extremely valuable.

5. The lawyer, who prepared your contract, is no longer with our firm.

6. "Who wrote this report," the manager asked?

7. Its time for management to speak it's piece.

8. Congratulations on your recent promotion.

9. If prices come down I plan to invest in the stock market.

10. Will your downtown office be open on Saturday!

11. Our president is a well known man in banking circles.

12. They opened stores in Gulfport, Mississippi, Mobile, Alabama, and Tampa, Florida.

13. Our topcoats come in four colors: blue, tan, brown and charcoal.

14. Two-thirds of the day's output was spoiled by the water.

15. The question remains: Who shouted, "Fire"?

4–10. For one reason or another, the following sentences are defective in the mechanics of language. Rewrite each sentence correctly.

1. The high cost of maintainance was the deciding factor.

2. We gathered these opinions by means of a house to house survey.

3. Burns-Ohio requests that their goods be held in storage.

4. This was a special shipment made via air express.

5. His prophesy of a strike this year has not come true.

6. Containing only college graduates, the office manager believed his department would win the efficiency prize.

7. The watchman reported a strange occurance that happened in furnace room.

8. By who's authority was this piece of equipment installed?

9. Perserverance is a mark of the successful businessman.

10. Two officers are striving for reelection, the president and the treasurer.

11. My drill press is different than his.

12. Mr. Hartley, rest his soul! introduced me to my first employer.

13. The mine office is still in good condition although some minor repairs will have to be made to the roof.

14. The largest model priced at $900 would not be good for our purposes.

15. We are confident that once you have tasted this candy that you will prefer it over any other kind.

···

CHAPTER 5

TRANSMITTING THE MESSAGE

The final area of consideration in the development of a business communication is that of form. In its relationship to the business communication process, form has some important roles to play. It is first of all the transmitting device by which the message is made accessible to the reader. Since it moves from our hands to the reader's hands, although with the help of some carrier, it functions (in the sense of being a document or medium) as a major element in the channel of communication. Once in the reader's hands, it becomes the equivalent of a receiving instrument, from which he begins his task of extracting our message. Unlike most other media, a business letter is not subject to distortions or noise from the time it takes the form of a document to the time the reader examines that document. But we, the fabricators of the document, if we are not careful, could build into it something that might become noise to our reader.

Because form, especially that of the business letter, has been long established, there has been a tendency to give only cursory attention to it in many modern textbooks. Possibly this attitude is due to the division of labor involving correspondence: executive personnel compose the letters; lower-level personnel take care of the form. But a chain is no stronger than its weakest link. A letter defective in form can undermine our purpose, just as can a letter defective in language or content. As the writer of a letter, we are held finally responsible for that letter in all its aspects—form, language, and content. To do a really good job we must have a sound basis of judgment in each of these aspects.

Before examining the specific elements of form, we can list a few general criteria:

1. *Form should be conventional.* Form should be used in keeping with the standards in effect at the time it is being applied. This criterion suggests that we keep alert to the gradual changes taking place and make whatever adjustments are needed to keep our form as typical as possible. We should be neither the first to jump at a new fad nor the last to give up a dying practice.

2. *Form should help create interest.* In essence, form concerns the placement of our message on paper. This can be done in an attractive way or in a discouraging way, as judged by our reader. If we use an attractive form—for example, generous side margins, ample vertical spacing, short opening and closing paragraphs, moderate-length middle paragraphs, listings when several points are involved, and a generally uncrowded appearance—we tend to stimulate our reader's interest. Thus, even before he begins to read our message, he feels encouraged to do so.

3. *Form should be inconspicuous.* The function of form is to present our message to the reader. It is therefore a means to an end, not an end in itself. Since the reader has only so much attention he can muster at any given time, we should prefer that he put all of it on what we have to say. Anything about our form—strangeness, gaudiness, blunders, messiness, unnecessary parts (printed or typewritten), dense paragraphs, and the like—that captures any of his attention is actually a type of noise. We should guard against implanting distractions when we apply form.

Business-letter form may be viewed as a twofold element. One part concerns subjective aspects, which actually comprise a planning task more than one of production. We who compose letters must make certain decisions about form, regardless of who does the production work. Whoever types our letter must reflect these decisions, as well as all standard matters of form, in the final document. The other part of form concerns the objective aspect, as evidenced by the body of rules and conventions concerning the physical preparation of letters and envelopes.

SUBJECTIVE FORM

There is little doubt that we all know what a business letter looks like. It has an identifiable appearance which makes it recognizable without our needing to examine it closely. If we were sitting in an office across from a person who was reading a business letter, we should not have to be told what he was doing. And, if that person were to hold the letter up with the typewritten side toward us, the positioning of the parts, the number of paragraphs, the density of each paragraph, the proportionate width of the margins, and the like would also be discernible. But, if the distance between us were rather great, we probably could not make out the words.

The same kind of situation would exist if the letter were written in Spanish or Russian, or any other language that we happened not to know. Even up close, if it followed conventional form, such a letter would *look* all right, except that we could not read the date, address, salutation, or anything else. We certainly could not appraise its content; but neither could we fully appraise its form—because part of form is subjective and must be read before it takes effect.

The following elements of form have this subjective aspect. They may be present in a letter, even positioned according to the best of rules for form; but they would not function correctly unless their subjective aspects were handled in the right manner.

DATE

This part of the letter provides it with meaning in time. Undated letters are fortunately rare; obviously, they are difficult for us to relate to events and other letters as far as time sequence goes. Every year, after January 1, we experience a flurry of letters dated with the wrong year. While this fact can easily be lived with at the time of receipt, such letters sometimes get filed uncorrected and cause confusion at a later time.

Also, some people practice antedating or postdating their letters for devious reasons. Whenever that is done, something tends to be out of alignment with the facts; and the reader is likely to experience some noise.

ADDRESSEE

When we write a business letter, we ordinarily address either an individual or a group. The individual might be an officer of a company; the group might be the company itself or a division thereof.

If the addressee is an individual, we should try to obtain and use his full name. When he uses a special title in front of his name—such as *Dr., Captain, Professor,* etc.—we should address him in that manner. Otherwise, we should use the applicable courtesy title: *Mr., Mrs.,* or *Miss.*

Sometimes we write to a person as the holder of a position in the company for which he works. We should include his position, and we should theoretically place it in front of, and on the same line with, the name of his company. The reason is that the position accrues to the company, not to the man. However, this placement usually results in an undesirably long line. Thus, for practical purposes, we place the position after, and on the same line with the person's name, in the case of a short title (*President*)—or on a line by itself between the person's name and the company name, in the case of a lengthy title (*Assistant Office Manager*). At other times, we write to a person by his position only, because we do not know his name. Thus, while *Personnel Manager* is really the designation of a position, we recognize that a person is filling that position.

When our addressee is a group concept, it could be either the company itself or merely a division of the company. In the latter case, of course, the company name would be included in the address, also.

Whether we address an individual or a company, we should take care to spell our addressee's name correctly. Also, we should express it in the same words as the addressee expresses it. To misspell our addressee's name even before beginnning our message would certainly be taken as noise by him, if not as an unpardonable error. To tamper with the wording of an addressee's name—a deed often done through laziness—is equally unwise. Thus, we should not use initials instead of a person's full name. Nor should we abbreviate parts of a company name which the company itself does not abbreviate.

SALUTATION

In a business letter, the salutation is a logical follow-through of the address. Thus, if we have addressed our letter to an individual by name, it is consistent and friendly that we greet him by name. A letter in which we have used "Mr. Joseph R. Brown" as the first line of the address would take "Dear Mr. Brown:" as its salutation. In some instances, we could be even more personal and use "Dear Joe:"—and at other times the relationship between our reader and ourselves might compel us to use the "Dear Sir:" variety. When the situation is such that we must address the person's position because we do not know his name, we have no choice but to use the "Dear Sir:" salutation.

In addressing either a company or one of its divisions, we must remember that such an addressee is considered to be a plural concept. There is only one salutation that is ordinarily applicable, "Gentlemen:" —and this holds true even when an "attention" line is used. Such a device merely invites the attention of a specific person to this letter, but the first line of the address still shows the name of the actual addressee. And, a plural-concept addressee calls for a plural-concept salutation.

ATTENTION LINE

If, as just suggested, we decide to include an "attention" line, the question arises as to its proper placement. One thing is certain: we should not bury it or submerge it so that it cannot perform its intended function. We should put it someplace where the eye will be attracted to it—someplace above the start of the message. In practice there are three workable positions for an attention line:

1. At the left-hand margin, between the end of the address and the salutation, with a line skipped both above it and below it.
2. On the same line as described in (1), but centered on the page.
3. On the same line as the salutation, and centered on the page.

Because of the limitation of space, the third-named position is probably the least practical.

SUBJECT CAPTION

Another device used in some business letters is the "subject" caption. This is a reference to the general topic, previous correspondence, a purchase order, an invoice, or something else recognizable by our reader. It helps us establish the subject matter before we get into the body of the letter. It lets us get right down to business without the preliminaries of an uninteresting or stereotyped opening sentence.

A subject caption is more closely related to our message than is an attention line. Therefore, we do well to place it somewhat near the body of the letter. A very good position is between the salutation (any variety) and the first line of the body (text), centered, and with a line skipped both above it and below it.

COMPLIMENTARY CLOSE

Whereas the first line of the address controls or restricts the choice of salutation to be used, the salutation has a bearing on the complimentary close to be used. In a simple, general classification we have two kinds of complimentary close for use in business letters. These are:

1. The formal variety, embracing:
   a) Very truly yours,
   b) Yours very truly,
   c) Yours truly,
   d) Respectfully yours,
2. The informal variety—all the others, but especially:
   a) Sincerely,
   b) Cordially,
   c) Sincerely yours,
   d) Cordially yours,
   e) Very sincerely yours,
   f) Very cordially yours,

The first three (a, b, and c) of the formal variety are standard usage in the following situations:

1. A letter between two companies.
2. A letter from a company to an individual, whether he be addressed by his name or by his position.
3. A letter from an individual to a company.

4. A letter from an individual to another individual, the latter being addressed by his position and not by name.

They are optional usage in one additional situation:

5. A letter from an individual to another individual, the latter being addressed by name.

The fourth complimentary close of the formal variety is limited to a letter from one individual to another, whether the latter be addressed by his name or by his position—provided the implied inferior-to-superior relationship actually exists.

The best choice of complimentary close for a letter we write to an individual whom we address by name is, of course, one of the informal, friendly types. If we have been personal and friendly in the salutation ("Dear Joe:" or "Dear Mr. Brown:") we should continue to be friendly in the complimentary close ("Sincerely," etc.). But, if by requirement or option we have used "Dear Sir:" as our salutation, we should continue the formality in our complimentary close. Also, because of the personal relationship that is implied by closings of the informal variety, we ordinarily should not use them in letters we address to companies or in letters signed by our company name ahead of our own name. In such cases, we should select one of the three standard formal closings.

SIGNATURE

Depending on the circumstances, the signature of a business letter may vary from four lines to two lines. At the top of the scale, we have the full signature, which begins with the name of the company sending the letter. This name serves as the legal signature and is usually typewritten in capital letters. A few lines below it is the longhand signature of the person who composed the letter. Beneath that signature, on consecutive lines, are the typewritten identification of the signed name and the signer's position in the company.

Although in proper form and legally correct, this full signature is sometimes subject to criticism on logical grounds. The question arises: If the first person singular is used in the letter, is it logically correct to use a plural-concept signature? Remember, we noted that the reverse situation—that is, addressing the letter to a company, but using a singular-concept salutation—would not be right. Would our reader detect such an inconsistency as our using a first-person-singular subject in the text of our letter and ending with a plural-concept signature? If so, the usage could result in that undesirable thing we call noise. It might be prudent, therefore, for us to limit the full signature to those company letters we write without using the first person singular.

A three-line signature occurs in a business letter when, having type-written it on letterhead stationery, we sign it without including the name of the company we represent. In such a case, the signature block, as this section of the letter is called, consists of our longhand signature, our typewritten name, and the position we hold in the company. In some instances, wherein a note of familiarity is especially applicable, the longhand part could consist merely of our first name or nickname.

Some business letters are prepared on plain stationery. There is no letterhead because the situation is not one of company business. Yet, such a letter may be written to a business house—for example, an in-quiry about a product or service, a credit application, an order, a com-plaint, an application for a position, and so on. Although probably typewritten, such a letter would never call for a company signature or for the position of the writer. The signature block would contain only the longhand signature and the typewritten name beneath it.

GUIDE FOR SUBJECTIVE FORM

From this discussion, we can see that the subjective elements of form are to a considerable extent interrelated. Except for the matter of the date and the possibility of a subject caption, the various choices we must make concerning these subjective elements require consistent de-cisions. The address of our letter (specifically, the inside address) con-trols the salutation and affects the complimentary close. Hence a guide, on the order of the accompanying chart, can be useful in helping us make the correct selections.

As mentioned earlier, we sometimes use attention lines in business letters. Regardless, the addressee as stated in the first line of the inside address controls the salutation to be used. Thus, if "Attention of Mr. Hawthorne" were used in either Case III or Case IV of the foregoing guide, the proper salutation would still be "Gentlemen" (not "Dear Mr. Hawthorne" or "Dear Sir").

While the guide illustrates the choices generally available, it is possible that we might be addressing our letter to a woman at one time or

GUIDE FOR SELECTING THE PROPER
SALUTATION AND COMPLIMENTARY CLOSE

CASE	If the first line of the inside address is	The proper salutation is	The proper complimentary close is
I	A person by name: Mr. John A. Hawthorne Assistant Secretary Interior National Bank 1100 Erieview Avenue Cleveland, Ohio 44114	In order of preference: Dear Mr. Hawthorne: Dear Sir:	(A friendly form)[1,2] or, in order of preference: Very truly yours,[2] Yours very truly, Yours truly,
II	A person by position: The Assistant Secretary Interior National Bank 1100 Erieview Avenue Cleveland, Ohio 44114	One form only: Dear Sir:	In order of preference: Very truly yours,[2] Yours very truly, Yours truly,
III	A division of a firm: Office of The Secretary Interior National Bank 1100 Erieview Avenue Cleveland, Ohio 44114	One form only: Gentlemen:	In order of preference: Very truly yours, Yours very truly, Yours truly,
IV	A company name: Interior National Bank 1100 Erieview Avenue Cleveland, Ohio 44114	One form only: Gentlemen:	In order of preference: Very truly yours, Yours very truly, Yours truly,

[1] *Sincerely, Cordially, Sincerely yours, Cordially yours*, and other such forms are appropriately used in business letters. The usage is limited, however, to Case I only, and even then *both* of the following conditions must exist:
   a) The addressee's name is used in the salutation.
   b) The writer's company name does not appear above his longhand signature.
[2] *Respectfully yours*, may be used when it is justified by the obviously superior status of the addressee over that of the writer.

another. Most likely, however, this fact would affect a Case I situation only—that is, a letter addressed to a woman by name. The implication is that knowledge of our addressee's being a woman would usually carry with it the additional knowledge of her name and marital status. Except in rare situations, our source of information would be a letter we had received from her; otherwise, our ordinary assumption would be that the addressee is a man. In Case III and Case IV, moreover, "Gentlemen" is the proper salutation, even though the attention line mentions a woman's name.

OBJECTIVE FORM

The last step in the preparation of a business letter is the typewriting or production activity. Usually we who have attended to the other steps turn this part of the work over to someone trained especially for it. When the document is finished, it is returned to us for scrutiny and signature. When we have signed the document, it is supposedly approved in every way and ready for mailing to our intended reader.

Matters which we have controlled all along—the points to be covered, their sequence, the matter of finesse, readability, language expression, and the subjective elements of form—must appear in the document according to our instructions. The objective elements of form, which we place under someone else's control, must measure up to the standards of current usage. And we become responsible for this aspect, too, when we validate the letter with our signature. Thus, we must be fully aware of what is good, conventional form for today's business letter.

At the present time we are in the midst of an evolutionary change in letter form. Before the advent of the typewriter, letters had to be prepared in longhand; and there was just one "business letter form." To the untrained eye, this form was not greatly different from what we regard as the typical form today. In fact, it was still fairly common as recently as 25 years ago. In today's terms, we might describe it as the "indented style, with closed punctuation." This means that in the heading, address, and signature block, each new line was indented from the previous line and each was punctuated by a comma, except the last, which took a period. In the body of the letter, the first line of each paragraph was indented. Another difference was that the inside address, then known as the "superscription," was placed below the writer's signature at the left-hand side of the page. Actually, the term "superscription" referred to the outside address; and this inside notation was a kind of memorandum to an assistant who would prepare the envelope.

When typewriters and stenography moved into the business office, and a greater division of work in preparing letters became practical, it was inevitable that changes in form would occur. The inside address became a more significant identification of the message for both the dictator and the stenographer, and it moved to its present position above the salutation. Although at first the longhand form was imitated, this practice was wasteful of typewriting time. Punctuation marks at the ends of the lines in the heading, inside address, and signature block began to disappear. Instead of being indented, the inside address became blocked at the left-hand margin; the signature block, at or near the center of the page. With single-spaced text and double-spaced paragraphs, there was little reason to indent the first line of a paragraph.

Of course, these improvements in office procedure did not come about abruptly or even simultaneously. In fact, other changes have been advocated and are being tried. The trend is toward aligning all parts of the letter at the left-hand margin and eliminating the salutation and complimentary close. But people traditionally resist change. Some people subconsciously fear change as a force undermining the things they believe in and rely on. Other people like change but prefer to move slowly because of the possible adverse effect it might have on the public with whom they deal. As a result, we find that some companies have moved further along in modernizing their letter form than have others. It is now necessary for us to have a number of designations to label the significant varieties of letter forms in the range from the oldest to the newest.

Not all of the varieties within this range are equally popular; and some are coming in, while others are fading out. Currently, the *block* and the *modified-block* (also known as semiblock) forms are the representative types. Of these two, the block form is probably gaining favor. Within the next several years, it is possible that we shall see the *full-block* form (all parts included, but aligned at the left-hand margin) become one of the leaders. If so, the modified-block form will have definitely lost its popularity. In the long run, we can expect not only that all parts of the letter will be blocked at the left-hand margin, but that an amount of simplification will be introduced. Ultimately, there will be but one "business letter form" again—and it will have its basis in office efficiency.

Objective form, the physical aspects of the business letter, will be discussed in the following paragraphs. First, we shall analyze the regular business letter, as prepared both on printed stationery and on plain stationery. Then, we shall illustrate both the block and modified-block forms. The envelope and such matters as the folding and inserting of the letter will be considered. In addition, we shall examine two other aspects: the memorandum form used for intracompany correspondence and the two-part (or multipart) form used when one or more supporting documents are sent with a letter of transmittal.

Throughout these analyses, we shall try to set up measures or criteria consistent with our fundamental premise that form is part of the process of communicating and not an end product. Earlier we made a comparison to another medium of communication—namely, television. Letter form is to the reader what a television picture tube is to the viewer. Each reveals the visual communication to the person at destination. Each is intended to provide maximum reception of the letter content or of the video portion of the telecast, as the case may be. But neither is to be so attractive, or distractive, that it borrows from the person's attention.

An unusual design of letter form or of a television viewing device does tend to be distractive and undesirable to the person at destination.

It can interfere with his appreciation of the message or enjoyment of the program. For example, some years ago when home television receivers were first being introduced on a large scale, customers were offered a circular picture tube. Television as a new medium supposedly had no precedent to go by, and this "lens-eye" design could have become the standard for television receivers. But the fact was that the buying public shied away from it in favor of a somewhat rectangular design. Even though the quality of engineering, fidelity of image, clearness, and other features might have been superior in the receiving sets with the circular picture tubes, the customers passed them up to have the other design. Perhaps they were influenced by the mental association that rectangular design has with motion pictures, but they were clearly basing their decision on external appearance or "form." In short, the circular tube seemed strange and distractive, whereas the rectangular tube seemed conventional and "friendly." Similarly, in letter writing, an unconventional form tends to make our reader feel uneasy—and that will do neither him nor us any good.

LETTER ON PRINTED STATIONERY

1. *Paper Stock.* As with so many other matters about which we must make a choice, the selection of the paper to be used for our business letters is based on convention. There are a number of different sizes, colors, weights, and qualities of paper in use today, but not all enjoy the same popularity. Our choice of paper should be one that carries out its function well, yet does not particularly draw attention to itself. In keeping with present-day usage, our writing paper should meet the following specifications:

   a) Color: white.
   b) Size: 8½ by 11.
   c) Weight: 20- or 24-pound.
   d) Quality: rag content, 25 percent or somewhat more.

2. *Letterhead.* In effect, a letterhead is the printed or engraved portion of the heading of a business letter. It contains information about the writer's company which is of a relatively long-term nature. Details such as the company name, its full mailing address (including the street or box number, city and state, and postal ZIP code), and some indication of the nature of the company's activity are considered basic parts of a letterhead. The company's activity can be brought out in a number of ways: it can be implied by the company name (e.g., Interior National Bank); by illustrations; by wording (e.g., Hardware . . . Paints . . . Elec-

trical Supplies); or by combinations of these devices. Frequently the business telephone number is included; and sometimes, the cable address. A company which has become identified by a trademark or symbol often displays this device in its letterhead.

In designing our letterhead, we should not be misled by the tendency of some companies to go overboard on letterhead styling. We should realize that gaudy colors, *avant-garde* art, superfluous information, marginal listing of board members, and the like are more likely to distract than to serve the reader.

Conveying information is the function of the letterhead, and its elements should serve that purpose. Certainly an attractive letterhead may incidentally be good advertising, and convey a good impression of our firm; but it will do neither unless it primarily fulfills its role of communicating pertinent and necessary information to the reader.

The following criteria, therefore, should guide us in the designing of a proper letterhead:

a) Color: black or other suitable color.

b) Lettering: clear and distinctive, but not ostentatious.

c) Process: printing or engraving.

d) Standard parts: Name of company.

   Full address (including street or box number, city and state, and postal ZIP code).

   Indication of company's activity.

e) Optional parts: Telephone number.

   Long-distance area code.

   Cable address.

   Trademark or symbol.

   Designation of branch or office.

f) Punctuation: open.

3. *Date.* The date of the business letter completes the heading and, on printed stationery, is the only typewritten portion of the heading. Because it is not in the same type style as either the printed or the engraved portion, as the case may be, we place the date two lines below the letterhead. We thereby avoid a clash of type styles. In both the block and modified-block forms, we may center the date beneath the letterhead or place it so as to end at or near the right-hand margin of the letter.

Sometimes the letterhead includes a telephone number or an office designation which has been placed at the left-hand margin about two lines below the city-and-state wording. If so, we can get a well-balanced appearance by typing the date on the very same line but ending at the right-hand margin. Whatever position we select, however, we do not abbreviate any part of the date. We use the month-day-year sequence and open punctuation.

August 15, 1966

4. *Inside Address.* Nowadays, the inside address serves as an identification of the person or group to whom our letter is officially directed. It does, of course, still serve as a guide for the preparation of the outside address (the address on the envelope).

The inside address is typed in block form at the left-hand margin of the letter. It is begun four, six, or eight lines (i.e., turns of the typewriter platen) below the date—according to whether the letter is long, medium, or short, respectively.

We always single-space the inside address and use punctuation for it. Usually, we have no problem with the number of lines in the inside address; but we should have at least three lines. In rare cases, when we have only the addressee's name and post office, we arrange this limited information into three lines for the sake of a satisfactory appearance. The following examples show us the handling of the inside address under different circumstances.

MANY LINES	THREE LINES	FORCED THREE LINES
Office of The Secretary	Mr. Henry C. Wagner	Mrs. Mary Terzano
Interior National Bank	6870 S.W. 26th Street	Vineland
1100 Erieview Avenue	Miami, Florida 33155	New Jersey 08361
Cleveland, Ohio 44114		

5. *Salutation.* Based on the official addressee of our letter, as indicated by the first line of the inside address, the salutation is a courtesy greeting to the reader. It is one of the parts of the business letter that is being threatened by the efficiency moves to do away with unnecessary details. Yet what is the final measure of "necessary"? Should a necessary part be only a functional part—or can it be one that serves an intangible purpose, such as pleasing our reader by according him a traditional courtesy? One of our aims in all business letters is to cater to our reader's

goodwill; so dropping the nicety of a salutation would seem to be unwise. In fact, so touchy are some people concerning this part of the letter that we retain the colon after the salutation even when we are otherwise using open punctuation. The typical reader tends to miss the colon, although he probably cannot say why, just as he would miss the buttons if they were omitted from the sleeves of his business suit.

Experiments to drop the salutation have frequently centered on the technique of including the reader's name in the opening sentence of the letter. For example, it is suggested that the letter begin along the lines of "Good morning, Mr. Jones . . ." or "Your ties, Mr. Barlow, are being mailed today." While these beginnings do sound appealing, we can cite several reasons why they do not justify the elimination of the salutation:

a) The absence of the traditional salutation would already have had its effect on the reader before he began to read the message.

b) Despite their cheerfulness and sparkle, these substitutions are not conventional procedure, and thus would tend to be a distraction (noise) to the reader.

c) The same wording, except probably for the reader's name, can be used just as effectively at the beginning of a letter that does have a salutation.

Perhaps it does cost us a few cents more to put in a salutation—but we should look upon it as the cost of some worthwhile merchandising on behalf of our letter.

As already discussed among the elements of subjective form, the form of the salutation follows from the first line of the inside address. If we have addressed a plural concept, we used the "Gentlemen" form. If we have addressed an individual, we preferably include the person's name in the salutation—"Dear Mr. (Mrs., Miss) White." And, if we do not know his name and must address him by his position only, we use the "Dear Sir" form. As for placement, the salutation is typed two lines below the inside address at the left-hand margin. As noted above, we use a colon as end punctuation.

6. *Body*. Regardless of length, the body of a business letter is started two lines below the salutation. As we have seen, the choice of dropping down four, six, or eight lines from the date to the inside address is intended to provide for proper vertical positioning of our letter. However, the placement of the body of the letter on the page

does permit us an amount of horizontal adjustment. The general aim is that we have equal margins, left and right, within the range of 1 to 2 inches. For most of our letters, we can use margins of about 1½ inches. When our letter will be lengthy, we can adjust to 1-inch margins; when it will be very short, to 2-inch margins.

If we use the block form, all the lines of the paragraphs begin at the left-hand margin. If we use the modified-block form (semiblock), the first line of each paragraph is indented. While there is no set rule on the number of spaces to indent, we should avoid anything that would be a distraction to our reader. Current practice, which is our safest guide, finds the five-space indention and the ten-space indention leading the other possibilities.

In the matter of typewriting details, we use standard punctuation throughout the body of a business letter. We use single-spacing within each paragraph and double-spacing between paragraphs. If we are preparing a very short letter—say, two or three sentences at most—we may decide to double-space the body. This practice is proper, but we must be careful about two things:

a) *Only the body* is double-spaced. All other parts of our letter are to be handled in the regular way.

b) If we have more than one paragraph, we still double-space between them. Since every line of our letter is then double-spaced, *we must use the modified-block form.* Otherwise, our letter would not have clearly defined paragraphs and could be troublesome to our reader.

Sometimes we must write a letter of such length that more than one page is needed to present it. Here again, we should use good judgment in carrying the last part of the letter to a final page. The following criteria are involved:

a) Cutoff. At the end of each full page of typing we should leave a bottom margin of about one and one-half inches.

b) Stationery. Each additional page of our letter should be typewritten on plain paper of the same color, size, and quality as we used for the first page.

c) Heading. A three-part heading—consisting of the addressee's name, the page number, and the date—should be placed at the start of each additional page of our letter, approximately one inch down from the top edge of the sheet. The date should be complete and should agree with the one we use on the first page.

Because there is no really traditional pattern concerning the formation of this heading, we may exercise a fair amount of personal judgment. But we should keep within the margins and not try for the bizarre. This heading is intended merely to assure the proper matching and sequencing of the pages of a particular letter. Two common arrangements, illustrated below, are the balanced heading (addressee's name at the left-hand margin, page centered, date at the right-hand margin) and the blocked heading (continuous from the left-hand margin, with commas separating the parts).

```
Mr. John A. Hawthorne              -2-            February 9, 1966
Mr. John A. Hawthorne, Page 2, February 9, 1966
```

d) Body. The margins of the additional pages should be the same as those we selected for the first page of the letter. We should begin three or four lines down from the heading and should use the same typewriting form (block or modified-block) as we used for the first page. We single-space the paragraphs and double-space between them.

e) Text. The final page should contain at least three lines of text matter. Anything less than three lines would not look pleasing to the reader and would suggest to him that we had been guilty of careless planning with regard to form.

f) Other matters. We handle the remaining parts of the letter, such as the complimentary close and signature, according to the accepted usage. These matters, which are taken up in the following sections, are generally the same for both the one-page and the multipage letter.

7. *Complimentary Close.* Another part of the business letter often charged with being unnecessary is the complimentary close. Admittedly, like the salutation, it is a trimming; but it is frequently a subtle way of embellishing goodwill. This is especially true when we use one of the very friendly forms (*Sincerely, Cordially,* etc.). Such a closing tends to confirm our attitude toward our reader. Moreover, a similar situation appears to exist with regard to punctuating it as exists with punctuating the salutation. The reader probably will expect to see a comma used after the complimentary close, even when we use open punctuation elsewhere in the letter.

As for position, the complimentary close is typed two lines below the end of the text matter, starting at the center of the page or a few spaces to the right. We capitalize only the first word of the complimentary close and, of course, use a comma as end punctuation. As we saw in the section on subjective form, we must use a *formal* variety of complimentary close when we address a company; but we should try to use a friendly, *informal* variety when we address an individual. The choices, discussed earlier, are outlined in the chart on page 124 for easy reference.

8. *Signature Block.* In a business letter prepared on letterhead stationery, the signature section is composed of either four elements (when the company name is included as the primary signature) or three elements (when the company name is omitted). In matters which are strictly company responsibility—such as negotiations, bids, or quotations—we should use the company name (preferably typed entirely in capital letters) ahead of our own name. The legal relationship is that the first signature on the letter establishes the responsibility for the message. Thus, when we use the company signature, a plural concept, we do better logically not to use the first person singular in the text.

Whether we use a four-line or a three-line signature section, we block these parts with the first letter of the complimentary close. If we include the company name, it is typed in capital letters two lines below the complimentary close. Depending on the boldness of our handwriting, we allow four to six turns of the typewriter platen for the longhand signature. Our full name is typed below, as a positive identification, and on the next line we state our position in the company. We sign the letter as a final indication of approval after we have checked it for overall suitability.

The following examples illustrate the two kinds of signature blocks we have just analyzed.

FOUR LINES   THREE LINES

Very truly yours,   Sincerely yours,

INTERIOR NATIONAL BANK   *John A. Hawthorne*

John A. Hawthorne   John A. Hawthorne
                                              Assistant Secretary
John A. Hawthorne
Assistant Secretary

9. *Miscellaneous Parts.* In addition to the foregoing parts, which are present in a regular business letter under all conditions, we often have need for other parts under specific conditions. Some of these extra parts are included primarily for the benefit of the reader; others are included mainly to aid our operations at the source. *Reader-oriented* parts include:

a) Attention Line. This device helps the receiving company place our letter in the hands of the proper individual or department. It is particularly useful when we must address the company rather than a person. It is handy also when we do not have our intended reader's full name and, therefore, cannot very well write directly to him. As for placement, we may select any of three positions: either blocked or centered between the inside address and the salutation, with a line skipped both above it and below it—or centered on the line used for the salutation. The following are typical examples of wording used.

```
Attention: Mr. C. R. Brown

Attention of Mr. Sorenson

Attention of Miss Tillman, please

Mr. John Underwood, please

Attention: Purchasing Agent

Attention of Shipping Department
```

b) Subject Caption. We often can get a business letter off to a refreshing start if we can avoid bogging down the first sentence with reference matter. A subject caption—placed between the salutation and the body of the letter, preferably centered, and with a line skipped both above it and below it—can alert our reader to the main topic before he begins reading the message proper. The following examples show various phrasings of this part.

```
Subject: Your Order No. 10792

Subject: Our Invoice No. L-611

Your Inquiry of May 25

Answer Reference: File No. 6-82

Subject: Your File No. 6-82
```

c) Footnote. Not to be confused with a term-paper or thesis footnote, this is a device for helping our reader answer a limited number of objective-type questions. Spaced proportionately between the signature block and the bottom edge of the sheet, this footnote contains ready-to-answer questions. Our reader need only check a box, fill in a space, encircle a word, etc. He can then return the letter to us. He is not required to compose a letter of his own.

Source-oriented parts which are used in some but not all business letters include:

a) Reference Initials. Whenever there is a division of work in turning out a business letter, it is customary to use some system of identification of the persons who participated. The signature is already part of the system; and, if we have done every bit of the work ourselves, no further reference is needed.

Along theoretical lines, if we only compose the letter and a typist puts it into finished form, the initials of the typist would be placed at the end, blocked at the left-hand margin. They could be typed on the same line as our position in the company, or two lines lower—depending upon whether it is desirable to expand for eye appeal. If an administrative assistant composed the letter for us, the reference would show his initials first and then those of the typist. The composer's initials would be typed in capital letters and the typist's initials in lowercase letters, to show a suitable contrast. In neither case would periods follow these initials, but some mark of punctuation—usually a colon or a virgule—would separate the two sets.

JSS:ab

JSS/ab

Common practice departs from theory in one respect. We find that the dictator's or composer's initials appear in the reference even when he is also the signer of the letter. Although a duplication of sorts, it is the conventional method, and we should go along with it.

b) Enclosures. Sometimes we send an enclosure with our letter, such as a purchase order, a check, or a reply envelope. Whenever there is a division of work in processing the letter, we should take necessary precautions to assure that the proper thing is enclosed:

1. We should mention the enclosure(s) in the text of our letter. This should be done in a regular place, if possible (such as the last paragraph), so that our clerical help can, if necessary, find out easily what should be enclosed.

2. A reminder to the person who places the letter in the envelope should be indicated—usually at the left-hand margin on the line below the reference initials. The two customary forms for this reminder follow.

SPELLED OUT	ABBREVIATED
Enclosure	Encl. 1
Enclosures 2	Encl. 2
etc.	etc.

c) Carbon Copies. Another helpful instruction to our clerical staff concerns the distribution of one or more carbon copies of our letter to persons who should be informed of the communication. Such an instruction is typed at the left-hand margin, usually on the line below the reference initials. If both enclosure and carbon-copy reminders are used, of course, the latter is typed on the line below the enclosure designation.

Since this is not a regularly used part of a business letter, we do not have a set pattern to follow for coding or wording. The purpose is fulfilled if the part alerts our clerical help to make the distribution and indicates the recipient(s). We should find the following form suitable.

```
cc: Mr. Roger Horton
    Miss Wanda Sill
```

We might consider having the original of the letter removed from the typewriter and the notation typed only on the carbon copies. Since it rarely concerns our reader—and sometimes should not be revealed to him—the reminder about carbon copies tends to add clutter to our letter. It is also a hint of "over-management," a somewhat irksome thought.

d) Postscripts. In former days—especially in places where mail service was infrequent—a new matter arising between the completion of a letter and the collection of the mail might have been added sensibly as a postscript. In this day and age, the use of a real postscript is almost an admission of faulty planning of our letter program. It would be better to rewrite the letter than tack on a left-out part.

Sometimes, however, we intentionally use the postscript form to achieve a desired effect. For example, in a collection letter or in a sales letter, a postcript could be a handy means of repeating a key point for emphasis or of stating something which could not well be brought into the text. We should realize, though, that such letters are special productions and not ordinary correspondence.

If we include a postscript, it is typed two lines below the last marginal notation, which would usually be the reference initials. Ordinarily, we introduce it with the abbreviation, P.S., which is either blocked or indented consistently with the form of the letter. If we use the introductory abbreviation, we space twice after it before beginning our message.

```
JSS:ab

P.S. You'll find free parking for 100 cars in the new lot behind
our store—another Martin service for your shopping convenience.
```

On the following four pages, we have illustrations incorporating the important features of the foregoing discussion. In each letter, the body gives a point-by-point review of the significant parts that are included. The first example shows us a two-page letter prepared in the block form. The second example shows us a one-page letter set up in modified-block form. The third uses a double-spaced body and, because it contains more than one paragraph, is necessarily typed in the modified-block form.

LETTER ON PLAIN STATIONERY

Not all of our business letters are prepared on letterhead stationery. Acting as private individuals, we may have to write to business firms for any number of reasons: to inquire about their goods or services, to place an order, to seek an adjustment, to request credit, to obtain an employment interview, and so on. Letters of this nature are certainly business letters, but they are not "company business" at the source. Therefore, we should use our personal address in the heading of the letter. This requirement usually leads to a fully typewritten letter on plain stationery.

In general, the rules of form applicable to this kind of letter are the same as those for the regular business letter, including the option of using either the block or the modified-block arrangement. A few of the details, discussed below, are adjusted to fit the situation.

Academy of
Consultants

AC

970 ABBEY ROAD,
COLUMBUS, OHIO 43204

February 9, 1967

Interior National Bank
1100 Erieview Avenue
Cleveland, Ohio 44114

Attention of Mr. Hawthorne

Gentlemen:

This letter is an example of the block form with open punctuation. You will notice that the date is double-spaced below the letterhead and that it ends at the right-hand margin.

The inside address is blocked at the left-hand margin. In this letter the inside address begins six lines down from the date. In long, one-page letters, it might begin four lines down; in short letters, eight lines down.

The attention line and the salutation, in that order, are each down two more lines and blocked on the left-hand margin. The entire body of the letter is blocked on the left-hand margin also. Single-spacing is used within the paragraphs; double-spacing is used between them.

The complimentary close, which is double-spaced below the last paragraph, begins halfway across the page. The signature section is blocked with it. Our company name is typed first, two lines below the complimentary close. The typewritten signature identification is four to six lines lower, with the dictator's position placed on the line immediately following.

Since this letter uses open punctuation, you will notice that no marks of punctuation follow the date, the lines of the inside address, the attention line, or the lines of the signature block. A colon, however, is used after the salutation; and a comma is used after the complimentary close.

Whenever a letter requires more than one page, the additional pages are set up according to this example. Plain stationery, of the same color, size, and quality as the letterhead, is used. Margins, punctuation, indentions, and size of type also conform to those used on the first page.

A one-line heading is typed on each additional page, about one inch below the top edge of the sheet. It consists of the name of the addressee, which begins at the left-hand margin; the page number, which is centered; and the date, which ends at the

Interior National Bank   -2-   February 9, 1967

right-hand margin.

The continuation of the letter begins about four lines below the heading. Good styling requires that 1½ inches of margin be left at the bottom of every full page, and that at least three lines of text appear on the last page. It is never correct to place only the complimentary close and the signature block beneath the heading of the last page.

                              Very truly yours,

                              ACADEMY OF CONSULTANTS

                              William F. Reinhart

                              William F. Reinhart
                              Communications Adviser

WFR:pd

Academy of
Consultants

AC

970 ABBEY ROAD,
COLUMBUS, OHIO 43204

February 11, 1967

Mr. John A. Hawthorne
Assistant Secretary
Interior National Bank
1100 Erieview Avenue
Cleveland, Ohio 44114

Dear Mr. Hawthorne:

Here is another letter that I am sure will interest you. It is an
example of the modified-block form with open punctuation.

It follows the same general rules as the block form, except that the
first line of each paragraph is indented five spaces. Because the letter
is rather short, I have used wider margins than I did for my previous
letter. However, the spacing between the date and the inside address
has been kept the same. I think that you will agree that this form is
both attractive and businesslike.

Incidentally, I have some notes on folding letters and addressing
envelopes. If you would like to have a copy of them, please let me
know. I have enclosed a stamped, addressed envelope for your convenience in answering.

Sincerely yours,

William F. Reinhart

William F. Reinhart
Communications Adviser

WFR:pd
Enclosure

Academy of
Consultants

970 ABBEY ROAD,
COLUMBUS, OHIO 43204

February 16, 1967

Mr. John A. Hawthorne
Assistant Secretary
Interior National Bank
1100 Erieview Avenue
Cleveland, Ohio 44114

Dear Mr. Hawthorne:

Your Letter of February 14

Yes, it is proper to double-space the body of a short letter;

but do not double-space any of the other parts.

If you use more than one paragraph—as I am doing here—you

will have to follow the modified-block form. Otherwise, your para-

graphs will seem to run together.

Cordially,

William F. Reinhart

William F. Reinhart
Communications Adviser

1. *Heading.*   Although the paper we use should meet the regular standards for business letters, it will not be imprinted with a letterhead. Therefore, we type the entire heading, including the date, on consecutive lines within the area constituting the top fifth of the page. We set this heading in block style with open punctuation and plan it so that the longest line will just reach the right-hand margin. We accomplish this in the following manner:

    a) Count the typing units needed for the *longest line* of the heading.

    b) Backspace that number of units from the right-hand margin.

    c) Type the *first line* of the heading.

    d) Block all other lines with the first line.

2. *Signature Block.*   In a letter prepared on plain stationery, our signature block contains but two elements: our longhand signature and our typewritten name. Neither the name of our company (if any) nor our position in that company applies in this kind of letter.

3. *Miscellaneous Parts.*   The possibilities of using reader-oriented extra parts (attention line, subject caption, footnote) remain unchanged. But virtually all need for source-oriented extra parts drops out of the picture. In this situation, we are supposedly on our own in composing, typing, and mailing the letter and distributing carbon copies, if any. Thus, we have no staff to refer to and no one to remind about enclosures and carbon copies. All notations for these purposes become useless.

Perhaps there is a remote chance of our using a postscript for a special effect. In such an event, we should follow the standard procedure as already given.

The example on page 144 illustrates a business letter prepared on plain stationery.

ENVELOPE

Our customary choice of envelope for mailing business letters is the Number 10 (4⅛ by 9½) size. The envelope should be of the same color and quality of paper as we used for our letter, and should be either printed or plain to match the letter. If the envelope is printed, the wording would duplicate the styling of our letterhead (probably on a slightly

1836 Indianola Drive
Columbus, Ohio 43204
February 17, 1967

Mr. John A. Hawthorne
Assistant Secretary
Interior National Bank
1100 Erieview Avenue
Cleveland, Ohio 44114

Dear Mr. Hawthorne:

Sometimes I must write a letter on plain stationery instead of printed stationery.
This letter illustrates the procedure that I follow in such a situation.

I place the heading near the upper right-hand corner, making sure that I do not end
more than 2¼ inches below the top edge of the sheet. I make the longest line of the
heading end at the right-hand margin. I block all remaining lines with the first letter
of the longest line. The fact that some lines are short and do not reach the margin is
unimportant.

After typing the heading, I merely follow the general rules for either the block form
or the modified-block form. That's all there is to it. Because I am typing this letter
myself, there will be no need for typist's initials at the left-hand margin afterwards.

If I may be of further help to you in the matter of letter forms, please let me know.

Sincerely yours,

William F. Reinhart

William F. Reinhart

smaller scale), would include our company name and full address, but would not show such extra details as the telephone number, cable address, etc. If a plain envelope is called for, we must type our return address in the upper left-hand corner. Whether this address includes our name is usually an optional matter when we write from our personal residence. But we should include our name and/or box number whenever we write from a multiple dwelling such as a hotel, apartment house, or condominium.

The front of a business envelope contains three regular elements, as follows:

1. *Return Address.*   For business-writing purposes, the return address (also called the "return card" or "corner card") appears most often on the front of the envelope in the upper left-hand corner. Sometimes, however, it is placed on the flap of the envelope. When we must type it on the envelope, we should use our full mailing address exactly as we did in the heading of the letter. If we use our own name with it, we do not have to use *Mr.;* but whenever a special title is applicable, we assist our reader by showing such a designation.

2. *Postage.*   Whether we use a regular stamp or metered postage, we should reserve the upper right-hand corner of the envelope for this purpose.

3. *Address.*   The outside address is based on the inside address of our letter. Therefore, there is little justifiable reason why we should ever have a difference between the two. As for placement, we find our guide in the combination of appearance and function. A skillful typist should have no difficulty arranging the address so that the center of the block will be slightly to the right and slightly below dead center on the envelope. This, of course, means adjusting to the height and width of each address. The following procedure is suggested for a permanent position which will nevertheless produce satisfactory results:

    a) Block the outside address, starting 12 turns of the typewriter platen down from the top edge of the envelope and 4¼ inches in from the left-hand edge.

    b) If the address contains three lines, optionally single-space them or double-space them.

c) If the address contains more than three lines, single-space them.

The following illustrations show (1) a printed envelope with a three-line outside address and (2) a plain envelope with a five-line address.

Academy of
Consultants

AC

970 ABBEY ROAD,
COLUMBUS, OHIO 43204

Interior National Bank

1100 Erieview Avenue

Cleveland, Ohio 44114

Attention of Mr. Hawthorne

[1]

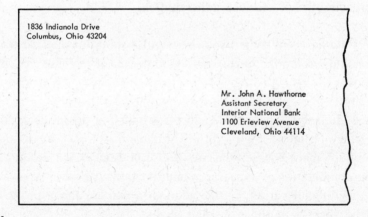

1836 Indianola Drive
Columbus, Ohio 43204

Mr. John A. Hawthorne
Assistant Secretary
Interior National Bank
1100 Erieview Avenue
Cleveland, Ohio 44114

[2]

In addition to the regular elements which appear on a business envelope, we sometimes have reason to use some of the following miscellaneous items:

1. *Attention Line.* If we have used an attention line in our letter, it makes sense to duplicate it on the front of the envelope (see envelope illustration [1], above). This step can save time at the destination. Our

letter can be delivered straight to the person designated, rather than having to be opened first and sent along the next time mail is distributed.

The outside position for the attention line is the lower left-hand side of the envelope about ½ inch in from the edge. The wording, of course, would be the same as our wording in the letter.

2. *Instructions.* By means of typewritten words, rubber stamps, or printed stickers, we sometimes alert the post office personnel to special things we want them to do. Such instructions are usually expressed in brief phrases along the lines of "First Class," "Airmail," "Special Delivery," "Please Hand Cancel," and so on. Preferably, they are placed slightly below the postage section, where they will be easily seen.

3. *Overprints.* If our company uses metered or prepaid postage for all of its first-class mail, a question arises as to whether the persons receiving it might fail to realize its importance and delay in opening it. We can eliminate this risk by having our envelopes imprinted with the wording, "First-Class Mail."

A similar risk is involved when we send out a large mailing of sales letters using a postage rate other than first class. We might overprint the envelopes with a phrase, possibly in a bright color, aimed at arousing the recipient's curiosity. Such phrases as "Coupon Enclosed," "Special Offer Inside," "U.S. Postage Stamp Enclosed," etc. are often used to get the intended reader to open the envelope as soon as possible.

FOLDING AND INSERTING LETTERS

Among the final steps in our letter-writing activity is that of bringing together the business letter and its envelope. To prepare the letter for the Number 10 envelope, we need to make a two-stage fold, in the following manner:

1. Bring the bottom edge of the sheet up over the typewritten side approximately two thirds of the way to the top edge.
2. Square off the corners of the upturned portion with the side edges of the sheet, and crease the fold. This step will leave about 3⅔ inches of the top part of the letter still visible.
3. Bring the top edge of the sheet down toward the crease, but stop short by about ¼ inch.

4. Square off the corners of this downturned portion with the rest of the letter, and crease the fold.

As for putting the letter into the envelope, the going way seems to be "cup up," with the heading portion against the back of the envelope. This conclusion is based on a year-long study, just completed by the author, in which five out of every six letters were found to be inserted this way. Only one sixth of the hundreds of letters checked were inserted "cup down," although most manuals recommend that method.

We have no knowledge at the moment of any trend that might change this ratio in either direction. The likelihood is that the typical reader will continue to receive letters inserted either way—but he should always be able to open his letter with the heading up. If the letter comes out of the envelope "cup up," he can tilt it slightly with his working hand and flip it open with the thumb of his other hand. If it is "cup down," he can lift the letter out, grasp it in both hands, and open it with his working hand.

Of greater concern is the situation regarding enclosures. Our guiding rule should be that the enclosure(s) and letter ought to come out of the envelope as a unit. In the case of a single letter, it is practicable to fold the letter around the enclosure so that the enclosure is locked within the folds. Then it would not matter whether the letter were inserted one way or the other. In mass mailings, however, we usually do our folding by machine. It would be a waste of time to unfold all these letters to insert enclosures. Instead, we should place the enclosures in the V-shaped cup of the folded letter—in which case inserting the letter into the envelope with the cup upright would be sensible.

THE MEMORANDUM

A number of the business communications we write are addressed to individuals within our own company and may or may not have to be delivered by the U.S. Post Office. Regardless, it does seem wasteful to use expensive letterhead stationery and fully executed form. Consequently, there has evolved a simplified form called the *memorandum,* which is especially suited for intracompany (or interoffice) correspondence. Although we find many designs in current use, the tyical features of the memorandum are listed on page 149.

1. *Paper*. Customarily, an inexpensive paper is selected. Often it is tinted in a pastel shade to help set it apart from the regular stationery. This paper may be the regular 8½-by 11-inch size or a smaller size, such as a half or two-thirds sheet.

2. *Heading*. The memorandum form contains a streamlined heading, set up primarily for function. The regular parts of the heading are the introductory words, *Date:, To:, From:,* and *Subject:*—after which the details applicable to the given situation are typed. The heading itself may be either printed or typewritten.

3. *Body*. In the memorandum, the body may be typed in either the block or the modified-block form as in a regular letter; and all the other rules are followed also. The typing should begin about ½ inch below the subject caption; or, if there is a ruled line beneath the caption, the typing may begin two lines below the ruling. In effect, it is as though we were to cut the body off a regular business letter and paste it onto a memorandum sheet. There would be no effect on the composition— only on the overall appearance.

4. *Marginal Notes*. Reference initials, whenever a typist shares in the work of preparing a memorandum, are used. These initials are placed two lines below the end of the text and are blocked at the left-hand margin. Other notations, such as enclosures and carbon-copy reminders, if used, are placed immediately below the reference initials in the regular manner.

5. *Signature*. Being a simplified form, a memorandum does not contain an inside address, a salutation, or a complimentary close. The longhand signature is written slightly to the right of the center of the page a short distance below the end of the text. Since the writer's full name is shown in the heading, there is usually no typewritten name beneath his longhand signature.

The illustration on page 150 shows a memorandum which incorporates the features just discussed. A two-thirds sheet has been used.

The matter of envelopes for use with memoranda has also been resolved. Regular envelopes are used for sending memoranda through the mail to plants and branches away from the source. But sturdy, re-

INTEROFFICE MEMORANDUM

DATE: February 24, 1967

TO: John A. Hawthorne, Assistant Secretary

FROM: Walter M. Landry, Executive Vice President

SUBJECT: Selection of block form for correspondence

You may go ahead with your plans to revise our Correspondence and Reports Manual.

The suggestions presented by Mr. Reinhart of the Academy of Consultants have been very helpful to Mr. Thomas and me. We have decided to select the block form as our standard way of preparing letters. You should make certain that our revised correspondence instructions are consistent in explaining and illustrating this style.

I am enclosing the two model letters that you prepared on our letterhead stationery. The block-form version should be useful to you as an illustration in the Manual.

WML:mn
Encl. 2
cc: Mr. E. R. Thomas

Walter M. Landry

usable envelopes, usually imprinted with as many addressee lines or panels as possible, are available for memoranda which are to be delivered by a company's own mail distribution system. Often, these envelopes are punched with widely separated holes so that something inside will be detectable.

In recent years several types of "snap-out" memorandum forms have appeared on the office-supply market. With built-in carbon paper, these forms permit the typing of the message and the detaching of a file copy before the memorandum is sent in duplicate to the intended reader. The recipient can later answer on the bottom portion, keep a file copy, and send back a copy. Some of these forms are designed to hold a regular address and then to fit into a window envelope for mailing.

THE TWO–PART LETTER

In preparing a business letter, we sometimes choose to set it up in a two-part (or multipart) form. In a sense, this kind of letter functions as a letter of transmittal, yet it is not exactly the same thing. We might say that anything enclosed with a letter makes that letter a transmitting instrument; but certain other conditions must be fulfilled before we could properly call it a two-part letter.

Letters of transmittal, considered from our reader's viewpoint, consist of five varieties:

1. The kind in which both the letter we send and the thing we enclose are expendable. For example, our sales letter may include an order reply card. If our reader responds, the card is returned and the letter is probably thrown away. If our reader does not respond, both card and letter are thrown away.

2. The kind in which our letter might be kept, but not the enclosure. This could be the situation when we send our reader a reply card or envelope, a check or money order, etc.

3. The kind in which the enclosure might be kept, but not our letter. This is the situation when we send a booklet, catalogue, or other requested materials and use a covering letter aimed at scoring some goodwill points with the person at destination. Usually, after he reads such a letter, it is of no consequence to him.

4. The kind in which both our letter and the enclosure are worth keeping. Each part has its own value, and so do the two in combination. Moreover, the recipient can choose to file the parts separately or jointly.

5. The kind that appears as a prefatory part of a formal report. This, of course, is a considerably different concept and is aside from the present discussion. This kind of letter of transmittal will be taken up in a later chapter.

Under the foregoing classification, the fourth variety applies to the two-part letter form in which we are interested. When we choose to use the two-part form, we should be striving to produce benefits at both the source and the destination. Advantages at the writing end include:

a) Material that requires special preparation—such as tables of statistics, charts, and graphs—can be presented separately. In this way, they do not create new problems in connection with the body of the letter.

b) A greater division of work is made possible. The skills of different kinds of typists, draftsmen, and other specialists, can be utilized under ideal conditions and be brought together at the end of the project.

c) Writing is often made easier—because instead of trying to discuss certain types of things, we simply let our reader see them for himself. We can limit our discussion to the highlights and make helpful references to significant sections of the enclosure.

Advantages at the reading end include:

a) Our reader can more easily maintain his interest. Psychologically, it is better that he see a one-page letter plus a sheet of facts than a two-page letter that embodies the facts.

b) He can observe the actual document, rather than try to visualize it from our mode of expression. Moreover, our references to the enclosure will help him know what we are trying to emphasize.

c) He can take advantage of a greater flexibility in using our letter when it is in two parts. For example, he can retain the letter and send the enclosure along to someone who is in need of it; he could show someone either part without necessarily having to show the other part; he could file both parts together or each part separately; and so on.

A note of caution regarding two-part letters is in order. Some people tend to forget that the reader's needs should take precedence over their own. They begin to overuse the two-part technique because it is convenient, and they often neglect to do everything that should be done. The reader, as a result, receives a letter that basically does not do its job; and this defect is not remedied by the two-part form.

We should observe the following suggestions when we decide to use a two-part business letter:

1. Be sure that the letter follows what would have been a suitable program for a letter prepared *without* the two-part form.

2. Be sure that the message is sensible and complete *without* the enclosure. The important facts should be included in the body of the letter so that all analyses and conclusions are logical.

3. Be sure that the second part or enclosed document will be self-explanatory. If it becomes separated from the letter at the destination, the people there should not have a problem understanding what it is supposed to mean.

SUMMARY
· · · · · · · · ·

Form, which serves as the transmitter-channel-receiver link of the business communication process, has both subjective and objective aspects.

The subjective elements of form concern the things which the recipient of a business letter reads as well as sees. Thus, we must make sure that they are combined in a logical and consistent manner. Otherwise, our reader is likely to be distracted or annoyed by some communication noise caused by our carelessness or ignorance.

Objective form pertains to the physical layout of the business letter, including the parts involved. Here, too, we strive to keep distractions out of the letter by sticking to the conventional way of doing things. The stationery, letterhead, date, inside address, salutation, body, complimentary close, and signature are the primary considerations here. Miscellaneous additional parts are often included, but only when they are needed. Typing is done in either the block form or the modified-block form, with open punctuation. Variations of form—as evidenced by the letter on plain stationery, the memorandum, and the two-part letter—serve special purposes in given situations.

In the final analysis, letter form is needed to make our message visible to our reader, but we should not let it attract particular attention to itself.

QUESTIONS
· · · · · · · · · ·

1. What are the roles played by form in the business communication process?
2. State the three general criteria for judging the proper function of form.
3. What principles are involved in *objective form?*
4. What evolutionary change has been taking place in the matter of objective form?
5. If, as some people say, the salutation is an antiquated element of form, is there any justification for retaining it in present-day letters?
6. Why is modified-block (semiblock) form needed when the body of a letter is double spaced?
7. Under what conditions should a so-called informal complimentary close be used in a business letter?

8. If the company name in first position in the signature block constitutes the legal responsibility for the message, why should the writer sign his name afterwards?

9. In the context of business letter writing, what is a *footnote?*

10. Would it be correct to say that marginal notations at the end of a letter (e.g., reference initials, enclosure references, and carbon copy distribution) are used primarily as a service to the reader?

11. Does a postscript signify faulty planning of the letter?

12. Is it likely that a business letter would be prepared on plain stationery rather than letterhead stationery?

13. What are the kinds of miscellaneous notations which can appear on the outside of an envelope beyond the expected addresses?

14. Are any purposes served by folding a letter carefully and inserting it in the envelope according to a certain fashion? Explain.

15. Define the term *memorandum.*

16. Is a signature identification (typewritten name) called for at the end of a memorandum? Explain.

17. Distinguish between a one-part letter (or memorandum) and a two-part letter (or memorandum).

18. What advantages does the two-part letter offer to both the writer and the reader?

19. What danger exists in the use of the two-part letter form?

20. Give the guidelines for the proper use of the two-part letter.

EXERCISES

5–1. Present the information given below as a typewritten business letter in block form with open punctuation (except for the salutation and complimentary close, which should be punctuated). Use letterhead stationery, if available; otherwise, set up a simulated letterhead as directed by your instructor.

Body: We received your shipment of sugar on Purchase Order No. 1494. All your previous shipments have arrived in excellent condition. However, this time the sugar has come in a damp state. Some bags are so wet that the contents is hardening into blocks. Naturally, we cannot use sugar of this kind.

So that we may continue to enjoy excellent relations, it is desirable that this sugar be exchanged for a fresh supply. May we expect a new quantity by December 6?

We will keep the questionable bags aside so that you may inspect them at your convenience.

Complimentary Close: Very truly yours,

Date: November 21, 1967

Firm Signature: The SILVER BELL CANDY COMPANY

Inside Address: Dixie Sweets Corporation, 1100 Prudential Building, Jacksonville, Florida 33014

Letterhead Data: The Silver Bell Candy Company,
2790 Lincoln Boulevard,
Rochester, New York 14612, Telephone 527-5200

Reference Initials: DFD:ph

Salutation: Gentlemen:

Signature Identification: Dennis F. Dorsett

Writer's Title: Director of Purchasing

5–2. Present the information given below as a typewritten business letter in modified-block or semiblock form with open punctuation (except for the salutation and complimentary close, which should be punctuated). Use letterhead stationery, if available; otherwise, set up a simulated letterhead as directed by your instructor. Indent the paragraphs five spaces.

Attention Line: Attention of Sales Manager

Body: Same wording as appears in Exercise 5–1.

Complimentary Close: Yours very truly,

Date: November 21, 1967

Inside Address: Same as that used in Exercise 5–1.

Reference Initials: DFD:ph

Salutation: Gentlemen:

Signature Identification: Dennis F. Dorsett

Writer's Title: Director of Purchasing

5–3. Present the information given below as a typewritten letter which you are supposedly sending from your residence. Use modified-block or semiblock form with open punctuation (except for the salutation and complimentary close, which should be punctuated). Type a complete heading on the right-hand side of plain stationery; indent the paragraphs 10 spaces.

Attention Line: Attention of Order Clerk

Body: My mother is having a party next Friday night and has found that she is short of her favorite candy. She will need a five-pound box of your assorted dark chocolates. The candy is to be sent to the following address:

Mrs. . . .
(To be completed
by the student)

Also, I would like a three-pound box of this same kind of candy sent to my sister, Helen, at the following address:

Miss Helen . . .
(To be completed
by the student)

Enclosed is a money order for $12.50—enough, I am sure, to cover all charges on both boxes of candy. Please have my order attended to in time for my mother's party.

Complimentary Close: Yours truly,

Date: January 16, 1967

Inside Address: Any retail candy story of your choice.

Salutation: The proper selection.

Return Address: The address where you are now residing.

Signature Identification: The same as your longhand signature. [Note that a married woman signs her given and last names, but types or writes "Mrs." and her husband's name below her signature: Mary Smith (Mrs. John Smith). An unmarried woman may use (Miss) before the signature identification, as a helpful indication of her correct return address.]

5–4. Prepare a typewritten second page of a business letter in the modified-block or semiblock form with open punctuation (except in any part that customarily retains closed punctuation). Indent paragraphs five spaces. Select the necessary parts from the information given below.

Complimentary Close: Very truly yours,

Date: September 9, 1967

Enclosure: One

End of Body: Actually, users have reported good results from all of these methods. Probably the best results, however, can be expected from the third recipe, which requires refrigeration of the dough for eight hours.

I am enclosing a complimentary ticket for our annual baking demonstration, which will be held in our seventh-floor auditorium on March 4. The program begins at 1:00 P.M. We hope you will be able to come!

Inside Address: Mrs. Joseph H. Cleary, 19320 Lake Shore Drive, Euclid, Ohio 44123

Reference Initials: BB/ac

Signature Identification: Betty Best

Writer's Title: Home Economist

5–5. Present the information given below as a double-spaced, typewritten business letter with open punctuation (except in any part that customarily retains closed punctuation). Use letterhead stationery, if available; otherwise, set up a simulated letterhead as directed by your instructor. Because this letter contains two paragraphs, do whatever is proper to give each paragraph its separate identity.

Complimentary Close: Cordially,

Date: December 1, 1967

Inside Address: Mr. Herbert J. Russell, Vice President, Peters Advertising Agency, 61 Madison Avenue, New York, N.Y. 10017

Letterhead Data: The Silver Bell Candy Company, 2790 Lincoln Boulevard, Rochester, New York 14612, Telephone 527–5200

Message: Congratulations on becoming Vice President of Peters Advertising! You are certainly spearheading the progress of our Class of '48.
Best wishes for many more successes!

Reference Initials: DFD:ph

Salutation: Dear Herb:

Signature Identification: Dennis F. Dorsett

Writer's Title: Director of Purchasing

5–6. Present the information given below as a typewritten memorandum. Use a memorandum heading, if available; otherwise, devise a simulated heading as directed by your instructor. You may use either block form or modified-block (semiblock) form, as you please.

Carbon Copy Distribution: J. P. Davis
Oliver Shaw

Date: June 19,1967

Message: There will be a final meeting of the 1967–68 advertising campaign committee on Monday, June 26. All members of this group are required to attend, so that the budget figure for the upcoming fiscal year can be settled.

Please bring along the briefs of your plans for all types of media. Mr. Davis will then be able to examine them before rendering his decision. Whatever plans are approved in the name of the Sales Department will be covered by the budget under the direction of Mr. Shaw.

The meeting will convene in the conference room at 1:00 P.M., as usual.

Reader: Stanley Walsh, Advertising Director
Reference Initials: RHK/pn
Topic: Meeting to Settle 1967–68 Advertising Budget
Writer: Robert H. King, General Manager

PART II

....

PLANNING AND
ORGANIZATION

In the next two chapters, our attention centers on reassembling the theoretical matters which we analyzed in Part I of this book. We discuss the forward flow of steps we must take before, during, and after we construct a business letter.

For convenience, our approach in Chapter 6 is that of turning out a business letter as an individual effort. We see that a business decision of some kind is to be reached and that we are selecting the device of the letter as the means of pursuing the problem or conveying the solution.

Planning our letter consists of gathering the facts, identifying the situation, recognizing the basic needs of the situation, visualizing our intended reader, alerting ourselves to the possibilities for applying finesse, and constructing a program. Composing our letter is done on the basis of the program, with readable and accurate language, and with finesse. After the composition effort, we must place our letter in the customary form—and then begin to test for feedback. This testing is an inspection of our finished document in the order our intended reader will use—form, language, content. If everything is up to desirable standards, we are ready to mail our letter.

In Chapter 7, we consider the production of a letter when the work is shared with others. Typically, we continue to do the planning and composing phases; but a stenographer (or the combination of a dictating machine and a typist) takes over the physical aspect.

For our part, since we do not prepare a preliminary draft, we must learn to think out our message promptly and to dictate with confidence and skill. Also, since someone else interprets our voiced message, we must be especially alert when we do our testing for feedback. This chapter contains helpful suggestions for successful dictation.

....

CHAPTER 6

COMPOSING A
LETTER

In the first part of this book our study concerned the principal components that are involved in a business communication, particularly a business letter. We analyzed or broke down those components into smaller elements so that we could gain a keen understanding of their importance and function in a letter. At this point, however, we are interested in applying theory to the production of a business letter. From now on, we deal with synthesizing or building up a finished letter from its various parts. In short, having disassembled the business letter to study its theory, we now see how it is reassembled on the job as an important tool of business administration.

SOLVING BUSINESS PROBLEMS
....

We should recall, at the outset, that a written communication is a medium for transacting business. It is selected when other media, such as the personal conversation and the telephone call, would not work so well or are actually impractical. But it nevertheless is just a method of carrying on a matter of business. As such, it must measure up to good business practice; it does not enjoy a special or exempt status because the reader is some distance away.

The question arises: Aside from the fact that the reader is not present, why are we writing him a letter in the first place? Obviously, there must be a reason for communicating with him. That reason, if we get down to fundamentals, arises from the fact that a management decision is pending or has been made. The business letter is an instrument for pursuing facts needed in making the decision (when it is pending) or for evidencing the decision (when it has been made). The choice of a letter, instead of another medium, is a matter of circumstance.

For example, suppose that our company became interested in buying an electric typewriter. We might send out inquiry letters to a number of suppliers. Such letters would be in quest of facts upon which we might base our decision to buy a specific model of typewriter. In response we might receive explanatory letters, quotations, printed information, visits from salesmen, and even demonstrations of some of the machines. Finally, if we reached a decision to buy, we would send a purchase order or an order letter to the supplier of the model chosen. This communication would be evidence of our business decision.

The reaching of a business decision is the theoretical solving of a business problem. The field of management has systematized the procedure for us to use in seeking a solution to a business problem. It is as follows.

DEFINE THE PROBLEM

Before we can hope to solve a problem, we must have a reasonably clear picture of what that problem is. Attention can then be focused on the proper thing and a specific solution looked for. Otherwise, a supposed solution might be only a partial solution and might in turn create new problems—for example, deciding to install a piece of machinery that turns out to be too expensive for its purpose, larger than necessary, of limited use, etc.

In our previous example, we cited the problem of selecting from among different models of electric typewriters. But why did it have to be an *electric* typewriter? Would not a manual typewriter be just as satisfactory—and less expensive? Such questions would be rather alarming if they were not considered until after the purchase of the electric machine. But, if the problem were properly defined at the outset—probably as the result of other business decisions—the question of which model of electric typewriter would be valid. The point is, our statement of the problem should not bypass any logical determinations that are needed.

GATHER THE FACTS

It is quite clear that we can make only as good a decision as allowed by the adequacy of the facts we have available. If some important fact or facts are missing when we make our judgment, we could easily come up with a wrong decision. We should, therefore, make every effort to accumulate all the facts and then appraise them objectively as to quality before arriving at a business decision. An unwise decision, instead of solving a problem, can create new and bigger problems. Where large outlays of money are concerned, a wrong decision can sometimes cripple a company for years to come.

"NOW YOU KNOW WHY THEY CALLED HIM LONGSHOT."

STUDY POSSIBLE SOLUTIONS

A study of the accumulated facts, in the light of the definition of the problem to be solved, will usually result in our finding two or more possible solutions. Sometimes one of these solutions will be vastly superior to the others. Often, however, each possible solution will present certain advantages and disadvantages. Our task is to study and compare these offsetting features. We must determine both immediate and long-range implications, if possible.

SELECT THE BEST POSSIBILITY

Finally, we must make our decision. It should be made objectively —that is, it should be consistent with the facts, not influenced by personal bias. In our honest judgment, it should be the best solution we can find to the problem as defined. It might be a wrong decision as events later show; but it should be a good and reasonable one on the basis of the facts available at the time we made it.

PRODUCING BUSINESS LETTERS

Turning out an effective business letter substantially parallels the solving of a business problem. Actually, it *is* a problem to be solved— in fact, a continual number of problems, from the time our message is born until it is in final shape for our intended reader.

Because of the complexity involved, our aim is to develop an approach to the problem of letter writing that is time-saving, yet fruitful. Here again, we can apply a management concept to good advantage. This is the so-called "exception principle," under which we let routine talent or systems take care of routine operations, thus permitting key personnel to devote their attention to nonroutine or exceptional matters.

As details tend to become repetitive, so do they tend also to become reducible to routine. And routine encourages the formation of habit— which, if good, provides a standard solution to a recurring problem without much conscious effort being expended on our part. Accordingly, we are freer to place attention on the nonstandard, nonrecurring, or exceptional aspects of the problem with reasonable certainty that the other aspects will be handled properly. This approach requires that we have a reliable classification of what is standard and what is variable. Otherwise, we run many risks: sequencing our intended points in a standard order, but not in an order suitable to our reader; failing to observe specials calls for finesse; failing to express ourselves in a way that is best for this particular reader; and so on. But with a basic understanding of what is essentially nonstandard in a letter-writing situation, with the realization that the standard things apply to unknown readers more generally than they do to a known reader, and with a willingness to cater to the needs of any given reader, we should be able to keep a proper perspective.

As we have seen, the stages of development of our business letter are:

Content

The content of our letter is actually the message we wish to communicate. Our first concern with it, of course, is in the planning stage of our project. At this point, we set up a program—the topics that we wish to cover arranged in a sequence that will be best for our reader. We also anticipate the opportunities for applying the principles of finesse.

Language

The language step is the so-called encoding of our message, in keeping with our program and the principles of finesse. This encoding requires us to use a readable level (ordinary language) and accurate mechanics of expression (correct language) so that our reader, in decoding, can translate back to our intended message.

Form

The various components which make up the document are known as form. In our study, the characteristics resulting from the application of form give rise to the identifying term, *letter*. We use the letter to make our encoded message visible. Since it is physically sent to our intended reader, it functions as transmitter, channel, and receiver in our chain of communication. Depending on how it is used, form can do its job smoothly and inconspicuously—or it can cause noise or interference.

In diagram form, this three-stage development builds up as follows.

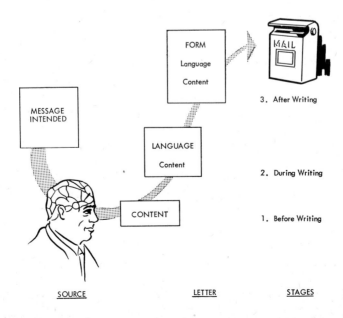

Our discussion will follow the order of development shown in the diagram. To keep it from getting needlessly complicated, we shall go on the assumption that we are to handle the entire problem on our own, without the assistance of clerical staff.

BEFORE WRITING

How should we go about the task of planning a business letter? This indeed is a problem, and it should be solved in a systematic manner. As we have seen, the first step toward a solution is to define the problem. After that, we can look for and find a solution. Therefore, when we plan a letter, we should proceed as follows:

1. *Identify the Situation.* In discussing content, we established that there are basically four situations involved in business-letter writing. All business letters should cater to the reader's goodwill, and one variety —the simple goodwill letter—does that and nothing more. But there are three multipurpose varieties, which carry some other message in addition to goodwill. These are known as the request letter, the good-news letter, and the bad-news letter. Our definition of the problem, therefore, is limited to one of these four possibilities—and most often to one of the three multipurpose varieties. In any case, we should be able to detect whether we shall be limiting our message to goodwill, or going on to ask for something, tell something pleasant, or tell something not so pleasant.

We can usually make such a determination quickly—in a matter of a few seconds, most of the time. Yet, this identifying of the letter-writing situation involved—the defining of the problem—is actually a major bit of progress toward the solution we are seeking.

2. *Recognize the Needs of the Situation.* As soon as we have identified the situation, we can confine our attention to the basic requirements demanded by that situation. These basic requirements have become standardized into general frameworks for writing business letters. We can use a standard framework successfully for almost every intended reader, but we should be alert to the possibility of an even better way when we write to someone we know rather well. We should play it safe, however, and use a standard framework for our letter whenever we write to someone not well known to us.

A simple goodwill letter is characterized by good timing, a sincere tone, and unity of content. As far as a standard framework is concerned, the last-named point, *unity*, tells the story. This kind of letter is intended solely for goodwill purposes—not to sell, or collect, or transact any other matters of regular business.

A request letter, regardless of the complexities arising out of the business at hand, calls for a definite request, motivation, and ample assistance. All of these qualities apply to the standard framework of a request letter, but the order of their appearance in the letter is not prescribed. The main thing is that we include all three requirements when we make a request of our reader. We must be clear and definite about what we want done; we should give our reader an appealing reason why he ought to do it; and we should do all that we can to make it easy for him to comply with our request. If we have handled these steps well, we have maximized our chances for success.

In the remaining two letter situations, not only must certain requirements be observed, but they must be included in a psychologically proper sequence. A good-news letter, especially if it is an answer to a request, would seem to work best if it gives its main message near the beginning. If there is any need to offer explanations, we can add them concisely afterwards. The reasoning is this: Most readers are interested in getting their answer above anything else. If the answer is a favorable one, they appreciate getting it at once; they do not like to be kept waiting while we bore them with an explanation or a sermon. Once we have given the favorable answer, however, our reader has what he was after and probably does not want to read much in the way of explanatory material. But, if the explanatory material is helpful to our reader—to clear up a doubt, to give needed instructions, and so on—a sufficient amount of it to do the job is acceptable.

A bad-news letter calls for delaying tactics at the beginning. It is better that we present our explanations and reasons before we let our reader know we are turning him down. Our discussion may not be particularly interesting to the reader, but he must read on if he wants his answer. Our words serve as a means of slowing his inevitable psychological plunge. On the other hand, were we to lead off with our bad-news statement, the impact on our reader would be sudden and abrupt. Having been smitten by our main message, our reader would probably tend to resist or dispute any following explanations. Our task of convincing him as to the reasonableness of our position would be more difficult. Our hope of breaking even on the goodwill relationship would certainly be dimmed. So we should prefer the gradual-letdown approach. Even then, we should not adjourn from our letter at the point of issuing bad news. Our reader should at least be headed upward psychologically by the time we end our letter. We need to append an encouraging ending—a goodwill gesture of some kind—to repair any possible damage done.

With a small amount of experience, we should find that recognition of the needs of the situation will occur almost simultaneously with our identification of the situation.

3. *Gather the Facts.* Having defined our problem and found a ready-made framework for solving it, we are ready to get specific in terms of whatever case we are handling. Now we need to gather the facts—the who, what, when, where, and why that will apply to the case. Because the writing of a business letter is connected with a business decision in one way or another, the principal source of facts is likely to be the same for both. Recurring or routine cases usually have been decided before they come up—by the establishment of what is known as *company policy.* Thus, the facts for many answer letters are obtainable simply from the reader's request and our knowledge of company policy regarding such requests. Obviously, other cases are more complex. Some require perusal of company records and files; some call for interviewing people inside and/or outside the company; some lead to various kinds

of research—public opinion, laboratory, library; and some even require assistance from professional consultants—accountants, engineers, lawyers. In most instances, of course, extensive fact hunting is not required, nor are all the facts gathered necessarily pertinent to the letter. But the likelihood of having all the necessary facts increases with the thoroughness of the fact-gathering effort.

4. *Visualize the Intended Reader.*   The better a picture we have of our intended reader, the easier it should be for us to write him an effective letter. The following points are among the many which we should try to consider:

a) *Sex.*   Whether our intended reader is a man or a woman has a bearing on what we can do, what we can say, and how we can express our message.

b) *Marital status.*   This knowledge is useful, of course, when we are addressing a letter to a woman. But it has deeper implications in that it can tell us something about the reader's probable daily routine, his needs, his motivations, and so on.

c) *Age.*   Even the simplest of age groupings—children, young adults, middle-aged persons, golden agers—can be helpful to us when we write to them. Each such group is of a different generation. Each grew up, formed likes and dislikes, and formed habits under a different set of historical and economic circumstances. We have a better chance of pleasing our reader if we have knowledge of his group and its peculiarities.

d) *Education.*   We can communicate effectively with someone if we can aim our language expression at his comprehension level. The person we address will not have to strain to understand us. Thus, if we can obtain some measure of our intended reader's level—such as his educational advancement—we are in a position to communicate with him in a more satisfactory manner.

e) *Temperament.*   Naturally, we wish to keep on our reader's good side. We are striving to create, enhance, preserve, or rebuild his goodwill in every letter that we write to him. Therefore, if we know something of his present temperament or attitude toward us, we are in a reasonably good position to know what to do. Sometimes we can tell from a letter we are answering whether our reader is agitated or calm. At other times, we must operate in the dark; and our best safeguard is being careful not to blunder into something antagonistic.

f) Mores.   Because people come from different cultural and social backgrounds, many of them have bound their lives by a set of conventions that is out of the ordinary. Hence, there are things which we may or may not say to a given reader, requests we may or may not make, and explanations we may or may not give —not because of any real rule, but because our reader has a special code of ethics or pattern of behavior. We are at a distinct advantage when we are aware of his viewpoint.

g) Occupation.   What does our intended reader do as his or her main occupation? Is he a banker, lawyer, doctor, salesman, machinist, laborer? Is she a housewife, receptionist, secretary, teacher? The answer will give us some added insight to our reader's needs, daily routine, vocabulary, and other variables. Such insight can be an asset to us in writing to his specific taste.

h) Income bracket.   Knowledge of our reader's probable income bracket adds dimension to our knowledge of his occupation. Affluence varies widely among persons even though they pursue the same basic occupation. Not all bankers, lawyers, and doctors are equally successful—nor does every housewife manage on the same size of budget. Inequalities in income result in people having different needs and interests, socializing at different levels, acquiring different tastes, and so on.

i) Business relationship.   No matter what particulars we accumulate about our intended reader, we should not overlook the role he plays in his business relationship with us. Whether he is a prospect, a customer, a supplier, an employee, or a competitor has a bearing on the perspective we need in writing him a good business letter.

5. *Construct a Program.*   We have selected the word *program* to describe the working outline of a business letter. Our choice of word is based on the necessity of placing the topics into a sequence which will best fill the psychological needs of our intended reader. We release the word *outline,* therefore, for use with other kinds of writing, in which the author's preference may dictate the sequence of topics.

A start on the construction of a letter program is already provided us in the four standard frameworks discussed above. These frameworks, however, contain only the irreducible minimum number of points in each situation and present them in somewhat vague, general terms. It follows that even when we write to an unknown reader and stick closely to the indicated standard framework, we must still put our program into specific terms applicable to the case at hand. For example, the favorable answer to a request for a department-store charge account fits the good-news framework: good news early; then concise explanatory material, if needed. In terms of our program, these parts would become more specific: charge account approved; how the credit system works.

Yet, the mere conversion of standard framework terms to specific program terms does not ordinarily do the full programming job needed. The standard framework contains only the minimum possible points, whereas a well-developed business letter must cover all points raised by the given case and must attend to the matter of goodwill. Thus, our accumulated facts about the problem and our knowledge of the intended reader are important. We should give these matters proper consideration when we construct our program.

As a general approach, we should begin our letter in a way that will create interest for our reader. This is best done by means of a short, eye-appealing first paragraph which is phrased to place the reader in a receptive frame of mind. After such a beginning, the main structure of our program can usually be fitted in smoothly.

In the case of a simple goodwill letter, however, the unity concept often forces us to lead off with the main message. But this occurrence is not troublesome to us, because little else remains to be said anyhow. In some good-news letters, the first part of the standard framework *can be* used as the beginning; but the effect is to make further discussion rather difficult. If we give our reader the good-news message immediately, we run the risk of dampening instead of kindling his interest in what follows. The recommended procedure, when we want our reader to keep his interest up, is this: Plan an interest-creating beginning which does not yet contain the main message. Then, convey the good news. After that, concisely give the explanatory material. Such a procedure takes advantage of momentum, which could not build up if we gave our main message at the very beginning. This way, our reader should become interested first, get his good news next, and then slacken off somewhat—but probably not enough to stop altogether, especially if what follows is useful to him.

When it comes to ending a letter, we face another problem. The ending is an important part of communication because it tends to linger on in the mind of our reader. The program we construct should provide for an ending that will be satisfying to our reader in the case at hand: a helpful suggestion; an offer of further help; a polite, yet climactic statement or question; a promise of appreciation; or simply a gesture of goodwill.

Two of the standard frameworks fit themselves naturally to this re-requirement. The simple goodwill letter by its very nature begins and ends with something of comfort to our reader. The bad-news letter situation calls for the inclusion of an encouraging ending so that our reader will not be left in a psychological trough. But the other patterns usually need to be fitted with an appropriate ending step as a part of their program.

To illustrate, let us pursue the situation of the good-news credit letter mentioned earlier. Suppose that this letter were being written from the credit department of Martin's Department Store. Our intended reader is a housewife, newly married, who filled out a credit application a few days ago. Our credit investigation has verified all of her statements; her rating is fair, but the future is promising. We have decided to grant her a charge account. In programming an answer letter to her, we might expand the standard framework of a good-news letter as follows:

> CHEERFUL GREETING.
> CHARGE ACCOUNT GRANTED.
> HOW THE SYSTEM WORKS.
> INVITATION TO USE ACCOUNT.

As an afterthought, we might wish to mention our new parking lot as extra encouragement for the reader to become an active credit customer. But this is a step removed from the charge account itself, and might be difficult for us to blend into the program. But how about a postscript, as a deliberate part of our plan?

From what has been said, we should not conclude that a program is necessarily something written down. A mental plan can be and often is used successfully. The advantages of written programs are that they can be seen, they can reveal their weaknesses more readily, they can be followed more surely, and they do not let steps evaporate after a period of time.

6. *Become Alert to Finesse.* Knowing the problem, the specifics of the case with which we are dealing, something about our reader, and the plan of action we intend to use, we are ready to consider the matter of finesse. We use finesse—diplomacy, service attitude, and positiveness —to achieve a smooth, satisfying reception of our letter.

The need for finesse naturally varies with the basic situation, the facts of the case at hand, and the peculiarities of the person to whom we are writing. Our letter program merely shows us the points we wish to cover in our message and the sequence in which we plan to go. Finesse is concerned with how we should put those points across. If special reminders and cautions will help us know when finesse is to be observed, we should try to arm ourselves with them before we begin our actual writing. Scanning or reviewing our program to gain such insight is a last-moment step before we put our message into words.

DURING WRITING

At first glance the phrase, "writing a letter," would give us the impression that it is chiefly a matter of composing a few paragraphs of written work. We have seen through the foregoing discussion, how-ever, that it represents a substantial amount of preparation. Gathering and organizing facts, knowing as much as possible about our intended reader, constructing a suitable program, and getting ready to use finesse must precede writing if we are to compose efficiently. After all that has been done, we have a message rather well worked out in our mind. If there were some other way of sending it to its destination—such as men-tal telepathy—we should have no need for "writing" at all. The writing of the message, therefore, is forced upon us by existing conditions—our message must be written (encoded) if it is to be transmitted.

We do not imply any minimizing of the role writing plays in the process of business communication. It is the sole means we have of sending our programmed message, of giving life to finesse, and of attain-ing a specific readability level. We definitely need it; and we must handle it competently. Our reader depends on the readability and accuracy of our writing when he tries to decode it and extract the message we intend for him. Hence, the following suggestions are offered as guidelines:

1. *Relax.*   Following the effort we put out taking the preparatory steps, a pause of some kind is usually a good idea. If we have built up any stress or strain, such a pause will relax us for the writing job ahead.

If we are confronted with but one letter, we might perform a brief task—such as getting a telephone call out of the way—before going on with the letter. This short intermission between the preparation and the writing will serve as a breathing spell. Each task calls for clear, crisp thinking, and we will avoid mind-dulling fatigue if we can break them apart. Sometimes we type our letter directly from our program, without the benefit of a rough draft. If so, we might be able to use the time of setting up the paper and typewriter as our diversion.

If we are handling several pieces of correspondence at one sitting, we have another means of separating the programming and writing of each letter. This is to set the first program aside to work on the second program, and so on. When we are ready to start writing, we can begin with our first program—and usually feel completely relaxed with it. It might be a good suggestion, though, to postpone our getting in touch with the aspects of finesse until we are ready to write. Then there will be less likelihood of forgetting anything as we put our thoughts into words.

Whatever we do, we should not attempt to write when we feel tense and nervous. Our "thinking muscles" should be limber so that our composition can be at its best.

2. *Write an Understandable and Agreeable Message.*   We must remember the following things about the letter we are trying to produce: It should be easy to follow and understand, and it should be acceptably and agreeably worded from our reader's point of view. It goes without saying that we should abide by the generally accepted standards of language. But aside from the strictly mechanical correctness of expression, there are certain requirements to be observed for effective business communication. The following is a résumé of the more important matters:

To be understandable: Our goal in the language phase of our letter lies beyond merely being understood by our reader. It calls for expressing ourselves in such a way that we cannot be misunderstood, which is a higher aim. Thus, we should:

a) **Go in a straight line.**   We should follow the program or plan we so carefully devised for our letter. It does not really matter whether each point in our program is handled in a separate paragraph, whether several are combined in one paragraph, or whether a point is discussed during more than one paragraph. The main thing is that our thought flow remains in the planned sequence and does not begin to zig-zag or backtrack.

b) **Prefer to use simple sentences.**   A good letter will contain sentences of varying lengths. It will also have a mixture of sentence types. But our preference should be toward the simple sentence, which has but one main thought. It is easier for our reader to understand than the more complicated types. Of the latter, the complex sentence (one main thought and a subordinate thought) makes a better second choice than the compound sentence (two main thoughts).

c) **Use the personal tone.**   Because readability is enhanced through the use of personal pronouns, we should take advantage of natural opportunities for using them. Letter writing is ideally suited for use of the personal tone, which introduces personal pronouns freely and easily.

d) **Use the informal style.**   Letter writing has been compared to conversation in writing. Within sensible limits, this comparison is appropriate. It implies that we should be friendly and informal in writing a letter—just as we are when we speak to someone in person or over the telephone. The informal style of writing, therefore, permits us to use ordinary contractions and slang of the everyday variety—the kind anyone should be able to understand.

e) **Use the active voice.**   Since the active voice goes naturally with the personal tone and the informal style, we ordinarily should use it when we write a business letter. At times, we might phrase something in the passive voice—such as to avoid antagonizing our reader or to cut down on the use of the first person.

f) **Use ordinary words.**   For the sake of reading ease, we should phrase our letter in words that will be easy for our reader to handle. If we know our reader well, we can make a reasonable adjustment to his level of vocabulary. If we do not know much about our reader, we should take no chances. We should always choose a familiar word at least; a *short,* familiar word if possible. Our purpose, remember, is to communicate a business message important enough to be writing about—and to be clearly understood.

g) **Employ eye appeal.** The element of eye appeal enters the communication process as the letter is being put into its final form. It nevertheless has a retroactive influence on the readability of our message. We should always take advantage of the possibilities of physical layout making our message more attractive and easier to read and understand. Good arrangement of parts, an uncluttered appearance, ample margins, and tabular listings are among the important considerations in this area.

To be agreeable: The matter of writing an acceptable and agreeable business letter is accomplished through the use of finesse. With it, we endeavor to keep our message from being misconstrued by our reader. We want him to accept what we say at face value and with a feeling of goodwill. We do not want him to develop any doubts about our sincerity, intentions, motives, attitudes, friendliness, or anything else as a result of reading our letter. While our program has headed us along a satisfactory route, we still need guidance along the way to include certain things, to say certain things in a certain way, and to leave certain other things unsaid. Such guidance becomes available through the three elements of finesse, which are:

a) **Diplomacy.** If we desire to create goodwill, we must be polite, courteous, and tactful when we write a letter. We should remember to use the so-called magic words, "please" and "thank you," whenever they are appropriate. As standard procedure, we should try to have the noun that follows "your" and the verb that follows "you" be complimentary to our reader.

b) **Service attitude.** To show sincerity and cooperativeness, we should be as helpful to our reader as possible—in word, deed, and attitude. If possible, we should do more than the minimum that is expected of us. As the name implies, this quality is an attitude which should permeate our letter, not just fulfill a step of the program.

c) **Positiveness.** When it comes to discussing something in a letter, we should remember that most things have a pleasant side as well as an unpleasant side. Our reader will find our letter more agreeable if we can write from the pleasant side. If an unpleasant occurrence pertaining to the reader must be referred to, we should try to use neutral terms, touch on it only lightly, be somewhat vague or devious about it. If we must report an unpleasant occurrence pertaining to ourselves, we should state the facts plainly; but we need not embellish it. We should prefer positive constructions to double negatives.

By way of illustrating the full development of a business letter, let us again turn our attention to the credit situation we introduced earlier in this chapter. In that case, Martin's Department Store had received an application for a charge account from a woman customer. Let us call her Mrs. Paul R. Elston. Although her credit rating checked out as only fair, we decided to go ahead with a credit approval for her. Thus, our letter of notification to her will be of the good-news variety: the main message early; concise explanations, if needed, afterwards. Furthermore, we decided that the program for the letter should contain more than these minimal parts. We added an interest-creating beginning and a goodwill type of ending. Our program became:

CHEERFUL GREETING.
CHARGE ACCOUNT GRANTED.
HOW THE SYSTEM WORKS.
INVITATION TO USE ACCOUNT.

We now review the program to see how finesse can be applied. One big thing is apparent—we shall make no mention of her marginal credit rating. Now we pause for breath. Then, following the suggestions for writing an understandable and agreeable letter, we compose a message somewhat like the illustration on the next page.

The statements made in this letter, of course, are based on our knowledge of the workings of our own department. The postscript, as mentioned before, is an intentional device to present material which would not be too easily includable in the body of the letter without deviating from the "straight-line" concept. The reference initials and enclosure designation may be regarded as window dressing in this letter, because we have been going under the assumption that we are without clerical help.

This illustration gives us a good view of a letter program in opera-

Martin's Department Store

20 RUNNYMEDE CIRCLE, ST. PAUL, MINN. 55177

August 25, 1967

Mrs. Paul R. Elston
1103 Archwood Road
St. Paul, Minn. 55143

Dear Mrs. Elston:

Best wishes to you from Martin's—as you begin a new era in shopping pleasure and convenience.

Your plastic Credex Card is enclosed—fully approved for use. It needs only your signature to become your most valued shopping partner. Carry it in your purse— it can help you to own a rare objet d'art or to pick up an unexpected bargain. Buy what you want, when you want it, with the regular privilege of delivery service as always.

Charges are summarized once a month, and statements are sent out under our cycle-billing system. Your regular closing date will be the seventh of each month, with your statement and itemized sales slips scheduled to arrive about a week later. On open account, payment is due within five days after the receipt of your statement. Because it is rather late in the month, your first closing date will be extended to October 7.

Do come in soon and enjoy the prestige of your new charge account.

Very truly yours,

MARTIN'S DEPARTMENT STORE

Myron T. Jackson

Myron T. Jackson
Credit Manager

MTJ:cj
Enclosure

P.S. You'll find free parking for 100 cars in the new lot behind our store—another Martin service for your shopping convenience.

tion. By following the steps laid out in the program, we were able to move from point to point in a forward flow of thought. We were kept on the track, so to speak—kept from wandering and floundering. Yet— and this is a significant feature—we were in no way controlled by our program in the matter of expression. We remained free to choose our own words, phrase our own sentences, and build up our own paragraphs. Our program merely prescribed the points to be covered and their sequence.

By coincidence, the program contained four steps, and the letter contains four paragraphs. This, however, need not have been the case. Someone else might compose this letter with a different number of paragraphs just as easily as he would use different words, a different writing technique, more or fewer sentences, and so on. In fact, dozens of writers composing a letter from this same program would likely come up with vastly different results. But, if we were to pare each such letter down and down, until only the barest gist of each point remained, we should arrive back at our original program.

AFTER WRITING

Whether we prepare a rough draft of our letter before typing the final copy or actually typewrite it as we compose it depends upon our personal choice and ability. The rough-draft method permits us to make revisions before the final typing and is recommended for beginners and for people handling troublesome cases. No matter which approach we use, however, we should subject our finished product to a test for feedback.

In Chapter 2 we identified feedback as something which gives us an indication of the success or failure of our letter. It could be in the nature of a letter from our reader, word through the "grapevine," observation of our reader's subsequent behavior, and so on. Naturally, we want our letter to do its full job as planned, including the observance of goodwill matters. Thus, before we mail a letter we should give it a careful inspection to see how it might be taken by its intended reader.

If we are engaging in a mass-communication effort, such as a public-opinion survey or a sales promotion, we possibly can run a test by means of an advance mailing. If the response from a representative sample mailing measures up to our expectations, we may go ahead with the quantity mailing. Otherwise, we should try to remedy the defects or weakness before committing a sizable amount of capital to the project.

Most of our letter writing does not lend itself to trial runs beforehand. We usually are writing one letter at a time—it will be either a success or a failure. There will be no such possibility as, say, a 50-percent response or acceptance; it will be 100 percent, or it will be nothing. To be on the safe side, we had better test the letter on ourselves before we send it out. We should assume the role of our intended reader, try to clear our mind of what our message says, and read the letter as though we had just received it. If we are up against a ticklish case, we might ask an associate or a secretary to read the letter and give us an opinion. Any defects spotted or suggestions received should lead us to make adjustments, because in this work we write to the needs of our reader.

" WELL, AT LEAST NO ONE CAN SAY OUR LETTER DIDN'T GET A RESPONSE . "

Let us examine the following diagram, which depicts the activity surrounding our letter at destination.

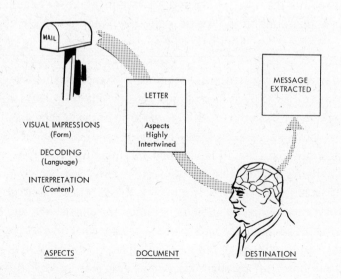

In a sense, our last stage in the development of the letter—form— is the first thing our reader encounters. Then comes language, as our reader begins to read and decode our message. As his decoding continues, he begins to interpret our thoughts; and, by the end of the letter, he has extracted the message—presumably the one we intended him to receive. This process is not exactly a direct reversal of our building-up stages of content, language, and form. Our reader experiences our letter as a continuous flow, with form, language, and content substantially unfolding together.

When we apply our test for feedback, therefore, we should consider our letter in terms of the various challenges it faces at destination. These challenges and some useful suggestions for meeting them are presented below.

1. Will our intended reader see our letter?

Since our business letter is mailed in an envelope, a great deal of work on our part can be wasted if the document inside never appears before the intended reader.

Most business letters are opened once they reach destination. But sometimes they are not opened promptly, or they are not opened by the right person. If our letter is delayed for any reason, it might not reach the intended reader soon enough to fulfill its assigned purpose. Much of the time our intended reader will be attending to his own business, unaware that we are writing to him. We cannot expect him to be chasing down a letter he does not even know is coming. It is strictly our responsibility to get the letter into his hands, ready to read.

We should always make sure that our letter is addressed properly. We should use the addressee's name correctly and show the complete address, the names of the city and state, and the postal ZIP code.

If we use an attention line in our letter, we should use it also on the envelope to save steps and time at destination. In the case of an order, an inquiry, or other routine letter, we are wiser to address the company or a department rather than an individual. By that approach, our letter should be opened even if the regular person is absent.

We should be careful to use the correct amount of postage. For regular mail, postage stamps are high in eye appeal, with the commemorative issues being best of all. We can resort to air mail whenever quick long-distance delivery is desirable. If we are writing to someone who did not provide us with his full mailing address, we can increase the chances for prompt delivery by adding special-delivery postage. In cases calling for proof of delivery, registered mail is at our service.

If we are involved in mass mailings and are using a bulk rate, we should do something to overcome the addressee's coolness toward this class of mail. As mentioned during the discussion of form, we can have our envelopes overprinted with a curiosity-arousing remark to get the reader to look inside the envelope.

If our company uses metered or prepaid postage for its first-class letters, we can choose to have "First-Class Mail" printed on our envelopes. Both stamped and metered postage are accepted usage, and both kinds can be affixed to envelopes by mechanical means.

2. Will he actually read it?

Once the envelope is in the hands of the intended reader and actually opened, our business letter must be read from beginning to end. Unfortunately, some letters are only half-read—either put aside before they are finished, or glanced at so carelessly that little of our message gets through. In such cases nothing was really done to whet the reader's interest. He was bored to begin with, and he stayed bored the full time he looked at the letter.

To assure that our letter will be read, we should check whether we have created a good first impression through our overall neatness and application of form. Among the important considerations are good-quality stationery; clean type; and a generous use of white space, particularly at the margins.

As for subjective interest, we can begin by addressing the letter to the reader, and greeting him by name in the salutation. Our opening statement should be calculated to create interest in reading what follows. Some types of letters, such as sales letters and collections, can be anticipated by our reader as soon as he sees the envelope. Thus, because we must overcome an amount of resistance or prejudice, we may have to expend some extra effort to inspire reader interest.

Once we have our reader started, we want to keep him reading the entire message without a letdown in interest. Sticking to our program is a decided advantage: a well-organized letter has continuity, a quality which helps to maintain interest.

In the presentation of our message, we should use familiar words. Most readers have a tendency to pass over any difficult words they encounter. This is a type of half-reading, and it results in a decrease in the meaning of our message. As the meaning deteriorates, certainly so must our reader's interest.

In lengthier letters, we can use eye appeal and/or the two-part form to overcome a drop in interest. Sales letters, for example, can be dressed up with variations of form and different colors of ink to reinforce interest. Job-application letters regularly make use of a letter of moderate length coupled with a summary sheet of the applicant's qualifications. This technique reduces what might otherwise be a forbidding and boring-looking letter.

3. Will he understand it?

In business communication, the burden of being understood falls directly upon us at the writing end. It is we who have a message to deliver, and we should make every reasonable effort to get it through to our reader.

As we have already seen, a letter that follows a well-planned program is off to a good start. Its straight-line sequence should be of help to our reader. Then, by using the conversational devices of active voice, informal style, and personal tone, we provide extra assistance.

In the matter of mechanics of expression, we should especially check our spelling—there is no compromise here. In general, we should favor easy-to-read language; it is also easy-to-write language. Emphasizing simple sentences, we should strive for a pleasing blend of short and medium-length sentences. We should use definite, clear phraseology; be specific in all requests that we make; and be complete on every point.

As for the words used in our letter, there are three aspects for us to check. First, we should do a thorough job of defining or translating into ordinary words all technical terms and expressions. Second, whenever possible, we should use short, familiar words in place of long, strange words. Third, we should make sure that our words are used correctly. Even ordinary words are often misused, especially where homophones (affect, effect; principal, principle; etc.) are concerned.

If added eye appeal will help the reader understand our message, we should take advantage of it. Underlining key words and phrases, placing items in tables, numbering questions, and the like are useful for gaining emphasis and understanding.

4. Will he believe it?

We may follow a good letter program and make some very nice-sounding statements in easy-to-understand language—but what effect will all this have on our reader? If he is like most of us, he will probably be skeptical about what he reads and hears. In fact—the taller the story, the louder the talking, the bigger the promises the more wary and doubtful the reader is likely to become.

If we want our reader to believe what we write him in our letter, we must use a presentation which fosters credibility. For one thing, we must be dependable. We should practice restraint and sincerity whenever we state our facts. Otherwise, we appear to be overemphasizing; and our reader's reaction is to become defensive and discount what we say. For example, inflated statements in a claim letter tend to cast doubt on the validity of the claim.

Another important thing for us to consider is our use of logic. If we draw conclusions from stated facts, such conclusions should be consistent with the facts. Explanations why our reader's request cannot be granted should make sense to him. Reasons we offer for the granting of our requests should be plausible. Sometimes we can use comparisons or analogies as a technique to associate something we want our reader to believe with something that he already believes. In such a case, the relationship itself must be believable, not flimsy or forced.

In some instances, it is even possible for us to offer proof to substantiate what we have said. As a matter of fact, in the highly de-

veloped request letters—such as sales letters and application letters—
some form of proof is expected. We could not expect our reader to believe
our sales talk about a new product unless we capped it with a guarantee,
a report of independent laboratory analysis, or some other form of proof.
Nor could we expect to be considered seriously for a position on the
strength of boastful statements of what we are able to do.

5. Will he be convinced by it?

Let us assume that we have written a letter
to a person in another company. In it, we have
asked for some information on their policy regarding the separation of workers at retirement
age. Our reader has opened, read, understood,
and believed our letter—but will he agree to
send us the information we have requested? The
answer will be favorable if we have convinced him that he should do it.
To convince him—to get him to agree—we need to have applied finesse.

In checking our letter, we should satisfy ourselves that the elements
of finesse have been applied properly to win approval, foster goodwill,
spark motivation, and render assistance.

> *a*) *Diplomacy.* Courtesy, tact, and getting in step with our reader's
> temperament help create the feeling that he and we are pleas-
> antly allied. Obvious flattery can be just as objectionable as
> bluntness or tactlessness. We should look for words that have
> doubtful connotations and discard them in favor of "safe"
> words. Furthermore, we should use the passive voice and neutral
> words to soften the impact of unpleasant but necessary dis-
> cussions.

> *b*) *Service attitude.* Our letter should be designed to interest our
> reader. Depending upon the given case, our reader's self-interest
> should be catered to, his problems solved, his company's name
> promoted, his peace of mind assured, and so on. On the other
> hand, the things of interest to us should be subordinated.

> *c*) *Positiveness.* Pleasantness, comfort, satisfaction—these are the
> flavors that appeal to our reader. Most situations can be found
> to have a good side about them, however slight. Our reader will

like to hear things from that good or pleasant side, and we should play them up that way for him. Sometimes just the way a thing is stated will make it sound much better: "as soon as" is more promising than "not . . . until"—yet the situation remains unchanged. Generally, the happier our reader feels, the more likely he is to cooperate with us.

6. Will he happily behave as we intend him to?

In the final analysis, our business letter can be termed a success only if it accomplishes everything it started out to do. Even though our test for feedback up to now has revealed everything to be in smooth working order, we might still have to make sure of a few more details.

Business letters of the simple goodwill, good-news, and bad-news varieties do not require this extra checkout. They will have reached the point of success through the process of being received, read, understood, believed, and agreed with. Our reader is not ordinarily expected to write back or take any other physical action. He needs only to accept our message as the proper one in the given case, and this acquiescence has certainly been encouraged.

Our request letters, however, call for more than our reader's mental act of agreement. They will not have succeeded if he stops there. They require that we take measures to prod our reader into prompt action—so that he does not postpone, forget, or change his mind. We must see to it that the essential features of a request situation have been adequately developed in our letter, not merely given token coverage.

a) Definite request. We should state the desired action clearly and precisely. If it is important, we should give the date by which action is needed.

b) Motivation. Some requests (orders and inquiries, for example) are often self-motivating, but ordinarily we need to provide some form of inducement in our request letters. Mild requests (such as in introducing someone or in seeking a favor) may get by on a promise of appreciation. More serious requests (collection letters and sales letters, for example) need special appeals—

urgency, time limits, quantity limits, and the like. In confidential matters, an explanation of the use we plan to make of the information could be helpful in getting action out of our reader.

c) *Ample assistance.* Whenever we make a request in a letter, we should make a thorough search for ways and means of helping our reader comply. We should remove all apparent obstacles, so that action is almost as easy as inaction.

The following sampling of cases should demonstrate this concept. If we are asking for information, we should use specific questions, preferably number them, make provision for easy answering (such as in a questionnaire), and supply an envelope and postage for our reader's convenience. Sometimes, providing for the answers at the bottom of our letter is helpful. If we are applying for a position, we should tell our reader where and when we can be reached, state when we can come in for an interview, and provide our telephone number and/or a stamped, addressed envelope. If we are trying to sell by mail, we should provide all the instructions and physical means needed for our prospect's effortless response. If we are asking for clarification of an unclear order, we should provide an easy-to-use form and a means of returning it. If we are trying to collect an account, we should state the amount to be paid and enclose a remittance envelope. All of this actually is commonsense application of the service attitude.

SUMMARY

The full preparation of a business letter may be divided into three phases: before writing, during writing, and after writing.

Before we get down to the work of composing our letter, we go through a preparatory stage somewhat paralleling the process for reaching any business decision. We must define our problem, gather the pertinent facts, and ultimately decide upon the best of several possible solutions. In letter writing we are able to build on the framework of one of four standard situations. Using the facts of the case and whatever knowledge we have of our intended reader, we work out a plan for our letter. It includes the points we wish to cover (the intended message), the sequence we will follow (the program), and an anticipation of how we will put our message across (priming for finesse).

As we compose, we follow our program, express ourselves in language that is both within our reader's grasp and in good usage, and apply the principles of finesse—diplomacy, service attitude, and positiveness. In business communication, it is our responsibility at the source to make certain that our message cannot be misunderstood or misconstrued at the destination.

Tangible shape is given to our message, sequence, level of readability, accuracy of language, and matters of finesse when our letter finally appears on paper. We should then examine it to see that it is adequate for its purpose.

In writing our letter, we were able to attend separately to content, language, and form. Our reader, on the other hand, will consume our letter one piece at a time. Each piece he reads will contain aspects of form, language, and content. In testing our letter for probable effectiveness, we should read it as our intended reader would. Above all, we should see that everything necessary has been done to have our letter be opened, read, understood, believed, agreed with, and (if applicable) acted upon.

QUESTIONS

1. Under what general condition is a written communication used as the medium for doing business?
2. Give the four general steps in the systematized procedure used for solving business problems.
3. What is meant by the *exception principle* of management?
4. Describe the cumulative buildup which occurs between the time the intended message is conceived and the time when the finished document is ready to be sent to the reader.
5. State the characteristics of a simple goodwill letter.
6. What three things are required in request letters, regardless of the complexities arising from a given problem?
7. What is behind the recommendation that in a good-news letter explanatory matter be minimized, and sequenced after the good-news statement?

8. Why, on the other hand, should there be abundant explanation in a bad-news letter, with placement ahead of the bad-news statement?

9. Are these two recommendations binding in *all* good-news and bad-news letters?

10. What is needed following the bad-news statement in a bad-news letter?

11. List the many details about the reader which, if known to the writer, will make the composing of a communication easier to handle.

12. What is behind the suggestion that the writer *relax* between getting set to compose and beginning his composition effort?

13. What are the basic suggestions for writing an understandable message?

14. In a word, what element especially contributes to making a business communication acceptable and agreeable to the reader?

15. How reliable is the statement, "The number of steps in the program indicates the number of paragraphs to be used in the message"?

16. What is meant by the phrase, *test for feedback?*

17. Suggest some methods that might be used to test for feedback.

18. Besides the fact that the reader receives a message somewhat in the reverse order of its preparation (form-language-content vs. content-language-form), what else is different about his extracting the message as against the writer's input of the message?

19. What are five challenges which must be overcome by every business letter?

20. In the case of request letters, what is a sixth challenge that must also be met successfully?

....

CHAPTER 7

DICTATING
A LETTER

In practice, the preparation of a business letter is usually not the sole effort of the person sending the message. If we serve in an executive capacity, our employer expects us to attend to activities on an executive level. We are supposed to be involved in such matters as making plans, directing personnel, studying problems, and making decisions. Of course, we do have to answer letters we receive and, at times, initiate correspondence ourselves. Our personal performance, however, should be with the executive aspects of the letter—the planning and the composing. Someone at another level can carry on with the typewriting work and other purely clerical details. The link between these two levels of activity is dictation.

To see dictation in its proper light, we should recognize that it is an application of one of several industrial management principles which have been adopted by office management. This is the principle of *division of labor,* under which a job is shared by several workers. Each worker attends to a special phase of a job according to his own trade or skill, instead of attempting to parallel the activity of each other worker on an entire, separate job.

In letter writing, proper application of the division-of-labor principle makes it possible for us to omit rough-drafting or typing our own letter. Instead, when we are ready to get our words down in writing, we do our composing orally. We speak our message either to a stenographer who takes it down in shorthand, or to a recording device for subsequent transcription by a typist. In either case, we should have the document returned to us for final approval and signature.

PRODUCTION CONTROL CONCEPT

The division of work through dictation does not alter our "before, during, after" problem of preparing a business letter. It merely allocates a part of the problem to someone besides ourselves. When dictation is used, the stage-by-stage build-up of the letter proceeds as shown in the following diagram.

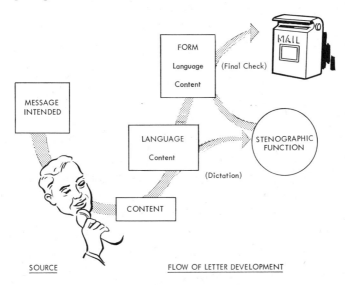

The overall preparation of our business letter can now be likened to an industrial production process. For production control, the principal functions are known as routing, scheduling, dispatching, follow-up (or expediting), and inspection. A parallel for each of these functions can be found in the letter-writing process when dictation is part of the preparation.

ROUTING

In industry, routing is the planning of the flow of work. In letter writing, we must decide on various priority sequences concerning the letters to be dictated first, those to be typewritten first, and those to be mailed first. As we have already seen, we have a kind of routing problem with the flow of thought through a given letter. Once we have settled the question of the situation we are facing, we plan a sequence for the points in our message—the letter program.

SCHEDULING

Assignment of times for the starting and accomplishing of different phases of the overall production is called scheduling. In letter writing, there will be occasions when priority letters will be needed by a definite time. Also, there may be need for time coordination with other departments in connection with enclosures needed for certain letters. For example, we may need to send a check with our letter—but we must depend on the financial department to provide that check by the time we need it.

DISPATCHING

A line of communication—of a different order, however, from the kind we are investigating—is needed to get the scheduled plans into operation. Whatever means are used for this purpose, the activity is known as dispatching. In our type of work, dispatching is present; but it is rather routine. If we have dictated our correspondence to a stenographer, all that we need tell her at the end is that she may return to her desk and begin on the work. Our dictation itself should have already keyed in any special instructions regarding priorities and special scheduling. Under the dictating-machine method, we might be able to depend on a systematic delivery service between offices and the secretarial pool. Otherwise, we can either telephone the pool for a courier or dispatch someone from our office to deliver the recordings. Priorities and special schedulings are best handled by our dictating them ahead of routine letters and then sending a note along with the recordings.

FOLLOW–UP

Production managers know that they cannot be satisfied with the mere planning and dispatching of work. The fact that they have ordered work into production does not mean that it has started on schedule—or if started, that it will stay on schedule. There has to be some kind of expediting or follow-up activity if plans and schedules are to be realized. So it is, too, in the matter of dictation. Especially if our letter output is more than just a trickle, we should have some dependable system for keeping track of letters in process. Otherwise, some of the letters we have dictated could lag behind schedule—or possibly never be typewritten, for one reason or another. Probably the best system would be to use a dictation log, showing the date dictated and the addressee of the letter and providing for the entering of the date that the letter is returned for signature.

INSPECTION

In any manufacturing operation, it is not the total number of units produced that is significant; it is the number of good or acceptable units that counts. The remaining units are not immediately useful, and may never be good for anything but scrap. The aim is to hit an optimum wherein both the production rate and the acceptable units produced are high. Control over this aspect is maintained through various kinds of inspection and testing, ranging from sampling and statistical quality control to 100 percent inspection. By comparison, in letter writing we almost always need 100 percent inspection—even when we do the entire job ourselves. In such a case, assuming that routine matters are in proper order, we still have to make our test for feedback. We want to satisfy ourselves that the letter will have the proper effect on the intended reader and will, therefore, produce the results we desire. When dictation enters the picture, we cause the routine matters to be shifted to someone else. We must now check these matters carefully, also. If form, neatness, spelling, punctuation, and such details are not the way they should be, we ought to reject the work. Perhaps only a minor correction is needed and can be made; perhaps the entire letter must be retyped. But, if we sign the letter and let it go out with mistakes in it, we assume the responsibility for those mistakes.

ADVANTAGES AND DISADVANTAGES

There are some important advantages to be gained from the sharing of the work of letter writing through dictation. We who manage can get our correspondence taken care of sooner, and thus have more time to devote to our primary work of managing. Other personnel, with training in secretarial work, can be expected to turn out finished copy at a faster rate and with greater skill than we. The salary differential between our two levels has the effect of bringing down the overall cost of producing a letter. This sharing of the letter-writing work would appear to be an ideal arrangement for the business firm.

There are, however, some pitfalls to be guarded against. One is the multiplication of the human factor, which is ever prone to error. When we do our own work, we are solely responsible for careful handling of spelling, capitalization, punctuation, and other such details. When we dictate our message, these matters for the most part are left to the secretary or typist. It frequently happens that a transcriber, while expert at verbatim copying, is erratic in spelling, capitalization, and punctuation when there is nothing to copy from. Sometimes the error is caused by carelessness—such as an entire sentence being overlooked, or the start of one sentence becoming joined with the end of the next sentence, with the intermediate parts left out. Thus, we cannot assume the accuracy of deputized work; we must check it carefully before we allow it to be mailed.

Then there is the possibility of misinterpretation. The secretary or typist must rely on sound to pick up the message we are sending. We may say one thing, but it could be interpreted as something else. The fault could be ours because of our manner of enunciation, or it could be that of our secretary or typist on account of not listening attentively. Whatever the reason, we can again see why a careful checking of the finished product is necessary.

A third danger is one to which we must be alert during the act of dictating. It is the tendency to violate readability. Unfortunately, this tendency is stronger when we dictate than when we do actual writing. One reason is that we do not see what our words look like or what length our sentences are reaching. Another is that we can more easily lose sight of the fact that we are addressing our letter to someone not in fact present—our intended reader. Physically, we may be speaking to a stenographer or a dictating machine; but it is up to us to keep firmly in mind that we are conducting business  with the reader, and he is the one to whom we are addressing ourselves.

Some of us become tense when it comes to dictating. In the preceding chapter, we cautioned against trying to compose a letter while under stress or strain. Our thinking ability and alertness will not be at their peak. We will have difficulty finding the best words we need for expressing our message and may have to settle for a number of second bests. Worse, we will often get stuck—and rather than see a stenographer's pen held in midair or a dictating machine going but not recording, we will begin to add "fill." These unmeaningful words, phrases, and sentences contribute little or nothing to our message, but they give us time to think. Again, what about our intended reader?

Many of the difficulties, we will find, tend to be magnified in our first attempts and disappear as we become more experienced. While we are acquiring skill and confidence, it might be a good idea to do a more thorough job of programming than will be needed when we are more practiced. We may need, like the "unaccustomed-as-he-is" public speaker, specific notes of the main points and a strong reminder to be brief, stick to the point, and stop talking as soon as possible. These matters will soon become routine as we form good dictating habits.

In importance, the advantages to be obtained from the dictation process heavily outweigh the disadvantages. Once the teamwork between the dictator and the stenographer is in smooth running order, dictation is superior to either rough-drafting or total preparation of the letter by the correspondent. Although some of us might prefer to rough-draft our copy, this work is time consuming. It ordinarily is not justified in light of the benefits available through dictation.

THE DICTATION PROCESS

In the production of a business letter by teamwork, dictation takes the place of the "during writing" activities which were discussed in the preceding chapter. All other activities remain substantially the same. Therefore, by the time we are ready to compose our letter, be it a written or an oral process, we have identified the basic situation involved, recognized the standard framework of the letter to be written, visualized our reader, devised a program to follow, and prepared ourselves for the application of finesse. In essence, we have cleared all hurdles concerning what we plan to do and can now put our full attention on doing it.

The act of dictation is similar to extemporaneous speaking. A message must be composed as we go along. The program keeps our thoughts from wandering about, but the build-up of sentences, paragraphs, and overall message occurs as we speak. While there is no substitute for practice and experience, the following guidelines should help us do a successful job of dictating a letter.

ESTABLISH A ROUTINE

For the best operation of a business office, we should have a regular period each day for dictating our letters. In that way we can depend on the availability of a stenographer or a dictating machine; can foster cooperation toward a daily "do not disturb" period; can probably answer most of our mail the same day that it is received; and can have our work arrive at its typing station as an expected thing, not as a surprise.

BE PREPARED

Before plunging into dictation, we should have everything in readiness. Important items include each letter we are answering, together with the program we have worked out for answering it and any forms, cards, clippings, and so on which are to be quoted in our answer. Programs for originating letters would also be included, accompanied by their supporting papers. Such preparedness will permit us to move along with our dictation without interruptions to hunt for something needed. It will also have everything set to move on to the typing station when the dictation has been completed.

RELAX

Just as for actual writing, we must be relaxed to do a good job at dictation. Any feelings of tenseness arising from the effort of making preparations should be removed before we attempt to dictate. When we are ready to start, we must be mentally and emotionally equal to the task of blending our program, the needed finesse, readability, and language accuracy into a suitable communication—preferably on the first try. We should overcome any tendency toward stage fright or freezing up. We need only remember that we and our secretary or typist are team-mates. We are simply going to tell our teammate what we otherwise would have jotted down. Whether we are seeing a stenographer or a microphone, we are just voicing our message to an assistant, not to an audience. There is nothing whatever for us to be nervous about.

USE A CLEAR, NATURAL VOICE

When we speak our message, we should neither shout nor use a strained, falsetto tone of voice. Whether we are speaking to a stenog-rapher or to the microphone of a dictating machine, we should use a normal, conversational tone. If we are working with a stenographer, we should speak openly, with our chin up and no hand covering our mouth. If we are using a microphone, we should speak straight into it and hold it as stationary as possible. Our rate of speed should be steady and set at a slightly slower pace than usual. We want to avoid spurts when an easy passage comes along, in contrast to the slowdowns which occur when we find the phrasing difficult.

ENUNCIATE CLEARLY

Because what goes down on the stenographer's pad will be symbols representing sounds and what goes onto a recording will be a representa-tion of our voice, we want to guard against errors that might occur during the transcription step. Our best safeguard is to speak clearly and deliberately, pronouncing each syllable with care. This process is known as enunciation—speaking so as to be heard correctly. We must not slur words, skip over syllables, chop off word endings, or commit any other acts of carelessness in voicing our message.

GIVE NECESSARY INSTRUCTIONS

When we have someone assisting us with our correspondence work, we should make certain that they know what they are supposed to do. Therefore, at the point of beginning the dictation of our letter we should give instructions concerning the number of copies to be made, the distribution of information copies, special mailing instructions, and whatever else is especially applicable to this letter. Whoever does the typing should be aware of the full situation before starting.

During the course of dictation, we should be on the lookout for matters which call for additional instructions or help. We should spell people's last names—and their other names, too, if these can be spelled in more than one way. We should always express figures digit by digit. We should always indicate when we are beginning a new paragraph. As for corrections, if we are dictating to a stenographer, we usually can handle the situation on the spot. If we are doing machine dictation, we should try to make each correction at the point needed. But, in any event, we should follow the equipment manufacturer's instructions for marking the place where a correction is to be made.

As part of our leadership responsibility, we are expected to give directions for using capital letters where there may be some doubt, to help with the spelling of troublesome words, and to indicate special punctuation and markings. For this latter purpose, we may find the following summary useful:

1. *Colon.* We ordinarily use a colon to introduce a listing or enumeration, or some other material that is dependent on the sentence that precedes the colon. In such cases, the word following the colon is not capitalized.

2. *Dash.* A dash is used to mark a rather abrupt shift in thought or expression. It can set off part of a sentence, when we want to do that more emphatically than with commas, or more informally than with a colon.

3. *Parentheses.* We use parentheses to enclose side remarks, clarifications, special references, instructions to the reader, and so on.

4. *Quotation Marks.* We make use of quotation marks to enclose direct quotations and also words and phrases which we wish our reader to take in a special sense. The latter group includes technical terms, coined expressions, and sometimes slang. We should be alert, too, to the combining of other punctuation with ending quotation marks. Following an arbitrary rule, commas and periods are always placed inside the quotation marks. Other marks of punctuation should not be placed inside unless they are a part of the quotation.

5. *Semicolon.* Ordinarily we consider the semicolon to be routine enough for the stenographer to handle without special instructions. But in at least one case we will probably need to indicate it. In enumerating a series of items, one or more of which already contain commas, semicolons are needed between the items of the series. It would be difficult to make such a complex listing clear by voice inflections and pauses; we should alert the secretary or typist to the punctuation needed.

6. *Diagonal.* Occasionally we find it possible to avoid a complicated construction by using the diagonal (or virgule) to stand for *or,* as in the expression "and/or." We are wise to make this clear, lest either a hyphen or nothing at all be the typewritten result.

7. *Other Punctuation.* Other marks which may require a mention from us during dictation are the hyphen and the period. As discussed in Chapter 4, we should have a fairly consistent style of hyphenating compound words. We may find that our typists routinely do a good job in this area; if not, we should indicate our preferences until we have established an understood usage. In special or doubtful cases, we should stay on the safe side and indicate the spelling.

Ordinarily, no specific instructions are needed for commas and periods; the transcriber infers these from our pauses and voice inflections. However, in some localized situations we are expected to dictate the periods; if that is the case, we will include this mark in our dictating. We dictate the question mark and exclamation point when they are called for.

8. *Underlining.*   To add particular emphasis and eye appeal to captions, phrases, or passages of our letter, we may wish to have such a part underlined. Our secretary or typist would never be able to guess at this intention; we must be sure to make it known. Underlining is done as a continuous line typed beneath the words and spaces involved.

9. *Italics.*   If we need to mention the name of a book, magazine, or newspaper; to use a phrase from a foreign language; or to add emphasis to an important word or term, we should make use of italics. Some people merely underline to show italics, but this procedure could lead to confusion with any regular underlining. The better method of show-ing italics is to underline each word separately. We are wise in specify-ing both the words to be italicized and the method of doing it.

CHECK AS NEEDED

While we are dictating, we may want to find out exactly what we have said at one point or another. There are many possible reasons. We may wish to collect our thoughts before going on; we may want to test a passage for accuracy of expression, readability, or finesse; we may wish to avoid sounding repetitious; we may be trying to avoid a contra-diction or inconsistency in our message; and so on. If we are dictating to a stenographer, we can have her read that part back to us. In the case of using a dictating machine, we can turn back the recording and listen to our own voice. Such checking is very helpful. It can result in changes before the letter is typed, with the result that a rerun is avoided. It is a good way of minimizing errors that would turn up during our inspection of the typewritten letter.

ILLUSTRATION

To get an impression of how dictation might be carried out, we can make use of the credit letter we developed in the preceding chapter. We can assume the conditions to be the same, except that we are going to compose orally instead of in writing. The following presentation shows how the letter and pertinent instructions might be placed on a recording. The diagonals indicate the slight pauses we insert after units of thought to help the typist keep up with us. The bold type in brackets represents the instructions to the typist. In giving our dictation, we should use a conversational tone of voice for the instructions as well as for the message. It might be helpful to the listener, however, if we were to use a slightly different vocal texture.

[Operator please type this letter with one carbon copy / address it to] / missus paul r elston e-l-s-t-o-n / 1-1-0-3 archwood a-r-c-h-w-o-o-d road / saint paul minnesota 5-5-1-4-3 **[salutation]** / dear missus elston / best wishes to you from martins / **[dash]** / as you begin a new era / in shopping pleasure / and convenience / **[exclamation point / new paragraph]** / your plastic / **[capital C]** / credex / **[capital C]** / card / is enclosed / **[dash]** fully approved for use / it needs only your signature / to become / your most valued / shopping partner / carry it in your purse / **[dash]** it can help you to own / a rare / objet d'art / **[that term is to be shown in italics / so underline each word separately]** / or to pick up / an unexpected bargain / buy what you want / when you want it / with the regular privilege / of delivery service / as always / **[new paragraph]** / charges are summarized / once a month / and statements are sent out / under our cycle **[hyphen]** billing system / your regular closing date / will be / the seventh of each month / with your statement / and itemized sales slips / scheduled to arrive / about a week later / on open account / payment is due within five days / after the receipt of your statement / because it is rather late in the month / your first closing date / will be extended / to october 7 / **[new paragraph]** / do come in soon / and enjoy the prestige / of your new charge account / very truly yours / **[set up the signature block with our company name first / indicate one enclosure / then add this postscript]** / you'll find free parking / for 1-0-0 cars / in the new lot behind our store / **[dash]** / another martin service / for your shopping convenience

AFTER DICTATION

Following dictation there is an interval of time during which the transcription work is done. Then the finished letter should be returned to us for inspection, final approval, signature, and mailing.

If inspection of the letter—the test for feedback, as we call it—was important when we did the entire job ourselves, it is even more important when we have someone else sharing the work. As for the message itself, we still must satisfy ourselves that it is likely to fulfill its entire mission. But, besides checking what we have dictated, we must look for "slippage"—any possible deterioration or misinterpretation of our voiced statements occurring as a result of the dictation process.

'IS THIS THE WAY YOU MAKE CORRECTIONS ON ALL YOUR LETTERS, MISS PIMPEL ? "

As for form and the mechanics of expression, matters which we placed to a large extent under the control of our secretary or typist, we must see that they have been handled as well as, or better than, we might have done ourselves. If we feel the need of some kind of reinforcment, we should have available our dictionary and a dependable reference book on business communication.

In general, our check for feedback after dictation follows the usual approach. Our primary concern is to test whether our letter will be opened, read, understood, believed, agreed with, and (if applicable) acted upon. It is necessary for us momentarily to play the role of the intended reader—to go through the letter from start to finish as he probably will. The purpose is to ascertain that everything we dictated is there, that it is just the way we said it, and that it will be suitable for our reader. In this set of circumstances, however, we must also be alert for errors which may have crept in because of the division of work. The following are some of the more important things to look for.

FORM

Because the physical aspects of the letter, as typified by form, will be the first to come to the attention of the reader, this area is a logical one for beginning our inspection work.

1. *Proper matching.* Our first task is to check that all pieces to be packaged together are assembled and in good order. We need to come up with affirmative answers to these questions:

Are all necessary parts—letter, envelope, carbon copies, and enclosures—gathered together in a folder, or fastened with a paper clip?

Is the enclosure the *correct* enclosure?

Does the address on the envelope match the inside address of the letter?

If an attention line is used in the letter, does it also appear on the envelope?

If any special postal service is needed—such as air mail, special delivery, or certified mail—has an indication of this been placed on the envelope?

If the letter is longer than one page, is the continuation page (or pages) properly matched with the first page?

2. *Objective form.* In the matter of how our letter is presented on the page, we need favorable answers to the following questions:

What is the overall eye appeal—will it entice the reader or will it discourage him?

Is the type clean and sharp?

Have corrections, if any, been made neatly?

Are the side margins approximately equal?

Has good judgment been used toward keeping the right-hand margin from becoming too ragged?

Has open punctuation been used consistently in the heading, inside address, signature block, and miscellaneous parts?

Has a colon been used after the salutation; a comma after the complimentary close?

Has either block or modified-block form (as selected) been followed consistently throughout the body of the letter?

3. *Subjective form.* Concerning the aspects of form which the recipient of the letter must read as well as see, we may add the following questions:

Is the date of the letter correct?

Is the addressee's name spelled correctly?

Does the salutation combine properly with the addressee as named in the first line of the inside address?

Does the complimentary close fit with the relationship established by the salutation and signature of the letter?

Is the first person singular entirely omitted from the letter, if the official signature is that of our company?

Are our name and position given correctly below the space where we are to sign the letter?

LANGUAGE

Fundamentally, the language of our business letter is our own responsibility. As the source of the message, we planned a program for presenting the points to be included in the letter, and then expanded these points into a full composition during dictation. Now, at the inspection stage, our words are being *seen* for the first time. Taking the reader's viewpoint, we should examine the letter on its readability and on its overall conformity to good usage in language. This latter part bears close watching. In the dictation process, the message is composed orally. Our secretary or typist does the actual "writing," including much of the spelling and punctuation. Whether these matters have been handled correctly remains to be seen. Hence, we should seek favorable answers to the major questions in each significant area.

1. *Spelling.*   This area is rather inflexible. Moreover, errors are relatively easy for a reader to spot and are a reflection on the source of the letter.

   a) Have all words been correctly spelled? We should check the spelling in all doubtful cases. Sometimes we find that a challenged word is spelled correctly after all—thanks to a dependable secretary.

b) If two spellings are possible, is the preferred choice used? Our dictionary will show the preferred spelling first—e.g., *acknowledgment, acknowledgement; analyze, analyse.*

c) If two spellings are possible, is the word consistently spelled the same way throughout the letter?

d) Is every word that is divided between two lines hyphenated at one of its syllable breaks?

e) If a word is divided between lines, are at least two letters retained at the end of the one line, and are at least three typewritten characters carried down to the next line?

f) As a rule, are abbreviations and symbols excluded from the body of the letter?

2. *Use of words.* Because of the existence of homophones—that is, words which sound a great deal alike but which have different meanings—our secretary or typist can introduce vocabulary mistakes. Although we may practice alerting the typist during dictation, it is not likely that we will be able to anticipate every possible homophone that comes along. Moreover, there is no assurance that the typist will always comply with every instruction we provide. Thus, as we see our letter, we should examine each word that fits the homophone category to be sure it is the word we intended. Also, we should look for other signs of misinterpreted speech.

a) Have any errors crept into the letter because of homophones? If we see the word *accept,* should it have been *except?* Should *do* have been typed *due?* Do we want *hoard* or *horde? Principal* or *principle? To, too,* or *two?*

b) Are there any other words or phrases which have been misinterpreted? Some unexpected typewritten versions have been known to come back to the dictator. For example, *default* instead of *the fault, a proxy mate* instead of *approximate,* and *the light* instead of *delight.*

3. *Grammar.* If we are regularly correct in our grammatical usage, it would seem unlikely that the dictation process could account for mistakes in this area. Yet, some secretaries and typists are not beyond a bit of editing at times. They are the first ones to come in contact with

what we have spoken and are in a fine position to make sensible changes immediately. We can often be thankful for that kind of help. On occasion, something they supposed to be incorrect was perfectly all right; and their revision may result in something not as good as the original or in something actually incorrect. Also, there is the possibility of their omitting an entire sentence or section while typing. Even though what remains may be grammatically correct, the meaning of our message may have been changed or obscured.

4. *Sentence structure.*   As with grammar, the matter of sentence structure is more our doing than that of our secretary or typist. Nevertheless, the same opportunities for making a change from right to wrong exist. In addition, there is the possibility that the typist might do some "telescoping." This fault is the result of omitting the last part of one sentence and the beginning of the next sentence. Such merging generally affects sentence structure more readily than it does grammar; and certainly it has an adverse impact on our message.

5. *Punctuation.*   When we dictate a business letter, it is only proper that we give an indication of any out-of-the-ordinary punctuation we wish to have used. We generally leave routine punctuation to our secretary or typist, and we should keep aware of it as we read through our letter. All necessary punctuation should have been used; and any punctuation used should have been used correctly.

a) **Comma.**   It is easy enough to state that, in general, a comma is used to indicate a place where we would naturally pause in speaking, to distinguish between parts of a sentence. It is much more difficult to state rules for comma usage; and it is to some extent a matter of personal choice between a "closed" and "open" style. Consistency in use and clearness to the reader are the overriding considerations. We can refer to dictionary sections on punctuation for help. Briefly, chief uses of the comma are:

> To set off the elements in a series; direct quotations; appositives, dates, place names, and the like.
> Between the clauses of a compound sentence when they are joined by a conjunction such as *and, but, or,* and *nor.*

To set off introductory words, phrases, and clauses, unless they are short and closely related in thought to the main clause.

To set off subordinate clauses, parenthetic phrases, and contrasting words or phrases, within the sentence. The determining element in such cases is whether the matter is restrictive or nonrestrictive. Restrictive parts are essential to the sentence, so that its meaning would be lost or badly warped without them. Nonrestrictive elements are additions to the main thought.

b) **Question mark.** As a general rule, in a business letter we should have an interrogation mark after every sentence that is phrased on the order of a question. This rule applies even when the so-called "polite command" technique of using a period might seem to be permissible. We must bear in mind that it is our responsibility to keep our reader from misconstruing our attitude. An interrogation mark will rule out the possibility of our sounding "bossy."

```
Will you please return the enclosed form?
```

c) **Period.** The punctuation mark to be used at the end of a declarative sentence is a period, and it is not too likely that it will be incorrectly used. Of course, what precedes a period in that usage should really be a sentence—not just a phrase or a dependent clause. We use a period also to punctuate permissible abbreviations. If such an abbreviation occurs at the end of a declarative sentence, one period is used to punctuate both the abbreviation and the sentence.

d) **Semicolon.** In judging the correct usage of the semicolon, we may consider that it is just about as strong a mark of punctuation as the period used at the end of a declarative sentence. If a period could have been used at the point where the semicolon appears, we may consider the semicolon to be used correctly. There is also an exceptional use of the semicolon, as we have noted previously: a semicolon is used at the major breaks of a series when there is already a comma in one or more of the parts of the series.

A moderate amount of experience in checking our letters should make us appreciate why simple language is a boon to communication.

We, as the dictators of letters, can expect these immediate benefits when we stick to simple language:

Familiar words tend to be used correctly.

Simple sentences present fewer problems with grammar and sentence structure.

Our secretary or typist can also derive benefits:

Short, familiar words are easy to receive by ear and are easy to spell.

Simple sentences present fewer problems with punctuation.

Our intended reader is the ultimate beneficiary. One of our aims is to present him with a letter that is easy to read. As we have seen, the systems for testing readability consider various factors—but all assume that language itself has been handled correctly. In effect, the systems attempt to give simplicity to writing that is already mechanically good but too complex for business usage. We are much better off if we write simply in the first place. Accuracy is more easily achieved that way, and the combination of simplicity and accuracy usually places our writing at a readable level without the need for adjustment. Our reader will easily assimilate it the way it is.

CONTENT

As we read our letter, we should try to let the message unfold, point by point, with or without the requisite finesse, just as our intended reader will do. We must not read with bias, with conscious knowledge of what meaning we intended, or with imaginary voice inflections to soften or shade certain words and phrases. We should look objectively at the typewritten words and let them speak for themselves. If we detect something that could be misunderstood or misconstrued, we must make the necessary revision.

Although our test for feedback is rather comprehensive in the number of things we might have to consider, in practice it is easy to apply. In checking our finished letter, we again invoke the exception principle of management. We go through our letter just as our intended reader is expected to do. As we read, form, language, and content unfold more or less together. Irregularities of form might be spotted first, then the errors of language, and finally the unclearness or unsavory aspects of content. Actually, we do not expect to find an excessive number of mistakes after all the care and preparation we have put into the letter. We just read on through the letter until we come to something that does not look right or read well; that is the sort of thing that requires checking. If, in playing the role of reader, we get completely through the letter without noticing anything amiss, we can approve the work as it stands.

FORESHADOWS OF THE FUTURE

Dictation is an outgrowth of the division-of-labor concept, which is by no means the only modern management principle or innovation to be applied to the work of letter writing and handling. We have ample evidence that such matters as simplification, standardization, interchangeability of parts, mass production, and mechanization are becoming increasingly useful in communication work. The indications are that our letter writing of the future will be fortified by far-reaching improvements in systems and procedures.

SIMPLIFICATION

The process of cutting out unnecessary adornments and reducing the number of varieties of something is known as simplification. We may or may not have a scientific basis for any simplifying that we do, but we arrive at a basically simpler thing, or fewer varieties of it, or both. In the letter-writing field we have already applied some simplification and are trending toward much more. In the area of form, we have gone to open punctuation and the left-side blocking of such parts as the inside address and the paragraphs. We are moving gradually toward the left-side blocking of all the parts and the possible elimination of the salutation and complimentary close.

The U.S. Post Office, which functions as the physical carrier of our letter, has also entered the simplification picture. As one in a series of steps to be taken, the Post Office has issued regulations banning the use of certain tiny, large, and odd-sized envelopes. The remaining sizes are within tolerance limits which simplify the handling operation. To facilitate sorting of letters by machine method, further simplification and standardization will undoubtedly be needed.

STANDARDIZATION

While standardization usually results in fewer varieties, it is not the same thing as simplification. Standardization is the adoption of the best variety or selection of varieties. It sometimes results in an entirely new variety coming into existence instead of merely cutting down from a large number of existing varieties. In letter writing, for example, a suggestion has been made to use the standard abbreviation *Ms.* in place of *Miss* and *Mrs.* when we are addressing women. This idea has been slow in catching on, but perhaps some day it will be in general use. Mostly it is being used as a hedge in those cases when the woman's marital status is not known. Thus, although a form of standardization, Ms. is actually causing an increase, not a decrease, in the number of designations for women.

A time-saving, money-saving idea for mailing letters has been suggested, although it also has met heavy resistance. It is that we use

window envelopes and fold the upper portion of the letter opposite of the way we now fold it. The theory is that the inside address should show through the window of the envelope and become the outside address, too. Duplicate typing of the reader's address would be eliminated, and there would be practically no envelope spoilage. To be functional, this plan would require an amount of standardization: in the size, shape, and location of the window; in the positioning of the inside address and (if applicable) the attention line, possibly by having marks printed on the stationery; and in folding the letter rather precisely, again possibly by having marks printed on the stationery.

The U.S. Post Office has long been interested in standardization. More than twenty years ago, it set up its system of zones. Mail could be sorted quickly by zone number and delivered to substations for prompt distribution. A standard position for the zone number was prescribed:

between the name of the city and the name or abbreviation of the state. Under its zone improvement program, the Post Office has now made a revision in the procedure, aimed at ultimate, nationwide, machine sorting. Under this revision we use what is known as the ZIP code. It is a five-digit number; the first three digits represent the postal district and state, and the other digits equate to the old-style zone number. A new standard position, moreover, must be used. The ZIP code is to follow the name or abbreviation of the state. A timetable has been planned for the compulsory conversion of the various classes of mail to ZIP coding. When all classes have been converted, we can look for additional improvements and further standardization. (See Chapter 20 for ZIP code information.)

INTERCHANGEABILITY OF PARTS

Whenever we have standardization of the components of something to be assembled, we can choose a needed part from any quantity that is available. This interchangeability of parts gives us a great measure of flexibility and removes our dependence on finding the one right part to fit another part.

Routinely, we rely on this principle every time we mail a letter, because it has been in force even from the time we stocked our stationery. As long as our supply of standard stationery lasts, we take it for granted. But, should we run out of Number 10 envelopes, for example, the lack of that standard part could immediately prove troublesome. If the window-envelope plan should become common usage, we should certainly expect any sheet of stationery we happened to choose to fit any of our envelopes, without the need for preliminary measuring or testing.

By the same token, we should use discretion in selecting a size for our business reply envelopes. At present, there does not seem to be much sign of standardization in general, although a specific company may have simplified to one size for its own use. A good recommendation for flexibility is to adopt a Number 9 envelope for this purpose. Being almost as large as a Number 10 envelope, it has initial eye appeal and a tendency to stay in sight. It can be sent out in a Number 10 envelope without having to be folded. It will accept our original letter or our questionnaire, requiring only that they be refolded at their original creases. It will accept an answer letter that is folded in the ordinary, two-fold manner.

MASS PRODUCTION

An understanding of these matters—the division of labor, simplification, standardization, and the interchangeability of parts— leads us to the concept of mass production. In industry, through the proper layout of a production line, either moving or stationary, we can bring workers and materials together effectively. We set time schedules for the different activities and coordinate the various phases of production so that, in a sense, the entire complex functions like one great machine. As for the finished product, the impression created is that the great machine routinely dispenses a unit of product after each regularly occurring interval of time.

In our area of activity, we also have made use of mass production. For example, let us look at the large-scale mailing of a sales letter. To begin with, the letter itself, the envelope, and the various enclosures would be mass-produced by a printer. The addressing of the envelopes, probably by machine, would be a kind of subassembly. The folding of the letter in quantity, also probably by machine method, would be another subassembly. Then some kind of assembly line would be used to put together the various parts and subassemblies of the mailing piece: enclosures, folded letter, addressed envelope. Probably inserting of the contents and sealing or tucking of the envelope flap would follow in line. Additional stages might include sorting, tying into uniform bundles, and filling mail sacks with such bundles.

MECHANIZATION

Today's business literature deals extensively with the terms *equipment, automatic equipment, automation,* and *cybernetics.* All of these terms are related in that they have to do with mechanization—that is, the using of equipment time in place of human time. They are somewhat different to the extent that, in the order listed, each represents a fuller replacement of the human element.

In the preparation of business letters, we already have been enjoying the benefits of both manned equipment and automatic equipment. Our manual typewriters, electric typewriters, dictating machines, postage machines, addressing machines, envelope sealers, office copiers, string-tying devices, and so on are examples of equipment in regular use. Other types of equipment—usually more automatic, and, once set up for a job, less dependent on human participation—include automatic typewriters, letter-folding machines, envelope openers, and duplicators.

As might be expected, the U.S. Post Office is interested in the savings available through the use of equipment. Machines to cancel postage were introduced long ago. Some postal stations supplement counter sales with stamp-vending equipment as a means of meeting peak-activity hours without unnecessary increases in personnel. Now being tried in selected cities is a machine that can pick out airmail letters for speedier service. Perhaps unbeknown to most users, airmail stamps are being printed with a special ink which the machine can recognize. In this way, letters bearing a proper airmail stamp are separated automatically and rapidly from the other classes of mail. The government is also experimenting, in several locations, with completely automated, unattended post offices—in shopping centers, for example.

"GET UP HERE QUICK AND FIX OUR AIRMAIL SORTER."

Automation is basically the use of automatic equipment in a continuous flow throughout the production process, including the movement of materials and work-in-process. Cybernetics is a further refinement of this concept. It places the automated process under the control of a computer which is set up to exercise certain options, somewhat as the human mind decides among various courses of action. Accordingly, if something begins to stray outside the established tolerance limits, the computer can correct the situation without further human help.

Some applications of automation and cybernetics have been made in the field of letter writing, and the outlook is for much more to come. For example, some companies have been able to use a computer for sending reminders automatically to credit customers who have become delinquent in their payments. While the computer is being used for the billing of monthly statements, it can add a collection message to the statements which contain overdue balances. In a more elaborate hookup, the computer can choose from among several complete collection letters, on the bases of size of balance, periods past due, type of credit risk, and so on. Delinquent customers thereby receive an appropriate collection letter instead of a routine statement of account—yet, once the instructions have been fed into the equipment, human decisions are not required.

Further applications are under development. The Post Office, for instance, has been running tests of automated processing of parcel post, including movement of the packages into railroad cars. It has also taken steps toward the use of OCR (Optical Character Recognition) equipment in the sorting of mail. The ZIP code is one of the necessary preparations. OCR is no mere pipe dream. It is already being used by some public utilities, oil companies, insurance companies, and department stores. Such equipment "reads" an invoice or sales slip and automatically produces a punched card for use in the company's computer. The early models required a distinctive type face for recognition and also the use of fixed positions on the invoice so that the information could be read. Already, improvements have done away with both of these limitations. In fact, we are now at the point of having equipment that can read almost any kind of print—even longhand figures—appearing anywhere on almost any size or shape of paper. The remaining obstacle to be overcome is the recognition of the figure 4 in longhand. Some people make an open 4, and others make a closed 4; and this difference has been troublesome. The effect of OCR is to eliminate the need for key punch operators, a field which is still regarded as new itself. The U.S. Department of Labor, however, has already concluded that there is no longer any prospect of growth in key punch employment—because OCR is here and it is here to stay.

The process of dictation also has entered an era of impending changes. The present method of dictation requires that our message be sent twice—first by voice, and then by typewritten letter. An intermediary—our secretary or typist—receives the oral version and prepares the typewritten version. The question arises: Is there some way of eliminating that intermediate step?

In a sense, we have the means available now. But some advantages would be sacrificed in order to gain others. The procedure would be to send the dictated recording directly from source to destination. The recipient could play back the recording on a machine in his office, and hear the message exactly as the sender intended it, complete with voice inflections and other tonal effects. There are drawbacks, of course: the method represents a drastic change from tradition; there is no guarantee that a voiced message would be as easy to interpret as a typewritten letter; neither end of the communication process has anything in writing—indeed, the sender might not even have a duplicate recording; information copies would be hard to provide; referring back to a part of the letter would not be convenient for the recipient; and certain legal questions might arise.

Another approach is that of having a typewriter which would be activated by the dictator's voice. This method has been tried, but some problems need to be overcome before it can be used on a large scale. Among the difficulties are the undependable pronunciation of the words in our language, enunciation faults on the part of a given dictator, and the different regional accents that exist. For example, let us suppose that a person wanted to speak the following sentence to the machine with the expectation that the machine would respond by typing the words:

The effect of the new law is being felt.

Pronounced correctly, this sentence would sound somewhat as follows:

Thee eh-fehkt uhv thuh nyu law iz bee-ing fehlt.

We see, however, that the first and fourth words of the sentence, *the,* are not pronounced the same way. This sort of thing could cause some strange-looking words to be typed by the voice-activated machine.

On the other hand, let us suppose that the speaker had a tendency to favor the "uh" sound, as some people do. His voiced sentence might sound something like this:

Thuh uh-fehkt uhv thuh nyu law iz bee-ing fehlt.

In this version, the first and fourth words have the same sound. The second word, *effect,* however, intensifies the problem of homophones. It now sounds exactly the same as *affect.* A human typist could make a distinction on the basis of reasonableness; but which word would the voice-activated machine type?

While some method of simplifying and/or mechanizing the production process of letter writing is desirable, there are still obstacles to be overcome. Still, the history of progress is that solutions are eventually found. Whenever a suitable one turns up in this area, we should be ready and willing to take advantage of it.

SUMMARY
· · · · · · · · ·

When we compose a letter by dictating it, we are applying the division-of-labor principle of management. The preparation of our letter can be likened to an industrial process under production control. The key activities are technically known as routing, scheduling, dispatching, follow-up, and inspection.

Before dictating, we must take the same preparatory steps as always to develop a program for the letter we wish to compose. The dictation process is a departure from actual "writing" to composing orally, after the fashion of an extemporaneous speaker. For successful dictation, we have these guidelines: establish a routine; be prepared; relax; use a clear, natural voice; enunciate clearly; give necessary instructions; and check as needed.

After dictation, our letter is typewritten and then returned to us for final inspection. We should examine it objectively, much in the manner that our reader will, and check all important matters of form, language, and content. We must be especially careful now, because another person participated in the work and may have introduced errors.

The division-of-labor principle, as evidenced by dictation, is not the only management concept that has been applied to letter writing. We already find many instances of simplification, standardization, interchangeability of parts, mass production, and mechanization. The outlook is for even fuller application of these concepts in the years ahead. The process of dictation itself is on the threshold of dramatic change.

QUESTIONS
· · · · · · · · · ·

1. In managerial terms, what principle is demonstrated by the communication activity of *dictation?*
2. Name the five principal functions of production control.
3. What are advantages and disadvantages of having dictation as a stage in the development of a business communication?
4. List seven guidelines that are of help in the process of dictation.

5. Generally speaking, what are four remaining tasks after the dictation and transcription steps have been completed?

6. If the writer (dictator) uses familiar words and relatively uncomplicated (simple or complex) sentences, what are the benefits that accrue to his composition (message)?

7. Under these conditions, what benefits should accrue to the stenographer and, ultimately, to the readability of the typewritten message?

8. In what ways are such modern developments as OCR and automation entering the U.S. Post Office's participation in the business communication process?

9. To what extent has mechanization (chiefly the use of computers) already entered the production of a business communication?

10. Is it likely that the future will see the ultimate elimination of the dictation process?

EXERCISES

7-1. Following the illustration given in this chapter on page 201, type the letter given below so as to depict how it might be recorded on a dictation tape by oral presentation.

```
Mr. John R. McDonough
Chairman, Accounting Department
Columbus Community College
Columbus, Ohio 43205

Dear Mr. McDonough:

Harrison Chemical Company will be happy to honor your request
for 250 copies of our annual report for 1966. It is one of our
public relation activities to provide copies of our reports
to interested parties, especially educational institutions.

You may expect the package of reports to be delivered to your
school, postage paid, within three days. If there is any
other published material which we can make available to you,
or information which will be helpful in your work, please let
us know of your needs.

                        Yours very truly,

                        HARRISON CHEMICAL COMPANY


                        Donald D. Netherton
                        Director, Public Relations

DDN/rr
```

7–2. Following the illustration given in this chapter on page 201, type the memorandum given below so as to show how it would sound when recorded on a dictation tape.

TO: C. T. Hesberg, Plant Manager /

FROM: Roy C. Baines, General Manager /

SUBJECT: Changes in the Method of Processing Travel Vouchers/

As a company grows,/it becomes necessary to adjust/certain operating procedures/to keep in step with the quickened pace of business./ Such is the case now/in our method of processing travel vouchers./ ⁊

Heretofore,/ each person entitled to reimbursement/for travel expense/had only to submit receipts/and an informal accounting summary./ The work of the cashier's department, however,/ has grown to such a point/that some degree of standardization) is needed to reduce the time/taken by each transaction./⁊

Effective January 1, 1967,/all requests for travel-expense reimbursement/are to be made on standardized form/No. TR-107,) which is obtainable at the cashier's window./ This form is designed to control the terminology used/as well as the sequence of the expense items/ It should help to simplify the accounting operation./⁊ /

Will you please call this change/to the attention of the personnel/in your division/who will be affected by it?

PART III

BUSINESS LETTERS

In the eight chapters of this part of the book, we are going to examine 24 typical business applications of the principles we have been discussing. These applications will include all four of the recognized business-letter situations: simple goodwill, request, good-news, and bad-news. In each instance, the requirements of the situation—that is, the standard framework of the letter to be written—will be expanded into what can be termed a "general program." In many cases, such a general program is adequate for immediate use in letter writing. Sometimes, however, the standard framework must be enlarged into a final, specific program which is needed for best results.

LETTER TYPES

The order of presentation is basically according to letter "types"— and wherever applicable, according to pairs of related types. This is the traditional approach, and probably the most satisfactory one.

To understand this point of view, we need only remember that business-letter writing amounts to the transacting of business through one of several possible media of communication. The overriding problem is the business problem; the communication problem depends on the medium selected. The businessman, therefore, is operating in a specific business setting: he is seeking information; he is filing a claim; he is granting or refusing credit; and so on. Knowing what activity he is performing and desirous of information on how to handle it in a letter, he may turn to his reference book on business communication. If the information he seeks is classified according to the business setting, he will be able to find it easily; and he will have the opportunity to review the related coverage at the same time.

LETTER SITUATIONS

It should be pointed out that there is another popular approach to the study of business letters—the so-called "situations" viewpoint. This approach is to classify letters under their respective situational headings: goodwill, request, good news, and bad news. It is a logical method, and it is consistent with the basic theory of business letters. But it cuts across the grain of the business setting in most instances.

The student after college days as well as the established businessman will sooner or later have to write a letter which is outside his usual specialty. If so, he will likely prefer his reference book to be organized in keeping with the business setting. When his reference book is designed in such a manner, he should be able to find the information he wants—quickly and directly.

A UTILITARIAN APPROACH

Regardless of individual preference for letter types or for letter situations, the 24 practical applications presented in this part of the book have been planned for utility. Each discussion provides the background of the business setting involved, develops a typical program, gives guidelines for incorporating the matters of finesse, and adds suggestions toward helping us meet all of the challenges along the way to a successful business letter.

. . . .

CHAPTER 8

SIMPLE GOODWILL LETTERS

A viewpoint often voiced by businessmen is that every business letter is a *sales letter*. In some respects, that statement is correct. If we consider that getting our reader to "buy" our message, our decision, our attitude, and so on is "selling," we could say that the business letter is always a sales letter. But we customarily apply the term "sales letter" to the attempted selling by letter of a specific product or service. The less rigid concept that these businessmen wish to convey is more likely that every business letter has a persuasive aspect—that it is always a *goodwill letter*. With this slight change in terminology, we can heartily agree.

Even though goodwill should be present in every business letter, we do not automatically include all categories when we use the term "goodwill letters." We limit this term to two general classes of letters. The first is a multipurpose letter (goodwill plus something else) in which the goodwill aspect is emphasized as the main theme. Such is the case, for example, with a number of so-called public-relations letters aimed at selling the house (a form of institutional advertising). These letters have a dual purpose. Structurally, they are similar to other letters of their type. The chief difference is one of emphasis on the goodwill portion and a subordination of the other part(s) of the message.

The other class of goodwill letters is the one we shall discuss in this chapter. Letters of this class are called *simple* goodwill letters; they are single-purpose letters. The reason for sending them is that something has been accomplished by, or has happened to, the reader. In most instances, there is no requirement that such a letter be sent—and, as a result, not too many are sent! Their entire mission is to create goodwill, not to carry an additional, separate message. These letters place maximum attention on the reader, practically none on the writer.

Because content is confined to the goodwill message, the writing program is necessarily uncomplicated and the letter rather short. Fundamentally, two approaches are possible: a brief introductory discussion climaxed by the main goodwill message; and the main goodwill message followed by a secondary goodwill gesture, which arises out of the main message.

In this chapter, our discussion will include simple goodwill letters of three types: (1) appreciation, (2) congratulations and commendations, and (3) condolence and sympathy.

APPRECIATION

A letter of appreciation is a kind of written "Thank you" we send to a person who has done something for us. In some cases, such a letter ought to be sent, whether we feel inspired to do so or not, just because common courtesy calls for it. In such instances, the person probably expects that we will show appreciation in some way; he may be disappointed if we neglect to follow through. Our best course of action is to be one of those—the knowledgeable and well-mannered—who respond with a letter of appreciation.

In other cases, however, the person might have no expectation, conscious or subconscious, of our going to any lengths to show appreciation. His performance may have been strictly within his line of duty, and, accordingly, nothing special. Yet, if we do recognize what he has done by sending him a letter of appreciation, we can bolster goodwill immensely.

The time to write a letter of appreciation depends somewhat on the nature of the performance being recognized. If the person is being thanked for a specific deed, our letter should be written as soon as possible afterward. Promptness in writing is one indication of our sincerity. If the person is being thanked for a continuing performance—such as being a regular customer in our store—a different timing must be considered. We probably would select some convenient occasion of the year—for example, Thanksgiving or New Year's—and use it as an opportunity for writing.

The program to be used for a letter of appreciation is simple enough because of the requirement of unity, which applies to all simple goodwill letters. Everything in this letter will be related to appreciation—leading up to it, communicating it, following it up. There are, however, some variations of programming possible, one of which is undoubtedly the best choice in a given case.

When we write a letter of appreciation that is consciously expected by the recipient, we do well to lead off with our main message. Also, we should let our reader know exactly what we are thanking him for. This handling immediately satisfies his desire or yearning and constitutes a beginning of high interest value. If we have any comments or observations to make, we can add them in a brief discussion section. We should, of course, end with a secondary goodwill statement, for a well-balanced letter. If we were merely to have a statement of appreciation, our letter might seem to be abrupt and to imply a lack of effort on our part. If we add some discussion, this part will be of diminishing interest; a goodwill ending will tend to bring about a psychological upturn. Thus, we might mention the possibility of reciprocating, of remembering his deed, of mentioning his name favorably to others, and so on. In program form, this approach appears as follows:

APPRECIATE.
DISCUSS (IF HELPFUL).
EXTEND GOODWILL.

The following letter was written on the basis of this program. The writer had previously requested a favor of his reader. Not only was the favor granted but also certain additional services were performed. The letter of appreciation is owed to the reader in this case, and the reader is very likely expecting it. If he receives it, he will feel happier than he does now; if he does not receive it, he may feel somewhat let down.

Dear Mr. Davenport:

Thanks sincerely for the hospitality you gave Bob Chambers last week.

When I asked you to meet him at Kennedy International and see that he got off to a good start in the big city, I never intended more than just that. Bob's glowing account of every-thing else you did for him—including the dinner at Begley's, the Broadway play, and the introduction to Harvey Wilcox—was indeed amazing.

Since your schedule usually brings you here in October, don't be surprised if the red carpet is rolled out in a special way.

Sincerely yours,

Sometimes a person does something for us entirely on his own initiative. For example, knowing that we are in a certain line of work, gathering material on some topic, or trying to solve a business problem, he might send us some helpful data or suggestions. Besides the require-ment of courtesy, there is the likelihood that our benefactor will be expecting, subconsciously if not consciously, some kind of acknowledg-ment from us. The following letter was written under these conditions; it follows the same general program as did the previous letter.

Dear Raymond:

Thank you for sending me the clippings from Tuesday's <u>Times</u>.

It was considerate of you to remember my interest in mutual funds. As of now, my report is about two-thirds finished. With voluntary research help, such as you have given, I am making excellent progress.

You may be sure that a copy of my report will be earmarked for you.

Sincerely,

When the deed done for us is in the normal line of duty or comes under the heading of "occupational hazard," the performer would not seem to be owed a special act of appreciation. Yet, when we seek con-tinued goodwill and understand something about human nature, we know the benefits to be obtained by an extra measure of thoughtfulness.

While another person may rationalize why he does not have to acknowledge the deed, we shall have already written a letter of appreciation and enhanced good feeling and cooperation with the recipient. Having a sense of direction for handling these letters and a sensitivity for opportunities to send them paves the way for future benefits.

In the following letter, a college graduate shows his appreciation for a recommendation letter written on his behalf by his former academic adviser. The fact that he was applying for admission to a graduate school is incidental; the principles involved would be the same if he had been seeking regular employment. The professor in the case, however, did only what he would have done for almost any of his former students; writing recommendation letters is a natural extension of his professional activity. As a general thing, he would not be expecting any special thanks.

Under such conditions, the program of the letter could be the same as that called for when thanks is definitely expected. But, an effective letter of appreciation can also be written from this alternate program:

CREATE INTEREST.

IDENTIFY CIRCUMSTANCES.

DISCUSS (IF HELPFUL).

APPRECIATE.

This program does not start with the main message. It leads up to the message of appreciation after an interest-creating beginning and a coverage of the pertinent facts of the case. It is the general program the college graduate followed in writing his letter.

Dear Dr. Whitehead:

Here is a bit of news I know will interest you.

Dean Jaekel of the Graduate School at Great Lakes University has awarded me the teaching assistantship which I need to see my way clear financially. He made a point of mentioning that I was the only applicant who had been given a truly adequate recommendation from his major adviser. All the other candidates had been discussed in generalities and stock phrases which could have applied to almost anyone.

I'm indebted to you for helping make a dream come true. Please accept my sincerest thanks.

Sincerely yours,

This same method of sequencing the program has proved to be effective in appreciation letters of the public relations variety. In the following letter, the president of a department store extends a periodic statement of appreciation for business done at his store. His purpose is to add a personal touch to what otherwise might have become a less-secure, impersonal relationship.

Dear Mrs. Bell:

In Paris, they say "Once a Frenchman, always a Frenchman."

At Martin's, we say: "Once a customer, always a friend"—and we try to observe this slogan in everything we do.

That is why, throughout the year, Martin's buyers are end-lessly searching for choice purchases of apparel, furniture, appliances—and luxury items, such as furs and jewelry. That is why Martin's planners are continually studying floor lay-outs, sales areas, parking facilities, delivery schedules, and other customer services. And why our interior designers work around the calendar to keep our store attractive and gay for your shopping pleasure.

To be sure, most of these activities pass unnoticed—going on behind the scenes, as they do. But they are among our ways of showing appreciation to our ever-growing following of friends. Another way, of course, is to tell you personally.

So—thank you, for letting us be of service during this past year. We look forward to serving you again in the days ahead.

Cordially yours,

CONGRATULATIONS AND COMMENDATIONS

In the course of our business careers, we are almost certain to receive news of an accomplishment on the part of someone we know. A friend may be elected to public office, a fellow businessman may be promoted to a high position in his firm, an associate may get married, a former college chum may become a father, a lodge brother may win some competitive event, and so on. Such events are usually given some kind of news coverage, so that a number of the person's friends will be aware of his achievement. But only a relatively small number of them will think to send congratulations; and because of human inertia, only a still smaller number will do anything about it. We should always try to be among this latter group, because the circumstances are ideal for scoring points toward goodwill.

Congratulations really can be sent in other ways than as a business letter. We could send a stock greeting card, a telegram, or a personal letter. Any of these methods would communicate our basic message and would win us a measure of goodwill—personally. But, a letter of congratulations prepared on our business stationery silently includes our company as well. It has continuing value in that such letters are so rare and so favorably received that our reader usually keeps them on file. Thus, every time he happens across ours, he tends to be pleased all over again—and our company name as well as our own name is brought to his attention.

To do an effective job of preparing a letter of congratulations, we must be extremely careful about what we include and how we phrase it. First of all, of course, we should write promptly—preferably the same day we receive news of our reader's happy event. A letter that is sent out quite some time after the fact is not usually effective, because the delay implies indifference and a lack of all-out sincerity.

In the further interest of sincerity, we should try to sound enthusiastic—that is, happy for our reader. To show the right spirit, we can open our letter with an elliptical sentence punctuated by an exclamation point. Handling the sentence this way gives it a convincing ring—as opposed to a formal sentence of some kind or even to the same words punctuated by a period. Having set the pace, we should continue the letter in an informal, conversational style. We should tell our reader what he is being congratulated for. Of course, he knows—but, some years hence, when he might see our letter again, it should still be meaningful to him.

If it is permissible under the relationship that exists between our reader and us, we should use the psychology of warmth in both the salutation and the signature. For example, we might be able to call him by his first name or nickname in the salutation; we might be able to use our first name as the longhand signature above our fully typed-out name.

A danger area connected with a letter of congratulations stems from our striving to maintain an informal, conversational style. In trying to extend best wishes, we could fall into the trap of mentioning the term, "good luck." In oral conversation, the wording is sufficiently safe because our meaning can be brought out by the tone of our voice; but appearing on paper, it could be misconstrued by our reader and cause him to cast doubt on the sincerity of our message. We should avoid any use of the word "luck" in a letter of this kind.

The program for a letter of congratulations is simple, in observance of the requirement of unity. In fact, some people write a poor letter of congratulations because they do not know how to hold to a simple program. They seem to think that this would be a fine opportunity to bring the reader up to date on their own activities during the past several years or to match his accomplishment with one of their own. The correct viewpoint should be that in this letter the spotlight is on the reader—period. The general program, therefore, is:

CONGRATULATE ON . . . !
EXTEND GOODWILL.

Following this program, our letter of congratulations leads off with the main goodwill message. It carries on with one or more secondary gestures of goodwill which are related to the main message. In a sense, when we include more than one such sequel to the actual congratulations, we appear to be carrying on a kind of discussion. Yet, we prefer not to include "discuss" as a step in our program, because it would be a misleading temptation for us to develop it into something more than a gesture of goodwill.

In the following letter, a businessman congratulates a friend who has earned a promotion. The first sentence takes care of the main message. The second sentence is already an extra goodwill statement. The elliptical sentence which constitutes the last paragraph is another such statement.

```
Dear Henry:

Congratulations on your promotion to Vice President of Belmore
Products! It's another milestone in your outstanding business
career.

Best wishes for continued success!

                         Sincerely,
```

A letter program obviously acts as a control over some of our thought processes during our composition effort. It is intended to keep us moving according to our previously decided plan. In the letter of congratulations, it is intended also to hold us down to writing a short, crisp, effective message. Were we to write substantially more than the program allows, our letter would lose much of its sharpness. However, the program should not be viewed as a restriction to our personal writing style; it governs only the number and sequence of the topics to be covered.

In the letter that follows, a businessman congratulates another on the birth of a son. His letter follows the same general program as did the preceding letter, but his own manner of expression shows through. In this case, the giving of the main message uses up the first sentence and the first portion of the second sentence. From then on, the statements follow along with secondary expressions of goodwill.

```
Dear Tom:

    So it's a boy! Congratulations, Dad; and best regards to
Alice!

    See you Friday at the luncheon—cigar on you; meal on me.

                    Cordially yours,
```

Both of these example letters possess the flavor of sincerity—which is conveyed by having the right tone for the type of letter involved. Actually, this flavor is mainly achieved by the use of exclamation points. If we were to read both letters again, but imagine periods in place of the exclamation points, we would see a dramatic change. The letters would suddenly sound flat and ineffectual. They would appear to have been written as a necessary chore instead of as a voluntary expression of gladness for the reader.

A letter of commendation is handled somewhat differently from a letter of congratulations, although both types have similar backgrounds. In either case, our intended reader has done something noteworthy. In one case, he has received some kind of reward or benefit; and our letter is really in recognition of that fact. In the other case, he has done something outstandingly well; and our letter of commendation is itself a kind of reward sent to him in recognition of his deed. For example, we may praise an employee for a job well done; we may laud an acquaintance because of a topical article he has written; we may commend a person for an act of heroism; and so on.

To be highly effective, our letter of commendation should be written promptly. We should further indicate our sincerity by displaying a high level of enthusiasm. We should write the letter in an informal, conversational style. As for content, we should be guided by the following program:

REFER TO PERFORMANCE.
DISCUSS (IF HELPFUL). *(Deed evaluated)*
COMMEND.
EXTEND GOODWILL (OPTIONAL).

This program uses the approach of leading up to the commendation · message. The reader's deed is identified, and possibly evaluated, during the first part of the letter. After we have given the main goodwill message, we can decide whether anything more is needed for a graceful ending. If necessary, a secondary goodwill statement can be used to round out our letter.

In the following letter, one member of a civic planning commission commends another member on a report. His letter leads up to the main message, but ends immediately after conveying it.

Dear Mr. Lahr:

Copies of your report on water conservation were distributed to the members of the planning commission last week. Until I read the facts you have accumulated, I did not realize how bad local conditions had become. Something will have to be done immediately, if we are to have enough safe water for our needs.

You are to be complimented on a thorough research study, an enlightening report, and helpful recommendations.

                              Sincerely yours,

CONDOLENCE AND SYMPATHY

Another occasion when we can demonstrate goodwill is at the time of the death of a colleague, business associate, the wife of a client, and so on. As thoughtful individuals, we should rise to the occasion by sending an expression of sympathy. We may choose to send flowers as well as a message. If the relationship is purely a business one, our message of condolence or sympathy may be expressed in a letter prepared on our business stationery. In this way we express the company's concern over the loss of a friend or associate, as well as our own.

Basically, condolence and sympathy mean the same thing. The distinction we are making here is solely one of convenience, because there are two general programs that can be used for this kind of letter. It is helpful to have a separate name for each.

We use "letter of condolence" to describe the traditional pattern. This approach finds us opening with a reference to the event that has occurred. Then we express our main message—our sympathy to the reader. To align ourselves in grief with our reader we next offer some kind words or eulogy concerning the deceased person. At the end of the letter, we offer a goodwill statement in keeping with the case and somewhat attuned to the future. The following program has been developed along these lines:

REFER TO CIRCUMSTANCES.

EXPRESS SYMPATHY.

EULOGIZE THE DECEASED.

EXTEND GOODWILL.

A letter of condolence must be written promptly, of course. Moreover, it should be characterized by simplicity; it should use neutral phrasing, to avoid unpleasantness; and it should be sincere—that is, use a serious tone, not a flippant one.

The following letter was prepared according to this traditional viewpoint. It was written from the president of the local advertising club to the man who had been the deceased person's employer.

Dear Mr. Thomas:

You must know how distressing it was for us to read of John Preston's accident. We offer you and your associates our heartfelt sympathy on his untimely passing. He was a diligent worker and a winner of friends, a combination hard to equal these days.

We at the ad club will miss his spirited participation in our affairs. But his memory will live in our hearts.

Sincerely yours,

An approach used much less frequently is designated here as a "letter of sympathy." The basis for this variation comes to us from a source that is well informed in the matter of dealing with situations surrounding death. This source is the clergy—whose very profession includes consoling people when a dear one has passed away. They have not surprisingly come to the conclusion that the deceased person is beyond needing kind words. They have found that it is the survivors who need consolation and reassurance. Often, for example, a surviving spouse is far from certain that he (or she) behaved properly toward the deceased during the latter's time on earth—and craves some words that might put his mind at ease.

Accordingly, we have developed an alternate program which substitutes "Console the reader" for "Eulogize the deceased." If we can offer some tangible help, we can use the offer as an appropriate ending. But we should not be vague or indefinite in making such an offer lest it be taken to be insincere. Incorporating these concepts, the letter program would appear as follows:

REFER TO CIRCUMSTANCES.

EXPRESS SYMPATHY.

CONSOLE THE READER.

EXTEND: OFFER OF HELP

OR

GOODWILL.

We cannot use this program indiscriminately. It is essential that we be sufficiently familiar with the people involved and that we understand all of the circumstances of the case. If we do not have a clear and safe course of action, we should fall back on the traditional pattern.

The following letter of sympathy illustrates the newer approach. In it, an employer tries to console the widow of a deceased employee and also offer her some kind of help.

Dear Mrs. Patton:

We were sorry to learn of Howard's unexpected passing. You have indeed suffered a grievous loss. I can but offer my sincere sympathy to you and the children.

Howard served us well, and many were the times when he credited his achievements to happiness at home. He certainly appreciated how helpful a wife could be to a man's business

career. I'm sure he is counting on you to meet the challenge
now, just as you always met his need for inspiration and
comfort.

We should like to offer our help, if there is anything we
can do for you at this time. Our personnel counseling service
is at your disposal. If you will be in need of employment,
you certainly have priority status here. To reach me, please
call 771-9800, my private line.

Cordially yours,

The next letter was prepared from the same basic program. It was
written from a businessman to a customer whose wife had passed away
after a lengthy illness. The ending consists of a general goodwill statement instead of an offer of help.

Dear Mr. Santelle:

All of us here at Superior Investment Service are saddened
by the news that Mrs. Santelle has passed on. Please accept
our deepest sympathy in this trying hour.

The faithful devotion you accorded your wife during her
months of illness has been inspiring to all who knew about
it. What a joy and consolation you must have been to her!
Truly, you have earned the respect and admiration of your
friends everywhere.

May your consideration of her be rewarded in the days that
lie ahead!

Sincerely yours,

SUMMARY
· · · · · · · · · · ·

Simple goodwill letters have but a single purpose; their mission
deals only with matters of goodwill. Our success in fulfilling this purpose
arises from winning the approval of our reader for an act of thoughtfulness. Our writing approach is to focus practically all attention on our
reader, and little or none on ourselves. We must have good timing, of
course; and we should use a sincere tone.

Throughout this chapter we examined several types of simple goodwill letters. The following pages show the essential features of each type,
in capsule form, for ready reference.

LETTER OF APPRECIATION

(Expected or Unexpected)

Intended
Reader
Reaction:

from this   to this

Program: Appreciate.
Discuss (if helpful).
Extend goodwill.

Pointers: Write promptly.

Open with "Thanks" or "Thank you."

If a specific deed is involved, single it out.

Consider "Discuss" an optional step; if there is nothing to discuss, omit it.

End with an applicable gesture of goodwill: an offer to reciprocate; a mention of new services; a promise to remember his deed; etc.

LETTER OF APPRECIATION

(Unexpected)

Intended
Reader
Reaction:

from this   to this

Program: Create interest.
            Identify circumstances.
            Discuss (if helpful).
            Appreciate.

Pointers: Write at an appropriate time: promptly, if a specific deed is
            involved; timed with some occasion, if it is of a general nature.

            Open with a statement that will arouse the reader's interest.

            Mention the action being appreciated.

            Consider "discuss" an optional step; if there is nothing to dis-
            cuss, omit it.

LETTER OF CONGRATULATIONS

Intended
Reader
Reaction:

from this   to this

Program: Congratulate on . . . !
          Extend goodwill.

Pointers: Write promptly.

          If permissible, use the reader's first name in the salutation.

          If proper, use your first name for the longhand signature.

          Be enthusiastic (!).

          Use informal, conversational language.

          Be brief; stick to the program.

          Let the reader know what he is being congratulated for.

          Avoid any use of the word "luck."

LETTER OF COMMENDATION

Intended
Reader
Reaction:

from this   to this

Program: Refer to performance.
Discuss (if helpful).
Commend, compliment, or praise.
Extend goodwill (optional).

Pointers: Write promptly.

Be sincere (sufficiently enthusiastic).

Use informal, conversational language.

Consider "Discuss" as an optional step; if there is nothing to discuss, omit it.

Decide whether "Commend" itself functions as a goodwill ending. If more is needed, add something along the lines of best wishes, an expectation of new accomplishments, etc.

LETTER OF CONDOLENCE

Intended
Reader
Reaction:

from this   to this

Program: Refer to circumstances.
Express sympathy.
Eulogize the deceased.
Extend goodwill.

Pointers: Write promptly.

Use neutral phrasing to avoid words that are not pleasant to read.

Be sincere; the circumstances call for dignity and respect.

Be concise; hold down the length of the eulogy.

Attend to goodwill by an encouraging reference to the future.

LETTER OF SYMPATHY

Intended
Reader
Reaction:

from this   to this

Program: Refer to circumstances.
Express sympathy.
Console the reader.
Extend—offer of help.
         —or goodwill in general.

Pointers: Write promptly.

Use neutral phrasing to avoid words that are not pleasant to read.

Be sincere; the circumstances call for dignity and respect.

Bolster the spirits of the *survivor*.

If tangible help can be given, offer it as the goodwill ending.

Do not offer vague or indefinite help. It is better to end with a goodwill statement that refers encouragingly to the future.

QUESTIONS

1. Is it literally true that every business letter is a sales letter?
2. What is the common denominator of all business letters, be they single-purpose types or multipurpose types?
3. Identify three types of simple goodwill letters.
4. From a purely objective viewpoint, is there any requirement that a simple goodwill letter ever be written?
5. What guidelines exist regarding the timeliness of sending a simple goodwill letter?
6. What is the suggested program (points in sequence) for a letter of appreciation?
7. How might the program proceed in the event the reader had no reason to expect a letter of appreciation?
8. What is the suggested program for a letter of congratulation?
9. Distinguish between the concepts, *congratulation* and *commendation*.
10. Give the suggested program for a letter of commendation.
11. How can enthusiasm be implanted in letters of congratulation and of commendation?
12. What distinction is made between the concepts, condolence and sympathy?
13. Give the traditional program for a letter of condolence.
14. What is an alternate program that has been suggested for a letter of condolence?
15. Which of these programs is stronger from the standpoint of finesse? Explain.

PROBLEMS

Some of the following problems are to be typewritten on business letterhead; others, on plain stationery. If a letterhead is indicated but not available, set up a simulated letterhead in accordance with directions issued by your instructor.

8–1. (Letterhead.) Assume that you are the office manager of the Tru-Mold Plastic Products Company of Indianapolis, Indiana. For years you have been an active member of the National Office Management Association. This season you have been in charge of program arrangements for your chapter's monthly meetings. Your principal speaker for this month's meeting, held last evening at a downtown hotel, was Dr. Otis Glenmore, professor of management at a nearby university. Write Dr. Glenmore a letter of appreciation for addressing your NOMA chapter.

8–2. (Letterhead.) Central Industries, Incorporated (a manufacturer of packing cases, bookcases, cabinets, chests, and other wood products), is located in the capital of your state. Last week the president of the firm wrote a letter to Donald J. Conway, vice president of Jefferson Aviation Corporation in St. Louis, Missouri. He asked Conway to extend courtesies to Central Industries' new regional sales manager, who was visiting customers in his territory. Since then, the sales manager has returned to headquarters and has given an oral report in praise of Mr. Conway's cooperation. Assuming the role of president of Central Industries, Incorporated, write a letter of appreciation to Mr. Conway.

8–3. (Plain stationery.) As a college student studying business administration, you have been assigned to do a research project on the organizational structure of several companies in this part of the state. One respondent to the many questionnaires you sent out was Mr. Michael Shelton, the public-relations director of a local radio station. Mr. Shelton added something extra—a brochure about his station —which promises to be very helpful to you. Write the gentleman a prompt thank-you letter.

8–4. (Plain stationery.) During a counseling session with your college adviser, you happened to mention that you were in need of summer work to earn expense money for the fall school term. Your adviser made a notation on the back of one of his business cards, gave the card to you, and told you to get in touch with a Mr. Roy H. Pardee of the local telephone company. You have pursued this lead and have been offered summer work in the telephone company's maintenance department. In the meantime, your college adviser has taken a three-month sabbatical leave to finish a manuscript he has been writing. Write him a letter of appreciation for having helped you find summer employment.

8–5. (Letterhead.) The Midtown Department Store of this city has a practice of keeping the personal touch in its relations with customers. For several years now it has sent a letter of appreciation to its customers just before Thanksgiving. The avowed purpose is to thank customers for their business during the past year—but a touch of goodwill on the eve of the big Christmas selling season may be more than mere coincidence. Assuming that you are one of the store's public-relations writers, prepare an appropriate letter for this year. When actually used, the letter will be signed by the president of the store.

8–6. (Letterhead.) The Tru-Mold Plastic Products Company of Indianapolis, Indiana, has a system for paying an annual Christmas bonus to its employees at all levels. The bonus is determined as 2 percent of the employee's annual earnings plus $10 additional for each full year of service with the company. Checks are mailed to the employees one week before Christmas. They are accompanied by a goodwill letter from the president in recognition of the employees' loyalty and performance. Prepare this year's letter. *Goodwill*

8–7. (Letterhead.) In appreciation of the past year's business, the Global Travel Agency of your city annually sends its customers an attractive wall calendar. Each page of the calendar contains a color picture of an interesting tourist spot in some distant part of the world. A letter of general appreciation is sent along with the calendar. Suppose that you are the owner-president of the Global Travel Agency. Prepare a suitable letter, to be printed in quantity for the next mass mailing.

8–8. (Letterhead.) Assume that you are the office manager of the Tru-Mold Plastic Products Company of Indianapolis, Indiana. Information has reached you that Edgar Maxwell, who was a close friend of yours during college, has been promoted to the position of controller of his company. He is employed by Ferris Match Corporation of Chicago, Illinois. Write Maxwell a letter of congratulation.

8–9. (Letterhead.) Beverly Philips is the widow of Jerome L. Philips, late treasurer of Central Industries, Incorporated, which has its home office in the capital of your state. After her husband passed away, Mrs. Philips was given a secretarial position at the company. Next month she will retire and move to Port Charlotte, Florida. As executive vice president of Central Industries, write Mrs. Philips a letter of congratulation and good wishes.

8–10. (Plain stationery.) Imagine that yesterday was election day in your city. In a bid for the mayor's chair, independent candidate Arthur St. John nosed out the incumbent mayor as well as the contender from the principal opposition party. St. John has been a successful lawyer; he has promised positive reforms in the city government. As a public-minded citizen, write St. John a letter of congratulation on his victory at the polls.

8–11. (Letterhead.) William (Billy) Henderson is the son of an important customer of the Tru-Mold Plastic Products Company of Indianapolis, Indiana. Billy is about to be graduated from a well-known liberal-arts college in the East. This news, together with the information that the youth plans to enter law school next fall, has reached you, the firm's sales manager. Write Billy a letter of commendation.

8–12. (Letterhead.) Mr. and Mrs. Henry Galan of your city have spent their vacation visiting in foreign lands during each of the past four years. This year, however, they stayed at home because of a forth-coming blessed event. About 10 days ago, Mrs. Galan presented her husband with a bouncing baby boy. According to the birth announcement you have received from the Galans, the baby is to be named after his father. Assume that you are the owner-president of the Global Travel Agency and that the Galans have regularly given you their travel business. Write a letter of congratulation to Mr. Galan.

8-13. (Letterhead.) The latest casualty list released by the Defense Department appeared in this afternoon's local newspaper. Captain Chester B. Miljencic was identified as one of three airmen killed on a helicopter mission in Southeast Asia. Captain Miljencic was the son of Stanley Miljencic, a foreman at the main plant of Central Industries, Incorporated, in the capital of your state. Assume the role of president of the firm and write a letter of condolence to the elder Miljencic.

8-14. (Plain stationery.) Assume that you are an attorney practicing in this area of the state. Gerald Roskamp, a client and personal friend of yours, has been caring for his invalid wife for the past several years. Now you have learned that the sick woman has passed away. Write a letter of condolence to Mr. Roskamp. In it, use the approach of reassurance to the surviving spouse.

8-15. (Letterhead.) Suppose that a flash flood has struck a low-lying section along the White River in Indianapolis, Indiana. Several hundred families have been forced to vacate their homes until the waters subside. The Red Cross has acted swiftly to set up shelters for the people at the State Fairgrounds. As the president of Indianapolis-based True-Mold Plastic Products Company, write an open letter of sympathy to the editor of the *Star*. In your letter, promise to provide free plastic meal trays to the Red Cross for use during this emergency.

· ·

CHAPTER 9

BASIC REQUESTS
AND REPLIES

The vast majority of business letters that we write are either requests or answers to requests. As such, each letter is rather easily identifiable with one of the three categories of multipurpose situations: goodwill plus a request, goodwill plus good news, goodwill plus bad news. Because of the common and essential element of goodwill present in each, we customarily speak of them by their distinguishing purpose only.

In this chapter we are going to take a look at some of the simpler types of requests and answers to requests. In so doing, however, we shall have had a sampling of every one of the basic multipurpose letter situations. In other chapters, we shall discuss the more complicated and specialized request and answer letters. Actually, the advanced types of letters are based on the same standard frameworks as the simpler types we shall examine now. The differences are those incidental to the presentation of specific details.

REQUESTS
· · · · · · · · · · ·

In considering request letters, we should recall that the standard framework from which our program will be developed has three requirements: a definite request, motivation, and ample assistance. The situation does not prescribe the sequence of these parts—only that they be provided for. We may reserve our decision as to sequence until we know the circumstances prevailing in a given case. Moreover, the matters of motivation and assistance do not always have to be clear-cut steps in the program. In some cases, the message is self-motivating; we may then decide whether to add anything else or to leave things as they are. "Ample assistance" suggests an amount of help corresponding to the need. Sometimes the very clearness of the request, the providing of information, and the presence of motivation would constitute all the assistance that is really needed.

The following chart shows an analysis of the principal types of request letters used in business:

SELF–MOTIVATING REQUESTS

Order Letters.
Inquiries with Sales Potential (solicited or unsolicited).

BASIC (FAVOR) REQUESTS

Inquiries for Information.
Requests for Assistance (courtesies or aid).
Letters of Introduction.

SPECIAL REQUESTS

Sales Letters.
Claim Letters.
Collection Letters.
Job Applications (solicited or unsolicited).

SELF–MOTIVATING REQUESTS

If ever there was a request letter that should be able to arouse our reader to action, it would be one in which we place an order for his merchandise or services. Motivation is part and parcel of the very nature of such a letter. An order helps fulfill our reader's purpose for being what he is and where he is. Nevertheless, our preparation of an order letter must not be done after a hit-or-miss fashion. Clearness and completeness are necessary if we are to receive satisfactory results from our order. So that we can cover all of its aspects thoroughly, we shall take up our discussion of the order letter in a later chapter.

Another request letter which should be self-motivating is an inquiry which carries with it a hint of sales potential. An alert firm would immediately sense this condition. Not only would it send us the information we requested about its merchandise or services, but it would also follow through with some attempt to convert our interest into desire, and our desire into a sale.

The inspiration for our inquiry might have been an advertisement of some kind about the company's product or service. If such an advertisement invited inquiries, we should expect that the company would have some facility ready and waiting to answer them. Certainly, motivation would be automatic. If inquiries were not solicited, or if we were simply writing "blind," the company might not be quite so ready, but still they should be sufficiently sales-conscious to respond. We might, however, add some motivation to our request, for good measure—such as a promise of appreciation. This statement would be suggesting to them how they might obtain our goodwill—a mild, but definite inducement.

The program for this type of letter would contain our request and up to three additional, but optional steps:

REQUEST POLITELY.
EXPLAIN (IF HELPFUL).
ASSIST (IF NEEDED).
PROMISE APPRECIATION (IF NEEDED).

The explanatory step of the letter might identify the lead we are following, the use we might make of the information, the gist of the problem we are having, and so on. But if the request requires no explanation, we do not have to offer any. In this type of letter, special assistance is not ordinarily needed. If the information is to be sent to us at an address other than the one we have used in the heading of our letter, or is to be sent to another person, the circumstances are different; and we should give full particulars. Even the motivation step is optional, as this type of request is supposedly self-motivating. We may include it, of course, if we judge that it is needed.

The following inquiry letter was written to the local gas company by a customer after he had read an advertisement. The tone is informal, courteous, and persuasive—not blunt or demanding. The letter contains two program steps: request and explain. It would seem to be self-motivating.

Gentlemen:

Will you please send me the booklet on gas-operated central air conditioning, which you advertised in Sunday's <u>Press</u>?

I understand that it is being sent free to anyone who heats his home with gas.

Very truly yours,

The next letter illustrated is also an inquiry with sales potential, but it was written under a different set of circumstances. The writer had no knowledge whether the desired information would be available; his inquiry was what we call "unsolicited." His request was that the information be sent to someone other than himself. Therefore, he provided assistance as well as a bit of information concerning the need. As an added precaution, he included a mild motivation step at the end of his letter. We observe, therefore, that his letter contains all four of the possible program parts.

Gentlemen:

Do you have any printed material explaining the features of your YARDMASTER power mower?

If so, would you please send it to my father, at the address shown below?

> Mr. Paul W. Carey
> 9848 Fairfield Road
> Kansas City, Mo. 68439

He has about two acres of land, including a large section of lawn. I believe he would be interested in learning more about tractor-type mowers.

I'll be grateful for any information you are able to send him.

Very truly yours,

Our chief interest in requests at this point is in connection with what we shall call *basic requests*. These would be in the nature of asking our reader to do us some kind of favor. In such letters, we cannot show our reader any sales potential—at least not in the foreseeable future. Instead, we encroach somewhat on his time and patience; we ask him to do something he probably is not ready to do. In many cases, all we can offer him in return is our goodwill (appreciation). To write successful requests in these cases, we must do a thorough job of persuasion. We must take advantage of every opportunity to use more than nominal motivation. We must make action as easy as possible. We must blend positiveness and diplomacy in our overall approach.

Basic requests can be considered according to a threefold classification: (1) requests for unpublished or restricted information; (2) requests for assistance—either to render a service or to make a handout; and (3) letters of introduction, in which we ask a favor for the benefit of someone unknown to our reader. The distinctions are more apparent when we look at the finished letters than they are when we see only the programs upon which the letters are based. In the case of the request for information, we in fact use the same general program as we do for a request for assistance. As each letter develops, however, the difference becomes evident. The request for information requires that we make a special effort to make action easy for our reader. We must anticipate and provide for his answering our questions easily and also for sending those answers to us. On the other hand, when we ask a reader to spend some of his time or money to do us a service or give us some material aid, we should expect to be concerned relatively more with motivation than with making action easy. In the case of the letter of introduction, we can see that its essential mission is just about the same as that of a request for assistance. But a letter of introduction requires an above-average amount of explanation. Because the general program for an ordinary request does not convey this impression, a person might be misled in trying to follow such a program in connection with an introduction. Thus, it is better that we follow a request program more specialized for the purpose involved.

1. Requests for Information

There are times when we desire to obtain information from a business firm, a governmental unit, an institution, or an individual. Such information usually is not available to us through published sources, such as we would find in a library. It may or may not be of a confidential nature; and sometimes we can only guess how the possessor might regard it. In any event, we need to write a letter that holds no promise of an eventual sale or of profit for the reader. We offer him some other kind

of inducement—often, only the opportunity of winning favor with us—
to comply with our wishes. We must use both persuasion and finesse.

The general program we follow for this type of letter contains
five steps:

CREATE INTEREST.
EXPLAIN (AS NEEDED).
SPECIFY.
MOTIVATE.
MAKE ACTION EASY.

Except for the obvious position of the interest-creating beginning, the
sequence of steps in this type of letter may be varied to suit the needs
of the case. We do not have to hold to a sequence prescribed by the
basic situation when we write request letters.

Create interest.   In the preceding part of this chapter, when we
developed our program for the type of inquiry that promised sales potential for our reader, we let the request be our opening step. This approach
was sensible, because the request was self-motivating and consequently
had high interest value. In our present circumstances, we seldom would
deem it wise to lead off with the request; it is a type of imposition, and
needs to be put across persuasively. Our guideline for deciding upon
the placement of the request might be this: If the specific request can be
effective for instilling friendly interest toward our problem, it may be
used as the opening step of our letter. Our program will be simplified
from five steps to four steps. It will become substantially the same as
the program for a self-motivating request letter.

Our usual procedure is to stick with the five-step program, wherein
the request appears after an appropriate introduction. The reasons are
that our request is not self-motivating and that often it consists of several
points or questions, a fact that interferes with its use as a crisp, interest-
creating beginning.

The measure of a good, interest-creating beginning is its ability to
command the maximum available attention of our reader so that his
mind is uncluttered enough to receive our message. Such a beginning
should "clear the atmosphere" for easy reception. Our best approach,
therefore, is to make a statement which sets his mental processes into
motion, but leaves our reader in need of more information before those
processes can run full cycle. The sort of statement made to order for

this purpose is the rhetorical question. We ask a rhetorical question mainly for creating an effect—interest, in this case. We do not intend the reader to give us an answer to the question; rather, we desire that he give himself the answer after reading our message.

The following are a few rhetorical questions that have been useful in creating interest at the beginning of a request letter. As examples, they are intended merely to stimulate our imagination—not to be used indiscriminately in any case that happens along. We are encouraged to seek ideas from many sources, but we should always express ourselves according to our personal, original style.

```
May I have a moment of your time?

May we have your help in an important study?

Will you have five minutes to spare this evening?

Would you consider trading a few minutes of your time for an
industrywide report?
```

Each of these beginnings creates interest politely and soberly—not clownishly. Each asks something, but leaves the reader somewhat unable to answer without having more facts. His mental processes have started to function, but they need material to work on. Psychologically, our reader tends to "lean" toward our message, in search of just such material—we have induced him to read on. Unless we ourselves do something to break the spell, he should get completely through our letter.

Explain.   Having sparked our reader's interest, we are ready to lay the groundwork for our request. We do this by means of a concise explanation to help the reader appreciate our problem and the reason we have for coming to him with our request. If necessary, we can go into the uses we plan to make of his information, with assurances that will appeal to him. In this way, our explanation can function as both a low-pressure sales talk and a mild inducement. As for phrasing, we should avoid obvious or thinly disguised flattery. Our reader would easily see through it and take it as a sign of insincerity.

In presenting our explanation, we must be careful to observe the quality of conciseness, which combines briefness with completeness. Our reader must have enough background to enable him to understand our situation, but he should not become bored reading it. In our explanation step, we are deliberately holding our reader in a kind of suspense. He is looking for the material he needs to answer our rhetorical-question beginning, but we are giving him only a portion of it here. If we are concise, his interest should mount; if we are long-winded, he is likely to turn cool.

Specify. For our reader, the awaited climax comes when we state our request. Here will be the key piece of material that he has been needing in order to evaluate our opening question. For our part, it is the main message in this kind of letter; and we must take every measure to assure that it cannot be misunderstood.

Our first consideration is to frame an effective question. We must be sufficiently abreast of our own problem to know what this question is. If we can ask only a vague, general question, we probably have not progressed far enough with our work to be asking questions of specific individuals or organizations. Our reader must know exactly what we need if we expect him to help us. It would not be proper for us to ask him an all-inclusive question which would take him hours of time and pages of copy to answer. For one thing, we could not use everything he provided. For another, he might still not cover the point we are most keenly interested in. Worst of all, the task of answering would be so forbidding to our reader that he might prefer to beg off with a polite, "Sorry." To improve our chances of an answer and to safeguard getting the information we really need, we must ask a specific, understandable question.

Our second consideration concerns our reader's ease of answering. Although we are dealing with the request step of our letter, we should already begin to anticipate the difficulties our reader is likely to have in answering and try to reduce them as much as we can. The method we use for stating our request has a bearing on the ease or difficulty of answering. Overall service attitude requires that we render assistance not only as a step of our letter but also wherever possible throughout the letter.

Subjective questions. Often, we ask a question or a number of questions which require our reader to respond by writing us a letter. On the surface there might not seem to be much we can do to make his answering especially easy—but let us consider the possibilities. When we ask a single question, there is little else we can do beyond being clear and specific. Yet, a single question is relatively little to ask of our reader; and because it is the essence of our message, our reader will not have a complicated job of identifying it in his answer. As for presentation, we could introduce it at the end of our explanatory material as a natural continuation. For better eye appeal, however, and for ease of reference by our reader after he has finished reading all of our letter, we might set the question off by itself. For example,

```
. . . Our question, therefore, is this:

What specific means are you using to make your factory
employees safety-conscious?
```

If we ask more than one question, we should definitely present them in a list. Such a list should be set apart from the rest of the text matter, and each question should be numbered. This procedure will give maximum eye appeal to our questions and make them easy for our reader to find when he is ready to answer. It will permit him to refer to the number of the question rather than repeat each question as he answers. It will probably control the sequence of his answers—a fact that could be useful to us in comparing answers from several respondents. Moreover, if we have used a logical sequence—in which a foundation question precedes one that is based on it—our reader should be able to answer in a concise, uncomplicated manner. On the other hand, if we have used an illogical sequence, our reader may get entangled in giving an explanation—and realize that had we asked the questions properly the tangle could have been avoided. Such a situation would not contribute to the feeling of goodwill which we should be trying to cultivate.

Objective questions. The more familiar we become with the precise nature of our own problem in a request situation, the better able we are to pinpoint the questions for the reader. If we carry this line of reasoning to its logical conclusion, we arrive at what are known as "objective questions." We have worked out our questions to such a degree that our reader need provide only a word, a date, an amount, or an age; respond with a *yes* or a *no;* or choose from a list of possible answers. Also, a new technique has opened up for us: We can make a physical presentation of our questions which will let our reader answer without having to write us a letter. By providing a place for each answer, we can invite him to insert the word or other fact called for on the very document we have sent him. When he has completed this easy answering work, he can simply send our document back to us—no fuss, no bother.

There are two effective ways of presenting objective questions. One method is to take advantage of the empty space that appears beneath the signature block of our letter. This space will usually be ample enough to hold as many as three objective questions and their answering spaces. Because of the location of the questions, we call this system the "footnote method." It does not affect our program to any great extent, however. The only incidental variation is that the request step asks the reader to answer the questions shown at the bottom of the letter and to return the letter to us.

Under the footnote method, our reader is asked to relinquish our letter together with his answers. Courtesy requires that we send him a copy of the letter for his files. Actually, he can enter his answers on both copies and return either copy to us. All we really want from him is his answers, not necessarily the original copy of our letter.

When we have four or more objective questions, it is not likely that there will be enough space available at the bottom of the letter for us to use the footnote method. In such a case, we should change over to a second method—the use of a separate question-and-answer sheet, or questionnaire.

Because of this change, we are confronted with a number of new considerations. First, the usage calls for the two-part letter form. This difference requires us to ask our reader to answer what we have listed on a separate document. We should mention the questionnaire as we would any other enclosure, and include it in the total number indicated in the enclosure reference of our letter. We must convert completely to a questionnaire presentation—not place some questions at the bottom of the letter and the remainder in the questionnaire. We should see to it that our questionnaire is self-explanatory—that is to say, it should contain all necessary notations as to topic, purpose, source of inquiry, and whatever else might be important for identification. In short, it should be understandable and returnable even if it becomes separated from its covering letter. As for arrangement, we should consider both eye appeal and logical sequence, as with all other lists of questions. Finally, we should keep within the psychological limitation on length. There is no absolute limit on the *number* of questions that may be asked, but results are known to drop off drastically whenever a questionnaire exceeds *one page*. By this indirect means, therefore, we can estimate that about 10 objective question-and-answer units, including subsections at times, would fill a page and be the probable maximum. In most cases, by careful structuring and economical use of our questions, we should be able to obtain the information we need.

Under the questionnaire method, there is no point in sending the reader an extra copy of our letter. He will either keep our letter or discard it as he pleases, but he is not expected to return it to us. We give serious thought to sending him a file copy of the questionnaire—especially if we believe we have produced a good one. Many businessmen have "idea files" in which they accumulate all sorts of forms, art work, and other material for future reference. It is just possible that, being impressed with our design of questionnaire, our reader might decide to keep it rather than return it. If we are foresighted enough to send him a "courtesy copy," we neatly avoid such a development.

Motivate.   Once we have asked our question or questions, by whichever method is most appropriate, we have technically delivered our main message. But we are not finished with our overall campaign, which must include our reader's agreement with and compliance with our request. To persuade him to act, we must show him that favorable action will be worth his while. This is our motivation step.

In every request letter, the very minimum we can do is promise our reader appreciation. As we have seen, such a statement indicates that his compliance will earn our goodwill. Of course, if this is to function best, we should show the increased goodwill to be contingent on his performance—that is, we should use the future tense. Some examples would be as follows.

```
Your cooperation will be greatly appreciated.

I'll appreciate your returning the questionnaire by the
fifteenth.

Because my sources of information are limited, I'll really
be grateful to you for answering this question.
```

Promises of appreciation along this line do not thank the reader "in advance" or even here and now; they use the possibility of future reward as leverage for inducing action. Moreover, the examples shown above have avoided "it if" (also, "it . . . if"), a commonly used expression for referring to the future. This construction is somewhat awkward, even in speech.

Aside from a promise of appreciation, we can usually find something else that can be used as motivation. It is possible that we could promise our reader:

> To keep the information confidential—when the reader or his company might hesitate to give out facts they consider to be of a restricted nature.
>
> To give publicity—when we have reason to believe that our reader would expect full credit for any information he provides.
>
> To reciprocate—whereby both sides could exchange information for mutual benefit, or whereby we could offer a copy of an extensive report in gratitude for some contributory information our reader might provide now.
>
> To reimburse—when a request would cause our reader or his company some measurable expense to answer.

At times, it is possible for us to combine more than one of these additional promises with the promise of appreciation. Of course, having an abundance of motivations should not be one of our aims; quality, not quantity, is important. If we do have a combination of motivations, the selections should be individually appropriate and certainly not in conflict with one another.

Make action easy.   The third basic requirement of a letter in a request situation is ample assistance to the reader. In the basic, or favor, request under discussion we apply service attitude as each opportunity for doing so presents itself. We strive for clear, specific questions. We place them in a logical sequence and in an eye-appealing form. We simplify the answering of subjective questions by numbering them. We number objective questions and provide for their answers on the same form that contains the questions. What remains now is to render assistance to our reader in the matter of sending the answers to us. Our final touch, therefore, is to give him an addressed, postage-free envelope. We can use a business reply envelope for this purpose—or simply an envelope which is addressed back to us and provided with adequate stamped or metered postage. Our best choice, if we have one, is a Number 9 size envelope; it will fit into our Number 10 envelope and yet it will hold regular 8½ by 11 stationery without special folding. But the unmentioned purpose behind the return envelope is a show of sincerity

—evidence that we are really trying for an answer. Many firms actually prefer to use their own stationery for outgoing mail—but still they are impressed by our earnestness in sending an addressed, postage-free envelope.

Summary and examples.   In a brief summation of these program steps, we see that our information request letter develops in a positive, straight-line fashion. We open with a suspenseful, interest-creating question. We hold our reader in suspense while we explain the circumstances of the case. Then we state our request in a businesslike way—politely, not bluntly, not apologetically. We present our questions with a view to making response easy. We induce action by promising appreciation and whatever else might be considered appropriate under the prevailing circumstances. We further assist action by providing a return envelope.

The following letters are all based on the same general program. Each illustrates a different handling of the request step, owing to the kind or number of questions involved.

EXAMPLE 1—A SINGLE SUBJECTIVE QUESTION

Dear Mr. Walsh:

Would you please give me your expert opinion on a storage problem?

Our company has a large number of steel castings which we acquired at a foreclosure sale in May. These castings are expected to be sufficient for our needs during the next three years. So far, they have been sheltered in our factory warehouse; but the steady expansion of our business is putting pressure on our storage space. Our stores superintendent has suggested that we move the castings outdoors to make room for other kinds of material.

Although I am considering this suggestion, I am somewhat fearful of the effects of rust and the danger of pitting. Since your company sometimes stockpiles metal castings outside, perhaps you can tell me what to expect. In your judgment, is there any serious risk in exposing steel castings to weather conditions for as long a time as three years?

I'll certainly appreciate getting your opinion, and I know my associates will echo my sentiments. For your convenience, I've enclosed a business reply envelope. May I hear from you soon?

Sincerely yours,

EXAMPLE 2—SEVERAL SUBJECTIVE QUESTIONS:

Dear Mr. Krieger:

May we consult you on a matter of importance to Baileyville?

We have received reports at the Chamber of Commerce that a
group of appraisers from Washington have been making inquiries
among several of the farmers near Tipton Junction, about 20
miles south of here. The rumor is that they are studying the
practicality of acquiring land for a military installation—
probably a supply depot. If such an installation should be
built, it would be staffed by military personnel numbering in
the thousands—and Baileyville would be the nearest town with
recreational facilities.

As president of our largest bank, you will agree that our community should start planning now for such an eventuality.
Would you think over the following questions and send us your
opinions, please?

   1. What are the implications of a nearby military base—
      in terms of jobs, prices, incomes, and other economic
      conditions in Baileyville?

   2. What impact would all this be expected to have on our
      social, cultural, and religious institutions?

   3. What stand should the Chamber of Commerce take if the
      rumor concerning the military installation proves to
      be correct?

We'll greatly appreciate your responses to these important
questions. The enclosed envelope is stamped and addressed back
to us for your convenience.

                      Very truly yours,

EXAMPLE 3—OBJECTIVE QUESTIONS IN A FOOTNOTE

Dear Mr. Hennings:

Would you be willing to give me the benefit of your experience?

Three years ago, as I recall, you changed your office air conditioning from individual units to a central system. My company is considering a similar move before the hot weather sets
in this summer. As purchasing agent, I have listened to conflicting statements from salesmen concerning the effectiveness
of central air conditioning.

Since you have used both kinds of equipment and can make an impartial statement, would you help me by answering the three questions listed at the bottom of this letter? I've enclosed a business reply envelope for your convenience and an extra copy of this letter. You may simply fill in your answers, send one copy to me, and keep the other for your records.

I'll appreciate your sharing your knowledge with me.

Sincerely yours,

Thomas R. Prell

Thomas R. Prell
Purchasing Agent

TRP:ml
Enclosures 2

1. What is the average monthly difference in electrical consumption with a central air-conditioning system as against individual units?

   _____ KWH more   _____ KWH less

2. What is the average monthly difference in maintenance costs?

   $_____ more $_____ less

3. How often, if ever, has a breakdown occurred in the central system?

   _____

EXAMPLE 4—OBJECTIVE QUESTIONS IN A QUESTIONNAIRE

Mr. Edward L. Cochrane
14407 Rockledge Drive
Montpelier, Vt. 05601

May I have a few minutes of your time?

As research editor for Him, the national magazine for the man of the house, I am interested in your preference in a shaving instrument. I am preparing a report to appear in the March issue of Him. My hope is to give our readers a representative cross section of masculine shaving habits and possibly point out a trend that might be developing with regard to the choice of instrument.

I've enclosed a brief questionnaire in duplicate and a business reply envelope. All I ask is that you jot down your answers on one copy of the questionnaire and return it to me in the convenient envelope. The duplicate is a courtesy copy for your own use.

Your answers will be an important contribution toward my research. I'll be grateful for your cooperation in sending them.

Sincerely yours,

James J. Bascomb

James J. Bascomb
Research Editor

JJB/cj
Enclosures 3

Please return this form by January 7, 1968, to: Research Editor, HIM Magazine Fifteenth Floor, Bond Building New York, New York 10017	(This space for office use only)	Project No. 1967-72 Topic: Shaving Instruments Investigator: J. J. Bascomb

QUESTIONNAIRE

1. Which type of shaving instrument do you regularly use? (Check one)

   ___ Straight razor ___ Safety razor ___ Injector ___ Electric ___ None

2. Which type did you use regularly before you obtained your present shaving instrument? (Check one)

   ___ Straight razor ___ Safety razor ___ Injector ___ Electric ___ None

2. What was the chief consideration involved in the choice of your present shaving instrument? (Check one)

   ___ Initial cost ___ Cost of using ___ Shaving satisfaction

   ___ Other, as follows: _____

4. Which type of shaving instrument do you recommend for a young man who is just beginning to shave? (Check one)

___ Straight razor ___ Safety razor ___ Injector ___ Electric shaver

5. In your opinion, is a shaving instrument suitable as a gift for a man, or is it something he should always select for himself?

_____

_____

6. If you had to get yourself a new shaving instrument today, which type would you choose? (Check one)

___ Straight razor ___ Safety razor ___ Injector ___ Electric shaver

The specific physical features of the two-part arrangement will be based on the number of questionnaires we plan to send out. If we are dealing with but one reader, we would have both the letter and the questionnaire typewritten. Up to a practical limit, we might use automatic typewriters for the letter part and an office duplicator for the common questionnaire, when we conduct a small or moderate-sized mailing. This approach would still permit an individually typed letter with a specific inside address and salutation. If a large mass mailing is involved, we undoubtedly would have to resort to a processed letter and forego individualized parts. Our salutation would become a standardized variety, such as "Dear Sir" or "Dear Friend."

2. Requests for Assistance

Another type of basic request, closely related to the request for information, is one in which we ask our reader to perform some courtesy or to give us some material aid. As in a request for information, often we can promise our reader little more than appreciation—except perhaps something equally intangible. Yet we earnestly desire his help and must do our utmost to obtain it from him. Examples of this type are requests that our reader write a letter of reference on our behalf, or a letter of introduction; join a committee; be a speaker or a panelist at a meeting; arrange a trip through his factory for our group; send us a quantity of annual reports, pamphlets, or reprints; donate a prize for a fund-raising cause; give money to a deserving institution or fund.

In general, our writing of this type of letter follows the sequence of steps we discussed above for requesting information. The program, which contains only a few negligible adjustments, may be stated as follows.

CREATE INTEREST.

EXPLAIN.

SPECIFY.

MOTIVATE.

ASSIST (IF POSSIBLE).

We should begin our letter on a positive note, never with an apology. Our aim is to put our reader in a receptive frame of mind—not to cloud his thinking by causing doubt or suspicion. We should try to trigger a "Tell me more" response from him as he reads our opening statement. If our request is merely that he perform a courtesy, the rhetorical-question technique should serve our purpose; but it might seem weak if we are seeking some kind of handout. In such a case we might consider something closer to the kind of opening used in a sales letter. The following are examples.

```
If you're like most of us, you appreciate the recognition
you get when you do something out of the ordinary.

To make a long story short, I have a favor to request of you.

Right now, about 50 students at Great Lakes University need
your help.
```

After our interest-creating beginning, we should give our reader a brief but complete explanation of the situation confronting us. This background will help our reader evaluate our request and will sometimes help to motivate him.

In this kind of letter we usually ask for one specific action and do not have to choose from among several possible arrangements of questions. We may place our request as a concluding statement winding up the explanatory section of our letter. Or, we may give it individual eye appeal by setting it off in a separate paragraph. We should be clear and specific about what we desire—yet polite and persuasive, not blunt and demanding.

Motivation—a reason why our reader should grant our request—is very important; we should be as convincing as we can. In all such requests, a promise of appreciation is a must. At times, we might be able to promise something additional, such as publicity or reciprocity. We must remember, too, that a promise implies a future action; we should not phrase it as something over and done with even before our reader has obliged us. Also, there are times when we may be able to use some kind of emotional appeal to induce action. For instance, we might go to work on his sympathy, altruism, or pride—things which could activate our reader from within.

Because of the nature of our request, that our reader do something that usually he alone can do, our assistance step cannot conform to any pattern. We can make sure, though, that the other steps have been handled well so that our letter as a whole will be easy to understand. As a given case requires, we should be ready to meet the challenge: enclose addressed labels for packages, names and addresses of persons to whom he is to write, pertinent instructions, pledge cards and return envelopes for fund drives, and so on.

The letter shown below, seeking a plant tour, is a request for a courtesy. It was sent to the general manager of a commercial bakery by a college professor.

Dear Mr. Stone:

Have you any appointments scheduled for the afternoon of November 4?

This fall I am teaching a course in industrial methods at Summit College. One of our study topics is modern production, with an emphasis on automation. Because Millstone Bakery uses automated facilities and is located right here in town, I am hoping that a plant tour might be arranged. My 33 students and I would be interested in the baking and slicing of bread and in seeing the cookie machine that does everything between the flour barrel and the delivery truck.

Would you be able to arrange a tour of your bakery for my group—starting, say, at 1:00 P.M. on Friday, November 4?

I'll certainly appreciate your approving this request. You
would be adding a practical touch to my educational effort—
and perhaps a few converts to Millstone products!

Sincerely yours,

In the next letter, the purpose is to obtain the donation of a prize
for a charity raffle. The writer made a special effort to create and maintain interest.

Dear Mr. Ritter:

This is a request with a sporting proposal attached. I've used
a comma in the body of this letter. Find it if you can—and
I'll withdraw my request.

The Sponsors of Future Citizens are planning their annual benefit raffle for May 20. All proceeds are pledged to maintain a
summer camp for the needy and deserving youngsters of our
city. Each such child will be eligible for an expense-paid
two-week vacation at the camp. This project has the solid support of Mayor Kline and other city officials.

In my capacity as chairman I am asking you and other merchants
to donate a piece of merchandise as a prize for the raffle.
Ritter's Radio Store could help appreciably by providing a
record player or a clock radio.

Our plan is to tag each prize with the name of its donor. We
would also publicize the donors on all placards and signs listing the prizes being raffled off. It goes without saying that
the gratitude of every member of our group would be extended
to you.

Won't you please help us help our future citizens this way?

Sincerely yours,

Conrad A. Armstrong

Conrad A. Armstrong
Activities Chairman

CAA:ln

P.S. Have you found the comma? So . . . be a good sport and
donate the prize anyhow!

This letter used what is known as a "gimmick"—an ingenious device (such as a change of color, change of type style, merchandising scheme, clever statement, picture, or attachment) slipped in to help captivate the reader. In this case, there is a good chance that the reader will have to go through the letter a second time. Thus, he will receive a double exposure to the request message.

Subsequently, the writer of the request letter sent the following note of appreciation.

Dear Mr. Ritter:

Thank you very much for your donation. The portable shortwave radio is an even better choice than either of my suggestions. All of us on the committee are grateful for your generous help.

About the riddle: You certainly are entitled to know the answer! Look carefully and you'll see "a comma" in the second sentence of that letter. But let's keep it a trade secret, please!

Sincerely yours,

3. Letter of Introduction

A third variety of favor-type request is a letter of introduction. Because it requires more explanatory material than the ordinary request, we do well to use a program designed especially for the purpose. The first three steps of this program deal with different stages of the background material, with the first step also serving to create interest. In all, the program has six steps:

INTRODUCE.
STATE PURPOSE.
GIVE PERSONAL DATA.
REQUEST.
ASSIST (IF APPLICABLE).
PROMISE APPRECIATION.

In this type of letter we are introducing someone we know to someone else we know, but the two do not know each other as yet. A ready-made element of human interest is available to us by this very fact, and we usually can capitalize on it by making it our opening step. If possible, we should use an original, informal style; we should revert to a formal style only if it is necessary. The reason is that our beginning rather sets the pace for the rest of the letter; and the informal, conversational style is to be preferred. We can compare the two styles below.

Formal: The purpose of this letter is to introduce Mr. John Flynn.

Formal: This letter will introduce Mr. John Flynn, who . . . .

Informal: At last, I'm getting my chance to introduce Mr. John Flynn.

Informal: The young man who handed you this letter is John Flynn, a business associate of mine.

Typically, the person being introduced is engaged in some activity which will bring him into contact with our reader. It is natural, therefore, that we follow up the introduction step with some explanation of the person's objective. As with explanations in other types of requests, such background often helps motivate our reader. But we should be concise; we weaken our hold on our reader if we bore him with nonessential details.

To complete our picture, we should include a brief business description of the person we are introducing. This summary should be limited to things which could be helpful to our reader: the person's profession, position, affiliations, experience, reputation, etc. Because we are writing in a request situation, we have considerable leeway in sequencing our program steps. We could, if we found it more practical, put the personal data ahead of the statement of purpose.

Besides there being the mission of the person introduced, we have a definite purpose in mind when we write this type of letter. It is to request our reader to extend a courtesy to this person as a favor to us. After our explanatory paragraphs, we must come to the point and state our request clearly and courteously—and in a positive, businesslike manner. According to the case at hand, we ask our reader to give the person some needed information, introduce him to other businessmen, show him a production process, help him plan a work itinerary, and so on. Then we add whatever could or should be provided to help our reader carry out our request. Many times, there is nothing that we can do, except rely on the clarity and effectiveness of our other steps. In some cases, though, we can add some helpful information, instructions, or suggestions. For instance, if the person is to be met somewhere, we should give our reader information on the date, time, place, and means of identification.

About the only motivation available to us in a letter of introduction is the promise of appreciation. By placing it in last position, we can make it serve also as a goodwill ending. To make it effective as a sincere inducement, we should use wording that suggests the future. An expression such as "Thanks in advance" is not good, because it suggests that we have closed our side of the case regardless of what our reader actually does.

In the matter of form, we sometimes face a decision on how to address a letter of introduction. Under ordinary conditions, whether the letter is to be mailed or is to be carried by the person being introduced, we address a specific reader. We use a conventional inside address and salutation for the letter and a conventional outside address for the envelope. Sometimes it is our intention that the letter be carried from place to place as part of the person's credentials. Under such an arrangement, we have to use a general form of address. In the letter, we omit an inside address entirely; and at the left-hand margin, about six lines down from the date, we place one of the following salutations.

```
To whom it may concern:

Introducing Mr. John Flynn:
```

We omit a specific address from the envelope, too; but, about 14 lines down from the top edge, we center a one-line description, such as one of the following.

```
              A Letter of Introduction

              Introducing Mr. John Flynn
```

The next illustration is a letter of introduction. It was mailed to the reader in advance of the arrival of the person being introduced. The informal beginning paves the way for an easy-to-read style throughout the letter.

Dear Mr. Lester:

Next Tuesday morning a friend of mine, Herbert C. Talmadge, will visit your office at my suggestion.

Herb is sales manager of Benson Industries, Inc., whose home office is here in Cincinnati. He is a graduate of Harrison College, a real comer in sales and merchandising, and a very likable person. He has only one "weakness"—devotion to his wife, Alice, and their two daughters.

Herb's purpose in going to Houston is to lease building space for a regional sales office. I thought it possible that you might know of two or three suitable locations in the downtown area. If so, would you put Herb on the right track to help him get started?

I'll consider whatever you can do for Herb to be a personal favor for me. Your help will be long remembered.

Sincerely,

SPECIAL REQUESTS

Regardless of any sorting of request letters into types, we always find that the basic requirements remain the same. A request letter must contain a definite request, motivation of the reader, and ample assistance. Because of the incidentals of a certain type of request, we may need some additional ingredients, but never are the basic three dropped or replaced. We understand, of course, that some requests are self-motivating and that some do not require a great deal of assistance.

There are four special types of business requests—sales letters, claim letters, collection letters, and applications for employment—still to be discussed. Being of a somewhat advanced nature, they are not appropriate for inclusion among the "basic" request types. We shall take them up in later chapters of this book.

ANSWERS

· · · · · · · ·

In all likelihood, as businessmen we are going to find that most of the letters we write will be in answer to correspondence we receive rather than in the nature of requests that we originate. The reason is that a large number of request letters are written by people who either are not businessmen or are acting as private individuals. Doctors, lawyers, teachers, students, housewives, retail customers, and prospective customers originate business correspondence which usually takes the form of a request. Such correspondence converges on a company, and someone must respond with an answer.

If we make a simple classification of answer letters, we see that there are three basic kinds. The first kind, which we have already discussed in Chapter 8, is the letter of appreciation—a simple goodwill variety. We do not count it as of great importance in our present discussion, because to become an "answer" letter, such a letter would have to be in response to correspondence from our benefactor, in which he told us about the favor he performed.

The two other basic answer letters are the good-news and bad-news varieties—each of which is a multipurpose letter that combines goodwill with its main message. In a good-news answer, we should make no bones about our message; we come right out with it and follow with explanation only if it is helpful to our reader. In a bad-news letter, we should prepare our reader through ample explanation, issue the main message as painlessly as possible, and add an encouraging note before ending.

The simple, black-and-white classification of multipurpose answer letters into good-news and bad-news varieties is somewhat inadequate for practical application. Even in a discussion of basic replies, we need to recognize types that are a bit more sophisticated. In later chapters, further variations will become apparent as we encounter the more specialized answer letters. Of the six multi-purpose letters described in the table (see next page), two are in the good-news situation, and four are in the bad-news situation. They probably cover the minimum number of combinations required for our ordinary purposes. Each is described by an informal designation of the specific letter type and a brief summary of the message features that distinguish it from the others. All of the types, of course, are expected to cater to the reader's goodwill.

We should clarify our thinking at this point by making a few observations about these reply letters. The first good-news type, "yes," and the first two of the bad-news types, the qualified "nos," are final answers. We tell our reader definitely whether his request is being honored or refused. These clear-cut replies are the ones we shall take up in this chapter.

MULTIPURPOSE ANSWER LETTERS

(REPLIES)

Situation	Informal Designation of Letter Type	Message Features Goodwill, Plus:
Good News	Yes	Grant
Good News	Yes, If	Agree, Request (clarification of details)
Bad News	No (expressed), But	Explain, Decline, Assist
Bad News	No (implied), But	Explain, Assist
Bad News	Maybe, If	Explain, Request (clarification on a large scale)
Bad News	Somewhat	Explain, Counteroffer

A further observation of the two bad-news types shows us that there is no such thing as a plain "no" business letter. The requirement of the bad-news situation is that we bolster our reader's feelings at the end of our letter. We cannot do this for him if we stop at the announcement of our bad news, no matter how gently we break it to him. He will be disappointed, and we cannot afford to leave him feeling that way.

While the three remaining types will turn up in later chapters, we can make some judgments about them, too. In the first place, they are not supposed to be final letters. Each of these replies contains some kind of request or proposal for the reader to consider. More correspondence is obviously indicated before we reach a final-answer stage. The "yes, if" type is considered to be all but fulfillment of our reader's request. In such a case, we have what he wants and are willing to provide it. The only technical difficulty is that we are not quite certain about one or more of the details of his request. We must ask him for clarification so that we can follow through.

The "maybe, if" and "somewhat" types cannot be considered as good news. In neither type of reply do we give our reader what he has sought from us. Therefore, these two types must be varieties of bad-news letters. We send our reader a "maybe, if" reply when his request was so inadequate that we are unable to say whether we can grant it or not. We need a large amount of additional information before we can even reach a decision. We write him a "somewhat" reply when we turn him down on his specific request but are willing to grant him something less. Naturally, we cannot force him to accept our counteroffer; we must await further word from him.

GOOD–NEWS REPLIES

For an experienced letter writer, answering a request under a good-news situation is scarcely a challenge. Even for a beginner, the job is relatively easy, provided he sticks to the requirements and is mindful of the matters of finesse. In fact, as we have already suggested in our discussion of request letters, some replies can be made without our having to write a letter. All we need do, if we are granting the request, is fill in objective-type answers on a questionnaire or at the bottom of a letter and mail the completed form to the questioner in the envelope he has provided.

When subjective answers are called for, we generally find it necessary to write a letter in reply. The same would be true in the case of granting requests for assistance; we probably would reply by letter in order to explain and confirm the various details involved. The general program for such a letter is as follows.

INDICATE YES.
FILL REQUEST.
ADD EXTRAS (IF HELPFUL).
MAKE GOODWILL OFFER.

In applying this program to a specific set of circumstances, we may find it necessary to use all four steps. Sometimes, by opening our letter with the actual filling of our reader's request, we combine the first and second steps. Our letter will then be made up of three steps instead of four. Furthermore, not all cases will require anything extra—not even an explanation. Thus, if we use a combined opening, we can compose a letter with only two steps—the first and the fourth. Usually, though, we are in a position to know something our reader did not anticipate—an explanation of how to use what we are giving him, an admonition about the confidential nature of certain information, the shipping data on a package being sent, an answer to a secondary question that our reader did not think to ask, and so on. If so, we should include such things as extra material, in keeping with service attitude.

To end our letter gracefully rather than abruptly, and to leave our reader with a favorable goodwill impression, we can close with an offer to help him again sometime. This is not meant to be taken too literally. We do not specify how or when—and we do not enclose a reply envelope! Our statement is mostly a gesture of goodwill. If some other approach seems better—such as to offer him our best wishes in what he is doing—we should use it.

In the following reply letter, the writer answers a simple request for information. He has followed a three-step program: a combined good-news beginning, something extra, and a goodwill ending.

Dear Mr. Carleton:

Subject: Your Letter of September 10

Yes, I'm sure that you can store your steel castings outside for three years. We have used that method three times since I've been here, and each time the results have been satisfactory.

A coating of rust will form on the metal, but ordinary machining will remove all of that, and more. In case your operations require only light machining, I'd suggest that you cover the castings with a tarpaulin. This precaution will help retard the rust; yet it should not run you a great deal of expense.

I'm happy to give you this information and pleased to learn that your company is doing so well.

Sincerely yours,

In the next letter, the writer found it necessary to use the full program of four steps. Because he had to reply to three subjective questions, he could not very well use a combined opening. His letter has to start out with an indication that the request is being granted and then follow with the individual answers. The answers are numbered and are further identified by descriptive wording. Something extra has been added, in the form of a suggestion; and a standard goodwill ending is used.

Dear Mr. Maloney:

You and your associates in the Chamber of Commerce are to be commended for your prompt concern over the prospects of a military depot being opened at Tipton Junction. I'm pleased to give you my opinions as you requested.

1. <u>Economic</u> <u>Factors</u>. In general, I don't think we should expect any economic upheaval. Some of our local firms would benefit temporarily by participating in the construction work. Later on, restaurants, cafes, and amusement places would undoubtedly experience some kind of boom. Real estate business might pick up a little bit, too. But our overall, basic activity would not be affected.

2. <u>Impact</u> <u>on</u> <u>Community</u>. With proper precautions, we should be able to adjust amicably to the numbers of military personnel likely to visit Baileyville. Our best approach is to have enough planned activities to fill their needs.

3. <u>Chamber's</u> <u>Stand</u>. There is no justifiable reason for us to be opposed to a military depot. The Chamber of Commerce should go on record as being in favor of such a proposal.

I do suggest, however, that a committee be assigned to prepare the local merchants for such an eventuality and to check into the facts concerning recreation. Perhaps we can get some group to set up a servicemen's center as a supplement to existing facilities.

Please call on me, should any new questions arise.

Sincerely yours,

The writer of the following letter was able to give his good-news reply with a three-step program. With granting a request for classroom copies of the company's annual report as the first step, the letter goes on to give the shipping data and a gesture of goodwill. While not strictly required, the shipping information is a courtesy to the reader. It has service attitude and contributes toward goodwill.

Dear Professor Hargar:

Yes, we're happy to fill your request for 50 copies of our annual report for 1966.

The booklets were mailed this morning under the special fourth-class postage rate. They are in a single package addressed to the college and marked for your attention. You should receive them by the end of the week.

If we can be of further assistance along this line, please let us hear from you.

Very truly yours,

BAD–NEWS REPLIES

We face a stiffer challenge when we must write a letter to someone and turn down his request. The basic requirements are different and so is the sequence of the basic framework of the letter. Moreover, we do not have a ready-made, interest-creating beginning as we do when we write a good-news reply. Thus, we must devise something that is appropriate to the given set of circumstances, that makes our questioner feel that his request is welcome, that is not so enthusiastic as to raise false hopes—in short, something that will open our letter and serve as a prelude to our explanation step. We must, of course, give our reader a plausible explanation before we decline his request; and we must do whatever is practical afterwards to generate goodwill.

There are two methods of communicating the turndown of a request. One way is to express it in so many words; the other way is to imply it by making a skillful change in the thought direction of the message. If we express the turndown of our reader's request, our program will be of the following type:

INDICATE FRIENDSHIP.
EXPLAIN CIRCUMSTANCES.
DECLINE.
SUGGEST.
MAKE GOODWILL COUNTEROFFER.

As noted above, our opening step in such a letter is a goodwill gesture to pave the way for our explanation of why a turndown must be given. What we tell our reader must be friendly, yet restrained—usually an appreciative acknowledgment of his request. The following are a few examples of how we might phrase such a beginning.

We appreciate the confidence you have shown in us by your letter of August 27 requesting a donation.

Thank you for considering me as a possible speaker for your regional conference.

Many thanks for the kind words that accompanied your inquiry of May 11.

We are pleased that you have come to us with your request for educational material.

What we offer our reader as an explanation should be something believable and convincing. A pitfall to be avoided is using a reason that is absolute enough for us, but not at all satisfactory to our reader. For instance, our company may have a flat rule against granting our reader's kind of request. This rule tells company personnel how to respond—but it should not be used as *the* reason we give our reader. If we write "It's against our rules" (or "policy" or "practice"), our reader is apt to become disgruntled. His reasoning could be, variously: "If they make a rule, they can break it!" "Are they telling me that I've overstepped my bounds?" "Why, they've never even considered my reasons!" Such reactions would not be in keeping with the goodwill we should be trying to instill. Our solution, then, is to find out the reason for the rule or policy, so that we can give a plausible explanation.

After we have given our reader an adequate explanation, we break the bad news as gently as possible. We should never bluntly "refuse" his request. We should take a milder stand. We are not against his request; we are just not in a position to grant it. The following examples show the mild tone needed for declining a request.

```
We regret that these reasons prevent us from helping you in
your study.

Under these conditions, you can understand why we must decline
your request.

For these reasons, we are unable to send you the budget data
you have requested.

We are sorry, therefore, that the personnel records cannot be
made available to you at this time.
```

At this stage of our message, our reader is at a low point, psychologically. He has received a turndown of his request, a letdown of his hopes. In the interests of goodwill, therefore, we must at least start him on the road to recovery before we end our letter. If possible, we may suggest another solution—perhaps a different source of information or supply or a different means of going about his stated task. As a final step, we make a standard goodwill gesture. It will probably be in the nature of a counteroffer to his request—to help him at some other time or in some other way. We could not sincerely offer to help him "again," because we have turned him down on this request. We should not try to take credit for something we did not do.

In the letter which follows, the writer applied this five-step program in turning down a request for a sample of his company's cost accounting form for reporting departmental overhead expense. His turndown is expressed as a definite step. His helpful suggestion is given an extra amount of service attitude because it is supported by a complete mailing address.

Dear Mr. Nelson:

We are flattered that you should think of us in connection with the modernizing of your cost accounting records.

From what you have explained, your most pressing need is for a sample form for a standing order of departmental expense. At Moreland Products we use a pegboard system for this purpose. The account titles are printed permanently on pegboards, along with the number of each line.

The accounting department enters the respective figures on a columnar sheet, which is then removed from the pegboard and sent to the department manager. While off the pegboard, this sheet contains only a meaningless list of figures and numbered lines. But on the department manager's pegboard, it again shows the financial facts opposite the account titles. In this way, only authorized personnel are able to make use of the standing orders.

So, you see, we are unable to fill your request for a sample standing order. Our form is just an ordinary columnar sheet, perforated to fit a pegboard.

There must be some manufacturers in the area who use the kind of form you require. One suggestion would be to check with Ed Lambert at Hillside Machine. The address is:

> Mr. E. J. Lambert
> Hillside Machine & Tool Co.
> 9200 Airline Highway
> Waterloo, Iowa 50701

If there is some other way in which we can help you with your cost accounting project, please let us know.

> Sincerely yours,

The expressing of bad news in this situation is not considered to be a violation of positiveness. It is the main message of the letter and is justifiable if for no other reason than that. But there is an alternate approach that we can use in many instances. It is to stress positive values all the way through our letter, and to imply the main message by changing the subject at a strategic moment. Our reader gets the message clearly enough, but he does not have to see it spelled out. Our early words let him down gently, but not all the way to rock bottom; our later words bolster him psychologically. The program for such a letter omits the "Decline" portion and contains only the remaining four steps:

INDICATE FRIENDSHIP.

EXPLAIN CIRCUMSTANCES.

SUGGEST.

MAKE GOODWILL COUNTEROFFER.

If we can handle this technique competently, we can produce a letter that seems more pleasant to read. We must be certain that the circumstances provide us with something helpful to suggest and that we do not leave our reader confused about our answer. To illustrate how effective this approach can be, we shall now see it applied to the case shown in the preceding letter.

Dear Mr. Nelson:

We are flattered that you should think of us in connection with the modernizing of your cost accounting records.

From what you have explained, your most pressing need is for a sample form for a standing order of departmental expense. At Moreland Products we use a pegboard system for this purpose. The account titles are printed permanently on pegboards, along with the number of each line.

The accounting department enters the respective figures on a columnar sheet, which is then removed from the pegboard and sent to the department manager. While off the pegboard, this sheet contains only a meaningless list of figures and numbered lines. But on the department manager's pegboard, it again shows the financial facts opposite the account titles. In this way, only authorized personnel are able to make use of the standing orders. So, you see, our form is just an ordinary columnar sheet, perforated to fit a pegboard.

There must be some manufacturers in the area who use the kind of form you require. One suggestion would be to check with Ed Lambert at Hillside Machine. The address is:

> Mr. E. J. Lambert
> Hillside Machine & Tool Co.
> 9200 Airline Highway
> Waterloo, Iowa 50701

```
If there is some other way in which we can help you with your
cost accounting project, please let us know.

                    Sincerely yours,
```

This four-step letter makes no different statements from those of the five-step letter. The only adjustments were to drop out 12 words ". . . . we are unable to fill your request for a sample standing order") and to move the remnants of the third paragraph to the end of the second paragraph. The result is a letter that tells the reader "no" without using a negative construction.

SUMMARY

Most of our business letters will be either requests or replies to someone else's requests. The chances are, moreover, that many more will be replies than will be requests. At the moment, we are concerned with the simpler varieties of request letters (inquiries for information and requests for courtesies or aid) and the replies that such requests normally demand.

Requests may be of self-motivating or of favor-type varieties. The former are relatively easy to prepare, requiring principally that we be clear and complete about what we want. The latter usually are more difficult, because they impose some kind of burden on our reader. We need to provide motivation and assistance according to the needs of the given case.

Replies to request letters may convey either good news or bad news. A good-news reply is rather easy to write; it is naturally in tune with our reader's goodwill. A bad-news letter requires more planning and care, because our reader will experience a letdown and must be restored to a proper degree of good feeling. An implied turndown, if handled skillfully, can help keep unpleasantness out of a bad-news reply.

For ready reference, the letter types covered in this chapter are summarized on the next several pages.

INQUIRY FOR INFORMATION
(Self-Motivating)

Intended
Reader
Reaction:

from this   to this

Program: Request politely.
Explain (if helpful).
Assist (if needed).
Promise appreciation (if needed).

Pointers: Be courteous and persuasive—not blunt or demanding.

Be sure the request is clear and complete.

Give explanatory material if it will help the reader understand
or evaluate the request.

If assistance is needed—such as a special mailing address to
be used—be sure to provide it.

Consider a goodwill ending, even when it is not absolutely
needed. It provides a smooth finish to the letter.

INQUIRY FOR INFORMATION

(Favor-Type Subjective Questions)

Intended
Reader
Reaction:

from this   through this   to this

Program: Create interest.
Explain (as needed).
Specify.
Motivate.
Make action easy.

Pointers: Be tactful—avoid obvious flattery and apologetic expressions
as well as bluntness.

Use clear, specific questions only.

Arrange questions in a logical sequence.

Consider eye appeal:
Set off a single question by itself.
Number plural questions and place them in a list.

Motivate the reader by promising appreciation and whatever
else is appropriate: secrecy, publicity, reciprocity, reimbursement, etc.

Express appreciation as a future concept, but avoid the "it if"
construction.

Provide a return envelope.

INQUIRY FOR INFORMATION
(Favor-Type Objective Questions)

Intended
Reader
Reaction:

from this   through this   to this

Program: Create interest.
Explain (as needed).
Specify.
Motivate.
Make action easy.

Pointers: Be tactful—avoid obvious flattery and apologetic expressions
as well as bluntness.

Use clear, pinpointed questions.

Arrange the questions in a logical sequence and number them.

Use a footnote presentation for 1 to 3 objective questions; send
a duplicate of the letter.

Use a questionnaire for 4 to 10 objective questions; send a
courtesy copy. Be sure that the questionnaire is self-explanatory.

Motivate the reader by promising appreciation and whatever
else is appropriate: secrecy, publicity, reciprocity, reimbursement, etc.

Express appreciation as a future concept, but avoid the "it if"
construction.

Provide a return envelope.

REQUEST FOR ASSISTANCE
(Courtesies; Material Aid)

Intended
Reader
Reaction:

from this   through this   to this

Program: Create interest.
             Explain.
             Specify.
             Motivate.
             Assist (if possible).

Pointers: Create interest with an opening sentence that commands the
             reader's attention:
                 If requesting a courtesy, use a rhetorical question.
                 If requesting material aid, use either a rhetorical question
                    or a dramatic affirmative statement.

             Be positive and tactful—not apologetic, not blunt.

             Be sure the request is clear and complete.

             Motivate well. Promise appreciation; and
                 If requesting a courtesy also promise reciprocity, publicity,
                    etc.
                 If requesting material aid, promise publicity and sound an
                    appeal to altruism, pride, sympathy, etc.

             Provide assistance, if possible:
                 If requesting a courtesy, give necessary instructions.
                 If requesting material aid, send an address label, pledge
                    card, envelope, etc.

LETTER OF INTRODUCTION

Intended
Reader
Reaction:

from this   through this   to this

Program: Introduce.
            Explain purpose.
            Give personal data.
            Request.
            Assist (if applicable).
            Promise appreciation.

Pointers: Prefer to use the informal style; be formal only if necessary.

            Be clear and concise.

            Assist the reader with necessary instructions and/or helpful
            suggestions.

            Express appreciation as a future concept, but avoid the "it if"
            construction. Prefer to use a possessive construction, as in
            "I'll appreciate your showing Mr. Brown the storage facilities."

            If the letter is to be mailed, use conventional addressing.

            If the letter is to be carried, decide between the conventional
            method of addressing and one of the following:

ON THE ENVELOPE	A Letter of Introduction *or* Introducing Mr. John Flynn
IN THE LETTER	Introducing Mr. John Flynn: *or* To whom it may concern:

GOOD–NEWS REPLY
(Yes)

Intended
Reader
Reaction:

from this   to this

Program: Indicate yes.
Fill request.
Add extras (if helpful).
Make goodwill offer.

Pointers: In replying to a single question, fulfill the first two steps of the
program by opening letter with the answer.

Be sure that everything asked for is covered in the reply.

If extra information, instructions, suggestions, additional
sources of supply, and the like would be helpful, provide as
much of such material as possible.

The ending offer may be to help him again some time or simply
consist of a few kind words.

BAD–NEWS REPLY
(No [Expressed], But)

Intended
Reader
Reaction:

from this   through this   to this

Program: Indicate friendship.
Explain circumstances.
Decline.
Suggest (if possible).
Make goodwill counteroffer.

Pointers: At the start, make the reader feel that his request is welcome.

Give the explanation before the turndown.

Be sure the reason(s) are plausible. Do not state, "It's against our rules" or "policy" or "practice."

Express the turndown as a regret or inability—never as a blunt refusal.

Try to suggest an alternative—a different source of supply or a different approach.

End with a goodwill counteroffer to help at some other time and/or in some other way.

BAD–NEWS REPLY
(No [Implied], But)

Intended
Reader
Reaction:

from this   to this

Program: Indicate friendship.
Explain circumstances.
Suggest.
Make goodwill counteroffer.

Pointers: At the start, make the reader feel that his request is welcome.

Be sure the reason(s) are plausible. Do not state, ''It's against our rules'' or ''policy'' or ''practice.''

After explaining, change the topic quickly but smoothly to a helpful suggestion—such as a different source of information or aid, a different way of approaching the problem, and so on.

Make sure that the implied turndown is self-evident even though it is not spelled out.

End with a goodwill counteroffer to help some other time and/or in some other way.

QUESTIONS
· · · · · · · · · · ·

1. How is the output of business letters divided between single-purpose and multipurpose varieties?
2. What are the principal types of request letters?
3. Identify the ingredients needed when a request tends to encroach upon the reader's time and patience.
4. How does a rhetorical question differ from an ordinary question?
5. What technique is recommended when more than one question, subjective or objective, will be asked in a request for information?
6. What two further techniques can be applied to objective questions for easy answering by the reader?
7. State reasons for the enclosing of a *courtesy copy* of any questionnaire that might be used.
8. Suggest five possibilities for motivating a reader to fulfill a request for information.
9. List the essential criteria for a sensible and effective questionnaire.
10. Would a request for assistance vary much in program from a request for information?
11. What are the suggested steps in the program sequence for a letter of introduction?
12. Name the three basic kinds of answer letters.
13. In a breakdown of multipurpose answer letters (goodwill plus something else) into six types, how many would be good-news and how many bad-news?
14. Would it be a sound idea to regard an answer that spurns a request as being a "no" answer?
15. State the suggested program for an answer which conveys bad news by implication only.

PROBLEMS
· · · · · · · · · ·

Some of the following problems are to be answered in typewritten form on business letterhead; others, on plain stationery. If a letterhead is indicated but not available, set up a simulated letterhead in accordance with directions issued by your instructor.

9–1. (Letterhead.) Wilson J. Cassidy is the chairman of the Urban Development League in the city where you are employed. Cassidy is making plans to visit Miami, Florida. His purpose is to meet Metropolitan Dade County officials concerning the problems they have experienced since instituting the METRO form of local government some years ago. He has asked you, the secretary of the Commerce National Bank, to write a letter to Henry P. Crandon, a bank president with whom you are acquainted in Miami. He would like to be met at the airport; put up in a suitable, but not too expensive hotel; and placed in touch with the proper METRO officials. Write such a letter for him; be sure to include all necessary details.

9–2. (Letterhead.) Matthew Smith is the buyer of men's furnishings for the Midtown Department Store of this city. Recently he was injured in a traffic accident; he will be incapacitated for an indefinite period of time. The store has appointed Lamont Clark as temporary buyer, to serve until Smith is able to return to work. As merchandising manager of the store, write a letter of introduction for Clark. The letter is to be mailed to Mr. Clyde Hanover, the buyer of men's furnishings at the Manhattan Department Store, 500 Fifth Avenue, New York City. Mr. Hanover is a personal friend of Smith's; the two men always got together when Smith made a trip to New York. They often traded business ideas during these visits. In your letter, ask Mr. Hanover to help Clark carry on for Smith—specifically, to take him to the various suppliers and see that he meets the right people. It might be a good idea to give Mr. Hanover the latest report on Smith's progress.

9–3. (Letterhead.) The Bonnie Lass Candy Co., 1500 Briarslope Drive, Cleveland, Ohio 44131, ran an ad in *The Wall Street Journal* publicizing the business opportunity available in a dealership it plans to franchise in a downstate city. Of the applicants who have responded so far, only James V. Prescot has had lengthy experience in retail sales. He also appears to have the minimum amount of capital that The Bonnie Lass Candy Co. requires for investment. Prescot has furnished references and a certified statement of his financial condition. One of his references is the Householders Savings Association of his city. Assuming that you are the general manager of the candy company, write to this reference concerning Prescot. Ask several pertinent questions.

9–4. (Plain stationery.) Suppose that you have been appointed this year's picnic chairman for an orphanage which is the favorite charity of your lodge. Part of your job will be to appeal to various local firms for their help in donating free food items, confections, and soft drinks for the event. Write a request to the local bottler of a nationally known cola beverage. Play up the good to be achieved by such a donation, as well as the obvious public-relations aspect.

9–5. (Plain stationery.) Assume that you are a graduate student in marketing. You are preparing a paper dealing with new trends in the television market. Write a letter to the Midtown Department Store of this city. Request information concerning the numbers of black-and-white and color television receivers sold in each of the past five years. Explain that the answers will be kept confidential and will be used for classroom purposes only. Enclose a return-addressed envelope.

9–6. (Letterhead.) Paramount Builders, Inc. is a developer of real estate in this area. Its latest undertaking has been the erection of Paramount Plaza, a large suburban shopping center. Now that the tenants have moved into the various stores and offices, Paramount Builders, Inc. is planning to have an "official" opening of the center. There is to be a celebration ceremony at noon of the 15th of next month. In the evening there will be a dinner for the tenants and their wives and for a number of civic dignitaries. As owner-president of Paramount Builders, Inc., write a request to Chester W. Addams, the mayor of the suburb in which the center is located. Ask him to attend the celebration ceremony and to be guest speaker at the dinner.

9–7. (Letterhead.) The Tru-Mold Plastic Products Company of Indianapolis, Indiana, has received a request from a professor at a nearby college. The request asks for 50 copies of the company's annual report for last year; the explanation is that they would be distributed to the students enrolled in a course in financial analysis. It so happens that one of Tru-Mold's public-relations activities is to send copies of its annual report to all stockholders and employees of the company, to all public officials in the state, and to many other people on a special mailing list. Also, it prints several thousand extra copies to take care of requests from schools and other organizations. Thus, the company will gladly honor the professor's request. As the firm's director of public relations, write a letter to that effect and include whatever else that might be helpful information to the professor.

9–8. (Letterhead.) Assume that you are the internal auditor for Central Industries, Incorporated, which has its main office in the capital of your state. Jerome Coughlin, a former bookkeeper at your company, has applied for a position as a junior accountant with Rutland and Beane, Certified Public Accountants. Coughlin gave Central Industries' name as a reference, and the accounting firm has written to you for work and character information. The letter was opened by mistake in the office of the general manager, but it has finally been forwarded to you. You remember Coughlin rather well. He worked under you from February 1, 1963, to March 31, 1966. He incurred no black marks on his record, was never absent from work, and never had any difficulties with his co-workers. He was reasonably competent; in fact, you would have been happy to have him stay on your staff. He left for what he thought would be a better opportunity —a position in the trust department of the Interior National Bank. Write a favorable letter on Coughlin's behalf.

9–9. (Letterhead.) A private investigator, who is working for a lawyer in another city, has written an inquiry letter to the Best Manufacturing Company of this city. He is trying to trace a certain Alvin Corley, who owes the attorney's client, State Jewelry, Inc., $75 for a watch he bought six months ago. Rumor has it that Corley is working in this city as a machinist, possibly at the Best Manufacturing Company. As personnel manager, you have looked into the matter. There *is* a man named Alvin Corley working in your company's machine shop. His social security number is 295-07-0408. He listed his age as 48 and his address as 813 Westbrook Road in this city. Answer the investigator; give him all the information that you have.

9–10. (Letterhead.) The Bonnie Lass Candy Co., 1500 Briarslope Drive, Cleveland, Ohio 44131, has received an interesting letter from the Midwest Novelty Co., 454 Taft Street, Cincinnati, Ohio. Thomas Blesing, their sales manager, writes that they specialize in costumed dolls representing the major countries of the world. Desirous now of expanding their production, they are contacting firms which have symbols that could be characterized through dolls. They are interested in making "Bonnie Lass" dolls which the candy company could sell at its retail stores. These dolls would capture the facial likeness of the current Bonnie Lass symbol and would be costumed in kilts. Blesing believes that a large number of young girls would persuade their mothers to buy such dolls. Taken home, the dolls would become constant, subtle reminders of Bonnie Lass candies. As sales manager for Bonnie Lass, write an answer letter to Blesing. Show interest; request that a representative be sent out to discuss the matter in greater detail.

9–11. (Letterhead.) Assume that you are the general manager of the Tru-Mold Plastic Products Company of Indianapolis, Indiana. You have just received a request from Professor Hermine Holdan, head of the business education department at a women's college located about 20 miles from your company's plant. Professor Holdan would like to bring a group of some 40 girls for a tour of the plant. It seems that she arranges a monthly field trip for her students so that they can see firsthand the operations of a variety of industrial firms. This would be their first glimpse of plastic manufacturing. Turn down Professor Holdan's request. We have never before conducted tours of our plant, and are not prepared to handle groups of visitors. Also, some of the processes require extremely high temperatures; even seasoned workers have been known to complain about the heat.

9–12. (Letterhead.) A college student, Ambrose T. Milunis, has written an appeal to the president of Pioneer Catalogue Sales, Inc., which is located in your home town. Although he wants help in a research project, his own letter is not at all helpful. He has asked for "all the data you can send me on direct-mail selling." Realizing that he cannot honor such a vague request, the president has forwarded the letter to you, the sales manager. Write the necessary reply. If Milunis would ask for specific information, perhaps Pioneer could be of some assistance.

9–13. (Letterhead.) The Midtown Department Store of this city has received a request from a graduate student at the state university. This student is preparing a report in marketing and wants information concerning the numbers of television sets (both black-and-white and color) sold in each of the past five years. There is nothing in the company policy against giving out this kind of information. In this case, however, sales records have been kept in dollar amounts only. Actual units involved could be determined, but only upon an analysis of all purchase invoices and inventory figures for these years. The cost of such work, measured in money and time, would be prohibitive. Turn down the request, in your capacity as controller. If possible, suggest another source for obtaining such information.

9–14. (Letterhead.) Suppose that you are the vice president for sales of a local soft-drink bottling company. Your firm is franchised by a nationally known cola beverage to operate in this county. Your firm has received a request from the picnic chairman of an orphanage, asking that you donate 25 cases of soft drinks for this year's outing. Write an answer in which you refuse the request. Your policy forbids donations of this kind. If you were to give free soft drinks to one group, you would soon have to extend the practice to all groups.

9–15. (Letterhead.) National Vend-o-matic Corporation of New York City has made a proposal to The Bonnie Lass Candy Co., 1500 Briarslope Drive, Cleveland, Ohio 44131. National is planning a new venture wherein they would syndicate the vending machines in all the major truck stops through the nation. Each stop would use National's equipment and would offer the truckers the same variety of products: hot coffee (in all combinations), cold milk, cold orange juice, iced soft drinks, candy bars, cigarettes, and chewing gum. Earl P. Bransin, vice president of National Vend-o-matic Corporation, asks that Bonnie Lass put up a "twin pack" of fudge to be sold through his machines at a dime apiece. The fact is, however, that the high-quality ingredients in Bonnie Lass Fudge are too costly to make this proposal worthwhile. As sales manager for The Bonnie Lass Candy Co., write to Bransin and turn down the request.

CHAPTER 10

CREATING SALES BY LETTER

We have already seen that every business letter requires our attentiveness to goodwill and the inclusion of the right amount of persuasion to get our reader to accept our message. We are, in effect, transacting business through the medium of writing; and we need to maintain a good business relationship with our reader. It is easy to see, therefore, why a viewpoint has developed that regards every business letter as a sales letter.

In a more precise framework, we prefer to define a *sales letter* as one of many methods of direct-mail selling of a product (or service). It is in fact a very significant form of direct mail—the "package" of a sales letter, an illustrated leaflet or brochure, and a reply form being both popular and successful. In the larger field of advertising, direct mail in turn represents a specialized selling attempt directed to a selected group of prospects. It is often compared to the precise aim of a rifle as contrasted with the unselective aim of a shotgun. Furthermore, advertising itself is an important activator in the marketing process. Although some abuses and excesses have been ascribed to it, advertising keeps consumers informed of the wonders of our productive capacity; it serves to keep our overall economy healthy and on the move.

MANAGERIAL ASPECTS
· ·

A manager of advertising is faced with a number of decisions regarding the use of his budget appropriation. He must work out a priority system for the products that will be advertised. He must make preliminary decisions concerning available advertising media: newspapers, magazines, radio, television, billboards, direct mail, and so on. He must decide what kind of agency help is needed to handle the various media he selects.

Some of the available media are better than others for certain purposes: Radio nowadays is strong at the local level and enjoys a virtual monopoly among people traveling in automobiles. Television plays to a vast audience and has the advantage of both sight and sound appeals. A newspaper can reach thousands—even hundreds of thousands—of people daily. A magazine can reach millions on a general basis—or thousands on a specialized basis. Billboards have a much smaller audience, but command attention and achieve emphasis by remaining on the scene for extended periods of time. Yet, for the most part, these media are rather typical of the "shotgun" approach to advertising. Even though the cost of such advertising may be small when divided among the numbers of prospects it reaches, much of it may be wasted on huge numbers of nonprospects. The same charge can be leveled at some types of direct-mail advertising, too—especially those which are sent out unselectively, such as to "Occupant" or "Resident." But, when it uses a carefully selected list of prospects and a well-prepared package, direct mail can produce profitable results.

A decision to use direct mail as a method of advertising should be based on a study of costs and an estimate of orders needed to justify such costs. For example, let us suppose that we wished to use a sales-letter campaign to promote a product retailing at $5.00. Suppose also that it costs $3.00 a unit to produce this item. From a careful analysis, we have determined that the mailing pieces (letter, brochure, order-reply form, outside envelope, addressing, postage, etc.) will cost $90 a thousand. In terms of one thousand pieces mailed:

1. How many orders must we receive to break even on our costs?
2. What is this performance expressed as a response percentage?
3. Is such a response percentage considered attainable?
4. Suppose we were to use the arbitrary ratio of 3:1 as a performance

goal for the campaign—that is, $3.00 of sales brought in for each
$1.00 in advertising costs paid out. What would be the necessary
response percentage now?

5. Is this response percentage reasonably attainable?
6. If this goal were reached, what would be the profit realizable from
   1000 mailing pieces?
7. In light of desired profits, is this method of doing business sufficiently
   attractive to be used?

Needless to say, the answers to these questions should hold forth
promise of success if we are to be justified in launching a sales-letter
advertising campaign. Under the conditions described, the answers
would be as follows.

1. The break-even point is simply the amount of sales needed to
produce a margin large enough to cover the expenses of the sales campaign. This figure can be determined in two steps: (a) dividing the cost
of 1000 mailing pieces by the amount of margin for one unit of product,
and (b) multiplying this figure by the sales price of one unit of product.

$$\text{(a) Break-even volume} \quad \frac{\text{Advertising cost per M}}{\text{Margin per unit}}$$
$$= \$90.00 \div \$2.00$$
$$= 45 \text{ units of product}$$
$$\text{(b) Break-even point} \quad = 45 \times \$5.00$$
$$= \$225.00$$

Proof:

Sales	$225.00
Less: Product costs	
(45 × $3.00)	135.00
Margin	$ 90.00
Less: Advertising costs	90.00
Net profit	–0–

2. In terms of response to the mailing, we should need 45 orders
from each 1000 letters mailed—or a response of 4.5 percent.

3. A response percentage of this size is to be considered attainable,
although by traditional standards it would be an above-average performance. But, at this point, no profit will have been earned, only the
break-even point will have been reached. It should become obvious to
us that, as postage, printing, addressing, and other costs rise, products
of a low price structure will require a greater and greater response percentage. In some cases, the challenge may become too great to overcome.

4. Since a company is in business to earn a profit, not merely to break even, it must be able to realize more than 45 orders under the conditions being discussed here. Often, a target ratio is established between dollars of sales generated and dollars of advertising cost expended. Such a ratio serves as a focal point for measuring the overall success of the campaign after the actual results are known. If a ratio of 3:1 were used:

1 . . . would be the $90 of cost for 1000 mailing pieces
3 . . . would be $270 of sales needed ($90 × 3)
Units sold would have to be 54 ($270 ÷ $5)
And, the response percentage would be 5.4 percent (54 ÷ 1000)

5. This higher response percentage is still within the realm of attainability. The challenge has grown stiffer, however; now 54 orders are needed from the 1000 pieces mailed—45 just to break even, and 9 additional to reach the pre-set goal.

6. The net income would be measured as follows.

Sales	$270.00
Less: Product costs	162.00
Margin	108.00
Less: Advertising costs	90.00
Net profit	$ 18.00

7. Our big managerial decision now comes to a head. How do we regard a net profit of $18 on sales of $270? If being able to retain 6.67 percent of our sales dollar (before taxes) is adequate, we can get it by this method of selling. If we want a larger percentage, and cannot confidently raise our 3:1 ratio (which already demands a 5.4 percent response), we should investigate other media in search of a satisfactory answer.

THE CHALLENGE OF SALES LETTERS

In our present sphere of interest, we are confronted with the problems arising once the decision to send a sales letter has been made. So complex is the process of turning out the sales letter package, that we probably face the ultimate challenge in letter writing when we take on this work. We are required to give exhaustive attention to all of the many details that can be involved in letter writing—before, during, and after the actual composition work.

We must conduct thorough research, leading to a comprehensive understanding of both the product and the prospective customers. We must match an appropriate quality possessed by the product against a timely need of these prospective customers. We need to present a vivid, positive sales message to get and hold interest, to create desire, to persuade our reader to follow through by placing an order. We need to check out our composition to be sure that it is complete, well assembled, readable, and capable of inducing action. We then must attend to the full mailing package, including typography, design, choice of colors, illustrations, and enclosures.

Because sales letters are in a special category apart from "correspondence," few of us will actually have to do much writing of this kind. But a study of this type of letter, plus some experimental practice, can be of significant value to us. For one thing, by measuring up to the superior challenge involved in writing a sales appeal, we should find that other request letters become relatively easy to write. For another thing, as we become familiar with the requirements of sales-letter writing, we can make sound appraisals of the service performed for us by professional agencies. Moreover, knowledge often leads to opportunity; we may be able to capitalize on our knowledge of sales letters in a number of practical applications, and thereby enjoy an advantage over someone less prepared.

PRODUCING A SALES LETTER

In adjusting to the preparatory stages of producing a sales letter, we can easily identify the underlying situation as that of a request. We are, therefore, alerted to the basic requirements of all request situations— that there be a clear, definite request; appropriate motivating power to obtain a favorable response; and ample assistance to make action easy for our reader. Everything else that happens to enter into consideration because of the specific sales situation—such as eye appeal, devices for gaining and holding interest, building of desire, and the like—must be considered to be over and above these basic elements. No matter how elaborate we make our superstructure, we cannot produce a truly effective sales letter if we omit one or more of the basic requirements.

GATHERING THE FACTS

The gathering of facts for use in writing a sales letter is somewhat different from that for ordinary letters. We are neither answering a reader's request nor simply creating goodwill. Instead, we are originating a request of our own; yet we are not seeking information for other uses or favors of some kind from a sympathetic reader. We are attempting to market our product (or service) by direct mail to a prospect. Thus, we must inform ourselves fully about what we are trying to sell and the people who will receive our letter.

Product Research

It stands to reason that the more we know about the thing we are trying to sell, the better equipped we are to select a sales appeal that will be effective with our prospects. In our sales appeal we must tell about our product descriptively and also functionally.

Through the descriptive part, we treat of what the product is like: size, shape, color, design, and other physical qualities. Such information helps our prospect get a mental picture of what is being offered to him. It is an important part of the sales presentation, but it is not so meaningful to our prospect as the functional explanation, which states what our product will do for him. Neither part alone is able to carry the full message; both are needed, with each giving meaning to the other.

There are three general resource areas available to us for gathering facts for possible use in a sales letter. These are the product itself, in its ready-to-use state; the process of manufacture; and the materials that go into the fabrication of the product. Usually, the product itself provides the most useful information; but this fact does not rule out the other areas. Sometimes a unique appeal can be developed from something taken from these other areas, and often secondary or reinforcing data can be cited to clinch an appeal taken from the product area.

Examples of useful information which we can obtain from a study of the finished product are appearance, shape, size, unique features, variety of styles or models, durability, capabilities, observed performance, price range, and the like. From an investigation of the manufacturing operations we may be able to compile such information as the location and type of plant, the production phases, the kinds of equipment used, the skills required, patents involved, sanitation, safety precautions, number and kinds of inspection, and packaging. By researching as far back as the materials from which the product is made, we may be able to get valuable facts on the variety used, the sources of supply, the methods used to obtain them, transportation used, and the like. Although some steps removed from the product itself, this kind of information can be useful in gaining understanding, in promoting confidence, and in developing an interesting presentation.

Prospect Research

Before we can make a satisfactory decision on selecting an aspect of the product to describe and explain to our prospect, we need to know quite a bit about him. Most often, our prospect is a member of a group of similar persons whose names have been compiled into a mailing list. Such lists are discriminating in nature; they are put together on the basis of a definite common denominator. Thus, we find lists comprised of accountants, of college graduates, of doctors, of homemakers, of lawyers, of purchasing agents, of retirees, of sportsmen, and so on. Some such lists can be purchased from firms that specialize in producing them for mass mailers. And, of course, we should have a list of our own customers—people who have already been cultivated by us and who often are good prospects for repeat business.

"BE THE FIRST TO TRY OUR NEW DIAPER SERVICE!"

Other lists may be rented. For example, a professional society or a college might possess a selective mailing list which the administrators would be unwilling to sell to mass mailers for unlimited use. They might, however, agree to an occasional use of the list. For a fee, they might take over the physical mailing operation for the mailer. They would address and mail the sales "packages" provided by the mailer and thereby maintain control of their list.

Once we have selected the mailing list that will be used in a given effort, we should learn all we can about the typical individual representative of the list. We need to know the role he will play—whether he is the actual user of our product (or service) or is the buyer or purchasing agent of that user. We must especially acquaint ourselves with his probable background, his likes and dislikes, and his needs with regard to what we are trying to sell. Such information will help us narrow down to the few best pairings of qualities of our product with the needs of our typical prospect. It will also help us reach decisions about our overall approach, style, reading level, motivation effort, and the like. We will send our letter to everyone on the selected list. But in it, we should appear to be writing especially to each reader. Hence, we must be thorough in our search for effective common denominators.

CONSTRUCTING A PROGRAM

As a preparatory step before developing a program for a sales letter, we must make our final selection of the approach to be used. Timeliness —that is, appropriate regard for the buying season involved—enters the picture here, and is often a determining factor.

Overall Theme

Coupled with our selection of the best approach is our deciding upon a theme which will prevail throughout our sales letter. Such a theme can be related to the matched-up consumer need we have selected as our main selling point, or it can be somewhat independent. By having a theme we coordinate the various steps of our letter for the purposes of maintaining interest, sticking to a consistent viewpoint, and producing a smooth flow of thought. For example, if an "economy" theme is used, references to economy and related terminology will appear as opportune points, not merely in a somewhat isolated section of the letter. The same would hold true of themes embracing status, comfort, security, and so on. On the other hand, we may choose a theme simply for effect. Some examples of these independent themes are a humorous style, a dialect (such as an Irish brogue), an activity (such as baseball, fishing, motoring, and so on), a fictional or comic-strip personality (Peter Rabbit, Alice in Wonderland, Happy Hooligan, etc.), and a slanted vocabulary.

The Traditional Viewpoint

Once we have settled on the overall approach and theme, we are ready to set up a program to guide the actual writing of the sales letter. In this respect we might note that the literature of sales writing contains an abundance of material on planning a sales letter. In essence, the authors of journal articles and textbooks are in agreement as to the ingredients of such a letter. By far the most famous of all recommended plans is the one known as AIDA. These initials represent the words Attention, Interest, Desire, and Action, and they have a memory-helping association with the name of the opera *Aida*. The reference is a way of saying that a sales letter may be considered as comprising four elements or stages. In effect, such elements or stages are like the steps of a program, which would take shape along the following lines:

A—GET ATTENTION.
I—CREATE INTEREST.
D—IMPLANT DESIRE.
A—CALL FOR ACTION.

This four-part breakdown of the structure of a sales letter is adequate for use by the professionals. It is their accustomed way of looking

"THEY MAKE A GREAT
COMBINATION."

at the problem. It serves them well whether they are writing a sales letter or discussing the subject with their peers. But to the ordinary person trying to understand exactly what he must do in a sales letter, this analysis leaves much to be desired. For one thing, it tends to mislead a would-be writer into supposing that there should be separate compartments in his letter for each of these four stages, instead of the smooth, coordinated flow that is really desired. For another thing, these stages are presented as simple points, whereas in reality they are complicated. They leave too much unsaid for safe use by an ordinary person or beginner in the field. The instruction, "implant desire," for example, does not begin to cover the things that have to be done in this stage of the letter. The statement is akin to many another unhelpful bit of advice— e.g., "You'd better strike this batter out."

Attempts at Improvement

Some efforts have been made by various textbook authors to remedy the shortcomings of the AIDA approach. As we might expect, rewording and reshuffling has accompanied these efforts; and a limited amount of clarification has resulted. Strangely enough, practically all of these revisions have ended up with the same number of stages as the AIDA plan, although not necessarily the identical ones. The reason for this occurrence is not readily seen. It could be that the original four steps have had their influence on the decision regarding the number to be stated. Or, possibly, a desire to have a minimum number has resulted in holding the steps down to four.

Whatever the explanation, our current sales-letter literature contains several statements on the handling of this type of letter. In the following chart we compare five representative models, including the AIDA plan. Each plan contains four steps; but these are not uniformly the same nor are they expressed in exactly the same terminology. Each would be clear, however, to an expert in the field.

The table shown on p. 301 is significant; its information leads us to an interesting conclusion. We see that three of the stages (interest, desire, and action) are common to all five of the letter plans. Plans which use *interest* (I) as their first stage really imply the concept of attention with it. Plans which use the concept of *desire* (D) as their stage necessarily include the concept of proof. And, plans which do not

Stages of a Sales Letter	Symbols			
1. Attention, Interest, Desire, Action	A I D			A
2. Interest, Conviction*, Proof, Action	I D P			A
3. Interest, Desire, Conviction†, Action	I D P			A
4. Interest, Desire, Proof, Action	I D P			A
5. Interest, Desire, Motivation, Action	I D		M	A
Stages common to all phases	I D			A

* Intended to mean "Desire."   † Intended to mean "Proof."

mention motivation actually embrace it in their *action* (A) stage. Our logical conclusion is that a sales letter, reduced to its minimum number of stages, would consist merely of:

I—create Interest.
D—implant Desire.
A—call for Action.

A Workable Program

From our point of view, the program or working outline of a sales letter is not to be governed by a minimum number of stages, a traditional number of steps, or even the spelling of the name of a famous opera. Nor is it to be chiefly meaningful to professional writers in the direct-mail field. We need a guide that will help us include all that is required and put us on the right track toward producing a polished, resultful sales letter.

With reference to the minimum sales-letter components we observed through our chart analysis above, we can expand each general component into its essential phases. "Create interest" (I) includes the need to get attention as well as create interest. "Implant desire" (D) contains three vital subdivisions: a description of the product, an explanation in terms of filling a selected need of the prospect, and some kind of proof to substantiate our allegations. "Action" (A), the third stage, actually embodies the entire basic set of requirements of a request letter: a definite request, motivation, and ample assistance. But it is not at all certain that an ordinary person would instinctively recognize all of these needs when his writing program has been pared down to three or four general stages. Therefore, we do better to spell out all of the requirements in a fully developed, eight-step program. Such a program is presented below.

I $\begin{cases} \text{ATTRACT ATTENTION.} \\ \text{CREATE INTEREST.} \end{cases}$

D $\begin{cases} \text{DESCRIBE THE PRODUCT (OR SERVICE).} \\ \text{EXPLAIN (MEET THE SELECTED NEED).} \\ \text{OFFER PROOF.} \end{cases}$

A $\begin{cases} \text{SPECIFY ACTION.} \\ \text{MOTIVATE PROMPT ACTION.} \\ \text{MAKE ACTION EASY.} \end{cases}$

This eight-step program is more realistic than any of the shorter models. By giving separate identity to each component of the sales letter, we lessen the chances that something important might be overlooked. Also, we increase the number of gradations between the beginning and the end of the letter, and thereby tend to have a smoother transition from step to step. Nevertheless, we should be fully informed as to the meaning of each step and the variables involved. The following analyses bring out such considerations:

1. *Attract attention.* The first job of our sales letter is to command the attention of the reader—that is, to arouse a sufficient amount of curiosity to get him to read at least the beginning of the message. Curiosity is aroused if the reader is made to ask himself, "Now, what's *this* all about?" The only possible way for him to arrive at an answer is, of course, to read some of what we have written in our sales letter.

Our method of getting the reader's attention may be anything ranging from a novel (unusual) opening statement all the way to a three-dimensional device (called a gadget) attached to the top of the letter. Most often, the attention-getter will incorporate an amount of eye appeal along with some attractive wording. Some of the possibilities are:

a) A stirring or novel statement in color or boldface type, as the opening words of the letter.

b) A similar statement, in color or boldface type, set up to resemble the form used for an inside address in ordinary correspondence.

c) A banner or headline, in large type and probably in color, running across the page above the text of the letter.

d) A similar banner or headline, printed above and at an angle to the text of the letter.

e) An illustration of some kind—photograph, drawing, sketch, cartoon, etc.—printed above the text matter.

f) A gadget—such as a coin, plastic device, button, stamp, feather, cartoon, etc.—attached to the paper.

g) A combination of two or more of these ideas.

Whatever wording accompanies—or comprises—our attention-getting step should, of course, be worthy of the prominent position we are assigning to it. It should be positive, agreeable, and inviting to our reader.

"IT'S EYE-CATCHING, BUT WILL IT SELL WIDGETS?"

2. *Create interest.* Despite all of its sparkle, our attention-getting device cannot be depended upon to provide more than a momentary effect on our reader. It can ignite a spark, so to speak, but it does not really enkindle interest. It is necessary that we act quickly to see that our reader does experience a surge of interest before the initial spark dies out.

Possibly we have already introduced our central theme in the course of attracting attention. If not, certainly now is a good opportunity for us to do so. In any case, we should proceed along the lines of continuing or clarifying our attention-getting step. We should be sure to "tie in" that step—to form a connection or bridge—with the sales message that is to come.

Because we have aroused our reader's curiosity, we should begin to satisfy it, to answer his question, "What is *this* all about?" Needless to say, the more unusual our attention-getting device, the more intently will our reader be looking for a possible "connection." A gadget, for example, has a high potential for attracting attention; but interest will not be achieved if our early statements in the letter do not put it to use. The purpose of the gadget is to lead our reader down a carefully laid-out path; it is not an end in itself.

Thus, by using our attention-getting device as a lead, by giving it a tied-in meaning, and by introducing our overall theme, we have a reasonable chance of securing the reader's interest. To maintain it throughout the letter is still another challenge. It can be met by effective description and explanation of the product, by imaginative handling of the main selling point involved, by keeping the theme alive, and by various visual techniques (which will be discussed later in this chapter).

3. *Describe the product.*   We are now set up to deliver the main body of our sales message. One portion of this message should cover the physical, external, and objective characteristics of our product (or service). Our reader should be given a reasonable description of what we are offering him so that he can appreciate, or at least comprehend, the explanatory material when we begin to present it. He should have a clear picture of the nature of the product; the brand name; the available models; and such particulars as size, shape, color, style, design, attachments, and the like.

4. *Explain value to reader.*   Creating a desire on the part of the reader for our product is the joint mission of our description and explanation steps. Both steps are needed, but explanation is decidedly the more important of the two. Our descriptive part lays the ground work, but it is our explanation which translates our product into terms of value to our reader. Our particular effort in this step is, of course, to press firmly and positively on our central selling point—that quality of our product which fills a specific, timely need we have found to exist on the part of our reader. We emphasize how what we are selling will fill his need or solve his problem—that is, what it will do for *him*. From our

viewpoint, we are supplying our reader with a reason why he should obtain our product. We have begun to instill motivation, a prime requirement of all request letters.

5. *Offer proof.*   Although our description and explanation steps may be interesting and enticing, we should not consider that we have implanted desire by our words alone. Too often, products do not live up to the high-sounding sales presentations prepared about them. Consequently, a large number of our readers may remain skeptical rather than convinced by what we have stated. Can they be made to put more faith in what they have read?

An affirmative answer to this question is possible, but it must be brought about by the introduction of some form of proof. If we can show effectively that our statements are believable, we have advanced to the point of having eliminated distrust as a factor entering our reader's final decision with regard to action. Thus, we should make a deliberate effort to convince him that the information we have given him is reliable. We can offer evidence that constitutes real proof (such as independent laboratory tests, performance records, endorsements, and testimonials). Or we can offer something more suggestive than real, but nonetheless effective (such as guarantees, samples, and free trials). Above all, we should make a definite point of whatever proof we offer, so that it will register properly with our reader. It is not enough to cover it casually, as an almost invisible clause in one of our sentences.

6. *Specify action.*   From the very beginning of the sales effort, we probably have had a good notion of how the marketing aspects of ordering and delivering the product were to be accomplished. Not always will we expect our readers to buy by mail, because some products cannot be handled that way, even though the advertising can. For example, the action desired might be for the reader to come to our place of business. It is conceivable that telephone ordering might be stressed— if for no other reason than to introduce customers to that possibility for placing hurry-up orders. Sometimes, we ask readers to respond by mail, but not actually to place orders. We might offer to send a sales representative, someone who is able to demonstrate how our product can be applied to their operations. Or, we might ask our readers to send for a booklet, catalogue, or "full details." In such a case our sales letter may

be a device for simplifying our mailing list to the most interested prospects, in anticipation of other appeals to be made later on.

In any event, we should know exactly what we want our reader to do; and we should ask him precisely for that action. The method used will depend somewhat on the aggressiveness of our letter up to this point. Probably the best phrasing is that of a command, because it is positive and stirring. If the buildup has been mild (the soft-sell approach), a suggestion or question can be appropriate. But these variations would appear timid or lacking in confidence if they were to be used with a hard-sell approach.

Furthermore, we should in any one letter call for just one course of action. People traditionally dislike making decisions. It is bad enough that they are faced with a basic decision about our product (buy or not buy). We should not befuddle them by tossing in extra decisions concerning *how* they might best go about buying after deciding to do so. We should call for a direct mail order, or a visit to our store, or a telephone order—but not for a choice among these possibilities. Such a choice invites the reader to put off action instead of taking action. It is possible, therefore, that he will forget to act, change his mind, or even be intercepted by an aggressive competitor—none of which spells success for us. Thus, if there is but one course of action possible, the decision to buy just about sews it up.

7. *Motivate prompt action.*   Earlier in our letter we moved through three stages of our program which, taken together, provided a certain amount of motivation for our reader. These stages were the description, the explanation, and the proof. In the sense of creating a desire for our product, they were intended to provide a convincing reason why our reader should buy our product. But, that is about all they could be expected to do. At the time we sound our call to action, there is need for a new kind of motivation—a reason for our reader to act at once or at least within a narrow time allowance. His desire will usually be at its highest pitch while our letter is still in his hands. Once he puts it down, a cooling-off phase begins to set in. The longer he waits before taking action, the less likely he is to take action. For a high measure of success, therefore, we should induce him to act as soon as possible.

Promotions carried on by sales letters have come up with a great number of methods for motivating the reader to act promptly. Among them are such inducements as introductory prices, a free trial period, a free trial sample accompanying the regular package, a combination offer at a price more attractive than the ordinary price, a "bonus" or premium added at no extra cost to the customer, a chance to get in on a "free shopping spree" or other type of "sweepstakes," and so on.

An important thing has been learned about such inducements, however. Without special handling on our part, they may amount to just so much additional information. They may intensify our reader's desire, but still there is no assurance that they will speed him up. Something else is needed if promptness is to be induced. So far the only things which have been truly effective along this line are a limit of time and/or a limit of supply. If our offer can incorporate one of these limitations, our note of urgency takes on a realistic meaning for our reader.

8. *Make action easy.* In addition to a definite call for action and an inducement to promptness, we should provide abundant help to our reader. The exact nature of this help will be governed by the kind of action we have called for. Part of this help may even be coupled with the call to action (as in "Place your order early—initial and mail the enclosed card *today*."). But, however we include the help, it should be adequate for the purpose. Our attitude should be that we have convinced our reader—or else he probably would not be reading this part of our letter. We should size up his situation and remove every conceivable obstacle that could be standing in his way. Sometimes financing the purchase is an obstacle, even when the price of the product is low; perhaps our reader does not have his checkbook handy. This obstacle can be removed by offering charge privileges, a payment plan, an option to send the payment with the order or to be billed later—whatever is appropriate. Other obstacles are more closely related to the kind of request we have made.

" JUST SIGN AND RETURN
BY CARRIER PIGEON "

A response by mail is made easy if we provide an addressed business reply envelope and a convenient order form. The less our reader has to put on this card, the better. Preferably, it will already contain his name and address and the wording that places his order. All that remains for him to do is to return it in the envelope with his check. Furthermore, if the other side of the order card is also a business reply device, our reader can simply validate the card with his signature or initials (thus exercising an option to be billed) and mail the card without the envelope.

A telephone order can be simplified in a number of ways. Although our telephone number may be somewhere in the letterhead we do well to state it for the reader's benefit following the request. We should size up the lack of confidence likely to be felt by the reader in trying to place his order by telephone. He will be reassured greatly if we add at least the extension number of the department that is set up to handle telephone orders. It would be even better if we could add the name of a competent person who is fully informed on this particular promotion.

A personal visit to our place of business is not always going to be easy. If our store is not a landmark in its own right, we should try to relate it to something that is. The address helps somewhat, of course, but it does not register with everyone. In fact, most people will not even know which side of the street we are on, unless we say something about it. If we are a large department store, the problem of which floor or area of the floor could discourage anyone who must shop in a hurry. We should analyze the entire situation to identify likely obstacles to action. Then, we should knock down at least the more significant ones by giving necessary instructions and playing up appropriate conveniences: special store hours, parking, public transportation, delivery services for large items, and so on.

SALES LETTER FORM

Behind the original decision to use a sales letter as the specific application of the direct-mail approach to selling is an understanding of what our reader rather expects to receive in his mail. If we were to mail him a flyer, a broadside, a brochure, or a leaflet—we would be neither showing much selectivity nor greeting our reader with what he is normally anticipating when he opens an envelope. Under varying circumstances, the element of surprise can be good or it can be bad—yet how is one to predict? We can sell nothing to our prospect if he tosses out our material because to him it seems to be just "another ad." But when he opens an envelope and sees a *letter,* he might give it a moment's attention because he rather expected that he would find a letter. That moment's attention is our opportunity to infiltrate his defenses.

Because a sales letter is usually a mass-produced document used in a large-scale mailing effort, it will have to be printed; thus it is necessary for us to make certain compromises on letter forms, although we should try to keep from deviating unnecessarily. Our letter will probably be dated; but the date ordinarily cannot safely be narrowed down to a precise day. More likely it will embrace a whole month (March, 1968) or a season (Fall, 1967).

While the text of our letter is individualized for the reader (insofar as he typifies his selected group), it is rare that we can do much to personalize our letter. Accordingly, we usually find it impractical to have an inside address—or even a personal salutation—in a sales letter. Instead, we resort to something that will attract attention and follow with a general salutation, such as "Dear Doctor," "Dear Homemaker," "Dear Reader," and so on.

When we speak in terms of maintaining interest in a letter, we normally think in terms of the composition. In a sales letter, however, we do not rely solely on words to do this job. Eye appeal is readily available to supplement the text matter as regards interest. Three frequently used forms of eye appeal are as follows:

1. *Layout.* We can vary the widths of the margins and change the styling used for different paragraphs (some blocked, some indented, etc.) The contrast between one paragraph and the one that follows it is noticeable—but not readily explainable. Our reader's curiosity is again aroused ("Now, what is *this* all about?") as he ends the one paragraph, and he is enticed to look into the next one. Then our copy can take hold until he reaches the end of that paragraph, where the cycle is repeated.

2. *Special printing.* Another approach we can use is to vary the details of the printing. A different color of ink, underlining, boldface type, capital letters, and extra-large letters are attention getters and, therefore, devices for keeping our prospect reading.

3. *Marginal signs.* There is also the possibility of our placing such marks as stars, pointing fingers, arrows, and brackets in the margin of

our letter to draw particular attention to the key points involved. Not only can this technique keep the reader going, but it can help us put our message across to people who are too much in a hurry to read our letter in full or with attentiveness. Such a reader is provided with a guide to the key statements of the letter and can by "skip-reading" extract enough to know what is afoot. He is always free to read the letter more carefully if it holds forth some promise to him.

Most of the other parts of the sales letter are present in order to maintain the semblance of a regular piece of correspondence. They may not actually be more than window dressing in many cases. The complimentary close occupies the standard position for such a part, and is usually a friendly form—"Cordially yours," "Sincerely," and the like. Perhaps the company name is used, perhaps not. The supposed writer's name and position in the company are found in their ordinary places; and the longhand signature is usually printed in a blue or green ink to give it the appearance of authenticity. Typist's initials and enclosure references, if they appear, are strictly for the overall effect, however; they could not possibly perform their ordinary functions. All in all, a large number of slight deviations from regular form creep into a sales letter. But the outward appearance of the document is still recognizable as a letter.

ILLUSTRATIONS

From the foregoing discussions, we are able to appreciate the complexities of the sales letter. The program for such a letter is the most extensive we have seen; its eight steps must receive attention and must be blended together into a smooth-flowing, coordinated, cohesive presentation. Each of the steps provides for variability and is flexible as to the manner in which it may be handled. We have open to us an almost unlimited number of possibilities for putting together a sales letter. A few examples, representing somewhat different approaches, are presented below by way of illustration.

The following letter was sent out by a department store. It was accompanied by a multipage schedule of merchandise, showing the exact quantity offered for sale, the regular price, and the special price for the sale. The letter was addressed to the store's charge-account customers only; the specified action was a visit to the store.

Martin's Department Store

20 RUNNYMEDE CIRCLE, ST. PAUL, MINN. 55177

November, 1967

Dear Charge Customer:

We are both pleased and excited to invite you to a unique PRIVATE AFTER-HOURS SALE of top quality home furnishings at truly exceptional savings!

THE PLACE: MARTIN'S DEPARTMENT STORE

THE DATE: TUESDAY, NOVEMBER 23rd

THE TIME: 6:15 P.M. TO 10:00 P.M.

ENTRANCES: RUNNYMEDE CIRCLE AND PARKING LOT

Please note that this is a private, after-hours event! There will be no announcements in the newspapers and no merchandise will go on sale before 6:15 P.M. And, of course, prices will return to normal as of Wednesday morning. However, during this four-hour extravaganza you'll find a marvelous choice of everything you want and need for the home on our 2nd, 3rd, and 4th Floors. Included are furniture, floor coverings, draperies, curtains, lamps, china, glassware, gifts, silver, pictures, mirrors, linens and domestics, appliances, TV, stereos, radios, records, housewares, cameras, sporting goods, luggage, toys and other household wares. Some of these items are limited in quantity, as you'll note from the listing inside. Still hundreds of other items are not listed here, but you'll see them when you shop.

We suggest you make the most of these thrilling savings opportunities by using any of Martin's easy credit plans. And don't forget! This sale is on Tuesday, which means you get DOUBLE BONUS STAMPS to add even more to your savings!

This is the story and these are the savings. . . the rest is up to you! Plan now to make it a date and bring the whole family. You'll be glad you did!

Cordially yours,

Lloyd H. Selby

Lloyd H. Selby
President

P.S. Please bring this letter with you, as it is your ticket of admission.
Families are welcome! Friends will be admitted as your guests.
Free parking in our convenient lot behind the store.

This letter may have been unselective in approaching all the store's charge-account customers, but nevertheless it limited the sales opportunities to them and their guests. The products were diversified, but an appeal of savings, or economy, was used as a common denominator. The promise of double trading stamps was an added inducement in tune with this concept. Proof was seemingly covered through the listing of dependable name-brand products on the enclosed schedule.

The following sales letter was fashioned after a noticeably different pattern. It attempted to sell the reader on a single item—a subscription to a new publication. The mailing list obviously was selected so that it would include prospects more likely to be interested in the kind of magazine being promoted. The sales talk matched the content of the magazine with the need this type of person would have for keeping up with the latest developments in management planning and control. A direct mail order was called for, and the means of ordering were provided. A free trial offer was included as a "prove it to yourself" device.

Illustrated on p. 316 is a gadget-type sales letter. It used a plastic heart (in red), which was fastened to the sheet partially over a printed red heart, as a primary attention-getting device. This gadget also served to introduce the notion of a prevailing theme—that is, a tenuous relationship drawn between the symbol and the name of the product. The text of the letter gave a minimal sales talk about the product, because a number of models and styles were offered. An enclosed brochure, however, was to carry on with illustrations and detailed descriptions. The action specified was for the reader to place his order by mail, and a bonus incentive for doing so promptly was included. Apparently all parts needed for easy fulfillment of the request were included.

The use of a gadget in a sales letter is almost certain to take care of the problem of attracting attention. But in doing so, it may open up or intensify other problem areas. For example, the gadget should complement, not dominate the sales message. It would be unfortunate for our purposes if our gadget attracted too much attention to itself and kept our reader from receiving the full force of our message. Because our gadget is a relatively unusual attention-getting device, the problem of connection becomes intensified. It is necessary that we fill our reader in on this connection as early in the letter as possible lest he become annoyed at us for not coming to the point.

Management Planning
111 FIFTH AVENUE, NEW YORK, N.Y. 10003

Fall, 1967

A WORD ABOUT A NEW BUSINESS MAGAZINE

*

AN OPPORTUNITY FOR YOU TO EXAMINE IT

WITH NO OBLIGATION ON YOUR PART!

Dear Sir:

Your undoubted interest in the new developments and techniques of modern business planning -- particularly as affected by the "EDP revolution" -- can be served in a unique and very practical way by Management Planning.

In order that you may see this for yourself, we are offering to send you our current issue.

If you agree that Management Planning can make a valuable contribution to your work--both now and in the future--you can authorize us to send you the magazine regularly. Otherwise, we will stop right there and thank you for this chance to prove our point.

There is every reason to expect that you will profit from Management Planning. All you need do is consider the exciting advances that are being made in the development and application of EDP systems as a basis for successful business management.

It is becoming more and more evident that, if you are to serve top management as effectively as possible, you can no longer measure and communicate data in the traditional ways and come up with the kinds of facts, figures, and recommendations that are needed for sound business decisions.

(next page, please. . . .)

- 2 -

To meet the challenges of modern business, today's professional person--the accountant, business executive, or management expert--should have a highly special-ized knowledge of planning and controls, and also be familiar with the sophisticated approaches made possible by computer technology.

Management Planning will help you acquire this greater competence. It is a magazine for the seasoned professional. It is designed for readers who are generally familiar with the basics of EDP, systems design, and control techniques. (We have tried to be selective in our distribution of this announcement and believe that you qualify in this respect.)

Every month--twelve times each year--Management Planning will bring you a selection of articles in specialized areas of management systems and procedures. It will put you in touch with new and original thinking as well as with the practical experiences of leading management services specialists from the fields of public accounting, government, and industry.

The magazine will also cover, in a more basic way, important subjects in which you may feel the need to expand your knowledge and competence. On the strength of this expert coverage of such vitally important subject matter, it stands to reason that every accountant, every management consultant, and every executive who must provide management with the best possible information and tools for decision making and control can benefit from this important new publication.

We urge you, therefore, to let us send you the current issue of Management Planning for your appraisal. We will enter your subscription with the clear under-standing that you may cancel if you find the magazine does not fill an important need in your business and professional life.

If you like what you see, you will have an opportunity to continue receiving Management Planning regularly. Otherwise, you will owe us nothing.

Please initial and return the enclosed form soon, to get this month's issue. Open up for yourself the limitless new horizons of your professional future.

Sincerely,

Vincent R. Higgins

Vincent R. Higgins
Manager of Circulation

VH:ms

Moreover, the gadget should be of a pleasant and appealing nature —a matter which depends to a great extent on our readership. We might successfully use a plastic or rubber worm in a letter to male fishermen— but we ought not to consider it as a possibility to be used in a letter to housewives. In addition, our gadget should comply with safety precautions and with postal regulations; some things are mailable only under certain circumstances and others may be prohibited altogether. Another consideration would be the matter of physical handling of the gadget (fastening, letter folding, inserting, etc.) in a mass-production situation. Our gadget should lend itself to physical handling without causing confusion or loss of time.

Last, but not least, we must consider the economics of the gadget approach. The cost of the gadget will be multiplied by the size of the mailing. We should determine what increase this will have on the package cost of 1000 mailing pieces, calculate the response percentage needed to earn a reasonable profit, and estimate the likelihood of such a response being attained. Like everything else involved, our gadget is justified only if it is likely to improve the performance as measured in the profit column.

In these respects, the illustrated gadget seems to fulfill the necessary requirements. The "heart" gadget is a reasonably pleasant device, and its connection or tie-in was made almost immediately. As a wafer-thin piece of plastic, it should be easy enough to fasten to the sheet and process through the various remaining phases of handling. The cost of such a gadget would seem to be a very small addition to the overall cost of the direct-mail package.

For a final illustration, let us consider the fund-raising letter. This sales letter differs from the standard varieties to the extent that it does not promise our prospect a direct benefit in the form of a product or service. The reader is offered an opportunity to support a cause that is probably in the nature of a general benefit. His principal motives would be the chance to align himself with a worthy cause, demonstrate his altruistic or philanthropic leanings, or perhaps someday be able to qualify for the services of the particular establishment. The intangibility of such appeals at once limits us with regard to the range of possibilities in such areas of our letter as the building of interest, description and explanation, proof, and an inducement for prompt action.

The overall mailing package of a fund-raising letter may well be

EMPIRE IMPORTS, LTD.

510 MADISON AVENUE, NEW YORK, N.Y.   10022

Christmas, 1967

LET'S HAVE  A "Heart-to-Heart" TALK

Dear Sir:

   Yes, with the holiday season fast approaching, it would be a good idea to get ready.

   Let's have a heart-to-heart talk about your Christmas shopping and how we can help you with it. Many of the question marks on your shopping list will be solved when you look over our wide selection of dependable HEARTHSTONE cigarette lighters.

   HEARTHSTONE lighters are imported from the British Isles, where they have provided flame for milord's tobacco and milady's hearth as well as warmth in the hearts of thousands of satisfied users. Here indeed is a welcome Christmas gift. You may choose from 37 models, including both men's and women's styles--the newest of which is a gold-filled combination lighter and cigarette case, complete with an attractive leather cover. All of our models, with their postpaid prices, are illustrated in full color in the enclosed brochure. You will soon agree that there is a HEARTHSTONE lighter for every man and woman on your Christmas shopping list.

   And we mean everything that we say about our HEARTHSTONE lighters. You must be completely satisfied with the value, beauty, and performance of your HEARTH-STONE--or receive your full purchase price plus handling costs of returning. Ours is an unconditional guarantee of satisfaction.

   We have a bonus for you, too, if you act promptly! Your purchase will be monogrammed free of charge if we have your order by December 10.

   An order form and a postage free envelope are enclosed for your convenience. So--check your Christmas list and place your order early.

Sincerely,

Paul J. Ramsey

Paul J. Ramsey
Sales Manager

PJR:mb
Enclosures

"Heart to heart--let HEARTHSTONE be your heart-warming gift."

put together in the same manner as a regular, commercial promotion. It would include a letter, an illustrated brochure, a sign-up card (for bookkeeping purposes only in the case of an accompanying gift—or to serve as a pledge card, if the "pay later" option is preferred), and a business reply envelope.

Because of the nature of the promotion—it will probably involve a hospital, school, church, health foundation, or similar organization— the general tone of our letter will have to be relatively tame. Our flashy beginning will have to yield to something more dignified, but still sufficiently attractive. In the development of our sales presentation, we are somewhat confined to the following kind of pattern:

1. We should identify the problem as it shapes up now, and tell our reader what has been done and is already under way toward solving that problem. To get off to a good start, we should try to involve our reader, so that the problem is partly his as well as ours.

2. We next should tell our reader what things remain to be done and how we (the organization involved) intend to go about doing these things.

3. Finally, we should point out how our organization is basically prepared to tackle these remaining aspects of the problem— assuming, of course, that the necessary financial support (which we should state) can be provided.

Such a sales presentation is capable of appealing to a sizable number of potential supporters, whose names should be on our mailing list if we have been selective in compiling it. But this type of motivation is only an initial breakthrough. We must be able to add the necessary clinchers. One need is the element of proof, and the usual methods are not available to us in this situation. Almost our only recourse is to get across the point that we have widespread support among our constituency. Our hope is to instill in our reader a feeling of wanting to be a part of something successful—that is, to apply a bit of the so-called "band wagon" approach.

As in all requests, we should be careful to make it clear to our reader just what it is we expect him to do. We should suggest an amount to be given and provide all necessary instructions. In addition, as an attempt at inducing promptness, we should set a target date for returns. This deadline need not be hard and fast, but it should serve the purpose of combating the tendency many prospective contributors have of putting off and forgetting.

The fund-raising letter which appears on p. 319 conforms to this basic strategy.

CHECKING THE TOTAL PACKAGE

We shall have solved a large portion of the problems involved in a sales-letter situation by the time we have completed the drafting of our composition. There still remain some important details, however, including our testing for probable feedback, selection and design of enclosures, printing, addressing, envelope stuffing, and all the postal requirements of mailing. Some of these matters are strictly procedural; but others have a bearing on the planning and development of the parts that go to make up the mailing package. We do well to look for satisfactory answers to the full set of test questions applicable to letters.

1. *Will the prospect actually see our letter?* This question includes such points as proper addressing and postage, of course. But the chief consideration in practice is the prospect's attitude toward the external appeal of the package. We want to be sure that the prospect will at least open our letter, not discard it as soon as he identifies it with advertising. Thus our job is to get him inside no matter how prejudiced he might be—and it calls for starting our strategy on the envelope itself.

Several viewpoints are possible. One is that if third-class mail is made to resemble first-class mail, it will be more inviting to our prospect. Therefore, the prepaid postage may be indicated in a way that resembles actual stamps or at least metered mail. Sometimes precanceled stamps are used. Another approach is to have no return address, or at least not have it on the front of the envelope. The approach here is to create an air of curiosity or mystery which can be solved only by opening the envelope. Another is to use a tan-colored window envelope with the prospect's name showing through. This could be a bill, a bank statement, a check; regardless, the prospect is likely to investigate before he throws it away. Still another approach is to address the envelope in longhand to reduce the suggestion of mass production. One variation of this idea is to mail the hand-addressed letters, with real stamps affixed, from some

GREAT **L**AKES **U**NIVERSITY

100 COLLEGE PARKWAY, PORT HURON, MICHIGAN 48245

November 10, 1967

Dear Alumnus:

You can almost see the way it happened, along about noon on Homecoming Day.

The men, some young and some not so young, had begun to gather at the campus sundial. A few puffed on their cigars; others stood in groups of twos and threes as they took long, approving looks at the new face of our campus. As if by signal, they formed a circle around one other person--Alumni Secretary Bill Wilson--who was last to appear.

Then, falling in behind Mr. Wilson, the men walked across the leaf-covered lawn to a spot midway between the observatory and the faculty parking lot. Again they crowded around Mr. Wilson as he unrolled a large pen-and-ink drawing. Your alumni trustees were getting their first collective look at the architect's drawing of Great Lakes' new library.

Thus opened the alumni phase of our current development campaign-- a $7,500,000 project--to build a new home for our overcrowded library and to set up an endowment fund to assure a steady influx of reference material. Since then, the backing of leading Michigan businessmen, grants from educational foundations, and pledges from individual alumni have already accounted for $4,100,000 of our goal. A project so well begun deserves to succeed.

You, as an alumnus, can help assure this success by the end of the year. The alumni phase of the campaign must be counted on for $2,000,000. I am asking you to consider the need--as you yourself have come to know it--and help out with a contribution, say, of $100. Outside sources may still be tapped, but only if our own constituents are behind us.

The enclosed leaflet explains the library situation in full and our plan for taking care of it. The leaflet also shows the architect's drawing of the exterior and the proposed floor plans of the new building. You will agree that this will be a Great Lakes dream come true.

May I count on you for a check or a pledge--mailed postage-free in the envelope provided--by December 1? Let's hope that there will be another gathering at the sundial next spring, with a ground-breaking ceremony to follow.

Sincerely,

J. Maxwell Barber

J. Maxwell Barber
Chancellor

JMB/ms
Enclosures

foreign country. Rare is the person who can resist the temptation to see what is inside.

In general, however, mass mailers have come to recognize that prospects are hard to fool when it comes to the class of postage use. Rather than depend on such window dressings as those summarized above, they prefer to be frank about the class of mail, but resort to another device to get their prospects to look inside. They make use of an attention-getting statement printed on the envelope. Some examples are the following.

AIRMAIL REPLY REQUESTED

INVITATION ENCLOSED!

An Invitation and a FREE Gift . . .

CERTIFICATE ENCLOSED

U.S. COIN INSIDE

MONEY–SAVING COUPON ENCLOSED!

FOREIGN STAMP ENCLOSED

IMPORTANT: About Your Subscription

OPEN IMMEDIATELY!

You Have Been Selected by UNIVAC to Receive . . .

What Will YOU Do When the
Revenue Agent Audits YOUR
Tax Return?

Such a statement whets the prospect's curiosity but requires him to look inside the mailing piece for the "connection" or the full story.

2. *Will the prospect actually read our letter?*   Or, once he has opened it, will he merely shuffle through the sheets of paper and throw them away? Obviously, the attention we are able to command and the interest we can develop rapidly through our opening words hold the key to the answer here. Attention, as we have already seen, combines

words and eye appeal (color, design, layout, typography); and the more unusual our approach, the greater is the need for a tie-in with the sales message. Once we have our prospect reading, however, we can keep him going by the use of well-slanted copy and well-placed eye catchers which tempt him to read on.

3. *Will the reader understand what we have written?* We have moved in the direction of a common ground for understanding by the careful selection of our mailing list and the matching of a quality of our product with a probable and timely need of the people on this list. But much more must be done before we can expect that our message will be easy to understand. We must, of course, use correct spelling and generally accepted grammar, sentence structure, and punctuation. We should encode our thoughts in words that are likely to be familiar to our readership. We should do a thorough job of clarifying all technical terms, and avoid using trade or professional jargon. In short, we should strive for accuracy of expression and adherence to a suitable readability level.

Such precautions will overcome the reader's tendency to bypass strange and difficult words and thereby miss out on the full meaning of our message.

4. *Will the reader believe our message?* The matter of belief is somewhat accentuated in a sales letter, because of our reader's defensive instinct to resist any assault on his pocketbook. Although our presentation may be registering with him, he still may be looking for a way out or a flaw to pick on. Our sales talk should be phrased in a believable manner, without exaggerations or sweeping statements which our reader would find incredible.

We have a ticklish job facing us here. At one and the same time we need to inspire our reader to buy, we need to sound believable, we need to attain a preestablished response from our sales letter, and we need to stay within the boundaries of governmental regulations and the ethical codes set by various groups. Even when we seem to have complied with all such requirements, our reader may experience the reaction, "Yes, it *sounds* good—but how can I be sure?" Therefore, we must include another ingredient—some form of proof—to overcome this kind of thinking.

5. *Will the reader be convinced by our message?*   In other words, will he conclude that he should go along with our offer or proposal? To be reasonably confident of a favorable answer, we should ascertain that all of our solutions to the above-mentioned questions are handled in a smooth, well-coordinated presentation. If one part of our letter leads easily and logically to the one which follows, and each part bears on the central selling point and theme, we have used a sensible sequence. If we have correctly singled out a timely need of our reader at the outset, the chances are that we have a meaningful message to give him.

6. *Will the reader act on our request?*   There is a difference between selling a prospect on the idea that our product is what he needs and getting him to buy it promptly. To be able to measure the effectiveness of a sales letter, we must have responses which can be traced back to it. For practical purposes, we must receive the reader's order on the form we sent him in our letter. If our prospect just eventually buys, we cannot be sure whether our letter or some other type of promotion should be given credit.

Our wrap-up of the sales message, therefore, should include a specific request (preferably a positive statement or command) related to a single method of performance. A date for action carries a suggestion of urgency, and should be included. We can make it especially effective by incorporating a time limit for the offer or a limit on the supply of the sales item. Then, we should provide for ease of compliance by our reader —so that ordering is almost as effortless as not ordering.

Naturally, we should give proper attention to the various enclosures which are to be used. Even when someone else is responsible for the brochure that might be included, we are still somewhat involved. Any references we make to the brochure in our letter must be consistent with the facts shown in the brochure. Another enclosure, the order form, should be sufficiently self-explanatory so that if it becomes separated from the rest of our material it will still be meaningful and useful to our prospect.

The preparation of a sales letter is a job that requires abundant research, sound basic decisions, careful planning, skillful writing, and attentiveness to many other details. Before it goes to press, we must give the copy a thorough check-out along the lines just discussed.

As for results, we must be satisfied with a percentage of the original mailing which might seem to be rather small. The reason is that there are still too many unknown factors involved for us to be able to count on a high response percentage. Some of the people on our list may not really belong there, in spite of the care with which the list was compiled. Some of the prospects may move away before our mailing is made. Others may already own the product we are trying to sell, or one similar to it. Still others may be sold in concept, but somehow keep putting off action or let it slip their mind. And there may be some people included who cannot be oriented to mail-order transactions, no matter what appeal we use.

In the final analysis, therefore, if our sales letter at least brings in our preestablished quota, we may rate it as a success. And not all persons who did not answer should be written off as a total loss. A surprising number may belong to the slow-moving categories—the stallers, the forgetters, and perhaps the resisters who were merely softened by our first approach. We should always be willing to give our mailing list more than a single try.

SOLICITED SALES LETTERS

Although most of us will not get the opportunity to prepare the type of sales letter described above, there are times when we may be called upon to demonstrate some degree of our sales-writing ability. One such occasion is that in which an interested person solicits information concerning our company's product or service.

In strict classification, our answer granting a request of this type can be regarded as a good-news basic reply letter. But that tag does not begin to describe the challenge that is involved. The inquirer in such a case is to be considered actually as a hotter prospect than any individual picked at random from our general mailing list. This person is clearly interested in what we have to offer, and he is coming to us for more information. Surely, we will welcome him, supply him with the information he desires, and do all we can to complete the sale.

The program for a good-news answer, as stated in Chapter 9, is:

INDICATE YES.

FILL REQUEST.

ADD EXTRAS (IF HELPFUL).

MAKE GOODWILL OFFER.

The third step, "Add extras," obviously becomes an essential (not optional) part of the response program. The situation has definitely taken on many sales-letter characteristics.

This point is illustrated in the following example.

Dear Mr. Lockwood:

Your inquiry concerning electric carving knives is well timed.

We have just placed on the market our new Ness 220, the ultimate utensil for your kitchen or dining room. Many new features have been included in this new model—our response to the suggestions passed along by users of introductory makes. These are:

1. <u>Variable</u> <u>speed</u> <u>regulator</u>—for light or heavy cutting jobs.

2. <u>Thickness</u> <u>controller</u>—for selective slicing of different kinds of meat: ham, roast beef, sirloin steak, turkey, etc.

3. <u>Two-notch</u> <u>blade</u> <u>channel</u>—for a quick and easy change from vertical to horizontal cutting.

4. <u>Perma-grip</u> <u>handle</u>—for a safe, sure grip by any size of hand.

5. <u>Choice</u> <u>of</u> <u>colors</u> (coral, gold, and ivory)—for easy matching with modern decorator tones.

Our Ness 220 electric carving knife is described in full in the illustrated leaflet I am enclosing. This model is popularly priced at $13.95 plus local taxes, if any. It is, of course, covered by our traditional money-back guarantee of satisfaction.

Your local dealer is Thomas Hardware, 1805 Pier Street. For a free demonstration—no strings attached—just drop in at the store and show this letter to Jim Thomas.

Sincerely yours,

SUMMARY
. . . .

A sales letter is one of the most elaborate types we can expect to find in the area of business letters. It belongs to the request category;

thus it requires the basic elements of a definite request, an inducement to action, and ample assistance to our reader so that he can perform that action. Because of its specialized nature, the sales letter thrusts upon us the full force of the many challenges that are possible in letter writing.

First of all we must decide upon the feasibility of using the sales letter for promotional purposes. We can use such a letter to make a direct-mail sale, to precipitate a telephone transaction, to induce a visit to our store, or to prompt a request for further information. But in each instance we must narrow down to the best approach and check out that approach for profit potential.

In the least number of terms, a sales letter may be regarded as consisting of three phases: developing interest, creating desire, and calling for action. To be useful, these phases must be broken down into

their significant parts—with the result that an eight-step program emerges and affords a better understanding of what should be contained in a sales letter. After composing our letter, we still face the task of putting together all the parts to be included in the overall mailing piece. These considerations include the outside envelope, the graphics, whatever brochure might be included, the order form, and the means of return mailing.

The structure of a sales letter is generally the same whether we are trying to sell a product or a service, or are trying to raise funds for some beneficial cause. On pages 326 and 327, in capsule form for ready reference, are guidelines applicable to a sales letter.

SALES LETTER

Intended
Reader
Reaction:

from this   through this   to this

Program: Attract attention.
Create interest.
Describe the product (or service).
Explain (meet the selected need).
Offer proof.
Specify action.
Motivate prompt action.
Make action easy.

Pointers: Consider an overprint on the envelope to spark the prospect's curiosity to see what is inside.

Be sure that the attention-getting device complements, but does not dominate, the message.

Be sure that the attention-getter is tied in with the sales message, and that this connection is made early.

Use typography, color, indentions, underlining, and other visual aids to supplement an interesting writing style.

In one letter have a central selling point. Let other advantages be subordinate to it.

Use a theme as a means of blending the various sections of the letter and thus attaining continuity as well as interest.

Use clear language—steer clear of technical terms and trade jargon.

Sound believable—that is, avoid exaggerations and outlandish assertions about the product or service.

Slant explanatory statements in terms of a definite benefit to the reader.

Decide on a course of action for the reader to take—and tell him (command preferred) what it is.

Don't confuse the reader by having several possible courses of action. He will be tempted to delay rather than act. Let the decision to buy coincide with the manner in which to place the order.

Sound a note of urgency; set a deadline for action. If possible, strengthen it by adding a time or quantity limitation.

Remove all possible obstacles standing in the way of action. Solve the payment problem. Provide all the means of responding if a mail order is called for. Give detailed instructions and helpful information (store hours, parking, department location, etc.) if a store visit is required. For a telephone response, consider all that the prospect must contend with. Give him the telephone number and the extension of the department telephone. Better still, add the name of the trained employee who handles such transactions.

QUESTIONS

1. Why would a cost study be needed before sending out a *sales letter* when such a study is not used with other varieties?
2. What is the general nature of the cost study made in connection with a proposed sales letter?
3. Why is it improbable that many businessmen will be called upon to write an actual sales letter?
4. What two general groups of facts need to be gathered before a solution to a sales letter problem can be pursued?
5. State the traditional four-point program for writing a sales letter.
6. What would be a theoretical sales letter program using only the barest minimum number of steps?

7. List the steps of a truly workable sales letter program—that is, one which spells out everything, leaving nothing to be assumed.

8. In the context of a sales letter, how should a *gadget* be defined?

9. Does the program step, "create interest," become more crucial or less crucial to a sales letter when an attractive gadget is used?

10. Which of the following steps is of greater importance to the *sales presentation* of a sales letter: description or explanation (of the product)?

11. What is meant by the concept of one *central selling theme* in any one sales letter?

12. In the call to action in a sales letter, what are the possibilities other than a direct order by return mail?

13. Point out variations from ordinary business letter form which may be necessary in the case of a sales letter.

14. How does a fund-raising letter fit into the general classification of sales letters?

15. Give the three elements contained in the basic strategy recommended for fund-raising letters.

16. Since most sales letters are recognizable as such even before the envelope is opened, how can the intended reader be enticed to look inside instead of discarding the letter unopened?

17. How can the call for action in a sales letter be made especially meaningful?

18. What influences often result in the response from a theoretically well-done sales letter being something less than excellent?

19. Define a *solicited sales letter*.

20. The outward appearance of the program for a solicited sales letter is the same as the program for what other type of letter?

PROBLEMS

Since the following cases deal with sales letters, the message involved will come *from* a company and move *to* a prospective customer. Although the ordinary expectation is that such letters will be prepared on letterhead stationery, there is always the possibility that something other than the customary letterhead might be used. Accordingly, before using letterhead (if available), simulated letterhead, or some other approach, check with your instructor for his specific instructions.

10–1. Assume that you are a staff writer in the advertising department of The Bonnie Lass Candy Co., 1500 Briarslope Drive, Cleveland, Ohio 44131. You have been assigned to write a sales letter to go out above the signature of the sales manager. This letter will go to all businessmen now on the mail-order lists. It will accompany an illustrated leaflet showing a special 1½-pound box of the company's creamy nut fudge and a similar box of assorted chocolates. This latter assortment includes butter creams, nuts, and fruits—all hand dipped in the highest-grade milk chocolate. The letter will seek to induce the businessmen to buy substantial quantities of these candies for their business gift-giving this Christmas. It will be mailed on November 10; the offer will be effective between November 15 and December 10. The candy will be specially priced at $1.95 for the fudge and $2.25 for the assorted chocolates. The purchaser may send a supply of his own shipping labels to The Bonnie Lass Candy Co. when he places his order. He is to provide a mailing list of the people who are to receive the gifts; if he desires, he may also provide an enclosure (such as a business card) to be packed with each box. The candy company will take care of direct mailing to the receivers of the gifts, but only the giver's labels and enclosures will be used. The offer is backed by a money-back guarantee of satisfaction.

10–2. The merchandising manager of the Midtown Department Store of this city wishes to contact the store's entire customer list for a special Christmas promotion. A sales letter will be mailed along with an enclosure illustrating a package known as a "Gourmet Tower." This is really a four-in-one package consisting of boxes of edible treats, each box of a different size and design. One box is wrapped in gold paper, one in green paper, another in striped red and white, and the fourth in white decorated with silver snowflakes. The boxes are stacked in a pyramid and are tied overall with a bright red ribbon. The pyramid cradles safely in a custom-made shipping carton. The contents of the respective boxes are fancy imported smoked cheeses, a chocolate cream torte, mixed salted nuts, and select hard candies. The price is $5.00, with a guarantee of money back in full if the customer is not satisfied. The recipient of the sales letter will be encouraged to buy one or more of these "Gourmet Towers" for use as gifts. However, mail order (either payment with the order or C.O.D.) is the only channel for this offer. The deadline for ordering will be December 16. As the store's chief ad writer, prepare the necessary sales letter. It will carry the signature of the store's sales manager.

10–3. Assume that you are the managing editor of the *Great Lakes Business Journal*. The *Journal* is a quarterly magazine published as a service of Great Lakes University (Port Huron, Michigan) to its alumni and students of business administration. It contains articles in such fields as accounting, economics, finance, general management, marketing, and personnel administration. Contributors include many of the university's own faculty members, as well as prominent businessmen and well-known professors from other leading colleges. The *Journal* has been favorably received since its inception six years ago. Now a campaign is to be launched to open the readership to the public, especially to businessmen in the Midwest. An annual subscription fee of $2.00, payable in advance, will be charged. Write a sales letter which can be used to solicit such subscriptions.

10–4. Pioneer Catalogue Sales, Inc., a mail-order house located in your home town, has acquired the exclusive rights to market a new product known as the "Porto-Pak." This is a zipper-fastened folder, made of soft, leather-grained plastic. Inside the folder are a standard, three-ring fastening device for loose-leaf paper and a hinged arm which can be turned under and behind the unit to convert it into a portable lectern. Formerly, the manufacturer tried to handle the marketing function himself; but the volume has grown so that he has decided to put the product on franchise to an established direct-mail handler. The retail price is to remain at $15.75, which apparently has been popular. Satisfied users include: Howard Burrows, sales manager of Watson Power Company ("The Porto-Pak is a great aid in our training of salesmen"); J. P. Hinckley, president of Universal Air Lines (". . . tremendous for conventions and meetings"); and Perry H. Andrews, independent manufacturers' representative ("It's just the thing for putting across a sales presentation"). Because it is too late for Pioneer Catalogue Sales, Inc. to list this item in its upcoming quarterly catalogue, a special sales letter will be mailed to all businessmen on the customer list. As chief ad writer for Pioneer, write an effective sales letter.

10–5. The Midtown Department Store of this city is planning to hold a sale of odd-lot merchandise. Such goods are to be found in all departments of the store, and include lamps, rugs, appliances, pieces of bolt cloth, hardware, furniture, jewelry, clothing, and the like. All goods are in first-class condition, but represent the tail end of merchandise purchased for last season. Now, with new shipments of goods on the way, the management wishes to dispose of all leftovers. The first day of the sale will not be announced to the general public. Instead, a sales letter will be sent to the store's charge-account customers so that they will have first choice of the many bargains available. Only then will the general public be invited by means of newspaper advertisements. As the store's merchandising manager, write the kind of sales letter that should be sent to the charge-account customers.

10–6. The Commercial Supply Company has its main office and warehouse in the capital of your state. The purchasing agent of this company recently made an opportune buy of 500 Moderne postal scales, which could be retailed easily at $3.00 apiece. The president of the company believes that an initial attempt should be made to sell these scales by mail, the offer to be presented as a service to established customers in recognition of their past dealings with Commercial Supply. Any scales not sold by this approach would be stocked as ordinary merchandise, list priced at $3.98. While there is nothing unusual about these postal scales, the special price would be a definite attraction. As sales manager of the Commercial Supply Company, write the necessary sales letter, which will be sent to all business houses that buy their supplies from your firm.

10–7. Do some investigating into the features offered by a current model of one of the makes of popular-priced automobiles. Then as "Bargain Bill" Bluefield, a local dealer of this make of automobile, write a sales letter to be sent to all persons who ever bought a car, new or used, from your outlet in past years. Play up the features that apply to this year's model and make mention of the new-car warranty. Of course, your letter will be printed in quantity for the mass mailing; but the intent is to have a girl use a Magic Marker to place a personalized "Yes, Mr.   (Name) " across the top of the letter. Your message will carry on from such a lead.

10–8. Select a product from the following list of possibilities: automatic washing machine, clothes dryer, refrigerator, or stove. From current issues of magazines and newspapers, obtain a number of advertisements relating to a specific make of one of these products. Then, using information thus accumulated, pick out a central selling theme which could be used as the basis for a sales letter. Assume that you are the advertising manager of an appliance distributor in your home town. Prepare a conventional sales letter to be sent to prospective customers; your request should be for the reader to visit the store to see the product for himself. Be sure to include all the necessary requirements of an effective sales presentation.

10–9. Select a product from the following list of possibilities: color television console, portable radio, stereophonic record player, table model television set (black and white), or tape recorder. Check into current advertisements of such products, and compile a quantity of information about a specific make of the product you have selected. Out of this information, choose a central selling theme that could be used for a gadget-type sales letter. Assuming the role of owner-manager of a radio-television store in this city, prepare a gadget sales letter. This letter will be mailed to prospects whose names are contained in a special mailing list which you have purchased. Be sure to include everything that is needed for an effective sales presentation; tell your reader exactly what you want him to do. As for the choice of gadget—remember that it should be safe, practical, and economical; it should catch the reader's eye initially, but it should not outweigh the message.

10–10. Assume that you have been out of college for 10 years or more. With the passage of time, you have become interested in a number of civic organizations. At present you are on the board of trustees of one of the hospitals in the city where you live. The hospital administration is planning a much-needed addition to its plant. So far, it has been able to buy a parcel of land adjacent to the existing site. Through pledges by industrial and business firms, it has lined up approximately half of the money needed for construction. The rest, it believes, must be raised by public subscription. Since you are in the advertising profession, it is only natural that you be expected to help out on this phase of the work. Prepare a sales letter of the fund-raising type.

· ·

CHAPTER 11

EFFECTIVE LETTERS IN THE MARKETPLACE

ORDER LETTERS
· · · · · · · · · · · · · ·

Raw materials, subassemblies, parts, supplies, merchandise for resale, repair work, transportation, personal services—these are among the many things for which we may expect to place orders in our day-in, day-out business activities. Sometimes we order in the name of our company, sometimes in our own right as individuals.

In the modern way of doing business, it is very likely that our company will use a system of centralized purchasing. Such a system is set up to have one officer primarily responsible for the purchasing function, to provide a standardized method of placing orders with suppliers, to authenticate such orders, to make possible economic lots through consolidation of small requests clearing through a central office, to assure prompt processing of invoices subject to cash discounts, to have a means of ascertaining commitments made against the budget, and so on. In short, the system is aimed at purchasing in an orderly, economical manner, and at safeguarding the financial interests of the company which relate to purchasing.

PURCHASING PROCEDURE

Basically, control enters into the purchasing routine through a system of records and forms. A storeskeeper of some kind is designated for each department. His job includes keeping records of increases, decreases, and quantities on hand of the various materials and supplies used by his department. When a preestablished level is reached, he issues a purchase requisition for replenishment, which may be approved by the department manager before it is sent to the purchasing office. Such a form would probably be prepared in duplicate, with the copy retained as a reminder by the issuing office.

When the requisition is received at the purchasing office, it can be consolidated with any similar requisitions received from other departments. At times, acting on the possibility that such requisitions are about due, the purchasing office can inquire of various other departments about their needs. Then, the total picture being seen, a purchase order is prepared and sent to an outside supplier. Such an order, signed by the responsible officer, commits the company in the manner of a contract—provided, of course, that it is accepted by the supplier. The forms used for this purpose are usually serialized so that each can be accounted for. They are of standard design, so that the clerks will be able to use them rather routinely; and they contain blanks and columns for all necessary information, so that nothing is likely to be overlooked. Additional information, concerning procedure that applies in all cases, is included somewhere, possibly on the reverse side. In general a purchase order form will provide the following:

"SHIP TO .... WHERE ?
FEED IT .... WHAT ? "

1. Date of order.
2. Date desired.
3. Place of delivery.
4. Method of delivery.
5. F.O.B. point and responsibility for transportation.
6. Method of packing.
7. Price.
8. Quantity discounts, if applicable.

9. Terms of payment.
10. Copies of invoice required.
11. Mailing address for invoices.
12. Claims and adjustment procedure.

The purchase order is issued in a number of copies, according to the complexity of the purchasing system. A recommended minimum is four copies. The original (signed) goes to the vendor, with one copy each going to the controller's office (for budgetary control) and to the requisitioning department (for feedback). A final file copy is kept in the purchasing office (as a reminder). Under this arrangement, three copies of the vendor's invoice are often requested. The original serves as the basis for payment, after being certified as to the satisfactory delivery of the order. The second copy is used in the purchasing office, to complete the file on the order; and the third is sent to the requisitioning department for their file or to serve as a source of cost data if records are kept along that line.

Whatever the mechanics of the system, however, centralized purchasing practically does away with the need for the company to write order letters. There are only a few exceptions—such as requests for bids, with lengthy specifications, or orders of an unusual nature—wherein a letter would be more suitable than a regular purchase order. Yet, even then, a purchase order would probably accompany the letter just to keep the "system" intact.

On the other hand, we still find that a number of sole proprietorships, partnerships of professional men, and other businesses small in organizational structure have not felt the need for a formalized purchasing system. Then, too, there are untold millions of people who, at some time or another, will have to place an order in written form as part of their personal business activity. Perhaps they will have an order form handy, perhaps not. The main thing in any of these situations is that the person ordering be careful to do everything necessary to obtain fulfillment of his order—even when he is not automatically reminded through a printed form.

PROGRAM FOR AN ORDER LETTER

An order letter is easily recognizable as a type of request letter. Certainly, therefore, it should contain a clear and definite request of what is wanted—in all of its aspects. The situation, however, is really

self-motivating; a supplier should not have to have a fire built under him
to act when an order comes in. As for the third basic requirement of a
request—ample assistance—nothing of a physical nature is necessarily
called for. Thorough attention to all details of the order by the purchaser
tends to make action easy for a supplier.

When it comes to working out a program or working outline for an
order letter, we should emphasize clearness and completeness. We should
be sure to include everything our supplier will need to give us prompt
and satisfactory service. Our steps, exclusive of incidental trimmings of
a given situation, are as follows:

REQUEST.
INSTRUCT.
PROMISE.

Significance of the Program

The *request* step is the actual placing of our order. In it we should
give the complete specifications of the item or items we want. The points
includable are:

1. Quantity: number and unit of measure (e.g., 1 qt., 1 doz., 10 ea.,
   1 pr.).
2. Description:
   a) Name of product.
   b) Brand name, if applicable.
   c) Size (all aspects).
   d) Color.
   e) Style.
   f) Trimmings, if applicable.
   g) Initialing, if applicable.
3. Catalogue references (issue and item).
4. Approximate unit price.
5. Approximate value (price times quantity).

It is likely that some of these details will not be involved in a given
case; but we should always be aware of the possibilities. The catalogue
references (if available) help clarify the description should our verbal

efforts be somehow lacking. For example, the item number can be verified—or, if a catalogue has been superseded by another, the supplier might still be able to identify the proper item by knowing which issue we have used. Our stating an approximate price can be helpful in much the same way. If our description should fit an item that is stocked in several prices, some inkling of our intended price range will help identify the proper kind. We extend (that is, work out) the value of the order for at least two reasons: it arithmetically tends to verify our intention with regard to quantity and price, and it permits a final totaling to obtain the approximate monetary amount of the order.

The manner in which we display our itemized request depends on what would be easy at the processing end and also at our end. In any event, eye appeal will be helpful. We might have but one item, which, if very simple, could be described in ordinary text matter. Usually, however, it will be a better plan for us to set this part off by itself, because of the many descriptive parts that are needed. Whenever we have more than one item, we should use some kind of tabular form, which necessitates itemizing this part and setting it off from the rest of the letter.

Generally, there are two approaches to the tabular form available to us—the full table and the modified table. The full table is a layout very similar to the styling of a purchase order form. It has a column heading for each significant piece of information needed, and is easy for our supplier to use. It requires a little extra work for us to set up, however; and it has its best eye appeal when all or most of the spaces are in use—that is, when the items are rather similar in the way they are described. The modified table is of simpler design, and especially suitable when there are only a few items or dissimilar items. It has just two columns, neither of which requires a caption. The left-hand portion contains all of the descriptive information (including the unit price, when more than one of an item is being ordered). The right-hand portion contains the value of the items so described (price times quantity). Each item is single spaced, and double spacing is used between the items. Leader lines (dots) usually run from the end of the item to the related amount. A total is shown at the end.

The *instruct* step is a matter of giving necessary explanations to the vendor so that he can perform according to our needs or wishes. As the request took care of the "what" this step takes care of the "who," "where," "when," and "how" details. The points to consider are:

1. The person to whom the merchandise is to be sent. If we have written, "Please send me . . . ," it is obvious that we ourselves are to be the recipient. But, if we want the items as a gift, for example, we should be sure to state clearly the name of this different recipient.

2. If delivery is to be made to us at the address shown in our letterhead or other heading, there is no need to repeat the address in our letter. On the other hand, if we want it delivered to us or to someone else at a different address, we should provide the necessary details. The best way of doing this is to set it off by itself in regular address form.

3. It is desirable that we review the facts regarding the date the items will be needed. If mentioning a specific date will help our supplier fill the order in time for our needs, we should include a mention of it in the instructions. For example, if a production schedule must be met or someone's birthday present is involved, delivery by a specific time could be a crucial point. But under ordinary business conditions, with sensible lead times in effect, we should expect that the processing of our order will be done promptly. In such cases "prompt handling" and "as soon as possible" are unnecessary, if not irksome; and "immediately," "at once," and "today" could backfire on us. Such could be the case if we were to put in an urgent request when we really did not need the items that soon. A supplier who might have helped us in the real interval might not be able to do so in the speeded-up interval.

4. The question of shipment has some practical considerations, too. If we know that one carrier is better for us than another, we are wise in stating which is to be used. For instance, a package sent parcel post might be delivered to our mailbox, whereas our address is outside the local express delivery zone. The nearness of freight terminals and local policies concerning deliveries from terminals also have their bearing on the matter. When it really does not matter, we could settle for a general remark, such as "Ship by the cheapest method." In such a case, we rely on the greater experience of the shipper to make this decision for us.

"I DON'T CARE IF IT DID SAY 'SHIP CHEAPEST WAY', SMEDLEY!"

Although an order is considered to be a self-motivating request, there is usually some need for us to mention something about the financial arrangements. This is what the *promise* step of our program is all about. It serves to add a bit of inducement by way of an assurance to the supplier that he will be paid. Ordinarily, this is a relatively simple step. We may specify that the invoice be charged to our account; we may request delivery C.O.D.; we may enclose a down payment and ask that the balance be handled C.O.D.; we may send payment with our order— especially if the amount is definitely known.

ILLUSTRATIONS

The order letters shown on pp. 340–42 offer a cross section of the various possibilities which we have just discussed. The first letter orders a single item as a gift to be delivered to a person at a different address from that of the writer. Full payment is enclosed.

The next letter is an example of an order from a professional firm. It makes use of a full table for the descriptive information of the items being ordered, and asks that the total of the invoice be charged against the firm's account.

The third example shows the use of a modified table in an order letter. By this method, the merchandise is described in an enumeration of the specifications for each item instead of being organized under column headings of a regular table. The preparation work is much simpler; yet the processing work at the supplier's end is not proportionately complicated. In this illustration, the writer wants the merchandise sent directly to him on a C.O.D. basis.

ACKNOWLEDGMENT LETTERS

The concept underlying the term "acknowledgment" is that of giving recognition to something we have received. In a literal sense, therefore, we include an acknowledgment in the structure of an answer letter whenever we relate it to our reader's request letter. But, in the field of business communication, we have come to use the term *acknowledgment* as the identification of a letter written in answer to an order. The situation implies that we write such letters only in our capacity as an actual or would-be supplier.

414 Park Avenue West
Mansfield, Ohio 44838
August 16, 1967

Mail-Order Department
The Bonnie Lass Candy Company
1300 Briarslope Drive
Cleveland, Ohio 44131

Gentlemen:

Your advertisement in last Sunday's Herald described a three-pound box of assorted
chocolate creams, shown as item "B." I'd like to have a box of this candy sent
parcel post to my sister, at the following address:

Miss Rosemary Nelson
873 Laverne Avenue
Cleveland, Ohio 44129

Because this will be a birthday gift, will you please enclose a Bonnie Birthday card--
"To Ro, From Tom"--and mail the package so that it will arrive by Tuesday, August 23?

I'm enclosing a money order for $3.90 to cover the price of the candy. I understand
that the courtesy card, handling, and postage will be assumed by your company, since
my payment accompanies my order.

Yours truly,

Thomas G. Nelson

Thomas G. Nelson

Rutland & Beane

Certified Public Accountants

211-220 SEGOVIA BUILDING   CORAL GABLES, FLORIDA 33134

June 3, 1967

Southern Office Supply, Inc.
619 DuPont Palm Terrace
Miami, Florida 33132

Gentlemen:

Will you please send us the following items, which are listed in your Spring, 1966, catalogue:

| QUANTITY | | | ITEMS | | Unit | |
No.	Unit	Cat. No.	Description		Price	Amount
1	ea.	441	Desk blotter, 36" x 42"		$3.75	$ 3.75
1	ea.	192	Journal binder		3.50	3.50
6	ea.	500	Apex ball-point pens, black ink, auditor's point		.69	4.14
1	dz.	78	Tuffy ink erasers		1.20	1.20
2	dz.	85	Hawkeye pencils, No. 3		1.10	2.20
6	pkg.	803	14-column analysis sheets		1.00	6.00
				Subtotal		$20.79
				Add: Postage		.55
				Total		$21.34

The parcel-post charges are in accordance with the rate table which appears in the catalogue. Please charge this order to our regular account.

Very truly yours,

RUTLAND AND BEANE

Charles J. Rutland

Charles J. Rutland
Partner

CJR:pgs

146 West Arnold Road
McKeesport, Pennsylvania 15245
March 21, 1967

Lee's Book and Browsing Shop
6722 Nottingham Place
Pittsburgh, Pennsylvania 15212

Gentlemen:

Please send me the following articles, if they are still available. The prices shown are only tentative estimates, as they are based on notations I made during a shopping trip to your store about two weeks ago.

One dispatch case, Morocco-grained vinyl, brown color, brass fittings, lock	$7.95
One Lester postal scale, one-pound capacity, first-class and airmail indicators	2.75
Two copies of Gerity's Pocket Dictionary, paperback edition, 1965 @ $1.75	3.50
Total	$14.20

I'd appreciate your sending these items C.O.D., including postage and customary handling charges, so that I may have them by March 31.

Yours truly,

Kenneth R. Gibson

Kenneth R. Gibson

As we have seen, orders may be sent out by various means: purchase-order forms, order blanks, and letters. The letter may be written as a matter of either company business or personal business. Acknowledgments, on the other hand, would seem to be rather limited to company business. Most likely they will tend to be handled by some kind of form, ranging from a simple post card to a document mechanically produced as one of the steps in a computer setup. Such forms are sent out promptly upon receipt of the customer's order. In essence, they have a built-in "thank you" as well as a standardized method of notifying the customer that his order has been received and how it is being handled. Their purpose is twofold: to create goodwill and to reduce the natural concern of the customer during the interval between his ordering and receiving the goods. Such forms usually restate the order as we have interpreted it, and add information that is useful to the customer: scheduled date of shipment, name of carrier or mode of transportation, probable time and date of arrival, back-ordered items, and so on.

There will be times, however, whether we regularly use forms or not, when prompt acknowledgment by letter will be the indicated action. In the case of a good-news situation, in which we can accept the customer's order, we might choose to write a personalized letter. In the case of an unclear order in which we must ask for additional descriptive details, we usually have to resort to a letter. And, in a bad-news situation, whatever our reason for declining the order, we may find that we can do a better job with a letter than with a printed form. As with other types of business letters, our preference should be for using a friendly, personal tone. In general, we should be sure to include the following ingredients:

1. An expression of appreciation.
2. Specific and complete information.
3. An effective portrayal of service attitude.

GOOD–NEWS ACKNOWLEDGMENTS

There are a number of circumstances under which we may sense the wisdom of writing an acknowledgment letter, even though the processing of the customer's order will be handled in a routine manner. Some of these circumstances are explained as follows:

1. *First Orders.*   When a customer comes to us with his first order, it does seem that we are a bit unappreciative or aloof if we do not give some special recognition to this fact. Here is a golden opportunity to strengthen relationships, win confidence, and create goodwill by giving our new customer some personal, long-term attention.

2. *Renewal of Goodwill.*   Our printed acknowledgments may contain "thank you" or some other statement of appreciation, but there is a danger that this notation may get lost amidst the other details. Moreover, some other company may have begun a serious effort to cut in on our business activity; our customer may find his overtures flattering as compared with our mechanically produced forms.

Thus, from time to time, we can overcome the impersonal approach by acknowledging an order by means of a letter.

3. *Change in Customer Habits.*   Sometimes, after a customer has been dealing with us for a period of time, he makes a significant change in his buying habits. He may have been buying in dozen lots, and suddenly places an order for a gross. Is this a sign that he is allocating us a greater share of his business? If so, is a printed form to be used this time? Or—suppose he cuts down from tonnages to hundredweights. Should we routinely acknowledge his order by a form, or should we become energized enough to recapture his business or at least learn the reason for the change? These certainly would be opportunities for writing acknowledgment letters, even though the order will be routinely filled.

Program Requirements

Our program for a good-news type of acknowledgment letter would be constructed as follows:

THANKS.
ORDER RESTATED.
SHIPPING DATA.
ASSURANCES.
SALES TALK.

Because this is a good-news situation, there has been some difference of opinion as to the placement of the "thanks" (or appreciation) step. Logically, the opening spot in the sequence is proper. Placing an order with us will be viewed by the customer as something good for us, and therefore something for which he is entitled to proper recognition. By giving this recognition to him immediately, we satisfy his craving and, in effect, finish "old" business before going on with "new" business. Our customer, being satisfied that we have shown appreciation, can clear his mind of that point and pay attention to what we tell him next. That next part, of course, contains information which he needs to know from a more practical standpoint.

This line of reasoning is not shared by all analysts of business communication. Some maintain that the good-news acknowledgment should open with what is being done about the customer's order—because that question is the really important one. They believe that a more imaginative beginning is accomplished this way. The appreciation step would then appear at the end of the letter.

While both viewpoints have their strengths, it does seem that delaying the "thanks" is subject to two serious weaknesses: (a) some readers will not be satisfied until they have read it—and many will miss much of what is being said up to that point, and (b) it tends to appear somewhat as a tacked-on afterthought, instead of being a sincere, coordinated culmination of the "old" business. The real test, of course, is how the intended reader is likely to react; and we should let his preference override ours.

Restating the order is no more than would be done by a standardized acknowledgment form. The purpose is to let our customer know how we have read his order and to give him a chance to make corrections, if necessary. The shipping data also are pieces of helpful information concerning packing, carrier, shipment date, estimated arrival time and date, and so on.

The last two steps of the program, "assurances" and "sales talk," are directed toward the aspects of confidence and goodwill. The first of these steps refers to the business organization itself, and the second step refers to the item (or items) ordered. The opportunity to include these steps is one of the big advantages in writing an acknowledgment letter. To be successful in the long run, we must depend on repeat business—

which, in turn, depends on satisfied customers. In reaching decisions, people generally do not select a choice that is overwhelmingly obvious. After appraising the facts involved and weighing the advantages and disadvantages, they may still feel that the decision could go either way. Their actions, therefore, may well be accompanied by deep shadows of doubt and feelings of uncertainty. Whenever buying merchandise, supplies, and equipment is involved, such misgivings may apply to both the supplier and the product.

To put our customer's mind at ease that he came to the right business house when he came to us, we inform him of—or review for him, if he is a regular customer—the advantages, services, prestige, and so on which we offer. By the time he has assimilated these facts, he should feel assured that we are a good choice of company with which to do business.

To convince him that he has made a good choice of merchandise, we can also add some sales talk—on the articles he has already ordered! The philosophy behind this effort has often been stated as, "Sell 'em— and keep 'em sold." We should remove any possible doubt from our customer's mind concerning his purchase, so that he will enjoy it more, tend to be satisfied with it, and come back for more. The concept is well established; a great number of things we buy contain leaflets, flyers, instruction sheets, etc., all designed to sell us on the very thing we have already bought. In many instances, we do not see these messages until we open the box or carton; obviously, therefore, they do not influence us in making our original purchase. But, they sell us on liking what we bought, so that we will buy it again when we are again in need of such a product.

ILLUSTRATION

The letter on p. 347 is an example of a good-news type of acknowledgment. It is addressed to a first-time customer who ordered some articles for his personal use. The appreciation step is placed at the beginning and the restatement of the customer's order follows the modified-table variation. Goodwill aspects applicable to the company round off the paragraph that gives the details on how the physical handling is done. The goodwill aspects applicable to the purchases, in general terms, are given in the final paragraph.

Hartlander's Men's Shop

1666 CAMBRIDGE ST., BOSTON, MASS. 02210

September 1, 1966

Mr. William Bennett
12616 Shaw Avenue
East Cleveland, Ohio 44112

Dear Mr. Bennett:

Thank you for your order of August 30--and a hearty welcome into Hartlander's circle of friends!

As you requested, we are packaging the following items for parcel-post delivery:

3 ea. Hartline white dress shirts, size 16-34,
monogrammed WB, @ $6.25 . . . . $18.75

2 ea. Hartline all-Dacron men's ties; one
maroon, one blue; @ $1.65 . . . .   3.30
$22.05

Postage and handling charges . .   .45
Total $22.50

Your goods will be sent to you C.O.D., and should arrive on Tuesday, September 6. As with all of our merchandise, we stand behind these goods with a guarantee of complete satisfaction or your money back.

Your shirts and ties are products made in our own factory, in accordance with our own high standards and original design theories. You may be sure of getting good taste in styles, top-quality materials, and expert workmanship. Add to these features the prestige value of the name "Hartline," and you have a combination that is hard to beat.

Sincerely yours,

Jerald P. Revere

Jerald P. Revere
Manager

JPR:vn

REQUESTS FOR ADDITIONAL INFORMATION

Whether our customers use forms or letters for placing their orders, it is reasonable to expect that some of these orders will turn out to be unclear. Perhaps a customer forgets to give part of the needed specifications—such as color, size, or style. Or, perhaps he omits necessary handling instructions or has stated them ambiguously. Such a situation boils down to the following facts:

1. We have in stock the merchandise that he wants.
2. We are glad to accept his order.
3. But, we need some additional information before we can complete the transaction.

The Nature of the Problem

In this set of circumstances, we recognize elements of all three of the basic multipurpose letter situations: good-news, bad-news, and request. The letter we write in response to an unclear order will carry a certain amount of good news—namely, we do have the merchandise our customer desires, and are happy to send it to him. But there is also some bad news, implied more than expressed: our customer will not receive his merchandise at this time; instead, he is merely getting a letter concerning his order. Finally, however, there is the request aspect, the real reason for our writing this letter.

With all these elements involved, we must decide on a suitable approach to use in programming our letter. Our solution will be to incorporate some aspects of all three of these basic frameworks, with priority assigned to each on the basis of importance. Because a request calls for a clear statement of what is wanted, motivation, and ample assistance, we should see that a letter asking for clarification of an order does, above everything else, contain these elements. But, because getting such a request in place of the merchandise he ordered will have a psychologically adverse effect on our customer, we do well to get him ready before we come to the point. Our sequence of steps, therefore, will be along the lines of the sequence we regularly use in a bad-news situation. Nevertheless, we do not regard bad news as the principal or overall message in this kind of acknowledgment. To overcome any likelihood of misinterpretation by our reader and to keep his hopes high, we should express our thoughts with an abundance of pleasantness and service attitude. Our net result is a special acknowledgment letter that is:

1. Based on the steps of a request program.
2. Sequenced along the lines of a bad-news message.
3. Expressed in the mood of a good-news message.

The Typical Program

The acknowledgment of an unclear order is best handled along the lines of the following program:

THANKS.

SALES TALK.

TIED-IN REQUEST.

HELP TOWARD ANSWERING.

The significance of these parts is readily explained. No matter what our viewpoint might be regarding the position of "thanks" in a good-news acknowledgment, for a straight-line flow of thought here we are virtually required to put our appreciation statement at the beginning. Such a beginning clears our reader's mind for paying full attention to the things which follow. It gives him something pleasant to read at the outset, and thus encourages him to read on.

The sales talk is a step intended to strengthen our customer's desire for the product which he has ordered. We know that a delay is in progress and that we could lose the sale if our customer is allowed to cool off, back down, change his mind, or become discouraged. We attempt to intensify his craving for fulfillment, even though ultimately he will have to do something in order to achieve it.

Our statement of the request is the heart of our letter. We must be careful to pack it with diplomacy and service attitude. To begin with, we should lead into the request with some preliminary wording that suggests a positive reason for our asking. In so doing, we must be careful to avoid scoldings, accusations, and anything else that might be untactful or antagonistic toward our reader. It is bad enough that he did something wrong; we have nothing to gain by rubbing it in or making him feel guilty, foolish, or ashamed. We are interested in his goodwill and in the information needed to process his order to his complete satisfaction. We should stick to the pursuit of these objectives, to the exclusion of anything negative or undiplomatic.

A subtle method of skirting trouble is to place special emphasis on *the present situation* as we lead into our request. Very likely, all that we need do is add a word or phrase to what would have been an ordinary introductory clause. By this method we remain truthful, yet we allow our reader to rationalize that circumstances may not always have been what they are now—that he therefore can be excused for not knowing—and that he therefore did not really err. Our customer is let off painlessly; and both of us get what we want. An example of this wording, in which the strategic element is "now," is shown below.

```
     As this style of jacket now comes in three popular
colors, we'd like to know your preference.
```

Our request itself should be clear and complete, so that one such letter will be sufficient. Included with our request should be a provision for answering; and some reassurance can be imparted if we mention that the clarified order will receive prompt handling.

It would be a mistake to ask our reader to write us a letter. Such a request would put the burden of work on the reader, a move that is contrary to service attitude. Moreover, he has already botched the order using his own methods; he could do so again in his second attempt. Thus, an easy-to-use form, worked out in maximum detail, should be our choice. Our reader can check off his preference from possibilities we have listed and return the form to us in a reply envelope which we have provided. To him, answering becomes almost as easy as not answering —and we have a reasonably good chance of salvaging the sale.

ILLUSTRATION

The letter on p. 351 is an acknowledgment of an unclear order for a sweater. The program is in accordance with the points we have just discussed. In this case, the accent is placed on the present through the use of the phrase, "this season." On the one hand, interest is built in to sustain the customer during the necessary waiting period. On the other hand, tactlessness and negative suggestion are carefully kept out so that the customer will be neither embarrassed nor discouraged.

Martin's Department Store

20 RUNNYMEDE CIRCLE, ST. PAUL, MINN. 55177

December 1, 1967

Mr. Delmar C. Cooke
202 East Market Street
Rochester, Minnesota 55404

Dear Mr. Cooke:

Thank you very much for your mail order of November 29. It's always a pleasure to be of service to our out-of-town charge customers.

We're happy to say that we have a new supply of "Matterhorn" heavy-knit sweaters, including the large size in your choice of burgundy and white. As these sweaters are designed for roominess and warmth, you can expect to get a lot of pleasure from yours-- whether you are a participant in winter sports or a spectator who likes to be up front where the action is. Observers at the popular resorts are saying that the "Matterhorn" is ahead of the pack for style.

This season the "Matterhorn" comes with a choice of three neck styles, to suit all tastes and needs. So, you may have your pick for complete satisfaction--turtleneck, crew neck, or V-neck. Just check your preference on the enclosed card, slip it into the postage-free envelope provided, and mail.

We will reserve a sweater of each style in your size and colors for ten days. You may be sure that we'll take care of your order the same day your answer arrives.

Sincerely yours,

Joseph P. Jurgens
Mail-Order Manager

JPJ:mg
Enclosures 2

THE TURNDOWN ACKNOWLEDGMENT

Among the various orders we receive, there will probably be some which we will be unable to fill, even though they are clear and complete. Sometimes the reason is that we do not have the product desired by the customer. In certain cases, we may be out of stock with regard to some or all of the items specified. In other cases, it may be that we do not even deal in the merchandise which has been ordered. Or, while we carry such merchandise, we do not handle the brand our customer has ordered. On the other hand, we may have exactly what our customer wants; but we are restrained from selling it to him. Our task in any of these situations is to write an acknowledgment which declines our customer's order —or at least a portion of it.

Stock Depleted

In routine situations, when we are temporarily out of stock on the merchandise ordered, we may be able to send a form acknowledgment which indicates this fact. The quantity and description of the goods are listed as being on "back order," and an expected completion date is given.

When our customer is in urgent need of his order, a more individualized handling is called for. Preferably, we try to find a solution to his problem. Perhaps we have a similar product to offer—although it may carry a different price tag or have some peculiarities not found in the product ordered. In any event, an acknowledgment would be needed; and we should try to make a sale of some kind.

Different Brand

If our customer has specified a product by brand name, it may be that we do not handle the make he has named. Very likely the brand line we carry includes a product that competes with the product our customer has ordered. As in the case of being out of his precise product, we should try to satisfy his needs with something else. We should add some sales talk to our otherwise bad-news acknowledgment letter.

Not Our Line

In some instances, would-be customers come to us in the mistaken belief that we are suppliers of the merchandise they want. Possibly our company name has suggested such a possibility to them; or, possibly we once did deal in such a product but have discontinued such activity.

There is little likelihood that we can salvage the sale in any such case. But, we still should not lose sight of the fact that we are in some line of business and that goodwill alone is worth shooting for. Some day this would-be customer may need our products, or may be in a position to recommend us to someone who does. The least we can do is write a courteous acknowledgment. If we can make a helpful suggestion as to a source of supply, so much the better.

Other Barriers

The basic reason for sending a turndown acknowledgment in any of the situations just mentioned—our stock depleted, the brand not handled, and the product outside our scope—is that we do not have the merchandise which has been ordered. There are other situations, however; these come under the heading of impediments to our filling the order, even though we have the goods in stock. One such impediment is the lack of credit on the part of the orderer. This reason, in fact, is so serious and delicate that we shall give it special coverage in a later chapter.

Aside from credit problems, the major barriers to our accepting a customer's order are as follows:

1. *Prohibitions.* It is possible that we simply are not allowed to fill certain orders. Laws or government regulations may prohibit our selling to minors, to people who do not present prescriptions, or to anyone at all (such as during a temporary ban on a medicine, drug, or insecticide). A contract with our dealers may preclude our entering the retail field. A territorial franchise may require that we confine our operations to a specific geographical area.

2. *Organization Problems.* Even though there may be no outside factors preventing us from accepting an order, we may be

set up to handle wholesale business only. Thus, it would be impractical for us to break open case lots to service retail customers. Or, it may be that we have no facilities to handle mail orders and not enough traffic to get us interested. Also, to engage in retail sales, we may need to acquire a license to collect, report, and return state sales and use taxes; and we might prefer to go about solving our customer's problem some other way.

3. *Product Problems.*   Sometimes the product itself becomes a factor in our deciding whether to accept a customer's order. If the distance involved is rather great and the product is of a highly perishable nature, we might choose to turn down the order. If the product should be of a particularly delicate or breakable quality, we may not be willing to accept orders which specifiy an unsuitable mode of transportation. Or, the article may be dangerous or otherwise unacceptable for handling by the post office or by a common carrier. It would be one matter if the customer would come and get the product, but an entirely different matter if he were to want it sent.

In the event we are prohibited from selling the merchandise which has been ordered, we may be able to suggest something; a different product or a somewhat different way for our customer to approach his problem. When the other conditions prevail—that is, our organizational setup or our product is not suited to the filling of the customer's order—we should at least help him find whichever dealer of ours is in best position to serve him.

Programming the Turndown

Whatever the circumstances for turning down an order, our acknowledgment in such a case will follow the pattern of a bad-news letter. The steps and their sequence should be as follows:

SHOW APPRECIATION.
EXPLAIN CIRCUMSTANCES.
DECLINE THE ORDER.
SUGGEST SOMETHING HELPFUL.

The turndown acknowledgment, much in the manner of the request for clarification of an order, almost has to begin with a statement of appreciation. In this position, the appreciation step seems to finish off the old business before the other parts of the letter get on with the new business. Our reader is at least made aware of our attitude toward his order. He can tune in attentively on the remainder of our message—all of which is arranged in a straight-line flow of thought.

Our explanation paves the way for the turndown, and also lays the foundation for what will be our goodwill ending—a suggestion of something helpful. The explanation identifies the problem involved, and the suggestion attempts to provide service to our customer by finding a solution to that problem. Our suggestion, therefore, should always be well matched with our explanation; it should be a logical follow-through.

ILLUSTRATIONS

The letters shown on pp. 356–57 are bad-news acknowledgments. The first letter turns down the customer's order for a power tool because the supplier does not carry the brand which has been specified. An effort is made, however, to save the sale by stressing the positive qualities of a competing product which the supplier does have in stock. This product is not held forth as a substitute, because the word "substitute" somehow connotes inferiority and would have a negative effect on the reader. Rather, the product is discussed forthrightly from the standpoint of its various qualities and advantages. Moreover, the suggestion is clearly related to a desired action, with ample assistance provided to the reader. Perhaps the customer will still prefer to have the brand he originally requested; but the supplier has at least tried to point out an effortless solution to the problem.

The second letter turns down the order because the product is distributed through a network of dealerships. The manufacturer sells to regional wholesalers who service the individual dealers. Despite the fact that the manufacturer does not know the name of the dealer nearest the would-be customer, it does make a reasonable effort to bring dealer and customer together.

In this letter, the step declining the order is implied rather than expressed. As a result, there is a positive flavor throughout the message. Emphasis is placed on the things the company does, can do, and will do —not on its inability to fill the order. The fact of the turndown gradually

7080 MICHIGAN BLVD., MILWAUKEE, WIS. 53212

May 11, 1967

Rockwell Fabric Company
829 Tecumseh Street
Milwaukee, Wisconsin 53219

Gentlemen: Attention of Purchasing Department

Thank you for your order of May 9 for an electric knife-and-scissors sharpener.
In a business such as yours, sword-edge cutting tools are indeed of prime importance.

Some years ago we decided to simplify the varieties of electric sharpeners we handle
and to stock only the very best brands made. We narrowed down to the Simplex (which
you have ordered) and the Emery. More recently, we discontinued the Simplex. So,
while we cannot send you this make of sharpener, we can acquaint you with the ever-
dependable Emery.

Here is an electric sharpener, in the popular-priced range, which is ideal for counter-
top operation. The Emery has special honing action which gives the sharpest edge
possible to almost every size and contour of knife, shears, and scissors. Its AC electric
motor is backed by an 18-month guarantee of satisfaction. And, there is a bonus feature--
a pencil sharpener, at no extra cost to you.

Surely, you will want to consider the versatile Emery! To confirm your order, just initial
inside the box on the enclosed business reply card, and mail the card to us. We'll be
waiting to give you prompt and courteous service.

Yours very truly,

MIDTOWN OFFICE SUPPLY, INC.

Harold K. Peters

Harold K. Peters
Sales Manager

HKP:jj
Enclosure

lemane
paint company

4145 PROSPECT AVENUE, PATERSON, NEW JERSEY 07508

June 17, 1967

Mr. Louis G. Young
2613 Broad Street
Richmond, Virginia 02512

Dear Mr. Young:

Thank you for your check and order of June 15 for two gallons of Lemane Pure-White outside house paint. We agree that this quantity is a good estimate of the requirements for the job you are planning.

You may have heard that paint chemistry is a demanding business. Primary attention must be directed toward continual research projects and the translating of new discoveries into dependable production methods. Because we wish to bring you the newest and best in paints, we have become manufacturing specialists. To serve your personal needs, we have enlisted the help of another group of specialists--the wholesalers and retailers who market our paints. We rely on them completely to perform this function.

Within a few days you will receive a card from our wholesaler for Virginia, Old Dominion Distributors, Inc. They will tell you the names of Lemane dealers in your area who can give you prompt service and free delivery.

We are, of course, returning the prepayment check you so thoughtfully sent-- and wish you success in your renovation activities.

Yours very truly,

LEMANE PAINT COMPANY

Barth L. Fuller

Barth L. Fuller
Sales Manager

BLF/ew
Enclosure

dawns on the reader; it does not hit him with force. Moreover, the reader will be receiving word on the remedy planned for his problem by the time he becomes aware of the turndown. Thus, the letter ought to succeed, without risking gloominess or friction.

SUMMARY

Orders and acknowledgments document the central activity of our commercial institutions. Often, this documentation is achieved through the use of standardized forms—purchase orders and order forms, in the case of the customer; acknowledgment forms, in the case of the supplier. In some instances, particularly those in which something out of the ordinary is encountered, a letter is called for. It can add a personal touch, and it can treat of things which a routine form was not designed to handle. Our aim, therefore, should be to accomplish *more* with a letter than we could with a printed form.

The crux of the matter in an order letter is that we be attentive to details. We must be clear in our specifications and instructions. Generally speaking, an order is considered to be self-motivating and thus presents few if any difficulties in the area of getting action.

In an acknowledgment letter, we need to be appreciative of the order, clear and complete as to information given, and responsive to opportunities to be of service to our reader. These matters are important whether we are accepting or declining the order or are requesting clarification of an unclear order.

Here, in condensed form for easy review and reference, are the recommended programs for the order letter and the various types of acknowledgment letters.

ORDER LETTER

Intended
Reader
Reaction:

 from this   to this

Program: Request—Quantity (number and unit of measure).
                       —Full description (size, color, style, etc.).
                       —Catalogue references.
                       —Limitation on price.
            Instruct—To whom.
                       —Where.
                       —When (if helpful).
                       —How (if important).
            Promise—Method of payment.

Pointers: Be clear and complete on all specifications and handling in-
            structions.

            For more than one item, favor the use of a visual appeal—full
            table or modified table.

            Don't sound a note of urgency unless it is necessary; then, be
            specific by mentioning exact date that the goods are needed.

            Include a mention of the proposed method of payment.

GOOD–NEWS ACKNOWLEDGMENT
(Yes)

Intended
Reader
Reaction:

from this   to this

Program: Thanks.
Order restated.
Shipping data.
Assurances.
Sales talk.

Pointers: Show appreciation somewhere in the letter, preferably at the
beginning.

Give enough information about the items to show that the
order has been interpreted correctly.

Take advantage of all opportunities to be of service to the customer—especially in the steps giving shipping data, assurances, and sales talk.

In the *assurances* step, strive to build confidence in the vendor,
with an eye to future business.

In the *sales talk* step, strive to strengthen the customer's belief
in the product ordered, with an eye to repeat sales.

REQUEST ACKNOWLEDGMENT
(Yes, If)

Intended
Reader
Reaction:

from this   through this   to this

Program: Thanks.
Sales talk.
Tied-in request.
Help toward answering.

Pointers: Show appreciation at the beginning of the letter.
Strive to sustain the customer's desire for the product even though there will be a waiting period before he can receive it.

Be clear and complete in requesting the information that is needed to complete the transaction.

Give the customer a chance to save face. Avoid accusations, scoldings, or anything else that might be antagonistic.

Consider the possibility of emphasizing the present-tense concept, by a modifying word or phrase to allow the reader to excuse himself for committing an oversight.

Do all that is possible to make answering nearly as simple as not answering.

Encourage cooperation by a promise of prompt handling.

TURNDOWN ACKNOWLEDGMENT
(No, But)

Intended
Reader
Reaction:

from this   through this   to this

Program: Show appreciation.
            Explain circumstances.
            Decline the order.
            Suggest something helpful.

Pointers: Show appreciation at the beginning of the letter.
            Give an adequate and plausible explanation before declining
            the order.

            Consider the use of an implied turndown instead of an ex-
            pressed turndown.

            Even when an expressed turndown is used, be sure that it is
            subordinated to positive values of what, in fact, can be done.

            End with a suggestion of some kind that will help the customer
            solve his problem. If nothing tangible is possible, at least
            provide a token of goodwill.

QUESTIONS
· · · · · · · · · ·

1. What is meant by *centralized purchasing?*
2. Outline a purchasing procedure planned for internal control.
3. In general, what information is typically shown on a purchase order form?
4. Why has the need for writing order letters continued to exist now that centralized purchasing has arrived?
5. Give the suggested program for an order letter.
6. Which step of this program really provides the motivation for action by the reader, and which step reinforces it?
7. What aspects of the message are taken care of through the "instruct" step?
8. State the differences between the full table and the modified table as methods of listing an order.
9. In business communication, what has come to be the specialized meaning of the term *acknowledgment letter?*
10. Are forms ever used for acknowledgments?
11. What is the two-fold purpose behind such acknowledgments?
12. If a personalized letter is chosen for the acknowledgment of an order, what general ingredients should be worked into it?
13. Which of the multipurpose basic frameworks would seem to apply to acknowledgment letters?
14. State the suggested program to be used for an acknowledgment when the customer's order is to be filled promptly.
15. Why should the appreciation step be placed at the beginning of an acknowledgment letter?
16. Give the suggested program to be used when the customer has submitted an unclear order.
17. What is the purpose of presenting a sales talk before asking for a clarification of the unclear order?
18. Give several reasons why a supplier might turn down an order for goods or services.
19. Give the suggested program steps to be used in an acknowledgment which turns down an order.
20. What would be some helpful suggestions to give a reader whose order is being turned down?

PROBLEMS
· · · · · · · · · ·

Some of the following problems are to be typewritten on business letter-head; others, on plain stationery. If a letterhead is indicated but not available, set up a simulated letterhead in accordance with directions issued by your instructor.

11–1. (Plain stationery.) Assume that you are a resident of a small town about 60 miles away from this city. Write an order letter to the Midtown Department Store here. Ask that they send you the following merchandise by parcel post and that they charge your account for the total amount of the billing.

> 2 bedspreads, chenille, white, for twin beds
> 1 pair of men's blue denim work trousers, size 33–30
> 1 pair boy's summer pajamas, blue color

11–2. (Plain stationery.) The Bonnie Lass Candy Co., 1500 Briarslope Drive, Cleveland, Ohio 44131, does an extensive mail-order business. Assume that you have received one of that company's candy brochures and that you have been attracted by certain of the items illustrated. Place a C.O.D. order for two 1-pound boxes of assorted milk chocolates at $1.60 a pound and a 1-pound box of chocolate nut fudge at $1.35. Write the letter from your home address.

11–3. (Letterhead.) The Tru-Mold Plastic Products Company of Indianapolis, Indiana, is planning to introduce a new line of nonbreakable dinnerware. As the firm's buyer of packaging materials, prepare a letter to be sent to the Western Plains Paper Co., P.O. Box 400, Rocky Bend, Iowa. In it, request a bid on designing and producing a box to hold one complete place setting. The manufacturer will have considerable leeway in the design, according to his own production needs. Your chief specifications are that the Tru-Mold name by displayed prominently on the lid and that there be a cellophane window to let the contents be seen. Suggest that 10,000 boxes be used as the basis for making estimates.

11–4. (Letterhead.) At the start of this year, Central Industries, Incorporated, which is located in the capital of your state, renewed its agreement with the Commercial Supply Company. This latter firm is also in the state capital, at 930 Chatham Avenue. Under the agreement it will continue to supply Central Industries' needs for stationery, ink, pencils, erasers, and other such items. For this purpose, Central Industries issued Purchase Order No. 1556—a blanket order to which all acquisitions of office supplies will be related. As Central Industries' office manager, write an order letter to Commercial Supply Company for one dozen No. 2 pencils, six boxes of paper clips, one box of No. 3 wire staples, and one pint of rubber cement. Include a reminder that our billing should be figured at 10 percent below the current list price, according to the agreement.

11–5. (Letterhead.) One of the services at the Midtown Department Store in your city is on-the-spot roasting of plain and fancy nut meats. The inventory clerk has now reported that the supply is running low on peanuts and pecans. While each variety has been assigned its own order quantity, more peanuts are used than pecans. As the store's purchasing director, use a letter and a confirming purchase-order form to place a first-time order with the Old South Nut Meats Co. of Atlanta, Georgia. This supplier has been suggested to you by the president of the store, who was recently on a trip to Atlanta.

11–6. (Letterhead.) As controller of Pioneer Catalogue Sales, Inc., a mail-order house in your home town, write a letter to Ernest E. Rutland. This gentleman is the senior partner of the auditing firm of Rutland and Beane, Certified Public Accountants, which has certified your statements for the past several years. The firm is based in the largest city in your state. In your letter, tell Mr. Rutland that you wish to engage his firm for a balance-sheet audit again this year. Ask him to send you the customary acceptance letter, outlining terms and stating the number of accountants that will be required for the work.

11–7. (Letterhead.) The Bonnie Lass Candy Co. markets its products through a chain of retail outlets and also by mail-order sales. Its plant and mail-order facilities are located at 1500 Briarslope Drive, Cleveland, Ohio 44131. A customer has sent in an order letter for a 2-pound box of chocolate creams and a 1-pound box of dark-chocolate cherries. His personal check for the correct amount, including postage, was also received. As the company's mail-order manager, send this customer an acknowledgment letter; enclose a small supply of order blanks for his future convenience.

11–8. (Letterhead.) The Midtown Department Store of this city has received a letter from an irate customer in a neighboring town. This man is provoked about the fact that the company did not send him the transistor radio he ordered by mail two weeks ago. Although he originally placed his order on a C.O.D. basis, he has now enclosed a check for $12.50—since the store apparently does not trust him! As assistant sales manager in charge of mail orders, you have checked into the matter; but you can find no record of this man's first order. Write to him; show proper concern for his situation. To spare him any further inconvenience, you will rush his choice of radio by parcel post, special delivery.

11–9. (Letterhead.) Physicians' Hospital, 200 River Boulevard, Evansville, Indiana, has sent a purchase order to the Tru-Mold Plastic Products Company of Indianapolis. It is Tru-Mold's first order from this customer, but there is no question about the hospital's credit standing. The order requests 150 plastic serving trays and 200 plastic 8-ounce coffee cups. The goods are to be shipped by the least expensive common carrier. As sales manager of the Tru-Mold Plastic Products Company, accept this order and write an acknowledgment letter to the purchasing agent of the hospital.

11–10. (Letterhead.) A customer of Pioneer Catalogue Sales, Inc., a mail-order house in your home town, has written that he is going on a vacation trip next week. He has placed a last-minute order (with payment enclosed) for the following items, which were advertised in the firm's latest circular.

1 pair	Men's leather slippers, brown, size 11	$ 9.95
3 packs	DeLuxe 35mm. colorchrome film, cartridge type @ $3.50 a pack	10.50
		$20.45

The company's stock of this film is depleted, but a new supply is expected within 10 days. As the company's sales manager, write an acknowledgment letter to this customer. Tell him that you are sending the slippers immediately. Request that he give you his vacation address so that the film can be forwarded to him as soon as it becomes available.

11–11. (Letterhead.) The Midtown Department Store of this city has received an order from Oscar Straughn. Writing from a rural address, Straughn has enclosed a money order for $9.45 and has asked the store to send him a pair of all-purpose work shoes, brown color, size 9. The amount remitted is correct, but no mention has been made of the choice of heel, which can be either leather or rubber. As chief shipping clerk in the store's mail-order department, write an acknowledgment letter to Straughn. Have him clarify his order.

11–12. (Letterhead.) Central Industries, Incorporated, is located in the capital city of the state. Today it received an order from the purchasing office of an out-of-state school. The order calls for two dozen wooden bookcases which would be suitable for displaying periodicals in the school's library. No specifications for the bookcases have been included; and while the indication is that the bookcases will be used to line the walls of a large reading room, no dimensions of that room have been included, either. As sales manager of Central Industries, write an acknowledgment letter to the school. In it, request the information needed for filling the order.

11–13. (Letterhead.) Valley Steel Corporation is situated in western Pennsylvania, not far distant from Youngstown, Ohio. It has received an order for structural steel girders from the Metropolitan Bridge Company of New York City. Unfortunately, Valley Steel Corporation will have to refuse this attractive-sounding order. It seems that an extended labor dispute some years ago resulted in the loss of most of their customers in the heavy-steel field. Since that time, Valley Steel has had to cut back to lighter products, chiefly steel wire for fencing. Assume that you are Valley Steel's sales manager. Acknowledge the order, convey the bad news, but be as helpful as you can.

11–14. (Letterhead.) Pioneer Catalogue Sales, Inc. is a mail-order house in your home town. It has received an order letter for "Item 706, Home Bread Maker—$11.95." The letter is from an out-of-town woman; a check for $11.95 accompanies her order. Upon checking, it is discovered that Item 706 has been discontinued from the line of merchandise. Apparently, the woman has ordered from an old catalogue. As the sales manager of Pioneer Catalogue Sales, acknowledge the woman's order, return her check, and offer whatever suggestions you can.

11–15. (Letterhead.) An order for one plastic trash container, orange color, 20-gallon capacity, has been received by the order department of the Tru-Mold Plastic Products Company of Indianapolis, Indiana. This firm is not licensed to transact business with the ultimate individual consumer. It deals only with wholesalers and mass consumers of the tax-exempt variety (schools, hospitals, etc.). Other customers must obtain the firm's products through ordinary retail outlets. Fortunately, there are plenty of such outlets—supermarkets, hardware stores, department stores, and the like. As the company's assistant sales manager, turn down the customer's order; but try to be helpful in some way.

....

CHAPTER 12

WHEN SOMETHING
GOES AWRY

In business, as well as in other fields of human endeavor, something will sooner or later go wrong. No matter how carefully we manufacture our product, inspect it, or package it, the chances are that something unplanned will occur. No matter how faithfully our various personnel take down orders, count out quantities, or follow instructions, someone will make a mistake. No matter how trustworthy a mode of transportation, delays will occur and accidents will happen. And not always are the instances of human error confined to a relationship between a company and a customer. Sometimes a visitor or a passerby is injured on our grounds or by one of our vehicles, or we are held responsible for damage to someone's property. Whatever event has occurred, the person affected will probably file a claim against us and ask that we take appropriate action.

All things remaining equal, of course, we can expect that the same probabilities are in effect at the companies with whom we do business. We should be tolerant of human error on the part of others, just as we want them to be tolerant toward us. Letters written back and forth should reflect the attitudes of courtesy and patience, and should be pointed in the direction of an equitable solution to the problem. Claim letters alert the supposedly responsible party to the occurrence and request a desired action; adjustment letters convey the answer and make a bid for recovery of lost goodwill.

CLAIM LETTERS
· · · · · · · · · · · · · ·

In this country we have a time-honored saying, "The customer is always right." This statement,

OH, THE CUSTOMER IS ALWAYS RIGHT, SMEDLEY. STUPID, MAYBE, OR UNPLEASANT, OR IMPOSSIBLE, BUT ALWAYS RIGHT ! "

COMPLAINT DEPT.

of course, is not literally true. The customer is just as prone to errors, misinterpretations, and other imperfections as anyone else. Behind the words of the saying, however, is a clue to how we should behave when we deal with customers. Come what may, we should not lose sight of the fact that our success depends on their continued satisfaction with the services, goods, and treatment they receive from us. The latter is especially important, because there is no easy explaining it away when we are guilty of discourtesies or other antagonistic acts.

THE MATTER OF DIPLOMACY

During the course of our business activity, we very likely have to take amounts of rudeness, unreasonableness, and temper tantrums from some of the people who come to us with claims. If we control ourselves in such instances, we will keep an unruffled appearance and the claimant will be persuaded to accept a fair and peaceful settlement. There will come a time, however, when the situation will be reversed. One of our suppliers, for example, will make a mistake in connection with one of our orders. How great will be the temptation to reason that "the customer is always right"—and this time, *we* are the customer!

Such reasoning must not be allowed to replace common sense and good judgment. It is always improper to write an undiplomatic letter, even when we are filing a claim. The fact that the supplier is at a disadvantage is not license for us to heap abuse on him. There is no "turn" which is rightfully ours.

A number of practical reasons can be cited for our using diplomacy in claim letters we write. Some of the more important reasons are the following:

1. *Protection of source of supply.* We should realize that markets are somewhat fickle and unpredictable. Without warning, a strike, a national emergency, or a catastrophe of some kind can change a buyer's market into a seller's market. What may have been an adequate supply of a certain material or product might be slowed to a trickle almost overnight, with the result that users come crawling to suppliers. If only a limited number of users can be served, who will they be—those who have been fair and square right along, or those who have been nasty?

2. *Preservation of image.* Like other businesses, our company probably budgets a sizable amount of money each year for public relations. This activity is concerned with establishing and maintaining a favorable reputation for our company as viewed by the outside world. Ultimately, this reputation or image can endure only as long as it is confirmed by our own behavior when that outside world comes into contact with us. If we accuse, blame, or censure people when we write to them—even in presenting claims—we tend to punch holes in our image. Suppliers do not always play just one role in our lives. Often, they are users or potential users of what we sell. Moreover, they may enjoy positions of influence in areas which relate back to us. Thus, if any word-of-mouth campaigning about us originates with them, let us increase the chances that it will be good for our image.

3. *Credibility.* If we have a valid claim, we should state our case clearly and calmly so that our reader can understand what has happened. We should give him a chance to appraise the situation and give us a satisfactory answer. This is fair procedure, because our reader usually is just finding out that something has gone wrong. But to use strong language, exaggerated accusations, threats, or any other unnecessary tactics hints that we are not sure of our case and are trying to cover up. Our reader is almost certain to be suspicious.

4. *Prompt settlement.* If we arouse suspicion in the mind of our reader, we may be in for a delay. An inspection, a report, and more correspondence would likely be involved before a final settlement could

be reached. And, our best hope would be to get what we asked for in the first place; it could be much less. We should recognize, therefore, that a fairly stated claim can appear to our reader to be the simple solution. If so, the matter can be settled promptly and routinely.

ESSENTIAL QUALITIES OF CLAIMS

In order to be effective and to achieve the results discussed above, our claim letter has to be diplomatic, specific, fair, and positive. As applied to claim letters, these qualities are explained as follows:

1. *Diplomacy.* As we have emphasized right along, one purpose of every business letter has to do with goodwill. Whatever else is involved, we strive to come out of the situation with as much or more goodwill existing between the reader and ourselves as there was before our letter was written. Our manner of expression in a claim letter should be sufficiently controlled so that we do not antagonize the reader. There is no need to shout, so to speak, when we want a mistake corrected.

2. *Definiteness.* There are two sections of our claim letter which call for clear, specific statements. These are the explanation of the situation and the request we are placing before our reader. When something goes wrong, we should identify the event clearly and definitely by date, time, place, purchase order, invoice number, item description, names of personnel, amounts, receipt number, and anything else that will be helpful to our reader. In calling for action, we should always know what we want done and make that clear to our reader. He should not have to guess or ask for clarification.

3. *Fairness.* In giving an account of a situation, we should be as factual as possible. We should not make mountains out of molehills. In asking for satisfaction, we should consider what is fair and proper. The reader can subscribe to a realistic claim very easily, but he is likely to balk at one that is unreasonable. By the same token, he can be softened by whatever good things we can

observe about his product. Fairness suggests that we recognize, if possible, some good points as well as the bad points when we file a claim.

4. *Positiveness.*   In the context of business writing, positiveness has to do with pleasantness. On the surface, it may seem that a claim letter is basically unpleasant—but really it does not have to turn out that way. Although the cause of the letter is unpleasant or negative, our letter can be sufficiently positive. Our approach should be to hold emotions in check, neutralize things that may upset our reader, state things as unemotionally as possible, avoid repeating or prolonging the unpleasant news, and emphasize the advantages of a prompt solution. In essence, we wish to clear up old business quickly and simply so that we can move ahead with newer and more inspiring things.

PROGRAMMING CLAIM LETTERS

In setting up a program for a claim letter, our first step is to identify the underlying situation as being a request. Then, we should realize that to be effective a letter in this situation ought to contain the three basic elements of a definite request, motivation, and ample assistance. The first element must always be a stated step, but the other elements sometimes are built in—that is, provided for by proper handling of everything else that appears in the letter. Putting these concepts to work in planning a claim letter, we are able to set up a program such as this:

DESCRIBE THE SITUATION.
EXPLAIN OUR POSITION.
SOUND AN APPEAL.
SPECIFY WHAT AND, IF HELPFUL, WHEN.

This program is still in the nature of a general plan which must be fitted to the specific case involved. The first two steps are obviously explanatory; they identify the particular difficulty and translate it into an understandable and meaningful effect on us, our property, or our operations. Thus we have laid the foundation for presenting our claim, whether it be a routine matter or something out of the ordinary.

Routine claims are often approached as being self-motivating. They deal with things which understandably happen in the best of organizations, but which are routinely corrected when they are brought to light. Neither side gets excited, because each has a clear-cut, sensible course of action to take. The supplier needs to nurture goodwill and to keep his customers pleased with his service. This need is usually motivation enough for him—there is little need to sound a special appeal to get him to act.

Claims in unusual situations, however, are somewhat different. They may be more serious, for one thing—or just seem to be, because they do not conform to any familiar accustomed pattern. Also, there is apt to be less automatic understanding of responsibility on the part of the reader of a claim letter in such instances. Therefore, as claims become more serious or more unusual in nature, there is a greater likelihood that some appeal will have to be made to motivate favorable action. Typical appeals are aimed at our reader's:

1. Pride.
2. Honesty.
3. Sense of fair play.
4. Fear.

An appeal to pride is a mild chiding intended to make our reader conscious of his own enviable status and to induce him to keep up the good work. Appeals to honesty and fair play are a bit more serious. In using either of them, we alert our reader to the fact that his image is involved—and that to keep his reputation untarnished he should correct any wrong he has caused. An appeal to fear is strongest of all, whether it can be made directly or indirectly. It is a threat of drastic action to come unless he gives us a satisfactory answer. Such action could be in the form of decreased business, loss of business, or even a law suit in certain instances. Naturally, such an appeal is a desperate one; we should not bring it to bear until all reasonable appeals have been unsuccessful. To threaten at the very beginning is not only undiplomatic, it is unfair. Most of the time, the reader will be hearing of the difficulty only when we bring it to his attention. Therefore, common courtesy requires us to give him a chance to appraise the situation and give us an answer. If he turns out to be unreasonable about accepting a solution, we can apply some pressure; but even so, we do not have to be rude or obnoxious.

As for our request, we should make it clear to our reader *what* action will satisfy us. This step gives our reader some indication of how he can please us. It tends to minimize the need for drawn-out correspondence or investigations, neither of which contributes toward the betterment of goodwill. If we can give a convincing explanation and a reasonable request, we can usually expect a favorable answer. The fact is that a just request offers our reader an easy way out of a troublesome situation. He can settle the matter simply by agreeing.

Under ordinary conditions, our presumption should be that our reader will respond promptly. If our request is to be granted, our reader should act quickly because of his desire to protect the goodwill relationship. After all, the original transaction is still in an uncompleted state and will remain that way until a solution of some kind is worked out. Therefore, we usually do not have to get specific about *when* our reader should take action.

If, however, a mention of the time aspect will be helpful to our reader, we do well to include it in our request step. For example, an order may be filled incorrectly; but there may still be time for our supplier to make an exchange and save his sale, provided he acts with unusual speed. Such information might be gratefully received by him. Also, in the extreme case of a threat, we should always give a sensible time limit within which the reader can do what is needed to avert the threatened action.

ILLUSTRATIONS OF CLAIM LETTERS

A look at a few examples of claim letters will show us a cross section of the appeals and degrees of insistence used. The letter on page 375 applies to a routine situation. The tone is mild; the appeal or motivation is automatic—the natural urge of the reader to safeguard his relationship with the writer; and no urgency is indicated.

The letter on page 376 concerns a situation that is not routine. The appeal or motivation step is spelled out more clearly. Still, no particular deadline is laid down for compliance with the request.

The letter shown on page 377 resorts to the use of a threat. It is not the first letter which has been written in connection with this particular claim; rather, it arises as the result of an uncooperative attitude toward previous, milder letters. Nevertheless, the writer manages to keep his emotions under control.

Martin's Department Store

20 RUNNYMEDE CIRCLE, ST. PAUL, MINN. 55177

March 14, 1967

Mayodan Garments, Inc.
3990 Madison Street
Greensboro, N.C. 27404

Gentlemen:

The twelve boxes (total order, one gross) of Mayodan men's slacks, which you sent in response to our P.O. No. 4079 of March 4, arrived today. These slacks are exactly what we have been looking for to round out our selection of clothing items for men.

In adding the slacks to our inventory, however, we discovered that one box contained only eleven instead of twelve pairs. The seal on the box had not been broken; so all we can assume is that somehow only eleven pairs of slacks were packed. The packing slip refers to Inspector No. 17 as the person who approved the contents for shipment.

Will you please adjust our billing, or send us a credit memorandum, for $15.75--the wholesale price of one pair of slacks? There is no point in having you make a special shipment of one pair, since we are contemplating future orders.

Very truly yours,

MARTIN'S DEPARTMENT STORE

Edward T. Murphy
Edward T. Murphy
Purchasing Director

ETM:ln

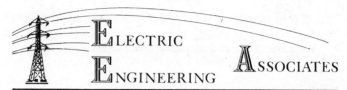

ELECTRIC
ENGINEERING   ASSOCIATES

11200 WAYNE BLVD., DETROIT, MICH. 48229

May 6, 1967

Harrington Manufacturing Co.
1020 Paulsen Building
Chicago, Illinois 60616

Gentlemen:

Subject: Our Order No. 3-314, of March 21

The electrical fixtures, which we wrote you about on April 10, have finally arrived.
Apparently they were delivered to a construction site in Dearborn before being re-
directed to our field office at the new "Mandalay" subdivision near Royal Oak.

In our April 10 tracer, we stressed the importance of having the fixtures in time to
complete installation in 62 new dwellings by April 30. When we saw that the order
was still undelivered on April 15, we had to obtain the fixtures from another supplier
rather than risk forfeiture of our bond.

We should have preferred to install Harrington fixtures, but had no choice in this
instance. Since our "Mandalay" project has been completed, we have no need for
the fixtures we received today. Under the circumstances it is only fair that we be
granted approval to return them to you in cancellation of our order.

Will you send an authorization, please?

Very truly yours,

ELECTRIC ENGINEERING ASSOCIATES

Herbert J. Black

Herbert J. Black
General Manager

HJB:ds

remote components inc.

4990 RIVERSIDE DR., LOS ANGELES, CALIF.   90010

August 15, 1967

Valley Electronics Company
1117 College Boulevard
Los Angeles, California 90024

Gentlemen:

You will agree, I'm sure, that it makes good sense to tie up loose ends.

There is one such loose end, however, which seems to be elusive. We first wrote you about it on July 5. That was when Jack Corley, your delivery man, caused a somewhat freak accident which resulted in 21 feet of our chain fence being pulled down. Because we are on a number of classified United States Government orders, we had to repair the fence immediately to comply with the security provisions of our contracts. The cost of this work came to $62.45, which we referred to you as a routine matter.

After no response was received from you, we sent a reminder on August 1. The next day, your attorney, William Harris, paid us a visit. He satisfied himself that our statement of the incident and charges was correct, and assured us that prompt settlement would be made.

Now two more weeks have passed, and we still have not heard anything further. May we receive payment by August 20, or should we have our attorney get in touch with yours?

Yours very truly,

Paul S. Houston

Paul S. Houston
Vice President

PSH:rb

ADJUSTMENT LETTERS
. . . .

If a lapse occurs in our phase of a business transaction or other event, or even appears that way to someone who stands to suffer a loss, the tables will be reversed. That other person will direct a claim toward us; and we will be faced with the job of straightening things out, probably through an adjustment letter. The difficulty of our job will depend partly on whether we can grant the claimant's request or must refuse it—and partly on whether the claimant showed himself to be calm and businesslike or to be highly distraught.

QUALITIES OF ADJUSTMENT LETTERS

In any case, we must bear in mind that the claimant has been worked up sufficiently at least to come to us with a claim. We should use an appropriate amount of delicacy and tact in dealing with him. Our general attitude in our reply to him should, therefore, contain the following elements:

1. *Promptness in giving an answer.* The claimant will only work into a deeper state of anxiety if he is kept waiting for an answer. If we cannot give a final answer immediately, at least we can acknowledge his communication.

2. *Attention to the claimant's state of agitation.* Our adjustment letter should open with a goodwill statement aimed at calming down the claimant. The more anger he has displayed in presenting his claim, the more effort we must put into this goodwill beginning.

3. *Finesse in discussing the situation.* We should especially be careful about applying diplomacy and positiveness (pleasantness). Our references to the claimant's communication should not appear to cast him in the role of a complainer or troublemaker. Our references to the situation involved should steer clear of unpleasant words or phrases that could revive the gruesome details

of what happened. We should use neutral terms: your letter, your report, last Wednesday's incident, the merchandise, the typewriter, etc. Such terms identify sufficiently well, but are harmless; they do not stir up undesirable memories and suggestions.

4. *Care in giving explanations.*   In any refusal-type adjustment letter, we should explain before giving our turndown. But we should offer a reasonable explanation—one that can be accepted by the claimant. We cannot afford to be argumentative or arbitrary. On the other hand, when we are granting the claim, we should add explanation only to the extent that it is needed or helpful. If, for example, the claimant would be more apt to desire an explanation because of some unusual occurrence, we should include it in our adjustment letter. But, if a claim is being granted out of deference to a special customer we should not get ourselves tangled up in any attempt at explanation.

In essence, these points amount to our having respect for the claimant's point of view. Whether he is right or wrong, the claimant has blamed something on us; and our reputation, in his eyes, has already become tarnished. Whether the matter is great or trivial in fact, the claimant has viewed it as serious enough to call for a protest from him. Whether our claimant has been polite or impolite in his communication to us, good business requires us to be polite when we answer him.

As a matter of fact, a healthy attitude on our part might be to welcome a claim letter as a ready-made opportunity for giving the writer of such a letter some personal attention. As we have seen earlier in this book, the businessman of today is often on edge because of the mechanical nature of his customer relationships. Businesses have become so large, that owners and top management have lost contact with their customers; and they often need to create situations so that they can inject a little of that desirable personal touch. Thus, we discover a certain amount of letter-writing activity aimed primarily at goodwill: the congratulation letter, the occasion-oriented appreciation letter, and the good-news acknowledgment of an order, to name a few.

When we have to write an adjustment letter, we do not have to contrive a situation to court goodwill—the situation is thrust upon us. Of course, we do not want anything to go wrong; but whenever it does, we should be glad that we have been notified about it. We then can do something to correct the situation, rebuild the goodwill, or both—instead of coasting along in the false security that all is well. Here is a golden opportunity for us to repair a relationship which has been damaged. We know the circumstances involved, the identity of the person concerned, his approximate state of mind, his wishes, and our own position in such a case as exists. Guesswork is reduced to a minimum; we should pretty well know *what* to say. If we are careful about *how* we say it, we should be able to come away from the encounter with a friend—or at least an understanding claimant, who likes us better after reading our answer than he did when he submitted his claim.

GOOD–NEWS ADJUSTMENT

One of the possible answers which we can give to a claim letter is the granting of the request in full. This is probably the easiest type of adjustment letter for us to write, because it is in the good-news situation. There are a few danger spots, however; and we should bear them in mind. We should avoid being too specific about the trouble which the claimant reported, and we should use neutral words in place of the unpleasant words which are naturally going to crop up during our thought processes. If we are at fault in the situation—which is likely to be the case—we should admit it and apologize. If we are not at fault, and are granting the claim for other reasons, we should be careful not to tip our hand. Once the executive decision has been made to grant the claim, we should follow through with an appropriate good-news letter. In that way we will not appear to be insincere or to be shaming our reader.

A Program for Good News

The writing program for a good-news adjustment letter takes shape along the following lines:

GET IN STEP.
GRANT.
EXPLAIN (IF NEEDED).
REBUILD GOODWILL (IF NEEDED).

Although this plan suggests that we have as many as four steps in the letter, we often can do some telescoping or bypassing. For instance, the opening step is intended to be a statement which puts our reader and us on the same side of the issue. In a serious situation, or one in which the reader is obviously angry, we should give special attention to smoothing things out before granting the request. Otherwise, our reader might just take the adjustment but still not calm down. In routine cases, especially when our reader has not displayed anything emotional, we often find that the granting act itself is sufficient for getting in step. Thus, the two parts are telescoped, and become one and the same.

As in good-news situations generally, explanation is a contingent step. If none is really needed, as would probably be the case in a routine matter, we do not put any in our adjustment letter. If some is needed, and has not already been taken care of through "get in step," we should put it in so that our reader will feel that he has been given full coverage.

The granting of the claim compensates our reader for whatever happened, but it does not necessarily restore his confidence in our company or operations. At the close of the letter we should do something to repair whatever damage has been done to our image. Whatever we say, however, should be convincing and pleasant sounding. For instance, we can promise to make improvements in our shipping department; but we should not go so far as to say that such an incident will never happen again. Or, we can assure the reader that we always stand behind our products; but we should not tell him to let us know *whenever* something goes wrong (suggesting a recurrence).

Illustrations

The letters on pages 382 and 383 are good-news adjustments. The first letter applies to a routine situation in which the customer used a calm approach in his claim letter.

The next letter applies to a situation of a nonroutine nature. The beginning, therefore, aims at getting the reader in a receptive mood so that the granting of his request will have maximum value. Some explanation is offered for the reader's satisfaction.

MAYODAN
GARMENTS , INC.

3990 MADISON ST., GREENSBORO, N.C.   27404

March 18, 1967

Martin's Department Store
20 Runnymede Circle
St. Paul, Minnesota 55177

Attention: Mr. Edward T. Murphy, Purchasing Director

Gentlemen:

Enclosed is our credit memorandum for $15.75. It will adjust the amount we
billed you for the Mayodan men's slacks which were delivered on March 14.

We are sorry that this incident occured, and appreciate the easy solution you
suggested to us. Thanks, too, for sending us the inspector's number. It should
help us as we follow through with a strengthening of our shipping-room function.

Very truly yours,

MAYODAN GARMENTS, INC.

Keith R. Sheldon

Keith R. Sheldon
Office Manager

KRS:mg
Enclosure

HARRINGTON **M**ANUFACTURING **CO.**

1020 PAULSEN BUILDING, CHICAGO, ILL.   60616

May 9, 1967

Mr. Herbert J. Black
General Manager
Electric Engineering Associates
11200 Wayne Boulevard
Detroit, Michigan 48229

Dear Mr. Black:

Please accept our sincere apologies on our handling of your March 21 order for fixtures. You had every right to expect prompt and proper delivery.

We certainly do authorize your returning the fixtures in cancellation of your order. Our local van will be dispatched to Royal Oak on Thursday, May 12, to pick up the fixtures. It should arrive at your field office about ten o'clock.

As far as we can determine, your fixtures were unloaded with another order at Dearborn. A construction foreman signed for both quantities, thereby giving the appearance of proper delivery to the papers pertaining to your fixtures. As you might expect, piecing together the puzzle some weeks later took considerable effort.

We appreciate your comments on Harrington fixtures, and are looking forward to serving you again when the opportunity arises.

Yours very truly,

James K. Harrington

James K. Harrington
President

JKH:kb

PARTLY–BAD–NEWS ADJUSTMENT

Most of the time when we are not responsible for the situation which has affected the claimant, we respond with a letter in the bad-news situation. Not always, of course, do we have to give the claimant an unqualified turndown. It may be possible that we are willing to make some kind of adjustment, although not exactly the one our reader has requested.

Such a situation is obviously a mixture of bad news and good news. Because our reader's precise request will not be granted, no matter what else happens he is likely to feel let down. Thus, we should proceed with caution, and use the bad-news sequence in our planning of the program. In this way our reader can be let down gently, and then have his hopes raised again by the positive offer of what we can do for him.

Programming a Counteroffer

The partly-bad-news, or counteroffer, adjustment letter is not intended to be the final piece of correspondence between the claimant and ourselves. He has written; now we are answering. But we cannot force a compromise solution down his throat. He must be given a chance to accept it or reject it, or perhaps counter with a second proposal of his own. The letter we write, therefore, can go only to a certain point, as follows:

GET IN STEP.
EXPLAIN.
COUNTEROFFER.

Our beginning is important now. It must be given thought and attention. We wish to show our reader that we have a proper attitude toward his request—that both parties are really going to work together to solve the problem involved. We should avoid apologies, even if offered supposedly as sympathy. "We are sorry," therefore, would sound somewhat like an admission of guilt; yet we are going to try to put across a turndown very shortly afterwards.

Our explanation will have to be realistic, diplomatic, and positive (that is, it should not dwell on gloomy concepts). We cannot get away with an arbitrary reason, such as "It's against our policy," because our reader will take it as a brush-off. Rather we should give a plausible, explanatory buildup to what will amount to a turndown of his request.

The final step is a statement of what we are willing to do for our reader, although it requires his concurrence before it becomes final. By careful phrasing of the transition from the explanation to the counter-offer, we should be able to imply the fact of the turndown. Examples of such phrasing are:

```
For these reasons, we can offer . . . .

You can see, therefore, that it is only fair that we . . . .

On the other hand, we suggest . . . .

Under these conditions, you will agree that . . . .
```

As for attending to goodwill in this kind of letter, we have to settle for the counteroffer step itself. But this step does serve to provide some encouragement to the reader. Possibly, leading out of a convincing explanation, it could even seem to be a generous proposal as compared to what might have been expected. In any event, we will have changed the direction of the request and must now await further word from the claimant.

Illustration

The letter on page 386 makes a counteroffer to a claim which seemed to be excessive. The writer does not, however, cast aspersions on the claimant. He merely applies common sense in setting the stage for his counteroffer.

BAD–NEWS ADJUSTMENT

Sometimes the situation will be entirely outside our area of responsibility. Whether we might still grant the claimant's request or suggest a counteroffer would be a matter of executive decision. Most likely, our response would be to decline the request. Ordinary causes for our turning down a claim are listed on page 387.

JEFFERSON COIN CO.

10350 KAHLMYER DR.   ST. LOUIS, MO. 63132

September 7, 1967

Mr. Gerald Fisher
972 Harold Street
Euclid, Ohio 44123

Dear Mr. Fisher:

You are right in wanting a top quality of coin for the price you pay. And that is why
we are careful to select only the choicest grades for our customers.

Our special mail offer of scarce U.S. $20 Liberty Head gold coins at $53 each arose
from our purchasing a sizable collection from the liquidator of an estate. We sorted out
the best of the collection for our sale and disposed of the rest to other dealers. For the
price advertised, you were assured a coin of beauty and lasting value. Orders had to
be filled on a first-come, first-served basis, of course, without reference to the coinage
date.

Although the advertised supply has been depleted, we still may be able to work out an
exchange of the 1913 coin you received for a 1907 coin of similar quality. We do have
a 1907 Liberty in our regular inventory; it is priced at $57.50. It can be yours if you
will send us your 1913 coin and the $4.50 price differential.

To provide time for your approval, we are placing the 1907 coin in our vault. It will be
reserved in your name for ten days.

Yours very truly,

Edward P. Weisbarth

Edward P. Weisbarth
Retail Manager

EPW:jh

1. The article was a final-sale item, not subject to a return or an adjustment.
2. Any warranty involved has expired.
3. The product has given all the service that reasonably can be expected of it.
4. The user is at fault in some way.
5. A third party (such as a common carrier) is actually at fault, and the claim should not have been made against us.

Our turndown letter in any such instance would be received as bad news by our reader. Our refusal need not be driven home, however. In fact, it can be implied rather than expressed. Either way, it will come after a diplomatic and plausible explanation; and it will be followed by a goodwill statement.

Our objective in the bad-news letter is to clear ourselves of any blame which the claimant has attributed to us. Included also is the goodwill aspect—to repair any lingering damage to our image. At the same time, we must not lose sight of the fact that the claimant is *our customer* and should not be left uncared for. It is one thing to be diplomatic in turning him down, but still another thing to make him feel that we have done whatever we could for him. In our final step, therefore, we should try to demonstrate our cooperative attitude as we try to rebuild goodwill. Perhaps we can suggest something that he can do to correct whatever is wrong. Perhaps we can suggest the name of a competent repairman—or even offer to do the work ourselves at a minimum cost to him. Sometimes it turns out that nothing is really wrong with the product; the purchaser just does not know how to use it properly. In such a case, we may be able to detect the fact and diplomatically put him wise. One tactic in this regard would be to send out an "inspector," who in reality is an "instructor." After getting the product working, this person could show the owner how to avoid a recurrence of the difficulty. And, if a third party is to blame, we should provide our customer with ample assistance in establishing contact.

Programming a Bad–News Adjustment

In keeping with the basic framework of a bad-news letter, our turndown adjustment letter would contain the following steps in the sequence shown:

Get in step.
Explain.
Decline (expressed or implied).
Rebuild goodwill.

Through the first two steps, this program is the same as that for the "partly-bad-news" adjustment letter. In this instance, of course, the steps are leading to a total turndown—not to just a counteroffer. Therefore, we must be especially careful of diplomacy, positiveness, and thoroughness in preparing our reader for such a finality. The turndown can be expressed, but it is less painful to our reader if it is merely implied. As a practical matter, the more helpful we can be in the goodwill step, the easier it will be to use an implied turndown. The technique for such a turndown is the same as that we use when making a counteroffer: a smooth but swift change of subject to something of a positive or constructive nature. Our reader will realize that the old subject has been closed in favor of a new subject which offers some benefit to him. The contrast between these two subjects communicates the turndown without our having to be explicit about it.

Illustration

The following is an example of a bad-news adjustment letter. Written to a customer who received in damaged condition a portion of the merchandise ordered, the letter gets in step with the reader. The beginning is properly sympathetic (not apologetic) and should put the claimant in a mood to pay attention to what comes next.

Two paragraphs are devoted to explanation, so that when the turndown comes the reader will be ready to withstand it. The danger of accusing the reader of misunderstanding the F.O.B. provisions is avoided by the writer's switching over to the impersonal tone.

The turndown is implied—nowhere in this letter does the writer actually decline to honor the reader's claim. But he moves deftly into a suggestion supported by appropriate assistance. And, he adds an encouraging statement—an extra bit of goodwill—as a finishing touch.

auditorium chair Company

2850 WOODWARD AVE., DETROIT, MICH. 48201

November 21, 1967

Capital City Music Center
1029 Scioto Boulevard
Columbus, Ohio 43204

Gentlemen: Our Invoice No. 11-72

    We appreciate your prompt and detailed report on the tubular chairs delivered to your warehouse on November 17. You may be sure that we understand your viewpoint entirely.

    Your order was loaded aboard a truck operated by Thruway Freight Lines, Inc., on November 16. It was signed for without qualification by Alex Waldeck, the driver. This acceptance supports our belief that the chairs were in good condition at that time.

    As a standard procedure, prices are quoted F.O.B. our factory. In that way, the basic charge is the same for all customers; but the delivery costs, billed separately by the transportation company involved, vary according to the service required. Technically, however, the carrier is agent for the purchaser, not for the shipper. Thus, the shipper cannot make any promises or adjustments that would be binding on the carrier--no matter how appropriate such action might seem to be.

    It is our suggestion, therefore, that you deal directly with Thruway Freight Lines, Inc. Describe the situation just as you did in your letter to us, and if you wish, mention that we are holding the signed receipt. Your letter should be addressed as follows:

        Mr. John J. Parnell
        Thruway Freight Lines, Inc.
        100 Terminal Center
        Toledo, Ohio 43616

We are confident that you will receive the adjustment you seek.

        Very truly yours,

        Glenn B. Macalester
        Sales Manager

GBM:md

SUMMARY
· · · · · · · · ·

Claim letters and adjustment letters are specialized requests and answers, respectively, which are written in connection with some adverse development.

If we have a grievance, we direct a claim letter to the company or person whom we suppose to be responsible. By its very nature, our claim letter must report something unpleasant; but it does not have to be an unpleasant communication. We can hold negative suggestion in check by factual rather than emotional reporting, and by minimal reference to the difficulty. We should not use threats, unless more reasonable motivations have failed. We should give clear and sufficient information. We should state exactly what we are after—with the expectation that our reader will probably go along with a reasonable request in a believable presentation.

If we must answer a claim letter, we should first decide on a course of action: to grant the request, to make a counteroffer, or to turn down the request. Then, we should write the type of letter that best conveys our decision. In any case, we need to get in step with our reader by beginning on an agreeable note. We should be patient with him no matter how aroused he has shown himself to be. We should use safe, neutral wording when referring to the difficulty; avoid apologies when there is no need for them; resist the temptation to argue; and strive to repair whatever damage has been done to our image.

The capsule summaries on pages 391–94 outline the plans for typical claim and adjustment letters.

CLAIM LETTER

Intended
Reader
Reaction:

from this   •   through this   to this

Program: Describe the situation.
Explain our position.
Sound an appeal—Pride.
                  —Honesty.
                  —Fair Play.
                  —Fear (threat).
Specify *what* and, if helpful, *when*.

Pointers: In giving the background, avoid stressing the gloomy aspects;
report in matter-of-fact tones.

Do not exaggerate—it will only arouse suspicion and tend to
lead to delays.

Give as much specific information as you can: purchase order
numbers, invoice numbers, product descriptions, etc.

In routine claims, generally consider that spelled-out appeals
are not needed.

In unusual and/or very serious cases, use an appropriate
appeal.

Do not use an appeal to fear (threat), except as a last resort—
never in a first notification.

Be sure to make it clear what action will satisfy you—such as
a refund, exchange, repair, inspection of the damage, etc.

Do not affix a deadline for action, unless (a) it will benefit your
reader, or (b) you have reached the threat stage.

GOOD–NEWS ADJUSTMENT

Intended
Reader
Reaction:

from this   to this

Program: Get in step.
Grant.
Explain (if needed).
Rebuild goodwill (if needed).

Pointers: Begin with a statement that wins the approval of the reader.

Consider that, in a mild situation, a single step can both win approval and tell the reader that his request is being granted. If the reader seems to be aroused, however, a preliminary step to calm him down is needed.

In a routine situation, expect that an explanation step should not be necessary.

In a serious or unusual situation, consider that an explanation is probably wanted and should be given.

In a routine situation, the granting of the reader's claim is usually sufficient to hold his goodwill.

When our reader has shown himself to be upset or when the situation is rather serious, our goodwill relationship has suffered somewhat. We should do our best to rebuild it to its former level.

PARTLY–BAD–NEWS ADJUSTMENT
(Somewhat)

Intended
Reader
Reaction:

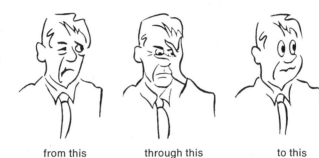

from this   through this   to this

Program: Get in step.
Explain.
Counteroffer.

Pointers: Begin with a statement aimed at winning the reader's approval.
In a mild situation, it could be as simple as a word of appreciation for his report. In a serious situation, it should be something with which he *has to agree,* thereby bringing us together
as partners to solve the problem.

Avoid a beginning such as "We are sorry"—unless it is a
genuine apology. Otherwise, it seems to imply an admission of
responsibility.

In this letter, the reader will be receiving some measure of bad
news, because his specific request will not be granted. While
the turndown is usually implied rather than expressed, the explanatory matter should precede it in sequence.

Provide a convincing explanation of our position concerning
the reader's claim.

Don't revive the ugly details of the situation.

Don't offer an arbitrary reason, such as "It's against our
policy."

Consider that the counteroffer is a tentative gesture of goodwill pending an answer from the reader.

BAD–NEWS ADJUSTMENT
(No, But)

Intended
Reader
Reaction:

from this   through this   to this

Program: Get in step.
Explain.
Decline (expressed or implied).
Rebuild goodwill.

Pointers: Begin with a statement aimed at winning the reader's approval.
This statement could be as simple as appreciation for his report; but because of the full turndown that is coming along in
the letter, it should definitely be something that aligns us as a
team searching for a solution to the problem.

Avoid saying "We are sorry," etc. It may sound more like an
admission of guilt than an expression of sympathy.

Give an adequate explanation *before* making the turndown.

Don't give an arbitrary reason, such as "It's against our
policy."

Don't revive the ugly details of the situation.

If possible, use an implied turndown. If it must be expressed,
don't dwell on it.

In the goodwill ending, try to be helpful. Suggest a remedy of
some kind; suggest a reliable repair shop; offer factory repair
at minimum cost; offer tactful instructions on using the product; or steer him to a third party who may be responsible—
giving details, of course.

QUESTIONS
• • • • • • • • • •

1. What is the attitude that the successful businessman has toward his customers?

2. Give some practical reasons why a customer should use diplomacy in a claim letter when he writes to a supplier.

3. Essentially, what are the four qualities desired in a claim letter?

4. Give the steps in the suggested program for a claim letter.

5. Do all claim letters need a spelled-out appeal to motivate the reader?

6. List four typical appeals which can be used to motivate the reader of a claim letter.

7. Under what circumstances would it be satisfactory to use an appeal to fear (a legitimate threat) as the motivation step in a claim letter?

8. In a claim letter, is it always necessary to state what is expected of the reader—or is it sufficient to leave that up to him?

9. Under what conditions would it be proper to mention a time limit within which action should be taken?

10. What influences have a bearing on whether an adjustment letter will be relatively easy or difficult to compose?

11. List the four elements which should be contained in the writer's attitude toward adjustment letters.

12. Whether or not the claimant is entitled to reparations, what fact makes the job of preparing an adjustment letter a serious matter for the writer's firm?

13. What opportunity is presented to a firm when it receives a claim letter, despite the fact that the firm is faced with a ticklish situation?

14. List the program steps for a good-news adjustment letter.

15. Give seven cautions applicable to the content of an adjustment letter, even though the letter fulfills the reader's claim.

16. Suggest a single word to describe an adjustment letter that conveys *partly bad news.*

17. What is the suggested program for a partly-bad-news adjustment letter?

18. State what is meant by the program topic, "get in step."

19. How is it possible to have a partly-bad-news adjustment letter when the program for such a letter does not contain a turndown of the reader's own request?

20. Name five ordinary reasons why a firm might send a bad-news adjustment letter—that is, an absolute turndown of the reader's request.

21. What important fact should be kept in mind by the writer when he has to refuse a claimant's request?

22. Give the suggested program for a bad-news adjustment letter.

23. How can an implied turndown be accomplished in a bad-news adjustment letter?

PROBLEMS
. . . .

Some of the following problems are to be answered in typewritten form on business letterhead; others, on plain stationery. If a letterhead is indicated but not available, set up a simulated letterhead in accordance with directions issued by your instructor.

12–1. (Letterhead.) The Midtown Department Store of this city advertised its annual sale of glassware in the local newspaper. To increase its normal inventory in this department, it placed an order (No. 1192) with Crystal Glass Company of Lancaster, Ohio; delivery was specified on a date which should have been sufficiently in advance of the proposed sale. As things turned out, however, the new glassware was not delivered until two days after the sale. During the course of the sale, the Midtown Department Store exhausted its stock of glassware and was obliged to turn away would-be customers. Now that the ordered glassware has arrived, there is no longer a need for so much of it. It is only fair that Crystal Glass Company, which had acknowledged the order but had not lived up to the delivery clause, do what is necessary to rectify the situation. As purchasing agent for the Midtown Department Store write a claim letter to Crystal Glass; ask that one half of the order be taken back for credit to the Midtown account.

12–2. (Letterhead.) Industrial Chemicals, Inc., of St. Louis, Missouri, filled an order for 100 gallons of resin distillates on the 10th of last month. The distillates were requested by the Best Manufacturing Company of this city; the purchase number involved was P–393. The related invoice, which billed Best for $232, bore the serial number 27 12 29. Delivery was made on the first of this month, as specified by the purchase order. Today, the first 5-gallon container of the distillate was issued from the storeroom to the production department. The foreman complained that the fluid, instead of being clear, was a rusty orange in color. A second container was issued, but the contents again appeared to be contaminated. Subsequently, three additional containers were tested with precisely the same results. This sampling has led the foreman to believe that the entire 100-gallon shipment is substandard and unsafe to use in the manufacturing process. Assume that you are the director of purchasing of the Best Manufacturing Company. Write to the supplier; request an exchange of this shipment of resin distillates, which is obviously below his regular standard.

12–3. (Plain stationery.) Ten days ago you mailed a letter, with a money order for $8.98 enclosed, to Metropolitan Book Sellers of New York City. You ordered a copy of *The Colonies in Revolt,* a documentary book edited by Paul Armbruster, Ph.D. Today you received a book from this supplier; but it is a copy of *The American Colonies,* also edited by Dr. Armbruster. The price appearing on the dust jacket is $8.98. Write the necessary claim letter to Metropolitan Book Sellers.

12–4. (Plain stationery.) The Commercial Supply Company, which is located in the capital of your state, placed an advertisement in the many Sunday newspapers throughout the state. One of the items in the advertisement was a "Diplomat" brand dispatch case listed at $10 plus 3 percent sales tax. You clipped the coupon which appeared in the advertisement and mailed it with your check to the address given. Upon receiving your case, however, you experience a disappointment. It is not exactly what you had pictured it to be; and it does not appear to be sturdy enough to stand rough treatment. As this case was advertised to "satisfy, or your money back," write Commercial Supply that you are returning it for a full refund.

12–5. (Letterhead.) This morning a tractor-trailer rig missed the turn at the driveway entrance of The Bonnie Lass Candy Co., 1500 Briarslope Drive, Cleveland, Ohio 44131. It collided with the gatepost and ripped out some 30 feet of chain fence. Upon investigation, it was learned that the truck driver was in a confused state of mind. He was neither making a delivery to Bonnie Lass nor coming to pick up a shipment. He could not explain why he was attempting to enter the grounds. The parking-lot guard called the police; but, since the accident occurred on private property, the officers declined to take action. As controller of The Bonnie Lass Candy Co. write a claim letter to the Kelly Transport System, 900 Livonia Road, Detroit, Michigan, owner of the tractor-trailer rig.

12–6. (Letterhead.) The Pioneer Catalogue Sales, Inc. mail-order house in your home town has received a letter and a package from one of its customers, Louis J. Halloran. The letter contains a request for an exchange of a large-sized bathrobe for one of medium size. Mr. Halloran says he actually ordered the medium size, but through some mix-up was sent the wrong size. Pioneer Catalogue Sales, Inc. recognizes that it is at fault in this transaction and will gladly make the exchange. The particular design of bathrobe is out of stock in the medium size, although a new supply is due to arrive within one week. As customer-service manager for Pioneer, write an appropriate answer to Mr. Halloran.

12–7. (Letterhead.) On a trip to Washington, D.C., Mrs. Leroy Palmer did some shopping at Milady's Fashions, an exclusive women's shop. Among her purchases was a stylish sweater of combed white lamb's wool, with cultured pearls adorning the front of the neck. Back home in Roanoke, Virginia, Mrs. Palmer discovered an unraveling strand of yarn on the left sleeve of the sweater. The more she tried to repair the damage, the more the yarn unraveled. In desperation, she mailed the sweater back to Milday's Fashions and asked them to determine the cause of the trouble. The store has arrived at the conclusion that the situation began as the result of a manufacturing defect. It is returning the sweater to the manufacturer with the request that a replacement be sent to Mrs. Palmer. As president of Milady's Fashions, inform Mrs. Palmer of this development.

12–8. (Letterhead.) Assume that you are the newly appointed adjustment manager of the Midtown Department Store, which is located in this city. You have just come from a special meeting attended by the president of the store, the merchandising manager, and yourself. The subject of the meeting was a mink stole which Mrs. Rene D. Bonville's maid brought back to the store on behalf of her employer. Mrs. Bonville's relayed message is that she has been unable to use the stole, because of poorness in the fit; she wants the $900 price credited to her account. Your investigation reveals that Mrs. Bonville bought the stole following a fitting given by Miss Welch, our expert in such matters; that the Civic Ballet performed *Swan Lake* two nights ago; that the society column of the newspaper mentioned Mrs. Bonville's presence at the performance "wearing a stunning mink stole"; and that the stole itself has a strong scent of perfume, an indication that it may have been worn. Your position has been that Mrs. Bonville should be given a polite "no"; but the other company officers have taken a more lenient attitude. After all, Mrs. Bonville is an important customer—year in, year out. Although admitting that she probably is not entitled to return the stole for credit, the president has ruled that her request will be honored anyhow. In an adjustment letter, convey the good news to Mrs. Bonville.

12–9. (Letterhead.) Paynter College for Women, located in Memphis, Tennessee, bought 250 compartmented plastic trays from the Tru-Mold Plastic Products Company of Indianapolis, Indiana. These trays were intended for use in the college cafeteria. However, on the very first contact with the hot, sudsy water of the dishwasher, the trays became badly warped. They would not rest flat on the surface of a table, nor could they be stacked in a satisfactory manner. The manager of the college cafeteria was so disgusted with this purchase that he wrote to Tru-Mold and demanded that the trays be taken back for full refund. He cited a guarantee clause in Tru-Mold's brochure advertising the trays. The fact is, however, that the guarantee does not promise a refund—only to replace trays which do not give full satisfaction. Assume that you are the sales manager of the Tru-Mold Plastic Products Company. Write to the cafeteria manager at Paynter College and tell him what your company can do in this instance.

12–10. (Letterhead.) The Work-N-Play Shop is located in a city with a population in excess of 100,000. It specializes in outdoor equipment of many kinds, such as power saws, light tractors, power mowers, lawn edgers, motorbikes, scooters, outboard motors, and so on. One day last week a suburbanite bought a rotary power mower and paid the full price of $59.95 in cash. Today a neighbor of his, who had business in the city, brought the mower back to the store in his station wagon. A note written by the purchaser of the mower stated that the equipment was unfit for use and that it should be taken back for a full refund. The attending clerk was not authorized to pay out refunds, but he gave the neighbor a receipt for the mower. A later inspection revealed that one of the blades was badly bent; it had become wedged in its housing and had thereby locked the entire mechanism. The diagnosis is that the mower had been pushed on top of a large rock or brick; but there is no positive proof. Since the damage can be repaired by the Work-N-Play Shop's own technicians, the request for a refund appears to be extreme. As the store's owner-president, write a letter to the customer and make your counteroffer.

12–11. (Letterhead.) Harley's General Store is located in a small community in the northern part of your state. Jasper Harley, the proprietor of the store, recently placed an order for billheads with the Commercial Supply Company, which is located in the state capital. He submitted a copy of his existing billhead as a sample of how he wanted the new ones printed. Earlier this week Commercial Supply Company mailed Mr. Harley his new supply of billheads. Today, however, a special delivery letter has been received at Commercial Supply. An irate Mr. Harley demands that the billheads be done over—and that this time his instructions be followed exactly. His complaint is that the wording "Established 1898" was not inserted between the name of the store and its mailing address. As adjustment manager you have gone to the files for Mr. Harley's order and the sample billhead. After several inspections of the sample you finally notice a scribbled-in-pencil notation at the bottom edge of the form. It is barely discernible as "Est. 1898"; however, there is no indication of where such wording should be placed. Under these conditions, Mr. Harley seems to be demanding too much. After all, the billheads are correct as they stand, and are perfectly functional. Write a reply to Mr. Harley. For goodwill purposes, you have decided to allow him a 5 percent reduction in the price but not a replacement of the forms.

12–12. (Letterhead.) In a special inventory-clearance sale of discontinued items, Pioneer Catalogue Sales, Inc., of your home town, filled an order from Mrs. Martha Lambert for a matched set of HIS and HER bath towels. The sale price was 30 percent lower than the price which had been listed in the company's catalogue. After she received the set of towels, Mrs. Lambert changed her mind. She mailed the package back to Pioneer Catalogue Sales, Inc. and also wrote the company a letter in which she requested a refund of her money. The company's stand in such cases is that an inventory-clearance sale is a final sale. Except in the instance of an out-and-out case of damaged merchandise, the customer gives up his right to a refund when he accepts the discounted price. As sales manager of Pioneer Catalogue Sales, Inc., write an explanation to Mrs. Lambert; return her towels.

12–13. (Letterhead.) "Bargain Bill" Bluefield of this city is an authorized dealer of a popular make of automobile. Four months ago, the Fred Donalds visited Bluefield's showroom and eventually bought a new four-door station wagon. Because they live in the village of Grantsville, about 40 miles from the city, they believed that such a model would be ideal for their purposes. Yesterday afternoon Mrs. Donald brought the station wagon to the service entrance at Bluefield's. She told the attendant that something was wrong with the automatic transmission, and that she would leave the station wagon there to be repaired. The costs of such repairs, she said, would be covered by Bluefield's new-car warranty. She then left for the bus terminal and home. Assume that you are Mr. Bluefield, and that your new-car warranties extend over a 90-day period only. Of course, you would be glad to undertake the repairs for the cost of parts and labor—estimated at $75. Your service garage uses only authorized parts and factory-trained mechanics. Write to the Donalds.

12–14. (Letterhead.) On February 1, the Tocqueville Hotel of Milwaukee, Wisconsin, issued its purchase order No. 1417 to Central Industries, Incorporated, a wood-products manufacturer located in the capital of your state. The order specified six four-drawer storage chests, birch wood, finished, with detachable casters. The size was stated in terms of the catalogue listing, "commercial." These chests were standard items which Central Industries had in stock; they were shipped F.O.B. from the factory by way of Kimball Truck Lines. Billing to the Tocqueville Hotel for $300 was made on the date of the shipment, February 4, on a serialized invoice—No. 119. On

February 11, Central Industries receives a complaint from Howard Josephus, the purchasing agent for the Tocqueville Hotel. He reports that two of the chests have arrived in damaged condition. Water has apparently soaked through the corrugated shipping containers. It has discolored the varnish finish and has caused large patches of cardboard to adhere to the sides and tops of the chests. Mr. Josephus believes that since Central Industries failed to use waterproof containers in the first place, and made the choice of carrier in the second place, the manufacturer should "make good" on these two damaged chests. As adjustment manager for Central Industries, refuse this claim. The shipping containers used were of a type generally recognized to be sturdy and safe. Any negligence on the part of the carrier is, of course, inexcusable. It is your belief, however, that legal title to the chests passed to the Tocqueville Hotel the moment they were loaded aboard the carrier's vehicle. In that case, Kimball Truck Lines acted as agent for the hotel and must assume full responsibility for the damage. Nevertheless, because the hotel is one of Central's customers, try to be as helpful as you can.

12–15. (Letterhead.) Mrs. Veronica Atwill, who describes herself as a "poor old widow living on a pension," has filed a claim with the Bonnie Lass Candy Co., 1500 Briarslope Drive, Cleveland, Ohio 44131. In a letter to you, the company's general manager, she is requesting reimbursement of $7.50, which is what it will cost her for a new pair of hose and for dry cleaning charges. Two days ago, while Mrs. Atwill was waiting for a bus near a shopping plaza in a west-side suburb of Cleveland, a panel truck roared by "like a drag racer" and threw mud and grease over her clothing from the waist down. She states that she saw the Bonnie Lass name on the side of the truck. Write to Mrs. Atwill and refuse her claim. Your company does not own a panel truck. There is, however, a firm named Bennie Lee Camera Co. which does have such a truck and which is located in the very shopping plaza mentioned in the complaint. Perhaps this is the truck which splashed Mrs. Atwill.

CHAPTER **13**

••

ANSWERING A
CREDIT APPLICANT

In the modern business picture, extension of credit to one's customers is a necessary requirement. We have rather permanently moved from the older concept of paying cash for purchases of all kinds to one that permits the accumulation of debts before payments are due. As much as we might prefer to operate on a pay-as-you-go basis, the willingness of our competitors to grant credit forces us to offer credit privileges, too.

There are some advantages and some disadvantages connected with the granting of credit. The advantages can benefit both ourselves and our customers. We as sellers can meet competition, increase our sales, and move our inventory at a faster rate than we could were we on a strictly cash basis. Our customers can take full advantage of "impulse" buying even when they are not carrying a large amount of cash, and they can own many items of a durable or luxury nature (automobiles, jewelry, appliances, etc.) much sooner than they could if they had to save the money first.

We can expect some disadvantages, however. First, there is the need to be organized for credit business. We must have staff to handle credit applications, to check on the applicants' suitability for credit terms, and to do the extra bookkeeping and billing that is involved. Then, too, there is the possibility of some loss because of uncollectible accounts. In the long run, though, assuming we have a well-functioning credit system, we should enjoy a net benefit. From our customers' viewpoint the chief danger is that some people are not capable of operating on a credit basis. They forget that credit is basically borrowing—a convenience of the moment—and that payment is still in the picture. They charge merchandise without regard for the consequences, and may be in financial difficulty when the bills come due.

TYPES OF CREDIT

In general, there are two types of business credit (as distinguished from direct loans such as would be obtained at a bank). These are retail credit, which is available to the ultimate consumer, and trade or mercantile credit, which is available to a middleman from his own supplier.

RETAIL CREDIT

Nowadays the identifying symbol of a retail charge account is usually the credit card or the charge plate. Such a device is a metal or plastic plate which identifies its owner as being approved for credit privileges. It usually contains a serial number as well as the name and address of the owner. The intention is that this identification plate be presented at the time a purchase is being made so that it can be inserted into an imprinter. Sometimes it is issued by a central agency and is notched to fit the imprinter at each store, in a given area, where credit privileges have been granted. The sales slip or invoice is then embossed with the information appearing on the plate to assure proper charging to the customer's account.

Before we issue such a plate to a retail credit applicant, we should obtain a credit rating. Usually this rating can be obtained from our local retail credit association. If it is not available, we can ask for references (names of persons qualified to comment on the applicant's past performance or his general eligibility for credit) and write to them for information. In issuing a credit card or charge plate, we can protect ourselves somewhat by including an expiration date—which, in effect, sets up a probation period.

A recent addition to the credit field is the bank chargecard. The card is issued by the bank at which the card-holder has a savings or checking account. Merchants who honor the cards receive an immediate (but discounted by 2 to 5 percent) payment from the bank, which takes care of collection and credit charges. These plans are almost certain to be a major factor in the future, particularly because they frequently have a small-loan feature (the holder may borrow perhaps $100 on the strength of the card alone) and because they bring the small merchant who could not afford his own credit setup into the credit buying field. It is widely predicted that the bank plans are only the beginning of a computerized system through which the public will be able to make purchases, travel, and even make telephone calls with a bank card; and payments will be deducted at the bank without even the necessity of writing a check!

VARIETIES OF RETAIL CREDIT

There are a number of different arrangements by which retail credit can be handled, depending on the nature of the business, the preference of management, the pressure of competition, and the credit capacities of customers. It is often found that a company will offer more than a single variety of retail credit, in order to meet the specific needs of its customers. The following are the better known varieties; they are given in the order of most liberal to least liberal.

Charge Account

The regular charge account is what most retail credit applicants seek. It permits them to use their identification plate at will. Although for high-priced articles, such as jewelry and appliances, a credit verification might have to be made, it is nevertheless possible for a customer to run up a very large overall bill through numerous routine purchases.

The usual procedure is that purchases made during a month's time are summarized on a statement. The total is payable when the statement is presented to the customer. As a means of smoothing out the busy and slack segments of the monthly work cycle, such billings are often made on a cycle basis. Certain letters of the alphabet are processed each working day to avoid a month-end crisis. Of course, a full month would be allowed between billings to any one customer.

Revolving Account

Because consumer buying can often have its own peaks and troughs —such as being high around Christmas and Easter—some customers can be served best by what is known as a revolving account. This arrangement has the same external aspects as a regular charge account, but an entire bill need not be paid upon presentation. Instead, the customer is allowed to make a partial payment and to defer the remainder. The amount to be paid may be a fixed amount, or it may be a fixed percentage of the total amount due. The deferred portion would be subject to a time-payment charge, made up of an interest figure and a service-charge figure.

Despite the disadvantage of the extra charge on the unpaid balance, the customer enjoys a number of benefits from such a plan. He can charge as much as he likes. He can buy certain things which he might never otherwise have because of his inability to hang onto available cash. And he need not fear becoming abruptly delinquent, because he can spread out his payments over a period of time. In effect, he is borrowing from the company and paying for the privilege; but he does so effortlessly, as against going to a bank or loan company. In fact, many companies provide for the converting of a regular charge account to a revolving account at any time the customer wishes to have it that way.

Layaway Plan

A much stricter method of credit is the layaway plan. Under this arrangement, the customer may not take possession of any merchandise until it has been paid for; but the company is willing to reserve an article specifically for him while he is making periodic payments on it. To many persons, this system may not appear to be credit at all; but we can see that it does conform to the original Latin meaning of *credit* (he trusts). The company acts on the expectation that the customer will eventually redeem the article and thereby consummate the sale. If he does not, the company may have to refund his payments. Then, it may suffer a loss in the sales column—if, for instance, styles or demands for the product have changed adversely while it was set aside.

C.O.D. Arrangements

For the customer who can scarcely be allowed credit of any kind, a C.O.D. arrangement is better than nothing. Here again, many people do not regard C.O.D. as a credit plan—but actually the company is trusting the customer to accept delivery of the goods and to pay the amount due, including the handling charges. If the goods are not accepted, the company does not make its sale, but has incurred expense in clerical work, packaging, and delivery expense of some kind—especially noticeable if the package went by express or parcel post.

The plan has definite advantages for the customer:

1. Convenience—the goods are brought to him.
2. Time—an extra cushion is allowed for raising the money between placing the order and receiving the goods.
3. Reputation—possibly, on the strength of several C.O.D. experiences, the customer can convince the company to grant him a somewhat better credit arrangement.

TRADE OR MERCANTILE CREDIT

An entirely different set of circumstances typifies the issuance of trade or mercantile credit. This form of credit is extended variously from a supplier to a manufacturer, from a manufacturer to a wholesaler or to a tradesman, and from a wholesaler (or jobber) to a tradesman. It is given in the form of a "line of credit"—that is, a specified limit up to which the grantor believes the applicant can safely be allowed to go.

In deciding whether to grant credit and, if so, what limit to set, the company must satisfy itself on the applicant's ability to meet his obligations. Enough information should be gathered so that these decisions will be made wisely. Such information should relate to the applicant's financial condition; the behavior pattern of the applicant in the conduct of business, including the experience and proven ability of the management; the future outlook, including location, competition, and trends; and integrity as evidenced by the applicant's record for honesty, payment of bills, and ethical practices.

Trade Credit Information

The sources of such credit information are usually within easy reach. Not all sources, however, are equally fruitful, and many are limited to certain phases of the desired information.

For instance, information concerning an applicant's financial position may often be obtained from national reports, such as those published by Dun and Bradstreet, Inc., as well as by numerous trade associations. In some instances, banks in the applicant's locality can be prevailed upon to give helpful information. And there is always the possibility of requiring the applicant to submit certified statements for scrutiny.

Information relating to the applicant's business acumen, experience, and integrity can be obtained from various people who have had dealings with the applicant. Some of these sources could be sales representatives in the field, references named by the applicant, and other suppliers known to have done business with the applicant. The latter are also a source of information on the applicant's bill-paying performance.

Economic facts about the applicant's industry and location are sometimes available from banks and governmental bureaus. Such facts, coupled with knowledge of what the applicant's competitors are planning, can have an important bearing on the decision to grant or withhold credit.

All available credit information concerning an applicant is accumulated, perhaps in a file folder, perhaps on punch cards or computer tape. It serves initially as the basis for the credit decision; but it is retained and expanded as additional information develops with the passage of time.

Features of Trade Credit

If the credit information gathered on an applicant is favorable, a decision to grant credit may be indicated. The next decision concerns the specific method of trade credit that is to be extended. Under the open-account arrangement, a limit is set on the amount of purchases that may be outstanding at any one time. The purchaser places his orders for materials, supplies, or merchandise during a one-month period. Amounts not paid for at the end of that time are usually sum-marized in a monthly statement, although there is a gradual trend to-ward omitting this step with customers who keep current in their pay-ments. A customary feature of trade credit is the provision for a cash discount—a savings over the regular price—if payment is made within a specified number of days. A familiar provision is stated, "2/10, n/30" —meaning that a discount of 2 percent is allowed if payment is received within 10 days, but that payment is due within 30 days otherwise. Such a discount is attractive to the purchaser and is decidedly an inducement to early payment of his account. This example is but one of many dis-count arrangements, some of which are unique within a certain field or trade. In some cases, extended periods are allowed for discounts, the percentage offered decreasing with the passage of time. Sometimes unusual percentages and time periods are involved, as in "1/30, n/31."

As with retail credit, there are substitute arrangements available in the area of trade or mercantile credit. These variations make it possible for a supplier to counteroffer with some form of credit when the ap-plicant's specific request cannot be granted. Thus, one approach would be to suggest a lower credit limit than the one sought by the applicant, even though the open-account arrangement might still be used.

A second possibility is the shipping of goods on consignment. Under this arrangement, title to the goods remains with the seller and the articles remain a part of his inventory. The receiver is required to submit periodic reports and make payment for the units which have been sold. The system has disadvantages to the supplier, who obviously is under-writing the whole operation. It is useful, however, when he is hard-pressed for retail outlets.

The almost negligible credit arrangement of collection upon delivery of the goods is another possibility. In trade credit, however, there are two approaches to this method: C.O.D. and S.D.–B.L. The C.O.D. approach is the requirement of payment at the time of delivery, either in currency or by check (possibly a certified check or money order). The S.D.–B.L. approach means that the carrier presents a sight draft along with the bill of lading. A sight draft, in effect, is a check; but it has been made out by the supplier and is presented to the purchaser for signature. Once signed, it functions the same way as a check issued by the pur-chaser. The only "credit" involved, of course, in either C.O.D. or S.D.–B.L. is the faith the supplier is placing in the purchaser to do his part when the shipment arrives. Otherwise, some loss may be incurred by the supplier.

PLANNING CREDIT LETTERS

The basic planning of a credit letter is not affected by general type of credit under consideration, be it retail credit or trade credit. We are confronted with a major decision on the kind of letter to be written. After our decision has been made, we can set up a program to be followed in communicating the message; all the rest constitutes the specific details of a given case.

Because we have restricted our study of credit letters to those given in answer to an applicant, we can draw some parallels between these letters and others we have already examined. Letters which grant credit, offer a lesser credit arrangement than the one requested, or which turn down a credit request, are structured in much the same fashion as adjustment letters. This may be regarded as an expected development, because both adjustment letters and credit letters of these types are in answer to definite requests. At the same time, a good-news credit letter is seen to resemble a good-news acknowledgment of an order. In both cases, the reader's request is being granted in full; and there is an ideal opening for added goodwill. Some of our credit letters may turn out to be similar to the acknowledgment of an unclear order. The reason is that the applicant has left out some information, and we cannot give him a final answer until he sends it along.

GOOD–NEWS CREDIT LETTER

If we decide to grant the exact type of credit which has been requested, we are in position to send out a good-news credit answer.

Program

The program for such a letter would be as follows:

WELCOME (PLEASURE TO GRANT).
TERMS, ETC.
GOODWILL STATEMENT(S).

Our opening statement should be properly enthusiastic. It should clearly indicate that the applicant's credit request is being granted and that we are happy to have him join our family of charge customers. Our degree of enthusiasm may vary somewhat with the applicant's credit rating, but it should be our basic attitude. We should not show doubt or display a grudging attitude in this letter. While we may have had a hard time reaching a favorable decision in this case, we should play up the positive in the letter which grants credit.

Whether we have rated our reader as a good, fair, or poor risk, the fact is that we have granted the credit he requested. A good credit arrangement, of course, depends on a clear understanding of the system involved and on prompt payment of bills as they become due. Our best safeguard in this respect is some educational effort at the moment of granting credit. We should be careful, however, to explain the terms in neutral, matter-of-fact tones, at worst—certainly not in severe or scolding tones.

To close our letter, we should make a play for the reader's goodwill. Usually we can point to the various advantages that will accrue to the reader in his role as our customer. For retail customers, we may offer convenience of location, parking privileges, late shopping hours, exclusive lines of merchandise, delivery service, store reputation (status), and so on, in addition to the basic convenience of the charge account itself. Here is a golden opportunity to put in an extra amount of "house" promotion. Similarly, in trade situations, we may be able to promote customer goodwill. We may have our product advertised nationally— say, on television or in magazines; have selling aids available—window displays, placards, leaflets, etc.; supply rack-service personnel, who stock and tidy up the dealer's shelves; have local warehouses for purposes of prompt service; offer free delivery; and the like.

Illustrations

The two letters on pp. 412–13 are good-news credit answers. Each could be used as either a personalized letter or a form letter, depending upon the approach favored by the company sending it.

The first letter concerns retail credit. It talks about the credit arrangement being provided and tries to encourage the customer to take advantage of his privileges.

The next letter grants credit to a trade applicant. From the size of the credit limit, we can surmise that the applicant's credit rating was rather good. But the tone of the letter would be much the same in any case, although the limit might be less. If credit is granted, it should be done graciously—not with a grudging, "Ordinarily, we wouldn't; but in your case, we'll make an exception."

REQUEST–TYPE CREDIT LETTER

We can expect that some of the credit applications we receive will be unclear or incomplete. As with other inadequate requests—such as orders from which needed details have been omitted—we must write back for clarification. In credit situations, we shall consider two sets of circumstances. First, there is the situation in which we already have enough information to make a decision to grant credit, but in which we need to satisfy some technical requirement before following through. Such a requirement might be something like the completion of a credit form or the obtaining of a guarantor's signature. Second, there is the situation in which we cannot make a judgment until the applicant supplies references, a financial statement, or other information that is required. In the first instance, we may indicate "yes" in our letter; but in the second instance, we should not go beyond "maybe."

TIDEWAYS
OIL   CO.

P.O. BOX 2900   NEW YORK, N.Y. 10017

May 1, 1967

Mr. Michael A. Tate
9510 Ranch Road
Brecksville, Ohio 44141

Dear Mr. Tate:

Your passport to highway traveling convenience is enclosed. With this plastic charge
plate, Tideways Oil welcomes you into its inner circle of credit customers.

For your convenience, itemized sales slips for your purchases will be sent to you with
your once-a-month billing. These slips may be useful to you when you prepare expense
accounts and other financial reports.

Above all, of course, you will enjoy the many privileges of being a credit card holder:

* Instant credit on all purchases on oil products at literally thousands of Tideways
  and affiliated service stations in the United States.

* Deferred payment (up to six months, interest-free) on tires, tubes, batteries,
  and parts.

* Travel routings for your trips.

* Special offers of name-brand merchandise at discounted prices.

* PLUS--by special arrangement, credit at all Homestead Motor Courts (for both
  rooms and meals)!

Just remember--whatever your traveling needs, you will find your Tideways credit card
at your beck and call.

Sincerely yours,

Leroy Pearson

Leroy Pearson
General Manager

LP:pn
Enclosure

Good News Credit

maple furniture co.

110 NORTH ILLINOIS ST., INDIANAPOLIS, INDIANA 46205

May 4, 1967

Harvey Interiors, Inc.
3320 Rutledge Avenue
Iowa City, Iowa 52240

Gentlemen:

Your application for open-account privileges has been approved. We are happy to include your name in our circle of preferred customers.

Under our credit system you will be able to charge your purchases of Maple furniture, up to a maximum of $5,000. Invoices will be mailed to you at the time shipment is made. Billings will be F.O.B. our factory, and transportation charges will be presented separately by the carrier. Our terms are the customary 2/10, n/30--so that a substantial savings can be yours simply by taking advantage of the cash discounts.

Maple furniture is not only an exclusive line, but also a profitable one. Our dealers in other cities have found that their customers are genuinely attracted by the prestige that goes along with the Maple name. Look for our advertisements in the leading journals for homemakers, and you will see how we keep the buying urge at high pitch. It's all a part of our merchandising program.

You are sure to be pleased with your new relationship with us. We'll be expecting to hear from you soon.

Yours very truly,

MAPLE FURNITURE COMPANY

James D. Parkman
Credit Manager

JDP:bw

Program

In either situation, however, the program structure of our letter is the same. The steps are as follows:

APPRECIATE.
EXPLAIN.
REQUEST.
ASSIST.

Our beginning should be a friendly acknowledgment of the reader's request for credit. As there will be a delay involved, we thus condition our reader to like what we are saying before we discuss the problem.

In giving our explanation of the situation, we should stick to a matter-of-fact approach. We should avoid raising issues, particularly accusations of scoldings of our reader because of anything he forgot to do. If only a technicality is involved, we can indicate that we have reached a favorable decision and are waiting to grant his request for credit.

Our request for clarification should be well thought out. Everything actually needed should be included the first time we write. We should not have to write the applicant a second time because we did not make a clear or complete request ourselves. And, of course, we should do all that is possible to make it easy for our reader to answer us. Forms to be completed and a return envelope should be sent along with our request letter.

Illustrations

The two varieties of request-type credit letter can be seen in the illustrations on pp. 415–16. They both have been developed from the same general program; the specific details of each case account for the different results. The first example applies to a retail credit situation. It concerns the technicality of a parent's signature, which is needed because the applicant is a minor.

The second example applies to a trade credit situation, wherein the applicant did not furnish enough information. A decision to grant or refuse credit cannot be made until the applicant complies with the request.

DISCOTHEQUE

236 STOCKTON ST.

SAN FRANCISCO,
CALIF. 94108

FASHIONS

June 14, 1967

Miss Pamela McMahon
745 - 92nd Avenue
Oakland, California 94603

Dear Miss McMahon:

It is always a pleasure to be of service to our friends across the Bay. We especially appreciate your interest in opening a charge account at our store.

The information supplied us in your letter of June 9 is indeed satisfactory. We have taken the preliminary steps toward opening your account, and need but one last item before completing the arrangements. Would you please have your father sign the enclosed contingent-responsibility form? It is a routine requirement for granting privileges to persons under 21 years of age.

Please use the postage-paid envelope which we've enclosed for your convenience. Your credit card will be on its way to you the same day we receive the signed form.

Yours very truly,

DISCOTHEQUE FASHIONS

Kirk Elliott

Kirk Elliott
Manager

KE:bf
Enclosures 2

B_{IG} S_{TATE} $I_{NSTRUMENTS}$ $C_{O.}$

1826 PEYOTE ST., SAN ANTONIO, TEXAS 78205

August 10, 1967

Phillips Tool Company
100 Robert Kerr Avenue
Oklahoma City, Oklahoma 94106

Gentlemen:

Your application for open-account credit is appreciated. We'll be glad to give it our careful consideration and to notify you promptly when our decision is reached.

As you are an out-of-state customer, we can't say how long it will take to complete a credit check. But you can help reduce the time involved by providing us with some of the information direct. Specifically, we'd like to have a certified copy of your July 31 financial statement (balance sheet) and three credit references. These references should be suppliers who have had recent dealings with your company.

If we can have your response soon, we'll be off to a good start in processing your application. We've enclosed an airmail reply envelope for your convenience.

Very truly yours,

BIG STATE INSTRUMENTS CO.

Wallace J. Smith
Credit Manager

WJS:ga
Enclosure

The Request as a Turndown

Strictly speaking, a skillful writer of business letters should be able to decline a request for credit. The fact remains, however, that a number of credit managers undergo uneasy moments when they have to write such a letter. Behind their concern is the problem of diplomacy. The applicant must be turned down—for a reason that may well reflect on his character, honesty, or integrity. Moreover, there is the fear that making adverse statements about a person's credit could involve the writer in legal complications. Rather than run any risks, some credit managers have gone so far as to check on the applicant's credit rating and to throw away his request if the report turns out to be unfavorable. The pretense is that the letter was lost in the mail; the hope is that nothing more will be heard from the applicant.

Such a practice seems to be unnecessarily crude and unimaginative. Assuming that fears or anxieties do cause the credit manager to become defensive, would it not be better to give the applicant the courtesy of an answer? One approach would be to send the applicant a "maybe, if" request letter. Enclosed with the letter would be a detailed questionnaire for the applicant to answer and return. But the nature of some of the questions, the vast number of questions, possibly the requirement that the form be submitted in duplicate, the absence of a return envelope, and the like could be made to appear unattractive to the applicant. The hope is that he will decide to give up his ideas about credit. But he will have done so voluntarily; he will not have been turned down by the company. In fact, the attitude of the company's letter would be pleasant and helpful; but the questions will be designed to lead him to realize on his own that he cannot qualify under the circumstances.

THE COUNTEROFFER CREDIT LETTER

Sometimes our credit investigation reveals that an applicant's rating is only fair, neither very good nor very bad. We are willing to extend some form of credit to such an applicant, but not the fancy kind he may have requested. In such a case, we can make a counteroffer which we believe to be more suitable.

Program

The program for a counteroffer credit letter contains four steps which are aligned in the following sequence:

Appreciate.
Explain tactfully.
Counteroffer.
Make action easy.

This program gives recognition to the fact that a counteroffer is a type of bad-news situation. The applicant is given an implied refusal of his specific request, although he is offered a different arrangement. It is best, therefore, that we get off to a good start with him and prepare him for the bad news by means of a plausible explanation. We should avoid showing too much enthusiasm in our appreciation step, because (1) it might mislead our reader and (2) it would tend to make our handling of the turndown a more difficult task.

Our explanation should be as tactful as we can make it, because the reader will be sensitive about any discussion concerning his credit shortcomings. If there is a possibility of selecting a reason for the turndown which is adequate but not especially painful to our reader, we should welcome it. There is no point in crushing the applicant with unfavorable evidence; a valid reason for a turndown is all we need. Of course, an arbitrary statement, such as "It's against our policy," would never convince our reader.

The counteroffer will depend on the applicant's credit rating and on the type of credit (retail or trade) that he needs. The better the rating, the better the counteroffer we can make. Retail customers, for example, may be offered a revolving account, a layaway plan, or a C.O.D. option. Trade customers may be asked to consider a lower credit limit; or they may be dissuaded from open-account credit to a consignment basis. At worst, they may be limited to a C.O.D. or S.D.–B.L. plan. Any of these arrangements are somewhat better than no credit at all—which would mean sending payment along with the order. Thus, a certain amount of goodwill is included in our counteroffer.

Since business can be transacted with our reader only after an agreement has been reached, we do well to make answering easy. Our minimum effort should be to enclose a postage-paid return envelope.

Illustration

The letter on p. 420 is a counteroffer made to a company that requested trade credit. As the applicant's credit rating was found to be only fair, the letter suggests a credit limit equal to one half of the amount sought.

BAD–NEWS CREDIT LETTER

When a credit applicant's financial picture is unworthy of even C.O.D. terms, no credit whatever can be offered. Obviously, a direct communication to the applicant on this subject will be in the bad-news situation.

Program

The letter program for such a case will be based on the basic framework of explanation, bad news, encouraging ending. In specific steps, it appears as follows:

APPRECIATE.
EXPLAIN TACTFULLY.
DECLINE (EXPRESSED OR IMPLIED).
SUGGEST CONVINCINGLY.
OFFER HOPE FOR FUTURE.

The first two steps prepare the reader for the turndown that is coming along. Here again, courtesy—not enthusiasm—should be the essence of the beginning of our letter. Our explanation should go easy on our reader—if possible, citing reasons strong enough to warrant a turndown but not too personal, harsh, or painful. As always, we should avoid being arbitrary or narrow-minded.

We will be better off if we can let our reader tell himself what the answer is. Thus, if we can, we should use an implied turndown in preference to one that is expressed. That way, we will be discussing positive

Western Garments Corp.

1360 COMMERCE ST., DALLAS, TEXAS 75201

April 20, 1967

Boot and Saddle Shop
6272 North Lincoln Ave.
Chicago, Illinois 60645

Gentlemen:

We appreciate your request to open an account to purchase your requirements of Western buckskin jackets. You are wise in starting your plans well in advance of the summer season.

Since you have only recently entered this specialty field, perhaps we can pass along a few suggestions. The experience of other dealers has been that a high degree of loyalty develops between their customers and themselves. Once they have won the confidence of a customer, that person usually comes back to them every time he needs something new--or even is just shopping for advice. On the other hand, the building of one's clientele is a slow, difficult job. Because of the loyalty factor, it is hard to win customers away from competitors. The main hope lies in the direction of new prospects, who, once satisfied, become steadfast customers.

For these reasons we believe it would be best for you to proceed slowly at the beginning. Stock a sufficient, yet moderate quantity of merchandise. As your business grows, you can take steps to increase your inventory.

Our suggestion is that you consider an initial line of credit up to $1,500 instead of the $3,000 limit you mentioned in your application. If this lower amount is agreeable to you, just sign the enclosed approval form and return it to us in the business reply envelope.

If we hear from you promptly, we can have your account ready by May 1.

Very truly yours,

WESTERN GARMENTS CORPORATION

Daniel P. Gibson

Daniel P. Gibson
Credit Manager

DPG:cb
Encl. 2

values by the time the bad news hits home; there is no chance for our reader to stay "down" emotionally.

About the only thing we can suggest in such a case is that our reader be our customer on a cash basis. But this suggestion will not have particular appeal unless we do some amount of selling or convincing. We can use *words* to make doing business with us look like an attractive thing, whether it be done for cash or credit. We can use *tone* and *attitude* to make our reader feel that he is putting himself into good hands.

" PERHAPS IF YOU CAME BACK IN A FEW YEARS ... "

Finally, we should not slam the door on the future. Times may change, the applicant may prosper, and we may wish we could have him as a loyal customer. It will be to our advantage to state our decision as of the present, and to keep an open mind regarding a possible review of the case some time hence.

Illustration

In the example on p. 422, a turndown is made to a couple who have been evacuated from Cuba. The husband, a lawyer in his own country, has had to take employment as a taxicab driver; the wife holds a part-time job as a waitress. Their combined income is below average for the area in which they live.

SUMMARY

Whether we are primarily concerned with retail customers or with trade customers, modern business practice almost requires us to grant credit—deferred-payment terms—to our customers. This fact opens up an entire area of activity in business communication. There will be request letters from people seeking credit, and inquiry letters to those

Biscayne Department Store
111 EAST FLAGLER ST., MIAMI, FLA. 33132

February 17, 1967

Mr. and Mrs. Emil Alvarez
7240 S.W. 8th Street
Miami, Florida 33144

Dear Mr. and Mrs. Alvarez:

Thank you for giving me this chance to say, "Bienvenidas! Welcome to the Magic City
of Miami!"

Biscayne Department Store has always been a friend of the Spanish-speaking community.
Long before Miami became a refuge for Cuban patriots, our store windows proclaimed,
"Se Habla Espanol"--a hint of the red-carpet service to be found inside. As a result
of this spirit, a bond of mutual respect has formed between our customers and ourselves.

From my vantage point, I am able to share some observations with you. As newcomers to
the United States, you can expect to go through a series of changes during the next year
or two. You will enjoy several improvements in employment. You will probably find
new and better living quarters, and eventually you will become a property owner.
But, to realize all this--to move from place to place--to take advantages of opportunities
as they arise--you should remain as financially flexible as possible.

May I recommend, therefore, that you stay on a cash basis until you are safely established?
As a customer of Biscayne Department Store you can count on good service, top-quality
merchandise, free delivery, and folks who stand behind the goods they sell. And, when
you become settled in your new life here, you and I can take up that matter of a charge
account.

Sincerely yours,

Bernard C. White
Credit Manager

BCW:cb

given as references and to other sources of information concerning the credit competency of the applicants. In turn, there will be letters of response from such sources, and answers of various kinds which will be written to the credit applicants.

Conceivably, all letters referred to above could be considered as "credit" letters, since credit is the underlying subject in each. The same might be said of a letter offering a credit plan to a deserving person who did not actually apply for credit. But most of these types are identifiable as either requests or replies, and conform to the programs and discussions already given for such letters.

The answer letters sent to credit applicants, however, present some special problems, and are our chief concern here. A good-news answer is pleasant enough to prepare—but its program should include a clear coverage of the credit plan so that there will be no complications or misunderstandings later on. A request for more information must be sufficiently diplomatic so that the reader does not feel blamed for being less than thorough in his original letter. Bad-news credit letters must be especially tactful in the matter of giving explanations, because the reason for a turndown bears directly on the applicant's character, past performance, and other touchy matters.

The letter types discussed in the chapter are summarized on pages 424–27 in capsule form, for ready reference.

QUESTIONS

1. List the chief advantages of credit in modern business practice.
2. What are the chief disadvantages of conducting credit business?
3. What are the two principal types of business credit?
4. How does credit to the ultimate consumer usually operate?
5. Name several varieties of retail credit.
6. What advantages are offered the customer under a C.O.D. plan?
7. How does trade or mercantile credit usually operate?
8. Point out some of the similarities that exist between adjustment letters and credit letters.
9. Give the suggested program for a good-news credit letter.
10. Is explanatory information an optional feature of a letter granting credit, as it is in a letter granting an adjustment?

GOOD–NEWS CREDIT LETTER
(Yes)

Intended
Reader
Reaction:

from this   to this

Program: Welcome (pleasure to grant).
Terms, etc.
Goodwill statement(s).

Pointers: Get off to a good start by showing an appropriate amount of warmth and enthusiasm.

Don't grant grudgingly—e.g., "Ordinarily, we don't; but in your case, we'll make an exception."

Be sure to explain the workings of the credit system, including presentation of statements, due dates for payments, cash discounts (if any), and so on.

In a retail situation, end with statements encouraging the customer to use his credit privileges. Emphasize other advantages, too: shopping convenience, delivery service, quality merchandise, exclusive lines, store reputation, etc.

In a trade situation, close on a goodwill note by stressing the positive values of the relationship: quality of merchandise, national advertising (if done), selling aids—racks, placards, display material (if provided), rack servicing (if done), delivery service, and so on.

REQUEST–TYPE CREDIT LETTER
(Yes, If)
(Maybe, If)

Intended
Reader
Reaction:

from this   through this   to this

Program: Appreciate.
Explain.
Request.
Assist (or seem to).

Pointers: Begin on a note of appreciation of the fact that the reader
came to us when seeking credit.

In the "yes, if" variety, indicate that in principle credit can be
granted.

In either variety, explain that additional information is needed
before a final (yes, if) or definite (maybe, if) answer can be
given.

Be clear and complete in requesting the information that is
needed to reach a decision.

Give the applicant a chance to save face. Avoid accusations,
scolding, or anything else that might be antagonistic. Discuss
what is needed—not what was omitted.

In the "yes, if" variety—and in the "maybe, if" variety when an
answer is desired—do all that is possible to make answering
as easy as not answering.

In the "maybe, if" variety, when an answer is not really wanted,
consider omitting assistance or giving only token assistance.
The hope would be to let the effort of answering, not our words,
cause the reader to discontinue his pursuit of credit. Thus, a
poor risk might be made to give up—yet would not have to be
told that his credit was inadequate.

COUNTEROFFER CREDIT LETTER
(Somewhat)

Intended
Reader
Reaction:

from this   through this   to this

Program: Appreciate.
Explain tactfully.
Counteroffer.
Make action easy.

Pointers: Begin on a note of appreciation of the fact that the reader
came to us when seeking credit.

Be careful not to go overboard with enthusiasm, however, because a partial turndown is to be given.

Since the reader's specific credit request will be declined and
another plan offered, this letter will be somewhat bad news.
Although the bad news will likely be implied rather than expressed, it should follow an appropriate explanation.

Explain, as tactfully as possible, our position with regard to the
reader's specific request.

If possible, use a valid reason, but not necessarily the strongest
reason for the turndown.

Don't use arbitrary wording, such as "It's against our policy."

Counteroffer a credit plan less than what was requested but
consistent with the explanation given.

Consider that the counteroffer is a tentative but sufficient expression of goodwill, pending an acceptance from the reader.

BAD–NEWS CREDIT LETTER
(No, But)

Intended
Reader
Reaction:

from this   through this   to this

Program: Appreciate.
Explain tactfully.
Decline (expressed or implied).
Suggest convincingly.
Offer hope for future.

Pointers: Begin on a note of appreciation of the fact that the reader
came to us when seeking credit.

Be careful to hold back on enthusiasm, because a full turndown is in the offing.

Explain slowly and tactfully *before* declining to grant credit.

If possible, use a sufficient reason, but not necessarily the
most serious or most painful reason for the turndown.

Don't use arbitrary wording, such as "It's against our policy."

If possible, use an implied turndown. If it must be expressed,
don't dwell on it.

In suggesting cash purchases, stress positive values: quality
goods, exclusive lines, reputation, shopping convenience, cash
discounts (if applicable), delivery service, etc. Buying from us
for cash must be made to look attractive.

Keep goodwill intact, by indicating willingness to review the
case at some future date.

11. What is especially important about the attitude involved in granting a credit request?

12. Give the suggested program for a request that the credit applicant submit additional information.

13. What possible approach can be used to curtail an undesirable request for credit without either expressing or implying a turndown?

14. Is a counteroffer permissible as an answer to a substandard credit applicant?

15. Why is it recommended that the beginning of a counteroffer credit letter be appreciative in tone, but not overly enthusiastic?

16. Why should the explanation step in any bad-news credit letter be especially tactful?

17. Give the suggested program for an absolutely bad-news credit letter.

18. What seems to be the only course of action that can be suggested to the reader in a bad-news credit letter?

19. How can the writer hope to convince the reader that a recommendation to trade on a cash basis is worthwhile advice?

20. If a credit applicant's financial picture is poor enough to cause a turndown of his request, is there any point in inviting him to apply again at some future time?

PROBLEMS

Some of the following cases deal with retail credit, others with trade credit. In either event, the solution should be typewritten on an appropriate business letterhead. If letterhead stationery is not available, set up a simulated letterhead in accordance with directions issued by your instructor.

13–1. Milady's Fashions is an exclusive women's shop located in Washington, D.C. Mrs. Hamilton Cobb, the wife of a dentist in Arlington, Virginia, has applied to the store for a charge account. As the Cobbs have an A–1 credit rating, the store is only too glad to extend credit privileges. Assume that you are the credit manager. Write an acceptance letter to Mrs. Cobb and enclose an identification card for her convenience. Explain that statements will be rendered once a month. The store uses a form of cycle billing whereby customers' accounts are worked on alphabetically but are spread out over the entire month.

13–2. Marvin R. Griswold is president of the University Savings Bank of this city. His various banking activities often require him to travel to cities within a 500-mile radius of his headquarters. A recent advertisement by Prairie Air Lines has aroused his interest. It told of an arrangement whereby businessmen could effectively "write their own tickets" whenever they needed to travel by air. By means of a checkbook-like packet of blanks, an approved customer could issue himself a ticket, check his luggage, and be on his way—no involved transactions with travel agents, no waiting in line at ticket counters. Mr. Griswold has applied to Prairie Air Lines' Chicago office for this credit privilege. As the airline's credit manager, you have approved the request. In an acceptance letter to Mr. Griswold, enclose his stock of blanks. Explain that a monthly statement will be sent to his bank.

13–3. The Suncote Paint Company is located in Wilmington, Delaware. It manufactures paints for indoor and outdoor use; both types are made with a latex base. The company distributes its products through retail dealers throughout the nation. It grants regular trade credit; the terms provide for a cash discount of 2 percent if payment is made within 10 days. In addition to national advertising in home-improvement magazines, the company aids its dealers by supplying window placards and hand-out color charts. Three days ago an order for paint and a request for a $500 line of open-account credit were received from Bixby's Hardware of Butler, Pennsylvania. A credit check indicates that this is a newly established store with no record of credit transactions. Wilfred Bixby, the proprietor, personally has a satisfactory credit rating. Moreover, he has had many years of experience in the hardware business. Before starting his own business, he had been a store manager for a hardware chain operating in Pittsburgh. As credit manager of the Suncote Paint Company, inform Mr. Bixby by letter that he is being granted the $500 line of credit.

13–4. Assume that you are the credit manager of the Commercial Supply Company, which is headquartered in the capital of your state. Most of Commercial Supply's business is conducted on a credit basis with various firms which are continually replenishing their office supplies. A sizable minority share of business, however, is transacted with individuals, in person and by mail. When Joseph Simms of nearby Ridgeville ordered an expensive desk set by mail and asked to be billed for the price and postage, you asked the Retail Credit Association for a rating of his credit position. The report is that there are blemishes on the applicant's record. Mr. Simms has often been delinquent and once was taken to court, where a judgment was obtained against him. On the other hand, his performance for the past two years has been above reproach. Although it is ordinarily against your policy to grant credit to anyone who has been sued for failure to pay a just debt, you have decided to take a chance on the apparently reformed Mr. Simms. Write him that his request is being granted.

13–5. As credit manager of the Midtown Department Store, located in this city, you have looked into the credit background of the Sebastian Cunninghams. The evidence indicates that Mr. Cunningham is employed as a clerk at city hall; he earns approximately $5,000 a year. Mrs. Cunningham, who has applied to the store for a regular charge account, contributes to the couple's income by means of a receptionist's job with a local physician. Her pay comes to about $2,000 a year. In your judgment, the Cunninghams should not become involved with a charge account. They could easily run up a monthly bill in excess of their ability to pay. Midtown has a second plan, however—a "revolving" account. Such a credit plan permits charge purchases, but requires that only a budgeted sum be paid each month. Interest charges, of course, are applicable to any unpaid balance which is carried into the following month. Write to the Cunninghams; indicate your willingness to open a revolving account for them.

13–6. Benjamin F. Weldon has written from his home in Davenport, Iowa, to Pioneer Catalogue Sales, Inc. of your home town. He has requested that the company open a charge account for him. It is against company policy to grant such requests. As a mail-order operator, the firm regularly expects to receive payment from the customer whenever an order is placed. It then mails the merchandise postage-paid. In some instances, it tolerates C.O.D. orders; but the customer himself must bear the cost of postage and handling charges. Assume that you are the sales manager of Pioneer Catalogue Sales, Inc. Write to Mr. Weldon; offer him C.O.D. privileges.

13–7. Prendergast's, located in Montgomery, Alabama, is a dealer in supplies and equipment required by various institutions, such as schools, hospitals, and libraries. Daniel Prendergast, Jr., the firm's general manager, has applied to Central Industries, Incorporated, which is located in the capital of your state; he requests an unlimited line of trade credit. For several years, Central Industries' salesman in Montgomery has been trying to land the Prendergast account. It is evident that he has at last succeeded; yet it is absolutely against sound business policy to allow unrestricted credit. A management discussion on the matter has been held at Central Industries. The decision is to make a serious try for Prendergast's business by offering a liberal $5,000 line of credit. As credit manager of Central Industries, Incorporated, extend this counteroffer in writing to Mr. Prendergast.

13–8. Except in rare instances, the customers of the Work-N-Play Shop depend on the store to deliver their purchases. The merchandise is usually of heavy weight, as the store specializes in such items as power mowers, motorbikes, and outboard motors. Located in a city with a population of more than 100,000, the Work-N-Play Shop uses a van type of truck to make deliveries within the general metropolitan area. Shipping orders and receipts are routinely kept in the files for all such deliveries made. When Roger Hilliard, an extremely poor credit risk who resides in an unincorporated area just north of the city, submitted an application for a charge account, the owner of the store turned thumbs down. As sales manager of the Work-N-Play Shop, you are to write Mr. Hilliard the bad news. If possible, however, suggest how he might qualify for a charge account at some later time.

13–9. Morgan Supply Company, located in a community in the Appalachian region, has requested trade credit from the Tru-Mold Plastic Products Company of Indianapolis, Indiana. The applicant wants an open account with a limit of at least $2,000. As credit manager of Tru-Mold, you do not favor granting any credit to the Morgan Supply Company. Its credit rating is minimal. The company itself is situated in an area known to be economically sluggish. It would be better for this company to proceed with caution, to stock moderately, to pay cash for its purchases. If current efforts to recharge the Appalachian region prove to be successful, a future credit application could be considered. Write to Morgan Supply and convey your views.

13–10. The Midland Petroleum Co. is an up-and-coming refiner of gasoline and related products. It has its headquarters in Dallas, Texas, and operates a chain of service stations throughout the immediate eight-state area. It extends retail credit to qualified motorists by issuing serialized "courtesy cards." Recently, Jeff Richmond of Backwater, Louisiana, wrote to the company's Dallas office and asked that he be issued a credit card. A prompt check of Richmond's past record for paying bills resulted in a very unsatisfactory report from New Orleans. Richmond is delinquent at several New Orleans department stores, and in danger of losing his house through foreclosure. As credit manager of the Midland Petroleum Co., you realize that you cannot issue a courtesy card to this applicant. Yet you feel that it would be unwise to state the reasons behind the turndown in a letter mailed to him. Think of a way to handle this situation without compromising your company or injuring the applicant. Then write an appropriate answer to Richmond.

• •

CHAPTER 14

PERSUADING A
CUSTOMER TO PAY

If a company has instituted a credit system, it is almost inevitable that it will find itself facing the problem of collecting from slow-paying customers. This problem will arise even in the most cautious of credit systems. It can be avoided only if all business is done on a strictly cash-on-the-line basis; and that approach does not contribute to the competitive well-being of a large number of business firms.

CONFLICTING GOALS WITHIN A COMPANY

Basically, a company is an economic unit, the various departments of which cooperate toward a common end—specifically, the making of a profit. The road to profitability, of course, is not always smooth. To succeed, the company must have good leadership to keep the ultimate goal in sight and to coordinate the activities of the various departments. Because of the immediacy of its distinct activities, however, each department tends to perform at its own level rather than performing in concert with the other departments.

For example, the sales department is constantly striving to attract customers and increase the size of orders. From the salesmen's point of view, it would be desirable to have a wide variety of models or styles to offer, a competitive price structure, and an assurance of prompt delivery. The production department might take a dim view of wide variety in the company's product. To people at this level, customer work or short runs of a given variety of product are inefficient. Purchasing must be done in small quantities, production setups must be changed often, and unit costs can mount. The hope of production people is for a small variety of product; then they can turn out finished goods at a rapid rate and at a low cost. Sales and production viewpoints need to be coordinated. A solution must be found that is best for the overall aims of the company.

In a similar fashion, there is a potential clash between the goals of the sales department and the credit department. Sales people would like to sign up as many customers as possible, and to secure from each a maximum-sized order. Credit people see it differently. They cannot grant credit privileges to prospects who do not show reasonable ability to pay for their purchases. And they cannot give an unlimited amount of credit to some of the customers. Their approach, therefore, will be to move cautiously and with somewhat less enthusiasm than the sales people. But they should be realistic in their decisions; they should not hold out for "gilt-edged" or top-grade credit customers only. The overall success of the company requires some amount of risk taking, although it does have its limits. A compromise between the differing goals of the sales and credit departments—that is, the exercise of good judgment— is required.

In like manner, there is a conflict of departmental goals between those who sell on credit terms and those who ultimately are faced with collecting amounts due. The aim of collections (often a function of the credit department) is obviously that of gaining possession of money that rightfully belongs to the vendor company. If performance could be measured on this point alone, collections of 100 percent would be the ultimate goal. But the sales department is naturally concerned about the collection tactics that are used. The sales people have spent much time and effort in developing the market, and need repeated orders from the customers to realize a profitable relationship. They cannot afford to have their work undone by harsh or imprudent collection activities.

Top management, of course, has the job of defining the overall company goals and coordinating the participation of the various departments. Individual officers in charge of the departments should be kept informed of the company goals so that they can regulate their activities cooperatively and consistently. As a result, marketing can meet competition by having an adequate product line; sales effort can be rewarded by acceptance of orders according to a sensible credit policy; and collections can be pursued on a systematic, but courteous, basis.

A MISTAKEN VIEWPOINT

From one point of view, we can recognize a collection situation as being similar to a claim. Somewhere in the past a business transaction has occurred; we have performed our end of the bargain, but the other party has not. There is no question as to our right to receive what is normally and legally ours. So far, so good—but there are overriding differences to be considered, differences which preclude our handling a collection along the lines of a claim.

As we have seen in our discussion of claim letters (Chapter 12), our program steps include statements of what has gone wrong and the effect the situation has on us. Having given a satisfactory account of this background information, we then sound an appropriate appeal for action and specify what action we believe to be proper.

When we analyze these steps, we can see then they fit a claim situation but are not so suitable for a collection situation. First of all, a claim letter generally comes unexpectedly; our reader is for the first time being alerted to the fact that something is amiss. Such is not the case in most collection situations. Here, our reader knows about the nonpayment even before we do, and is rather expecting to hear from us about it. There is little hope of our building interest through a review of what has happened. A routine beginning more than likely will discourage complete or attentive reading of the letter because our reader will tend to believe that he already "knows" its message.

Telling our reader what effect his nonpayment has on us is usually a wasted effort. In general such information has little interest value to him. He can probably match it or exceed it with aspects of his own situation—and accordingly will not be impressed. In fact, even if we do a thorough job of convincing him of our plight, we might unwittingly be downgrading our own image.

Sounding an appeal (that is, applying some effective motivation) and specifying what action is to be taken are basic ingredients of all request letters. So is the providing of ample assistance. In a *claim* letter, we render the necessary assistance when we give a thorough, definite account of the situation and its resulting effect on us; make a convincing appeal; and specify what we wish to have done. In a *collection* letter, we assist by identifying the transaction; specifying the amount to be paid, and including a remittance envelope.

Such an analysis shows us that there are enough differences between claim letters and collection letters to require a different psychological handling. For persons who have never considered these differences, however, the two situations may well seem to be identical. This fact may explain why so many dull, negative, offensive collection letters were written in yesteryear and why some continue to be written even today. Writers of such letters concentrate too much on the "right to receive" aspect and not enough on the "finesse" aspect.

If we can make a final, clear-cut distinction between a claim letter and a collection letter, we can get on the right track for the right purpose. Such a distinction is simply this: claim letters are usually written to suppliers; collection letters are usually written to customers—the very life blood of our business. In writing claim letters, we properly expect our reader to please us—satisfy us—perpetuate our goodwill—by granting our request; but we are exhorted to use courtesy and restraint. How, then, should we behave when we are dealing with one of our own customers?

Granted that we have a right to seek what is ours, granted that our customer appears to have violated his agreement regarding payment; but in a collection situation, relationships do not change. We are still the vendor; our reader is still the customer. Our purpose still includes catering to our reader's goodwill. So, our tendencies toward anger and displeasure must be held in check even though we are basically in the right. We should try to collect our due without disturbing the status quo; and we should begin our message with something that encourages our customer to read it through to the end.

A PROPER COLLECTION ATTITUDE

It is not suggested that collection efforts be conducted along weak, hit-or-miss lines. A very real business problem exists, and it must be solved in a businesslike manner. Such a solution calls for a well-defined collection program which is followed systematically and applied with finesse.

Strictly speaking, the term *collection,* although traditional, is somewhat of a misnomer in this usage. Collecting suggests a physical act—the accumulating, amassing, or gathering of something of interest or value to the person or persons performing the act. It generally involves purpose, seeking, finding, and obtaining, but does not necessarily require cooperation (in the sense of joint action toward a recognized goal) from other people.

In the matter of what we call collecting accounts receivable, the action is shared. The creditor requests; and, if all goes well, the debtor responds by making payment. Unless the debtor pays, however, there is no collection—the creditor depends on the debtor's ability and willingness to make payment. Otherwise, the full action cannot be achieved, no matter how hard the creditor tries. Even when a case is taken to court, there is no assurance that a ruling in favor of the creditor will result in a so-called collection. The debtor cannot make payment if he is entirely without funds!

As soon as we realize that we are powerless to *collect* money that is owed to us—except through such illegal means as theft or burglary—we can begin to view a collection letter in its proper perspective. The challenge is to persuade, to sell our debtor on the notion that paying us is something he should do promptly and amiably.

We should bear in mind that a sermon will bore our customer, that a scolding will harm our goodwill relationship, and that nastiness will alienate him. Such approaches do not produce the full results desired. Thus, we must proceed with diplomacy and subtlety.

Collecting really amounts to a program of education which we conduct for a slow-paying customer. It is based on the trust we had in granting him credit in the first place. It is aimed at developing improved paying habits on the part of such a customer, at the same time keeping him satisfied with our business relationship.

THE COLLECTION STAGES

In a well-rounded collection procedure we may expect to find six stages of activity. These are:

1. A sound credit system.
2. A positive system for billing.
3. A provision for follow-up.
4. An impersonal appeal stage.

5. A personal appeal stage.
6. A termination stage.

SOUND CREDIT SYSTEM

As we have seen earlier, modern business depends on the granting of credit to customers. Yet some selectivity must be used. Not everyone who comes to us seeking credit deserves to have it; and not every customer granted credit is necessarily entitled to the same terms as everyone else.

Actually, a great deal of the problem of collecting from customers has its roots at the credit-granting stage. It is important, therefore, that we have an effective credit department. This department must be able to get reliable credit data on applicants. It must be able to weed out applicants with hopeless credit ratings and to classify the remainder into at least good, ordinary, and poor categories. It must be careful to grant credit terms that are consistent with its own findings about each accepted applicant.

Such activity is an important determinant of the collection work that we will face at a future date. Primary credit controls tend to match customers with credit terms they can handle; secondary credit controls (such as those made in connection with large orders and expensive items) tend to keep customers from exercising credit beyond their ability to pay.

POSITIVE SYSTEM FOR BILLING

Although sweeping statements are never quite true, it would not be a bad idea for us to regard our credit customers as being "hand-to-mouth" in their cash position. It certainly is a safer point of view than to assume that they have excess cash and are just waiting for us to send our bill. Most tradesmen depend on credit in both directions. They must collect from debtors in order to satisfy their creditors—and the latter had better bill promptly if they want to be paid promptly. Retail customers often live from paycheck to paycheck. Sometimes they find themselves "robbing Peter to pay Paul"—that is, paying the more urgent bills by hedging a little on others. In dealing with them, we invite trouble if we are slow or casual in our billing procedure.

Further, nowadays we find more and more companies applying the principle of "ample assistance," even with the first billing. This means enclosing a remittance envelope with the invoice (trade accounts) or monthly statements (retail accounts). Such a remittance envelope bears the return address of the payee company and any pertinent handling instructions to assure delivery to the proper person, desk, or office. It may require the user to provide the postage or it may be postage-free to the user (business reply mail), according to the policy of the billing company. In either case the envelope serves as an extra reminder that a payment is due, that the creditor is asking for payment, and that the mechanics of remitting are readily at hand. The expectation is that payment will be made somewhat more promptly because of this assistance, rather than having the debtor find his own envelope and making him address it himself.

PROVISION FOR FOLLOW–UP

Effective collection procedure has merely cleared the launching stage at the time we have billed a customer for his purchases. Under ideal conditions—that is, a proper respect for credit by our customer and his positive response to our initial billing—we should expect payment by the established due date. Not always, however, will ideal conditions prevail. Sometimes a customer grows careless or runs short of enough funds to cover all bills he receives, or wishes to dispute our bill (time permitting), or for some other reason neglects to send us payment. If so, we have encountered the first malfunctioning of our collection procedure and we have to do something about it.

"IF WE DON'T GET RESULTS ON OUR FIRST TWO COLLECTION LETTERS, WE'LL LET OLD DUKE HERE DELIVER THE THIRD ONE ... "

It is now necessary that our system contain some mechanism for correcting the malfunction. Such a mechanism is called *follow-up*. In its early stages, follow-up consists of rebilling the customer who has not responded to the original billing. At the end of each billing period (usually a month), we should send statements to all customers who owe us money. Included, of course, will be the large group of customers who have made charge purchases during the current period. But also included will be any customers carrying over a balance from a previous billing period. In the case of these latter customers, the monthly statement is both:

1. Another request for payment.
2. A reminder that the overdue account is under routine surveillance.

To apply follow-up, even in this routine fashion, we must be equipped to make prompt postings of all payments received. Furthermore, we must be set up to get all statements out on time, on a definite date each month. This work is best taken care of by having bookkeeping operations mechanized or even automated in keeping with the volume of work involved. Also, some system of cyclical billing (billing different segments of the customers, alphabetically, on different days of the month) may be needed.

IMPERSONAL APPEAL STAGE

It is our hope, through the routine follow-up stage, either to collect outstanding accounts or to receive some explanation of why payment was not being made. In some cases, the desired results will be achieved; but in others, more effort will have to be exerted. Depending on how we have rated these customers according to credit performance, impersonal appeals are as follows:

1. *Rubber stamps.* An easy way of indicating urgency is to sort out all monthly statements which are overdue. Before mailing, we can stamp a reminder across the face of each such statement to impress the customer with the seriousness of his situation—yet fall short of making a personal matter of it. Illustrations of rubber-stamp reminders are shown below.

> **Your account is Past Due.**
> **We ask for payment.**

> **PLEASE REMIT**

2. *Stickers.*   Another easy way of showing that an overdue account has begun to draw the attention of the creditor is that of using stickers (gummed labels) instead of rubber stamps. Such stickers can be designed specifically for our company or they can be selected from stock designs sold by suppliers of this sort of thing. They are available in many models, ranging from the gentlest of reminders to last-ditch appeals. They have the added advantage of adding several colors for eye appeal—and being printed, they tell the delinquent customer that he is not necessarily being singled out. Illustrations of reminder stickers follow.

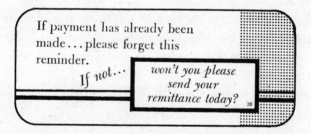

3. *Inserts.*   Some companies prefer to enclose inserts with their statements to delinquent customers instead of using either rubber stamps or stickers. If we follow this method, we simply add

a small card or slip of paper before mailing our statement. Such an insert contains a mild, but definite reminder that payment is past due and expected. The following illustration is an example of a reminder card sent out by a large urban department store.

> *We invite your attention to the enclosed statement which shows an overdue balance. If payment has already been made please disregard this notice.*

The next illustration shows a similar insert used by the publisher of a professional journal.

> Please take a look!
>
> Somewhere on your desk is that check for your BULLETIN subscription.
>
> Send it along in the enclosed reply envelope--today, please!

In both instances, the practice is to enclose the card with the customer's periodic statement, which identifies the date and amount of the debt. At this stage of the collection effort, a remittance envelope most certainly would be included.

4. *Greeting cards.* A relative newcomer to the collection scene is the specialized greeting card. Supplies of such cards, printed in a variety of styles and slanted specifically for collection purposes, are available from specialized publishers. Of amusing design,

greeting cards add a touch of color and wit—and they can be expected to serve as a reminder without straining the business relationship. If we adopt this device, we can go so far as to address the envelope by hand and use a commemorative stamp. At the receiving end, this mysterious piece of mail will arouse curiosity and probably be given prompt attention. The mystery will be solved upon the opening of the card, but our message will have been put across.

On the outside, these greeting cards seem to be much like the humorous birthday and anniversary cards we see in drugstores and card shops. The inside message, however, applies the theme to a collection appeal and contains a slot for showing the amount to be paid. The following examples are illustrative of this approach:

a) Alligator Theme. The face of the card has a head-on drawing, printed in green, of an alligator, its jaws open wide to display sharp teeth, red mouth and tongue. A caption reads, "Not later, Alligator. . . ." Inside, the message continues ". . . We need your payment NOW!" The sender's name and address are printed below, and there is a line for inserting the amount involved.

b) Antique Theme. The face of the card has an illustration of an old-fashioned hurricane lamp with a tag attached reading "Antique." Inside the card, a brief message states, "Some antiques are stylish—but not antique accounts. We'd appreciate your check for $____ now."

c) Dragon Theme. A fierce-looking Chinese dragon in red and gold covers the face of the card. Oriental style letters spell out the words, "Is this a Dragon?" Inside, the question is answered: "Yes —and so is your account *a-draggin'*. Please send us your payment of $____ today."

d) Gadget Theme. Sometimes an adaptation of the gadget approach of the sales letter is put to work in these collection greeting cards.

The outside of one such card contains a drawing of a man's hand. An aspirin tablet is glued between the thumb and forefinger of the hand, the impression being that the tablet is being offered to the reader. The wording reads: "Headache? An aspirin could be the remedy." On the inside of the card, the wording goes: "We have an ailment, too—an overdue balance in your account. Your check today for $____ would be the perfect cure."

Another gadget card also uses a drawing of a hand, but has a bow of colored string fastened to the forefinger. The wording on the face of the card begins a sentence, "That string on your finger . . . ," which is completed on the inside of the card, ". . . should remind you that this is the day you intended to settle your account with us: $_____."

5. *Form letters.*   Still another approach to the impersonal collection appeal is the form letter. There are two general varieties: (a) the preprinted letter and (b) the individually typewritten letter which uses standard, predetermined wording.

Preprinted letters (sometimes even produced by an office duplicator) can be either brief or full-blown. The main thing is that they are ready for use and need only to be rounded out with a date, inside address, and the amount being collected. The wording has been approved in advance by all personnel who should have a say in the handling of collections. As seen by the reader, such a letter is obviously not too personal—yet it is a positive step forward in his creditor's effort to collect.

The individually typewritten form letter is a variation of the preprinted type. It may be turned out mechanically, as happens when a robotypewriter or an electronic computer is used. Or, it may be prepared manually by a clerk-typist. In the latter case, for practical reasons, the letter may tend to be of medium or short length. It has the advantage of a possibly neater appearance; but it begins to imply that the reader is being singled out. The wording, of course, would still be clearly applicable to debtors in general. In fact, it often has a "canned" flavor which gives away its form-letter origin.

The following examples illustrate various lengths and styles of form collection letters.

```
Gentlemen:
```
We remind you that our invoice _____ amounting to $____ is now past due.

Prompt remittance of this amount will be appreciated.

Yours very truly,

Gentlemen:

Is it <u>check</u> or <u>cheque</u>?

Right now, .we'd like one of each from you. A <u>check</u> in one of the boxes below will tell us where we stand. A <u>cheque</u> for $____ will clear up that overdue balance in your account.

Please "check" on the situation, and then let the enclosed envelope be your messenger.

Very truly yours,

☐ What cheque? We mailed it on _____
☐ Calm down! Cheque enclosed.
☐ Waiting, because _____

Gentlemen:

This is our second letter reminding you that $____ is past due.

Please remember that we filled your order promptly with the expectation that payment would be made under terms of "Net 30 Days."

We expect an early remittance of the above-listed amount.

Very truly yours,

PERSONAL APPEAL STAGE

Although we should hope that one or the other of the above-mentioned stages will prove successful in inducing payment from a given customer, it is inevitable that some debtors will still need more prodding. When this situation becomes apparent, we can resort to one or more of several means of communication. Two obvious, straight-forward methods involve speaking personally with the customer. We could meet with him to discuss the situation or we could give him a telephone call. Both methods, of course, have the limitation of being practical only if the customer is not too far distant from us.

Another approach is that of sending a telegram. By this device we most certainly will get attention and impress our customer with the seriousness of his credit situation. A telegram of this kind should be confined to either a request for payment or a request for explanation. By no means should it sound like a libelous message. Here are two examples of telegrams written in the proper tone.

URGENT. MAY WE HAVE $_____ PAYMENT BY MARCH 5?

PLEASE CLARIFY STATUS OF $95 PURCHASE JULY 10.

The usual means of personal communication, of course, is the business letter. As with telegrams, the matter of distance is no particular problem when we choose to write letters. The cost of each letter, however, is more fixed than variable—that is, it does not mount in direct ratio to the length of our message. Thus, from a managerial viewpoint, the letter has certain advantages over other types of media.

We have already seen that it is not advisable to write a collection letter along the lines of an ordinary claim letter. The debtor is our customer; but, in the final analysis, the customer is also our "boss." True, he may be wrong in not paying his bills; but we serve no purpose in proving that to him. The aims of our collection effort should be purely positive: to persuade him to pay, to have him continue liking us, and to educate him to keep his account current henceforth.

Conventional Collection Letters

The conventional program of a collection letter designed to get favorable action without offending the customer is as follows:

CREATE INTEREST.
SOUND AN APPEAL.
SPECIFY WHAT (IF HELPFUL, WHEN).
MAKE ACTION EASY.

Interest can be created at the outset by the simple means of doing something unexpected, yet not objectionable. In this situation, only one thing is really expected, however; almost anything else is apt to catch the reader off-guard and thus spark some interest.

We should remember that sometime in the past this reader bought something from us and has not paid for it. He was billed at the regular time and again later on. He was sent some kind of reminder and possibly a form letter. All of these collection attempts have been ignored. Now he receives a first-class letter from us—what does it contain? Our

debtor knows, even before he opens the envelope. Moreover, he can venture a guess as to its wording: "According to our records, you . . . ," "Although we have sent you several statements, we . . . ," "Our records show that you . . . ," "In going over our accounts today, we . . ."—ho hum!—his suspicions are confirmed. It is just another routine reminder, not worth reading seriously. It lands on a pile of others—unless perhaps the reader has spotted something he considers libelous and is reading it over the telephone to his lawyer.

There is little point in our rehashing the mechanical or historical steps which have occurred. If anything, our reader knows about them better than we do, since he is the one who brought them on. Instead, we should open with a statement which will arouse some interest and at the same time serve as an introduction to the motivation and request which are to follow.

As we do in other request letters, we need to supply motivation in a collection letter. We try to sound an appeal that will arouse his cooperative instincts. The exact nature of the appeal will depend on the degree of relationship existing between us and the debtor, the size of the amount involved, the length of time the debt is overdue, and the number of previous messages we have sent. The better we match our appeal to these matters, the better chance we have of success. Some of the frequently used appeals are the following:

1. *Sympathy.* Under the proper conditions, an appeal to the reader's sympathy can motivate action. It works best with customers who are also personal friends, have the ability to pay, and simply allowed the payment to slide. We can safely tell such debtors, "We need

the working capital." But we should not use this appeal to debtors of a more general kind. It would not be effective as motivation—after all, it probably covers their own reason for not paying us. Moreover, we risk broadcasting the impression that we are in financial difficulty, and invite stepped-up pressure from our own creditors.

2. *Fairness.* A somewhat stronger appeal is one which stresses fair play between the transacting parties. We involve our reader by the simple logic of showing him that a business transaction is a fair exchange and that in this case we alone have done our part. Our emphasis on the need for him to fulfill the conditions of fair play implies that delaying payment is unfair. Our reader senses that his ego is in danger of attack. He can ward off this possibility by making his payment.

3. *Pride.* Another approach available to us is that of appealing to the debtor's pride. We comment favorably on his reputation and show appreciation for his past record of prompt payment. Then we urge him to keep his image intact by settling his account in the present instance.

4. *Self-interest.* There are at least two variations of an appeal to the debtor's self-interest. One variation is somewhat similar to the appeal to pride. However, it goes a bit further; we call the debtor's attention to the value of a good credit rating and the wisdom of preserving it.

The other variation is related to benefits that can accrue to the debtor if he settles his account. For example, we may be planning a special sale, or we may be obtaining a desirable stock of merchandise. Our debtor could capitalize on such events, we suggest, if he clears up his overdue balance. Or, it may be that a special season is at hand, such as Easter or Christmas. If so, whether the debtor be a trade customer or a retail customer, we should be able to appeal to his naturally increased self-interest.

5. *Cooperation.* Sometimes we can reach the debtor with an appeal for cooperation, especially when he can recognize a further benefit in it for him. In one such appeal we call upon him to save us trouble and expense by making payment now. On the surface, this appeal seems to stress our needs rather than his. But the thinly veiled implication is that

both parties would be involved in the trouble and expense. Very likely the debtor would come out second best. Obviously, there is good motivation for him to cooperate.

Another approach to cooperation is that of inviting the debtor to present his side of the case. This is often the approach used in the first personal letter. Let us suppose that the debtor has financial problems and cannot make a full payment. Perhaps he can make a partial payment, but is fearful of an embarrassing situation. He prefers to "overlook" our payment as long as possible. By showing him that we are open-minded, we can encourage him to explain his situation. Then, we are in position to consider an extension of time, revised terms, acceptance of a note receivable, or some other solution to the problem.

It sometimes happens that we are in the wrong somehow. Our customer, however, has not filed a claim; he has simply held up payment of our bill and possibly has stopped doing business with us. If we can get such a customer to state his case, we may be able to make a satisfactory adjustment, settle the account, and resume doing business with him.

6. *Fear.*   When ordinary appeals have failed, we reach a point where drastic action is called for. This action may be cancellation of credit privileges, reporting the case to the credit bureau, turning the collection job over to an outside agency, placing the account in the hands of an attorney, repossessing the goods, or various combinations of these possibilities. We do not directly threaten our reader; we merely inform him that such action is imminent, and is the logical conclusion to our collection effort. We do provide a final escape route, however, by means of a time interval before the drastic action goes into effect. Our debtor is thus given time to settle his account and make it unnecessary for us to carry out the drastic action.

7. *Combination of Appeals.*   To distinguish the different kinds of appeals ordinarily used, we have considered them individually. But in a given situation, we may find it helpful to use more than one appeal. For example, we might combine sympathy and cooperation, fair play and pride, fair play and cooperation, pride and self-interest, and so on. Our choice of a single or combination appeal is based on an overall appraisal of our reader and the facts of the case at hand.

Because a collection letter is a request letter, we should be clear as to what we want our reader to do. In the personal letter, therefore, a mere notification or reminder about the past-due amount is insufficient. We want an explanation at least, if not payment in full. We must face this issue squarely, so that our reader cannot conveniently "misinterpret" our message as just a reminder.

Our request for payment should specify the *what* of the situation— that is, the amount due and sufficient identification of the transaction behind the debt. We can mention the date and invoice number, or we can specifically describe the product or service which we provided.

It is not always necessary for us to specify a date by which payment is to be made. Since the account is past due, the assumption of immediate or prompt payment is in effect. Sometimes we may wish to emphasize this point by means of a general reference such as "by return mail," "prompt attention," or "today."

If, however, giving a specific date would be helpful to our reader, we should put it in our letter. Such could be the case when we have sounded an appeal to self-interest wherein some benefit can be enjoyed if the account is settled by a definite date. Also, any notification of impending drastic action should contain a deadline for payment. In this way we provide a final interval during which our debtor can make payment and avoid unpleasantness. After all, we want to collect the money if possible; we should prefer not to get involved in drastic-action situations.

Providing ample assistance is a must in a collection letter. We will have already helped somewhat by identifying the transaction by invoice number and date and by specifying the amount to be paid. Such information simplifies the debtor's work of verifying the details preparatory to making payment.

Physical assistance is also indicated—namely, a remittance envelope enclosed with our collection letter. We can choose from three common varieties: an addressed envelope which requires the user to affix the postage; a business-reply envelope; and a stamped, addressed envelope. These varieties are listed according to their popularity; but it remains our choice as to which we should use in a given situation. A remittance envelope is unquestionably a boon to a retail customer and is at least an extra reminder to a trade customer.

The following examples illustrate the conventional collection letter in keeping with the suggested program. In order of presentation, the appeals used are cooperation, self-interest, and fear.

Gentlemen:

Is there something we should know about?

If so, we'd welcome your comments or explanations. We have not received your payment for $125 worth of envelopes billed last June 14 on Invoice No. 4719. The amount is past due; but a few words from you might work to our mutual advantage.

We've enclosed a business-reply envelope for your convenience. Won't you use it today to send us your check—or at least a note of explanation?

Very truly yours,

Gentlemen:

Here is an item of news for you.

With a big Christmas selling season in the offing, we have acquired a wide selection of specialty items for our trade customers. For the first time, jade jewelry and world-famous Hummel figurines have been included.

You will want to be ready for the most profitable Christmas season ever predicted. So start now to list your needs and lay in an ample stock. And, be sure to keep your credit channel clear, to assure smooth handling of your order.

A check for $250, sent in the enclosed envelope, will clear up the August 10 balance on your account. You will then be able to get the jump on competition whenever you please.

Yours very truly,

Gentlemen:

This is an important message that calls for your full attention.

Next Thursday, November 17, has been set as the deadline for receiving an answer from you or, better still, your check for $107.50 on Invoice No. 877 dated August 1. Our job, you know, is to safeguard the assets of our stockholders; and we cannot do so by letting unpaid accounts linger indefinitely. Our only recourse is to enlist the help of an outside agency.

We hope that you will choose to settle your account directly with us, by sending your check today in the enclosed envelope.

Very truly yours,

Collection letters written in this fashion have a reasonably good chance of being read, understood, agreed with, and acted upon. They are persuasive and polite—not at all "two-fisted" in attitude. Even the third letter, with its reference to drastic action, exercises customer-oriented restraint.

Psychological Collection Letters

A trend which has been noticeable since the end of World War II is the use of a psychological approach to the writing of collection letters. In essence, the aim is to have the very letter itself "appeal" to or motivate the reader, whether or not a regular appeal is used. Not only does the beginning arouse interest, but an effort is made to maintain a high degree of interest throughout the entire letter. Thus, the letter is usually somewhat unconventional, out of the ordinary, entertaining, or even humorous.

Often the psychological collection letter is kept as brief as possible by implying whatever can be omitted, so that the reader can finish it before his interest lets down. Brevity, however, is not a requirement; many a longer collection letter has been developed along psychological lines.

Psychological collection letters embody features of the greeting cards and form letters already discussed. In our present context, however, they are understood to be typewritten on company stationery and addressed to a specific debtor. In practice, they are probably most effective when the amount is relatively small or when the account is not long overdue. In the more serious situations, a conventional collection letter would seem to be the better choice.

The suggested program for the psychological collection letter is as follows:

CREATE INTEREST.
APPEAL PSYCHOLOGICALLY.
SPECIFY THE AMOUNT.
MAKE ACTION EASY.

The text of our psychological collection letter would necessarily include the first two steps of this program. But it could omit either or both of the remaining steps. We do not have to give text coverage to these points if we have provided for them adequately some other way. For instance, we might show the transaction date, invoice number, and amount as a footnote. By this method we bring these facts to the attention of our reader but do not clutter our psychological message with details. Similarly, the presence of an addressed remittance envelope is sufficiently self-explanatory. We need not slow the pace of our psychological appeal in order to include a mention of the envelope.

The following examples illustrate a cross section of collection letters prepared along psychological lines. The first letter sticks rather closely to the program.

```
Dear Mr. Wallis:

    This is not a request for payment—unless you still owe $22
on the Lane hat we sold you on September 6.

    In that case, simply mail your check in the enclosed en-
velope. Presto! No request then!

                             Yours truly,
```

The second letter is streamlined. Its text incorporates only the first two steps of the suggested program. The other two steps, however, are not left entirely to the reader's imagination. The footnote calls attention the past-due balance, and an enclosed remittance envelope speaks for itself.

```
Dear Mr. Andrews:
    Who is admired more than a promising businessman?
    Why—a paying one, of course!

                             Yours very truly,

$12.50
                 (Inv. No. 115-E)
                             Promised June 30, 1967
```

The third letter is another which conforms to the suggested program. It demonstrates that a collection letter need not be extremely short to hold the reader's interest to the end.

Gentlemen:

Have you heard the Parable of the Postponer? It goes something like this:

In those days there was a Postponer who delayed in paying his just debts.

"Behold," he said; "I have gold in my treasury and many flocks grazing on the hills. It is known that I have wealth; so why should I hasten to make disbursement?"

And a certain wise man, hearing him speak, replied to the Postponer, saying, "Master, thou hast spoken truly; thy fortunes have flourished even as the bay tree. But thy distant creditor knoweth only that thy account remaineth unpaid. How can he judge thee save as one who doth withhold payment?"

When he had pondered these words of wisdom, the Postponer summoned his steward saying, "See to my just obligations—for lo! my good name shall remain untarnished." And so it was done.

Won't you do as the Postponer did, so that your "good name shall remain untarnished"? A check for $102.75 will cover Invoice No. BL-5880, now 60 days past due. Mail it in the enclosed envelope today.

                    Very truly yours,

TERMINATION STAGE

The number of attempts we will make at collecting an account will be determined by a number of factors. These include the credit rating of the customer, the size of the amount due, competition, prevailing economic conditions, and our own financial status. We might show a great deal of patience with a prime-rated customer by moving through all the available stages: billings, reminders, impersonal appeals, and personal letters. Real letter writing occurs only at the last-named stage, and it is often more than a one-shot approach. Although we should hope that each letter sent out will be the successful one, we should still allow that another may be needed. As time goes on, the interval between letters can be speeded up and the urgency of each message intensified. Both of these activities can be carried on with diplomacy.

Ultimately, however, we will reach the end of the line. We will notify our debtor of a necessary action to be taken if he does not respond within a specified period of time. Our "countdown" is on; and if our debtor chooses to let it go full term, we have little choice but to carry out the action. This is an important stage of a well-run collection system. While we should not give a deadline angrily, we should not back down from one after we have given it. Otherwise, we begin to build for ourselves the image of "bluffer"—a concept that could weaken our entire collection program.

In the termination stage, therefore, we carry out the drastic action, be it notifying the credit bureau, repossessing the merchandise, engaging a collection agency, or whatever. There is no point in writing a post-deadline letter to tell our delinquent debtor that such action has been started. Such a letter would be a waste of time and money. Our debtor will learn about the action soon enough, another way.

SUMMARY
. . . .

The dual function of our collection effort is to motivate our credit customers to pay their bills and, at the same time, to retain the goodwill of those customers. To neglect the second aspect of this function would undo much of the work of our sales department, discourage repeat business, sometimes lead to repercussions.

In a sense a collection effort resembles a business claim. But the direction of our message is from vendor to customer, not vice versa. As claimant, we cannot afford to talk from a position of strength lest we damage the goodwill relationship we enjoy with our customer. We must look upon collecting as an educational task, one calling for persuasion rather than pressure.

There are six stages in a well-rounded collection procedure: a sound credit system; a positive system for billing; follow-up (continual monthly statements); impersonal appeals (rubber stamps, stickers, inserts, greeting cards, form letters); personal appeals (visitations, telephone calls, telegrams, personal letters); and termination (drastic action).

Personal collection letters are of two main varieties: the conventional letter and the psychological letter. These letters are briefly reviewed on the next two pages.

CONVENTIONAL COLLECTION LETTER

Intended
Reader
Reaction:

from this   through this   to this

Program: Create interest.
Sound an appeal.
Specify *what* (if helpful, *when*).
Make action easy.

Pointers: Begin with something unexpected, but agreeable. Avoid talk of ledgers, records, bills sent, etc.

If possible, let the beginning set the theme of the letter.

Motivate by stressing an appeal that is meaningful to the reader. Useful appeals are:
Sympathy.
Fairness.
Pride.
Self-interest.
Cooperation.
Fear.
Various combinations of these.

Reserve the appeal to fear for the last letter to be written.

Specify the amount to be paid; identify the transaction involved.

If it will help the reader (as with appeals to self-interest and fear), specify a payment date.

Enclose a remittance envelope.

PSYCHOLOGICAL COLLECTION LETTER

Intended
Reader
Reaction:

from this   to this

Program: Create interest.
Appeal psychologically.
Specify the amount.
Make action easy.

Pointers: Begin with an attention-getting statement or question.

Motivate by entertaining the reader—use a story, play on words, humor, etc.

Consider holding down the length of the text to sustain the reader's interest. The third and fourth program steps need not be worked in the text. Instead,
a) The amount due and transaction identity can be shown as a footnote.
b) The enclosed remittance envelope can be considered as being self-explanatory.

Limit the use of this approach to a debtor who either owes a relatively small amount or is not long delinquent.

While the number and frequency of collection attempts we will make will vary with our different classes of customers, one fact is certain: continued nonpayment by a customer will lead to drastic action of some kind. Our final letter will give him a final chance to preclude such action. If the deadline expires, we act; there is no longer a reason to write.

QUESTIONS

1. Identify the almost inevitable problem that arises when a firm enters into the practice of extending credit. •
2. Give examples of conflicting goals within a firm, even though all departments are supposedly working toward the same overall goal.
3. In what regard is a collection situation similar to a claim situation?
4. What important differences enter the scene to make the handling of a collection situation *unlike* the handling of a claim?
5. As a matter of fact, is there really such a thing as a *collection* letter? Explain.
6. What is the dual role of a so-called collection letter?
7. List the six stages of activity in a complete collection procedure.
8. Name five devices that are useful during the *impersonal appeal* stage of a collection procedure.
9. What are four media of communication open to a creditor who wishes to use a *personal appeal* to make a collection?
10. Give the suggested program for a conventional collection letter.
11. Why is it necessary to create interest at the beginning of a collection letter?
12. Name the various appeals which are frequently used in collection letters to motivate the reader.
13. When should a *specific deadline* be mentioned in a collection letter?
14. Point out some of the characteristics of the *psychological* collection letter.
15. Give the suggested program for a psychological collection letter.

PROBLEMS

Some of the following collection cases deal with retail accounts, others with trade accounts. In either event, the solution should be typewritten on an appropriate business letterhead. If letterhead stationery is not available, set up a simulated letterhead in accordance with directions issued by your instructor.

14-1. Nearly three months ago, Mrs. Burgess Somers purchased a Duchess cocktail dress at Milady's Fashions of Washington, D.C. After her fitting, she had the dress delivered to her home in Silver Spring, Maryland. That is the last that the store has heard from Mrs. Somers, although it billed her, as always, at the end of the first month, and has sent bills twice since then. As credit manager of the store, you are puzzled by her behavior. Her financial status has always been first-rate. Undoubtedly there must be some special reason behind the nonpayment of her account. Write a first-time collection letter to Mrs. Somers.

14-2. The Midland Petroleum Co. of Dallas, Texas, uses electronic data processing equipment in billing its credit-card customers. As invoices come in from the company's service stations, an electronic scanning device reads the information which has been imprinted by the individual customer's credit card. A punched card is automatically produced by the equipment. Then a key punch operator fills in the rest of the data—namely, the amount of the invoice. Payments made by customers are accompanied by a remittance notice in each case. This notice is really a punched card itself; a key punch operator can easily add in the payment data. Cards representing each customer's previous balance, new charges, and payments are fed into a computer which does the bookkeeping work. It prints out a punched card which goes to the customer as his monthly statement, and which is to be returned by the customer with his payment. In the event that a certain customer's statement shows a balance remaining from the previous month, the computer automatically ejects that card into a separate bin. A reminder slip is then enclosed with each such statement. Until now, the Midland Petroleum Co. has had success with this system. But it is beginning to look as though an additional step will have to be added to the process. A few customers have been ignoring the reminder slip and have fallen two months in arrears. In their case a letter will have to replace the reminder slip. As credit manager of the company, prepare a form letter which would be suitable for this purpose.

14-3. The Commercial Supply Company, located in the capital of your state, is in the business of selling office forms, typewriters, adding machines, and other items needed in administrative work. Three months ago, it received an urgent order from a long-standing customer, the All-American Life Insurance Company of East Boston, Massachusetts. The insurance company was opening a huge branch in this area and was in immediate need of 50 standard typewriters

and 22 full-key adding machines. Commercial Supply could not fill
this order from stock; but it was able to shop around and, by paying
cash, accumulate the requisite number of items. Delivery was made
to the new branch of the All-American Life Insurance Company,
and invoice No. 3304 was submitted for $7,385. So far, the insurance
company has not paid for this purchase, although two monthly billings and two impersonal-type reminders have been sent to the main
office in East Boston. Having paid cash in acquiring the equipment,
Commercial Supply is running low on working capital. Assume
that you are the president of the Commercial Supply Company.
Write a collection letter to the insurance company; make an appeal
to fair play.

14–4. Samuel Westmore is a charge-account customer of the Work-N-Play
Shop, which is located in a city of more than 100,000 persons. The
store features various pieces of power equipment for yard maintenance and also such recreational items as boats, outboard motors,
and motorbikes. On May 1, the store sold a Tech electric chain
saw to Mr. Westmore, on credit. The sales price was $25 plus state
sales tax of 3 percent. It is now July 15; and, although he has always
been punctual with his payments in the past, Mr. Westmore has not
responded to any of the store's billings regarding the chain saw.
As proprietor of the Work-N-Play Shop, write a personal collection
letter to Mr. Westmore, who lives at 377 Winding Road in suburban
Chesterton. Use an appeal to pride.

14–5. The Suncote Paint Company of Wilmington, Delaware, manufactures latex-base paints for both interior and exterior use. With
spring in the offing, the management is interested in clearing all
unpaid balances in its trade accounts receivable. The various paint
dealers and hardware stores who carry the Suncote line will likely
want to put in new stocks for the clean-up, paint-up season. It would
be in their own self-interest, therefore, if they kept themselves eligible for extended credit. Assume that you are the credit manager of
the Suncote Paint Company. Prepare a form letter which will embrace the self-interest concept. The plan is to send each customer
an individually typewritten copy of the letter, so that he will not
know that he is getting a form letter.

14–6. Alton B. Charles, president of the ABC Manufacturing Co. of Du-
luth, Minnesota, is a credit customer of Prairie Air Lines. He carries
a packet of ticket forms and issues his own ticket whenever he needs
to go to a distant point on business. Suddenly he has stopped making
payments, although he has been billed for his tickets in the customary
manner. At present, he owes Prairie Air Lines for two months' worth
of service—and today another current voucher has come in against
his account. Assume that you are the airline's internal auditor and

that you are headquartered in Chicago, Illinois. Write a self-interest collection letter to Mr. Charles. Stress the convenience of your credit-ticketing arrangement and the importance of retaining one's right to use it.

14–7. For six months the Best Manufacturing Company of this city has been trying to collect a trade account from the Tefla Tool Co., also of this city. There is an unpaid balance of $117.50 on 50 gallons of a solvent which Best Manufacturing prepared according to specifications set by the purchasing agent at Tefla Tool Co. During all this time billings, reminders, and collection letters sent out by Best Manufacturing have fallen upon deaf ears. The time has come for Best Manufacturing to resort to drastic action. The question is: will Tefla Tool Co. send its payment within the next five days, or must Best Manufacturing turn the account over to a collection agency? As manager of accounts receivable at the Best Manufacturing Company, write a final collection letter to the Tefla Tool Co.

14–8. Suppose that you are the credit manager of the Midtown Department Store, which is a large retail establishment in this city. At a credit-men's convention held recently in New York City, you heard it said that accounts which were not cleared up within 90 days of the sale were likely to become uncollectible. You also heard it stated by a number of the speakers that a humanistic approach tends to win more cooperation than a hard-fisted approach. After considering these views for several days, you have decided to try something new in your collection procedure. You will make use of a "gadget," as is sometimes done in the case of sales letters, to attract attention and arouse interest at the beginning of the collection message. Some of the possibilities you have in mind include a patch of terry cloth ("Here's a piece of our crying towel"), an aspirin tablet ("This will take care of *your* headache"), and a three-cent stamp ("We'll meet you more than halfway"). Give the matter some further thought; then prepare your gadget collection letter. Ultimately, it will be printed for use as a form letter.

14–9. The Ferris Match Corporation of Chicago, Illinois, manufactures advertising book matches according to specifications laid down by its customers. Some of these customers, however, are not so exacting when it comes time for them to settle accounts with the Ferris Match Corporation. Usually, the cause can be traced to oversight, carelessness, or a lackadaisical attitude on the part of such customers. The best handling, it has been learned, is persistence—regular billing and reminders. In difficult cases, a collection letter series is used; the first letter in this series has been a short, humorous letter of the so-called psychological variety. The current version of this letter seemingly has outlived its effectiveness. As a correspondent in the collection department, prepare a new version. It will eventually go out above the signature of the sales manager.

14–10. Assume that you are the credit manager of Central Industries, Incorporated, which has its offices and factory in the capital of your state. You are a believer in the psychological approach to collection letters and have, in fact, an entire series along this line. The first two letters are of a short variety, but the third makes a more thorough presentation. It regularly includes a story that will entertain the reader and also express a moral of some kind. As might be expected, this letter has a relatively short life and must be changed several times a year. Since the next replacement date is approaching, prepare a new narrative-type, psychological collection letter.

....

CHAPTER 15

SUCCESSFUL WRITING
FOR AN EMPLOYMENT
INTERVIEW

One of the most important business letters we will write is the application letter. Through it we will try to win consideration for a position we want in a firm we have selected as a particularly desirable employer. In the present labor market there is an ample supply of job opportunities for college-trained people, but getting the right position takes some doing.

Nowadays companies of all sizes send recruiters to the larger colleges and universities, wherever they may be situated, and to those smaller institutions which are in or near metropolitan areas. In fact, probably every school experiences some amount of visitation each year from recruiters. Arrangements are generally handled through the campus placement office, which schedules the visitations and gives notice of them to the student body. Interested students place information on file with the placement office and ask to be included for an interview whenever they are attracted by the company name, the type of positions, or some other aspect of an announced visitation.

The practice of campus recruiting introduces both advantages and disadvantages. To the prospective employer, it provides for the screening of a large number of possible candidates from a wide range of educational backgrounds well in advance of the hiring period. But, because recruiters are probably more interested in the prospect with a high achievement record, they often find themselves up against stiff competition. They are under pressure to offer rather lucrative starting salaries in their attempt to sign the top seniors. In the end, however, the best prospect can join only one of the bidding companies. The other firms have to settle for second best, third best, and so on—at somewhat inflated salaries.

From the student's standpoint, the work of job hunting seems to be simplified. A student may be able to land a position without really trying. A student with an impressive record may be able to choose from among several attractive offers. An ordinary student may get his name on a large number of interview lists, and rely on the law of averages to bring about a satisfactory offer. Yet, throughout it all, the student sacrifices his initiative, and therein is a danger.

It is possible that a more positive attitude could have resulted in the student's obtaining a position at a company which did not visit that particular campus. It could be that the position foregone would have been a better overall choice in considerations such as starting salary, personal satisfaction, and potential for the future. Some companies have been accused of luring top students by means of overly generous starting salaries, while not mentioning that promotions and pay increases may be almost nonexistent. By the time the young person becomes aware of this fact he is in a dilemma. He probably has become accustomed to a standard of living higher than he could maintain with a starting job in another company, but he is relatively "frozen" at that level in his present company.

Campus recruiting, of course, appears to be here to stay. In general, it is a service that has benefits for both the college student and the prospective employer. But it does not solve all problems for either side. The alert student should take some initiative on his own behalf if what ought to be his first choice of position and employer is not among the offerings of his school's recruitment program. His customary medium for taking this initiative is the application letter.

Classified according to general physical characteristics, the application letter may be either a one-part or a two-part letter.

THE ONE-PART LETTER

One approach to the application letter is to prepare a rather long, all-inclusive narrative about the applicant's qualifications. This possibility is suitable in specialized or infrequent application situations, but does not enjoy wide popularity. To the writer, it is a time-consuming task, certainly no help in an emergency situation. Moreover, the entire letter has to be redone—or at least retyped—before it can be used a second time. To the reader, the great distance between the salutation and the complimentary close tends to discourage reading. Pertinent data are too often obscured by narrative presentation whereas they stand out in a tabular presentation. Moreover, flexibility of handling is lost. The whole letter would need to be circulated if some routing among executives is to be carried on, simply because there is no easy way of separating the objective information from the subjective.

THE TWO–PART LETTER

A second possibility consists of a relatively short request letter accompanied by a detachable summary of qualifications. This summary is often reproduced by some mechanical process; it can be stocked in quantity for instant use as the need arises. The two-part letter is popular with both writers and readers of application letters. The job applicant can file an application letter on short notice because preparation time has been reduced. His main work is the writing of a selling type of letter which matches his key qualifications with the requirements of the position being sought. Because his compiled list of data is subject to gradual change only, the printed summary is probably ready for immediate use. On the reader's end, a two-part letter appears inviting to read. The narrative part is held to a moderate length; the summary of data has good eye appeal. Flexibility is available, because the summary is distinct from the letter itself and can be handled as a separate document.

Another classification made of application letters is according to whether one is:

1. *A solicited letter,* written in response to an advertisement or a feeler extended by the company.

2. *An unsolicited letter,* written without there being an indication from the company that an opening is available. Writing this type of letter is sometimes referred to as "writing blind."

The above-mentioned classifications indicate that there are four kinds of application letters.

Application Letters

One-part . . . . 1. Solicited.
                                   2. Unsolicited.
Two-part . . . . 3. Solicited.
                                   4. Unsolicited.

In the discussion which follows, we shall consider the two-part application letter, as it is to be handled in both solicited and unsolicited situations.

GETTING STARTED

Producing a summary of our overall qualifications for employment is a somewhat time-consuming task. At least, we should not expect to turn out an adequate summary in just one sitting. It usually takes us awhile to compile a full list of items to be considered for inclusion and to sift them down to what will be our final selection. Occasionally, we recall things of value some time after we supposedly had exhausted the possibilities. Often, we need time to research precise information such as names, dates, and places. We are wise, therefore, to start our task well in advance of the period when we will begin sending out application letters.

EVALUATE YOUR QUALIFICATIONS !

Our first activity is accumulating facts about ourselves. We should do a thorough job of fact finding so that we are not likely to overlook something valuable. We should prefer to come up with more facts than we may finally need. It is easier for us to trim down an abundant supply than it is to find new facts, on short notice, to bolster a skimpy supply.

To compile an inventory of our employment qualifications, we should place various general headings on sheets of paper or card stock. These general headings identify the nature of the information which we will note on the respective cards; and they will roughly correspond to the sections appearing in our final summary of facts. The following headings are suggested:

1. Education.
2. Work experience.
3. Other qualifications.
4. Personal data.
5. References.

Taking each sheet in turn, we list as much information as we believe to be of use. If we remember something else about a certain area after we have gone on to a different area, we can easily go back to the proper sheet to make an addition.

Now, let us consider the kind of information that should appear beneath each of our general headings.

EDUCATION

As college-trained people, we usually do not have to go back to our primary and secondary educational records for important facts. Nor is it necessary that we state the names of the schools we attended at the primary and secondary levels. If, however, such a school happens to have a significance of its own (such as a nationally respected military school, or a high school which is acclaimed tops in its district), we can see advantages in listing it.

Under college, we should include our degree and our major field of study, and then support these major items with specific courses, grouped as follows.

1. *Major courses:* the specialized courses or electives which are characteristic of our major field of study.

2. *Related courses:* the more important of the core courses, or prerequisite courses. While all students may have taken the same courses in this grouping, not all of these courses will be listed. We should pick out those which have the most bearing on our major field and our intended area of employment. For example, if our major were accounting, we should be able to find supporting value in courses such as business communication, business law, business policies, finance, and statistics.

3. *Background courses:*   the more significant of the nonprofessional courses which were included in our curriculum. Business firms are looking for trainable, flexible, and promotable employees taken from college ranks. Most collegiate business schools have adjusted, and are continuing to adjust, their programs so that their students will not be overly specialized. Once-slighted courses in the liberal arts have returned, making for a better educational package. Accordingly, we should select a number of these nonprofessional courses for listing. Certainly worthy of consideration are those in the areas of English, history, mathematics, psychology, public speaking, science, and sociology.

4. *Honors and Awards.*   A review of our files, school records, souvenirs, and so on, can sometimes uncover long-forgotten distinctions we earned during our college career. When we add these to others we may have recalled easily, we may have an attention-getting collection. Items for us to check include:

a) Dean's List (Honor Roll)—frequency and dates.
b) Awards in specified subject—such as mathematics, science, foreign language, public speaking, accounting.
c) Achievement awards—for being top student in a class or in a major field of study.
d) Scholarship—partial or full.
e) Graduation honors—cum laude, etc.
f) Election to honor societies.

5. *Activities.*   Prospective employers regularly take the view that there is more to going to college than taking courses. They like to see some evidence of a well-rounded individual—one who has good social adjustment, who can work with other people without being compelled to, and who has at least the attitude of leadership. For this reason, we are urged to take advantage of some of the many activities which are available to us. Then, in compiling facts about ourselves, we can profitably list some cocurricular and extracurricular activities.

Cocurricular activities is the term that refers to organizations outside of class but still related to our academic discipline. Thus, membership in a management club, an accounting discussion group, or a business fraternity would constitute a cocurricular activity for a business administration student.

Extracurricular activities, by contrast, refers to organizations which are not related to our academic discipline. Specific examples, in the case of business administration students, would be varsity sports, the band, the glee club, the theatrical society, and the debating team.

WORK EXPERIENCE

The amount of work experience accumulated by an individual by the time he receives his college degree varies with the circumstances. In some cases it is negligible, if indeed there is any at all. In other cases, as with the person who has worked his way through school or the person who has held down a full-time job while attending evening college, work experience can be substantial and impressive. The typical college graduate, however, has had some job experience. The work generally has been done during summers, during short-term vacation periods of the school year, or even on a part-time basis after school hours.

We should make a record of such work on our inventory sheet, but we probably do not gain by going back to jobs we held at a tender age (such as serving a paper route). For each entry, we should list the name of our employer (company), the address, the job or jobs held, and the applicable dates.

OTHER QUALIFICATIONS

Under a caption for miscellaneous qualifications we list anything else which we are able to present as an employment asset. Our possibilities here include membership in worthwhile groups (e.g., the Junior Chamber of Commerce); hobbies and interests (e.g., bowling, coin collecting, golf, painting, photography, the stock market); acquired skills (e.g., typewriting, shorthand, computer programming, familiarity with general office machines); knowledge of another language; and travel (especially if it was extensive or to foreign lands).

PERSONAL DATA

In the category of personal data we list such details as date of birth, height, weight, general health, marital status, and draft status. In comparison to the other facts we have accumulated, such facts are of minor importance. But they do have some bearing on our case and definitely serve to round out the listing of data on ourselves.

REFERENCES

Strictly speaking, any references given do not fill the definition of "qualifications." They do, however, offer the names and addresses of people who can speak in our behalf. Good practice suggests that we name at least four references. Our best choice is to select people who have supervised us during our work experience. The employment personnel to whom we write our application letters usually place credence in the testimony of people who have witnessed our performance. For this reason, also, they are willing to accept recommendations from college references if we are short of work references. On the other hand, personal or character references are seldom useful; it does not pay us to list them in preference to other kinds. If we are asked to provide a character reference, we can place it in the body of our letter; otherwise, we should not list it.

We should bear in mind that it is always polite, although not always practical, to obtain permission from a person before using his name as a reference. This guideline holds true particularly with college professors. Other people—specifically, former employers and college deans —have easy access to records from which to draw needed information. The professor, however, may have to find and dig through old class records; he may not have a typist available; he may not have access to supplemental records; and he may not even lean favorably toward us. If we obtain his permission first, the professor has advance notice and time to collect his facts before a request comes in. Better still, if he agrees to write the reference, his code of ethics should require him to give us a *favorable* reference.

As thorough as we try to be, it is always possible that we may have omitted some significant detail the first time we list our qualifications. Our minimum double check should be a review of each group of items. Better still, we should let a few days go by, during which time our memories might improve.

THE DATA SHEET

Once we have satisfied ourselves that we have a complete listing of our qualifications grouped under general headings, we can prepare a summary for our application letter. Such a summary is often referred to as a *résumé*.

As college-trained personnel, in search of a position at or leading to the executive level, we should submit an extensive summary, which we will call a *data sheet*. It will be sufficiently detailed to show that we have the necessary qualifications expected of all applicants (neutral data) and also some talents or experience that may be unique (positive data). Moreover, our form will give names and addresses of people who can supply additional information.

To be effective, our data sheet should possess the following characteristics:

1. Instant identification.
2. Overall order of importance.
3. Adequate coverage.
4. Good organization of data.
5. Consistent presentation.
6. Eye appeal.

Our data sheet may be individually typewritten or it may be reproduced in some manner (e.g., printing, multilithing, mimeographing); but it should never be a carbon copy. Because typing each data sheet would be very time consuming, we should prefer to do it once and have a quantity reproduced for future use.

Identification of our data sheet is a prime requisite. If our application and data sheet should become separated, the latter will be self-explanatory if it bears our name, address, and telephone number at the very top. Moreover, we should display this information prominently so that finding it will be swift and easy.

Some decisions about our data confront us before we are ready to produce our final copy. First we must decide upon an overall sequence for our groups of data. In general, we will strive for the order of most important to least important, which is the order in which our inventory of qualifications was taken. In some cases, however, work experience may be considered of greater importance than one's education; if so, it should be listed ahead of education.

Within each group of qualifications we should list those which seem to be most significant. Sometimes our list will need all the facts we have accumulated; but usually, it will not. The following criteria will be helpful in our decisions concerning the key groupings:

1.   Under education, we may or may not want to list our high school; but we certainly should list colleges attended, degrees earned, and respective dates. A degree should be backed up by a stated major supported by some pertinent and background courses. Awards, honors, and participation in activities can follow in that order.

2.   Work experience since leaving high school should be listed. We should show part-time and vacation jobs, even though they are in no way connected with our education or with the field we wish to enter. Such jobs are taken to help defray college expenses or to make productive use of otherwise idle time. Prospective employers will likely interpret such activity as a plus factor that shows character, initiative, and willingness to work. Also they can extract a degree of confidence that we are somewhat in tune with the demands of employment. People without any experience, for example, sometimes must learn the hard way that:

a)   Absenteeism is taboo—no more authorized "cuts."

b)   Punctuality is important—no drifting in 15 minutes late.

c)   Alertness is required—no dozing on the job, or daydreaming while the boss is giving instructions.

d)   Full performance is required—no getting by with work only 75 percent completed by the deadline.

e)   Accuracy is demanded—no passing grade at 70, 80, or even 90 percent accuracy.

3.   A look at our tentative listing of miscellaneous qualifications should tell us whether there are enough data of a homogeneous nature to warrant our using a special caption to identify them. If there are only odds and ends of information, our best move is to list them under the general heading, "Other Qualifications." Our preference in this area should be things that could give us an edge over other applicants. If we consider that most of the applicants for the position we are seeking are likely to be close duplicates of ourselves in age, education, and experience, we may realize that we have yet to attract particular attention. The data in our "other" category, however, are not so likely to be duplicated

by anyone else. Thus, special skills, desirable memberships, hobbies, and travel experience do open up the possibility of a "plus" on our behalf.

Within each group of data, we should strive for good organization of our material. In a general sense we should lean toward the order of importance just as we do with the overall data sheet. Sometimes our choice is based on preference, but often it follows suggestions fed back to us from the personnel people themselves. The following guidelines will be helpful:

1. Education is shown in the chronological order. This arrangement disregards importance, per se. It places our most recent schooling, probably our most significant, in last position. However, it does trace our progress as regards education and sometimes indicates the turns we have taken.

2. Work experience is preferably shown in the reverse chronological order. This method, too, disregards importance; but since our present position, or one most recently held, is apt to be most fruitful for answers to inquiries, the method is regularly used.

3. In listing other qualifications we should definitely follow the order of importance. Of course, the judgment factor enters in here. For example, different people may favor slightly different orders of listing hobbies—say, golf, photography, and stamp collecting—and each could have a valid reason for his decision.

4. Our personal data would not seem to present any difficulties. In this area we usually have a limited number of points to cover. We should be careful to list our data in a "straight line"—that is, we should complete our treatment of a specific subdivision (e.g. physical details) before taking up something else (e.g., draft status).

5. The way of listing our references will depend upon the kind we are offering. If they are all work references or all school references, we can list them in a single alphabetical order. If some are of each variety, we could subdivide them accordingly and use a separate alphabetical arrangement for each portion.

The last, but not the least of our decisions concerning the data sheet will be its format. We should keep in mind that our data sheet is intended to convey an adequate amount of information, but is expected to display such information attractively. Eye appeal, therefore, becomes a rather important element of a good data sheet.

Our data sheet should be typewritten, reproduced, or printed on white bond paper, of 20-pound stock or better, and of 8½ - by 11-inch size. In the interests of eye appeal, we should use ample amounts of open space, clear-cut headings for all main groups of data, subheadings for larger groups of data, and parallelism in expressing items under each heading. If such usage causes our data sheet to lengthen—say, to two pages—we should be willing to accept that fact. It is better to have two pages of easy-to-find, easy-to-read data than to have either reduced data or cramped presentation on a single page.

While there is no rule concerning the matter, it also is better to use words and phrases as opposed to full sentences in our data sheet. Some applicants have found that the sentence approach removes the problem they might have had in listing data in parallel style. But, in the final analysis, it is the reader's comfort, not the writer's, which should be considered. Words and phrases are better for the reader, both in the initial reading and in any reviewing that may be desirable.

Under Title VII of the Civil Rights Act enacted by Congress in 1964, employers may not discriminate against applicants because of color, race, religion, sex, or national origin. Moreover, several of the states have passed fair-employment laws of their own; some of these prohibit *applicants* from mentioning such matters in any advertising they publish seeking employment. Thus, an interesting question arises: Does a photograph, an item traditionally attached to a data sheet, violate any of these statutes? This question is difficult to answer on a general basis. The problem could be that what is approved in one state (say, the state in which our college is located) is *not* in another (say, the state in which the job opportunity exists). Our best practice, therefore, would be to arrange our data sheet *as though no photograph were involved*. This is a departure from earlier stylings which recommended that we clear a box somewhere at the top of our data sheet to accommodate a photograph.

Presented on pp. 474–77 are two data sheets which incorporate the suggestions herein proposed. The first data sheet places greatest emphasis on the educational background of the applicant.

The next data sheet is more typical of a part-time or evening student. In his case, several years of work experience in his field of interest may well take precedence over his educational data.

DATA SHEET

PETER A. JAMIESON
2412 Piquette Avenue
Detroit, Michigan 48202

WAbash 1-4975

Major Interest   Basic Qualifications

Public Accounting   University training in accounting

EDUCATION

Graduate of Fort Dearborn High School, Detroit, Michigan. 1963

Bachelor of Science in Business Administration (Accounting Major),
    Great Lakes University, Port Huron, Michigan 1967

    Upper fifth of class; point average of 2.981 (maximum, 4.000)

Major Courses

    Advanced Accounting   Controllership
    Auditing Principles   Standard Cost Accounting
    Basic Cost Accounting   Tax Accounting

Supporting Business Courses

    Business Communication   Corporation Finance
    Business Law   Principles of Economics
    Business Statistics   Typewriting

Background Courses

    English Composition   Mathematical Analysis
    Ethics for Businessmen   Public Speaking

Extracurricular Activities

    Varsity track team. 1965-1967   Intramural basketball. . . . 1966

WORK EXPERIENCE

1966-1967 . . . . Junior Accountant (Part-time) . . . . Wilcox and Brownlee
                                                          Certified Public Accountants
                                                          1424 Book Tower
                                                          Detroit, Mich. 48202

1966 and 1965 . . Service Station Attendant
                   (During summer vacations) . . . . . . Phil's Midoco Service
                                                          282 Piquette Avenue
                                                          Detroit, Mich. 48201

Data Sheet of PETER A. JAMIESON   Page 2

OTHER QUALIFICATIONS

Acquired Skills: Typewriting (45 words a minute); familiarity with electric adding machines and calculators

Hobbies: Camping; outdoor sports, in season; stamp collecting

PERSONAL DATA

Date of birth: May 9, 1945
Height: 5 feet, 11 inches
Weight: 171 pounds
Health: Excellent
Marital status: Single; no dependents
Draft status: 2S, student deferment

REFERENCES

Dean William F. Chennaw
School of Business
Great Lakes University
Port Huron, Mich. 48247

John R. Pennick, Ph.D., C.P.A.
Associate Professor of Accounting
Great Lakes University
Port Huron, Mich. 42847

Clarence B. Schmidt, Ph.D.
Professor of Finance
Great Lakes University
Port Huron, Mich. 48247

Mr. Harrison Wilcox, C.P.A.
Wilcox and Brownlee
Certified Public Accountants
1424 Book Tower
Detroit, Mich. 48202

DATA SHEET

THOMAS R. CONNALLY

4701 Sanborn Street
Port Huron, Michigan 48217

Telephone: MAdison 2-5550

Major Interest
Marketing

Basic Qualifications
Experience in selling, sales correspondence, and public relations;
university training in marketing

WORK EXPERIENCE

1964-   . . . . Senior Sales Correspondent . . . Endicott Copper Corporation
1200 North Bay Road
Port Huron, Mich. 48225

1962-1964 . . . . Sales Correspondent . . . . Endicott Copper Corporation

1959-1962 . . . . Public Relations Trainee . . . . . Kendall Distributing Company
620 East 14th Street
Port Huron, Mich. 48225

EDUCATION

Diploma, Roosevelt Senior High School, Port Huron, Michigan 1959

Bachelor of Science Degree in Business Administration,
Great Lakes University, Port Huron, Michigan 1967

Major Courses in Marketing

    Advertising Theory and Practice   Market Research
    Marketing Management   Retail-Store Management
    Marketing Psychology   Sales Management

Related Business Courses

    Business Communication   Business Statistics
    Business Decisions   Principles of Purchasing
    Business Law

Supporting Courses

    English Composition   General Psychology
    English Literature   Public Speaking

Activities

    Evening Students Association 1960-1967
    The Lighthouse (campus newspaper), Reporter 1965-1967

Data Sheet of THOMAS R. CONNALLY   Page 2

HOBBIES AND OTHER INTERESTS

<u>Hobbies:</u> Golf, oil painting, and ballroom dancing

<u>Interests:</u> Civic improvement (member, Port Huron Jaycees) and do-it-yourself
projects

PERSONAL DATA

Physical Data:	Date of birth:	June 14, 1941
	Height:	5 feet, 10 inches
	Weight:	165 pounds
	Health:	Excellent

Other Details:	Marital status:	Married; one son
	Community status:	Homeowner
	Draft status:	4A, inactive reserves

REFERENCES

Mr. Joseph J. Dittrich
Director of Public Relations
Kendall Distributing Company
620 East 14th Street
Port Huron, Mich. 48225

Dr. George R. Franklin
Professor of Marketing
Great Lakes University
Port Huron, Mich. 48247

Mr. Raymond Eberhardt
Office Manager
Endicott Copper Corporation
1200 North Bay Road
Port Huron, Mich. 48225

Mr. J. Charles Richland
Instructor in Marketing
Great Lakes University
Port Huron, Mich. 48247

College and university placement offices often help job applicants in the preparation of data sheets. In fact, the *College Placement Annual* for 1967 advocates a standard format for the data sheet. An illustration, using the Jamieson data (pp. 474–75), is shown on p. 479.

We should recognize that there are both advantages and disadvantages connected with a form data sheet. A person who has but little understanding of what is needed is certainly better off when he follows a form. He is thereby guided on the important facts to be included; he is kept on the right track in the matters of organization and orderly presentation. It is likely, also, that his reader will be familiar with the format and will be able to extract information easily.

The chief drawback would seem to be the leveling effect a form has on all who use it. A person with superior training, skills, and experiences is often unable to present such facts in the best way possible. Sometimes he is misled into believing that only information which is common to everybody should be shown. Moreover, his creativity and originality tend to become obscured. Under such conditions, the use of a standard form would deprive the job applicant of much of his competitive advantage.

The fact remains, therefore, that a presentation made up in an orderly, logical manner, and designed specifically to fit the person involved, is to be preferred. But we do recognize that a form presentation is better than one which is ill conceived and poorly prepared.

THE COVERING LETTER

Accompanying our data sheet in a two-part application will be a letter of transmittal, or covering letter. In a number of ways, this letter is rather similar in nature to a sales letter—our own personal services being the "product" we are trying to sell. It is necessary, therefore, that we be sufficiently descriptive, explanatory, and persuasive in what we write. It is never enough to single out a position and then refer to the enclosed data sheet for a rundown of qualifications. Such an approach places the burden on our reader, whereas we should be telling him how various qualifications we possess actually fulfill the needs of the position at his company.

During the preparation of our data sheet, we gathered useful infor-

PETER A. JAMIESON

Home Address: 2412 Piquette Avenue
Detroit, Michigan 48202
Telephone: WAbash 1-4975

Campus Address: None

Personal Information	• Single – No dependents U.S. Citizen – Born 5-9-45 5'11" – 171 pounds
Job Objective	• Public Accounting To begin work as a junior accountant in a C.P.A. firm, qualifying eventually for a C.P.A. certificate.
Experience 1966 to 1967	• Wilcox and Brownlee, C.P.A.'s – Detroit Part-time work, after class hours, as junior accountant. Responsibilities included bank-reconciliation statements and inventory taking on audits.
Summer 1965 Work and 1966	• Phil's Midoco Service – Detroit Work as service-station attendant and mechanic, to help defray college expenses.
Education 1963 to present	• Great Lakes University – Candidate for B.S. in Business Administration in June, 1967. Major in accounting, with strong background in liberal arts and general business subjects.
Extracurricular Activities	• Varsity track team, 1965-1967 Intramural basketball, 1966
Military Service	• None; classified 2S, student deferment.
Personal Information	• In excellent health . . . able to operate typewriter (45 words a minute) . . . familiar with electric adding machines and calculators . . . hobbies of camping, outdoor sports (in season), and stamp collecting.
References	• References furnished upon request.

May, 1967

mation concerning ourselves. Now, at the actual letter-writing stage, it is reasonable that we arm ourselves with information concerning the

"I'VE JUST THE MAN
TO WASH YOUR
CEILINGS. "

EMPLOYMENT
AGENCY

requirements of the position we seek and, if possible, about the prospective employer. Such information will help us match our qualifications with the requirements and help us do an effective selling job. If we are writing a solicited application (for example, answering an advertisement), we are usually pressed for time and may have to settle for what we know to be the normal requirements of the position involved. If we are writing an unsolicited application letter, however, we usually have time to do some research. The more we can learn about the job requirements in terms of the operation of the specific firm we plan to approach, the better we can match our qualifications to their requirements.

Sources of information for this purpose are varied, but abundant. If we are still in college, we might turn first to our campus placement office. The counselors there should have been able to accumulate brochures, correspondence, pamphlets, and other written or printed material; and they should be willing to place such aids at our disposal. Next, there is our college library—or our local public library—where we can obtain facts on a company's history, development, structure, products and services, divisions, and plant locations, from that company's annual report and from summaries published by such organizations as Moody's, Standard and Poor's, and so on. In addition, the librarian can assist us in tracing information by way of the many periodical indexes. Another source would be faculty members who teach subjects in the field we are planning to enter. Finally, we may be able to use current newspapers and magazines. For example, company advertisements can tell us about product lines. Moreover, business and financial sections of newspapers reveal much about mergers, personnel changes, promotions, and the like. Specific publications, such as *Fortune* magazine and *The Wall Street Journal,* often contain an abundance of information about individual companies—and even are known to present feature articles highlighting one company or another.

If we are already employed and are looking for a better position, we can still look to many of these sources for information. But it is possible that we may have an additional channel not usually available to college students. Such a channel is opened by our membership and participation in professional societies, trade associations, and technical groups. We mingle with personnel from other companies, learn much about their employers, and even obtain leads about attractive job openings. However we come by our facts, we need to be well informed about our prospective employer.

A suitable program for the letter portion of an employment application is as follows:

CREATE INTEREST.
PRESENT SALES MESSAGE.
OFFER PROOF.
REQUEST AN INTERVIEW.
MAKE ACTION EASY.

This five-step program is very similar to the eight-step program we used for a regular sales letter in Chapter 10. The chief differences are that we omit the "flashy" beginning which is used in a sales letter to command attention, and we do not apply pressure on a would-be employer by using an urgency motivation.

We create interest in an application letter by one or both of two methods. In our opening paragraph we should identify the position we are seeking—e.g., junior accountant, management trainee, banking trainee. Moreover, in the case of a solicited application, we should give our source of information that the company has an opening. By identifying the position, we help the reader appraise our qualifications as he goes through our letter. Otherwise, he has to hold things in abeyance until he knows what we are aiming for; and this could be an irritating, if not impractical, approach. By stating how we learned about the opening (advertisement, inside lead, etc.), we alert our reader to the fact that he should be expecting such a letter and should give it his full attention.

There is a word of caution here for anyone who might try to do something unusual as a way of creating interest at the start of an application letter. A position in business is generally reserved for the stable, dependable, responsible individual. Thus, to try something unorthodox, risqué, or comical could be unwise. In fact, very few people are able to do a good job of humor when it comes to the written word. The best advice is: stick to the businesslike or conventional patterns.

In the middle paragraphs, we do our selling job. We show that we know what our field is about, that we know the specific requirements of the position we are seeking, and that we can meet these requirements. At the same time, we should avoid exaggerated statements about what we know or what we can do. Similarly, we should avoid "window dressing" our message by the use of trade jargon or technical terms which we barely understand.

Our letter presentation is aimed at our becoming at least one of the finalists, if not the outstanding candidate for the position. To attain this goal, we must introduce facts beyond the routine level of our competition, and we must express these facts in a way that points up their significance. For example, "I also took a course in public speaking," seems to be headed for the reaction, "So what?" But the following statement appears to place a value on this fact.

```
My course in speech communication taught me to be at ease
in talking to groups, a function expected of people in man-
agement.
```

Or, let us compare the neutral sentence, "I belonged to the Management Club" with the positive, meaningful statement.

```
As a two-year member of the Management Club, I met and
talked with local businessmen, and kept myself informed on
current issues in industry.
```

In a solicited application, we should heed all questions which the prospective employer has asked. If his advertisement asks us to state our willingness to travel and our salary expectations, we are expected to state them in our letter. If we omit such details, we stand a strong chance of eliminating ourselves from the competition. On the other hand, matters of this kind generally should be discussed at the interview. The salary figure is usually within the prerogatives of the employer, when it comes to making the first move. Let us not risk creating friction by introducing it ourselves. There is a possibility of our mentioning salary in polite, but very vague terms; yet such a treatment really does not accomplish much. For example, we could express our willingness to accept "the going rate" or "the beginning rate at your company." But we still have not expressed a tangible figure.

The number of paragraphs that we will need for this "selling" portion of our letter will depend on the quantity of data involved. Presumably, as college-trained persons, we should have at least two middle paragraphs in our letter: one for educational qualifications, one for other qualifications. If there are a sufficient number of homogeneous components among the other qualifications, however, we might discuss them in a separate paragraph. Thus, we might have a paragraph each on education, work experience, and other qualifications.

Behind the selection of the two-part application letter, of course, was the desire to make reading and handling easy for the recipient. To this end we should, when composing our sales presentation, strive for conciseness. If we can confine our letter to one page, so much the better. If we cannot hold its length down, we should at least make sure that interest is maintained all the way through.

In offering proof, we proceed along lines a bit more subtle than those we follow in a regular sales letter. A good portion of our proof is given through demonstration. We should be submitting a package that speaks well in our behalf. Neatness, good eye appeal, proper organization of thought, correct English, finesse, and completeness do tend to support our allegations that we have learned something in college. Beyond these measures, of course, we submit a slate of references who are in position to put in some words for us.

Our final paragraph is the action section of our application letter. Here is where we state our specific request, which usually is a request for an interview. We should realize that it is not likely that we will be hired on the strength of an application letter only. The personnel officer of the company involved, if he is interested in what we have written, will still want to see us in person before committing himself on the position. Thus, we should not expect a good letter to land us the job outright; but we might consider that a poor letter could easily ruin our chances.

Having requested an interview, we should follow through with ample assistance. We ask ourselves such questions as: On what days am I free for an interview? At what hours? How will they notify me? If by letter, how can I help? If by telephone, is my number handy?—when is a good time to call?—can a message be left for me? If we can answer such questions before they become a problem to the reader, we will have made his action easy.

In the event we require a response by mail, we should provide a stamped, addressed envelope. Although the firm may not ultimately use it, this envelope makes a favorable impression on our reader. He can see that when we ask for something, we have enough sense to follow through with some kind of assistance. In like manner, when a telephone response is desired, we should state our number and other helpful information right after our request. In all likelihood, we will have listed this number on our data sheet: but that does not make it overly convenient to our reader. We should not require him to search for it; we should put it at his fingertips, at the strategic moment. Here again is silent proof that we are the alert and desirable applicant we say we are.

Following the composition work, we still have the task of casting our letter into its final, tangible form. We should typewrite each application letter; reproduced letters and carbon-copy letters are not desirable. We should use a good-quality paper stock and a typewriter that has both a good ribbon and clean type. The stationery, of course, should be unprinted—not the letterhead of our present employer. We do not want to hurt our cause by implying that we may be stealing paper, envelopes, and stamps; typing our letter on company time; or using the company's clerical staff.

The form used may be of our choosing—usually block or modified block. We head our letter by placing our complete mailing address and the date at the right-hand margin. If we are writing a solicited application letter, we should address it according to available instructions. In the absence of instructions, however, and with unsolicited application letters, we do well to address the personnel officer by his exact name and title. We may have to do a bit of research to learn these details, but they are worth the effort. They please our reader, and they also help a letter come to his attention sooner than letters addressed any other way. If we cannot get this kind of information, we should address the letter to the man's position as best we can. At least, we are still writing to the right person even though we do not know his name. On the other hand, it is not recommended that we address the company in general. Our letter will go to some central office for opening and then have to be forwarded to its ultimate destination. The result can be only a slowing down of our message en route.

The next two illustrations are examples of the covering-letter portions of applications written at the college level. The first letter is of the *unsolicited* variety. It relates to the first data-sheet illustration (pages 474–75).

The second letter is of the *solicited* variety; it responds to a word-of-mouth lead circulated by the prospective employer. This letter relates to the second data-sheet illustration, which places greater emphasis on experience than on education (pages 476–77).

OTHER EMPLOYMENT LETTERS

Within the broad scope of employment letters, we can include such additional varieties as: a request to use a person's name as a reference, an inquiry concerning an applicant's qualifications, a recommendation letter on behalf of an applicant, a letter granting an interview, a letter in appreciation of an interview, a tracer letter on an application submitted some time ago, a letter promoting an employee, a letter discharging an employee, a letter of resignation, and so on. We can identify most of these situations with one of the four basic letter situations, and thus usually can proceed to devise a satisfactory program.

Four of the situations, however, will be discussed here—application follow-up letters, answers to interview invitations, recommendation letters, and resignation letters. Each has something specific to be noted, and each has a reason for being handled in the best possible manner.

FOLLOW-UP LETTERS

A question that arises after we mail an application letter concerns what follow-up, if any, we can prudently give it. There is no standard answer to this question, but there are a number of guidelines available.

Sometimes we receive a response telling us that the prospective employer does not have an opening in our interest area. If we are genuinely keen on working for this company, we may take this response at face value, although it is possible that it constitutes a polite turndown. In

2412 Piquette Avenue
Detroit, Michigan 48202
April 16, 1967

Personnel Manager
Gibbons, Ross & Sloane
Certified Public Accountants
1040 Williamson Building
Cleveland, Ohio 44114

Dear Sir:

From all reports, most professional accounting firms soon will be screening this year's college graduates for staff additions and replacements. May I present myself as a candidate for a possible opening at your firm as a junior accountant?

I am a senior at Great Lakes University, where I have been studying accounting as my major subject. I am academically in the upper fifth of my class and am expecting to be graduated on June 4.

Our business curriculum at Great Lakes combines both liberal arts and professional courses for the development of well-rounded students. Therefore, I shall come away with a sound preparation in the accounting field--reinforced by one or more subjects in each of the other important areas of business administration and a strong base of English, mathematics, ethics, public speaking, and other general courses. You may see this relationship on my enclosed data sheet of qualifications.

In selecting electives, I chose courses in auditing and tax accounting as being particularly valuable in professional accountancy. My recent part-time experience for the firm of Wilcox and Brownlee here in Detroit has introduced me to the duties expected of a junior accountant. I am enthusiastic about the accounting field, eager to enter it, and willing to apply all of my talents to become successful.

May I have an interview with you to discuss my qualifications more fully? I am free to travel to Cleveland any Friday or Saturday during the remainder of the semester.

I've enclosed a return envelope for your early answer.

Yours very truly,

Peter A. Jamieson

Peter A. Jamieson

4701 Sanborn Street
Port Huron, Michigan 48217
April 24, 1967

Mr. Alan S. Sampson
Director of Personnel
Starr's Department Store
1400 Michigan Avenue
Detroit, Mich. 48201

Dear Mr. Sampson:

Through Mr. Walter P. Carson of your Advertising Department, I have learned that your company will soon be expanding the scope of its public relations function. Would you please appraise my qualifications for the position of Assistant Public Relations Manager?

A recent survey of business executives, published in Business Scene magazine, concluded that the quality found to be most lacking among businessmen today is the ability to write a good business letter. Four years' experience as a sales correspondent for the Endicott Copper Corporation and a recent course in business communication at Great Lakes University have helped me develop this ability.

I enjoy meeting people and have been conducting visitors on tours of Endicott's home office for the past two years. This experience has enabled me to discuss problems with businessmen from many parts of the world and has taught me the art of dealing with people of varied backgrounds. For four years, 1959 through 1962, I worked in the field of public relations as an employee of the Kendall Distributing Company. I absorbed much "public relations thinking" through active participation in numerous promotions conducted by that company.

My membership in the Jaycees has taught me what can be done when a group of young people unite their efforts toward a common community goal. No matter what the project-- civic improvement, children's activities, or some phase of political activity--I feel that I have broadened my outlook on life, just by being a willing participant.

Mr. Alan S. Sampson   -2-   April 24, 1967

Rounding out my list of qualifications is a Bachelor of Science degree in Business Administration from Great Lakes University. This program of study has given me a liberal education and concentrated instruction in marketing. I'm certain that the knowledge gained from courses in advertising, marketing psychology, market research, English, general psychology, and public speaking provide a solid background for my reentrance to public relations.

You will find me eager to learn and to prove my worth, Mr. Sampson. I enjoy responsibility and have a definite interest in public relations. With guidance, I should be able to fit into your organization effectively. I've listed four references on my data sheet. These gentlemen have seen me perform, and they will be happy to answer any questions for you.

Will you grant me an interview? I'd welcome the opportunity to discuss my qualifications with you in greater detail. I have a week's vacation coming up during the first week in May, and could come to your office at a time you name. My telephone number is MAdison 2-5550.

Sincerely yours,

Thomas R. Connally

Thomas R. Connally

such a case we could send a follow-up letter, after a month or more has passed. It is not in the interest of goodwill for us to pressure prospective employers repeatedly or too soon.

Since a prospective employer is likely to keep the letters of promising candidates on file for several months to a year, our new letter will reactivate our application. We do not have to send another data sheet with our follow-up. We refer to our original correspondence, show continued interest in the position involved, and inquire about the prospects of an interview now that some time has passed. A slightly different guideline applies if we do not receive any response to our application letter.

It is hard to believe that a company would deliberately neglect its correspondence in this day and age. But oversights can occur, or files can be misplaced, because of human error.

If we send a follow-up to a company which has not responded, we should still allow a discreet interval of time (e.g., one month). Then, in writing to them, we may refer to our original letter at the beginning; but we should do another "selling" job just in case the earlier letter has disappeared. Logically, we should also include another data sheet.

Sometimes the company we apply to will send us one of its own application forms to complete and return. This form may not be vastly different from our own data sheet; but it is a standard form at the company, and it helps their staff find the information they wish to have. In such a case, we should not send a follow-up letter. The indication is that the company has our data in process and will call us in for an interview when the proper time comes. We gain nothing by sending follow-up letters. Of course, we could attach a brief letter of appreciation as we return their form to them.

Probably the most valuable variety of follow-up letter we can write is one in appreciation of an employment interview. The fact is that only a small number of applicants even think to write such a letter, and fewer still actually write it. At the same time, employment people are impressed by this type of letter and frankly admit that they do not receive enough of them. Accordingly, we should strive to be the one who submits such a letter following a given interview. It may be too much to expect that we could move from last to first position among all applicants being considered, simply because we have sent this follow-up letter. But, in the event of a close contest between us and someone who is not heard from again, it is likely that we will come out ahead.

As we identified it earlier in this book, a letter of appreciation is a simple goodwill type. The basic requirements are good timing, sincerity, and unity. Applied to an application follow-up, good timing means that we should write the letter upon returning home from the interview, certainly not later than the next day. If our follow-up letter is to influence our prospective employer, it must reach him before his decision has been made. Sincerity deals with the things we single out for appreciation and with the way we state our message. For instance, we can appreciate being called in for an interview and any out-of-the-ordinary courtesies extended us. These special courtesies might be a plant inspection, introduction to certain executives, or luncheon at company expense. Ordinarily, the time spent in interview is merely performance of duty and does not call for special mention. Exceptions would be an extra-long interviewing session and/or the absence of anything else to mention. Our tone of expression should be unaffected, not padded with superlatives and soft-soap expressions.

Unity, of course, means sticking to the main purpose of the letter's goodwill and not wandering into other subjects. At the end, we may express the hope of hearing from our reader without violating the concept of unity.

A concise follow-up letter might be written along the following lines.

Dear Mr. Nichols:

Please accept my thanks for the interview which you held for me this afternoon. I especially appreciate your taking me through the business office and introducing me to Mr. Shanks, the office manager.

The experience has left me with a stronger desire than ever to be of service to your organization. I shall be eagerly awaiting the outcome of your decision.

Respectfully yours,

ANSWERS TO INVITATIONS

Suppose that we have received a letter in which a prospective employer invites us to come in for an interview. If we are agreeable to such a meeting, we should consider writing a letter of acceptance and confirmation. If we do not wish to be interviewed, we should write a turndown letter.

The circumstances of a given situation will have some bearing on the exact statements that we must include in our letter. For example, the letter may come as a direct result of our application letter; or it may come after we have returned some forms sent to us by this company; or it may simply be a "next step" following a campus interview. Our main concern, however, should be to recognize whether we are giving out good news or bad news—and to program our letter accordingly.

A concise good-news letter (acceptance) might be written as follows.

```
Dear Mr. Jackson:

    Tuesday, June 6, definitely will be satisfactory for an
interview at your office. I am confirming the 9:00 A.M. ap-
pointment you have suggested.

    I appreciate this opportunity to discuss my qualifications
with you personally.

                    Sincerely yours,
```

A bad-news letter (turndown) would move more slowly and use subdued tones.

```
Dear Mr. Sanders:

Thank you for considering me for an employment interview. The
fact is that, with so many eligible students turning out for
your campus visit, I am really flattered to hear from you.

During the past several months, I have met with any number of
campus recruiters. Some of them made offers that were very at-
tractive indeed. A few weeks ago I committed myself to join
the sales department of Porter Plastics, Inc. I will begin my
work for them on June 16.

Although I cannot accept your invitation for an interview, I
do appreciate the interest you have shown in me.

                    Cordially yours,
```

RECOMMENDATIONS

Managers, department heads, supervisors, and teachers usually can count on being asked to write recommendation letters on behalf of their former charges. Because they possess firsthand knowledge of a given individual's actual performance, they are often asked by that individual's prospective employer to furnish pertinent information.

Recommendations may be given in a number of ways. Sometimes, the prospective employer is satisfied to make a telephone check. This approach is speedy and minimizes the work of the person who is being asked for his opinion. Its chief disadvantage is the lack of warning the respondent receives. Often he must rely entirely on memory and cannot do as thorough a reporting job as would be possible. Given time to go through his records, he might uncover something that had slipped his mind.

Sometimes the inquirer makes action easy by providing a form or questionnaire. The person answering merely answers each question that is applicable and perhaps appends a few comments at the end in a space provided expressly for that purpose. This system is often used by various branches of the United States government. A variation is to enumerate the points to be covered by the recommendation, but to let the respondent cover them in letter text according to his own manner of writing.

"THAT'S A GREAT RECOMMENDATION, DAD."

Probably the best thing for us to remember when preparing a recommendation is that our message should be sincere. Whether we are adding comments at the end of a questionnaire, covering points suggested in a request, or framing a letter entirely on our own, we should see to it that the message fits the subject individual in particular. If our remarks are of a general nature, they will tend to be applicable to any number of people and will not mean much to our reader. On the other hand, if we include a mention of something that applies to the subject individual only, we tend to sound convincing and sincere. In fact, even general statements in the same letter seem to take on individuality under these conditions.

Two other aspects of a recommendation are positiveness and definiteness. We are positive when we cite favorable things about or done by the person we are recommending—for example, his punctuality, his popularity among fellow workers, and so on. By contrast, we want to be careful to stay clear of "negative" suggestion—that is, stating that he never did such-and-such, which would have been a bad thing. Finally, we are definite when we make our stand clear to our reader. We should come out clearly with whatever kind of recommendation we are giving —qualified or unqualified. Our reader should not have to figure it out for himself.

As for structure, a letter of recommendation is a type of good-news reply letter. We are granting the reader's request for information. We should, of course, observe the suggestions which are given in the paragraphs above.

The following letter answers a request concerning a former employee of the writer. It conforms to the good-news framework, and is developed from the following program:

INDICATE YES.

FURNISH THE INFORMATION.

ADD EXTRAS, IF POSSIBLE.

END ON A POSITIVE NOTE.

Dear Mr. Praugg:

Yes, we had a Melvin Busch working for us from May 16, 1961, until December 3, 1965.

Mr. Busch started with us as a general clerk in our Accounting Department. In 1963, he was given a more responsible position in the accounts receivable section. A year later he was promoted to the management level as supervisor of that section. He resigned his position with us to fill an attractive opening in the systems department at American Electronics, Inc.

We were always pleased with Mr. Busch's performance and were sorry to lose him. He was an accommodating and trustworthy employee, a popular leader and a doer of commendable things. One of his notable achievements was transferring our accounts receivable records from manual to machine method.

Personally, I'm glad that he is getting a chance to join your growing concern. I wholeheartedly recommend him to you.

Sincerely yours,

LETTERS OF RESIGNATION

It is not unusual for a person to change jobs a number of times before he finds himself in a position which he is willing to regard as permanent. As likely as not, job-hopping is accompanied by a change of employers. If we are involved in such activity, how do we go about notifying our present employer?

Sometimes a letter is necessary, because of the distance involved or the difficulty of arranging an interview with the proper company official. If notice can be given in person, we should prefer to do so. It is a forthright, openhanded, and natural method. It usually takes little time of itself, but it affords the opportunity for a discussion which could lead to improved understanding, if not other advantages. Even so, we might still consider placing a letter on file following an oral statement. We should address it to the manager or department head nearest above us.

A good letter of resignation, including one that merely confirms a conversation, has many possible advantages. Written in a spirit of friendliness and cooperation, it can be a valuable addition to our personnel file. Later on, if supplying a recommendation, a supervisor may wish to see our file to refresh his memory about us. Our "exit" letter will show that we apparently left on amicable terms and gave notice in writing. Under the principle of "All's well that ends well," the letter may precipitate a better recommendation than would otherwise be written. It can also provide a favorable climate for our rejoining the company, if unforeseen events bring us back to their door.

In writing a letter of resignation, we should follow the general patterns of a bad-news letter. We imply that our departure will be taken as an inconvenience. To do the opposite would be derogatory of ourselves. The suggested program is as follows:

GET IN STEP.
EXPLAIN.
GIVE NOTICE.
GOODWILL STATEMENT.

The beginning step consists of some statement that will be of interest and appeal to our reader. We might show appreciation for the months or years of employment under this company's management. We might acknowledge the confidence placed in us by various advancements granted us; or we might comment on the rewarding experience we have acquired under their direction. The purpose is to place our reader in a relaxed frame of mind so that he will be receptive to the message to follow.

In the explanation step, we should try to put our cards on the table with regard to what we plan to do. We should give "positive" reasons for going to the new job—not "negative" reasons for leaving the old. We should mention the name of the new employer and the position we are to fill. After all, secrecy leads nowhere—and it could alienate someone to whom we might later turn for a recommendation. Whether we mention a salary figure is optional. If we choose to do so, we should not appear to be trying to get a higher bid to stay on.

The giving of notice includes an appropriate time interval as well as a statement of when the change will become effective. This time interval should be reasonable enough to allow the company to get a suitable replacement. There is no set time that can be quoted; sometimes two weeks is long enough, sometimes a month, sometimes an even longer period of time. Usually the higher we are in the organization, the more likely it is that we should give notice of a month or more.

Our last step, as in other bad-news letters, is to end on a constructive or encouraging note. In a letter of resignation we want to be certain that the last thoughts indicate a high degree of goodwill. Depending on the situation, we can:

1. Request a personal interview to explain in greater detail.
2. Offer to extend the departure date, if possible, while a replacement is being found.
3. Offer to help break in the replacement.
4. If not presumptuous, suggest a possible replacement.
5. Simply offer to be available to help in the transition, as needed.

An example of a letter of resignation which follows this program appears below.

Dear Mr. Neal:

Ten days ago I had no inkling that I might be writing you this letter. I must say that my association with Chroma Corporation has always been gratifying and rewarding. In particular, I appreciate the guidance you personally have given me since my start here in 1965.

Last week, however, I received a job opportunity which I
consider too good to pass up. National Steel Products is
staffing its new plant in Cincinnati, my old home town. I have
been offered the position of assistant office manager at an
attractive starting salary. Although the income part is important, the prospect of returning to the southern Ohio area is
irresistible.

I've decided to accept the offer from National Steel Products. As I am to report on June 1, this letter should give you
about four weeks' notice.

If there is anything I can do during the next few weeks to
help the office prepare for my departure, I shall be happy to
be of service.

Respectfully yours,

SUMMARY

Application letters are the principal variety of employment letters.
They may be classified as being either one-part or two-part, depending
upon whether they are developed as a relatively long, continuous narrative, or whether they are prepared as a relatively short narrative accompanied by a summary of qualifications (a data sheet). The two-part
presentation is usually preferred, by both writer and reader, over the
one-part presentation.

Before preparing a data sheet, we should do a thorough research job
on ourselves and compile an inventory of qualifications. We should
organize these qualifications into homogeneous groups and arrange them
in a sensible sequence within each group. In its final form, our data
sheet may be typewritten, reproduced, or printed; in any case, emphasis
should be on eye appeal, clear identification of sections, and ease of
finding information.

If possible, we should do some research on our prospective employer
before we compose the letter portion of our application. This study will
tend to help us match our qualifications with the requirements of the
position we are seeking. If we are answering an advertisement, we may
not have time for this kind of research. In that case, we must rely on our
knowledge of the generally recognized requirements of the position.

An application letter closely resembles a sales letter in the matter of
program. In fact, through an application letter we lay the groundwork

for the sale of our personal services on a continuing basis. The chief difference between the two letters is the intensity of the sales fervor; in an employment situation, we use a "soft sell" tone and do not try to motivate by stressing urgency. The program of our application letter is thus confined to the following five steps:

CREATE INTEREST.

PRESENT SALES MESSAGE.

OFFER PROOF.

REQUEST AN INTERVIEW.

MAKE ACTION EASY.

Among other varieties of employment letters are the follow-up letter, the letter of recommendation, and the letter of resignation.

The chief type of follow-up letter is the one we might write in appreciation of an interview. Only a few applicants will even consider the possibility of writing such a letter, and fewer still will actually write one. Because this kind of follow-up letter is known to impress personnel officers, we should be on our toes to write it. Being of the simple goodwill pattern, it calls for promptness, sincerity, and unity.

Sooner or later we can expect to do our share of writing recommendations for other people. Usually the programming presents no problem—the letter fits the basic reply, good-news pattern. But we do well to state our facts in such a way that they apply to the subject person specifically rather than to almost anyone who has his general background.

Then, too, there may come a time when we will move on to another employer. It can be a strategic move for us to place on file a letter of resignation. At a later date, this letter can show that we gave written notice, how adequate that notice was, and how amicable our relations with the firm were at the time of our departure. The suggested program for such a letter, which conforms to the bad-news pattern, is:

GET IN STEP.

EXPLAIN.

GIVE NOTICE.

GOODWILL STATEMENT.

The impression thus created can be favorable to our cause if and when we need a recommendation from our former employer.

QUESTIONS

. . . .

1. Cite some advantages and disadvantages to the employer arising out of the present-day practice of campus recruiting of personnel.

2. What are some of the advantages and disadvantages of this practice to the person seeking a position?

3. Distinguish between a *one-part* and a *two-part* application letter.

4. What is the particular advantage of using a data sheet, or résumé, in connection with an application letter?

5. Distinguish between a *solicited* and an *unsolicited* application letter.

6. What headings are suggested for sorting and identifying facts in the process of compiling an inventory of one's employment qualifications?

7. What are the characteristics of an effective data sheet?

8. In the data sheet, what order of presentation is recommended for work experience?

9. Is it wise nowadays to enclose a photograph with one's application letter?

10. Is it better to design one's own data sheet or to use a form data sheet such as one that may be obtained from a campus placement office?

11. Give the suggested program for the letter portion of a two-part employment application.

12. How does an applicant state facts about himself so that they will not appear to be routine or defensive?

13. What points need to be given particular attention in a solicited application letter?

14. How is the number of *middle* paragraphs in an application letter determined?

15. How is it possible to support statements with *proof* when one has not yet been tried out on the job?

16. Should a stamped, addressed envelope always be submitted with an application letter if a response by mail is indicated?

17. To whom should an application letter be addressed?

18. What is the advantage in writing a follow-up letter of appreciation immediately following an employment interview?

19. In a letter of recommendation, what kind of information should be included to make the letter sound sincere and convincing?

20. What are the suggested program steps for a letter of resignation?

PROBLEMS
• • • • • • • • • •

In most of the following cases, the solution is to be typewritten on plain stationery. In a few instances, however, either business letterhead or a memorandum form is required. If business stationery is indicated but not available, set up a simulated letterhead in accordance with directions issued by your instructor. If a memorandum form is called for, you may use either printed or typed-in captions.

15–1. (Plain stationery.) Using actual facts about yourself, prepare a complete data sheet of your qualifications for employment. Assume that you are in the second semester (or last term) of your senior year; therefore, include in your educational summary those courses which you plan to take between now and the actual end of your program. Fashion your data sheet after the regular "Jamieson" and "Connally" examples shown in this chapter. Write an application letter, which you will submit with your data sheet, in response to the following advertisement appearing in today's edition of the local newspaper: "COLLEGE SENIORS. Earn while you learn. Part-time positions now available in various departments of growing manufacturing firm. Could lead to permanent employment in management. Apply in writing, enclose qualifications. Address: College Trainee Director, Best Manufacturing Company, P.O. Box 1968."

15–2. (Plain stationery.) Using actual facts about yourself, prepare a complete data sheet of your qualifications for employment. Follow the form used in the regular "Jamieson" and Connally" examples shown in this chapter. Even if you are not in your last term at college, assume that such is the case; therefore, list any important courses called for in your program. In light of your major field of study, select a position in business for which you feel reasonably qualified. Then write a two-part application to a company which might have an opening for you in such a position. Your objective will be to obtain an interview so that you can discuss employment possibilities in greater detail.

15–3. (Plain stationery.) A standard format for a data sheet has been recommended in the *College Placement Annual*. An illustration, using the data for Peter A. Jamieson, is shown in this chapter. Set up your own employment qualifications in this manner. Then write an application letter, which will accompany your data sheet, in response to the following advertisement appearing in Sunday's edition of the local newspaper: "CORRESPONDENTS. Local department store now interviewing men and women to work as credit correspondents. Typing desirable but not necessary. Forty-hour week, regular hours, fringe benefits. College graduates preferred. Midtown Department Store, c/o Box 33, *Times.*"

15–4. (Plain stationery.) About six weeks ago you wrote an unsolicited two-part application letter to the local plant of the Ace Electric Company, a national manufacturer which has production facilities in many parts of the country. A few days after sending your letter, you received a reply from the local personnel manager of the firm. He informed you that the Ace Electric Company had no immediate opening in your particular field of interest. He implied, however, that you might inquire again sometime. During the past three weeks you have been away on a vacation trip with your parents. A visit to Mexico was included in your itinerary. Now back home, and still hopeful of obtaining employment with Ace Electric, you have decided to write a follow-up letter to your original application. The only significant change in your record is the fact that you now possess your college degree, which was merely pending at the time of your application letter. Write a suitable follow-up letter; assume that the firm still has your initial application on file.

15–5. (Letterhead.) Suppose that you are the man in charge of the campus recruitment program which is carried on each year by the Jarmin Publishing Company of Philadelphia, Pennsylvania. Your firm is a specialist in publishing product catalogues for industry, and at the moment is in need of a replacement in the cost-estimating department. Among the seniors at a nearby college who contacted you while you were on his campus this year was James Pierson. This student impressed you favorably at that time. Now, in reviewing his placement-office data sheet, you see that he has compiled a good academic record and that he has studied cost accounting. Write a letter to Pierson, who lives in Philadelphia, and invite him to come to your office for a formal employment interview.

15–6. (Plain stationery.) For general background information, read Problem 15–4. Suppose that you have sent a follow-up to your original application letter to the Ace Electric Company. Before hearing again from the personnel manager, however, you receive an invitation to report for a job interview at Central Industries, Incorporated, in the capital of your state. Your are not particularly interested in obtaining employment in the state capital, although you are not absolutely against the idea. Your real preference has been, and still is, to become associated with the Ace Electric Company—even though, in the end, it may mean moving to some other part of the country. You decide to stand pat until you hear from Ace Electric. Therefore, write to Central Industries. Thank the personnel people for remembering you from their campus interviewing, but decline their present offer.

15–7. (Plain stationery.) For general background information, read Problem 15–4. Suppose that you have sent the follow-up letter to the Ace Electric Company, and that this time they invite you to come to their plant for an interview with the local personnel manager. You have attended the meeting at the appointed time. You have had an enjoyable interview, have been shown portions of the firm's operations, have been introduced to several of the managers, and have been given some aptitude tests. You have been aware, however, that two other applicants are in the picture; yet there is only one opening to be filled. Assume that you have just returned home from your interview at the Ace Electric Company. Write a goodwill letter of appreciation to Ace's local personnel manager.

15–8. (Memorandum.) Roy Stark, long-time advertising manager of the Ferris Match Corporation, has turned 65 and will retire at the end of this month. He has recommended that his assistant, Jaime Procter, age 51, be appointed to take over the advertising department. Suppose that you are the president of the Ferris Match Corporation, and that you heartily approve of this move. Write a memorandum to Proctor; let him know that he will become the advertising manager as of the first of next month.

15–9. (Letterhead.) Assume that you are professor of management at Great Lakes University, Port Huron, Michigan. A request for an employment reference has come to you from Prairie Air Lines, Chicago, Illinois. A former student, now an alumnus of Great Lakes University, has applied for the position of assistant office manager at the air line. Your records show that this student, Terence Parsons, was of low-average performance. Judging from the fact that he was seldom absent from classes, you believe that he must have been one of those diligent individuals who manage to get through college while others of similar ability but less drive tend to drop out. In addition, you recall that Parsons held a part-time job to help support himself and his widowed mother. On a Great Lakes University letterhead, write as favorable a reference letter as you can for Parsons.

15–10. (Memorandum.) Suppose that you are the credit manager for The Bonnie Lass Candy Co., which has its main offices and kitchens in Cleveland, Ohio. Your duties have not been particularly demanding because this firm has followed a very limited credit policy. You have received an offer to join Hartline's, a department store located in

Buffalo, New York. The work promises to be challenging, and the salary will be $1,500 a year above what you now receive. Write a memorandum to the general manager of The Bonnie Lass Candy Co.; tell him of your decision to go with Hartline's. You will take up your new duties after one month.

PART IV

BUSINESS REPORTS

A second large area of business communication is that of business reports. People at all levels of management depend on various kinds of reports to keep themselves informed and to simplify the preparatory work of decision making. Good reports received from subordinates remove a great deal of burdensome work from executives up the line.

Those who have learned to prepare useful reports have a decided edge over other persons at the same level. This is true whether we are a junior executive writing to our department head, or an outside consultant writing to a client. In either case, our reader will judge us by what we have written—its accuracy, its clearness, its thoroughness, its value in helping him solve a problem. After all, these are the things that count. Possibly someone else may know more about a given matter than we; but where does he stand if he is not able to put his knowledge across to his reader? How would such a person be judged by his client or by his boss—people who have so much to say about his rise or fall? It should be obvious that the ability to communicate effectively through reports is, if anything, a more personally important skill to the writer than is the ability to compose a business letter.

In this section, we shall investigate the matter of business reports in three segments. Chapter 16 treats of basic principles applicable to report writing in general. Chapter 17 takes up the informal report, including typical programs and illustrations of the common varieties. Chapter 18 covers the subject of formal reports, with examples shown of the significant parts.

THE WHAT
AND HOW OF
BUSINESS REPORTS

Our English verb *to report* has its origin in the Latin verb *reportare,* which means "to bear or bring back." Herein we have a clue to the activity that is involved in the matter of report writing. In essence, someone goes after a desired segment of information and "brings it back" for the benefit of another person. The searcher may make his report either orally or in writing, the latter method of course, being preferred. The written report has permanency, and it can be re-communicated (by circulation) without distortion or loss of meaning.

KINDS OF BUSINESS REPORTS

CLASSIFICATION BY READERSHIP

In business communication, we are chiefly concerned with the written business report. In the broader sense of the term, written reports may move in any direction—that is up or down the line of responsibility, or laterally to personnel of comparable rank with the writer. For example, the controller of a corporation may issue a statement to his staff concerning the installation of a new computer. Included are new instructions for the preparing and routing of work that is to be handled by this computer. His statement constitutes a report written *downward*—to people responsible to the writer.

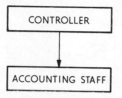

The same officer, however, might also write a report to the heads of other divisions or departments of the corporation. The controller might use this device for calling the attention of other executives to the fact that the company has such a computer, for letting them know what its potential is, and for inviting them to take advantage of this potential. A report of this nature would be written *laterally*—to people who should be informed, but who are not responsible to the writer.

Again, the controller may be required to submit a report to the general manager or to the president of the corporation. He may have to give facts on how the new computer is working out, how much use is being made of it by his own and other departments, how expensive the installation is to maintain, and so on. He may also be required to recommend ways of getting fuller use out of the equipment and what pieces of additional equipment, if any, might be needed soon.

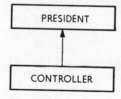

CLASSIFICATION BY PURPOSE

Another approach to the type-casting of business reports is for us to consider the purpose for which they are written. We can easily distinguish between such basic types as the informational report and the analytical report—the one which simply presents facts and the other which not only gives facts but also interprets them.

Informational reports can be of two kinds, identified as (1) periodic reports and (2) progress reports. Both subdivisions are reports written to cover a specified interval of time, but periodic reports would be of a regularly recurring nature. For instance, a report called for at the end of each year, or quarter, or month, or week—or even each day—would fit this description. We usually find that the recurrence of such a report leads to a "way of doing it," or pattern that tends to be consistently followed. On the other hand, a progress report would be written only when a significant milestone in a given project has been reached. The measurement here is really on the basis of accomplishment, even though a necessary time factor is involved. The chief difference is that the writing of the report is not related to that time factor.

Analytical reports are easily subdivided into two kinds also: (1) examination reports and (2) recommendation reports. Both kinds of analytical reports go beyond the normal stopping point of mere information reports. In the examination variety, the facts presented are analyzed and discussed. By these steps we interpret the facts into a meaningful message for our reader, rather than leave it up to him to know what is significant and what is not. In the recommendation report, we go a step further. We piece the significant facts together and express an opinion—or recommendation—as to what action the reader should take. Most of the time, the reader has asked us to make such a recommendation. Sometimes, we may provide one anyhow—but we should not be presumptuous. The better practice is to remain silent except in an instance where we see ourselves ethically or responsibly bound to make a recommendation.

CLASSIFICATION BY FORMAT

Another way in which we may distinguish between one kind of business report and another is by format—that is, physical construction and appearance. The two basic varieties are (1) the informal, or letter-type, report and (2) the formal report.

Informal, or letter-type, reports themselves are of two models: the conventional letter and the office memorandum. These two subgroups have given rise to the terms "letter reports" and "memorandum reports"; but this difference is really superficial and does not affect the writing function. The significance of the informal report is that it is allowed to develop in accordance with the needs of the situation; it does not have to conform to a rigid set of rules for its physical presentation.

Formal reports are so named because they are developed according to a prescribed formality or set of rules. First of all, there are a definite number of parts or general sections which even the lengthiest of formal reports may have. We need not use all of the possible parts, on the basis that some parts do not apply to certain reports. But each part that we do use must be handled according to some recognized standard. Moreover, there are a minimum number of parts (such as a title page, letter of transmittal, table of contents, summary, and fully developed text) in even the most humble of formal reports.

CROSS–CLASSIFICATIONS

Although we have seen several possible classifications of business reports, we should understand that a great number of opportunities exist for cross-classifications. For example, an information report can be written as either an informal report or a formal report. It can be directed down the line of responsibility, up the line, or laterally. It can also be either a periodic report or a progress report. By definition, however, it cannot be either an examination report or a recommendation report, as these are the distinguishing characteristics of an analytical report.

In theory, the analytical report, which goes on to interpret the information presented therein and sometimes to make a recommendation concerning it, can branch out to a maximum number of combinations. In practice, however, it is not likely that we will find an analytical report being written downward. The simple reason is that personnel down the line usually do not receive "recommendations" as such. Information comes to them after it has been reported as facts and analyzed for the higher-ups in the company. It has already been interpreted and restated in the form of instructions by the time it reaches the lower levels.

The following chart shows us a summary of the combinations we may reasonably expect to find.

	DOWNWARD	UPWARD	LATERAL	PERIODIC	PROGRESS	EXAMINATION	RECOMMENDATION		
INFORMATION	X	X	X	X	X				I N F O R M A L
REPORTS		X	X	X				FORMAL	
ANALYTICAL		X	X	X	X	X	X		
REPORTS		X	X	X	X	X	X		

THE PRELIMINARIES OF REPORT WRITING

As we saw in the case of the business letter, the preparation of a message entails the solving of many kinds of problems. What holds true for letters holds equally true for reports. Some of the problems have to be solved before we can even think about expressing our message in words. Each such preliminary problem, large or small, has to be settled in its own turn and all of them must be solved in a satisfactory manner. Here again, the traditional problem-solving formula plays an important part.

1. Define the problem.
2. Gather the facts.
3. Study possible solutions.
4. Select the best possibility.

DEFINING THE PROBLEM

Defining the problem in a report-writing situation helps get us off to a good start. At the beginning, most studies tend to be too broad or too far-reaching to be accomplished well or in a useful manner. Often if we examine a cumbersome problem, we find that there can be a narrowing down to something more specific. We can find some clues in the answers to such questions as:

1. Who will read this report?
2. What are the problems confronting this reader?
3. How much importance is the reader apt to attach to this report?
4. What is to be decided on the basis of this report?

Let us suppose that a study were to be made to determine the best of three possible locations for a new plant. Our beginning analysis based on such questions might very well be:

1. *Reader*—the company president.
2. *His problem*—acquainting himself with the facilities available for a new plant, as they exist at three possible locations; deciding which offers the greatest overall advantage to the company (with proper consideration given to initial cost, water supply, labor supply, tax structure, transportation facilities, access to suppliers and markets, etc.); making a convincing recommendation to the board of directors; answering questions in depth.

3. *Importance to the reader*—very important, because a decision must be reached soon; because the reader needs assistance in gathering the facts.
4. *Decision involved*—which of the three possible plant locations the reader is to recommend.

On the strength of such answers as these, we can begin to recognize the nature of the problem involved. If we can then state this problem in a sentence or a phrase for our own guidance, we can feel rather secure in the direction we must take. One of the best ways to express this idea is to draw up a title for our report. Even if this title is tentative, we can use it as a sounding board, provided we have built into it sufficient clues to the subject and purpose of our report.

For example, we might tentatively title our report, "A Report of the Comparative Advantages and Disadvantages of Three Possible Locations for the Proposed Plant of Seaway Products Corporation." Such a title would tend to keep our study objective and within its intended bounds. Later on, when preparing the final copy, we might decide to reword our title to read: "Recommendation of Cleveland, Ohio, as the Location for the New Plant of Seaway Products Corporation."

GATHERING THE FACTS

With our problem rather clearly defined, we next consider the ways open to us for gathering the facts that will be needed to reach a solution. Sometimes a single source of information is sufficient; sometimes many sources must be tapped before we have the facts that will be useful to us. Much will depend on how we have defined our problem.

Sources of data fall neatly into four groups: (1) records maintained by the company, (2) experimentation, (3) questioning of people (variously by questionnaire, interview, or telephone call), and (4) published material.

Company records are probably the easiest and handiest sources. We do not have to travel outside the company to inspect them; we do not have to plan a "fool-proof" questionnaire or interviewing system; and we rarely incur any accountable cost by using them. At the same time, however, we can depend on our company records for only a limited variety of report projects. If we are writing about occurrences or statistics relating to our company only—such as personnel matters, production figures, sales, inventories, and so on—company records may suffice. But, beyond that, we can expect to look elsewhere for our answers.

Experimentation may be a direct and scientific method of finding facts, but it usually is a costly method. Sometimes, however, it is the only way that can be used successfully to get a desired bit of information. For example, a customer may register a complaint about a shipment of our product—which is, say, an industrial chemical. If we are to get at the root of what may be wrong, we may have some laboratory tests run to analyze the substance.

Questioning of people covers a wide range of possibilities and is frequently resorted to when information is needed for a report. We might go about it in a casual, informal conversation; or we might stage an extensive, highly controlled campaign. For example, if we had to report on a work stoppage that occurred this morning in one of the departments of the factory, we might simply speak to the section superintendent about it. At the other extreme, if we needed to know the reactions of thousands of consumers to one of our new products, we might have to resort to an elaborate mailing project with questionnaires, return envelopes, explanatory letters, and a production-line operation for addressing and handling.

Each of the various methods of extracting information from people has its advantages and limitations. If we make personal inquiry of a supervisor in our plant, we have the advantage of speed and the possibility of probing more deeply if we believe there is more to be learned. But we are limited as to our source of supply. If we are not able to get what we want from this supervisor, we may not be able to get the desired information at all.

In another set of circumstances, we may desire statements from several people and still prefer the personal questioning approach. If so, we use what is known as the personal interview. We can prepare in advance for this kind of fact gathering. We decide on a definite set of questions which we will ask of each person; and preferably we will stick to a definite sequence in asking those questions. Then we will convert these questions to memory so that we need not be consulting a notebook as we go about our interviewing. The disadvantages or limitations of this method are readily seen. For one thing we can tackle only a relatively small number of questions, which must be of a rather uncomplicated nature. Otherwise, we can get tangled in our sequencing of questions and may even overlook one or more of the finer points. It fact, cataloging the answers becomes difficult in any case, because we should not intimidate our interviewee by taking notes on what he says. Thus, we must rely on our memory to bring back his answers for recording purposes after we have finished our interview.

"THEY WANT TO KNOW ABOUT THE LIFE SAVERS."

Certain advantages are available to us when we resort to fact gathering by questionnaire. It is possible for us to approach a much larger audience by this means than it is by the personal interview. There is no danger of our forgetting or confusing any of our questions, because they are set down in writing. Tabulating answers is simplified to the extent that a prescribed sequence and method of answering is controlled by our questionnaire. But there are some disadvantages involved, too. There is no compulsion that makes a recipient of our questionnaire respond to our questions. In a face-to-face interview, the same person often feels a greater involvement or an inner nudge to cooperate, with the result that he does give us his help. Also, with a questionnaire there is the possibility that one of our questions is not understood by a given reader. If we were there in person, we might be able to restate it for him; but being absent, we cannot help him help us. In such a case, and in instances wherein a reader does not want to answer a certain question, we may not receive any answers. The reason is that the would-be respondent becomes self-conscious and ducks the whole job rather than return an incomplete questionnaire.

In the final analysis, the mass gathering of information by questionnaire is no more than the making of an inquiry according to the two-part method which we studied in Chapter 9. The covering letter contains the subjective elements of our appeal for information. We should use it to spark the interest of our reader, to explain concisely what our project is about, and to win cooperation. Because the letter itself is a request—that our reader answer and return the questionnaire—we must give adequate instructions on what we want and provide ample assistance. Two methods of giving our reader such assistance are (1) devising a questionnaire that is easy to understand and (2) enclosing an addressed, postage-free envelope that is easy to use.

The following guidelines will help us prepare an effective questionnaire.

1. Our questionnaire should be self-supporting—that is, it should contain enough information in its heading to make it identifiable and usable even if it should become separated from the covering letter.

2. In general, our questions should be of an objective nature. They should be answerable with a minimum of effort on the part of the respondent. Thus, multiple-choice answering, fill-ins, and simple "yes–no" options are usually better than the essay-type approach. We should be careful, of course, not to force answers by giving a biased list to choose from, or sequencing a list so as to influence our respondent.

3. To the extent possible, we should arrange the questions so that they follow along in a logical, agreeable sequence. Our reader should experience a feeling of accomplishment as he answers our questions. If we skip about, or show poor organization of thought, he is apt to feel that the study is leading nowhere and give up in disgust.

4. We should ask specific questions, not vague or general questions. In this way we impress our reader that we know what we are seeking and accordingly tend to gain his confidence.

5. We should hold our questions to a minimum, to support our reader's interest and to forestall his balking at a project that could look formidable or time consuming. The best guide here is to limit our questions to those which can be fitted on one side of a

sheet of paper. Our maximum will therefore be about 10 questions (with subdivisions), but a surprising amount of information can be gathered by carefully prepared questions.

6. Numbering our questions is always helpful. Our reader can see at a glance that the questionnaire does have a limit. Also, he can sense his own progress as he answers; and he has a clear indication of what constitutes a subdivision of an old question and what is really the beginning of a completely new question.

7. If a subjective or open-end question is to be included, we should place it at the end of the list. We often can benefit from the unrestricted comments obtained through an essay-type answer. When we place it in last position, we allow our respondent to answer as he pleases and to continue on the back of the questionnaire, if need be.

In another approach to obtaining information from individuals, we may combine some of the features of both the questionnaire and the personal interview. We can prepare a set list of questions and then telephone the people from whom we desire answers. This method has been used in polling and in gathering data for the audience ratings assigned to television and radio shows. It has the advantages of control (coverage of all questions, preservation of the desired sequence, and the opportunity of entering responses promptly) and of probing (explanation of misunderstood questions and clarification of puzzling answers). It also permits us to conduct our research from a central location; we do not have to travel from place to place. As is to be expected, however, we are up against some inherent disadvantages when we use this method. There is a much lower limit on the number of inquiries that we can make this way as compared with mailed-out questionnaires. The cost element is likely to be higher, in terms of money and manpower, with this method than with a mass mailing. There is the likelihood of lost motion caused by wrong numbers, busy signals, and absence of the intended interviewee at the time of our call. Also, there is a risk that, unknown to our respondent or to us, some of the questions or answers may be misinterpreted and thus cause us to compile incorrect "facts."

Published material is another source of information which we can turn to in many situations. Often, someone else already has researched the very thing we are interested in, or a significant portion of it. Our own research effort can be reduced if we are able to read whatever has been published by those other people. At least we can see what has and has not been covered, and channel our research into those areas which do not duplicate studies already completed.

Areas of activity which definitely require reference to published material are legal matters (such as conflict of interest, employment, government contracts, labor relations, regulation of public utilities, taxation, and zoning for construction) and statistical data which are not limited to our own organization. On a somewhat lesser scale, we may need to consult published material when our study touches on something which has to be expanded or checked for accuracy. Then such aids as biographical directories, dictionaries (e.g., an unabridged English dictionary, a foreign language dictionary, a dictionary for a certain profession, etc.), encyclopedias, and industrial directories can be of benefit to us. In fact, we can even refer to a "directory of directories," if need be, as a way of getting started.

Ready access to a wealth of published material is provided by our community libraries. We usually can enlist the help of the reference librarian to find the periodicals and books which contain the information we need. If our activity takes us to a library regularly, we usually can gain time by becoming familiar with the various indexes which list subject matter by topic and list the specific names and numbers of the journals containing related articles.

STUDY POSSIBLE SOLUTIONS

Facts which we have gathered may have come to us by a number of the different methods which we have discussed. In many cases, we will end up with more facts than we can use, because of duplications, overlapping, and irrelevancy. Herein lies a challenge. We must be willing to edit the overall material to that which is really pertinent and useful. Sometimes this requires will power; we must counteract a desire to salvage material simply because of the work we did in accumulating it.

In terms of our main problem, we should retain and examine facts that lead to possible solutions. By describing these facts for our reader, we comply with the minimal requirements of an information report. If we carry on to evaluate the possible solutions by pointing out the advantages and disadvantages of each, we render a fuller service. In such an instance, we attain the minimal requirements of an analytical report.

SELECT THE BEST POSSIBILITY

Problem solving is not complete until a final decision has been reached concerning a course of action. The responsibility for such a decision lies with a definite individual in the organization, no matter who happens to be given the assignment of gathering, presenting, and interpreting the facts. But there is a reasonable expectation that, if we have been entrusted to do so many other phases of the work, we may be in a good position to state an opinion. After all, we have been in touch with the full facts, not just a review of them. In addition, we have had the advantage of seeing a wider range of facts than those finally appearing in our report. Although we have discarded the excess facts, we may still benefit from some insight gained by our having been exposed to them. If, therefore, it is our place to single out for our reader what we believe to be the best possibility for solving the problem, we can do him an added service. Our message would then qualify as a recommendation report.

COMPOSING A BUSINESS REPORT

A business report is one of the possible variations of a business communication. Thus we can expect to find a high degree of similarity between the composing of a report and the composing of a business letter. In fact, when we prepare an informal report we are preparing a business letter, except that the message or content is not of a type that we studied in the preceding chapters. The incidental problems of writing a business report exist in the same basic areas as they do in other varieties of business communication.

1. Content.
2. Language.
3. Form.

CONTENT

According to our way of looking at content, which deals with the message value, there are two general subdivisions that need to be handled carefully. These are (1) the program or working outline that we will follow and (2) the finesse which we will use in stating our thoughts.

Our investigation of program requirements for various kinds of reports will be taken up in Chapters 17 and 18. In essence, our objective is to find an order of presentation which will be best for our reader. In report-writing situations, this person is usually someone important to our well-being—for example, a client or the boss himself. Since we are in position to gather clues about our reader's likes and dislikes, we should gather all that we can. Then, if we know our reader's preference for one program or another, we should cater to his likes. We should never try to force our way, or anyone else's, on a reader who prefers something else.

Finesse in business reports is something we should include whenever possible. One of the chief criticisms about reports has been that they are devoid of feeling for the reader, not service oriented, and lacking in positiveness. Present-day report writers are conscientiously striving to exclude such defects from their work; we are well advised to develop good habits from the start.

Probably there are not so many opportunities for working finesse into a report as there are in a regular letter. But we should be alert to the possibilities whenever they arise. Most of the information we present and discuss in a report tends to be of a factual nature, and that fact reduces the potential for using diplomacy. Yet, in the beginning and ending parts of many reports, we come close to conversing with our reader. Here, then, are sections wherein we can try for some "plus" values in diplomacy, as contrasted with the neutrality of the rest of the report. Also, we can consider that our selection of a program that fits the likes and temperament of our reader is in itself a form of diplomacy.

Another area of finesse, the service attitude, is obviously a little easier for us to handle. We are on the right track when we select a suitable program. Our presentation will come across to our reader in a flow that he can follow. Service to our reader continues when we use a language level that is attuned to his own, when we translate all technical terms, and when we adjust physical form (e.g., layout, visual aids, etc.) specifically for his ease in extracting our message.

Positiveness, the third ingredient of finesse, should be a characteristic of our business reports. We can obtain this quality in a number of ways. We should prefer to write in the active voice. We should be specific, not vague, in presenting our facts. We should prefer to go all-out with a recommendation report, if permissible; next best, an examination-type analytical report; and at the bottom of our priority list, an information report. Moreover, in stating a recommendation, we should use language that is specific, definite, positive. It is a mistake to mince words or hedge our position when we are expected to recommend something that is indicated by our facts and our analyses.

LANGUAGE

Basically, in report writing, we are confronted with the same two aspects of language as in business letter writing. These are the matters of accuracy and readability. While correctness in all principal language details—spelling, word usage, grammar, sentence structure, and punctuation—requires our constant attention, report writing does not cause us any particularly new problems.

Readability in report writing, however, does present us with some special challenges. The general tendency is for reports to be harder to read than business letters. This tendency has a number of explanations, some of which are listed below:

1. The subject matter of a report often lies in a technical area which is more familiar to the writer than it is to the reader.
2. The content of a report is loaded with information and/or statistics, which rate as neutral in the finesse areas of diplomacy and service attitude. Positiveness, if any, arises mostly from the grammatical concept of "affirmative statement," not so much from the desirable additional quality of "pleasantness." A report, therefore, can be low on human interest, which is an important contributor toward readability.
3. Many reports turn out to be written in the impersonal tone instead of the personal tone (the conversational I–you language). Sometimes the impersonal is prescribed by the reader. At other times,

this tone is chosen by the writer, possibly in the belief that the reader expects it. In any event, use of the impersonal tone converts the reader from participant to onlooker. The work of holding his keen interest—another factor that helps in producing reading ease—tends to become increasingly difficult.

4. Letter-type reports are regularly written informally—that is, with natural slang and contractions—and thus enjoy an easy-to-read, conversational flavor. Conceivably, formal reports might be written this way, too; "formal" in this usage refers more to the physical makeup of the report than to the language. Very often this point is bypassed, and the writer of a formal report uses the formal style. The result is a certain lessening of readability. Worse still, some writers confuse formality with solemnity and go out of their way to produce a dull, drab report. If we must use the formal style, we should do all we can to keep our report lively and interesting.

In studying readability in Chapter 4, we noted that there are as many as seven separate factors influencing the overall readability of a given piece of writing. Only three of these factors, however, have been reduced to any kind of quantitative measurement that would tell us how readability is being affected. These factors are the length of sentences, the length of words, and the frequency of human-interest references.

By means of ordinary arithmetic, we can combine values representing sentence length and word length and subtract a value for human-interest words. The net result is a score by which we can judge the readability of a particular piece of writing. If the score turns out to be higher than it should be (that is, difficult for the reader), there are four things we might do to lower it. These are:

1. Make separate sentences out of the independent clauses of compound sentences.
2. Remove superfluous words and phrases from sentences of all kinds.
3. Replace long, strange words with short, familiar words.
4. Increase the number of human-interest words.

We usually have to pay closer attention to these suggestions when we write a report than when we write a business letter. For the reasons stated earlier, the mood of a report is rather serious, technical, and factual; and we are immediately confronted with the task of inserting "readability"—which will not automatically work itself in.

If we use the formal style of writing, we must resist a tendency to use lengthy sentences along with it. Our preference for simple and complex sentences should be applied as much as possible. Most of our compound sentences, except possibly those used for a desired effect on our reader, should be separated into simple sentences. Moreover, each sentence should be checked for redundancy. All nonessential or "dead-wood" phrases and words should be deleted.

The Word Sequence	Can Be Reduced To
at the present time	now
cooperate together	cooperate
despite the fact that	although
each and every item	every item
enclosed herewith	enclosed
first and foremost	foremost
first and only	only
for the reason that	because
inasmuch as	as
in order that	so that
in order to	to
in the amount of	for
in the event that	if
in the first place	first
in the neighborhood of	about
in place of	for
in view of the fact that	as, since
on the occasion of	on
one and only	only
please do not hesitate to	please
previous to	before
right and proper	right
subsequent to	after
under date of	on
without further delay	now

Whether we write formally or informally, we always face some problem with our choice of words. In report writing this problem has two facets: (1) the ordinary question of whether we are preparing our message at our reader's comprehension level and (2) the special question of whether our reader is familiar with the technical area under discussion. Here again, we must be alert to resist adverse tendencies. In general, we should strive to keep our vocabulary in tune with our reader's. We render a fuller service when we can convey our knowledge of technical matters in language which can be understood by someone who does not have a technical background. Sometimes, however, we know that our reader is well versed in the technical area; and in such a case we could use technical terms freely. In fact, we may win greater confidence from such a person by doing so. But there is still a danger. Because of yielding to the desire to use technical terms (which are often strange, if not relatively lengthy), we may find ourselves being carried past the safety point on other matters of vocabulary. We could end up by writing something which not only is technical but which is otherwise too difficult to be absorbed effortlessly. Our reader might feel at ease with the technical terms but still not be satisfied with our report.

Finally, whenever we write a report in the impersonal tone, we find ourselves severely restricted in the use of human-interest words. The fact is that the personal tone, with its abundant use of I–you language, virtually bulges with human interest and reader involvement. The impersonal tone lacks this advantage and makes for psychologically "deeper" reading. If we are denied the use of personal tone, we should be all the more conscientious in applying the other three steps available for achieving or improving readability.

FORM

When a written communication is put into its final physical state, it takes on what we call "form." The message is then contained in a more or less stable document, which performs three functions in the communication process. To the writer, it is the instrument for transmitting the message. To the reader, it is the instrument for receiving the message. In addition, because the writer releases the very same document that the reader receives, there is no need for facsimile communication. Thus, the document either becomes or displaces the customary function known as the "channel."

In written communication, "noise" cannot enter the process, as a responsibility of the writer, once the document is transmitted to the reader. But a great deal of noise can be introduced during the process of placing the communication into documentary form, if we as writer are not careful to follow conventional practice in routine matters and to use good judgment in unusual or nonrecurring matters.

Specific forms of reports.   When we turn out an informal report, we make a simple choice between the conventional business letter form and the office memorandum form. Specific guidelines for using these forms in report writing are given in Chapter 17.

When we produce a formal report, we abide by a set of rules and conventions that do not relate to letters or memorandums. The pertinent rules governing the mechanics of the formal report are given in Chapter 18.

Graphic aids.   Both kinds of reports, informal and formal, have the common requirement of clarity and eye appeal in the matter of presenting facts. To this end, we advocate the use of graphics—visual presentations such as tables, charts, graphs, and pictures—to supplement text matter. Our decision whether to use graphics in a given report should be based on their value to our intended reader. For instance, if graphics will help our reader understand the text coverage, see facts in their original context, or get a better appreciation of relationships—we do well to include them in our report. But we should not have them as an end in themselves or as a substitute for explanatory text.

Our handling of matter to be included in a graphic aid depends on a combination of things, including the space requirement, the nature of the data to be shown, and the kind of report we are writing.

As a general rule of thumb, we can plan to include a graphic presentation in the going text whenever it does not require more than a third of a page. The reason is that we will find it difficult to predict the point on a typewritten page where the graphic presentation will occur. If it happens to come so far down on a page that it will not fit, we should go to the top of the next page. Thus, when our graphic aid is at most a third of a page, the gap we leave at the bottom of the old page will be minimal. It should not be objectionable to our reader. Moreover, the odds are in our favor that the graphic aid will come due at some higher point. In that event, it will fit conveniently and possibly will even permit resumption of text matter on the same page.

When we have more than a third of a page of material to show in a graphic aid, we should not plan on having it built into the continuity of the text. Instead, we should be guided by the following suggestions:

1. In informal reports (letters and memorandums) we can present our graphic aid as a separate document. This arrangement converts our report to a two-part format—that is, a covering letter or memorandum with an enclosure.

2. In formal reports, we can show our graphic aid as an appendix. An alternative would be to present the aid on a separate sheet of paper and number it as the next page of our report following our first mention of it. As this method actually breaks into the continuity of the text pages, we should make sure that it is a satisfactory one in a given case. Our aim should be to help our reader, not to risk confusing him.

Although there are many ways of displaying data in a graphic aid, we face two practical limitations in selecting one to use in a given instance. One limitation arises from the data; not everything can be shown by the same kind of presentation. We must choose a method suited to the kind of data we wish to exhibit. The other limitation is imposed by the elements of time and talent, which often force us to choose the simplest of several possibilities.

The kinds of visual presentations most likely to be of practical value to us are the table, the scattergram, the line chart (or graph), the histogram, the bar chart (either grouped or ungrouped), and the pie chart. Other presentations, including pictorial symbols, can be very useful; but they may be beyond our reach, unless we have access to the services of a graphic-arts department.

The simplest of these possibilities is the table. It calls only for a sensible organization of the data beneath columnar captions. Of course, it should have an identifying number and a descriptive heading. "Leaders," or lines of dots between columns, help make it easily readable. An example of a table is shown on page 524.

Another relatively easy-to-do presentation is the scattergram. This form of graphic aid is useful when we wish to show the interplay of two elements of data. We either use coordinate paper or draw a series of intersecting horizontal and vertical lines when we present data in a scattergram. Our job is to indicate measures of one element along the base line of our form and measures of the other element along the left

TABLE I

PARKING FACILITIES AT
SCHULTZ METAL PRODUCTS COMPANY

Lot	Allocation	Spaces Available
1	Visitors	19
2	Officers	11
3	Office Staff	30
4	Research Staff	20
5	Factory Personnel	75
6	Factory Personnel	157
	Total Parking Spaces Available	312

sideline, and then place a dot to express the twofold value of each item of our data at the proper spot on the form. When all of the items have been plotted in this manner, we can draw a "regression line"—that is, a line that cuts through the field of dots to give a general impression of the expected change in one element of our data when there is a change in the other element.

The following scattergram, with a descriptive legend, shows the relationship between the age of 16 junior and senior executives and their score on a Management Achievement Test.

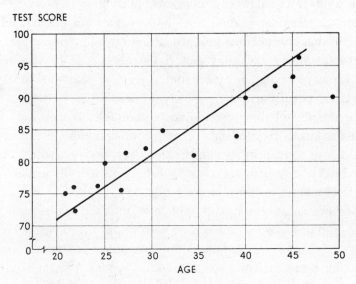

Figure 1. Scatter diagram with regression line. Age of executives and test scores received.

We can use a line chart or graph to show data which do not necessarily involve the influence of one set upon another. Thus, we can present a single series of data by means of a line chart known as a frequency polygon. The following illustration shows the results of a survey of 50 families concerning the number of radio sets owned.

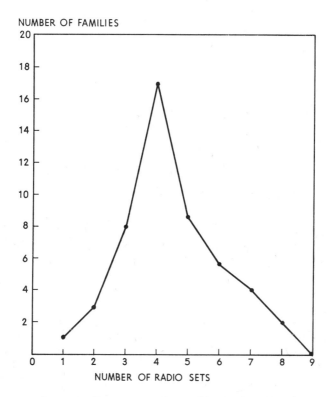

Figure 2. Frequency polygon. Distribution of 50 families according to number of radio sets owned.

Sometimes we can use a line chart to show comparative data. This device works best when we hold the comparison to two series of data, and becomes increasingly hard to follow when we try to display more than three series. The example on page 526 uses a solid line for one series of data and a broken line for the other.

NUMBER OF EMPLOYEES

Figure 3. Male and female workers employed, by years, 1961–66.

If we have a single series of data that is related to the time element (a time series), we can display it by means of a histogram. This device calls for the use of areas instead of points to represent the value belonging to a given segment of time. For example, the data for female employees shown in the preceding line chart would appear as follows in a histogram.

NUMBER OF WORKERS

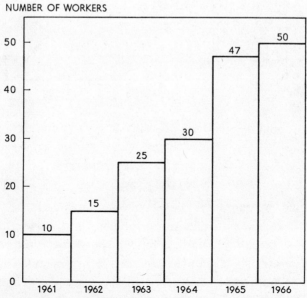

Figure 4. Female workers employed, by years, 1961–66.

We can show the comparative data for the male and female employees in a similar manner by means of a bar chart. In this instance, our presentation would be called a "grouped" bar chart, because more than one series of data would be shown. A bar chart differs from a histogram in that we allow a space interval between the display of data for one period and that of the following period. The following is a bar chart of our male/female employment statistics.

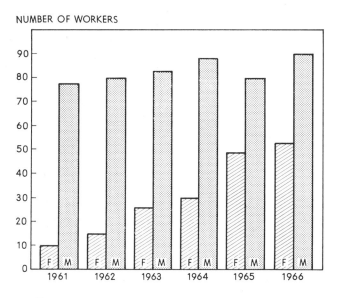

Figure 5. Male and female workers employed, by years, 1961–66.

When the data to be exhibited constitute a whole entity of some kind and we wish to show the relationships of the various component parts to that whole entity, we can use a pie chart. This kind of graphic presentation consists of a circle which symbolizes the whole value under study. Wedge-shaped areas are marked off within this circle to represent the relative value of each component of the whole.

In illustrating a table earlier in this chapter, we used data on parking facilities available at a certain company. If we wanted to show how the 312 spaces were allocated to different groups of people, we might use a pie chart. The data would then appear somewhat as follows:

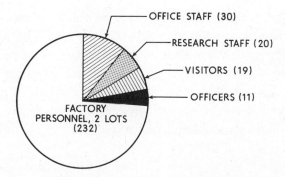

OFFICE STAFF (30)

RESEARCH STAFF (20)

VISITORS (19)

OFFICERS (11)

FACTORY
PERSONNEL, 2 LOTS
(232)

Figure 6. Allocation of 312 available parking spaces, Schultz Metal Products Company. Data from Table I.

SUMMARY

The basic function of a business report is the delivery of information to someone who is in need of it. We may prepare a report for a subordinate, for a person who is at our own level of responsibility, or for someone who ranks above us, such as a superior or a client.

Under a given set of circumstances, we may be faced with preparing either a periodic report or a progress report. Depending on the assignment, we may have to write only an information report, which is confined to the presentation of facts. However, we often are expected to produce either of two varieties of analytical reports. An examination report would be needed if we had to interpret the facts for our reader. A recommendation report would be needed if we had to suggest a remedy to a problem or advocate a choice of possible courses of action. Somewhere along the line, we must also select a format to use, usually a choice between the informal (letter-type) report and the formal report.

In getting ready for report writing, we should apply the time-tested formula for problem solving. First, we should define our problem—preferably by stating it in the form of a title for our report. Second, we should gather the facts that will be needed in reaching a solution. The means available to us include examining company records, conducting experiments, questioning people (by interview, questionnaire, or telephone), and consulting published material. Third, we have to look for and study possible solutions to the problem. Our work here includes sorting, editing, and reducing our accumulated data to those which are really pertinent. Fourth, on the basis of a careful evaluation of the useful facts, we select the possibility that appears to be best for solving the problem.

At this point we are ready to draft our report. The overall requirements are similar to those we have already studied for business letters. We begin with the area of content, which consists of what we will cover (program) and how we will fit it to our reader's psychological needs (finesse). This latter segment of content demands more of our attention in report writing than in letter writing. Next, we express our thoughts through language. In this area, both accuracy and readability are important, with readability being harder for us to achieve in reports than in business letters. Finally, we need to prepare the physical document which will carry our message to our reader. When we prepare an informal report, we simply apply the customary rules of form for the business letter. In the case of a formal report, we follow a different set of instructions, which apply specifically to this situation.

One matter that requires our careful consideration is the use of graphic aids in reports of any kind. Assuming that we are going to use a graphic aid, we can safely plan to have it appear in the going text if the space requirement will be a third of a page or less. Otherwise, we do well to plan it as an enclosure (in an informal report) or as an appendix (in a formal report). Our exact selection of the type of graphic aid will depend on the data involved and on what will be best for our reader. In any event, it should be a type that is within our ability to produce. Practically speaking, therefore, our choice is likely to be one of the following: table, scattergram, line chart, histogram, bar chart, and pie chart.

QUESTIONS

1. State whether the following is a reasonable definition of a written report: a message containing information compiled by the writer for the benefit of the reader.
2. Name two kinds of strictly *informational reports.*
3. Name two kinds of *analytical reports.*
4. What is the chief difference between informational reports and analytical reports?
5. From the standpoint of format, what are the basic kinds of business reports?

6. List four questions which need to be answered in the process of defining the problem in a report-writing situation.

7. What can be done to assure that the scope of a given report will not become distorted while the writer is composing the report?

8. What four general groups of data are possible sources of facts to be used in solving a report-writing problem?

9. List the various methods available for obtaining information from people in general.

10. Would a communication model applicable to a business report be much different from the model that applies to a business letter?

11. In a business report, what changes (if any) take place in the relative importance of the three components of finesse: diplomacy, service attitude, and positiveness?

12. What facts account for a tendency for reports to be more difficult to read than ordinary business letters?

13. What is meant by *deadwood* in language?

14. List some advantages in using *graphic aids* in a business report.

15. Why is it often wise to plan a graphic aid as a separate unit, referred to rather than presented in the text of the report, when it is expected to occupy more than a third of a page?

16. What is the simplest form of graphic aid?

17. Identify the chief advantage arising out of the use of a scattergram (scatter diagram).

18. What is a *frequency polygon?*

19. How can comparative data be shown in a *line chart?*

20. Distinguish between a *histogram* and a *bar chart.*

21. What is always under study when a *pie chart* is used as a graphic aid?

EXERCISES

16–1. Typewrite the following questions in a logical order which would be suitable for a questionnaire. Although it is not intended that you rephrase these questions, you may make incidental changes if you believe that such action will improve the presentation.

```
Generally speaking, do you think that the trading-stamp
movement is a good idea and should be continued?
          ____ YES ____ NO
What irregularities, if any, have you experienced with mer-
chants (such as their "forgetting" to give you the trad-
```

ing stamps, withholding stamps on certain items, etc.)?

What brands of trading stamps do you save?

_____   _____   _____

_____   _____   _____

Does the convenience of redemption-center locations have
any bearing on the brand of trading stamps you save?

_____ YES _____ NO

Has stamp saving caused you to favor those merchants who
issue the brands of stamps you save?

_____ YES _____ NO

At present, do you (or members of your household) save
trading stamps?

_____ YES _____ NO

What type of redemption arrangement do you consider to be
best?

_____ Selection of merchandise in redemption store only.

_____ Selection of merchandise in a department store.

_____ Other: _____

Do you think that there is any significant difference in the
number of stamps needed to fill a book under one stamp plan
as against another?

_____ YES _____ NO

Do you think that there is any significant difference in
the redemption value of a filled stamp book under one stamp
plan as against another?

_____ YES _____ NO

Do you think that prices are any higher at a place of business that gives stamps as against a direct competitor who
does not?

_____ YES _____ NO

16-2. The following information concerns the average first-mortgage interest rates on new houses during 1966 in 15 selected cities. In a
table with columnar captions, present these data in a sensible, organized fashion.

Seattle	6.84%	Cleveland	6.27%
Atlanta	6.80	Minneapolis	6.26
Denver	6.60	Chicago	6.16
New Orleans	6.57	Miami	6.15
San Francisco	6.54	Boston	6.04
Houston	6.53	Philadelphia	5.98
Detroit	6.41	New York	5.81
Los Angeles	6.40		

16-3. The following table shows the scores achieved on a logic-type in-
telligence test by 20 employees whose educational backgrounds varied
from eighth grade to the completion of college. Present this information in the form of a scattergram, and then rule in a regression line.

Employee Symbol	Education (Years)	Test Score		Employee Symbol	Education (Years)	Test Score
A	10	67		L	16	92
B	16	92		M	16	93
C	11	80		N	12	76
D	16	85		O	10	82
E	9	70		P	15	93
F	13	81		Q	8	70
G	15	81		R	14	84
H	12	70		S	8	50
J	12	86		T	12	80
K	11	65		U	16	82

16–4. From the information given below, prepare a frequency polygon to show the families classified according to the number of children they have.

Number of Children	Number of Families
0	10
1	13
2	17
3	22
4	18
5	11
6	5
7	2
8	2
	100

16–5. From the information given below, prepare a comparative line graph. The purpose is to show the changes taking place in the period 1956–65 with regard to the number of families in a certain community who owned two or more automobiles as against the families who owned none.

Year	Families with Two or More Automobiles	Families with No Automobile
1956	60	140
1957	65	139
1958	71	137
1959	76	130
1960	80	124
1961	87	131
1962	92	141
1963	110	132
1964	119	127
1965	138	125

16–6. The following table lists the amount of rain recorded by the U.S. Weather Bureau in Rockledge, Arkansas, for a 10-year period. Present this information in the form of a histogram.

Year	Rainfall (Inches)	Year	Rainfall (Inches)
1957	19.5	1962	20.5
1958	18.1	1963	20.7
1959	17.6	1964	18.4
1960	17.0	1965	19.1
1961	21.2	1966	18.5

16–7. From the information given below, set up a comparative bar chart. The purpose is to show the changes taking place in the period 1957–66 in the number of families of a selected community who owned two or more television sets as against other families who owned none.

Year	Families with Two or More Television Sets	Families with No Television Set
1957	28	110
1958	32	88
1959	45	70
1960	50	62
1961	61	59
1962	69	50
1963	78	42
1964	90	35
1965	111	35
1966	140	33

16–8. Prepare a pie chart to depict the following analysis of the personnel employed by the Enrod Engineering Company.

Clerical Workers	65
Corporate Officers	4
Day Laborers	141
Managers and Supervisors	23
Skilled Workmen	126

● ●

CHAPTER 17

STREAMLINED REPORTS FOR EVERYDAY USES

Informal reports as we shall view them are business reports which we present in the form of a simple document as distinguished from one of a complicated nature. Thus, it is the physical appearance more than any other factor that classifies a report as being informal or formal. Such matters as program, tone, and writing style are not necessarily a distinguishing characteristic—although certain combinations of these elements are often found to go along with one type of report or the other.

The length of a report also has but incidental bearing on whether a report is to be informal or formal. In practice, however, we find that short reports almost always are informal reports. On the other hand, a long report may be either informal or formal. Furthermore, while a formal report is likely to result when the material is lengthy, there still is no requirement that a formal report must be selected just because of the length.

Informal reports probably account for the bulk of the business reports that keep businessmen informed on matters of current importance. They are customarily used when the research effort is relatively light, when the text matter is brief, or when progress is being reported on matters that will be dealt with in a formal report at a later time.

COMMON VARIETIES

The types of informal reports most widely used are the letter report and the memorandum report. These types are often referred to jointly as "letter-type reports."

A letter report is simply a letter, the content of which is a report of some kind. The content can be informational only, or it can be analytical —that is, it can interpret the information and even state a recommendation. A letter report contains all of the elements of a regular business letter (heading, inside address, salutation, body, complimentary close, and signature). It may be prepared on either a business letterhead or on plain stationery, depending on its point of origin.

A *memorandum report* is really a second variety of letter report, even though it bears a separate label. After all, a memorandum is just a streamlined letter form which is used chiefly for interoffice communication. The identifying feature of the memorandum is the simplified heading. It consists of a date line and the following captions:

To:

FROM:

SUBJECT:

Often, a form with these captions printed at the top is available to us for the preparation of office memorandums and memorandum reports. Otherwise, we must have the captions typed on plain stationery when the report is being put into documentary form. In any case, we do not need an inside address, salutation, or complimentary close in a memorandum report. Moreover, since our name already appears in typewritten form after the caption "From:" we usually omit a typed signature identification on the end of the report. As far as the rest of the presentation is concerned, everything could conceivably be the same, word for word, as a letter report written on the same subject.

INCIDENTAL MATTERS

Other features that we must consider when we prepare an informal report are the matters of format, tone, and style.

As for the format to use in a given instance, we may choose between a one-part presentation and a two-part presentation. Our data provide some clues as to which would make the better choice. If everything (including any tables, charts, or graphs) can be presented handily in a continuous flow of text matter, we usually select the one-part format. If, however, the tables, charts, or graphs are too cumbersome to handle within the text matter, we can choose to place them on separate sheets of paper and make them enclosures to our report. This approach results in the so-called two-part format.

Either the personal tone (I–you language) or the impersonal tone (third person language) may be used in an informal report. We should consider, however, that in many persons' minds "personal tone" equates with "informal," and that such a tone is better for readability. Hence, we do see a possible preference for the personal tone whenever the choice is left to us.

In the area of style, we have a similar situation. There is no rule that an informal report has to be written informally (that is, using colloquial language and contractions). Nor is there a rule against such usage. We will have to make a choice each time we prepare an informal report. Our decision will be based on what seems to be the most acceptable style under the existing circumstances, including the preference of our reader, the subject matter of the report, and the full use to be made of the report.

PROGRAMMING

Whether we happen to choose the letter or the memorandum as the specific document to use in a given instance, we must still decide between two basic models for the programming of the content of our informal report. These basic models are known technically as the *inductive order* and the *deductive order*. These terms are somewhat suggestive of the reasoning process that might have been followed in our investigation of the facts presented. Most of the time, however, we solve our problems by the method described in the previous chapter, which typifies the inductive reasoning process. It is only because of our reader's preference —real or supposed—that we would arrange the sequence of our report in what is known as the deductive order.

To get a better understanding of the difference involved, we should recognize that research ought to be conducted in an open-minded, un-biased manner. We should gather as many facts as we can. We should analyze them carefully and evaluate them as weighted factors to be considered in arriving at a needed answer. Then, on the strength of the preponderance of evidence, we should select a logical course of action. This method of approach is called the inductive approach; and a report that presents its facts that way is said to be in the inductive order.

On the other hand, although our actual problem-solving activity was inductive in nature, we can write our report in a different sequence. Our reader may want an answer rapidly and prefer not to plow through explanatory material to get it. Thus, we might place the answer early in our report and follow it with the methods of approach and the factual details. The chief drawbacks of this method are (1) the suggestion that our research was carried on in this same manner—that is, we favored a course of action and set out to find data to support it; and (2) if the answer is not to our reader's liking, he may become prejudiced against us before we have had a chance to state our facts.

The words "inductive" and "deductive," although technically proper, have been criticized for weakness as descriptive adjectives. For one thing, they sound so much alike that many people are confused when they encounter them or try to use them. Also, unless one is well founded in matters of logic or reasoning science, there is not enough identity in either term to give a satisfactory indication of what is involved. Accordingly, we will find that several attempts have been made to develop a better pair of terms. Some of the results are as follows.

Inductive Order	Deductive Order
Logical Order	Psychological Order
Conventional Order	Inverted Order
Bad-News Approach	Good-News Approach

None of the new terminology has enjoyed widespread adoption; but it is well that we know how they substitute for "inductive" and "deductive" in case we encounter them. Each suggested pair is somewhat more specific than the technical pair, but none is free of some kind of limitation.

Logical and *psychological* are more easily kept separate than *inductive* and *deductive*. Yet, we have reasonable doubt that they are adequate replacements. From the viewpoint of logic, both inductive reasoning and deductive reasoning are considered to be logical processes; so how can we dub one as being logical and the other as not? In our earlier discussion of programming business letters, we recognized that the sequence of steps is attuned to the psychological needs of our reader. In some cases, the sequence should delay the answer; in others, it should expedite the giving of the answer. Thus, either sequence has its psychological application; and we should not try to show a difference by labeling one sequence as psychological in contrast to the other.

Conventional and *inverted* are fairly workable terms after we once become familiar with what is "conventional." The limitation is, there- fore, that the use of this pair depends on a specific clarification of the programming possibilities. After that, the words are very functional. Moreover, they do not cloud the picture by mixing in unneeded con- notations of research methods, logical processes, or psychological aspects.

Bad-news and *good-news* are terms which have the advantage of continuity in the application of knowledge we have already acquired. In our study of letter writing, we become well acquainted with these two terms. Now, we need only recognize that "bad-news" equates to the adjective "inductive" and that "good-news" equates to "deductive." From then on, we have terms that not only distinguish between the two basic concepts but even remind us of the program model to be followed in each case. As to be expected, we still are confronted with limitations. The terms are meaningful only when we have had exposure to them beforehand. Someone who has no knowledge of the basic frameworks for letters, for example, would not gain by a change from "inductive order" to "bad-news approach." In addition, we are not literally correct in suggesting that *all* bad-news reports are to be written in the inductive order or that *all* good-news reports are to be written in the deductive order. The fact is that our reader's preference will have much to do with our program sequence regardless of anything else.

We can see, therefore, that while some insight is provided regarding the differences in programming, the various substitute terms need to be used with judgment. Each of us may select one or the other pair of terms, as we prefer, to help us grasp the meaning of "inductive" and "deductive." In the long run, we stand to benefit most by accustoming ourselves to the technical terms.

PROGRAM FOR THE INDUCTIVE ORDER

In planning an informal report which we intend to present in the inductive order, we use a program consisting of at least four main steps —as would be the case in an information report. Sometimes, we will have six main steps—as might be the case in a recommendation report. The following pattern shows the possibilities.

Intended Reader Reaction

from this   through this   to this

Program: Statement of purpose.
Methods used.
Findings.
Analysis (if applicable).
Conclusions and recommendations (if applicable).
Goodwill statement (if needed).

The overall approach is persuasive in nature. The beginning calls for a statement of purpose, in which we identify the subject matter and the authorization of the report project. Such information tells our reader immediately what this report is intended to cover. Memorandum reports automatically give some of this information by means of the "Subject" caption in the heading; the rest must still be supplied in the opening paragraph. If we use a subject caption in a letter report, we can follow through in the same manner. In letter reports without such a caption, we should build all of the necessary identifying information in the opening paragraph.

The methods used in gathering and refining the data contained in the report are described next. Such coverage tells our reader how thorough we were in conducting our investigation and can serve to win his confidence in our sources of data and in the significance of our statements.

By *findings,* we mean a presentation of the information we have collected, organized, and edited for our reader. This presentation may be entirely text matter, or it may be text supported by tables, charts, or graphs. In an information report, this is the limit to which we would theoretically have to go. As a practical measure, however, we would probably end on some statement of a statistical nature; and this would sound rather abrupt. Thus, in an information report, we can usually expect to add a final statement, along the lines of a goodwill gesture, to achieve a graceful ending.

In some cases, of course, our assignment calls for an analytical report. If so, we may be required to interpret our findings and even make some kind of recommendation to our reader. The presence of such continuing information removes the likelihood of our report ending abruptly, because arriving at a conclusion or recommendation is a recognizable ending. But we still have the option of adding a courtesy or goodwill statement if we sense that such would be expected by our reader.

PROGRAM FOR THE DEDUCTIVE ORDER

When we prepare an informal report in the deductive order, we are up against a somewhat different set of circumstances. While we still need to identify our subject at the beginning, we have a greater number of steps to put into our program and a significantly different sequence to follow. The program is outlined below.

Intended Reader Reaction

| from this | to this | through this | to this |

Program: Statement of purpose.
Conclusions and recommendations.
Methods used.
Findings.
Analysis.
Goodwill statement.

The steps in the deductive-order program are not different from those in the inductive-order program. What makes the two programs distinct from each other is the sequence of those steps and the fact that all six steps are likely to be needed whenever the deductive order is followed. In addition, the deductive order does not seem to be useful in the case of an information report, which would contain neither an analysis section nor a recommendation section. Therefore, it would be rather impossible to sequence such a report in the deductive order.

SUBORDERS

Whether we follow the inductive order or the deductive order in report writing, we devote coverage to the matters of methods used and findings. Exactly how we will accomplish such coverage is something still to be considered.

If we have used but one method of research in obtaining our facts, which in turn comprise a single set of findings, we have no problem. For example, a telephone survey concerning the ownership of home air conditioners is uncomplicated as to methods and as to findings.

On the other hand, while one method of inquiry may have been used, the findings may consist of more than one series of data. Also, there is the possibility of further complication by having several sources of data and one or more series of data finally to be reported on. In such cases, we will have to select an order of presentation which will work best under the prevailing circumstances. Actually there are many possibilities from which to choose; but in most cases, one of the following will usually serve us best:

1. *Alphabetical order,* which works best with lists of names, places, companies, and so on—and when no other order seems to be justifiable.
2. *Order of importance,* which arranges items starting with the most important and moving down to the least important.
3. *Chronological order*—also known as the narrative order and the historical order. We use this order when we choose to report things in their order of occurrence.
4. *Climactic order,* which is somewhat the reverse of the order of importance. We can use this order when we wish to go through a process of elimination and arrive at a final, or best, selection.

5. *Logical order,* in which we present our facts in keeping with a coherent progression of thought.

FLEXIBILITY OF INFORMAL REPORTS

From what we have just seen, we can expect a high degree of flexibility to be available to us when we prepare an informal report. We have options in almost every area of reporting: form, format, tone, style, sequencing of the overall program, and sequencing of the methods used and findings. A summary of these possibilities is as follows.

Options—Informal Reports

FORM	Letter	or	Memorandum
FORMAT	One-part	or	Two-part
TONE	Personal	or	Impersonal
STYLE	Informal	or	Formal
PROGRAM	Inductive	or	Deductive
SUBORDER	Alphabetical		Climactic
	Importance		Logical
	Chronological		

ILLUSTRATIONS

In the following pages we have some examples of office memorandums, letter reports, and memorandum reports. These examples represent a cross section of the chief variations (including the different orders of presentation) discussed in the preceding portion of this chapter.

The first of three examples of memorandums is carefully programmed in the inductive order—to be as persuasive as possible, and to avoid any taint of coercion or pressure. It carries a message from top management to company personnel in general.

INTEROFFICE MEMORANDUM

DATE: November 1, 1967

TO: All Personnel, Seaway Products Corporation

FROM: John J. Malone, Executive Vice President

SUBJECT: Physicians' Hospital Development Campaign

A moment's reflection will show us the facts as they really are.

Sure, we have a group prepayment plan to protect ourselves and our immediate family. Sure, our old folks have their Medicare. Financially speaking, we are pretty secure should a medical emergency arise. But--what about the availability of hospital space?

In our city, hospital facilities are good, as those things go. Yet they are lagging behind the ever-growing demand. The population boom, the movement of people toward urban centers, the new discoveries in medical science--even the Medicare program itself--all these are putting pressure upon pressure. The need is clear: our city must enlarge its hospital facilities.

To this end, Physicians' Hospital has begun a campaign to underwrite a 200-bed expansion. Your Company has been asked to help, along with all other firms and the citizens of this community. As in every worthy cause, we want to do our fair share. Will you help us decide what that share should be?

If each employee will channel his personal contribution through the Company, we will match the total collected. Thus, every dollar you would have given anyhow will become two dollars by the time it reaches campaign headquarters.

Do think it over--and when a representative in your department approaches you some day soon, follow your heart.

JJM:amk   *John J. Malone*

The second memorandum is a directive from a company officer to a subordinate. It also is presented in the inductive order; the reason for the directive is explained before the principal message is stated. This sequencing is used to prepare the reader to receive an unexpected message without shock or a feeling of resentment.

INTEROFFICE MEMO

TO: Harvey Thorpe, Sales Manager   FROM: Roy C. Baines, General Manager   DATE: December 15, 1967

SUBJECT: Changes in the Method of Processing Travel Vouchers

As a business grows, its activities increase. Often, it becomes necessary to adjust certain operating procedures to keep in step with the quickened pace.

Such is the situation facing us in the matter of processing the travel vouchers of our many departments. Executive trips, buying expeditions, sales department travel, and convention attendance have been many times more numerous than they were a few years ago. Until now, each person entitled to reimbursement for travel expense had only to submit receipts and an informal accounting summary. The work of the cashier's department, however, has grown to such a point that some degree of standardization is needed to reduce the time taken by each such transaction.

Effective January 1, 1968, there will be a necessary change in procedure. All requests for travel-expense reimbursement are to be made on standardized form No. TR-107, which is available at the cashier's window. This form is designed to control the terminology used as well as the sequence of the items—thereby simplifying the accounting operation.

Will you please call this change to the attention of all personnel in your department?

Roy C. Baines

RCB:ms

It is possible, of course, that this same directive could have been presented in the deductive order. We should have to presume, however, that some previous explanatory foundation had been laid. Then, the message would become a formalizing of something that had already been brought to the attention of the reader. Under such conditions, the memorandum might be written along the lines of this third example.

INTEROFFICE MEMO

TO: Harvey Thorpe,   FROM: Roy C. Baines,   DATE: December 15, 1967
Sales Manager   General Manager

SUBJECT: Change in the Method of Processing Travel Vouchers

Effective January 1, 1967, there will be a necessary change in procedure pertaining to reimbursement for travel expenses. All requests for such reimbursement are to be made on standardized form No. TR-107, which is available at the cashier's window.

The accounting department has selected this form from the three possibilities suggested during our executive staff meeting of December 6. It is designed to control the terminology used as well as the sequence of the expense items--thereby simplifying the accounting operation.

Will you please call this change to the attention of all personnel in your department?

RCB:ms

Roy C. Baines

Our next illustrations deal with informal reports and show many of the options of form, tone, style, program, and so on. The first illustration is of a one-part letter report which uses the personal tone and formal style. It is programmed in the inductive order. While the research methods and findings are uncomplicated, the accumulated facts are tabulated in the order of importance.

independent
surveys

800 CENTRAL TRUST BANK   CLEVELAND, OHIO 44114

September 7, 1967

Mr. Allan Dodd, President
Dodd's Department Store
1200 Cuyahoga Street
Cleveland, Ohio 44115

Dear Mr. Dodd:

The study of women's attitudes toward the abbreviation "Ms.," which you requested of us in your letter of August 10, has been completed. In this report I am submitting a summary of that study and an analysis of the results.

During the week of August 22-27, we assigned a team of one man and three women to conduct personal interviews at the Femme Fashions Department on the third floor of your store. Two members of the team served as interviewers and operated at a table set up near the escalators. The other two members approached women customers as they stepped from the escalators, invited them to participate in the interview, and escorted them to the interviewers' table.

The women interviewed were simply asked to state their marital status and to give their opinion regarding the use of "Ms." as a standard abbreviation for addressing women in business correspondence in place of the customary "Miss" or "Mrs." Each interview was conducted on a friendly, unhurried basis so that the individual woman could speak freely and her questioner could probe as deeply as possible.

The tabulation of our week's interviewing shows the following data:

By Groups	For "Ms."	Against "Ms."	Neutral	Total
Single	115	137	15	267
Married	91	129	23	243
Widowed	36	37	8	81
Divorced	40	35	7	72
	282	328	53	663
Percentages	42.5	49.5	8.0	100.0

Mr. Allan Dodd   -2-   September 7, 1967

Before stating any conclusions, I shall comment on two elements of the data shown. First, our interviewers recorded more answers from single women than from any other group. By some standards, one might expect department-store customers to contain mostly married women. I believe, however, that more than the usual number of single women were coming to your Femme Fashions Department during the week in question. Your advertising in the Sunday newspaper was specifically aimed at the back-to-college trade, and it undoubtedly influenced the customer mix.

Second, our results include some "neutral" answers in all four of the groups--a total of 53 such answers being received. On the surface, such a category might appear to be of little value; to some observers it might indicate that the question was defective. However, I think we have exercised sound judgment in this study. We avoided forcing a woman to give a definite answer when she honestly did not have one. Also, since the proposal to use "Ms." represents a change, we should evaluate neutral answers as signifying open-mindedness--and therefore at least not hostile to the proposal.

In interpreting the results of this survey, please note that 328 women spoke against the use of "Ms." and only 282 women supported it. We should realize, though, that people traditionally are against change. Yet, if a good idea or a new product comes along, it is likely to catch on regardless. The critical point is, I believe, knowing how much avowed support one needs before introducing something new. Certainly, an overwhelming percentage of advance support is not required. If it were, might we not still be stranded in the stone age, waiting for a favorable opportunity to introduce the wheel?

The 53 neutral votes in our study combined with the favorable votes would recast the results as follows: not against, 335 (50.5 percent); against, 328 (49.5 percent). If you would begin using the abbreviation "Ms.," I am confident that many who have declared themselves against "Ms." would quietly change sides.

My recommendation is that you go ahead with your plans to use "Ms." on your new addressing tapes.

Sincerely yours,

Joseph P. Garth

Joseph P. Garth
Project Director

JPG:ln

The second example illustrates a two-part memorandum report, written in the personal tone and using informal style. The program follows the inductive order. The findings consist of one set, but they are restated from different viewpoints. Since each new version is based on the one that precedes it, we can recognize the logical progression of thought.

INTEROFFICE MEMORANDUM

DATE: October 17, 1967

TO: Mr. Harold B. Walsh, President

FROM: J. R. Pettigill, Controller

SUBJECT: Condensed Statement of Operating Profit for the Nine-Month
Period Ended September 30, 1966

Here are the accounting figures which you asked me to send you for use at the Board meeting on Friday, October 21.

I've taken this information from the detailed income statement for the first nine months of 1966. For present purposes, however, I omitted the individual expense items and used only the significant subtotals. In the enclosure accompanying this memorandum, I've arranged the data in the form of a single-column statement, with each amount further expressed as a percentage of the net sales figure.

Also, I've extended the study through two additional steps for you, by making a sales-dollar analysis and then showing this information in the form of a pie chart. You will note that our operating profit so far this year has averaged $.08 for each $1.00 of sales. As this is the proportion we had in mind when we set up our budget for 1966, I'd say that our operations are going along according to plan.

JRP:bk
Enclosure

J. R. Pettigill

WALSH SUPPLY COMPANY

Condensed Income Statement

For the Nine-Month Period Ended September 30, 1966

	Amount	Percent of Sales
Net Sales	$150,000	100.0
Less: Cost of Goods Sold	90,000	60.0
Gross Profit	$ 60,000	40.0
Less: Operating Expenses:		
Selling Expenses	$ 30,000	20.0
General and Administrative Expenses	18,000	12.0
Total Operating Expenses	$ 48,000	32.0
Operating Profit	$ 12,000	8.0

SALES-DOLLAR ANALYSIS

	Sales Dollar
Cost of Goods Sold	$0.60
Selling Expenses	0.20
General and Administrative Expenses	0.12
Operating Profit	0.08
	$1.00

PIE CHART OF SALES-DOLLAR COMPONENTS

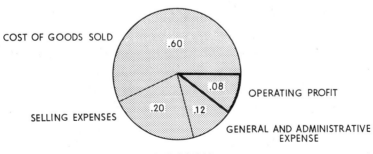

SALES DOLLAR

A few observations may be made concerning this memorandum report. The courtesy title of "Mr." was used with the name of the intended reader. Often, this detail is omitted on the ground that an internal communication need not have all the trimmings that would apply to a mailed-out letter. The best guideline for us to follow would be the current practice in effect at our own company. In the absence of an established pattern, we might prefer to use a courtesy title whenever we address someone above us in the organization.

The two-part format was used for this report even though the text matter was relatively short. The only alternative would have been to divide the graphic portions between two pages of a one-part memorandum. Such handling would interfere with the unity of the graphic portions, and would lessen the flexibility that is now provided by the existence of two separate documents. At the same time, there would be nothing of particular value gained by using a one-part format.

In the next example, we have an illustration of a lengthier memorandum report. It uses the one-part format and is programmed in the deductive order. It is expressed in language that is both impersonal and formal. It uses an alphabetical suborder in a table which presents information according to companies by name.

INTEROFFICE MEMORANDUM

DATE: May 15, 1967

TO: Mr. Charles C. Phelps, General Manager

FROM: John J. Woodruff, Personnel Manager

SUBJECT: Recommendation to Use Vending Machines for Employees'
           Coffee Breaks

The personnel department has completed its study of how best to handle the morning and afternoon coffee breaks authorized for Company employees under the contract which became effective in January, 1967.

The recommendation is that five vending machines be installed in the plant. Three of these machines would dispense coffee (with various options for cream and sugar) at $.10 a cup. The other machines would dispense an assortment of snack items such as candy bars, cookies, and crackers.

Information supporting this recommendation was obtained from the following sources:

1. A firsthand study of conditions at four firms located nearby.

2. Consultation with Atlas Vending Associates, who are the principal operators of vending machines in this area.

All four firms in the immediate vicinity of the Company have vending machines in use at the present time. Facts concerning the number and types to be found at each company are given in the following table:

Name of Company	No. of Employees	Coffee Machines	Snack Machines
Bantam Plywood Products, Inc.	61	2	2
Midway Ceramics Corporation	119	5	3
Southington Furniture Company	37	1	1
Turner Drill Press Co.	51	2	1
TOTALS	268	10	7
Ratio of Employees to Machines	27	1	.7

A study of the totals shows that a relationship exists between the number of employees at the four companies and the number of machines serving their needs. The ratio of employees to coffee machines is 27:1; the ratio of employees to snack machines

Mr. Charles C. Phelps   -2-   May 15, 1967

is 27:0.7, or about 39 persons to each machine. On these bases, the Company could install three coffee machines and two snack machines to take care of its present roster of 76 employees.

The Atlas people are willing to put in the equipment, stock it daily, and service it as needed. They would pay the Company a variable-percentage royalty; and this monetary potential has already been deemed excellent by the accounting department.

Mr. Bronson, the budget director, has worked out the income projections at different levels of activity. He is prepared to discuss them whenever such informa-tion is called for by the planning committee.

JJW:ft   *John J. Woodruff*

SUMMARY
· · · · · · · · ·

An informal report derives its name mostly from its physical appearance; it is a simple document as distinguished from a complicated one. Certain other features—such as personal tone, informal style, and relative shortness—are typical of informal reports, but they are not essential characteristics. The common varieties are the letter report and the memorandum report, known jointly as letter-type reports. The chief difference between these varieties is that the letter is suited for intercompany use and the memorandum is intended for interoffice use. Either may have a one-part format or a two-part format.

In planning an informal report we choose between two general programs or sequences: the inductive order and the deductive order. For a persuasive approach, wherein an adequate foundation is laid before our conclusion or recommendation is given, we use the inductive order. We can use this approach for either information reports or analytical reports. In the suggested program we have three steps which are to be followed regularly and three conditional steps, one or more of which may be sufficient in a given situation. This program appears below:

STATEMENT OF PURPOSE.
METHODS USED.
FINDINGS.
ANALYSIS (IF APPLICABLE).
CONCLUSIONS AND RECOMMENDATIONS (IF APPLICABLE).
GOODWILL STATEMENT (IF NEEDED).

When our reader wants his answer promptly, we use the deductive order, wherein we place our conclusion or recommendation ahead of the facts that support it. This sequence is workable only with analytical reports. The suggested program contains the following six steps, all of which are usually needed:

STATEMENT OF PURPOSE.
CONCLUSIONS AND RECOMMENDATIONS.
METHODS USED.
FINDINGS.
ANALYSIS.
GOODWILL STATEMENT.

In the parts of an informal report which deal with the methods used and the findings, we may have to decide on a suborder of presentation. We can choose from the following possibilities: alphabetical order, order of importance, chronological order, climactic order, and logical order.

QUESTIONS

1. What is the principal distinction between a *formal report* and an *informal report?*
2. In what way are informal reports of significance in the business world?
3. Give a popular synonym for informal reports.
4. Distinguish between a *letter report* and a *memorandum report.*
5. What preference (if any) is there for the tone to be used in an informal report?
6. Must an informal report be written in informal style?
7. What are the two basic models for programming the content of an informal report?
8. Is the order of presentation or programming of an informal report of itself indicative of the manner in which the applicable research was conducted?
9. Indicate two important drawbacks of the *deductive order* of programming a report.
10. Sort the following terms into two lists, the aim being to gather only synonymous terms in each list.

Bad-news approach	Inductive order
Conventional order	Inverted order
Deductive order	Logical order
Good-news approach	Psychological order

11. Give the suggested program for an informal report to be written in the *inductive order.*
12. What is the meaning of the program step, "Findings"?
13. Give the suggested program for an informal report to be written in the *deductive order.*
14. Name five suborders of reporting—that is, methods of giving specific information within the overall order of the writing program.
15. State what is meant by the *climactic order* of giving information in a report.

PROBLEMS
•••••••••

Solutions to the following problems are to be presented in typewritten form on business letterhead or on memorandum stationery, as indicated. If printed stationery is not available, set up a heading in each case according to directions issued by your instructor. Follow the suggestions given for the choice of tone, style, and program.

17–1. (Letterhead; personal tone, informal style, deductive order.) Assume that you are the senior partner of Management Associates, a consulting firm. Maxwell Presner, manager of a suburban shopping center, has requested your services in improving conditions at his parking lot. The area is 360 feet wide by 300 feet deep and is fenced on all sides. The lot is on the north side of the street; it has an entrance gate at the right, an exit gate at the left. Spaces for 422 parking positions have been provided. They are marked off by yellow lines painted on the black asphalt surface. Single-row parking is permitted against both the rear fence and the front fence. Double-row parking is permitted in eight blocks marked off within the central area. Driving passages are maintained at both sides of the lot and around the double-row parking blocks. A capacity sketch would therefore appear as follows.

After describing this layout, Mr. Presner has come to the specific problems that exist. Although each parking position is nine feet wide, customers of the shopping center have said that they cannot park easily. Sometimes drivers straddle the yellow lines and waste parking space in the most desirable locations. At times, someone gets into a tight spot and has a hard time getting in or out of his car. Minor accidents—such as scraped paint, broken tail lights, and dents from door handles—occur whenever the lot gets crowded.

Customers have complained to the merchants; the merchants, to Mr. Presner. At the moment, Mr. Presner is considering the idea of widening the parking positions to 10 feet. But before he takes action, he wants an outside opinion.

An on-the-spot inspection of the parking lot bears out Mr. Presner's description. It also reveals that the dividing lines are painted perpendicular to the front and rear fences. Because of the sharp turn needed for a car to enter a parking position, the driving passages are 20 feet wide. Prepare a report to Mr. Presner and recommend:

(a) That angle parking be instituted.

(b) That nine feet be retained as the width of a parking position.

(c) That a "buffer" line be painted 30 inches inside the left-hand boundary of each parking position, as follows:

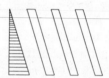

(d) That parking along the front fence be discontinued.

(e) That the double-row parking blocks be increased to 10.

(f) That the driving passages be narrowed to 16 feet.

Tell Mr. Presner that these recommendations, if followed, would lead to the following improvements:

(a) Through the "power of suggestion," the buffer lines would help keep drivers inside a given parking position.

(b) There would be a consequent decrease in minor accidents and customer complaints.

(c) Parking positions would be increased by 22 (from 422 to 444), because narrower driving passages would be practical under the system of angle parking.

17–2. (Memorandum; impersonal tone, formal style, deductive order.) A problem has developed in the office shared by four rate clerks in the traffic department of the Hendrix Appliance Corporation. Ramsey McClure, the traffic manager, reports that these men have been steadily dropping behind in their work. Yet on a number of occasions, either he or the assistant traffic manager has surprised these men in the midst of a talk session not related to their work. Each time the clerks would stop talking abruptly and make a pretense of being absorbed in their work.

There is no question as to the basic competence of each of the four rate clerks. The traffic manager prefers not to be overly strict with them. If one or more of them should resign (or be discharged), a suitable replacement would be hard to find right now. Mr. McClure has therefore referred the matter to you, the plant manager.

Suppose that you approach the problem by making an after-hours visit to the office in question. You observe that the desks are arranged as shown below.

Prepare a report for Mr. McClure. Suggest a new office layout, which will make use of opaque-glass dividers in the following manner.

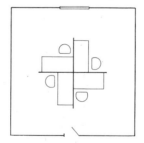

Point out the advantages to be obtained in reducing conversations and thwarting a quick cover-up of any nonbusiness talking.

17–3. (Memorandum; personal tone, formal style, inductive order.) *Lookout,* a monthly trade journal of the jalousie industry, renders a number of statistical services to its subscribers. Among them is an index of labor turnover for the industry. The index is a refined turnover rate, and it is published each February for the previous calendar year.

The Standard Jalousie Company usually computes a similar refined turnover rate for its own guidance. For several years it has enjoyed a lower rate than that published for the industry in general.

This February's *Lookout,* just received, states that the industry's labor turnover rate for last year is the lowest on record—an index of 17.31. This news comes as a shock to Cary Pendleton, the president of the Standard Jalousie Company. Mr. Pendleton's labor summary shows that his average working force for the year was 102 persons, whereas 26 separations were recorded. Mr. Pendleton has hurriedly figured his company's turnover rate as being in excess of 25 percent. He has summoned you, as acting personnel director, to explain why the company compares so poorly with the industry in general.

You find that no one has yet computed the company index for last year. Your personnel records contain the following facts about separations occurring during the year:

Separations	Reasons for Separation
6	Higher pay elsewhere for same work.
4	Disliked working conditions.
3	Retired at age 65.
3	Inducted into the U.S. Army.
2	Returned to college in September.
1	Argument with foreman.
1	Resigned because of ill health.
1	Died from injuries in auto accident.
5	Reason unknown—departed without waiting for exit interview.
26	

Lookout magazine's research department computes its refined turnover rate by using only those separations which could be attributable to managerial shortcomings. The computation does not include separations which are clearly "normal attrition"—that is, beyond the company's control. The index is determined as follows.

$$\frac{100 \times \text{Chargeable Separations}}{\text{Average Work Force}}$$

Write a report to Mr. Pendleton; give him an interpretation of how the Standard Jalousie Company compares with the industry in general.

17–4. (Letterhead; personal tone, informal style, deductive order.) As sales manager of the Regency Manor motor hotel, submit a report to Mr. H. H. Jackson, the purchasing agent of the Industrial Service Company. Jackson has asked for menus and prices applicable to a dinner his company is planning for its employees, who currently number 64 persons.

The dining facilities at Regency Manor include private rooms, at least one of which is large enough for a group of this size. A wide variety of dinner menus are available, but you are proposing the following possibilities as being appropriate to the occasion.

Menu No. 1. Roast beef, au jus—de luxe relish tray—hard rolls—fresh fruit cup—creamery butter—fresh green beans with mushrooms—chef's salad—Russian or French dressing—baked potato—chive sour cream— beverage—Dutch apple pie.

Menu No. 6. Baked boneless chicken—snowflake potatoes—giblet gravy —head lettuce salad—French dressing—chicken noodle soup—dinner rolls—whipped butter—relish tray—carrots and peas—ice cream snow- ball—beverage.

The chicken dinner is listed at $4.75 a plate; the roast beef, at $5.50. Your recommendation is the roast beef. It seems to be the better value in spite of the higher price, and it has an aura of "status" about it. Parking is ample at Regency Manor. Bar and checking facilities are available.

17–5. (Letterhead; impersonal tone, formal style, inductive order.) Floyd B. Henderson has written to you for advice. He hopes that you, the local representative of the Actuarial Assurance Company, will be able to help him work out a program for his retirement income. Henderson, age 60, is a bachelor. He has a job which pays him $7,200 a year. Because of gradually failing eyesight, he is convinced that he will have to retire at age 65.

Henderson's assets include a bank account of about $9,500 and a one-family brick house which he believes could be sold for $25,000. When he retires, he will have to provide for himself through social security and withdrawals from his savings account. He is interested in selling his house and investing in an annuity, but won- ders whether that would be a wise move. Future inflation could be troublesome if he were entirely dependent on fixed income.

In your opinion, the Actuarial Assurance Company has just the plan to solve Henderson's problem. It is an annuity arrangement under which the insurance company will deliver monthly shares of stock instead of a fixed sum of money. The shares can be either kept or sold at the discretion of the recipient. In case of inflation, the sales price should be greater than the fixed money payment would have been. In that way, the owner of the annuity could protect himself against a loss of purchasing power.

Write a report to Henderson. Recommend that he sell his house and buy a $25,000 Actuarial Cost-of-Living Annuity. In case the house does not bring in $25,000, Henderson could make up the difference from his bank account. He can be granted an annuity contract which will give him monthly shares of stock for life, starting on his 65th birthday. This stock will be of Henderson's choice, from a list of blue-chip securities compiled by Actuarial's investment experts. The number of shares to be delivered to Henderson monthly will be the number which $175 would buy on the date the annuity contract is signed.

17–6. (Memorandum; personal tone, informal style, deductive order.) Assume that you are the personnel manager of your company. The chief accountant is in need of a replacement for a junior member of his staff who has been drafted for military service.

When you ran an advertisement in the local newspaper, sixteen persons responded with application letters. Five of these persons were interviewed by yourself and one of your assistants. Three of the applicants came off poorly during the interviews; they are of no further interest to you. The remaining applicants appear to be alert, intelligent, and well versed in accounting.

Send a report to the chief accountant. Submit information on both applicants so that he can reach a final decision. The pertinent data are as follows:

HOPWORTH, WILLIAM P. Age 24, single. B.B.A., Lovett University; top third, class of 476 seniors. Major, accounting; specialties, auditing and tax accounting. Background courses: history, mathematics, physics, economics, business law. Experience: time keeper, Horton Construction Co., one summer; junior accountant, C. J. Blackwell (C.P.A.), two years, part time. Travel: New England and Canada. Draft Status: 2S (student deferment). Hobbies: tennis and water skiing.

WALKER, MILDRED. Age 26, married (Thomas J.). A.B. *cum laude*, Bella College. Major, English; minor, business administration. Special interest: accounting. Courses in accounting: principles, intermediate, cost, budgeting. Experience: bookkeeper, Central Hospital, two years; teller, City Savings Bank, three years. Familiarity with office equipment: typewriter, dictaphone, calculator, bookkeeping machine, office copier. Hobby: crossword puzzles.

Be sure to include your own recommendation based on how the qualifications appear to you.

17–7. (Letterhead; personal tone, formal style, inductive order.) Five years ago, Dr. Russell Overman, a psychologist, founded the Executive Placement Center. He persuaded you, then a personnel interviewer at the State Bureau of Employment, to join his staff. Dr. Overman's firm has since built a reputation for counseling and placing middle-management personnel who seek to upgrade themselves by changing their employers.

During the past half year, a number of complaints have been received from persons who have subscribed to this service at one time or another. These men have found that the grass is not necessarily greener in the next pasture. In some cases, they have lost out because the new employer was absorbed by a merger with a larger firm. Some men have been unable to measure up to the requirements of the new position and have been demoted—or even discharged. Others have learned of successes which might have been theirs had they not left their original employers.

Dr. Overman senses that a continuation of this trend could spoil his firm's reputation. He has appealed to you, because of your background and experience, to study the situation.

Your investigation shows that the firm could be more cautious in its counseling function. It could dig more deeply into each client's case—and under certain conditions, advise him not to make a change in employers. Until now, the firm has placed more emphasis on its other function—that of finding a new position for the client.

Write a report to Dr. Overman. Recommend that henceforth a two-pronged analysis, as outlined below, be made in the case of each new client:

(a) Factors pertaining to the client's present employer: movement in relation to competitors; personnel and promotion policies; atmosphere for employee satisfaction.

(b) Factors pertaining to the client himself: proficiency in his line of work; notable accomplishments, if any; desire to face new challenges; potential value to a new employer; adaptability to change, retraining, etc.

17–8. (Memorandum; personal tone, informal style, inductive order.) The Burns-Ohio Automotive Company operates a chain of retail stores. These stores specialize in automobile parts and accessories. The manager of the firm's Cincinnati outlet has given notice of his resignation. You, as sales manager, must recommend a replacement. The company policy is to make promotions from the ranks of present employees.

After carefully screening a dozen possibilities, you have come up with two promising candidates. Although you have had occasional dealings with both of these men, you cannot rate either as having the better personality. Your final choice between the two men will be based on interpretations of the following objective data which have been given to you by the personnel office:

VINCENT A. FORTUNA

Assistant manager of Burns-Ohio store in Dayton, Ohio. Age 34; married, two children. Education: graduate, Middletown, Ohio, Senior High School; has earned 78 semester credits (evening college) toward a B.B.A. degree. Personnel testing results: I.Q., 114; Leadership Index, 83d percentile. Experience: clerk, Dayton Auto Supply, five years; manager, Dayton Auto Supply, four years; assistant manager, Burns-Ohio Dayton outlet (following merger with Dayton Auto Supply), six years. Was draft-exempt because of dependency.

HERBERT PETTREY

Manager of Burns-Ohio store in Sandusky, Ohio. Age 30; single. Education: A.B., Great Lakes University (Michigan); major in sociology; minor in business administration. Personnel testing results: I.Q., 120; Leadership Index, 80th percentile. Experience: clerk, Burns-Ohio outlet in Toledo, Ohio, three years; assistant manager, Burns-Ohio Toledo outlet, two years; manager, Burns-Ohio Sandusky outlet, three years. Captain, inactive reserves, U.S. Army.

Write a report containing your recommendation to Mr. Chalmer C. Burns, the president of your company.

17–9. (Memorandum; impersonal tone, formal style, inductive order.) As a small manufacturer of high-quality cameras, Flexograph, Inc. specializes in two models: Serflex and Serflex, Jr. Serflex is made on a custom basis, the lenses and attachments conforming to customers' specifications. Serflex, Jr. is turned out on a continuous basis, and each camera of this model is fitted with a standard lens.

Among its equipment, Flexograph, Inc. has two lens-grinding machines which are used exclusively in the manufacture of Serflex, Jr. cameras. These machines will grind 1,000 lenses a year each—a total of 2,000 lenses. They were purchased for $6,000 apiece two years ago, at which time they had an estimated useful life of six years. At the present time, these machines have a trade-in value of $400 each; by the end of their useful life, they will have a scrap value of only $100 each. The total cost of operating both machines for one year has been analyzed as follows:

Direct labor	$3,000
Power	360
Maintenance	300
Taxes and insurance	100
Depreciation	1,967
	$5,727

The company has an opportunity to buy a new-style lens-grinding machine for $8,000. Although it would last only four years before it would have to be sold for scrap value estimated at $200, this new machine is capable of producing as many lenses a year as both old machines combined. Its operating costs would be computed as follows each year.

Direct labor	$1,800
Power	200
Maintenance	200
Taxes and insurance	225
Depreciation	1,950
	$4,375

Assume that there are no important side factors to be considered, such as a difference in the quality of the lenses produced. As plant manager, prepare a report for the president of Flexograph, Inc. In it, support a recommendation either that he buy or that he not buy the new machine.

17–10. (Letterhead; choice of personal tone or impersonal tone; informal style; deductive order.) Suppose that you are a personnel psychologist associated with an industrial-relations consulting firm. The Aluminum Container Company has asked your firm to design an effective suggestion system which it could institute for its factory and office workers.

Write an informal report to this client. State a reason for each point included in the following plan, which you are recommending.

CRITERIA FOR SUGGESTED SYSTEM

Full advance explanation to employees on how the plan will be operated. Prominent display of suggestion boxes. Access to the boxes by members of all departments. Anonymity guaranteed in the form that is used. Serialization of suggestion form and stub. Frequent collection from the suggestion boxes. Regular monthly meetings by the evaluation committee. Monetary awards, within announced limits, made in accordance with the worth of the suggestion. Recognition of employees who made acceptable suggestions. Some means of explaining why suggestions have not been accepted.

17–11. (Memorandum; choice of personal or impersonal tone; formal style; inductive order.) The Big Ben Discount Store operates in a leased one-story building. It pays a rental fee of $2,000 a month, and this cost is prorated among the various sales departments on the basis of floor space.

The department handling goldfish, hamsters, parakeets, and canaries has been put under scrutiny by the sales manager. A typical monthly operating statement of this department shows the following:

```
Sales .......................... $890
   Less: Cost of Sales .............  520
       Gross Profit ................. $370
Direct Expenses:
   Attendant's Wages .. $250
   Advertising ........    40   $290
Allocated Expenses:
   Rent .............. $150
   Miscellaneous ......   25   175   465
       Net Loss ...................($ 95)
```

Also, there is a storage problem in the garden department, which is adjacent to the pet department. If the latter were to be eliminated, sacks of lime and chemical fertilizer could be piled conveniently, out of the way of customer traffic.

Mr. Nathan Preiser, owner of the Big Ten Discount Store, has asked you, his accountant, to verify the wisdom of this supposition. Your interpretation of the facts is this: as long as the pet department has income to cover all of its direct expenses and some of the allocated expenses, it is really worth keeping as against converting the area to dead storage. Write a report to this effect to Mr. Preiser.

17–12. (Memorandum; personal tone, formal style, sensible choice of program.) The directors of Pontiac Cement, Inc. have voted to build a new plant for the production of concrete building blocks. As president of the company, you have appointed a committee to investigate several sites that might be used for the new facility. This committee has completed its work and has given you the following descriptions of two enticing possibilities.

MARSHALL, TEXAS. Size of parcel: 90 acres. Price: $100 an acre. Water supply: limited, but sufficient. Transportation outlook: railroad center; siding can easily be extended to plant site. Labor supply: adequate; rates average for South. Schools and churches: adequate. Tax situation: favorable.

MEMPHIS, TENNESSEE. Size of parcel: 60 acres. Price: $150 an acre. Water supply: unlimited. Transportation outlook: area is served by trains and boats. Proposed site is at edge of Mississippi River. Labor supply: adequate; rates average for South. Schools and churches: ample. Tax situation: favorable.

Prepare a report in which you recommend one of these locations to the board of directors.

17–13. (Letterhead; impersonal tone, formal style, sensible choice of program.) As an insurance adjuster, you have been sent by the Industrial Hazards Insurance Company to investigate and settle a claim entered by the Western Twine Corporation. This firm had a fire in the parking garage at its main warehouse. The fire was brought under control by quick-thinking employees who trained a wall-bracket fire hose on the flames. Nevertheless, an entire consignment of twine (packed in cardboard cases) was ruined; also, an interior door and wall were badly scorched.

You have appraised the amount of damage to be $417, which will have to be paid by the insurance company. You are inclined to believe, however, that some negligence may have been involved here. In transmitting the reimbursement check to the Western Twine Company, report some findings which have caused you to make the following recommendations: (1) flammable cases should not be stored against a wooden wall; (2) smoking should be banned inside the parking garage; and (3) burnable debris should be disposed of daily, and not allowed to accumulate inside the garage.

17–14. (Memorandum; sensible choices of tone, style, and program.) The majority of the depositors of the Patriots Savings Bank have their interest income posted to their passbooks during January. At that time, the teller gives the depositor an inexpensive token of the bank's appreciation. As the corporate secretary of the bank, you have the responsibility of selecting the gift. This year you have narrowed the possibilities to two articles: a ball-point pen and a glass ash tray.

The pen costs $20 a thousand. It has a metal cap and a barrel of blue-colored plastic. The purchase price includes printing of the bank's name on the barrel. The pen would make a popular gift; but it would probably run out of ink after about three months of use. Then, unless the owner would invest in a refill, the pen would cease to be of value.

The ash tray costs $22 a thousand. It is made of heavy-duty glass, and measures four inches square. Its price includes the embossing of an advertising message. Being sturdy, the ash tray can be expected to last for several years. Although not all depositors are smokers, they might still use the ash tray for guests of theirs who happen to smoke.

Make a final recommendation of one of these gift possibilities in a report addressed to Mr. Ward Webster, the president of the Patriots Savings Bank.

17–15. (Letterhead; sensible choices of tone, style, and program.) The Manhattan Cosmetics Company uses a special grade of lanolin in one of its products. The average daily requirement for this ingredient is 15 pounds.

The interval of time between the placing of a purchase order for this lanolin and the actual delivery at the Manhattan Cosmetics Company varies from 15 to 25 days. Despite peaks and troughs in production, the maximum requirement for a 25-day period is 475 pounds of this lanolin. The minimum requirement for the same period is estimated to be 275 pounds. The standard order quantity has been set at 1,000 pounds.

As a management consultant, you have been approached by the inventory controller of the cosmetics company, one Lamont Chambers. He would like your help in establishing maximum and minimum inventory points and a proper ordering point for this special grade of lanolin. With reference to the following formulas, recommend the necessary control quantities in a report addressed to Mr. Chambers.

Formulas:

Maximum Inventory = Quantity on hand at time of ordering (ordering point) — Smallest quantity to be used during waiting period (slowest consumption, fewest days) + Quantity ordered.

Minimum Inventory = An arbitrary quantity to serve as a safety factor —say, average needs for five days.

Ordering Point = Minimum inventory + Largest quantity to be used during waiting period (fastest consumption, most days).

. . . .

CHAPTER 18

COMPLEX
REPORTS FOR
FORMAL USES

A formal business report is basically a report that follows a pre-scribed or conventional set of rules concerning its physical appearance. Such a report has a noticeable degree of standardization in its construction; and this standardization tends to make the reader feel at home with the document. It enables the reader, for example, to know the probable sequence of the various sections contained in the report; to count on the existence of a summary or synopsis somewhere ahead of the main presentation; and to find a table, chart, or discussion that is of particular interest to him.

ASPECTS TO BE CONSIDERED
. . . .

Other than its physical construction, a formal report is simply another business report. Thus, it can be a periodic report or a progress report. It can be an information report or an analytical report. It can be long or short. It can be written in the personal tone or in the impersonal tone, with formal language or with informal language.

There are some practical indicators, however, to guide us in choosing between a formal and an informal presentation and also between various alternatives which may subsequently arise. These indicators are summarized below:

1. When time is not an overriding factor, we generally lean toward a formal report presentation if there is weightiness involved. In determining weightiness, we should consider such matters as the ultimate use to be made of the report, the amount of work that has been put into the investigation, the seriousness of the problem under study, and the importance of the specific subject matter of the report at hand.

2. From a practical standpoint, a formal report is easier to use than an informal report. Its various parts are in their expected places, and there are some built-in aids—such as a table of contents, list of illustrations, and index—to help the reader find a desired piece of information.

3. From a psychological standpoint, a formal report has several advantages over an informal report. For one thing, it is more apt to impress our reader because of its organization and orderliness. For another, it inspires confidence in our work because of its easy-to-find information and its systematic presentation. The tidy finished product implies careful research, good editing, and well-calculated conclusions and/or recommendations.

4. The formal report presentation is highly desirable when the report will be circulated beyond the initial reader. Its appearance permits it to cross many desks; there should be no cause for concern about its dignity.

5. The longer a report, the more likely it is to be presented as a formal report. This is not an absolute cause-and-effect relationship—it is just that long reports require better organization than short reports. Good physical presentation, in turn, is an essential feature of a formal report.

6. When our choice of document is the formal report, we have a tendency to extend formality into our style of writing. Some writers, in fact, overshoot the need in this regard. Our best approach to a writing style is the query: Under the conditions that prevail, what will be expected by our reader? If he seems to want the formal style (no slang, no contractions), we should write our report that way. But it does not mean that we must write in a somber, uninteresting way.

7. In composing formal reports, we also have a tendency to use the impersonal tone (third person only). Actually, there is no such requirement. In fact, many businessmen have voiced their dissatisfaction with the impersonal tone. Such businessmen say that it lessens the interest value of the report—and causes the writer to appear noncommittal at a time when the reader may prefer to learn his opinion. They are puzzled about how the notion could have spread that the impersonal tone was to be preferred in a formal report. It may be true, however, that the impersonal tone sounds more factual and less opinionated than the personal tone. We can justify its use on that basis at times—provided we do not go against our reader's announced preference. We should not choose it in the mistaken belief that it is required. If we can use the personal tone safely, we should do so. The personal tone is easier on both the writer and the reader.

THE PARTS OF A FORMAL REPORT

If a formal report has been constructed properly, its reader has a pretty good idea of what parts he will find inside even before he opens the cover. Of course, he will not have extracted the message yet—but he will know roughly how the reporting has been done. If it is a relatively long report, the reader will be expecting a maximum number of parts:

1. Title Page.
2. Letter of Authorization.
3. Letter of Transmittal.
4. Preface.
5. Table of Contents.
6. List of Illustrations.
7. Summary.
8. Text.
9. Appendix or Appendices.
10. Bibliography.
11. Index.

The *title page* is the first page of the overall report, and is also the first page of the preliminary sections (or preliminaries) which run in a series of lowercase Roman numerals. The title page itself, however, is not numbered physically; it is merely included in the count. It usually gives four pieces of information, as follows:

a) Title of the report.
b) Name of the intended reader.
c) Name of the author.
d) Date of presentation.

The *letter of authorization* is the letter (or possibly the memorandum) which called for the study and the resulting report. Physically, it could even be a typewritten copy of such instructions—or a facsimile made by an office copier. Whether a page number should appear or not is a matter of practicality and choice; but this part follows the title page in the same series of Roman numerals.

The *letter of transmittal* is a letter (or possibly a memorandum) which releases the report to the reader. It is much the same as any other letter of transmittal, which we have seen in situations calling for two-part formats—except that now it is part of the overall document rather than being a separate, covering document. In length, it can vary from one or two sentences to many paragraphs, depending on how much needs to be stated at this point. The essence of the letter of transmittal comes down to the concept, "Here is the report you asked me to prepare." This part of the report may or may not be numbered physically, but it follows the letter of authorization in the Roman-numeral series.

The *preface* is an introductory discussion of some kind. It is usually concerned with statements which the author believes should be made, but which he cannot easily work into the text of the report or even into the letter of transmittal. Such statements may be background material relating to the reason for the study, certain limitations of the study, some of the facts gathered but not put into the text of the report, or comments on the overall experience. Appropriate Roman numerals are used on the pages of the preface.

The *table of contents* is a listing of the things which are to follow. Basically, these items are the summary, text, appendix, bibliography, and index. Ordinarily, the text section is presented in outline form with its pertinent subdivisions. Each of the items listed in the table of contents is paired with the number of the page on which that item begins. Thus, the reader has a useful aid for finding the starting point of a discussion he might want to read, at any given time. As for page numbers, the table of contents falls within the Roman-numeral series.

The *list of illustrations* is another aid to the reader. It shows the number of the page on which each piece of illustrative material is to be found. Thus, it helps the reader find a given visual presentation easily, without requiring him to page through the report until he chances upon it. Being one of the preliminary sections, this list bears a Roman-numeral page number next after that of the table of contents.

The *summary* (also called the abstract or synopsis) is a condensed version of the text of the report. Being the last of the preliminary sections, its pages close out the Roman-numeral series. The summary may range from less than a page to several pages in length. As a minimum, it will include a statement of the problem, the highlights of the facts that have been uncovered, and the gist of the conclusions and/or recommendations of the report. In a longer version, it could include background material, the general approach(es) used in gathering data, a fuller disclosure of the findings, and some discussion and analysis. Whether it is short or long, it is a digest of the text of the report, positioned ahead of the report. In this position it becomes an additional aid to the initial reader as well as to subsequent readers. It highlights the problem under study and indicates a solution in a brief presentation. Thus, it conveys the message of the report with relative speed. The main body of the report can thereafter be meaningful to the reader whether he examines it hastily or studiously, whether he reads it through completely or merely spot checks the subdivisions of greatest interest to him.

The *text* is the main section of the formal report, the part wherein the subject matter is discussed and analyzed. Basically, the text of the formal report is patterned after the conventional English composition:

INTRODUCTION
BODY
CONCLUSION

The introduction contains a clarification of the background details of the problem under study, a statement of the purpose and scope of the study, and possibly a coverage of the methods used in gathering the data being reported. In some instances, however, the methods used are not introduced until the body of the report. Then each method of research can be paired with its resultant findings.

In any event, the body of the report presents the data which have been uncovered by the study, and it usually goes on to discuss and analyze them. The sequencing of facts within the body of the report will depend on the circumstances involved in each report situation. The general possibilities, however, are the same as those available for informal reports: namely, alphabetical order, order of importance, chronological order, climactic order, and logical order.

In essence, the conclusion of the formal report is the termination or ending. More specifically, this section functions in one or more of the following ways:

a) As a summary, to pull together the various highlights of the discussion.

b) As a statement of conclusions (logical judgments) drawn from the facts presented.

c) As one or more recommendations concerning the action to be taken.

The programming of the composition work of a formal report is concerned with the effective sequencing of the methods used, findings, and conclusions. The general aim is to have the thought processes move in a recognizable direction—that is, from a definite starting point to a definite conclusion, without unnecessary straying in between.

Sometimes the three elements will be simple, or uncomplicated; sometimes they will be complicated; and sometimes they will be partly simple and partly complicated. For example, a study that requires but one kind of research (say, interviewing by telephone) to gather one kind of information (say, whether the selected interviewees own or rent their living quarters) probably would lead to a single conclusion (say, a logical judgment drawn from the findings). The text of a report on such a study could be programmed as follows.

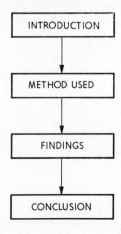

In another situation, the study might call for several approaches to research. Several different kinds of facts might be uncovered, and each type might lead to a separate conclusion. Such could be the case when both laboratory and library research are used. The findings obtained by each method could conceivably be different, because of different incidental conditions; and the conclusion to be drawn from each would be valid only under the pertinent conditions. Probably a summary type of general conclusion would be needed to round out the report. The program, then, would be of the following design.

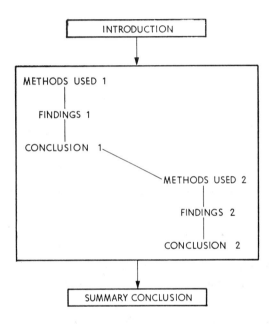

Later in this chapter, we shall examine a complete illustration of a formal report. The text of this illustration follows a program that is partly simple and partly complicated. The method used for gathering the information for the report was simple—a standardized questionnaire was mailed to a segment of the alumni of a certain university. The questions involved, however, were not homogeneous. Therefore, the findings had to be kept separate. They were reported upon individually in the body of the report, and each led to its own logical judgment, or conclusion. Following the individual presentations, a summary-type conclusion was used to round out the text of the report. Thus, the writing program was sequenced in the following manner.

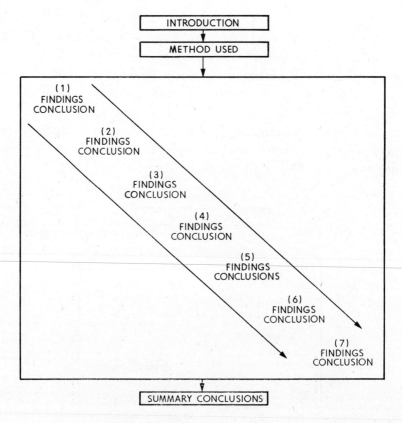

As for physical details, the first page of the text marks the beginning of a second series of pages, which will continue through to the back cover of the report. This numbering series will be in arabic numerals; and it will embrace the pages of the various supplementary sections of the report, such as the appendix, bibliography, and index.

The *appendix* (or *appendices,* when plural) is a supplementary section which is placed after the text of the report. It contains graphic aids —lists, tables, charts, pictures, maps, etc.—that cannot conveniently be presented in the body of the report. Data taken from such exhibits are highlighted in the body and are identified by number or letter with the appendix in which they are shown in their entirety. Not all graphic material, however, need be deferred to an appendix. Ordinarily, material that does not require much more than one third of a page can safely be planned for inclusion in the text of the report. In that way it is a greater convenience to the reader.

The *bibliography* is a list of books and periodicals which have a bearing on the subject matter of the report—especially those which were used as sources of information. Each item listed includes the author's name, the title of the article (if applicable), the name of the book or journal, and the appropriate identifying details—such as the publication date, copyright, volume and issue numbers, place of publication, and the name of the publisher.

The *index* is the final section of the supplements and of the overall report. It is an alphabetical listing of all the significant names, topics, and subtopics which appear throughout the report, together with a notation of the pages on which these details are mentioned. The index helps the reader pinpoint all references that have been made to a given topic, whereas the table of contents merely tells him where a certain area of the discussion begins.

INCLUSION OF PARTS

Not all formal reports need to contain all of the parts enumerated above. Sometimes circumstances relating to the assignment of the project, the nature of the problem, the methods of gathering information, and the decisions on what should be included and excluded will render one or more of these parts unnecessary or even impossible. Thus, if the assignment were to be given orally, there could not be a letter of authorization. If the letter of transmittal has already stated the preliminary comments of the author, a preface may not be needed. A report that contains no illustrative material certainly does not call for a list of illustrations. Also, since a report should not have an appendix section just for the sake of having it, a number of reports will not require this part in their format. If the research was carried on through experimentation, interviews, or questionnaires, to the exclusion of any previously published material, there obviously would be no need for a bibliography. This, in fact, is the case with a large number of business reports. Even an index is not a necessity when the report is short and uncomplicated. In such a situation, the reader generally will be able to find a desired topic or item by making use of the table of contents.

There is a limit, of course, to how far we can go in eliminating parts from a formal report. As always, it should be our reader's need, not our own, upon which a final decision is based. In short formal reports, it is conceivable that only the following parts would be used.

1. Title Page.
2. Letter of Transmittal.
3. Table of Contents.

4. Summary.
5. Text.
6. Appendix (if necessary).

ILLUSTRATION OF A FORMAL REPORT

Although the general format of our formal report may be in tune with our reader's expectations, we still have a number of minute details to consider. These details lie at the level of mechanics wherein several acceptable methods may be possible. Basically it will not matter which choice we make; but having made a choice, we should stick with it consistently. For example, a page number at the top of a sheet may be either centered or situated at the right-hand margin. The main idea is that we adopt a consistent way of showing it on every page—not sometimes centered and sometimes at the margin.

In order to get a clear impression of the mechanics of the formal report, we shall examine an illustration and discuss its various features. This illustration is a report of "moderately short" length. It contains seven principal parts: title page, letter of transmittal, table of contents, summary, text, appendices, and index. Although the text is organized according to the introduction, body, and conclusion pattern, the illustration is shown to clarify mechanics. It is not offered as a model for everything concerning the formal report.

GENERAL APPROACH

Our rough draft of a formal report does not have to be prepared in any particular sequence except that the *text* should be composed before the *summary* (which is a digest of the text). At the typewriting stage, certain parts (such as the title page and the letter of transmittal) can still be prepared at any time. But some of the flexibility disappears with regard to other parts. Because they are in an arabic numbering series, the text, appendices, and index should be typewritten in that order. Perhaps the index will turn out to be the next-to-the-last part put into final form. On the other hand, the summary will begin on the page following the table of contents, in the lowercase Roman-numeral series. Yet, the table of contents cannot be finished until the starting points of all its component parts (in the typewritten version) have been determined.

One of the qualities we should build into our typewritten presentation is attractiveness or eye appeal. Fundamentally, we achieve this quality by always double-spacing in the preface, summary, and text sections, and by using good judgment in the layout of other sections. The regular page of the report should be centered on the exposed portion of the sheet with margins of 1 inch at the top and sides and a margin of 1½ inches at the bottom. Most of the time our formal report will be bound in a cover, with the binding at the left-hand side. This binding will obscure about 1 inch of the sheet. Any centering, therefore, will have to be made on the basis of a visible page only 7½ inches wide. If we were to type our report on the basis of the real center of the page, the result would appear to be left of center, with a narrow left-hand margin, when the report was placed in its cover.

Probably the simplest way to cope with this problem is to draw a backing sheet similar to the model shown on the following page. It has a panel which provides a border of 2 inches at the left, borders of 1 inch at the top and right, and a border of 1½ inches at the bottom. In addition, it has a vertical line which divides the panel in half, thus providing a guide for centering headings, subheadings, and illustrations. This sheet can be placed behind the bond paper on which our report page will be typed, and both can go into the typewriter together. The lines will be sufficiently visible to serve as guides for margins and for centering.

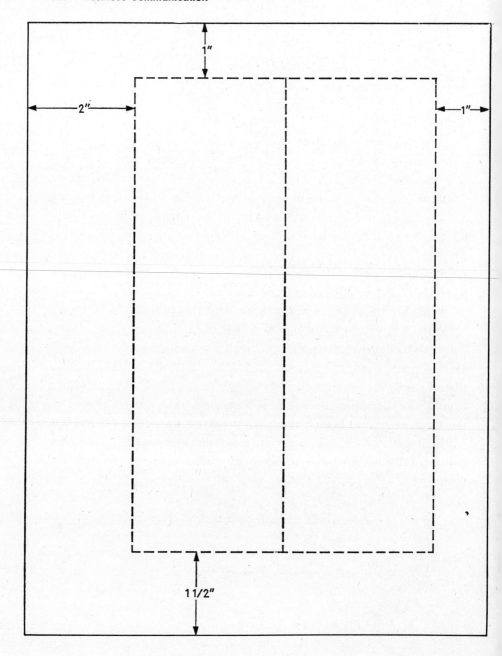

TITLE PAGE

The title page is the first page of the formal report. The information shown on the title page is divided into four parts: the title, the presentation, the authorship, and the date. These parts are centered and balanced (a guide would be the center line of the suggested backing sheet), and are separated by equal amounts of spacing.

The title is typed in capital letters; and if it requires more than one line, it is double-spaced and arranged in an inverted pyramid. The title should be conservatively, but attractively, phrased. If the outcome of the study involved is considered to be favorable to the reader, the title should preferably suggest that result. On the other hand, when the outcome is adverse to the reader or contrary to his leanings, it would be more diplomatic to suggest the method of approach in stating the title. We can see the difference in the examples given below:

Suggesting the results:

```
THE FAVORABLE REACTION OF CUSTOMERS
TOWARD THE PROPOSED RATE REVISION
```

Suggesting the method:

```
A SURVEY OF CUSTOMER OPINION CONCERNING
THE PROPOSED RATE REVISION
```

Our illustrative example begins with a title page set up in the manner shown on page 580.

BUSINESS ALUMNI COMPILE CREDITABLE RECORD

IN BUSINESS LEADERSHIP

Submitted to

MR. EDWARD P. HARRIS

Public Relations Director

Great Lakes University

by

Paul T. Winton

Alumni Secretary

Great Lakes University

January 10, 1968

LETTER OF TRANSMITTAL

This section follows the same general rules as those given for writing letters. Either block form or modified block form may be followed, and the customary personal tone (I–you language) is used. Complete heading, inside address, salutation, complimentary close, and signature block are included. If the letter is short, double-spacing may be used; for moderately long letters and two-page letters, single-spacing should be used.

Theoretically, letterhead stationery could be used for the letter of transmittal, although it complicates the job of centering. The printing is in a fixed position, probably centered. After binding, it will appear somewhat off to the left because of the inch of margin lost behind the cover. This lopsidedness could detract from an otherwise pleasing appearance.

When a typewritten heading is used, the only exceptions are these:

1. The heading often begins four lines below a page number, which is in the lowercase Roman-numeral series.
2. Regardless of length, the letter of transmittal has 1-inch margins, left and right, after it has been bound into the report cover.

Our illustration continues on page 582, with its version of a letter of transmittal.

19526 Gardenside Boulevard
Port Huron, Michigan 48247
January 10, 1968

Mr. Edward P. Harris
Public Relations Director
Great Lakes University
Port Huron, Michigan 48247

Dear Mr. Harris:

The alumni survey of the College of Business has been completed. This report presents a detailed account of the facts learned. Special emphasis was given to the numerical data and how these data depict the Great Lakes business graduate as a man on the move.

At your convenience, I shall be glad to discuss any parts of this report with you.

Yours very truly,

Paul T. Winton

Paul T. Winton

TABLE OF CONTENTS

The heading of this section is centered and typed entirely in capital letters, as follows:

TABLE OF CONTENTS

It is placed four lines below the page number, regardless of the length of the table. Each item of the table is identified by the number of the page on which that item begins. Leaders (alternate spaces and periods) extend from the end of each item in the direction of the page number, stopping short by a few spaces to allow for the building up of digits.

The portion referring to the text of the report (discussion and analysis) is subdivided into essential parts. The sequence of subdivision is handled in the following manner:

Roman numerals (uppercase)   I.
Letters of the alphabet (uppercase)   A.
Arabic numerals   1.
Letters of the alphabet (lowercase)   a.

The table of contents for our illustration appears on page 584.

SUMMARY

The last of the preliminary sections is the summary or synopsis. It contains a statement of purpose, whatever other information is considered necessary to familiarize the reader with the situation, and the conclusions or recommendations which are arrived at in the text of the report. If helpful, because of length or some other complication, subheadings may be used. Either the personal tone or the impersonal tone of writing may be used. The chief determining factors are the preference of the person to whom the report will be submitted and the matter of consistency—that is, using the same tone as that which was used in the text. In our illustration, impersonal tone and formal language style (no slang, no contractions) are used.

The heading of the first page of the summary is placed four lines below the page number, which is still in the Roman-numeral series. This heading is underlined, but only the first letter of the word is capitalized. The message begins four lines below the heading and is double-spaced (between the lines and also between the paragraphs). New paragraphs iii

TABLE OF CONTENTS

iv

Summary

In recent months, the Public Relations Department of Great Lakes University has had numerous requests for publicity data which would include facts about the alumni. Such information is needed for many purposes, including talks by officials of the university, development efforts in the local business community, placement activity, and student recruitment. The alumni records, however, have been of limited value in providing the necessary details. Not enough of these records are complete, up to date, or organized in a uniform manner.

As a possible solution to the problem of getting better information, the Alumni Office has agreed to canvass the alumni according to the different academic units within the university. It is the purpose of this report to discuss and analyze the information which was received during the third phase of the study, which concerned alumni of the College of Business.

Questionnaires were sent to all business graduates of record--the 20 classes from 1947 through 1966. The questions were neutral and general in order to eliminate any reference to personal information which might discourage a response. As a result, the survey proved to be very effective. Of 1190 questionnaires mailed out, 533 were returned--for a response of 44.8 percent. This return was better than those of earlier surveys made of the Law School and the College of Engineering.

Of the 533 alumni who responded, 497 were in regular employment.
Those in the armed services, in schools, and among the unemployed accounted
for only 36 persons. The number of unemployed was two--a mere 0.4 percent
of the persons responding. Of the 497 graduates in regular employment, 151
or 28.3 percent stated that they worked for national firms and organizations.
The federal government ranked first among 25 such employers; it has 29
business alumni on its payroll. It is interesting to note that of the 151 alumni
employed by these 25 national organizations, 97 persons or 66.9 percent have
received promotions. This fact shows the Great Lakes business graduate to be
a man on the move.

As for respondents working for other than the 25 major employers, 346
alumni accounted for 114 different occupational titles. Almost one fourth of
these titles denote some type of managerial position.

Bettering of oneself after graduation from college was clearly evidenced by the survey. Of the responding alumni, 143 or 26.8 percent hold
some kind of professional designation or license. Moreover, 84 respondents
or 15.7 percent pursued further education and earned a second degree. To
this number may be added 148 others who have taken graduate courses but
who have not yet earned a second degree.

In the final section of the questionnaire an optional, open-end question asked the commerce alumni to give their opinion on the matter of con=

⌐   ⌐
                                                                          vi

tinuing educational services available to the Great Lakes graduate. More

than half of the respondents, 52.9 percent, gave comments and suggestions.

Their statements indicate that the Great Lakes business graduate is constantly

looking for ways in which to better himself. In short, he looks to the future

for better positions by reason of continuing education and employment with

progressive firms.

L   ⌐

are indicated by indenting the first sentence. Good eye appeal is gained by making the indention ten spaces, although the use of five spaces is very popular.

TEXT

The main development of the formal report is known as the text. As with all regular compositions, it is basically organized according to the plan: introduction, body, conclusion. More specifically, however, these elements may be broken down into smaller segments, as follows: background information, purpose, methods used, findings, analyses, conclusions, recommendations.

The text begins the second series of page numbers, this series being in arabic numerals. The heading of this section is centered in what will be the *exposed portion* of the first page after binding. This heading is the title of the report, fully capitalized. The message begins four lines below the heading, is double-spaced both between sentence lines and between paragraphs, and contains subheadings to the extent that they will be useful to the reader. Such subheadings agree in wording with the subdivisions shown in the table of contents—but no numbers or letters are used to designate the various levels of importance. The first subheadings are centered in the same manner as the main heading. They are underlined, but only the first letter of each important word is capitalized. They are typed four lines below the previous text matter, and the new text matter is begun another four lines down. Thus, only by coincidence will a subheading appear at the top of a page. The following is a guide for presenting various levels of headings:

First-degree subheading

Introduction

Second-degree subheading

Methods Used

Third-degree subheading

Miscellaneous

Our illustration, using these principles, continues. It is written in both the impersonal tone and the formal style.

BUSINESS ALUMNI COMPILE CREDITABLE RECORD

IN BUSINESS LEADERSHIP

Need for Alumni Studies

Within the past year, a need has arisen at Great Lakes University for better, more current information on the alumni. The Public Relations Department has been besieged with requests for summaries of various facts involving alumni and their activities: How many alumni are there, identified by school or college of the university? Have they pursued studies beyond their basic college degree? How do they rate professionally? What kind of positions do they hold? Are they doing a good job? Who are their employers? What views do the alumni have regarding continuing education?

Such questions have been posed by numerous officials and departments of Great Lakes University. The answers are needed so that university representatives can talk knowledgeably about the alumni during speaking engagements, development and other fund-raising work, placement activities, and student recruitment.

Although the regular alumni records contain much helpful information, there are definite limitations. A large number of alumni have variously omitted segments of information, moved slowly to update the information they have on file, or allowed periodic inquiries to go unanswered. Moreover, a

2

lack of uniformity in the listing of information has made the work of compiling statistics difficult and time consuming.

By agreement with the Public Relations Department, the Alumni Office has begun a canvass of the alumni according to the various academic
units of the university. The plan is to cover one unit a month until the work
is done. In October and November, attention was given to the Law School
and the College of Engineering, respectively. These units, being relatively
new, have small numbers of alumni. Thus, the work involved in the initial
stages of the overall project was held to a minimum; and there was prompt
feedback by which to measure the effectiveness of the techniques being used.

In December, on the basis of experience gained, attention was turned
to the College of Business alumni. All business alumni of record--members
of the 20 senior classes from 1947 through 1966--were sent questionnaires on
their progress after graduation. It is the purpose of this report to discuss and
analyze the information which was received from this survey.

Survey Gets Results

The questionnaire was presented in a clear and concise manner. Most
of the questions were of an objective nature and were worded in a rather
general way in order to eliminate any reference to personal information. It

┌   ⌐3⌐

was felt that personal questions on such topics as salary, for example, might

cause a negative reaction and thus have an adverse effect on the number of

responses received.

The objective questions covered such matters as the name of one's em-

ployer, the position held, professional designation or license, and advanced

education. A single subjective question asked for an opinion on how Great

Lakes University could best continue educational services to its alumni. A

copy of this questionnaire is displayed in Appendix A.

The survey proved to be very effective. Of 1190 questionnaires mailed,

533 were returned with the three-week period provided. This is a response of

44.8 percent, the best obtained so far. Previous responses were: Law School

alumni, 33 percent; College of Engineering, 37.1 percent.

A rather even relative distribution of returns came from both local and

out-of-town alumni. Of the 711 graduates living in the Detroit area, 308 or

43.3 percent responded to the survey. Of the 477 graduates living outside

the Detroit area, 223 or 46.7 percent responded. Interesting, but of minor

importance, is the fact that the two alumni who happen to be living in foreign

countries responded within the time limit.

The following table shows the comparative figures for the mailing

pieces sent out, the number of questionnaires returned by the business alumni,

└and the response percentage obtained: ⌐

	TOTAL	LOCAL	OTHER U.S.A.	FOREIGN
Pieces Mailed	1190	711	479	2
Questionnaires Returned	533	308	223	2
Response Percentage	44.8	43.3	46.7	100.0

The pie chart below shows the proportionate share of the total response accounted for by each segment of the business alumni: local, other U.S.A., and foreign.

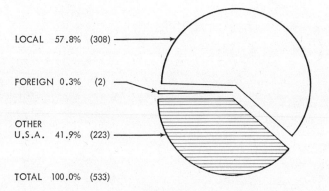

LOCAL   57.8%   (308)

FOREIGN 0.3%   (2)

OTHER
U.S.A.   41.9%   (223)

TOTAL   100.0%   (533)

51

Wealth of Information Received

Alumni Employment High

There do not seem to be any unusual patterns in the types of positions held by the business graduates of Great Lakes University. As might be expected, a large portion of the respondents (41.4 percent) work for general industry. As indicated in Appendix B, employment with accounting firms, marketing services (both wholesale and retail), and public administration is also popular. Also, significant employment is found in the transportation, insurance, and financial services. Out of the 533 alumni who responded to the survey, 497 persons hold regular employment. Other persons--who are in the armed services, in schools, or among the unemployed--are not considered to be in regular employment. There were only 36 alumni, or 6.8 percent of the total respondents, in this category.

A rather optimistic view of the employment potential of the business alumni is thus provided. The above-listed data show that 93.2 percent of the responding graduates are in regular employment. Most of the remainder-- those going to school and those serving in the armed services--will in all probability find some kind of employment when their schooling or service has ended. As a result, a truer measure of the employment situation might be 531 or 99.6 percent of the alumni who responded. Only two of the business alumni--a mere 0.4 percent--are clearly unemployed. No explanation as to the reason involved--such as injury, illness, or labor strife--has been received.

Prominent Employers Abound

The information gathered on the organizations who employ the business alumni shows that 25 major employers account for the employment of 151 graduates or 28.3 percent of those who participated in this survey. The United States government employs the largest number of these alumni; yet the total is only 29 individuals, or about 5.4 percent. Other organizations employing relatively large numbers of business graduates are General Electric Company, Ford Motor Company, and International Business Machines, Inc.

An examination of the names of the 25 major employers shows that 19 firms are large industrial and service organizations which add much to the national economic growth, and that 6 others are public accounting firms which have branches in the Detroit area. The remaining employer in this group is, of course, the United States government.

The general conclusion is that much of the business talent from Great Lakes University is being attracted toward large business organizations. Also, it may be seen that Great Lakes University is a large supplier of accounting personnel, especially to public accounting firms with offices in the Detroit

⌐   ¬

area and why so many of them work for these 25 employers.

Jobs Traceable to College Training

It would appear that the positions held by business alumni with the 25 major employers are consistent with the classroom training received by these persons while they were enrolled at Great Lakes University. Such positions lie in the areas of accounting, finance, management, marketing, and transportation. A certain number of the positions, of course, do not relate to business education; but they may have come about because of specialized training received after the person had graduated from college. Occupations in this category include those of engineer, instructor, and computer programmer.

Of the 151 alumni employed by the 25 major employers, 97 individuals or 66.9 percent are not occupying the same position as when they first started to work for their employer. This fact shows that the Great Lakes business graduate is on the move, and that the direction is toward newer and better positions. Additional optimism enters here, because many of the graduates who are included in the 66.9 percent are relatively new in their respective positions and have had neither the time nor the opportunity to move very far. Probably, if the 66.9 percent could be rated equally as to time and opportunity, the percentage of graduates who move upward would be even higher.   ⌐

└   ┘

Many Top Positions Held

The business alumni employed in other than the 25 major organizations numbered 346 persons, and they reported a total of 114 different job titles. At the top of the list were the occupations of attorney at law and corporation president, with 18 alumni holding each position. Other rather numerous positions were vice president, certified public accountant, salesman, and sales representative. There may be a degree of overlap between the designations salesman and sales representative; but the two positions were treated individually according to the answers received. In Appendix C, a chart is given containing the 22 most common positions held by alumni working for organizations other than the 25 major employers.

Also, Appendix C indicates that of the 204 alumni involved in these 22 positions, 56 individuals or 22.5 percent have a title which contains the word "manager" within it. Many others have titles which designate a high level of managerial responsibility, such as president, vice president, and treasurer. It is easily concluded that the Great Lakes business graduate is rather predominantly in a managerial position.

┌   9̄|

Many Professions Represented

Of the 533 responding alumni, 143 persons or 26.8 percent hold some type of professional designation or license. Appendix D discloses that 44 alumni are certified public accountants, 33 are members of the bar, 16 are registered public accountants, and 11 are licensed to practice before the Tax Court of Appeals. This table also shows a few unusual designations: a dentist and a licensed embalmer. Although these areas have no direct relationship to training in the College of Business, it does indicate that the persons involved remained flexible enough to change objectives.

Education Continues after College

After graduation from the College of Business, 84 persons or 15.7 percent of the responding alumni pursued further studies to the extent of earning a second degree. The following degrees occurred with the greatest frequency:

L.L.B.	34
M.B.A.	33
M.A.	9

Also, 148 additional alumni reported some amount of graduate work completed, but none of these has as yet earned a second degree.   ⌋

⌐   10̅|

Continuing Education Service Favored

In the final section of the questionnaire, a subjective question
called for the alumni to give their opinion on continuing educational
services for the Great Lakes graduate. Of those responding to the
survey, 52.9 percent answered this question. A summary of their answers
is presented in Appendix E. As may be noted, the answers were rated in
equivalent whole units. Each respondent to the question was allotted one
answering unit. If a given respondent gave two answers or opinions, each
was rated at half value. Similarly, if there were more than two opinions
given, each such answer was given its proportionate share of the respondent's answering unit.

Under this method of weighting, three suggested activities appeared to be the most popular forms for continuing education at Great
Lakes University. These were seminars, conferences, and the creation
of a graduate school of business administration. Other suggested educational services were special credit and noncredit courses, refresher courses,
and business publications. An alumnus serving in the Army suggested
refresher and summer programs, mentioning that they would be especially
helpful to men like himself who had been away from school for an extended
period of time. Another graduate suggested a set of condensed refresher   ⌐

courses, noting that many college graduates have only a limited amount of
time available for further study. Perhaps the most meaningful request was the
asking for creation of a graduate school of business administration at Great
Lakes University. In all, 56 individuals stated this request--indicating that
there is a substantial desire among the alumni to continue education through
a formal degree program.

Laudable Present--Bright Future

The College of Business alumni survey was the most successful of the
three studies thus far conducted at Great Lakes University.

From the data already analyzed, it can be concluded that the Great
Lakes business alumnus accounts for a very low rate of unemployment. Of
those graduates holding regular employment, a division is noticeable between
those who prefer to work their way up in a large organization and those who
prefer to assume a managerial capacity with a small organization. A heavy
concentration of alumni was found to exist within the bounds of 25 nationally
known employers. Other than the federal government, which is the largest
employer of business alumni, the employers were principally industrial enter-
prises or accounting firms. Of the graduates not included with the 25 major
employers, the top positions held were president, vice president, and treasurer.

12

The Great Lakes business graduate showed up as a man on the move.
He is increasingly meriting new positions at his place of employment. Also,
there is an emphasis on continuing education existing among the graduates.
Already, 84 alumni have earned a second degree, and 148 others have begun
graduate programs. Professional bettering of oneself is evidenced by the 143
alumni who have acquired some type of professional designation or license.
Further indication of positive thinking is seen in the opinions given on the
matter of continuing educational services.

In short, the Great Lakes business alumni are looking to the future for
better positions through continuing education and through employment with
progressive firms.

APPENDIX OR APPENDICES

An appendix is a section following the text of the report which contains information related to the discussion, but too cumbersome or extensive to be handled in the body of the report. Slightly different techniques are used for presentation, depending on whether one appendix or several appendices are used:

1. If there is but one appendix, the heading is placed four lines below the page number, which is the next arabic numeral in sequence. The heading is underlined and the first letter only is capitalized. The single word *Appendix* is used.
2. If there are several appendices, each is begun on a new page. Each heading is placed four lines below the page number and is underlined. With each appendix, a separate identifying letter is used: *Appendix A, Appendix B,* etc.

The method for handling each appendix will depend on the nature of the material involved. Charts, graphs, and tables should follow the conventional patterns; drawings, photostats, and photographs should be mounted on paper that corresponds in size to the other pages of the report; blueprints and maps should be mounted in such a manner that they can be folded neatly inside the report cover. Each appendix should be self-explanatory—that is, it should clearly inform the reader of its purpose and significance. Sources should be given for all compilations of data. If a physical document is used as an illustrative appendix, it should be introduced by a heading sheet placed in front of it.

The various appendices of our illustrative report may now be examined:

13

Appendix A

Copy of Questionnaire Used in Survey

GREAT LAKES UNIVERSITY
The Alumni Office
Port Huron, Michigan 48247

COLLEGE OF BUSINESS ALUMNI SURVEY

For Alumni
File of

Name of employer _____

Address of employer _____

City, State, ZIP _____

Your present position _____

Number of years   with this employer: _____ ; in this position: _____

Indicate the professional designations and licenses which you hold:

_____	Certified Public Accountant – State _____	Year _____
_____	Registered Public Accountant – State _____	Year _____
_____	Member of the Bar – State _____	Year _____
_____	Teaching Certificate – State _____	Year _____
_____	License to practice, Tax Court of Appeals – Year _____
_____	Chartered Life Underwriter – Year _____
_____	Chartered Property and Casualty Underwriter – Year _____
_____	Interstate Commerce Commission Practitioner – Year _____

Other (Specify): _____

Education received after graduation from Great Lakes University:
            Institution   Years Attended   Degree

_____   _____   _____

_____   _____   _____

_____   _____   _____

_____   _____   _____

In your judgment, how can Great Lakes University best serve its alumni in
the matter of continuing education? (Use back of page, if needed.)

⌐   15⌐

Appendix B

Employment Summary of Alumni

Type of Employment	Alumni	
Regular Employment		
Accounting Firms	49	
Advertising Services	4	
Attorneys at Law (In Practice)	18	
Educational Services	15	
Financial Services	22	
General Industrial Firms	221	
Health Services	8	
Insurance Services	27	
Marketing Services (Wholesale and Retail)	43	
Mining and Petroleum Industries	10	
Miscellaneous Employment	7	
Public Administration	35	
Public Utilities	10	
Real Estate Services	10	
Transportation Services	18	
Total in Regular Employment		497
Irregular Employment and Unemployed		
In U.S. Armed Services	26	
In Schools	8	
Unemployed	2	
Total Irregular and Unemployed		36
Total Responses		533

Source: College of Business Alumni Survey
         Great Lakes University

         December, 1967

L   ⌐

Appendix C

Top Positions Held by Alumni
(Smaller Employers Only)

Position	Alumni
Attorney at Law	18
President	18
Vice President	16
Certified Public Accountant	13
Salesman	13
Sales Representative	13
Treasurer	11
Manager	11
Controller	11
Accountant	10
Assistant Treasurer	9
Sales Manager	9
Registered Public Accountant	8
High-School Teacher	7
Branch Manager	7
Office Manager	6
Credit Manager	6
Manager of Accounting	6
Management Trainee	6
Internal Auditor	5
Auditor	5
Assistant Manager	5

Source: College of Business Alumni Survey
Great Lakes University

December, 1967

⌐   17⌐

Appendix D

Professional Designations and Licenses

Designations or Licenses Held	Number
Certified Public Accountant	44
Member of the Bar	33
Registered Public Accountant	16
License to Practice, Tax Court of Appeals	11
Holder of Teaching Certificate	8
Chartered Life Underwriter	5
Licensed Real Estate Broker	4
Holder of Insurance License	4
Holder of Securities Dealer's License	4
Licensed Real Estate Salesman	3
Chartered Property and Casualty Underwriter	2
Interstate Commerce Commission Practitioner	2
Licensed Embalmer	1
Holder of Counselor's Certificate	1
Notary Public	1
Registration, New York Stock Exchange	1
Licensed Securities Salesman	1
Dentist	1
Licensed Securities Trader	1
Total	143

Source: College of Business Alumni Survey
         Great Lakes University

December, 1967

∟   ⌐

Appendix E

Summary of Opinions on Continuing Educational Services

Type of Service Suggested	Answer Equivalents	
Seminars	77.0	
Creation of Graduate School of		
Business Administration	56.0	
Conferences	46.0	
Credit Courses	24.5	
Refresher Courses	21.5	
Publications on Current Business Topics	21.5	
Noncredit Courses	20.0	
Correspondence Courses	8.0	
Summer Programs	5.0	
Extension Courses	2.5	
Total Answers to the Question	282.0	52.9%
No Comment	251	47.1%
Total Questionnaires Returned	533	100.0%

Source: College of Business Alumni Survey
Great Lakes University

December, 1967

INDEX

The index is an alphabetical list of names, publications, topics, and subtopics used in the text of the report, together with the numbers of the pages on which they appear. Such a section is often used to round out a lengthy formal report, but it is omitted from shorter formal reports. The main reasons for its omission are:

1. The index cannot be made until the rest of the report is finished, but takes time to prepare. Often, a prompt report without an index is preferable to a late report with an index.
2. The work of indexing requires a degree of skill which many report writers have not developed. An extremely shallow or disorganized index would not be of much value to the reader.
3. When the report is short, the table of contents may serve the reader sufficiently well in his finding of desired information.

In preparing an index for a formal report, we may use cards or slips of paper. On each such form we set up a heading for the item to be indexed. Beneath this heading we make a record of the pages on which the item appears. When all significant items have been accounted for, we can place the cards or slips in final alphabetical order and use them as our source of information for the index.

The index for our illustrative report is shown on the following page.

┌   19⌐

Index

-A-

Alumni

   College of Business, 2, 8-11

   College of Engineering, 3

   Law School, 3

Alumni Office, 2

Alumni records, 1

Attorney at Law, 8

-C-

Canvass, 2

Certified Public Accountant, 8

Classroom training, 7

College of Business, 2, 11

College of Engineering, 2

Continuing education, 9-10, 18

Corporation president, 8

-D-

Degrees, additional, 9

Detroit area, 3, 6-7   ⌐

20

SUMMARY

• • • • • • • • •

Formal reports differ from other types of business reports chiefly in the area of physical presentation. The various informal report types are designed according to the circumstances existing under a given situation. Formal reports, however, follow a traditional, prescribed organization—which lets the reader anticipate where a certain section of the report will occur, even though he has yet to read it.

Other than this physical aspect, formal reports are much the same as other business reports. They may be informational or analytical. If analytical, they may simply interpret data or they may go on to a recommendation. They can be written in either personal or impersonal tone, and in either formal or informal style.

A formal report is composed of three main groups of elements. These groups, including their respective components, are as follows:

1. Preliminary Sections.
    Title page.
    Letter of authorization.
    Letter of transmittal.
    Preface.
    Table of contents.
    List of illustrations.
    Summary.

2. Report Proper.
    Text (introduction, body, conclusion).

3. Supplementary Sections.
    Appendix or Appendices.
    Bibliography.
    Index.

Two series of numbers are used for paginating a formal report. Lowercase Roman numerals are used in the preliminary sections; arabic numerals are used for the remaining pages. Each part of the formal report has its own incidentals of form. In cases of doubt, we can serve our reader best by handling repetitive matters consistently.

QUESTIONS
· · · · · · · · · ·

1. What is the general description of a *formal report?*
2. Discuss the practical indicators which help a writer decide when to use the formal-report approach and how to choose among incidental variables.
3. List the parts contained in a relatively long formal report.
4. What essential information is shown on the title page of a formal report?
5. What is the theme message of the letter of transmittal in a formal report?
6. In general, what matters are contained in the summary section of a formal report?
7. What are the possible functions of the *conclusion* portion of the body of a formal report?
8. Diagram the flow of thought in the body of an uncomplicated formal report.
9. Diagram the flow of thought which might be expected in a formal report analyzing responses to a five-point questionnaire.
10. Name the five or six elements which might be adequate for a rather short formal report.
11. State the general preference concerning the titling of a formal business report.
12. Describe the numerical-alphabetical system of classifying the various portions of the table of contents of a formal report.
13. What are *leaders?*
14. Give the similarities and differences that exist with regard to the items shown in the table of contents and the headings shown in the pages of the report proper.
15. Explain how an independent physical document may be put to use as an appendix in a formal report.

PROBLEMS
· · · · · · · · · ·

18–1. Rearrange the following items into a logical sequence for use as a program (working outline) for a formal report. Assign appropriate roman numerals, letters, and arabic numerals to designate the different degrees of importance.

Introduction
  Purpose of the Study
  Background Information
Outlook for the Future
Discussion and Analysis

Interpretation of Answers
Questions Posed
    Ownership of Color Television Set
    Color Brand Liked Best
    General Reaction to Color Television
    Ownership of Conventional Television Set
    Brand of Conventional Set Owned (if any)
    Conventional Brand Liked Best
Methods Used
    Supplementary Telephoning
    Personal Interviews

18-2. Suppose that an associate of yours has made a survey of 100 industrial organizations concerning the mandatory retirement age that each firm imposes on its workers. He has received completed questionnaires from 62 of the firms. A study of the answers shows that the average retirement age is 66, the actual range extending from 65 to 70. All responding firms have some kind of pension plan for their retirees. Also, 23 firms provide hospitalization benefits and a nominal amount of group life insurance. It can be concluded that older workers in general face mandatory retirement, but can look forward to some financial assistance through a pension arrangement. It could be recommended, however, that a greater number of the firms consider extending fringe benefits to their retirees.

Your friend intends to submit a formal report on this subject to the local management society. He has asked for your opinions regarding the title of his report and the various headings and subheadings to be used in the text. The following is his tentative list.

Title:

A STUDY OF MANDATORY RETIREMENT
FOR INDUSTRIAL WORKERS

Headings and Subheadings:

Purpose of Study
Methodology
    Number of Questionnaires
    Number of Responses
Points Considered
    Range of Retirement Ages
    Average Retirement Age
    Pension Arrangements
    Other Retirement Benefits
Conclusions
Recommendation

Rewrite the title, headings, and subheadings in a way that will be more informative and interesting.

18–3. Suppose that you have prepared a formal report on the subject, "New Trends in Banking Services." Write an appropriate letter of transmittal, addressed to the president of the local chamber of commerce. In your letter, give recognition to the fact that your research activities brought you into contact with a number of the leading bankers in your community. Mention also that you had the opportunity to witness various banking activities which go on behind the scenes. Make certain, of course, that your message retains all the necessary features of a customary letter of transmittal.

18–4. Gather information on price and on the features available in comparable two-door station wagons manufactured by Chevrolet, Ford, Plymouth, and Rambler. Your sources may include advertisements appearing in newspapers and magazines, brochures on these makes, consultations with dealers and salesmen, etc. On the assumption that you are the purchasing director for the Taylor Carpeting Company, write a formal report to Mr. Ross W. Taylor, the president of the firm. Include your recommendation of the best choice of station wagon, which is to be used on business errands by the top executives of the company. NOTE: Check with your instructor for any specific directions he may want you to follow.

18–5. Under directions issued by your instructor (e.g., he may suggest a group effort on the research portion of the project), write him a formal report containing conclusions arrived at as a result of following the procedure outlined below:

(a) Prepare a request letter to accompany a questionnaire. Use block form, but position the inside address in a way that will permit the use of a window envelope. Ask the reader to answer and return the questionnaire within a certain time limit. Provide a stamped return envelope.

(b) Design a questionnaire that will remain self-explanatory, even if it should become separated from your letter. Ask five objective questions which relate to the covering letter—such as the placement of the date, blocking of the paragraphs, width of margins, etc. Ask a final, subjective question which will allow the reader to comment on anything not covered by the objective questions.

(c) If possible, have the letter and questionnaire run off in quantity. In any case, mail out as many as suggested by your instructor; ask his advice on a mailing list.

(d) At the end of your established time limit, use the information received as the material for your report.

The undisclosed purpose of your study will be to test reaction to the window envelope, without enticing your readers to take sides.

18–6. By consulting sources on your campus (such as the admissions office, registrar's office, dean's office, etc.), compile a list of enrollment figures for entering freshmen applicable to the past 10 years. Determine the average change per annum. Then, project a trend into the future so that you can estimate the size of the freshman enrollment five years from now. The purpose of this forecast supposedly is to alert campus officials as to the planning needed between now and then. Write a formal report to your instructor. Include a statement of purpose, research methods used, facts learned, interpretations, and whatever conclusions or recommendations seem to be indicated. Use a histogram to lend visual acuity to the actual enrollment data for the past 10 years. Check with your instructor for any additional requirements.

18–7. Prepare a questionnaire, and have it run off in quantity, if possible. The following questions are suggested:

(a) Do you smoke cigarettes?

(b) If so, what is your usual brand?

(c) What is the name of the manufacturer of this brand? (Please answer from memory only.)

(d) List as many cigarette brands as possible beneath the names of their respective manufacturers, as follows:
American Tobacco Co.
Brown & Williamson Tobacco Co.
Liggett & Meyers Tobacco Co.
P. Lorillard & Co.
Phillip Morris, Inc.
R. J. Reynolds Tobacco Co.

Use these questionnaires during personal interviews with a representative cross section of adults, the number to be suggested by your instructor.

Write a formal report to your instructor. In addition to a direct analysis of the answers received from your research, draw a conclusion about a manufacturer's potential risk of "guilt by association." For example, if one brand of a company's line were to be condemned as a positive cause of lung cancer, might that company's other brands be boycotted by smokers?

NOTE: Check with your instructor for any specific directions he may wish you to follow.

18–8. (For students enrolled in a coeducational college or university.) By consulting sources on your campus (such as the admissions office, registrar's office, dean's office, etc.), compile lists of enrollment figures for men students and women students applicable to the past 10 years. Prepare a comparative line graph showing both series of data. Observe the behavior of the two lines, and look for any trend that may be developing. Determine whether the movement (if any) indicates a narrowing or widening of the gap during the next five years. Such a forecast could help campus officials plan for specific types of facilities needed for each component of the enrollment. Write a formal report on this subject to your instructor, after checking with him for exact requirements.

18-9. Have a quantity of the following brief questionnaire run off by some duplicating process.

---

1. Exclusive of any keepsakes, or pocket pieces, how many subsidiary coins of each current denomination are you carrying in your pocket or purse? (Please indicate numbers below.)

Half Dollar	Quarter	Dime	Nickel	Cent
_____	_____	_____	_____	_____

2. Which (if any) of the current denominations of subsidiary coins do you believe could be discontinued?

_____

As the first step in a research project, use these questionnaires during interviews with persons of both sexes and a general cross section of age groups. Then, inspect a number of coin-operated devices (such as telephones, vending machines, washing machines, parking meters, etc.) to ascertain which denominations of coins are really needed to activate them.

Write a formal report to your instructor. In addition to analyses of your gathered data, report on the typical composition and average amount of the change carried by a person. Include a final recommendation concerning the practicality of eliminating one or more of the present denominations of subsidiary coins.

NOTE: Check with your instructor for any additional details he may want you to consider.

18-10. Suppose that you are drawing up a syllabus for a course in business communication, which you will be teaching for the first time next semester. Using the facilities of your campus library, prepare a list of outside readings selected from journals and periodicals published during the past five years. Write a formal report to the chairman of your department. State a case for the value of such a list, and give the reasons behind the particular articles you have chosen. Recommend that the entire list (presented in an appendix) be approved for required reading.

18–11. (For students attending a college or university which has an evening division.) By consulting sources on your campus (such as the admissions office, registrar's office, dean's office, etc.), compile lists of enrollment figures for day students and evening students applicable to the past 10 years. Prepare a comparative line graph showing both series of data. Observe the behavior of the two lines, and look for any trend that may be developing. Determine whether the movement (if any) indicates a narrowing or widening of the gap during the next five years. Such a forecast may be helpful to campus officials in planning for specific types of facilities needed to accommodate both day and evening students. Write a formal report to your instructor, in accordance with his directions.

18–12. Following directions issued by your instructor (e.g., he may want you to conduct the research portion of this project as a team effort with two or more other students), write him a formal report on the study described below:

(a) Select at least nine hours of prime television time for the purpose of making a viewing analysis. If there are several television channels operating in your area, be sure that at least two hours are allotted to each channel.

(b) Design a work sheet (or sheets) upon which you will be able to make notations on the commercials which will appear during the viewing time you have selected. Provide for three kinds of information: length of time taken by the commercial, good or bad taste of the presentation, validity of any proof offered to substantiate an assertion. (In a team effort, each student could be assigned to cover one of these aspects exclusively.)

(c) After the observations have been made, analyze your notations to determine the number of commercials seen, the total time consumed by them, their average length, the ratio of commercial time to program time, the number and types of bad-taste presentations, and the number and types of inconclusive proofs.

(d) Draw a logical conclusion from the facts as you have analyzed them.

18–13. Under directions issued by your instructor (e.g., he may decide that the research portion of this project should be a joint effort of the entire class), write him a formal report on the study described below:

(a) Design a questionnaire which will call for the following points:

1. If both pieces of mail did not reach you on the same day, which one came in first—the metered mail or the stamped mail?
2. What was the interval (if any) between the arrival of the two pieces?
3. What was the date shown on the metered mail?
4. What was the cancellation date of the stamped mail?
5. In your opinion, which type of mail appears more impressive—metered or stamped?
6. In opening mail, are you inclined to give priority to either metered or stamped letters; if so, which?
7. Which of the two pieces of mail did you open first in this case?
8. What additional comments do you have concerning these two methods of posting mail?

(b) Prepare a request-type letter, asking the reader to complete and return the questionnaire. Explain that this is the first of two identical letters sent to him. One letter will be sent with metered postage and will contain a questionnaire. The other will be sent with regular postage and will contain a stamped return envelope. The purpose is to help you find out whether the kind of postage has any bearing on the speed of delivery and/or the attention commanded by the mailing piece in the hands of the recipient.

(c) Have the questionnaire and the letter run off in quantity by some duplicating process.

(d) Check with your instructor for suggestions on compiling a suitable mailing list and for any specific directions he may want you to follow.

(e) When your returns are in, tabulate the answers to questions 1 through 7. Also, analyze the subjective answers (if any) given to question 8.

18-14. (For students attending a university which has a graduate school.) Consult campus sources (such as the admissions office, registrar's office, dean's office, etc.) to learn the numbers of undergraduate and graduate students enrolled during the past 10 years. Construct a comparative line graph showing both series of data. Note the behavior of the two lines, and look for any trend that may be taking shape. Determine whether the movement (if any) indicates a narrowing or widening of the gap during the next five years. Such a forecast could help campus officials recruit a sufficient number of qualified faculty members to teach both the undergraduate and graduate courses needed at that time. Write a formal report to your instructor, in accordance with his pertinent directions.

18–15. Assume that you are a graduate assistant, assigned to any one of the following departments: accounting, finance, management, or marketing. The chairman of that department is interested in establishing a special self-study course to be offered to undergraduate seniors. His planned format for such a course is to issue an extensive list of required readings. Enrollees in the course would cover a definite number of these readings each week, and report orally once a month to a faculty coordinator. A term paper would be required, and a final examination would be given at the end of the semester or quarter.

You have been assigned the task of compiling the list of readings. Using the facilities of your campus library, prepare such a list by selecting significant material from reference books, professional journals, business magazines, and other publications. Write a formal report to the department chairman, and state reasons for choosing the articles you have listed. Recommend that the entire list (presented in an appendix) be approved for the self-study course.

18–16. Under directions issued by your instructor (e.g., he may suggest that a group effort be used for the research portion of this project), write him a formal report on the study described below:

(a) Design three simple work sheets on which you can list three general classes of coin-operated devices: PRODUCTS FOR CONSUMPTION (beverages, candy, cookies, etc).; SERVICES (washing machines, juke boxes, stamps, etc.); and MERCHANDISE (cigars, cigarettes, postcards, detergents, etc.).

(b) Do a thorough job of checking the situation with regard to coin-operated devices in your community. Visit a good cross section of supermarkets, filling stations, drug stores, restaurants, amusement centers, travel terminals, self-service laundries, and the like.

(c) Analyze your three lists to determine the extensiveness of coin-operated devices in present-day living and to see whether one of the three areas predominates the field.

(d) Reexamine the facts you have gathered in an attempt to find some applications of coin-operated devices which, as yet, seemingly have been untried.

(e) On the basis of what you have learned through this study, comment on the future outlook for the coin-operated industry.

18–17. Pick a topic from the following list, research it, and then write a formal report to your instructor in accordance with specific directions laid down by him.

(a) *Grade Labeling* (Does it make any impression on the buyer?)

(b) *Drive-in Post Offices* (Is there a need for them in our present-day way of life?)

(c) *Junk Mail* (What do people think about it, and what can be done to control it?)

(d) *Shabby Packages* (Do consumers buy packaged or canned food on the basis of external appearance of the container?)

(e) *Truth in Packaging* (What are the facts about allegedly misleading packages; is there justification for government intervention to protect the consumer?)

(f) *Television in Education* (How extensive and how effective is the use of closed-circuit television in today's schools?)

(g) *Discount Stores* (Are any trends noticeable in the service and/or quality of merchandise being sold through discount stores?)

(h) *Hospitalization Rates* (What are the factors causing the continual increase in the rates charged by Blue Cross and other cooperative hospital plans?)

(i) *National Debt* (What might be inferred from a comparison of the figures for the national debt, GNP, and population figures for 1945, 1950, 1955, 1960, and 1965?)

(j) *Market Research* (What recommendation will you make following a simulated market-research study performed on two possible locations for a variety store?)

PART V
· · · · · · · · · · · · · · · · · · ·

SUPPLEMENTS

Presented in this final section are three special supplements aimed at assisting the user of this book. Some of the information contained in these parts can be found among the regular chapters, but much of it is new or expansive in nature. In any event, various guides, rules, and suggestions have been assembled under appropriate headings.

In Chapter 19 we have a general language review. Aspects of language mechanics dealing with words, grammatical usage, sentence structure, and punctuation are discussed and demonstrated. Conventional terms are used in designating topics and subtopics.

Chapter 20 presents a special aid useful both to the dictator of a business letter or report and to the typist. It deals with stenographic matters—the problems to be solved in getting the final document in acceptable typewritten form.

Chapter 21 provides a unified, alphabetical, easy-to-use listing of the significant technical terms and phrases used in this textbook. Most of the time the terminology of this book coincides with that which is standard among practitioners of business communication. Whenever a difference occurs, it has been intended to achieve better logic or consistency. A newcomer to the field of written business communication should find his entrance made easier because of such improved terminology. Yet he will be fully in step with persons who already occupy this field. The listing of terms, or glossary, conveniently assembles concepts which are distributed here and there throughout the book.

....

CHAPTER 19

LANGUAGE
REVIEW

In written communication, business or personal, our message must be expressed by means of language. In essence, putting our thoughts into language is putting them into a transmittable code. To be effective in this step of the communication process, we must observe the following rules:

1. We must select a language, or code, which is common to us and our reader.

2. We must express, or encode, our thoughts in keeping with the generally accepted rules of that language.

3. If there are different choices or levels within the language selected, we should follow the one best suited to our reader's needs.

The second rule listed above deals specifically with accuracy of language in all its details: spelling and usage of words, grammar, sentence structure, and punctuation. Proper handling of these matters means technically correct encoding of our message. Of course, if several levels of reading difficulty are possible within the range of accuracy, we should choose the level that identifies with our reader.

In Chapter 4 we covered many of the highlights of language accuracy. There, we examined specific items as they might come to our attention during our composition work. In this chapter, we shall examine language accuracy from the viewpoint of important areas and terms within those areas. For example, *punctuation* in Chapter 4 was discussed in connection with what needs to be punctuated: a sentence, a clause, a phrase, etc. In this chapter, punctuation is discussed point by point: comma, semicolon, dash, etc. Thus, in a given situation, we should be able to refresh on a matter of punctuation regardless of how we happen to approach it.

WORDS

Our first consideration in the encoding of a message is that of choosing and handling the words we shall use. Words are the basic units of thought; on paper they are symbols by which we express a thought unit and from which our reader will extract a thought unit. Obviously, we need to have accuracy of spelling, usage, and form if we are to have a code which is easy to decipher. The following review is intended as a refresher on some of the important details concerning words.

ABBREVIATIONS

As a general rule, abbreviations are to be avoided. They tend to give the impression of haste, whereas our business writing should always seem cool, calm, deliberate—giving a full treatment, not a "once over lightly" treatment. There are, of course, some notable exceptions. Words like *Mr., Mrs., Dr., A.M., P.M.,* etc.—which are customarily abbreviated—would be included in this grouping of exceptions. But we should not abbreviate ordinary words just to save time or space. For further details, see Chapter 20.

CAPITALIZATION

Certain guidelines are available regarding the area of capitalization. Whenever we may exercise an option to capitalize or not capitalize, we should apply the rule of consistency. It would be confusing to our reader if, in a given document, we were to use different systems indiscriminately.

The rules of capitalization, for purposes of business communication, are summarized as follows:

1. We capitalize at the beginning of sentences and of direct quotations.

```
This sale will end tomorrow.
The manager said, "This sale will end tomorrow."
```

2. When items in a series are listed on separate lines, we capitalize the first word and put a period at the end for the sake of appearance, disregarding sentence structure.

```
The reasons for their delay in making payment to us are as
follows:
  1. Slow collections.
  2. Greater seriousness of other accounts.
  3. Irregularities in our latest shipment.
```

If the same series were given in running text, we would ordinarily enclose the numbers in parentheses and use commas and lowercase beginning letters.

```
The reasons for their delay in making payment to us are as
follows: (1) slow collections, (2) greater seriousness of
other accounts, and (3) irregularities in our latest ship-
ment.
```

3. We capitalize proper nouns—the names of person, places, and things. Within this area, there are specific matters of difficulty. Some of these are subject to style and taste, but general rules may be pointed out. Again, resorting to the punctuation section of a dictionary (Webster's, for example) will acquaint us with modern use and help to solve problems that arise.

   a) Titles. In book, magazine, and similar titles the major words are all capitalized; articles and prepositions are not, unless they are the first words in the titles. In referring to magazines or newspapers, within the text, *the* is usually not capitalized ("... in the *Herald Tribune* ...").

   Titles attributed to persons are usually capitalized only when they precede the name: President John Smith, etc. However, in the case of very high dignitaries, the title alone is usually capitalized when it refers to a specific person: the President (of the United States), the Pope, the Queen, the Prime Minister, etc. (But: ... kings and presidents are ...) In business use, we may prefer to adapt this rule to company policy, expected usage by the intended reader, or just personal preference; but we should avoid a policy which leads to an apparent and unsightly overuse of capitals.

   b) The names of specific departments, companies, institutions, organizations, governmental units, and the like are capitalized; but not a general reference to such a body. Ordinarily, for example, we would use the official title at first, but follow with lowercased second references (the Accounting Department . . . within the department. A meeting of the Committee on Safety . . . members of the committee.) In the case of governmental units, if this is a frequently encountered area, the Government Printing Office in Washington, D.C., publishes a *Style Manual* which is very helpful. As a matter of general usage, one does not capitalize *government, federal, state,* etc., unless they are used as the specific title (New York State).

c) We capitalize geographic areas when they are an integral part of a specific name (Biscayne Bay, Sun Valley, Niagara Falls) but not as a less specific reference (the Ohio and Missouri rivers, the California coast, the Sahara desert). Similarly, specific regions are capitalized (the South, the Midwest, the Western Hemisphere) but not references to a general direction (go due east, driving south).

d) A few other points: names of seasons are not capitalized unless they are personified (almost never in business use). Trademarks should be capitalized, and we may need to be aware of some that seem to be general words: Coke, Formica, Pliofilm, Kleenex. Words like Father and Mother are capitalized only if used as a name for a specific person: I saw Father . . . he is my father.

PRECISE USE OF WORDS

As mentioned in Chapter 4, we can communicate in a clear, decisive manner or we can do it in a blurry fashion. Part of the clarity we desire springs from selecting the precise word needed to convey a thought.

Ability—Capacity	A man has the *capacity* to receive knowledge and the *ability* to use it.
Almost	Never use *'most* or *most* for this adverb.
All right	Never use *alright.*
All-around	Is preferable to all-round.
Alternative—Choice	*Alternative* is a choice between two things only, strictly speaking.
Among—Between	*Among* refers to more than two things, while *between* refers to two only.
Anxious—Eager	*Anxious* implies concern, uneasiness. *Eager* implies desire, enthusiasm.
Apt—Likely—Liable	Formally, *apt* refers to a natural inclination and *likely* to simple probability or possibility. General good usage now tends to use the two inter-

changeably. *Liable,* however, retains its implication of being subject to something (usually something unpleasant) and should not be substituted for the other two terms.

As—Like	*As* is the preferable, and formal, conjunction in introducing a clause of comparison. However, *like* as a conjunction is used by some respectable writers, and may be considered a colloquial usage.
At your convenience	This expression is hackneyed and often superfluous. When a time element is important, indicate it naturally and specifically.
Awful	In formal usage, means awe-inspiring. *Awful* as an intensive, or meaning "very bad," is permissible in general use—but it is trite.
Badly	Do not use this to mean "very much."
Bank on—Take stock in	These slang expressions are poor usage.
Beg	*Beg* is not acceptable in business relationships.
Besides—Beside	*Besides* means in addition to; *beside,* at the side of, near by.
Both—Each	Use *both* for two considered jointly; *each* for one of two or more.
But	Never use "not but" in the sense of "only." Never use "but what" instead of "that."
Character—Reputation	A man's *character* is his real nature; his *reputation* is his supposed nature.
Continual—Continuous	*Continual* means prolonged repetition at intervals; *continuous,* without cessation.
Different from	Is preferred to *different than,* although the latter is permissible in constructions where it is obviously smoother.
Differ from—with	Person, things, and opinions differ *from* one another; persons differ *with* one another (argue).
Directly	Misused for "as soon as."
Disinterested—Uninterested	*Disinterested* means impartial; *uninterested,* apathetic.
Hanged—Hung	Only criminals are *hanged.* Pictures are *hung.*
Healthy—Healthful	*Healthy* means having health. *Healthful* means promoting health.
In—Into	Use *in* to express location (the place where); *into* to express motion from one place to another. Certain established phrases retain in when motion is indicated: fall in line, split in two, put in shape, and so on.

In re; re	These phrases are out of place in any letter. Use concerning or some other appropriate English equivalent.
Kind of—Sort of—Type of	*Kind of, sort of,* and *type of* should not be followed by *a* or *an.*
Last—Latest	*Last* means the final thing in a series. *Latest* means the most recent.
Leave—Let	*Leave* means abandon; *let* means allow.
Off of	Omit *of.*
Verbal—Oral	*Verbal* means in words; *oral,* by word of mouth.
Party—Person	*Party* as a substitute for "person" or "man" is a slang use.
Percent—Percentage	*Percent* is the form used when preceded by figures; otherwise, *percentage.*
Practical—Practicable	A workable plan is *practicable. Practical* is the opposite of theoretical.
Proposition—Proposal	A *proposition* is a specific proposal which stresses its advantageous nature.
Reason	The expression *the reason is* should be followed by *that,* not *because.*
Respectfully—Respectively	*Respectfully* means in a respectful manner. *Respectively* means in the order designated or as singly considered.
Same	This word is improperly used as a substitute for *it* or *they.*
Stop—Stay	To *stop* does not involve duration of time. Correct: We stopped when we saw his signal. Correct: We stayed in the car until help arrived.
Teach—Learn	*Teach* means to give instruction. *Learn* means to receive or assimilate instruction.
Till—Until	These words have the same meaning and use.
Up-to-date—Modern	These expressions are not interchangeable. Correct: Our records are up-to-date. Correct: Here is the up-to-date information. Correct: It is a city of modern buildings.
Where	*Where* is frequently misused for *that, in which.* Correct: I saw in your report that you recommend a new system.
Who—Which—That—What	*Who* refers to people. *Which* refers to things. *That* may refer to either people or things. *What* means *that which.*
Without	*Without* should not be used in the sense of *unless.* Correct: I told him not to do that unless he had obtained permission.

HOMOPHONES

By definition, homophones are words which are similar in pronunciation but different in meaning. Such words can cause misspellings and other confusion in a written communication, and they often lead to some humorous observations by the reader—at the expense of the writer.

Whether we write a rough draft of our message or dictate it for subsequent transcription, unexpected errors involving homophones can creep into our finished document. It pays us, therefore, to proofread carefully before we sign and release a communication. The following sets of homophones are some of the more troublesome along this line.

affect	all together	ascent	borne	capitol
effect	altogether	assent	born	capital
complement	confidant	council	discreet	its
compliment	confident	counsel	discrete	it's
principle	stationery	there	who's	you're
principal	stationary	their	whose	your

Besides the above, which many find difficult to distinguish in reading, the process of dictation introduces a great host of "sound alikes" which may be very easy to distinguish when we see them typed—which may not be true homophones—but which we are likely to *see* mistyped unless we are very careful in pronunciation and alert to the possible confusions. A few of the many possibilities follow.

accept	access	adapt	air	allowed
except	excess	adopt	err	aloud
		adept	heir	
ascent	attendance	bare	berth	billed
assent	attendants	bear	birth	build
brake	breech	buy	cell	cent
break	breach	bye	sell	sent
		by		scent
cereal	cite	coarse	dew	fair
serial	site	course	do	fare
	sight		due	

fate	feat	for	hail	hear
fète	feet	fore	hale	here
		four		
hole	hour	isle	knew	know
whole	our	aisle	new	no
lead	load	marry	mind	oar
led	lode	merry	mined	or
				ore
pair	patience	peace	peer	plain
pare	patients	piece	pier	plane
pole	precedence	presence	right	scene
poll	precedents	presents	rite	seen
steal	team	to	write	way
steel	teem	too	wares	weigh
		two	wears	

Then there are particularly troublesome areas in spelling. There are the words ending in the sound "sēd"; most of them end in "-cede," with exceptions such as proceed, exceed, succeed and supersede. We need to know when to drop the final *e* when adding suffixes—for example, that most final *e*'s are dropped before consonants (judgment, acknowledgment) but most final *ce*'s and *ge*'s retain the vowel before another vowel, to keep the "soft" sound of *c* and *g* (peaceable, knowledgeable). Is the final consonant doubled? In modern usage, many that may be single or double are preferably left single (canceled, totaled, traveled). Is the correct suffix *-able* or *-ible? -ance* or *-ence?* Is the correct plural *-os* or *-oes?* In brief, we will find a dictionary an indispensable tool of correct writing.

GRAMMAR

After choosing the words which will properly encode our thought units, we turn our attention to putting them into message units, or sentences. In so doing, we encounter some additional areas of language. One of these, grammar, has to do with the relation of words to each other—such as agreement of subject and verb, agreement of pronoun and antecedent, proper tenses, cases, idioms, and so on. The following review highlights the more important matters in this area.

Adjective—Adverb

1. An adjective is a descriptive word; it is used to modify a noun.

   This is a profitable investment.

2. An adverb adjusts a description; it is used to modify a verb, an adjective, or another adverb.

   Our funds are invested profitably.

   This is a very profitable investment.

Agreement of Case and Number

1. A singular subject takes a singular verb.

   Mr. Brown is the sole owner of the business.

   The president, as well as the production manager, is in favor of the plan.

2. A plural subject takes a plural verb, as does a compound subject.

   Both trucks are ready to be loaded.

   The sales manager and his assistant are attending a conference in Chicago.

3. A collective noun may be used as a singular or a plural, depending upon whether the word refers to the unit or to the various members of the unit.

   The committee is in the conference room.

   The board are talking informally while refreshments are being served.

4. Pronouns used as objects are placed in the objective case.

   We paid him in full.

   He issued us a receipt.

   They did not want her in the room.

   He will give you an answer tomorrow.

   He will give it to you tomorrow.

5. A pronoun should have a definite noun antecedent, and it should agree with that antecedent in number, gender, and person.

    ```
    Here are the cost figures; they are based on present
    prices.

    The attached memorandum is urgent; please read it at once.
    ```

6. When a collective noun is used, both the verb and any pronoun relating to the collective noun should be in agreement.

    ```
    Maston's is making this offer to all its regular customers.

    Maston's are making this offer to all their regular cus-
    tomers.
    ```

7. When a clause is introduced by the relative pronouns *who* and *whom,* the case is governed by role (subject or object) played by the pronoun.

    ```
    Notify those who you think will be interested.

    Notify whoever is available.

    Notify whomever you meet.
    ```

8. Words which are singular in concept—such as *each, every, everybody, everyone, either,* and *neither*—take singular verbs when they are used as subjects.

    ```
    Each of the applicants was interviewed.

    Everyone knows that the regulation is unfair.

    Either site is suitable for our new building.

    Neither is able to keep up his payments.
    ```

9. When *either* is coupled with *or* in a subject (also, *neither* with *nor*), the number of the verb agrees with the portion of the subject that is nearer the verb.

    ```
    Either Evans or Smith will be promoted.

    Neither the motor nor the housing appears to be damaged.

    Neither the carton nor the cans were missing.

    Neither the cans nor the carton was missing.
    ```

10. The words *all, none, some, any, most,* are types of collective pronouns, and follow this rule: if they refer to a singular or bulk concept, they take a singular verb; if they refer to a plural concept, they take a plural verb.

```
All of the workers are on the job.

Some of the work is done.

None of the packages have been mailed.

None of the merchandise has been sent out.
```

11. The possessive case of a pronoun should agree in number (singular or plural) with its antecedent.

```
My secretary has already finished her work.

The repairmen forgot their tools.

Each person's time is listed on his own card.
```

12. A pronoun used in a sentence which contains more than one noun should refer unmistakably to its antecedent. Otherwise, the reader may be confronted with an ambiguous reference.

```
The manager explained the pricing system to the clerk,
and showed him how to compute the sales tax.
```

Articles

We have three articles in English: the indefinite articles *a* and *an,* and the definite article *the. A* is used with a word that begins with a sounded consonant or with the vowel *u* when it carries the sound of "you." *An* is used with a word that begins with a silent consonant followed by a vowel (e.g., heir, hour), or a word that begins with a vowel (*a, e, i,* and *o,* as well as the vowel *u* when it carries the sound of "uh").

```
Your office is a good place to work.

This is an active stock.

We have been waiting for an hour.

It is not a universal condition.

They have given us an ultimatum.

The accounting department is short of help.
```

Idioms

Custom or usage, rather than formal language rules, sometimes governs the formation of a message unit. We should be alert to use the regularly accepted way, even though another way could be technically justified.

1. One area of idiomatic usage concerns the use of an infinitive or a gerund phrase with certain words.

   ```
   It is possible to get a discount on the price.

   There is a possibility of getting a discount on the price.

   He believes that trading stamps would aid in promoting
   business.

   He believes that trading stamps would help to promote busi-
   ness.
   ```

2. Another area concerns the preposition to be used for giving an intended slant to a prepositional phrase.

   ```
   We advertise in magazines throughout the country.

   Last year we advertised on radio.
   ```

3. In some cases, the choice is between the use of two prepositional phrases and the use of one preposition with a compound object. If we use two idiomatic expressions of exactly the same form, we need only one preposition; but if we use two different idioms, we must express both prepositions.

   ```
   We advertised in magazines and newspapers.   (compound object)

   We advertised in magazines and on radio.     (two phrases)
   ```

Perfect Infinitive

The perfect infinitive of a verb (e.g., *to have served*) is used only when the action it expresses happened before the action expressed by the main verb of the sentence.

```
We are glad to have served you in this manner.
```

Perfect Participle

The same rule holds for the perfect participle of a verb (e.g. *having completed, having been completed*). It should be used only when the action it expresses happened before the action expressed by the main verb of the sentence.

```
Having completed his talk, the attorney left the room.

Our deadline has been met, the final units having been com-
pleted yesterday.
```

Mood

Our regular manner of discourse is carried on in the indicative mood. When we state a supposition that is contrary to fact, we use the subjunctive mood. That is not to say, however, that every supposition is to be considered contrary to fact. The subjunctive mood is also used to indicate a polite "demand" or request, and a wish or hope.

```
If I were you, I would consult a lawyer. (Contrary to fact.)

If he was at the meeting, I did not see him.
(Not necessarily contrary to fact—possibly, he was there.)

Our concern is that our candidate be elected.
```

Shall–Will; Should–Would

Usage concerning these auxiliary verbs has been an area engendering more controversy than perhaps any other. Fortunately, in the field of business writing, we need to know only the highlights of the debate.

One usage indicates that "shall" denotes simple futurity in the first person, and denotes some sort of compulsion in the second and third persons. On the other hand, "will" in the first person indicates determination or volition; in the second and third person, simple futurity.

```
I shall go there tomorrow.

I will do it at all costs.

Curfew shall not ring tonight!
```

Other distinctions and special usages flowed from these premises; anyone adhering to this system must follow them all to be considered correct.

It is useful to know about this simply because one encounters it in British-style publications; in very formal writing; or simply in the writing of those who were drilled in it while American schools were still attempting to inculcate it. When it is found, we should know the general meaning the writer intends to convey.

However, standard American usage in our day simply uses "will" as the auxiliary verb in all persons. Use of "shall" and "should" is confined only to the indication of obligation, or of uncertainty.

Since business writing should be on the general, standard level of good usage—leaning much more toward informality than formality—good practice will lead us to follow the simpler style. The formal use of "shall" and "should" in a business letter will not only tend to make it sound stuffy or stilted; but it will fail in the areas of encoding our precise meaning and of readability.

Voice

When the active voice is used, the action of the verb is *performed by* the subject of the sentence.

```
Terrence Smith works in our accounting department.
```

When the passive voice is used, the action of the verb is *applied to* the subject of the sentence.

```
The burglar was caught leaving the building.
```

There should not be a needless change of voice within a sentence; active voice, of course, is to be preferred.

```
When we reduced the price, we expected a reaction from our
local competitors.
```

SENTENCE STRUCTURE

Even though we have selected our words judiciously and have used them in proper relation to other words in a sentence, we have a further matter to consider. This is the area of sentence structure, or syntax, which deals with how the various words, phrases, and clauses of a sentence are fitted into position. The important aspects of this area are discussed below.

MODIFIERS

1. An elliptical clause—that is, one in which some of the words are omitted—should refer to a definite noun or pronoun in the sentence. To do this, it must be positioned as near as possible to that word. Otherwise, it may appear to modify some other word and distort the meaning of the message involved.

```
Before making a decision, we will consider the alternatives.

While there, you should ask to see their plating process.
```

2. Modifying phrases which contain infinitive or participial constructions also follow this rule. They should be as near as possible to the word they modify. These phrases may occur at the beginning, in the middle, or at the end of sentences.

```
To hedge against possible losses, you should diversify your
investments.

The driver, believing his truck to be loaded, replaced the
tail gate.

Your postdated check will be held for five days before being
deposited.
```

3. Modifying words or word groups also belong as near as possible to the words they modify.

```
We have carefully examined the sample which you sent.

We deal in structural steel only.

They have finished almost all of their work.

Nearly all of the work is done.
```

4. Ordinarily, a word modifying an infinitive should be placed somewhere before or after the infinitive, not between the sign (*to*) and the verb form.

```
To wait patiently under those conditions was not easy.

I told him to pack the glassware carefully.
```

Sometimes, however, awkwardness can be avoided either by "splitting" the infinitive or by expressing the thought another way.

```
His policy was to never be conspicuous.

His policy was to remain inconspicuous.
```

PARALLEL CONSTRUCTION

When two or more concepts are joined in a series of some kind, all of the elements so joined should be expressed in the same grammatical form. This principle applies with equal force to series joined by conjunctions and to those joined by correlative conjunctions.

1. Examples using ordinary conjunctions are:

```
A tablet and a pencil were placed on each desk.  (nouns)

They specialize in making nuts, bolts, and washers.  (nouns)

Remove all the bent and broken pieces from the bin. (adjectives)

Please stamp and mail these letters.  (verbs)

When you enter, go quietly but confidently.  (adverbs)

He is in New York to attend the various style shows and to
buy a selection of dresses for our stock.  (infinitives)

Mr. Cardwell wanted to sign the papers today, and he was
waiting in his office for the lawyer to arrive.  (main clauses)

The Bactrian camel has two humps, the dromedary has one
hump, and the llama has no hump.  (main clauses)

He is a man who is able to come and who would be happy to
help.  (subordinate clauses)
```

2. Examples using correlative conjunctions are:

```
We learned that we could borrow the money from either a
bank or a loan company.  (nouns)

He is neither rich nor poor.  (adjectives)
```

```
They carry not only a full line of men's suits but also a
wide variety of shirts.  (noun phrases)
```

PUNCTUATION

In a sense, punctuation is a code within the overall code of language. Through punctuation, the writer is able to send signals to the reader to let him know when to pause, stop, imagine a rising inflection, and so on.

CHIEF MARKS OF PUNCTUATION

1. Comma. A relatively mild punctuation mark, the comma is used:

   a) Between the main clauses of a compound sentence which is of medium length and connected by *and, but, or,* or *nor,* and in which no other commas are used.

   ```
   Construction costs were high at the first location we
   checked, and labor shortages were acute at the second.

   There is a flaw in the veneer, but it is not a serious
   defect.
   ```

   b) After an introductory word, phrase, or clause appearing at the beginning of a sentence, except for short, closely connected words or phrases.

   ```
   Incidentally, these goods are on sale.

   In other words; they are planning to give us some stiff
   competition.

   Because the shipment was late, we could not hold the
   sale we had advertised.

   In some cases the rule does not apply.
   ```

   c) To set off nonrestrictive clauses and phrases.

   ```
   That particular drill, which was designed for softer
   materials, should not be used for masonry.

   Our newest clerk, who was hired yesterday, is doing
   well.
   ```

```
This sweater, marked down to $4.77, is an attractive
item.
```

(No punctuation is used with restrictive elements).

```
The man standing at the door is a customer.

The report which gives this data is now available.
```

d) Always, to set off a nonrestrictive clause in the inverted order (that is, in front of the main clause).

```
Because the shipment was late in arriving, we could not
hold the sale as planned.
```

e) To set off elements used in apposition, dates, and addresses.

```
John, my brother, went with me.

His check was dated January 10, 1967.

We met him in Austin, Texas, last year.
```

f) Provided they are nonrestrictive, to set off clauses introduced by *although* (*even though, though*) or using *for* (*as, since*) in place of *because*.

```
I believe that business is improving, although I may be
mistaken.

We decided to use plastic, since other materials were
in short supply.
```

g) To set off mildly parenthetical phrases and clauses, as well as various "asides" used in a sentence.

```
That price, of course, is for one week only.

Frankly, Mr. Brown, we are worried.

That, too, is an important consideration.

You will agree, we're sure, that all reasonable precau-
tions have been taken.
```

h) To separate the various elements in a series of three or more.

```
We ordered paper clips, pencils, and erasers.
```

```
Do not fold, staple, or tear this card.
```

i) To separate consecutive adjectives individually modifying a noun (or a term used as a noun).

```
He took a long, shiny object out of the box.

He used a short, blunt pocket knife.
```

2. Semicolon.   In general, a semicolon should be used only when a period (or other terminal punctuation) could have been used. Its main uses are:

a) To separate the main clauses of a compound sentence which is not joined by a conjunction.

```
Construction costs were high at the first location we
checked; labor shortages were acute at the second.
```

b) To separate the main clauses of a compound sentence when one clause is already broken up by commas, even though a conjunction is used.

```
Some days you feel that you will never be able to get
your work done; but, in spite of everything, you finish
exactly on schedule.

Burgess still had not paid his bill at the end of No-
vember; therefore, we decided to start proceedings
against him.
```

c) To separate the members of a series when one or more of the members contains a comma.

```
They have branches in Dayton, Ohio; Harrisburg, Penn-
sylvania; and Newark, New Jersey.
```

3. Sentence terminals.   Three marks of punctuation provide terminals for sentences. These are:

a) A period is used to indicate the end of an affirmative or declarative sentence.

```
I recommend that the New Haven site be purchased.
```

b) An interrogation mark is used to punctuate a question.

```
What do you suppose has been causing this shortage?
```

c) An exclamation point is used to punctuate a statement of unusual emotion or feeling (a brisk command, for example).

> Mail the card today!
>
> Congratulations on your promotion to the board!

MISCELLANEOUS MARKS OF PUNCTUATION

a) Apostrophe.   An apostrophe is used to mark the point of omission of letters in a contraction, the possessive case of a noun
(including various idioms), and the plural of letters or numbers
used as words.

> Your answer isn't important now.
>
> He was a member of the class of '65.
>
> Keith was the politicians' choice.
>
> This business comes within Jones's jurisdiction.
>
> We still had an hour's work ahead of us.
>
> It was Williams' turn to speak.
>
> The 1920's were called "the roaring twenties." (not '20's)
>
> He earned straight A's in college.

b) Colon.   The principal use of the colon is to introduce an enumeration or an explanation.

> His reasons for dieting were three, namely: (1) a dis-
> like of being teased by his associates, (2) a fear of
> high blood pressure, and (3) a desire to look trim.
>
> We want the complete outfit: the projector, the screen,
> and the extension cord.

It should be noted that the first word after a colon is regularly
not capitalized, whether or not it begins a new sentence, when
the following material is logically dependent on the preceding
material—which includes the great majority of cases. A capital
is used after a colon only when it introduces a new and inde-

pendent discussion, usually one which consists of several sentences.

c) Dash.   A dash is used to set off an element with special emphasis or clarity; to indicate an abrupt shift in mood or thought; to indicate a bridged construction; or to set off a summarizing or enumerating conclusion to the sentence.

> His boss—a Scrooge if I ever saw one—sat behind an
> ancient desk.
>
> We had planned to—well, perhaps we'd better not go
> into that.
>
> We want the complete outfit—the projector, the screen,
> and the extension cord.

d) Hyphen.   One use for a hyphen is to show the division of a word at the end of a line (see Chapter 20, "Hyphen"). Other uses are to form compound nouns and verbs, and compound adjectives (preceding the word modified, usually). In cases of doubt, consult dictionary listings.

> The older man is his father-in-law.
>
> Double-space within this letter.
>
> He is a well-known man in our city.
>
> He is well known.   (following adjective)
>
> I own a one-fourth interest in the business.
>
> One fourth of the responses were positive.   (noun)
>
> The electrician suffered first- and second-degree burns.
>
> We placed a person-to-person call to Mr. Walsh in At-
> lanta.

e) Parentheses are used to enclose remarks, clarifications, references, and instructions for the reader.

> The present situation (hopeless, I'd say!) did not come
> about by itself.
>
> His birthplace (Vincennes, Indiana) is steeped in Ameri-
> can history.

> Our sales for the second year have virtually doubled
> (see Appendix B).

f) Quotation Marks.   These are used for direct quotation. Sometimes it is necessary for us to indicate the use of a coined word, a
slang expression, an unusual term or meaning. In these instances,
we also make use of quotation marks. We should take care not
to overdo this, however; if a word is correctly used, do not
apologize for it by using quotation marks.

> "Finesse" is an overall word for such intangible qual-
> ities as politeness, courtesy, tact, friendliness, help-
> fulness, and positiveness.

> He was made the "fall guy" of every scheme.

> "Who wrote this letter?" the office manager asked.

> "If you don't hurry," he said, "you will miss the
> train."

> "There is no such thing as teaching," he murmured;
> "there is only learning."

QUESTIONS
· · · · · · · · · ·

1. Give the general rule for abbreviations in business writing.
2. State the principal rules governing capitalization.
3. If either of two words will actually communicate one's message, why
   should one be careful about choosing the word which is more precise in
   meaning?
4. What are *homophones?*
5. How does it happen that homophones tend to create problems for even
   a careful and competent business writer?
6. What specific aspects of language are governed by the rules of grammar?
7. How might the area of sentence structure be described?
8. Does punctuation exist only in written language?
9. Under what conditions may commas be used to punctuate the ends of
   sentences?
10. Other than at the end of a line, is it permissible to have a hyphen with
    nothing but spacing immediately after it?

EXERCISES
· · · · · · · · · ·

19–1. Type or write the following sentences, but be sure to use proper capitalization.

1. The Ambassador bridge connects Detroit, Michigan, with Windsor, Ontario.
2. We shall be driving East on Friday.
3. They do not seem to understand the significance of the constitution of the United States.
4. The South is undergoing a period of change.
5. Several New Products will be introduced during the summer.
6. He is a firm believer in the democratic way of life.
7. The middle-aged applicant was looking for a company that needed a purchasing agent.
8. "This sale," explained the clerk, "Will continue until Saturday."
9. Their wanderings took them to the brink of the grand canyon.
10. The rule may be stated as follows: Always space twice after completing a sentence.
11. Several firms have built new plants in the State of Ohio.
12. Miss Radcliffe, the company nurse, applied a bandaid to the typist's injured finger.
13. Let me give you this warning: don't drive through those hills at night.
14. The *Ariadne,* a luxury liner, departs weekly on cruises to the Caribbean sea.
15. He was able to get you a reservation on Midwest airlines.

19–2. Using the dictionary for reference rewrite the following sentences. Select the better choice of the words shown in parentheses.

1. The (above, foregoing) instruction applies to all of the sentences in this list.
2. We are (almost, most) ready to introduce our newest product.
3. Another (alternative, choice) would be to retrain some of our present workers.
4. The hospitals of a given community usually divide the various specialties (among, between) themselves.
5. They are (anxious, eager) to get the report on the storeroom fire.
6. Mrs. Wilson is (liable, likely) to be upset by this news.
7. We shipped two thirds of the parts this morning, and will send you the (balance, remainder) within one week.
8. Mail a catalogue to (both, each) of these prospective customers.

9. Their suburban store has a large parking lot for the convenience of their (customers, patrons).

10. The price was different (from, than) the one which had been advertised on television.

11. I think that the opposition should (leave, let) us state our case.

12. After much haggling, the bank finally (lent, loaned) us the money.

13. A significant (percent, percentage) of the responses were against the proposal.

14. The reason he was late was (because, that) a fog had grounded his flight in Jacksonville.

15. Please answer the enclosed questionnaire and return (it, same) to me.

16. They (stayed, stopped) at the Regency Manor for three days.

17. Brasilia is a city of (modern, up-to-date) buildings.

18. We read in the local newspaper (that, where) Villers has been promoted to a new position.

19. The contract will be awarded to the company (who, which) submits the lowest bid.

20. Please let us know (who, what) you are recommending.

19–3. Using a dictionary for reference, rewrite the following sentences. Select the correct choice of homophone from the words in parentheses.

1. There was no (access, excess) to the fire escape.

2. We'll have to (adapt, adopt) this plan to our needs.

3. The (affect, effect) was to cancel out the gains made during the previous day.

4. The trucks are (all ready, already) to depart.

5. They doubted that such a loss could be (born, borne).

6. He will have to make a house-to-house (canvas, canvass).

7. Hartford is the (capital, capitol) of Connecticut.

8. Most people agree that it is well to (complement, compliment) someone who has done an outstanding deed.

9. His success was (do, due) to his liberal education.

10. Their research center is guarded almost as though it were a (fort, forte).

11. Problem solving sometimes requires an extraordinary amount of (incite, insight).

12. The strike was (lead, led) by a few outspoken workers from the second shift.

13. They are fearful that the party candidate may (loose, lose) the election.
14. Miss Robinson is in charge of the (personal, personnel) in the stenographic pool.
15. Our (principal, principle) product is still the plain, old-fashioned chocolate bar.
16. The office manual specifies that letterhead (stationary, stationery) be used for all outgoing correspondence.
17. He has had more experience (than, then) anyone else in that department.
18. (Therefor, Therefore), I believe that he should be first in line for the promotion.
19. (Who's, Whose) pen is this?
20. When (your, you're) doing a good job goes unnoticed, you may have difficulty in getting a raise in salary.

19–4. In the following sentences, use the correct choice of word to fulfill the grammatical requirement of agreement of case (subject or object) and number (singular or plural).

1. The office manager, in addition to the plant manager, (was, were) invited to attend the conference.
2. Mr. Jensen, as well as all the members of his staff, (is, are) enthusiastic about the plan.
3. The advertising manager and his new assistant, Mr. Osborn, (is, are) attending a meeting this morning.
4. The committee (is, are) shaking hands with the union officials.
5. The drum-and-bugle corps (was, were) marching down the street.
6. They will issue you and (I, me) a receipt for the goods.
7. Politics (is, are) interesting to most of us.
8. LaTour's (is, are) planning a special sale for their charge-account customers.
9. There is the man (who, whom) we thought was the office manager.
10. Arrest anyone (who, whom) you see entering the grounds.
11. Give this information to (whoever, whomever) you believe can benefit from it.
12. Gregory's is opening a new store, which will be (its, their) fifth retail outlet in Tyler County.
13. Either of the locations (is, are) acceptable to the stockholders.
14. Neither of the men lived up to the promises (he, they) had made to the credit manager.

15. Neither the passengers nor the bus driver (was, were) aware of the smouldering fire.

16. None of the stores in this city (handle, handles) that brand of furniture.

17. Neither the shed nor its contents (was, were) damaged by the flood.

18. None of the office equipment (has, have) to be serviced this month.

19. All of the typewriters, in addition to the bookkeeping equipment, (is, are) beginning to wear out.

20. Each worker's absences are noted in (his, their) personnel file.

19–5. In the following sentences, use the correct choice of article (*a, an, the*) as required by the rules of grammar.

1. Football is (a, the) sort of game that I like.

2. Our creditors have given us (a, an) ultimatum.

3. Roger is planning to attend (a, an) university in California.

4. At five o'clock, there was still (a, an) hour's work ahead of us.

5. We'll have to put up (a, an) united front, if we are to succeed.

6. If you ask him for (a, an) honest opinion, I'm sure that he will give it to you.

7. (A, An) adding machine is (a, an) useful piece of equipment.

8. The only sound that we could get out of him was (a, an) *"Oui."*

9. The man dressed in the white suit is (a, an) Hindu.

10. He was just (a, an) humble monk from the monastery in the hills.

19–6. Rewrite the following sentences with the correct choice of *shall* or *will, should* or *would*.

1. I (shall, will) be glad to help you this afternoon.

2. We (shall, will) be happy to consider your application.

3. If I were you, I (should, would) report the incident to the police.

4. We (shall, will) gladly send you the free samples you requested. (Show promise.)

5. Our branch manager in Boston (should, would) appreciate your sending the answer this week.

6. I (shall, will) be awaiting your report. (Simple futurity.)

7. You (shall, will) agree, I'm sure, that appearances are sometimes misleading.

8. We (shall, will) expect Mr. Krause on Tuesday. (Simple futurity.)

9. I (shall, will) meet the publisher's deadline. (Emphatic.)

10. When (shall, will) your driver be able to come in to sign the release?

19-7. Rewrite the following sentences in accordance with the rules governing the various points of grammar involved.

1. His picture is often seen in newspapers and billboards.

2. Finish the work as speedy as you can.

3. The accounting office was laid out like sensible.

4. A special sale would aid to reduce our inventory.

5. Come as quick as you can.

6. If I was in his place, I'd ask for a postponement.

7. Finishing the lecture, Professor Hawkins dismissed the class.

8. If Carney were agreeable to the proposal, he was keeping the fact well hidden.

9. Because we had timed our advertising carefully, a much better response had been expected.

10. He would have preferred to have heard from you much sooner.

11. Our production schedule has been met, the last order being completed this morning.

12. There is a possibility to make a better decision after Robertson has made his report.

13. His health is not well this year.

14. Norris has proven himself to be a competent manager.

15. She most always can be trusted to do her work neat.

16. We would like to know your preference, and a return envelope is enclosed for your convenience.

17. He is one of the recent married men.

18. Our credit department should hear from you sooner than today.

19. These rules are to be subject to final review by the boards of both corporations.

20. He hung his work clothes into the closet.

19-8. Rewrite the following sentences so that any misplaced modifiers (words, phrases, clauses) are positioned in keeping with the rules for correct sentence structure.

1. We only distribute our products through bonafide wholesalers.

2. Before reaching a decision, we suggest that you reconsider the tax implications.

3. He has accepted the financial statement which you sent him without question.

4. Being recently reconditioned, she felt certain that the typewriter would be satisfactory for another year.

5. He seems to definitely favor our plan over the others.

6. While visiting in New York, Rockefeller Center would be an interesting place to see.

7. We have almost withdrawn all of our money from the bank.

8. Knowing that you were in need of the answers, the questionnaire was filled out and returned immediately.

9. To avoid embarrassing errors, each customer's balance must be verified at the end of the month.

10. He not only works on week ends but on holidays as well.

11. To protect yourself against a serious loss, your investment portfolio should contain securities of different types.

12. For the sake of good customer relations, we have to carefully check each person's account before we send him a statement.

13. He will either pay the amount in cash or by check.

14. The report neither mentioned the accident nor the circumstances which led to it.

15. When completed, Mr. Patterson will move into the new office.

19–9. In rewriting the following sentences, correct the faults in parallel construction.

1. I am 25 years of age, married, and have two children.

2. They earned expense money by repairing screens, fences, and doing other odd jobs for their neighbors.

3. He is neither rich nor is he poor.

4. They requested us to send the goods at once and that they be delivered to their warehouse.

5. He is in Washington attending a meeting and to discuss the economic situation with Senator Hastings.

6. For the benefit of our customers and to enhance our standing in the community, we will provide home delivery as a free service.

7. We read all of the inquiries received that morning and which, according to company policy, had to be answered immediately.

8. When you speak, make your words sound softly and clear.

9. He told us to borrow the money either from a bank or to get it from a commercial loan company.

10. They bought not only an accounting machine but installed an electronic computer as well.

19–10. Rewrite the following sentences with the correct or preferred choice (if any) between a *comma* and a *semicolon* as the internal marks of punctuation.

1. Because the shoes were the wrong size (, ;) I could not wear them to the dance.

2. Our new computer (, ;) which was being installed during your recent visit (, ;) is now in full operation.

3. Mr. Jaynes is not in the laboratory (, ;) perhaps he is out to lunch.

4. We sent them notices on November 30 (, ;) 1966 (, ;) December 31 (, ;) 1966 (, ;) and January 15 (, ;) 1967.

5. The man (, ;) who is talking to the manager (, ;) is a private detective.

6. Of course (, ;) when storing the boxes (, ;) you may be able to count the number on hand.

7. Naturally (, ;) he is not planning to reveal any secrets to our competitors.

8. We always try to please our customers (, ;) yet (, ;) some of them seem to doubt our sincerity.

9. Unfortunately (, ;) he did not get our message (, ;) and he was not in his office when we arrived.

10. Fraser did not get the position (, ;) even though he was one of the leading applicants.

11. If you pay the amount within 10 days (, ;) you will be entitled to a cash discount of two percent.

12. The shipment was delayed in Detroit (, ;) and the merchandise did not arrive in time for our sale.

13. In other words (, ;) we would appreciate your explaining the system to Mr. Sloane.

14. He was born in Salem (, ;) Oregon (, ;) but he moved to Los Angeles about 15 years ago.

15. You should be given an adjustment (, ;) as the warranty is still in effect.

19–11. Rewrite the following sentences and insert *hyphens* wherever they are required.

1. He received a well deserved promotion.

2. One fourth of the workers have been employed by our company for 20 years or more.

3. We forgot about the two percent cash discount.

4. Appleton is a man well known in the legal profession.

5. It was one of those off again, on again situations.

6. He has done well for a man with only a high school education.

7. I believe that these records are up to date.

8. The students conducted a house to house survey.

     9. They sell both medium and high priced suits.

    10. He expects to inherit a one third interest in the property.

19–12. In rewriting the following sentences, insert all necessary punctuation marks.

    1. Noise is anything which disturbs the smooth flow of a message from its source to its destination

    2. Who is there the guard asked loudly

    3. The trend shows that full capacity will be reached before 1970 see Appendix A

    4. Should the project fail which heaven forbid Plankton will lose his job

    5. The way I manage my office Im sure you will agree with me is none of Bayless business

    6. He will be transferred to St Louis Missouri next month

    7. We ordered blue pink and tan colors

    8. Naturally the frightened little girl did not know what to say

    9. Congratulations on your victory at the polls

    10. She was trying to write with a short dull pencil

    11. Its time to give the kitten its food

    12. The instructions are clearly stated do not fold staple or twist this card

    13. Mr Zuver is not here said the receptionist he has a cold today

    14. Her home town Chiswell Virginia is situated in the mountains

    15. Who cried Fire Fire

·······································

CHAPTER 20

STENOGRAPHIC
AIDS

In most instances, the final preparation of a business letter, memorandum, or report in typewritten form will be the problem of the typist or secretary. Each such person should own or have access to a manual of conventional typing forms, and in addition should be instructed on the overall form adopted by the company for each type of document.

The composer of the communication, however, is ultimately responsible for the perfection of the document once he has signed (approved) it. He should have enough knowledge of at least the commonly occurring forms to be able to distinguish the right from the wrong. He should insist on compliance with the ordinary procedures so that his reader will not be distracted by needless, though minor, imperfections. Whenever there are two or more acceptable ways of doing something, it is important that one way be adhered to exclusively in any one document.

Presented below are some of the stenographic matters with which a writer of business communications should be familiar.

Abbreviations

In general, words should be spelled out rather than abbreviated. A few exceptions exist, however, whereby the abbreviation *should* be used, not the word itself: *Dr., Jr., Sr., Mr.,* and *Mrs.*

In tables, charts, and graphs, abbreviations may be used when it is necessary to save space.

In addresses, street designations (not the names of streets) may be abbreviated, if better balance and eye appeal are thus obtained. The same privilege applies to directional portions of the street names.

STREET DESIGNATIONS	DIRECTIONAL PORTIONS
Ave.	N.
Blvd.	E.
Ct.	S.
Dr.	W.
Rd.	N.E.
St.	N.W.
Terr.	S.E.
	S.W.

In addresses, state names may be abbreviated, provided there is an official Post Office abbreviation and better balance and eye appeal are thus obtained.

LIST (DISTRICTS, COMMONWEALTHS, STATES, POSSESSIONS)

STATE	ABBREVIATION	STATE	ABBREVIATION
Alabama	Ala.	Montana	Mont.
Alaska	-	North Carolina	N.C.
Arizona	Ariz.	North Dakota	N. Dak.
Arkansas	Ark.	Nebraska	Nebr.
California	Calif.	Nevada	Nev.
Canal Zone	C.Z.	New Hampshire	N.H.
Colorado	Colo.	New Jersey	N.J.
Connecticut	Conn.	New Mexico	N. Mex.
District of Columbia	D.C.	New York	N.Y.
		Ohio	-
Delaware	Del.	Oklahoma	Okla.
Florida	Fla.	Oregon	Oreg.
Georgia	Ga.	Pennsylvania	Pa.
Hawaii	-	Puerto Rico	P.R.
Illinois	Ill.	Rhode Island	R.I.
Indiana	Ind.	Samoa	-
Iowa	-	South Carolina	S.C.
Kansas	Kans.	South Dakota	S. Dak.
Kentucky	Ky.	Tennessee	Tenn.
Louisiana	La.	Texas	Tex.
Massachusetts	Mass.	Vermont	Vt.
Maryland	Md.	Virginia	Va.
Maine	-	Virgin Islands	-
Michigan	Mich.	Washington	Wash.
Minnesota	Minn.	Wisconsin	Wis.
Mississippi	Miss.	West Virginia	W. Va.
Missouri	Mo.	Wyoming	Wyo.

A new list of state abbreviations has been introduced by the Post Office. It provides a two-letter abbreviation for each state; both of these letters are expressed in uppercase (capitals). The new abbreviations are allowed only in connection with ZIP code numbers. Some mailers, notably publishers of magazines and other periodicals, have already begun to change their addressing tapes to include the new abbreviations. Eventually, when ZIP coding becomes mandatory for all mailing, the new abbreviations will replace the old.

The two-letter abbreviations follow.

STATE	ABBREVIATION	STATE	ABBREVIATION
Alaska	AK	Montana	MT
Alabama	AL	Nebraska	NB
Arizona	AZ	Nevada	NV
Arkansas	AR	New Hampshire	NH
California	CA	New Jersey	NJ
Canal Zone	CZ	New Mexico	NM
Colorado	CO	New York	NY
Connecticut	CT	North Carolina	NC
Delaware	DE	North Dakota	ND
District of Columbia	DC	Ohio	OH
Florida	FL	Oklahoma	OK
Georgia	GA	Oregon	OR
Hawaii	HI	Pennsylvania	PA
Idaho	ID	Puerto Rico	PR
Illinois	IL	Rhode Island	RI
Indiana	IN	South Carolina	SC
Iowa	IA	South Dakota	SD
Kansas	KS	Tennessee	TN
Kentucky	KY	Texas	TX
Louisiana	LA	Utah	UT
Maine	ME	Vermont	VT
Maryland	MD	Virginia	VA
Massachusetts	MA	Virgin Islands	VI
Michigan	MI	Washington	WA
Minnesota	MN	West Virginia	WV
Mississippi	MS	Wisconsin	WI
Missouri	MO	Wyoming	WY

In text matter, certain abbreviations are also permissible. These abbreviations should be used when they are the ordinary method of presentation, not merely as an effort-saving device at the writer's side of the communication process. Included in this category are the following.

ABBREVIATION	SPELLED–OUT FORM
A.D.	anno Domini (in the year of our Lord)
A-1	first grade or quality

ABBREVIATION	SPELLED–OUT FORM
A.M. ... (or, a.m.) ...	ante meridiem (before noon)
B.C.	before Christ
C.O.D.	collect on delivery
C.P.A.	Certified Public Accountant
E.O.M.	end of month
etc.	*et cetera* (and other things)
F.O.B.	free on board
I.O.U.	I owe you
I.Q.	intelligence quotient
M.	meridian (noon)
N.B.	*nota bene* (note well)
No.	number
Nos.	numbers
N.S.F.	not sufficient funds
P.M. ... (or, p.m.)	post meridiem (after noon)
2/10, n/30	2 percent discount allowed for payment made within 10 days; net amount due in 30 days
U.S.	United States
U.S.A.	United States of America

Address Forms

Sometimes it is necessary to use a special form of address and salutation in keeping with the addressee's position or rank. Some of the important forms are presented below. (Substitute "Madam" for "Sir" as needed.)

PERSON	ADDRESS	SALUTATION
Ambassador, U.S.A.	His Excellency (or, the Honorable Name) The American Ambassador The American Embassy London, England	Sir: Excellency: Dear Mr. Ambassador:
Ambassador, Foreign	His Excellency (Name, if available) The Ambassador of the French Republic Embassy of the French Republic Washington, D.C. 20225	Sir: Excellency:
Archbishop	The Most Reverend (Name)	Your Excellency: Your Grace:
Bishop, Catholic	The Most Reverend (Name)	Your Excellency: My dear Bishop (Name):

PERSON	ADDRESS	SALUTATION
Bishop, Episcopal	The Right Reverend (Name), Bishop of (Name)	My dear Bishop (Name): Right Reverend and Dear Sir:
Bishop, Methodist	The Reverend Bishop (Name)	My dear Bishop (Name): Dear Bishop (Name):
Cabinet Officer	The Honorable (Name) Secretary of (Department) Washington, D.C. 20225	Dear Sir:
Cardinal	His Eminence, (First name) Cardinal (Last name)	Your Eminence:
Chief Justice of the Supreme Court	The Honorable (Name) Chief Justice of the Supreme Court of the United States Washington, D.C. 20225	Sir: Mr. Chief Justice:
Clergymen: Doctor of Divinity	The Reverend Dr. (Name)	Dear Dr. (Name):
Minister	The Reverend (Name)	Dear Mr. (Name):
Priest, Catholic	The Reverend (Name)	Dear Father (Name):
Priest, Episcopal	The Reverend (Name)	Dear Father (Name):
Rabbi	Rabbi (Name)	Dear Rabbi (Name):
Councilman	Councilman (Name)	Dear Councilman: Dear Sir:
Dean, College	Dean (Name) College (School) of (Name)	Dear Dean (Name): Dear Sir:
Governor	His Excellency (Name), or The Honorable (Name) The Governor of (State)	Dear Sir:
Judge	The Honorable (Name) (Jurisdiction) Judge	Dear Judge (Name): Dear Sir:

PERSON	ADDRESS	SALUTATION
Mayor	(The Honorable <u>Name</u>, if available) The Mayor of the City of ___	Dear Mr. Mayor: Dear Sir:
Member of Congress	The Honorable (<u>Name</u>) House of Representatives House Office Building Washington, D.C. 20225	Dear Representative (<u>Name</u>): Dear Sir:
Military Personnel	A military person is addressed by his rank and name. In general, the salutation would be one of the following: Dear (<u>Rank</u>) (<u>Last Name</u>): Dear Sir: Two exceptions are to be noted, however: (1) In the salutation, general rather than specific titles are used. Thus <u>Lieutenant</u> <u>Colonel</u> would become <u>Colonel</u>; <u>2nd</u> <u>Lieutenant</u> would become <u>Lieutenant</u>, etc. (2) Navy personnel below the rank of Commander are referred to as <u>Mr.</u>	
Monsignor	The Right Reverend Monsignor (<u>Name</u>)	Right Reverend and dear Monsignor: Dear Monsignor (<u>Name</u>):
Pope	His Holiness Pope (<u>Name</u>)	Most Holy Father: Your Holiness:
President (United States)	The President of the United States The White House Washington, D.C. 20225	My dear Mr. President: Mr. President:
President (University)	President (<u>Name</u>) (<u>Name</u> <u>of</u> <u>Institution</u>) —or : (<u>Name</u>), (<u>Terminal</u> <u>Degree</u>) President, (<u>Name</u> <u>of</u> <u>Institution</u>	My dear President (<u>Name</u>): Dear Sir:
Senator	The Honorable (<u>Name</u>) United States Senate Senate Office Building Washington, D.C. 20225	Dear Senator (<u>Name</u>): Dear Sir:
Vice President of the United States	The Honorable (<u>Name</u>) Vice President of the United States Washington, D.C. 20225	My dear Mr. Vice President: Mr. Vice President: Dear Sir:

Amounts

When showing monetary amounts, proceed as follows: Spell out an amount, regardless of size, when it starts the sentence.

Use the dollar sign ($) and figures for amounts appearing later in the sentence.

For even dollars below ten, use ".00" with the number.

```
$1.00
$9.00
```

For even dollars starting with ten (two or more digits), do not use ".00" as a general rule.

```
$10
$190
```

When amounts requiring ".00" or actual cents appear in the same sentence with even dollars of two or more digits, use a parallel style by adding ".00" to the round amounts.

```
The prices were $10.00 and $8.95, respectively.
```

Ampersand (&)

The ampersand should not be used in letter writing, except in company names, and then only when the company itself authorizes it.

```
McNeil & Ross, Architects
```

Apostrophe

Use an apostrophe to indicate the possessive case, when either genuine or idiomatic possession is to be indicated.

```
The man's hat.
The dog's tail.
Sunday's newspaper.
Today's output.
```

Prefer to use the genitive "of" in other situations.

```
The roof of the factory was damaged.
The point of the pencil is dull.
```

Use an apostrophe also to fill in the gap caused by the omission of letters in the formation of a contraction.

```
We're glad to have your report.
He hasn't been in his office this afternoon.
```

Apposition

When two adjacent nouns stand for the same person or thing, they are said to be in apposition. The appositive should be set off from the rest of the sentence by commas.

```
Our new salesman, Earl Swanson, has a suggestion.
Captain Palmer, the fire inspector, will send us his recom-
mendations.
```

City Names

Always spell out the full names of cities, with the exception of the word *Saint*. Never use *City* in place of the specific names of the city and state in an address.

```
St. Louis
San Francisco
University Heights
```

In addressing, always include the name of the state (or the correct abbreviation).

```
New York, New York
Pittsburgh, Pa.
```

Colon (:)

Double-space between a colon and the word that follows it.

```
The rule may be stated thus: double-space after using a colon.
```

Comma (,)

Single-space between a comma and the word that follows it.

```
It may be made of copper, silver, or gold.
```

When using a comma in conjunction with closing quotation marks, always place it within the quotation marks.

```
I said "and," not "or."
```

Dash (—)

To form a dash, use two hyphens without spaces before or after.

```
If the ship should sink—which God forbid!—Jones will be a
ruined man.
```

Dates

In letter writing always spell out the names of the months. Use a comma to separate the day of the month from the year.

```
October 1, 1966
```

In text matter, when the year is included in the date, use a comma to separate the year from what follows in a sentence.

```
I was born on March 4, 1952, in Cleveland, Ohio.
```

Diagonal (/)

Use a diagonal (also called "virgule"), without spaces before or after, to indicate fractions (in lists); to separate *and* and *or* to indicate the possible options; and to separate the components of reference initials.

```
1-3/4
and/or
JSS/ab (or JSS:ab)
```

Division of Words

Make it a practice to refer to your dictionary every time you must hyphenate a word at the end of a line—do not guess at the syllabication. For example, one might guess that the proper division of *knowledge* should be *know-ledge;* the dictionary shows that the correct division is *knowl-edge.* Moreover, do not divide a word by placing only the first letter on one line and the remainder on the next (wrong: *e-nough*); and do not divide a word by placing only two letters on the second line (wrong: *print-er*).

Ellipsis (. . .)

When portions of a sentence are omitted, a special procedure is used. Single-space after the word immediately preceding the omission, and then use three periods alternately with three spaces before starting the next word. When the omission occurs at the end of a sentence, a fourth period should be added.

```
The regulation clearly states, "Failure to comply with the
foregoing requirements will result in the suspension of the
driver's license of the operator . . . for a period of three
years . . . ."
```

Exclamation Point (!)

To form an exclamation point, first use a period; then backspace and use an apostrophe.

When using an exclamation point in conjunction with closing quotation marks, place it within the quotation marks when the quotation itself is an exclamation. Place it outside when the whole sentence is an exclamation. Double-space between an exclamation point that ends a sentence and the word that begins a new sentence.

```
He shouted, "Stop that man!"
Stop saying, "I don't know"! Someone will hear you.
```

Fractions

Use figures for fractions used with a whole number, otherwise spell out. If the keyboard has fractions, use them.

```
21¼
```

If the typewriter does not have fractions, improvise as shown in the next example. If it has some but not all of the fractions to be listed, improvise on all of them, for uniformity.

```
21-1/4
33-1/3
45-3/4
```

Hyphen

Use a hyphen to divide a word at the end of a line. Never use a hyphen at the beginning of the following line.

```
Something told Anderson that this was only the begin-
ning.
```

Indention

In a formal report, and in a letter if you use the modified block form, indent the first line of each paragraph 5 or 10 spaces.

Italics

To italicize a word, underline it. To italicize a series of words, underline each word individually.

```
I read about it in a recent issue of Time.

Do you read the American Business Review?
```

Numbering

In letters, do not number the first page. On the second and subsequent pages, center the number near the top of the page and use a hyphen before and after it. (-2-)

In formal reports, place the number at the right-hand margin near the top of the page. Use the figure only. (2)

Numbers

For numbers, the standard keyboard has the following figures: 2, 3, 4, 5, 6, 7, 8, 9, and 0. To make the figure 1, use the letter *L,* lowercase. Do not use a capital *I.* For further details, see *Rule of 10.*

Number Symbol

The symbol # should be used only in tabulations. In text matters, figures used to represent items, stock numbers, serials, policy numbers and the like, should be preceded by the abbreviation *No.*

Parentheses ( )

Use parentheses to enclose purely explanatory or instructional words, phrases, or clauses. Use capitalization and end punctuation if an independent clause is enclosed by parentheses but does not appear inside another sentence.

```
These facts have been grouped into five geographical areas
(see Appendix A).
```

```
These facts have been grouped into five geographical areas.
(See Appendix A.)
```

Percent (%)

The symbol % should be used only in tabulations. In text matter, the word should be spelled out.

```
You are all allowed a standard deduction of 10 percent.
```

Period (.)

Double-space between a period that ends a sentence and the word that begins the next sentence. When using a period in conjunction with closing quotation marks, always place it within the quotation marks.

```
Suddenly, a flock of ducks flew over our heads. Bob took
careful aim, and fired.
```

```
I said,"and," not "or."
```

Postal ZIP Code

Place the postal ZIP code after the name or abbreviation of the state. Use a comma to separate the name of the city from the name of the state.

```
Cleveland, Ohio 44118
```

Question Mark (?)

Use a question mark after all questions in direct discourse. Double-space between a question mark that ends a sentence and the word that begins the next sentence.

```
What is wrong with John? He seems to be letting his competi-
tors put him out of business.
```

Quotation Marks (")

The standard typewriter keyboard provides a double quotation mark to be used for ordinary quotations. For a quotation within a quotation, however, use an apostrophe (single quote).

```
Jack replied, "I said 'and,' not 'or.' "
```

When using a question mark or an exclamation point in conjunction with closing quotation marks, place it within the quotation marks if it belongs with the quoted matter.

```
He began to ask himself the question, "Should I go on to
graduate school?"
```

```
The stock boy ran into the room shouting, "Fire! Fire!"
```

When two punctuation marks appear to be indicated in combination with closing quotation marks, apply the following rules:

1. Only one of the two marks may be used. The question mark and the exclamation point are of equal rank; the period is inferior to each.
2. When the marks are of *equal* rank, retain the inside mark; drop the outside mark.
3. When the marks are of *unequal* rank, retain the stronger mark; drop the weaker mark.

Punctuation Indicated	Correct Punctuation	Explanation
."	."	Drop outside mark
."?	"?	Drop weaker mark
."!	"!	Drop weaker mark
?".	?"	Drop weaker mark
?"?	?"	Drop outside mark
?"!	?"	Drop outside mark
!".	!"	Drop weaker mark
!"?	!"	Drop outside mark
!"!	!"	Drop outside mark

Rule of 10

In business usage, the presentation of numbers follows the "Rule of 10." This rule is summarized as follows:

If a number begins a sentence, spell it out regardless of size. Also spell out numbers below 10. Otherwise, use figures:

```
Five hundred freshmen will be admitted.
We saw two men enter the warehouse.
There are 23 people on the payroll.
```

Additional notes: If in a given sentence two or more numbers used in the same context involve some ordinarily spelled out and some ordinarily shown as figures, use figures for all (except, of course, the one that might begin the sentence). If such numbers are not used in the same context, apply the regular rules.

```
They have inspected 15 houses and 4 school buildings.
He wants 24 five-cent stamps.
```

Semicolon (;)

Single-space between a semicolon and the word that follows it.

```
He tried to appear confident; however, his eyes gave him
away.
```

Spacing Rules

Single-space between each word not followed by a punctuation mark, after commas, and after quotation marks that follow commas.

```
Bob took careful aim, and fired.
I said "and," not "or."
```

Single-space after semicolons.
Single-space after periods that end individual abbreviations.

```
Mr. H. J. Dalton
```

Single-space after periods that end multiple abbreviations, but not between the integral parts. Do not add a period when an abbreviation appears at the end of a sentence, but do use other punctuation marks when necessary. (Many multiple abbreviations are preferably typed without periods or spaces: NATO, AFL–CIO, SEC, etc.).

```
Does he belong to any group besides the N.A.A.?
Yes, he belongs to the B.P.O.E. and to the K.C.
```

Double-space after colons.

Double-space after periods that end sentences, or after the parentheses or quotation marks that follow them at the ends of sentences.

Double-space after exclamation points or question marks that end sentences, or after the parentheses or quotation marks that follow them at the ends of sentences.

Do not space between an abbreviation and the period that punctuates it, or between a word and the punctuation mark that follows it.

Do not space between opening or closing quotation marks and the matter to be enclosed by them, or between opening or closing parentheses and the matter to be enclosed by them.

Do not space before a hyphen. Do not space after a hyphen when more is to follow on the same line, except when two or more compound words are to be used with a common base.

```
He is a four-year-old boy.
It is a fourth- or fifth-grade lesson.
```

Do not space before a dash, or after a dash if more is to follow on the same line.

State Names

When used in text matter with the names of cities, the names of states should be set off by commas.

```
He was born in Cleveland, Ohio, and lived there for at least
30 years.
```

Strikeovers

Never be guilty of strikeovers. Always be careful to erase neatly any typographical errors before correcting them.

Symbols (Misc.)

As a general rule, in text matter spell out such words as *percent, at,* and so on—even when symbols for these things are available. One notable exception is the dollar sign ($), which is regularly used when the amount does not appear at the beginning of a sentence.

In tables, charts, and graphs, symbols are permissible as space-saving devices. "Leaders"—lines of dots—between the columns of tables make them more readable.

Text Matter

In letters, single-space the lines of each paragraph, as a general rule. Double-space between the paragraphs. In very short letters, it is permissible to double-space between the lines, indent the paragraphs 5 or 10 spaces, and double-space between the paragraphs.

In formal reports, the summary (synopsis) and text sections should be double-spaced between the lines and between the paragraphs. Paragraphs should be indented 5 or 10 spaces. Headings should be "double double-spaced" from the text matter.

Type

Always make certain that the type is clean and unclogged. Make it a practice to clean the type daily.

Virgule (/)

Use a virgule (also called "diagonal"), without spaces before or after, to indicate fractions (in lists); to separate *and* and *or* to indicate the possible options; and to separate the components of reference initials.

```
1-3/4
and/or
JSS/ab (or JSS:ab)
```

QUESTIONS
. . . .

1. Under what conditions may abbreviations of state names be used in addressing business correspondence?
2. Give the general rule followed in business for expressing monetary amounts.
3. Although it is a symbol of long standing, the ampersand has limited usage in present-day business practice. When is it properly used?
4. What is the rule for using commas and periods in combination with closing quotation marks?
5. How is a dash formed when one's typewriter does not have a key for this mark of punctuation?
6. How is an exclamation point formed when one's typewriter does not have a key for this mark of punctuation?
7. Give the rule for showing several fractions in a table or list.
8. Give the instructions for showing italics—both for one word and for a series of words.
9. What procedure is to be followed when two end-punctuation marks appear to be indicated in combination with closing quotation marks?
10. Briefly state the "Rule of 10" for expressing numbers in business writing.

··

CHAPTER 21

GLOSSARY

In general, the terms used in this textbook agree with those regularly used in business communication. Sometimes, however, special terms have been introduced to achieve clarity, to avoid ambiguity, and to establish logical relationships which otherwise might be missing.

The following alphabetical list gives the meanings of the various terms as they have been used in this book.

Acknowledgment Letter.   A letter written in response to an order for goods or services.

Action Statement.   The specific request that is made in a request letter; it may be made in the form of a command, a question, or a suggestion.

Active Voice.   The ordinary grammatical behavior of a sentence, wherein the action signified by the verb is performed by the subject of the sentence.

Address (Inside).   The name and address of the intended reader of a business letter, placed at the left-hand margin above the salutation.

Adjustment Letter.   A letter written in response to a claim or complaint filed by a person reporting a supposed infringement of his rights.

A.I.D.A. Plan.   A traditional mnemonic (memory-aiding) designation of four major components of a sales letter: *A*ttention, *I*nterest, *D*esire, *A*ction.

Airwave Static.   Interference or noise caused by electricity and troublesome to communication by radio.

Allowable Syllables.   The number of syllables a word may contain without adding to its reading difficulty. Some measurement systems exempt two syllables; others, allow only one.

Alphabetical Order.   A method of sequencing a list, or items in a series, when there is no suitable value basis to go on. This order simply places the items in sequence according to letters of the alphabet.

Ample Assistance.   Doing, in words and/or deed, whatever is necessary to make the fulfillment of a request as easy as possible for the reader of a business letter.

Analytical Report.   A report which goes somewhat beyond the presentation of facts. It may interpret these facts for the reader, and it may make a recommendation on action to be taken.

Appendix.   A unit of material added after the completion of a formal business report. Usually, it consists of a table, chart, graph, map, blueprint, copy of the questionnaire used, or some other item of interest to the reader which happens to be unsuited to inclusion in the text of the report.

Application Letter.   A request letter in which a person seeks to whet the reader's interest and thereby get himself invited to an employment interview.

Appreciation.   The spirit (or expression) of grateful acknowledgment for a helpful act performed by another. If it is to reward a deed, it should be phrased in the present tense and appear early in the letter. If it is to be an inducement for future action, it should be phrased in the future tense and appear in association with the request.

Appreciation Letter.   A simple goodwill letter, written to show gratitude for a deed performed by the reader.

Background Courses.   A classification of courses taken in college: those which do not specifically relate to one's career but are helpful in broadening one's outlook on life.

Bad–News Approach.   The sequencing of program steps so that the explanatory material precedes the essential message conveyed by a business letter or report. See *Inductive Order.*

Bad–News Letter.   Any letter wherein the essential message can be considered as being adverse to the reader.

Bar Chart.   A graphic aid for showing comparative values for two or more series of data through side-by-side rectangles or bars.

Basic (Favor–Type) Requests.   A category of business letters comprising requests which do not have immediate sales potential and which have no special-purpose designation.

Bibliography.   In a formal report, a list of books and periodicals (including names of authors, dates of publication, etc.) which contain additional information about the subject, including those which were consulted during the research.

Budget Appropriation. Approval to a department to carry on a planned activity, stated in terms of the monetary requirement for that purpose.

Business Communication. The process of transferring a train of thought (message) from one person to another, usually by written means, within the framework of a business situation.

Business Report. A specific kind of communication, identifiable chiefly by its program and partially by its appearance, prepared to help the reader solve a problem.

Businesslike. In readability analysis, a term to describe the ideal level of a business letter—that is, effortless reading for the majority of American adults.

Campus Recruiting. The sending of representatives to college campuses, by business firms, for the purpose of signing staff additions and replacements from among the seniors and graduate candidates.

Centralized Purchasing. A system of internal control in a company whereby only a designated officer may issue purchase orders to suppliers.

Channel. The means by which a message is transferred from the source to the destination. In written communication, it is the document itself; in other kinds of communication (facsimile communication), it may be air-waves, electrical impulses, etc.

Charge Account. A form of credit whereby a customer may take possession of goods or services immediately, with the understanding that he will pay for them when billed.

Chronological Order. The method of sequencing information in the order accumulated; it is also known as the historical order and the narrative order.

Claim Letter. A letter written by someone who believes he has suffered an infringement of his rights to the person whom he believes to be responsible, in which he asks for recompense.

Climactic Order. The method of sequencing information in the order of least significant to most significant. In a process of elimination, the inferior facts or choices are discarded until only the best remain.

Cocurricular Activities. School activities which, although outside the regular curriculum, are nevertheless compatible wth a student's major interest.

C.O.D. Arrangements. A system of low-level credit whereby goods will be shipped at the seller's risk, but will not be handed over to the buyer until payment for both the goods and handling charges are received.

Collection Letter. A request for payment of an overdue balance, having the dual objective of collecting the money and maintaining friendly relations with the reader.

Commendation Letter. A variety of business letter which compliments a person on a particular accomplishment.

Communicate. Verb: to transfer a train of thought (message) from one person to another.

Company Policy. A prevailing understanding that exists in an organization whereby the personnel know how to respond to a specified occurrence.

Conceptual Negative. Something that causes an unpleasant or depressing effect on the reader of a business communication.

Condolence. Expression of sympathy to someone who has experienced misfortune.

Congratulate. To express happiness to someone because of his success or good fortune.

Content. In a written communication, the message that is being conveyed. It is partly the program and partly the matter of finesse (the *what* and the *how*).

Conventional Order. In a report, the inductive order of program; the persuasive approach obtained by placing the reasons in front of the conclusions and/or recommendations.

Correspondence. Communication by means of letter; collectively, the letters which pass between persons who write to each other.

Counteroffer. In an answer to a request, an offer to grant or do something less than was specified.

Courtesy Copy. A duplicate copy of a form (e.g., a questionnaire) which the reader of a request letter may keep for his own use.

Covering Letter. A letter of transmittal; specifically, the first part of a two-part business letter.

Credit Letter. In general, any letter dealing with a credit situation; specifically, an answer of some kind to an applicant for credit terms.

Credit System. The method available at a given company for administering credit, including provisions for terms and limits.

Cybernetics. A refinement of automation whereby electronic equipment can operate selectively, make various decisions, and exercise choice —much in the manner of the human brain.

Cycle Billing. A method of billing customers on a rotation basis, for the purpose of evening out peaks and troughs of monthly office activity.

Data Sheet. In an application, an organized summary of one's education, experience, and other qualifications for employment. It is usually a separate document—the second part of a two-part application letter.

Decoding. The process of reconverting a message from its transmittable form to the form it possessed before transmission. In written communication, it is the extraction of the message content from the message words.

Deductive Order.   In report writing, the program sequence which places the conclusion and/or recommendations in a prominent position ahead of the facts which actually led to them. It is substantially the good-news approach used in business letters.

Definiteness.   Concrete expression of one's thoughts; use of specific names, dates, and references instead of generalities.

Destination.   In communication theory, the end of the line for the message. Specifically, in written communication, it is the reader of the message.

Dictation.   An intermediate step in written communication, whereby the composer places his message into words by oral expression; these words are recorded by a stenographer or a dictaphone before being prepared in final copy.

Diplomacy.   A subdivision of finesse, embracing such matters as politeness, tact, and courtesy.

Direction of Thought.   The path taken by our message as it progresses step by step. It will be easy to follow if it goes in a straight line, does not zigzag or backtrack.

Direct–Mail Advertising.   Mailing of promotional material directly to the would-be consumer, usually with the intention that response will also be handled by mail.

Dispatching.   In a production situation, the giving of the go-ahead signal to carry out a plan.

Division of Labor.   The breaking down of a larger operation into small stages, so that a given workman can specialize on doing one job well instead of having to be sufficiently skilled to do an entire operation.

Elliptical Clause.   A clause from which an important, but readily under-standable, portion is omitted. Usually such a clause takes the form of an object (without a subject or verb), or a past-participle construction (without a subject or completion of the verb).

Elliptical Sentence.   A main clause from which an important, but readily understandable, portion is omitted.

Encoding.   Converting a message into a form that can be transmitted by a given means of communication.

Enunciation.   In dictation, the practice of speaking deliberately and clearly —especially when using words easily misspelled or confused with homophones—so that one's message will not be distorted.

Examination Reports.   A report in which facts are interpreted for the reader.

Exception Principle.   A managerial guideline which calls for bringing attention only to occurrences that are not according to plan—and not to the things that are going properly.

Expediting.   Taking necessary steps to assure that plans set into motion are kept on schedule.

Extracurricular Activities.   School activities which are both outside the regular curriculum and unrelated to a student's major interest.

Eye Appeal.   Psychological use of color, open space, layout, etc. aimed at attracting a reader's attention and interest.

Facsimile Communication.   A system of transferring a message through an image of, or substitute for, the communicator. Examples would be the telephone (impulses substituting for the speaker's voice), television (a visual image on the screen, but not the actual person), etc.

Fairness.   In collection letters, an appeal made on the basis that a business transaction is not justly closed until both parties have performed according to agreement.

Feedback.   Anything that informs us of the success or failure of our attempt at communication. Sometimes we get an answer from our reader, and can obtain a measurement rather soon. Sometimes we must wait a long time, and can get clues only from our reader's subsequent behavior.

Fidelity.   A high degree of similarity between the message intended and the message extracted.

Findings.   In report writing, the facts gathered through the study and presented in edited form in the body of the report.

Finesse.   That part of the content (message) of a business communication which pertains to making it acceptable to the reader. It embraces the three qualities of diplomacy, service attitude, and positiveness.

Follow–up.   An action taken to assure that something well begun is carried through to a successful conclusion. In the area of employment letters, a follow-up is a letter sent after the initial application—hopefully, to add weight to one's competitive position.

Footnote Method.   In a request letter, the listing of objective questions at the bottom of the page, so that the reader can give his answers without having to write a letter himself.

Form.   The physical aspects of a letter or report, as evidenced by the document which passes from writer to reader.

Formal Report.   A business report which follows a traditional manner of presentation, with no more than incidental differences, so that the reader can expect certain parts to be in certain places regardless of the subject matter or authorship.

Formal Style.   In written English, the style of composition that adheres to pure forms of expression and excludes colloquial terms, slang, and contractions.

Format.   The general makeup of a communication document: size, shape, physical assembly, etc.

Frequency Polygon.   A form of line chart used to illustrate the number of occurrences of each value contained in a series of data.

Full Table.   In an order letter, the organization of the parts of the order beneath columnar captions.

Gadget.   A three-dimensional device fastened to a business letter to attract the attention of the intended reader. It is used in some types of sales letters and even occasionally in collection letters. The hope is that the recipient will become sufficiently curious to start reading the letter to find out more about what is going on.

General Program.   The suggested program for a type of business letter, not yet reduced to the level of a given case or a given reader.

Gimmick.   Any device or scheme introduced into a letter to win the co-operation of the reader. Examples: use of colors, a "two-for-one" offer, a sweepstakes, a free sample, a free trial, free admission for a child accompanied by an adult, a gadget to attract attention—all these qualify as gimmicks of one kind or another.

Good–News Approach.   The sequencing of program steps so that the essential message of a business letter or report is given ahead of the explanatory material supporting it. See *deductive order*.

Good–News Letter.   Any letter wherein the essential message can be considered as being favorable to the reader.

Goodwill.   A classification of business letters comprising those which have no other purpose for being written except the catering to the reader's goodwill.

Grammar.   The technical area of language which deals with the relationships among words—e.g., agreement of subject and verb, agreement of pronoun and antecedent, correct formation of verbs, etc.

Grammatical Positive.   The attitude involved in an affirmative or declarative sentence.

Graphic Aid.   In a report, a presentation of data by some visual (illustrative) method.

Histogram.   A graphic aid for depicting data in a time series, wherein rectangular areas are used to represent the values measured by the various time intervals.

Historical Order.   In report writing, the sequencing of information according to the order in which it was accumulated; it is synonymous with the chronological or narrative order.

Homophones.   Words which are pronounced alike, but which differ in meaning and spelling.

Human–Interest Word.   A word involving a person in the presentation of a message—such as people's names, personal pronouns, and common nouns referring to human beings.

Idea File.   A collection of various worthwhile ideas being saved for possible future use.

Illustration.   A visual demonstration of a principle or procedure which supplements a written description.

Impersonal Tone.   A manner of writing which does not make use of first- or second-person references.

Importance, Order of.   In report writing, the sequencing of information in the order of most significant to least significant.

Index.   In a formal report, a supplementary section which alphabetically lists all important names and topics mentioned in the report, identifying each item by the page or pages on which it may be found.

Inductive Order.   In report writing, the program sequence which positions the parts concerning research methods and findings ahead of the conclusions and/or recommendations. This order tends to promote open-mindedness on the part of the reader and to gain his acceptance of the message.

Informal Report.   A business report, usually in letter or memorandum form, which is assembled in a manner inspired by the situation at hand rather than by a traditional or conventional set of rules.

Informal Style.   A manner of writing, especially appropriate for business letters and letter-type reports, in which everyday slang and natural contractions are used.

Informational Reports.   Business reports which simply provide facts for the reader to examine; they do not extend into interpretations or recommendations.

Inspection.   The process of checking something against its specifications.

Interchangeability of Parts.   As a result of standardization, the quality possessed by a component enabling it to fit any unit of product that would contain such a component.

Interview.   In an employment situation, a meeting of the applicant and a representative of the prospective employer during which requirements, qualifications, and other pertinent details are discussed.

Inverted Order.   Any sequencing that is opposite to the conventional or natural order generally expected.

Invoice.   The initial billing for goods sold in a trade or mercantile situation. It is the equivalent of the sales slip used in a retail situation.

Jargon.   The specialized vocabulary of a field of activity. Often it consists of ordinary words which are given an unusual meaning known chiefly by members of the trade or profession involved.

Language.   In general, the means by which thought is communicated from one person to another. In terms of the communication process as it applies to writing, it is the encoding of thought into a form that can be communicated by some medium.

Layaway Plan.   A credit plan whereby the seller agrees to reserve an object for the buyer but does not deliver it to the buyer until all payments have been received.

Layout.   The aspect of format which deals with spacing, margins, centering, balancing, and the like.

Letter of Authorization.   In a formal report, a section displaying the letter (or copy of it) which commissioned the writer to produce such a report.

Letter of Introduction.   A request-type business letter wherein the writer introduces someone to the reader and asks that some courtesy be extended to the person so introduced.

Letter Report.   An informal report which has been cast into the physical form of a business letter.

Letter of Transmittal.   In letter writing, the letter portion of a two-part format—that is, the covering letter that would accompany a data sheet, a questionnaire, a table of figures, or anything being delivered to and explained for the reader. In the case of a formal report, it is the section of the report which officially presents the finished document to the reader.

Line Chart.   A graphic presentation illustrating the number of occurrences of each value contained in a series of data, using points connected by straight lines.

Line of Credit.   A credit limit granted to a trade customer, whereby he may make purchases without payment up to a specified point.

List of Illustrations.   In a formal report, a preliminary section which indicates the pages on which the various illustrations will be found.

Logical Order.   An order of presenting information in a consistent, well-organized progression of thought. See *Direction of Thought.*

Major Courses.   College subjects which represent specific, in-depth training in a profession or area of interest.

Mass Production.   The assembly-line method of manufacturing, generally speaking. It is based on the principles of interchangeability of parts (standardization) and division of labor (specialization).

Mechanics of Expression.   The part of language which deals with the rules of spelling, word usage, grammar, sentence structure, punctuation, and so on.

Mechanization.   The use of machinery to do standard, repetitive work in place of personnel.

Memorandum.   A simplified or streamlined letter form, particularly useful for interoffice correspondence.

Memorandum Report. An informal business report presented in the form of a memorandum or interoffice letter.

Message. The subject of a given communication. In a sense, there are two messages discernible in a communication model: the intended message, as it exists at the source; and the extracted message, as it exists at the destination.

Messageless Communication. The "medium-oriented" concept of communication. The functions of encoding, transmitting, channel, receiving, and decoding are shown to be in good running order. But the value side has not entered in. Unless there is thought to communicate, there is no message in the real meaning of the word.

Modified Table. In an order letter, the listing of the items in the order by tabular means, but without using columnar headings.

Monthly Statement. A financial accounting submitted to a customer each month, summarizing his business activity (charges and credits) occurring during that month.

Motivation. In a request letter, a step which moves the reader to action. It is an application of the principle of service attitude.

Multipurpose Letter. A business letter which is written to accomplish more than one goal, one of which will necessarily be some aspect of goodwill.

Narrative Order. A sequence used for presenting information in the order of acquisition. See *Chronological Order* and *Historical Order*.

Noise. In the field of business communication, anything that interferes with or distorts a message between the mind of the writer and the mind of the reader.

O.C.R. Optical Character Recognition. This term applies to the field of reading or scanning equipment which is capable of preparing data for computers directly from original sources of information.

One–Part Letter. A business letter which, between the salutation and complimentary close, presents the entire message involved. There is no need, for example, to have a separate document to contain a certain portion of the message—such as the data sheet of an application letter.

Order Letter. A request letter in which the writer petitions the reader to sell him specified goods or services.

Outline. A list of topics and subtopics, in a planned order of presentation, set up to guide the writer in the preparation of a composition.

Parallel Construction (Parallelism). A system of expressing a pair or a larger series of thought concepts in a uniform fashion.

Passive Voice. A grammatical construction in which the action of the verb is performed on its subject.

Per Se.   Literally, by itself. It suggests an intrinsic value of some kind, independent of its relationship to something else.

Periodic Report.   A business report recurring after a specified interval of time, such as a year, month, week, etc.

Personal Appeal.   The quality of being capable of attracting the interest or gaining the responsiveness of a specific individual rather than people in general.

Personal Data.   In the data sheet of an application letter, such information as pertains only to the individual being described—such as height, weight, date of birth, etc.

Personal Tone.   The use of first- and second-person pronouns in written communication.

Pie Chart.   A graphic aid in the form of a circle (to represent the whole of something) with wedge-shaped partitions to indicate the relative shares of that whole accounted for by the component parts.

Positiveness.   A subdivision of finesse; it concerns the stressing of pleasant (positive) concepts and the neutralizing or excluding of unpleasant (negative) concepts.

Preface.   In a formal report, a preliminary section containing introductory remarks.

Preliminary Sections.   In a formal report, those sections which precede the main body of the report. These sections would include such elements as the title page, letter of authorization, letter of transmittal, preface, table of contents, list of illustrations, and summary. These sections are usually numbered in a separate sequence of pages from the rest of the report.

Program.   A list of topics and subtopics, in a planned order of presentation (as determined by the psychological needs of the intended reader), set up to guide the writer in the preparation of a business communication.

Progress Report.   A business report giving information on a project not yet completed. It differs from the so-called periodic report in that it relates to work completed rather than to a regular time interval.

Psychological Letter.   In the area of collection letters, a letter which appeals in total to the reader as compared with a conventional letter in which only one step states an appeal.

Psychological Order.   In report writing, the sequencing of the conclusions and/or recommendations ahead of the information supporting them. See *Deductive Order*.

Public Relations.   A function of a business enterprise aimed at creating or strengthening the public image of that enterprise.

Public Relations Letter. A letter written for the purpose of creating or strengthening the public image of an enterprise.

Purchase Order. A serialized, standardized form for ordering supplies or services from outside a company.

Questionnaire. In a request situation, a separate document asking for several pieces of information and usually containing a provision for answering.

Readability. The quality attributable to a piece of writing that is easy to read and understand.

Readability Score. A quantitative measure of how easy a piece of writing is to read and understand.

Recommendation Letter. A letter written on someone's behalf commenting favorably on his character and ability.

Recommendation Report. A type of analytical report which not only interprets the information presented but goes on to recommend specific action by the reader.

References. In the data sheet of an application letter, a list of names and addresses of people who are in a position to comment on one's character and ability.

Regression Line. A line drawn on a chart or graph to indicate the direction of a trend.

Related Courses. A classification of courses taken in college; those which relate to one's career in general but are not specifically within one's field of interest.

Remittance Envelope. An addressed return envelope sent by a creditor as a form of assistance to the debtor in making payment.

Request Letter. Any letter which specifically asks the reader to carry out a course of action.

Resignation Letter. A business letter, of the bad-news variety, giving notice of one's impending termination of employment.

Response Percentage. The ratio of responses received to requests sent out —usually measured in sales campaigns and surveys.

Résumé. In application letters, the second part of a two-part format. In most usages it is a synonym for the *data sheet*.

Retail Credit. Any credit arrangement which is made available to the ultimate consumer—especially applicable to some form of charge account.

Revolving Account. A system of retail credit by which a customer is required to pay only a certain portion of his balance each month, with the balance deferred but subject to carrying charges.

Routing.   In production control, the activity concerned with planning the flow of materials and parts through the manufacturing process.

Rubber–Stamp Words.   Words used by so many individuals in exactly the same places of their various messages that the reader practically can predict phrasing before he sees it.

Sales Letter.   A type of request letter in which the writer attempts to sell his product or service to the reader.

Scattergram.   A graphic aid which presents data as points plotted in a field of crossing horizontal and vertical lines. A solid line (called a *regression line*) can be inserted from left to right through the field of points. If this line conforms to the general rise or fall of the points, it will roughly define a trend in the data.

Scheduling.   In production control, the assigning of the time factors necessary to achieve and maintain a coordinated effort in manufacturing.

Score.   In readability analysis, the quantitative value assigned to a given piece of writing so that it may be interpreted.

S.D.–B.L. Approach.   In trade or mercantile transactions, a credit arrangement somewhat similar to C.O.D. In effect, a sight draft is a check already made payable to the seller; it is sent along with the bill of lading. To take delivery of the goods, the buyer must sign the draft (or check, as it were).

Self–Motivating Request.   A request which does not have to be fitted with a special message step in order to get action from the reader. For example, a person in business should not have to be told that an order for his product or service calls for action.

Sequencing.   The arranging of information in a planned order of presentation.

Service Attitude.   A subdivision of finesse concerned with emphasizing things which are within the reader's sphere of interest in preference to things which are more important to the writer. It is the slanting of statements, whenever sensible, in terms of benefits offered to the reader.

Simplification.   In management, the process of reducing the variety of anything to a minimal few.

Single–Purpose Letter.   A classification of business letters embracing those which have but one reason (that is, goodwill) for being written.

Slippage.   The amount of change occurring in a message from the time it takes shape in the writer's mind to the time it gets into the reader's mind.

Solicited Letter.   In the employment area, an application letter written in response to an advertisement or other lead put out by the prospective employer.

Source.   The point of origin of a business communication; specifically, the writer of a business communication.

Special Request.   In letter writing, any of a number of possible request-type letters which would call for more than routine handling or programming. Examples are the sales letter, the claim letter, the collection letter, and the application letter.

Standardization.   The reaching of a scientifically best way of selecting sizes, shapes, varieties, methods, etc. Standardization usually results in simplification, but not vice versa. A standardized selection may not even be one of the original varieties, but an entirely new one set up by a scientific approach.

Stenographic.   Of, or pertaining to, stenography: the art of writing in shorthand and then transcribing into typewritten form.

Subjective Form.   A subdivision of the form of a letter, referring to those details which must make for sensible reading as well as pleasant appearance. Thus, the correctness of a date, an address, a salutation, and so on would have importance beyond mere appearance.

Suborder.   In report writing, a sequence selected for presenting different pieces of information, within the framework of an overall *inductive order* or *deductive order* program.

Summary (Abstract, Synopsis).   In a formal report, a preliminary section in which the essential features of the report are presented in condensed form. A summary gives the reader a statement of the problem, a digest of the findings, and appropriate conclusions and/or recommendations.

Sympathy.   An alignment of one's feelings in harmony with those of someone who has suffered a misfortune.

Syntax (Sentence Structure).   The arrangement or manner of fitting together the parts of a sentence (especially modifying words, phrases, and clauses) so that the reader can extract a clear, unambiguous meaning.

Table.   A list of items, wherein those portions of the description of each item which are common to other items are placed in vertical columns.

Table of Contents.   In a formal report, a prefatory section consisting of a basic outline of the portions of the report which are to follow, together with the number of the page on which each such portion begins.

Tabular Form.   In the form of a table of some kind.

Termination Stage.   In a collection effort, the drastic-action stage which takes effect after the writing stage has been completed without success.

Text.   In general, material written in prose. In formal reports, the main body of the report, often called, "Discussion and Analysis."

Time Series.   A collection of data relating to a succession of specified intervals of time.

Timeliness.   The quality of doing the right thing at the right time.

Title Page.   A preliminary part of a formal report which gives the name of the report, the person for whom it is written, the author, and the date.

Tolerance Limit.   The boundary line between something that is acceptable and something that is not.

Tone.   In writing, the extent to which the first, second, and third persons are used in the construction of the sentences. *Personal tone* permits all three persons; *impersonal tone* allows only the third-person usage.

Trade (Mercantile) Credit.   Any form of credit terms made available to a person or firm at a level other than that of ultimate consumer.

Two–Part Letter.   A format for preparing a letter in two documents: one, a relatively short covering letter; the other, an enclosure of some kind. It is used to overcome some awkwardness which might arise in trying to put both in a single document.

Unsolicited Letter.   In the employment area, an application letter written without knowledge beforehand that the prospective employer has an opening or is even contemplating interviewing applicants.

Voice.   In a sentence, the formation of the verb to indicate whether the action is being performed *by* or is being done *to* the subject of the sentence. *Active voice* indicates action taken by the subject. *Passive voice* indicates something happening to the subject.

Wording.   The manner in which something is phrased in communication.

QUESTIONS

Give informal definitions of the following terms which appear in this textbook, using the restricted or specialized meanings which many of them have in reference to business communication.

1. Allowable syllables.
2. Ample assistance.
3. Businesslike
4. Channel.
5. Conceptual positive.
6. Cybernetics.
7. Decoding.
8. Destination.
9. Diplomacy.
10. Dispatching.
11. Encoding.
12. Facsimile communication.
13. Feedback.
14. Fidelity.
15. Finesse.
16. Footnote method.

17. Formal style.
18. Gadget.
19. Mechanics of expression.
20. Messageless communication.
21. Noise.
22. O.C.R.
23. Program.

24. Readability.
25. Rubber-stamp words.
26. Sequencing.
27. Slippage.
28. Source.
29. Suborder.
30. Tone.

CLASSIFIED
BIBLIOGRAPHY

AIDS FOR WRITERS
· · · · · · · · · · · · · · · ·

BATY, WAYNE MURLIN. *Business Communication and Typewriting,* Belmont, Calif.: Wadsworth Publishing Company, Inc., 1962.

DOUGHERTY, MARGARET M., FITZGERALD, JULIA H., AND BOLANDER, DONALD O. *Instant Spelling Dictionary,* Chicago: Career Institute, 1964.

EVANS, BERGEN AND CORNELIA. *A Dictionary of Contemporary American Usage,* Fairlawn, N.J.: Oxford University Press, 1959.

Manual of Style. Washington, D.C.: U.S. Government Printing Office, 1966.

New York Times Style Book for Writers and Editors. New York: McGraw-Hill Book Company, Inc., 1962.

PEARLMAN, DANIEL, AND PAULA. *Guide to Rapid Revision,* New York: The Odyssey Press, 1965.

RATHBONE, ROBERT R. *A Writer's Guide for Engineers and Scientists,* Englewood Cliffs, N.J.: Prentice-Hall, Inc., 1961.

SISSON, A. F. *Sisson's Word and Expression Locater,* West Nyack, N.Y.: Parker Publishing Co., 1967.

VAN HAGAN, CHARLES E. *Report Writer's Handbook,* Englewood Cliffs, N.J.: Prentice-Hall, Inc., 1961.

Webster's Seventh Collegiate Dictionary. 15th ed., Springfield, Mass.: G. C. Merriam Company, 1965.

COMMUNICATION FOR BUSINESS

AURNER, ROBERT R., AND WOLF, MORRIS PHILIP. *Effective Communication in Business,* 5th ed., Cincinnati: South-Western Publishing Company, 1967.

BRENNAN, LAWRENCE D. *Business Communication,* Paterson, N.J.: Littlefield, Adams & Co., 1960.

BROWN, LELAND. *Communicating Facts and Ideas in Business,* Englewood Cliffs, N.J.: Prentice-Hall, Inc., 1961.

DAMERST, WILLIAM A. *Resourceful Business Communication,* New York: Harcourt, Brace & World, Inc., 1966.

HIMSTREET, WILLIAM C., AND BATY, WAYNE M. *Business Communications: Principles and Methods,* 2d ed., Belmont, Calif.: Wadsworth Publishing Company, Inc., 1964.

MAYBURY, SALLY B. *Principles of Business Letter Writing,* New York: The Ronald Press Company, 1959.

MENNING, J. H., AND WILKINSON, CLYDE W. *Communicating Through Letters and Reports,* 4th ed., Homewood, Ill.: Richard D. Irwin, Inc., 1967.

PARKHURST, CHARLES CHANDLER. *Business Communication for Better Human Relations,* 7th ed., Englewood Cliffs, N.J.: Prentice-Hall, Inc., 1966.

SHEPPARD, MONA. *Plain Letters,* New York: Simon and Schuster, Inc., 1960.

SHURTER, ROBERT L., AND WILLIAMSON, J. PETER. *Written Communication in Business,* 2d ed., New York: McGraw-Hill Book Company, Inc., 1964.

WILLIAMS, CECIL B., AND GRIFFIN, E. GLENN. *Effective Business Communication,* 3d ed., New York: The Ronald Press Company, 1966.

COMMUNICATION FOR MANAGEMENT

BROWN, LELAND. *Effective Business Report Writing,* 2d ed., Englewood Cliffs, N.J.: Prentice-Hall, Inc., 1963.

COMER, DAVID B., AND SPILLMAN, RALPH. *Modern Technical and Industrial Reports,* New York: G. P. Putnam's Sons, 1962.

COYLE, WILLIAM. *Research Papers,* New York: The Odyssey Press, 1965.

FERBER, ROBERT, AND VERDOORN, P. J. *Research Methods in Economics and Business,* New York: The Macmillan Company, 1962.

GRAVES, HAROLD F., AND HOFFMAN, LYNE S. S. *Report Writing,* 4th ed., Englewood Cliffs, N.J.: Prentice-Hall, Inc., 1965.

HICKS, TYLER J. "How To Write Reports That Get Read," *Journal,* Society of Automotive Engineers, November 1960, pp. 75–79.

LESIKAR, RAYMOND V. *Report Writing for Business,* Homewood, Ill.: Richard D. Irwin, Inc., 1961.

MENZEL, DONALD H., JONES, HOWARD MUMFORD, AND BOYD, LYLE G. *Writing a Technical Paper,* New York: McGraw-Hill Book Company, Inc., 1961.

MERRIHUE, WILLARD V. *Managing by Communication,* New York: McGraw-Hill Book Company, Inc., 1960.

SHERMAN, THEODORE A. *Modern Technical Writing,* 2d ed., Englewood Cliffs, N.J.: Prentice-Hall, Inc., 1966.

SHURTER, ROBERT L., WILLIAMSON, J. PETER, AND BROEHL, WAYNE G., JR. *Business Research and Report Writing,* New York: McGraw-Hill Book Company, Inc., 1964.

SIGBAND, NORMAN B. *Effective Report Wriitng,* New York: Harper & Row, Publishers, Incorporated, 1959.

THAYER, LEO O. *Administrative Communication,* Homewood, Ill.: Richard D. Irwin, Inc., 1961.

COMMUNICATION THEORY
. . . .

BERLO, DAVID K. *The Process of Communication: An Introduction to Theory and Practice,* New York: Holt, Rinehart and Winston, Inc., 1960.

CHERRY, COLIN. *On Human Communication,* New York: John Wiley & Sons, Inc., 1957.

"Courtesy in Correspondence," *The Royal Bank of Canada Monthly Letter,* Vol. 46, No. 10, October 1965.

HANEY, WILLIAM V. *Communication and Organizational Behavior: Text and Cases,* Rev. ed., Homewood, Ill.: Richard D. Irwin, Inc., 1967.

HUGHES, JOHN P. *The Science of Language,* New York: Random House, Inc., 1962.

KNIGHT, W. R. "Getting Your Message Through," *The Atlanta Economic Review,* February 1965, p. 18.

MCLAUGHLIN, TED. J., BLUM, LAWRENCE P., AND ROBINSON, DAVID M. *Communication,* Columbus, Ohio: Charles E. Merrill Books, Inc., 1965.

OLSON, DEWEY E. "Six Steps to Better Written Communications," *The Office,* April 1966, Office Publications, Inc.

WRIGHT, CHARLES R. *Mass Communication,* New York: Random House, Inc., 1959.

YERIAN, C. T. "Check Your Communications I.Q.," *Northwest Business Management,* Vol. III, No. 1, School of Business and Technology, Oregon State University.

LANGUAGE AND EXPRESSION

HOOK, J. N. *Hook's Guide to Good Writing,* New York: The Ronald Press Company, 1962.

KEITHLEY, ERWIN M., AND THOMPSON, MARGARET H. *English for Modern Business,* Homewood, Ill.: Richard D. Irwin, Inc., 1966.

OSBORN, ALEX F. *Applied Imagination, Principles and Procedures of Creative Thinking,* New York: Charles Scribner's Sons, 1953.

PARKHURST, CHARLES CHANDLER. *English for Business,* 4th ed., Englewood Cliffs, N.J.: Prentice-Hall, Inc., 1963.

SHAW, HARRY. *Errors in English,* New York: Barnes & Noble, Inc., 1962.

STRUNK, WILLIAM, JR., AND WHITE, E. B. *The Elements of Style,* New York: The Macmillan Company, 1959.

READABILITY

FLESCH, RUDOLPH. *The Art of Plain Talk,* New York: Harper & Brothers Publishers, 1946.

————. *The Art of Readable Writing,* New York: Harper & Brothers Publishers, 1949.

GOWERS, SIR ERNEST. *Plain Words: Their ABC,* New York: Alfred A. Knopf, Inc., 1955.

GUNNING, ROBERT. *The Technique of Clear Writing,* New York: McGraw-Hill Book Company, Inc., 1952.

SHIDLE, NORMAN G. *Clear Writing for Easy Reading,* New York: McGraw-Hill Book Company, Inc., 1951.

READINGS AND VIEWPOINTS

BLICKLE, MARGARET D., AND PASSE, MARTHA E. *Readings for Technical Writers,* New York: The Ronald Press Company, 1963.

ESTRIN, HERMAN A. (ed.). *Technical and Professional Writing: A Practical Anthology,* New York: Harcourt, Brace & World, Inc., 1963.

JANIS, J. HAROLD (ed.). *Business Communication Reader,* New York: Harper & Row, Publishers, Incorporated, 1958.

VOYLES, JEAN. *An Evaluation of Written Communications in Two Atlanta Companies,* Atlanta, Ga.: Bureau of Business and Economic Research, Georgia State College, 1964.

WEEKS, FRANCIS W. (ed.). *Readings in Communication from Fortune,* New York: Holt, Rinehart and Winston, Inc., 1961.

Wilkinson, C. W., Menning, J. H., and Anderson, C. R. *Writing for Business,* Homewood, Ill.: Richard D. Irwin, Inc., 1960.

SALES PROMOTION

Buckley, Earle A. *How To Increase Sales With Letters,* New York: McGraw-Hill Book Company, Inc., 1961.

Dichter, Ernest. *The Strategy of Desire,* Garden City, N.Y.: Doubleday & Company, Inc., 1960.

Keyes, Langley Carlton. "Profits in Prose," *Harvard Business Review,* January-February 1961, pp. 105–12.

Yeck, John D., and Maguire, John T. *Planning and Creating Better Direct Mail,* New York: McGraw-Hill Book Company, Inc., 1961.

SPECIAL SITUATIONS

CREDIT AND COLLECTIONS

Eller, J. W. "Collecting Past Due Accounts Without Losing Customers," *Management Aids for Small Manufacturers,* No. 168, November 1964, Small Business Administration.

Morris, Richard H. *Credit and Collection Letters: New Techniques To Make Them Work,* Great Neck, N.Y.: Channel Press, Inc., 1960.

EMPLOYMENT

Pell, Arthur R. "Are You at a Career Crossroad?" *Purchasing,* January 2, 1961, pp. 55–57.

Weaver, Robert G., "Letters That Get Interviews," *Industrial Science & Engineering,* April 1960, pp. 11–13.

GOVERNMENT

Wnuk, Joseph J., Jr. *Communication and Government,* Cleveland, Ohio: Business Research Center, John Carroll University, 1965.

INTERNATIONAL BUSINESS

Lurie, Richard G. "Avoid the Wastebasket in Your International Business Letters," *Clipper Cargo Horizons,* May 1966, pp. 6–8.

POLICY AND PRINCIPLE

DOVER, C. J. *Management Communications on Controversial Issues,* Washington, D.C.: BNA, Incorporated, 1965.

NEWCOME, ROBERT, AND SAMMONS, MARG. *Employee Communications in Action,* New York: Harper & Row, Publishers, Incorporated, 1961.

INDEX

INDEX

••

Page numbers in boldface indicate illustration.

A

Abbreviations, 100, 138, 205, 207, 626, 655 ff
Accepting a job, 490 ff
Accuracy, 18, 20, 83 ff, 173 ff, 188, 198, 204 ff, 625 ff
Accusations (scoldings), 349 ff, 436
Acknowledgment letters: definition, 339, 670; basic ingredients, 343 ff; ready-reference capsules, 360 ff
Acknowledgments — bad news: reasons for a turndown, 352 ff; program, 354; **356 ff**; ready-reference capsule, 362
Acknowledgments—good news: use of, 343 ff; program, 344; **347**; ready-reference capsule, 360
Acknowledgments—requests for clarification: circumstances involved, 348; nature of the problem, 348; structure general, 348; program, 349; **351**; ready-reference capsule, 361
Action statement, 299 ff, 305 ff; definition, 670
Active voice, 61 ff, 175, 638; definition, 670
Active voice versus passive voice, 61 ff, 638
Address, inside: subjective aspects, 119 ff; combining with other parts, 124; objective aspects, 125 ff, 130; relation to outside address, 126, 145; problem with sales letters, 309; abbreviations permitted, 656 ff; definition, 670
Address forms: Ambassador, U.S.A., 658; Ambassador, foreign, 658; Archbishop, 658; Bishop, Catholic, 658; Bishop, Episcopal, 659; Bishop, Methodist, 659; cabinet officer, 659; Cardinal, 659; Chief Justice of the Supreme Court, 659; Doctor of Divinity, 659; Minister, 659; Priest, Catholic, 659; Priest, Episcopal, 659; Rabbi, 659; Councilman, 659; Dean (college), 659; Governor, 659; Judge, 659; Mayor, 660; member of Congress, 660; military personnel, 660; Monsignor, 660; Pope, 660; Presi-

Address forms—*Cont.*
dent (United States), 660; President (university), 660; Senator, 660; Vice President of the United States, 660
Adjustment letters: qualities of, 378 ff; goodwill opportunity, 379 ff; definition, 670
Adjustments — bad news: 385–89, 394; ordinary causes, 385, 387; program, 387 ff; **389**; ready-reference capsule, 394
Adjustments—good news: program, 380; routine cases, **382**; nonroutine cases, **383**; ready-reference capsule, 392
Adjustments—partly bad news: program, 384; **386**; ready-reference capsule, 393
Agreeable(ness), 16 ff, 21, 26 ff, 53, 174, 176 ff, 185 ff
Agreeable versus disagreeable, 43
Agreement: case and number, 90 ff, 633 ff; subject and verb, 90 ff, 633; pronoun and antecedent, 91, 634 ff; collective noun, 91 ff, 633 ff; either-or situations, 92, 634; pronouns, relative, 92, 634; pronouns, collective, 92 ff; pronouns, possessive, 93, 635; pronouns as objects, 633
AIDA sales letter plan: shortcomings of, 300; improving, 300 ff; definition, 670
Airwave static, 5, 7; definition, 670
Allowable syllables, 74; definition, 670
Alphabetical order, 541 ff, 550, **551**; definition, 671
Amounts, 661
Ampersand, 661
Ample assistance, 167, 187, 251, 256, 262, 265 ff; in sales letters, 301, 307 ff; in acknowledgments, 350; in credit letters, 414, 418 ff; in collection letters, 449; in application letters, 483 ff; definition, 671
Analysis: of finesse, 45 ff; readability measurement, 71 ff; of request-type letters, 245; of direct-mail costs, 292 ff; in body of reports, 571 ff
Analytical report: subdivisions, 507; cross-classifications, 508; definition, 671

This book has been set in 11 point Times Roman leaded 3 points, and 10 point Times Roman leaded 2 points. The word "Chapter" is 10 point Univers Bold No. 693 followed by 36 point Univers Medium No. 55 Arabic number; the chapter title is 24 point (small) Univers Bold No. 693 italic. The size of the type page is 27 x 45 picas.